Between Court and Confessional
The Politics of Spanish Inquisitors

Between Court and Confessional explores the lives of Spanish inquisitors, closely examining the careers and writings of five sixteenth- and seventeenth-century inquisitors. Kimberly Lynn considers what shaped particular inquisitors, the kinds of official experience each accumulated, and to what ends each directed his acquired knowledge and experience. The case studies examine the complex interplay of careerism and ideological commitments evident in inquisitorial activities. Whereas many studies of the Spanish Inquisition tend to depict inquisitors as faceless and interchangeable, Lynn probes the lives of individual inquisitors to show how their operations in their social, political, religious, and intellectual worlds set the Inquisition in motion. By focusing on specific individuals, this study explains how the theory and regulations of the Inquisition were rooted in local conditions, particular disputes, and individual experiences.

Kimberly Lynn is an associate professor of early modern Europe in the Department of Liberal Studies at Western Washington University. Professor Lynn has been awarded a William J. Fulbright Fellowship for research in Spain and an Andrew W. Mellon Fellowship in Humanistic Studies. She also won a Philanthropic Educational Organization Scholar Award, as well as short-term research fellowships to the Herzog August Bibliothek in Wolfenbüttel, Germany, and the Folger Shakespeare Library in Washington, D.C.

Between Court and Confessional

The Politics of Spanish Inquisitors

KIMBERLY LYNN

CAMBRIDGE
UNIVERSITY PRESS

32 Avenue of the Americas, New York NY 10013-2473, USA

Cambridge University Press is part of the University of Cambridge.

It furthers the University's mission by disseminating knowledge in the pursuit of education, learning and research at the highest international levels of excellence.

www.cambridge.org
Information on this title: www.cambridge.org/9781107507302

© Kimberly Lynn 2013

This publication is in copyright. Subject to statutory exception and to the provisions of relevant collective licensing agreements, no reproduction of any part may take place without the written permission of Cambridge University Press.

First published 2013
First paperback edition 2015

A catalogue record for this publication is available from the British Library

Library of Congress Cataloguing in Publication data
Lynn, Kimberly.
Between court and confessional : the politics of Spanish Inquisitors / Kimberly Lynn.
pages   cm
Includes bibliographical references and index.
ISBN 978-1-107-03116-6
1. Inquisition – Spain.   I. Title.
BX1735.L96   2013
272′.20946–dc23   2012048143

ISBN 978-1-107-03116-6 Hardback
ISBN 978-1-107-50730-2 Paperback

Cambridge University Press has no responsibility for the persistence or accuracy of URLs for external or third-party internet websites referred to in this publication, and does not guarantee that any content on such websites is, or will remain, accurate or appropriate.

For Jonathan,
senza parole di più

Contents

Figures

Acknowledgments

I am profoundly grateful for all of the support, encouragement, and assistance that brought this book into being. Richard Kagan has been the best of mentors; his creativity and range as a scholar, his generosity as an advisor, and his passion for research and for the field have been constant sources of inspiration. Lu Ann Homza's example made me want to become a historian, and I have benefited far more than I can convey from her exceptional dedication to the profession, her skill as a critic, and the warmth of her friendship. David Nirenberg has likewise generously shared his time with me, and continues to inspire me; I have learned much from reading and listening to him, and from his care and attention in reading and in questioning me.

On my first research trip to Madrid, now more than a decade ago, I had the very good fortune to become acquainted with Jim Amelang, whose extensive expertise, suggestions, and insights have helped me tremendously. Also at the Universidad Autónoma in Madrid, María José del Río Barredo welcomed me and generously shared her knowledge, as did Virgilio Pinto Crespo.

This project has also been possible because of the funding and institutional support I received from several sources. In its first form, as a dissertation, Johns Hopkins University; a William J. Fulbright Fellowship to Spain; the Program for Cultural Cooperation between Spain's Ministry of Education, Culture and Sports and United States Universities; and a P.E.O. Scholar Award provided essential support. I am also grateful to the institutions that afforded me invaluable time and space to rethink that initial work and conduct further research in the years that followed. I offer my sincere thanks to the Herzog August Bibliothek in Wolfenbüttel, Germany, the Gladys Krieble Delmas Foundation, the Folger Shakespeare Library, and for a Mendel Fellowship at the Lilly Library at Indiana University. Moreover, this project would not have been possible without the assistance and professionalism of the librarians and archivists at each of the many institutions where I have conducted research; in that regard, I am particularly grateful to the staff of the Biblioteca Nacional and of the Archivo Histórico Nacional in Madrid. At Western Washington University, I have appreciated the interest, patience, and encouragement of my students and colleagues, the invaluable assistance of the university's librarians, and the support provided by the Liberal Studies Department, the College of Humanities and Social Sciences, and the Office of Research and Sponsored Programs.

I am also particularly appreciative of the audiences who listened to me present various pieces of this project over the years, commented, critiqued, and asked questions. Collegial conversations at the EMERGE early modernist group at the University of Washington, at Johns Hopkins, as well as at the NEH Summer Institute in Venice in 2008 (directed by Murray Baumgarten and Shaul Bassi), were of great value. I also thank those who considered my work at the annual meetings of the Association of Spanish and Portuguese Historical Studies, the Renaissance Society of America, and the American Historical Association, as well as the Sixteenth Century Society and Conference, among other venues.

Whether or not they were aware of its importance, I am very grateful to all those colleagues who furnished assistance over the years or shared their work in progress, and whose questions, interest, and criticisms provided such encouragement. From my graduate work and dissertation defense to the rounds of research, conferences, and rethinking that followed, these included, among others: Katherine Aron-Beller, Jodi Bilinkoff, Marco Cavarzere, Christopher Celenza, John Chuchiak, Sabina de Cavi, Carrie Euler, Robert Ferry, Orietta Filippini, Mary Fissell, Clive Griffin, Renzo Honores, Thomas Izbicki, Guy Lazure, John Marshall, Robert Maryks, Peter Mazur, Clare Monagle, Macarena Moralejo Ortega, Martin Nesvig, Katrina Olds, María Portuondo, Allyson Poska, Conchi Redondo Moreno, Erin Rowe, Ana Schaposchnik, Anne Jacobson Schutte, Violet Soen, Gretchen Starr-Lebeau, David Tavárez, Molly Warsh, Daniel Wasserman, and Alison Weber. I would also like to thank Fernando Marías, in particular, for so kindly providing me with photographs from Córdoba's cathedral and allowing me to use them in this book.

At Cambridge University Press, I thank all the members of the editorial staff and production team who shepherded the manuscript along. I am especially grateful to Emily Spangler for taking an interest in this project and for her commitment to it, and to Eric Crahan, as well as to Debbie Gershenowitz for seeing it through to print. I am also indebted to the two anonymous readers for the press who devoted such time, care, and attention to reviewing the manuscript.

Finally, my heart is full of gratitude for those who lived the years of this book with me. Its footnotes remind me of the places where I researched, wrote, and revised it, and of the many joys I shared with others along the way. For Amanda Dotseth and Ry Kovar, my fellow travelers, treasured companions anywhere in the world. For Norma del Barrio Peña, Antonio del Barrio, and Ana Peña, who gave me a home in Spain and introduced me to so much there. For Jonathan Miran, who has been by my side with advice, reassurance, and love. And most of all, for my grandparents, John Lynn, Bill Hein, and the late Margaret Rest Hein, and for my parents, Tom and Sherri Lynn, who have always given me boundless love and unconditional support; to them I offer immeasurable thanks, and that on this page their names might always live on beside mine, on a library shelf somewhere.

Abbreviations

ACC	Archivo de la Catedral, Córdoba
ACM	Archivo del Cabildo Catedral Metropolitano de México, Mexico City
ACP	Archivo de la Catedral, Palencia
ACS	Archivo de la Catedral, Santiago de Compostela
ACZ	Archivo Catedralicio, Zamora
Add.	Additional Manuscripts
ADP	Archivo Diocesano, Palencia
ADPZ	Archivo de la Diputación Provincial, Zamora
AFZ	Archivo y Biblioteca de Francisco Zabálburu, Madrid
AGI	Archivo General de Indias, Seville
AGN	Archivo General de la Nación, Mexico City
AGS	Archivo General, Simancas
AHAM	Archivo Histórico del Arzobispado de México, Mexico City
AHDS	Archivo Histórico Diocesano, Santiago de Compostela
AHN	Archivo Histórico Nacional, Madrid
AHPM	Archivo Histórico de Protocolos, Madrid
BCS	Biblioteca Capitular, Seville
BL	British Library, London
BNE	Biblioteca Nacional de España, Madrid
BNF	Bibliothèque Nationale de France, Paris
BUS	Biblioteca General Universitaria, Salamanca
DHEE	Q. Aldea Vaquero and T. Marín Martínez, eds., *Diccionario de Historia Eclesiástica de España* (Madrid, 1972–75)

DSI	A. Prosperi, ed., with V. Lavenia and J. Tedeschi, *Dizionario storico dell'Inquisizione* (Pisa, 2010)
doc.	documento
EE	V. Guitarte Izquierdo, *Episcopologio Español (1500–1699)* (Rome, 1994)
Eg.	Egerton
exp.	expediente
HAB	Herzog August Bibliothek, Wolfenbüttel
HC	G. van Gulik and C. Eubel, eds., *Hierarchia Catholica Medii et Recentioris Aevi* (Münster, 1913–68)
HIEA	J. Pérez Villanueva and B. Escandell Bonet, eds., *Historia de la Inquisición en España y América* (Madrid, 1984–2000)
Inq.	Inquisición
IVDJ	Instituto Valencia Don Juan, Madrid
leg.	legajo
lib.	libro
OM	Órdenes Militares
PR	Patronato Real
r.	ramo
RAH	Real Academia de la Historia, Madrid
RB	Real Biblioteca, Madrid

A Note on Language

Unless otherwise specified, all translations are mine. In the notes, I have left the irregular orthography in the quotations from the original sources. I have, however, chosen spellings of names and places closer to modern usage, in the interest of clarity. I have also used the following abbreviations for university degrees: Lic. for Licentiate (*licenciado*) and Dr. for Doctor (*doctor*).

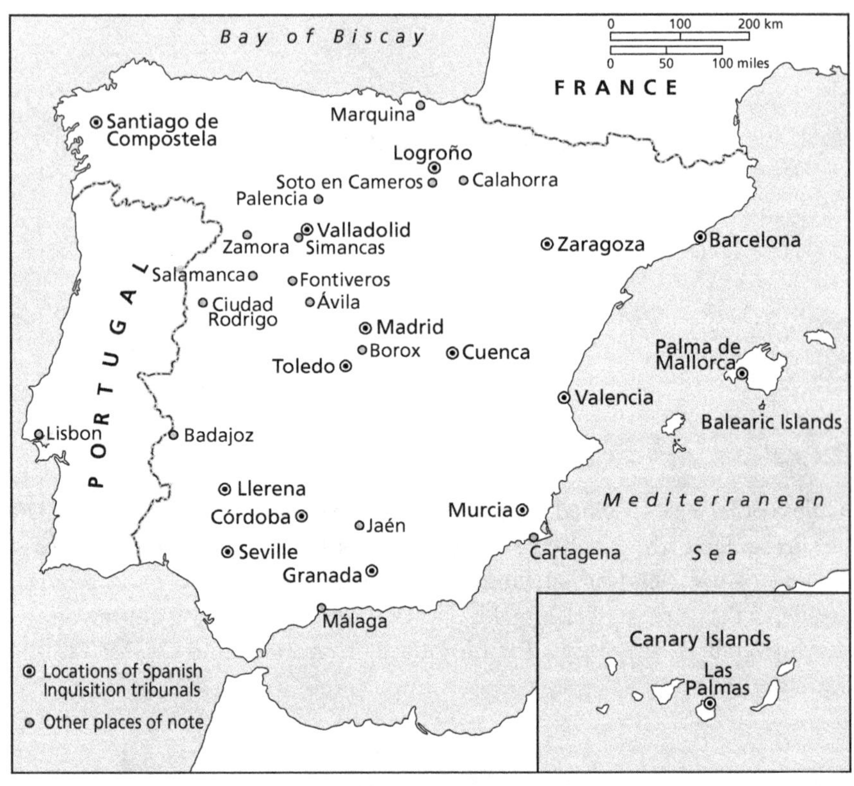

MAP I. Spanish Inquisition Tribunals in the Seventeenth Century

MAP 2. Spanish Inquisition Tribunals and Notable Cities in Italy

MAP 3. Inquisition Tribunals in the Viceroyalties of New Spain and Peru

Introduction

Arbiters of Faith, Administrators of Empire

Hard marble would soften at the cry, / And with it the fierce breast hardens, / O hard Office, *who calls you* Holy?[1]

Few historical figures are as iconic as the inquisitor, and few institutions are as infamous or reviled as the Spanish Inquisition. At its foundation in 1478, the Spanish Inquisition fit in the mold of established customs: a delegation of authority from the papacy to King Ferdinand and Queen Isabel to appoint inquisitors who would seek out heresy and conduct trials of faith in the lands under the authority of their recently conjoined crowns, powers that followed precedents set by earlier medieval inquisitions and drew on judicial practices with origins in Roman law. The initial focus of these inquisitors was the pursuit of *conversos* – Jewish converts to Christianity and their descendants – suspected of Judaizing heresy, that is, the conduct of practices or credence in beliefs identified as Jewish by baptized Christians. As the Spanish Inquisition soon included an Inquisitor General, a royal Council of the Inquisition (or *Suprema*), and a growing number of regional tribunals, each with inquisitors, lesser officials, and even buildings, it became clear that it was also something strikingly new. From the fifteenth century until its final abolition in 1834, the Spanish Inquisition developed a body of law and practice and an institutional framework that, by the seventeenth century, included twenty-one tribunals on two sides of the Atlantic; its targets and the frequency, intensity, and severity of its activities changed over time and varied across its wide

[1] I.S. Révah, "Autobiographie d'un Marrane. Édition partielle d'un manuscrit de João (Moseh) Pinto Delgado," *Revue des études juives* 119 (1961): 128.

geography. Much ink has been devoted to scholarship on the Spanish Inquisition; over the past four decades, there has been a flourishing of excellent revisionist studies that have charted the institution's history, excavated the identities of its victims, and read its archives in original ways.[2] Still, the inquisitors themselves have rarely been the focal point of this analytical work. In response, this book focuses on the multifaceted careers of Spain's inquisitors and the worlds they inhabited, and so it seeks to reexamine the Spanish Inquisition through the prism of some of the individual judges who sat on its tribunals and on the *Suprema* and who wrote its history and compiled its laws.

A series of questions lies at the heart of this book. How can we account for inquisitorial action? Or, how is it possible to explain the activities of inquisitors? What motivated Spanish inquisitors: that is, what made an inquisitor and what subsequently drove his decisions? On one level, these are questions that might be posed about an array of historical actors; questions that seek to probe the balance between autonomy, choice, or agency and social, institutional, or intellectual constraints in examining the past; questions that seek to consider how and why individuals behaved in certain ways vis-à-vis the systems of an earlier era. On another level, these are questions that have a particular potency when they are posed about those who have become the great villains of history.[3] In this book, I have sought neither to excuse nor to rehabilitate Spanish inquisitors, but rather to explore how their actions might be comprehended, to analyze what made their choices viable, their careers successful, and their writings persuasive – if never uncontroversial – within the logics of their social

---

[2] The best starting place for research on the Spanish Inquisition remains the magisterial three-volume *HIEA*. The *DSI* is now another fundamental resource. See also the approaches to the scholarship in Geoffrey Parker, "Some Recent Work on the Inquisition in Spain and Italy," *Journal of Modern History* 54.3 (1982): 519–32; Jean-Pierre Dedieu and René Millar Carvacho, "Entre histoire et mémoire. L'Inquisition à l'époque moderne: dix ans d'historiographie," *Annales HSS* 57 (2002): 349–72; Francisco Bethencourt, *The Inquisition: A Global History, 1478–1834*, trans. Jean Birrell (Cambridge, UK, and New York: Cambridge University Press, 2009), 1–34; Kimberly Lynn Hossain, "Unraveling the Spanish Inquisition: Inquisitorial Studies in the Twenty-First Century," *History Compass* 5.4 (2007): 1280–93.

[3] For some avenues into this vast body of theoretical work, see Anna Green, *Cultural History* (New York: Palgrave Macmillan, 2008). For explorations of how and why to study some of history's infamous "perpetrators," see Daniel Jonah Goldhagen, *Hitler's Willing Executioners: Ordinary Germans and the Holocaust* (New York: Vintage Books, 1997); Hannah Arendt, *Eichmann in Jerusalem. A Report on the Banality of Evil* (New York and London: Penguin Books, 1994); Elizabeth Fox-Genovese and Eugene D. Genovese, *The Mind of the Master Class: History and Faith in the Southern Slaveholders' Worldview* (Cambridge, UK, and New York: Cambridge University Press, 2005).

world. In sum, I would submit that inquisitors were motivated by a potent combination of careerism and ideological commitment, a blend that varied from judge to judge in balance and content and that, for each individual, was also liable to change over time and to develop in a dynamic relationship to his acquired experience and to the particular situations in which he found himself.

The judges' official ideals were delicately poised between belief in the fallen nature of humankind and in human perfectibility. They shared in the tensions of clerical life that proposed that a removal from the mundane concerns of family would better enable them to care for the world, a pastoral ideal that simultaneously advocated engagement with the flock and an exceptional position within it. They also experienced the tensions surrounding judicial action. Ideally, rendering justice was understood as the prudent exercise of judgment, the seeking out of the truth in a given matter, an operation in which the judge should be free of enmity, passion, and personal interests. As an arbiter of trials of faith, an inquisitor was thus expected, by his own ideals, to be doubly insulated from worldly concerns in order to best correct the religious practice and belief of his fellow humans. At the same time, an inquisitor understood his search for the truth of a case to require a capacity for discernment, an ability based both on more theoretical learning and on knowledge derived from experience of the world. It was for such reasons that the Inquisition's guidelines often recommended forty as the minimum age for appointment to the office. As arbiters and administrators, inquisitors were expected to be both set apart from their world and adept at navigating within it. The chapters that follow examine how individuals who became inquisitors sought to negotiate this tension and how they simultaneously elaborated the ideals of their office and exercised their authority on the ground.

No one was born an inquisitor in early modern Spain. Thus, this book considers what propelled a man into this peculiar judicial career through an examination of the lives of five men who were inquisitors. Each of the first five chapters charts the professional trajectory of a single individual, suggesting a method of approach that might be taken – to varying degrees of depth – to any Spanish inquisitor. Each of these chapters considers the inquisitor's origins, the kinds of offices he held and the cases in which he was involved, the places where he worked, and the political pressures to which he was especially subject. Each then traces some of the ways in which the inquisitor conducted his work, how he responded to the situations he encountered and the multiple constraints on his actions, and what might be gleaned from this about what kinds of ideals he drew from to give meaning to his office. This approach offers a way to explore the persistent negotiations that suffused inquisitorial careers and to which inquisitors' actions were subject. Simultaneously, it seeks to locate inquisitors – so often rendered as a case apart – more coherently as part of their society.

This study builds on prosopographies of judges in the Inquisition's district tribunals, councillors of the *Suprema*, and Inquisitors General.[4] Historians have established a standard social profile of inquisitors at the apogee of the Spanish Inquisition. By and large, they were so-called Old Christians, often from gentry families and with ties of kinship to other royal and ecclesiastical officeholders. It was common for them to have relatives who were Inquisition officials. Usually secular clerics, they were increasingly jurists by discipline, many educated at the university in Salamanca, where they had attained the degree of licentiate or doctor of laws – canon, civil, or both. Frequently shaped by initial appointments in universities, civil courts, and cathedrals or as lesser officials in tribunals of the Holy Office, while inquisitors they were often delegated to short-term inspections of other institutions. Increasingly, holding office in the Spanish Inquisition offered a route of social mobility within the Catholic Monarchy. There was crossover with the Chanceries (the royal appellate courts) and occasionally with the Rota in Rome (the papal appellate court). Being an inquisitor could be a stepping-stone to Court in multiple ways, more and less formal, in particular to nomination as a royal councillor – especially to the *Suprema* – and sometimes to council presidencies. It was often a path into the episcopate, and there were extensive connections – as well as persistent conflict and competition – between bishops and

---

[4] See, for example, Teresa Sánchez Rivilla, "Inquisidores Generales y Consejeros de la Suprema: documentación biográfica," *HIEA* 3:228–437; Solange Alberro, *Inquisition et Société au Mexique, 1571–1700* (Mexico City: Centre d'Études Mexicaines et Centramericaines, 1988); Jaime Contreras, *El Santo Oficio de la Inquisición de Galicia, 1560–1700: poder, sociedad y cultura* (Madrid: Akal, 1982); Jean-Pierre Dedieu, *L'Administration de la foi: l'Inquisition de Tolède, XVI-XVII siècle* (Madrid: Casa de Velázquez, 1989); Ricardo García Cárcel, *Herejía y sociedad en el siglo XVI. La Inquisición en Valencia, 1530–1609* (Barcelona: Ediciones Península, 1980); William Monter, *The Frontiers of Heresy: The Spanish Inquisition from the Basque Lands to Sicily* (Cambridge, UK: Cambridge University Press, 1990); Ángel de Prado Moura, *Inquisición e inquisidores en Castilla: El Tribunal de Valladolid durante la Crisis del Antiguo Régimen* (Valladolid: Universidad de Valladolid, 1995). For more recent summaries of these findings, see Helen Rawlings, *The Spanish Inquisition* (Malden, MA, and Oxford, UK: Blackwell Publishing, 2006), 25–26; Joseph Pérez, *The Spanish Inquisition. A History*, trans. Janet Lloyd (New Haven, CT, and London: Yale University Press, 2005), 116; A. Del Col, "Inquisitore," Dedieu, "Inquisitore di distretto, Spagna," and R. López-Vela, "Inquisitore generali, Spagna," *DSI* 2:800–808.

inquisitors. There were also regional variations in career patterns, as inquisitorial office in the Americas rarely led to appointments in the peninsula; over time, a relatively self-contained circuit of colonial promotions was established. Nevertheless, approaching inquisitorial careers in the aggregate or, occasionally, as brief sketches has its limitations. Julio Caro Baroja observed in a seminal 1968 essay a habit of depicting an "Inquisition without inquisitors," an imbalance that has yet to be thoroughly corrected.[5]

The collective treatment of inquisitors has tended to mute the differences between them. It has also played into a long-standing image of inquisitors as frightening by their very facelessness, by the disappearance of the individual human into the authority and power of his office. In undertaking a more detailed interrogation of a few inquisitorial careers, this book proposes that the particular experiences, ambitions, and beliefs of individual inquisitors were significant to how they constructed their writings, how they conducted trials of faith, and how the Spanish Inquisition took shape as an institution. To some extent, this approach is a response to a mechanistic vision of the Inquisition. From early modern polemic to more recent analyses of the Inquisition as proto-bureaucracy, the tendency has been to depict inquisitors as interchangeable. In one of the most sophisticated such formulations, Jean-Pierre Dedieu cast them as "the machine's essential cog."[6] There is much truth to this metaphor. The relationship between the individual and the corporate in early modern expressions of identity is notoriously fraught. The metaphor also captures something very important about inquisitors' self-perception; in a way, it mirrors their rhetoric of judicial dispassion. It indicates – as many institutional histories of the Spanish Inquisition have found – that their actions were constrained by procedure, by directives from their superiors, and by a host of political exigencies. Inquisitors' industriousness or lack thereof, vacancies in the office, and the deaths of its incumbents altered the conduct of business in a tribunal. At the same time, the inquisitor was more than a mere executor of predetermined procedures, and inquisitorial correspondence offers glimpses of the human dynamics of the tribunal, of how

[5] Julio Caro Baroja, *El Señor Inquisidor y otras vidas por oficio* (Madrid: Alianza Editorial, 1968), 15.

[6] I draw this phrase – "le rouage essentiel de la machine" – from Dedieu's masterful study of Toledo's Inquisition tribunal, *L'Administration de la foi*, 161. For one such more recent approach to the Inquisition as bureaucracy, see Irene Silverblatt, *Modern Inquisitions: Peru and the Colonial Origins of the Civilized World* (Durham, NC: Duke University Press, 2004).

procedural reform was often rooted in individual experience, and of how cases stalled or advanced as a result of the quality of interactions between inquisitors and their colleagues, other authorities, and defendants. Scholarship on medieval inquisitions and the Roman Inquisition has increasingly considered the working habits, pastoral impulses, and intellectual lives of inquisitors.[7] Histories of the Spanish Inquisition have ventured less into such questions, although there has been particularly suggestive work about how the personal dynamics between judges and accused affected the course and conduct of trials.[8]

Apart from those Inquisitors General whose names have taken on a mythic cast, Alonso de Salazar Frías has become arguably the most famous Spanish inquisitor.[9] Gustav Henningsen's extensive study of the witch

[7] There has been far more focus on the inquisitors in these studies, for example, Laurent Albaret, ed., *Les Inquisiteurs: Portraits de défenseurs de la foi en Languedoc* (Toulouse: Éditions Privat, 2001); Christine Caldwell Ames, *Righteous Persecution: Inquisition, Dominicans and Christianity in the Middle Ages* (Philadelphia: University of Pennsylvania Press, 2009); Michael M. Tavuzzi, *Renaissance Inquisitors: Dominican Inquisitors and Inquisitorial Districts in Northern Italy, 1474–1527* (Leiden and Boston: Brill, 2007); Adriano Prosperi, *Tribunali della coscienza: Inquisitori, confessori, missionari* (Turin: G. Einaudi, 1996); Simon Ditchfield, "Umberto Locati, O. P. (1503–1587): Inquisitore, Vescovo e Storico – un profilo bio-bibliografico," *Bollettino Storico Piacentino* 84 (1989): 205–21; Giovanni Romeo, *Inquisitori, esorcisti e streghe nell'Italia della Controriforma* (Florence: Sansoni, 1990); most recently, Karen Sullivan, *The Inner Lives of Medieval Inquisitors* (Chicago: University of Chicago Press, 2011). On the other officials who served the Portuguese Inquisition in Brazil, see James E. Wadsworth, *Agents of Orthodoxy: Honor, Status and the Inquisition in Colonial Pernambuco, Brazil* (Lanham, MD: Rowman and Littlefield, 2007).

[8] Sara Nalle has consistently attended to the place of inquisitors in a host of social, legal, and religious dynamics; see her "Inquisitors, Priests, and the People during the Catholic Reformation in Spain," *Sixteenth Century Journal* 18 (1987): 557–87; and *Mad for God: Bartolomé Sánchez, the Secret Messiah of Cardenete* (Charlottesville: University of Virginia Press, 2001). See also Richard Kagan, *Lucrecia's Dreams: Politics and Prophecy in Sixteenth-Century Spain* (Berkeley, Los Angeles, and Oxford, UK: University of California Press, 1990); Lu Ann Homza, "How to Harass an Inquisitor-General: The Polyphonic Law of Friar Francisco Ortíz" in *A Renaissance of Conflicts: Visions and Revisions of Law and Society in Italy and Spain*, ed. John A. Marino and Thomas Kuehn (Toronto: Centre for Reformation and Renaissance Studies, 2004), 299–336; Jaime Contreras, *Sotos contra Riquelmes: regidores, inquisidores, y criptojudíos* (Madrid: Anaya and M. Muchnik, 1992).

[9] Spain's Inquisitors General have received significantly more study than those below them; for the sixteenth century: José Luis González Novalín, *El Inquisidor General Fernando de Valdés (1483–1568): Su vida y su obra*, 2 vols. (Oviedo: Universidad de Oviedo, 1968); Maurice Boyd, *Cardinal Quiroga Inquisitor General of Spain* (Dubuque, IA: William C. Brown Co., 1954); Henar Pizarro Llorente, *Un gran patrón en la corte de Felipe II: don Gaspar de Quiroga* (Madrid: Universidad Pontificia Comillas, 2004); see also John Edwards, *The Inquisitors: The Story of the Grand Inquisitors of the Spanish*

trials of the Navarrese village of Zugarramurdi, between 1609 and 1614, gave Salazar Frías an enduring place in the historiography as a heroic skeptic whose thorough investigation, petitions, and remonstrances both halted a wave of persecution and forestalled further witch hunts in Spain. When Henningsen described an inquisitor whose doubt about the evidence before him caused him to urge caution and to oppose further prosecutions, he created a figure who has been perceived as exceptional.[10] Although the inquisitors treated in this book are far more likely to be classified as arch persecutors than as forward-thinking skeptics, their careers suggest that many elements of Salazar Frías's story were decidedly unexceptional. In the right circumstances, other junior inquisitors in district tribunals could, like Salazar Frías, trump their senior colleagues and persuade higher authorities of the validity of their opinions. Like his opposition to the Zugarramurdi trials, other particular local conflicts were also transmuted into legal precedent; he took his extensive consideration of a set of cases, his experience of visiting a tribunal's district, and his judicial practice and translated them into a broader theory. Through letters and first-person memoranda, he made that theory persuasive to an audience on the *Suprema*, ultimately altering the Spanish Inquisition's practices. Like some of the inquisitors examined in this book, he entered the Inquisition after holding ecclesiastical office in a cathedral, and he left a trail of writings in his wake. Early in his career, Salazar Frías wrote a local history; later, he wrote extensive memoranda in his inquisitorial capacities, including a brief autobiographical sketch, written in response to the *Suprema*'s request for reports of its officials' qualifications. While promoting reforms, he also promoted both the institution's judicial authority and his own; elevated to the *Suprema* a decade later, he remained a councillor until his death in 1635. The compelling tale of Salazar Frías hints at how much

---

Inquisition (Stroud, UK: Tempus, 2007), and, now, Eduardo Galván Rodríguez, *El Inquisidor General* (Madrid: Dykinson, 2010).

[10] Gustav Henningsen, *The Witches' Advocate: Basque Witchcraft and the Spanish Inquisition (1609–1614)* (Reno: University of Nevada Press, 1980); *The Salazar Documents: Inquisitor Alonso de Salazar Frías and Others on the Basque Witch Persecution* (Leiden and Boston: Brill, 2004); and "Alonso de Salazar Frías: Ese famoso inquisidor desconocido," in *Homenaje a Caro Baroja*, ed. Antonio Carreira, Jesús Antonio Cid, Manuel Gutiérrez Esteve, and Rogelio Rubio (Madrid: Centro de Investigaciones Sociológicas, 1978), 581–86. The following query exemplifies the way Salazar has entered recent historiography: "Whom should we regard as typical, the acutely sceptical Salazar or his two credulous and bitchy colleagues in the Logroño Inquisition?" Robin Briggs, *Witches and Neighbors: The Social and Cultural Context of European Witchcraft* (New York: Viking, 1996), 199. Caro Baroja also wrote about him. I am grateful to Lu Ann Homza for sharing with me her work in progress on this subject.

might be learned about the Inquisition by attending more closely to the individuals who staffed it.

This book spans the middle of the sixteenth to the middle of the seventeenth centuries – from the close of Charles V's reign through the first phases of Philip IV's – years identified as the height of the Spanish Inquisition's institutional influence and activity. The five inquisitors on whom it is centered – Cristóbal Fernández de Valtodano, Diego de Simancas, Luis de Páramo, Juan Adam de la Parra, and Juan de Mañozca y Zamora – were all born during the sixteenth century. For the oldest of them, the institution that they would serve had been established in their grandparents' time. Their lives offer glimpses of four overlapping generations of judicial practice, of how jurists made their careers in an institution that was already fairly well established within their society and its political order. As those who exercised the office at its apogee, their careers offer five approaches to examining a certain inquisitorial status quo, suggesting both the shared terrain and the variability in how they sought to voice, fit themselves to, and apply a fairly constant set of shared ideals and practices.[11] None were Inquisitors General, although three of the five sat on the *Suprema*. No selection of five such men can be representative of all Spanish inquisitors.

At any particular moment in the late sixteenth or early seventeenth century, between forty and seventy men were likely serving as inquisitors in the Spanish Inquisition's district tribunals and as councillors of the *Suprema*. In sum, I would estimate that a bit fewer than a thousand men – several hundred at the very least – were appointed to these offices between the 1540s and the 1650s.[12] Thus, the five subjects I have selected for study are meant to be suggestive of the range of inquisitorial experience. All had notable successes in their careers and brushes with life at

---

[11] For the characterization of the period 1569–1621 as "el apogeo del Santo Oficio," see *HIEA* 1:701.

[12] As the chapters that follow imply, in addition to the length of their service, the total number of individuals would be further reduced by the practices of transfer between tribunals and promotion to the *Suprema*. Although there were eventually twenty-one tribunals, several of them (including all three in the Americas) were founded during the century under consideration. For example, there were 158 appointments to the *Suprema* between 1539 and 1664, see n. 51. Thirty-seven inquisitors were appointed to Sicily's tribunal between 1543 and 1659, only sixteen were appointed to Mexico's tribunal between 1571 and 1642, while forty-two inquisitors were active in Valencia's between 1530 and 1609. Manuel Rivero Rodríguez, "La Inquisición Española en Sicilia," *HIEA* 3:1212–20; Martin Austin Nesvig, *Ideology and Inquisition: The World of the Censors in Early Mexico* (New Haven, CT, and London: Yale University Press, 2009), 274–75; García Cárcel, *Herejía y sociedad*, 127.

Court, although some also found their ambitions frustrated. Taken together, they illustrate possibilities for success and failure for that vast majority of inquisitors who never reached the helm of the institution. They held office in a variety of locales, each spending significant time in Castile, but their careers also encompass Rome, Sicily, and all three Inquisition districts in the Americas; three were promoted to the episcopate. In this way, they show the mobility and the polyvalence of inquisitorial careers, which served as vehicles to carry theoretical stances and practical experience between interconnected institutions and disparate places.

Following inquisitorial careers thus offers one way to bridge the gaps between studies centered on individual tribunals. Inquisitors operated in an argumentative culture that valued tradition and reviled innovation. When they confronted a new situation, they were charged to interpret the environment and to accommodate its peculiarities in a way that could fit within existing precedents, even as they might then use the experience of novelty to reshape practice and precedent. When inquisitors engaged in this negotiation between universal standards and local environments, between their experiences and the languages in which it was acceptable to communicate that experience, they drew together far-flung pieces of the Catholic Monarchy. They transported directives and their acquired knowledge between what is often referred to as center and periphery, but also from periphery to periphery, as, to take a particularly mobile example, in the early seventeenth-century career of Juan Gutiérrez Flores, who moved from the tribunal in Sicily to that on Mallorca, to Mexico City's, and finally to Lima's.

Each of the five inquisitors examined at length here has been offered as a face of the institution in some manner. Valtodano's contemporaries praised him as a model judge. Simancas was one of the foremost commentators on inquisitorial law; over the past century, he has attracted particular attention for his autobiographical *Vida*. Páramo gained fame for writing the first printed history of the Inquisition. Adam de la Parra has become known as a poet and propagandist, for his purported friendship with Francisco de Quevedo and his imprisonment in the waning months of the count-duke of Olivares's administration. Mañozca, on the other hand, has been depicted as an archetypal ambitious inquisitor, amassing power in colonial tribunals and driven by enmity, zeal, and greed. The chapters that follow seek, then, to assess what differentiated and what bound together these individual careers.

These inquisitors are also particularly apt subjects for study because each left a significant body of writings, albeit of varied kinds. Whereas three have become known to scholars, in large part, for what they wrote, the two with the most successful career trajectories – Valtodano and Mañozca, who sat on the *Suprema*, were nominated to be Chancery presidents, and ended their lives as archbishops – did not publish treatises. They established another relationship to the available modes of writing, producing extensive correspondence and substantive reports within their institutional contexts, some written in their own hand. When they appeared in print, it was as the objects of dedications, patrons praised as reformers by younger clerics. Thus, Mañozca took center stage in vernacular accounts of elaborate *autos de fe* and other religious celebrations. Attending to what inquisitors wrote, or did not write, provides an avenue to explore the complicated relationship of inquisitorial work to publicity and to secrecy; it illuminates both how they wrote their way into higher offices and also how too much writing – or writing of the wrong kind – could stall an inquisitor's professional ascent.

Inquisitors' work hinged, in part, on their writing abilities. Promotions were pursued, jurisdictional conflicts were argued, and a host of disputes were fought out in missives and memoranda, in print and manuscript compositions of greater or lesser formality, sometimes in Latin, usually in the vernacular Castilian Spanish. Judges in the district tribunals used letters to defend their judgments to the *Suprema*, the Inquisitor General, the king and his other councils, and even occasionally to the pope; the *Suprema*, in turn, communicated its decisions in the same manner. Inquisitors' writings form the backbone of this book. Although only Simancas has been perceived as writing an autobiography, all five constructed narratives of their lives as judges.[13] They turned to their pens to make their decisions comprehensible to their contemporaries and to supply their judgments with legitimacy. Hence, this study is based on their published writings and manuscript treatises, as well as the print and manuscript in which they or the cases in which they were involved appeared. It relies heavily on the Spanish Inquisition's internal correspondence sent between the *Suprema* and the district tribunals, as well as instructions, consultations, visitation and trial records, and accounts of *autos de fe*. It draws on other administrative documents as well, such as the reports of royal and ecclesiastical councils, the minutes of cathedral chapters, and the correspondence of bishops. Much has been written about the self-affirming

---

[13] I gesture here to Simancas's *Vida*, on that see Chapter 2, below. On autobiographical writing in early modern Spain, see especially James Amelang, *The Flight of Icarus: Artisan Autobiography in Early Modern Europe* (Stanford, CA: Stanford University Press, 1998).

qualities of the Inquisition's paperwork and the difficulties of using its trials as historical sources. Produced under significant duress, the testimony of defendants and witnesses was mediated by the notaries who recorded the proceedings and the inquisitors who posed the questions.

Yet it is also difficult to access individual inquisitors' experience of their work. Much of the correspondence of the tribunals and the *Suprema* was collective; it privileged consensus and was subject to the constraints of its institutional contexts and to rhetorical conventions. Used with caution, inquisitors' writings allow an examination of the idiom they created to make sense of their work and lend authority to it, individually and collectively. They can reveal elements of the judges' ideologies and the strategies they adopted to promote both what they perceived as reforms – religious, judicial, and administrative – and their material interests. They can indicate common patterns and refrains across an inquisitor's career and between inquisitors. Inquisitors drew on a language of virtue that repeatedly elevated prudence, justice, diligence, and conscience. They aspired, to varying extents, to the ideals of academic life, the lettered republic, the Tridentine pastor, the adept courtier, the wise councillor, the judicious administrator, the zealous inspector, the magnanimous patron, the devoted kinsman, the learned jurist, and the discerning judge. In sum, inquisitors' writings divulge the myriad negotiations that made up their careers. They indicate the multiple pressures that lay behind the scene of any trial, a scene that the judges framed as simultaneously an ideal site for administering religious justice and defending the faith and, like all worldly things, an arena susceptible to corruption. The office came with built-in tensions, and the humans who were appointed to it – who shaped it and were in turn shaped by it – further multiplied the negotiations inherent in any inquisitorial action. They navigated between their ambitions and the political possibilities, between laws and procedures and changeable human environments, and between the evidence of heretical threat and the politics of the courtroom.

In short, this book seeks to uncover the range of concerns that informed inquisitors' actions and the space that they had to maneuver in the world. It uses five case studies to explore how an inquisitor gained or lost authority, honor, and influence and to chart what he did with the social and political capital he acquired. Although careerism had a persistent presence in inquisitorial decisions, so too did varied ideals and the accumulation of practical experience, religious belief, and the hope of salvation. By focusing on the judges, this book suggests that the theory and regulations of the Inquisition were more rooted in local conditions, particular disputes, and individual experiences than has usually been asserted. Inquisitors were among their society's educated elite, men, some of them with considerable persuasive powers, for whom inquisitorial office was one piece of a varied career, and it was these characteristics that might account, in part, for their institution's surprising durability.[14]

A PECULIAR INSTITUTION: ORIGINS, PROCEDURES, TARGETS

The history of the Spanish Inquisition – as legal institution, social phenomena, or polemical tool – is both long and complex. Its roots stretch back into the juridical codes of Roman antiquity; more immediately, its practices were made possible by the revival and reworking of specific Roman legal procedures in courts across Europe, both secular and ecclesiastical, from the twelfth century onward. The law books prepared by inquisitors appropriated those precedents. Thus, when a Spanish jurist such as Simancas examined a point of inquisitorial law in the mid-sixteenth century, he did so with a reference to Ulpian (the highly influential Roman jurist and imperial officer of the third century), buttressed by a trio of legal authorities active in the late fifteenth and early sixteenth centuries (Philippus Decius, Andrea Alciato, and André Tiraqueau).[15] The institution took its name from a legal procedure, the *inquisitio*, or the searching for evidence in support of a formal charge. In medieval Europe, as Edward Peters has explained, it "came to designate the central role of the magistrate in all criminal cases – the obligation of finding out the truth in criminal matters."[16] In an inquisitorial system, the judge presided, investigated, and ultimately rendered a judgment. One effect of this legal revolution – in heresy inquisitions and elsewhere – was to increase the importance of the judge's role, to center the trial's progress on his exercise

---

[14] Cf. Henry Kamen, *The Spanish Inquisition: A Historical Revision* (New Haven, CT, and London: Yale University Press, 1997), 144; Bethencourt, *The Inquisition*, 442.

[15] The point being considered was what claim a spouse might lay to the confiscated goods of a heretic. Simancas, *Institutiones Catholicae* (Valladolid: Egidio de Colomies, 1552), fol. 32r. Another former inquisitor's library contained works of Decius, Alciato, and Tiraqueau. José García Oro and María José Portela Silva, "El arzobispo Valtodano (1570–1572). Un recuento de su Testamentaría," *Compostellanum* 50 (2005): 725–31. For more on the Inquisition's origins and its myths, see Edward Peters, *Inquisition* (Berkeley and Los Angeles: University of California Press, 1989); Doris Moreno Martínez, *La Invención de la Inquisición* (Madrid: Marcial Pons Historia, 2004).

[16] Peters, *Inquisition*, 17.

of discretion and pursuit of truth.[17] Heresy, moreover, came to be likened to treason against God, opening the way for the penalties for traitors to be employed in the pursuit of heretics as criminals.

From this twelfth-century legal ferment emerged heresy inquisitions: legal procedures governed by canon law and conducted by those holding delegated papal authority, designed to identify, investigate, and ultimately reconcile heretics (in this context, baptized Christians who had deviated from orthodoxy) to the Church. Although some of these investigations occurred on Iberian soil, the Spanish Inquisition did not have its specific incarnation until 1478, when Pope Sixtus IV authorized King Ferdinand of Aragon and Queen Isabel of Castile to oversee an inquisition in their crowns. The newly appointed inquisitors quickly initiated trials, and marked activity had already begun in the early 1480s, in Andalusia in particular. What distinguished the Spanish Inquisition, in part, was its surprising permanence. Despite significant resistance to its establishment – especially in the first decades, often from Catholic authorities – and persisting opposition, it was not abolished until 1834.[18] The pursuit of heretics had previously been undertaken on temporary delegations of papal authority, sometimes as a criminal matter by secular officials, or as a right and charge of bishops, who had the authority of inquisitors within their dioceses. In relatively short order, however, the Spanish Inquisition refigured this terrain, as it grew from a handful of inquisitor delegates into a regularized institution headed by an Inquisitor General and consisting of a royal council, numerous local tribunals, and a wide variety of official staff and loose associates; it became, in essence, a new branch of governance with a hybrid papal-royal mandate. Its foundation was thus also bound up with the new political equilibrium that Ferdinand and Isabel sought to establish in their kingdoms. King João III founded an institutionalized Portuguese Inquisition in 1536, and Pope Paul IV reformed the

---

[17] See also the superb explanation of arbitrative justice – a system predicated on the judge's capacity for reasoned deliberation – in William Monter, *Judging the French Reformation: Heresy Trials by Sixteenth-Century Parlements* (Cambridge, MA: Harvard University Press, 1999).

[18] On both dissent against the Spanish Inquisition – from an array of sources – and on the building of its institutional authority, see especially Stefania Pastore, *Il Vangelo e la Spada. L'Inquisizione di Castiglia e i Suoi Critici (1460–1598)* (Rome: Edizioni di Storia e Letteratura, 2003); Moreno, *La Invención*; Michaela Valente, *Contro L'Inquisizione. Il dibattito europeo secc. XVI–XVIII* (Turin: Claudiana, 2009); Peters, *Inquisition*. For another approach to the question of resistance to the Spanish and Portuguese Inquisitions, see Miriam Bodian, *Dying in the Law of Moses: Crypto-Jewish Martyrdom in the Iberian World* (Bloomington: Indiana University Press, 2007).

Roman Inquisition in 1542.[19] Although independent entities with distinct practices, these three early modern inquisitions also had complicated ties to one another through the papal authority by which they operated, as well as through correspondence and their corpus of legal theory.

Supposedly relapsed *conversos* comprised the bulk of those tried by the Spanish Inquisition in the first four decades, the most violent of its long history. The pursuit of so-called Judaizing heresy was central to the framing of the institution in the papal bull conceding its authority and the jockeying that led up to its concession, in the monarchs' instructions to authorities in Aragon and Castile, and in polemical histories that memorialized their reign.[20] Historians often chart the origins of these conflicts about the status of *conversos* in Iberian society to 1391, when anti-Jewish violence swept across the peninsula, violence that included a critical mass of forced baptisms and other conversions to Christianity under duress. The conflicts leading up to the foundation of the Spanish Inquisition and its initial decades, in particular, have produced a host of interpretive debates. At issue for fifteenth-century religious authorities was the very efficacy of conversion; one contemporary justification for the Inquisition was that it would prevent the "contamination" of sincerely Christian *conversos* by their Judaizing associates. Recent scholarship has, in turn, explored questions of how to gauge religious identity, the coherence of *conversos* as a group, the relationship between persecution and state formation, and whether racism was the principal motivation for the Inquisition's establishment. Historians have also shown how the Inquisition quickly came to be used as a tool in a variety of local conflicts and embedded in a host of social and economic rivalries.[21]

---

[19] I use the Spanish Inquisition, the Inquisition, and, occasionally, the Holy Office, interchangeably to refer to that institution and its constituent tribunals; when I mention other inquisitions, I specify which.

[20] See Miguel Jiménez Monteserín, *Introducción a la Inquisición española* (Madrid: Editora Nacional, 1980), 50–62; Lu Ann Homza, ed. and trans., *The Spanish Inquisition 1478–1614. An Anthology of Sources* (Indianapolis, IN, and Cambridge, MA: Hackett Publishing Company, Inc., 2006), 1–12. There is excellent and extensive scholarship on Catholic authorities' constructions of Jewish-Christian difference, including on the concept of "Judaizing"; the verb itself can be traced to the Pauline epistles, Gal 2:14.

[21] To approach these debates, see Benzion Netanyahu, *The Origins of the Inquisition in Fifteenth-Century Spain* (New York: Random House, 1995); R. I. Moore, *The Formation of a Persecuting Society: Power and Deviance in Western Europe, 950–1250* (Oxford, UK: Blackwell Publishers, 1987); David Nirenberg, *Communities of Violence: Persecution of Minorities in the Middle Ages* (Princeton, NJ: Princeton University Press, 1996); "Mass Conversion and Genealogical Mentalities: Jews and Christians in Fifteenth-Century Spain," *Past and Present* 174 (2002): 3–41; Pastore, *Il Vangelo e la Spada*; Renée Levine Melammed, *Heretics or Daughters of Israel? The Crypto-Jewish Women of Castile* (New York: Oxford University Press, 1999); Gretchen Starr-Lebeau, *In the*

What the conditions in fifteenth-century Spain catalyzed, to borrow David Nirenberg's formulation, was a "crisis of classification and identification": as the aftermath of the anti-Jewish violence of 1391 created an influx of *conversos*, the boundaries that divided religious communities grew less clear.[22] It was in this environment that Spanish inquisitors carved out their social role. Numerous scholars have shown how the Inquisition both played into and intensified categorical thinking. For example, Gretchen Starr-Lebeau found in her study of trials in Guadalupe in 1485 a transformation in the perception of religious identity: that the Spanish Inquisition created power in "its ability to construct difference out of ambiguity."[23]

Whereas the Spanish Inquisition construed its jurisdiction as extending only to those who could be classified as Christians, the study of it is bound up with that of other initiatives that dismantled the religious toleration that had existed in the polities of earlier medieval Iberia. So it is frequently connected to purity of blood statutes: regulations passed by a host of religious and secular bodies that prohibited officeholding by those who could not demonstrate the absence of Jewish or Muslim ancestry. Likewise, its foundation is often seen as intertwined with Ferdinand and Isabel's 1492 expulsion of Spain's Jewish population. The polemical literature of the era knitted these events together. The fifteenth-century chronicler and cleric Andrés Bernáldez, a partisan of Isabel, exemplified the stark dichotomies and poisonous stereotyping that fueled such actions, writing events from 1390 to the 1480s as a unified history of combat against "heretical Mosaic depravity."[24] Jewish expulsion chronicles also made the suffering from 1391 to 1492 and its aftermath all of one piece in their lamentations.[25]

Shadow of the Virgin: Inquisitors, Friars, and Conversos in Guadalupe, Spain (Princeton, NJ: Princeton University Press, 2003); Béatrice Perez, *Inquisition, Pouvoir, Société. La province de Séville et ses judéoconvers sous les Rois Catholiques* (Paris: Honoré Champion Éditeur, 2007).

[22] Nirenberg, "Mass Conversion," 11.

[23] Starr-LeBeau, *In the Shadow of the Virgin*, 6.

[24] Translated in Homza, *The Spanish Inquisition*, 1. On Bernáldez as a chronicler, see Richard L. Kagan, *Clio and the Crown: The Politics of History in Medieval and Early Modern Spain* (Baltimore, MD: The Johns Hopkins University Press, 2009), chap. 1; see also Nirenberg, "Mass Conversion," 27, 33.

[25] David Raphael, *The Expulsion 1492 Chronicles: An Anthology of Medieval Chronicles Relating to the Expulsion of the Jews from Spain and Portugal* (North Hollywood, CA: Carmi House Press, 1992); on the flourishing of Jewish historical writing after 1492, see Yosef Yerushalmi, *Zakhor. Jewish History and Jewish Memory* (Seattle: University of Washington Press, 1982).

What happened over the sixteenth and seventeenth centuries, however, was not inscribed before 1500, even when later actors justified their decisions by invoking the 1480s and 1490s. After the 1492 conquest of Granada, expulsions of the Muslim population of Castile and Aragon did not occur until 1500 and 1526. The expulsion of Spain's *moriscos* – the descendants of Christian converts from Islam – between 1609 and 1614 was, in contradistinction to what had occurred in 1492, of those at least nominally Christian. There was a tolerated Jewish population in Spanish Oran until the middle of the seventeenth century, and there were exceptional cases of Jews granted licenses to live in Spain.[26] Despite the extensive use of purity of blood language, only in the 1570s did the Spanish Inquisition set a standardized process for investigating the genealogies of those who sought its offices and jurisdictional protections. The purity of blood statutes were, moreover, subjected to serious and viable challenges, especially in the early decades of the seventeenth century.[27]

Eventually, there were twenty-one local tribunals of the Spanish Inquisition, seated in cities and each with a district subject to its jurisdiction. The first decade of their formation – 1482 to 1493 – spread a tribunal presence across much of Iberia; the districts and their headquarters were in flux, however, into the early sixteenth century. Over that century, some of the monarchy's frontier zones were incorporated into the institution:

[26] On the persistence, revival, and remembrance of Muslim communities in Spain, see A. Katie Harris, *From Muslim to Christian Granada: Inventing a City's Past in Early Modern Spain* (Baltimore, MD: The Johns Hopkins University Press, 2007); Kathryn Miller, *Guardians of Islam: Religious Authority and Muslim Communities of Late Medieval Spain* (New York: Columbia University Press, 2008). For exceptional instances of toleration, see Jean-Frédéric Schaub, *Les juifs du roi d'Espagne* (Paris: Hachette, 1999); Mercedes García-Arenal and Gerard Albert Wiegers, *A Man of Three Worlds: Samuel Pallache, a Moroccan Jew in Catholic and Protestant Europe*, trans. Martin Beagles (Baltimore, MD: The Johns Hopkins University Press, 2003); Gretchen Starr-LeBeau, *In the Shadow of the Virgin*, has noted the equally exceptional expulsion of *conversos* from Guadalupe, ordered unilaterally by the Inquisitor General in 1500. For an excellent approach to such questions, see Mercedes García-Arenal, "Religious Dissent and Minorities: The Morisco Age," *Journal of Modern History* 81 (2009): 888–920.

[27] Officials drew on old arguments; Eymeric's fourteenth-century manual had urged the exclusion of the descendants of heretics from inquisitorial office into the second or third generation, while late fifteenth-century inquisitorial instructions stipulated vaguely that officials be models of honorable conduct. J. Meseguer Fernández, "Las primeras estructuras del Santo Oficio," *HIEA* 1:370–79; López Vela, "Estructuras administrativas del Santo Oficio," *HIEA*, 2:226–71; Albert A. Sicroff, *Les Controverses des Statuts de 'Pureté de Sang' en Espagne du XVe au XVIIe Siècle* (Paris: Didier, 1960); Henry Kamen, "A Crisis of Conscience in Golden Age Spain: The Inquisition against Limpieza de Sangre," in Kamen, *Crisis and Change in Early Modern Spain* (Aldershot, UK and Brookfield, VT: Variorum, 1993), 1–27.

Navarre, Granada, Galicia, Mexico, and Peru. In the seventeenth century, a tribunal was founded in Cartagena de Indias – a nod to the importance of that port's location on the Caribbean – and, finally, after years of negotiations, at Court in Madrid. The result was fourteen peninsular tribunals, three in the Americas, and four island establishments (in the Canaries, the Balearics, Sardinia, and Sicily).[28] Tribunal foundation was also an important focus of dissent, often from other local authorities or those whose jurisdictions were liable to diminish. Naples, a Spanish viceroyalty, successfully resisted the establishment of a tribunal; rumors of plans to impose one were rife in the sixteenth-century Netherlands and informed civil unrest and revolt there.[29]

The institution's organization drew on a fundamentally urban model of life; even in Castile's farming regions, inhabitants tended to reside in a town from which they walked to the fields each day.[30] In theory, it also drew on an administrative model that assumed the possibility of replicating organs of governance across diverse geographies, human and physical. Or, as the revised legal code for the Americas put this mirroring principle: "Inasmuch as the kingdoms of Castile and of the Indies are under one Crown, the laws and the manner of government of the one should conform as nearly as possible to those of the other."[31] Each tribunal was subject to the complex and simultaneous interplay of a host of local circumstances and interests with more universal notions of law, justice, and orthodoxy, themselves in the midst of persistent renegotiation and reform.[32]

---

[28] Here I follow Jaime Contreras and Jean-Pierre Dedieu, "Estructuras geográficas del Santo Oficio en España," *HIEA*, 2:3–47.

[29] Each saw, instead, a variety of other kinds of anti-heretical operations: royal edicts and punishments by secular judges, papally delegated inquisitors, and episcopal inquisitions. Alastair Duke, *Dissident Identities in the Early Modern Low Countries*, ed. Judith Pollmann and Andrew Spicer (Farnham, UK, and Burlington, VT: Ashgate, 2009); Aline Goosens, *Les Inquisitions modernes dans les pays-bas méridionaux, 1520–1633*, 2 vols. (Brussels: Éditions Université de Bruxelles, 1997–98); Monter, *Frontiers of Heresy*; Peter Mazur, "Negotiating with the Inquisition. *Conversos*, the Holy Office, and the Viceroy of Naples, 1569–1582," *Archivio Italiano per la storia della pietà* 20 (2007): 39–54.

[30] Helen Nader, *Liberty in Absolutist Spain: The Habsburg Sale of Towns, 1516–1700* (Baltimore, MD: The Johns Hopkins University Press, 1990).

[31] *Recopilación de Leyes de Indias*, lib. II, tit. ii, ley 13, quoted in J. H. Parry, *The Audiencia of New Galicia in the Sixteenth Century: A Study in Spanish Colonial Government* (Cambridge, UK: Cambridge University Press, 1948), 4.

[32] For examples of such complex interactions, see Contreras, *Sotos contra Riquelmes*; Starr-LeBeau, *In the Shadow of the Virgin*. On how resistance to the Inquisition drew from currents both particular and universal, see Pastore, *Il Vangelo e la Spada*. For the centrality of the negotiation between the local and the universal to understanding early modern

Conditions on the ground were not, of course, equal. The district of Valladolid covered close to 90,000 square kilometers, that of Córdoba closer to 27,000, and the one based in Mexico City included the Philippines, a whole ocean away.[33] In such a landscape, the person who arrived bearing official authority and its signs did much to define the amount of inquisitorial activity and the character it assumed.[34]

The first decades of the Spanish Inquisition saw significant contestation of its institutional structure. After 1518, a single Inquisitor General was at its helm. Also above the local tribunals was a royal council, the *Suprema*, with several members (the number and their activity varied). It served as the tribunals' appellate court, ordering consultation on serious cases, and supervised the administration of the tribunals, including appointments to offices. It was a legal institution of mixed jurisdiction, straddling royal and papal authority. Thus, the king nominated the Inquisitor General, and a papal bull confirmed the choice. This mirrored the privilege of appointment of bishops and archbishops that Spanish kings had likewise acquired from the papacy. The Inquisitor General, in turn, recommended candidates for the *Suprema* to the king, although the precise relationship between the Inquisitor General and council was not codified. In the seventeenth century, for instance, councillors debated whether he had the right to preside in their sessions. Papal briefs also sometimes shaped the Inquisition's activities, for example, curtailing cases against Portuguese *conversos* in the early seventeenth century. In the famous sixteenth-century heresy trial of the archbishop of Toledo, the defendant managed to recuse the Inquisitor General and two councillors of the *Suprema*, papal legates were sent to Spain to investigate the case and negotiate with the king, and it was eventually revoked for judgment to the papal court in Rome.[35]

The jurisdictional relationships between inquisitors and bishops – who were the so-called ordinary (as opposed to extraordinary) inquisitors in their dioceses – remained a point of contention. Some crimes, moreover, were tried in secular, episcopal, and inquisitorial courts in early modern

Catholicism more broadly, see especially Sara Nalle, *God in La Mancha: Religious Reform and the People of Cuenca, 1500–1650* (Baltimore, MD: The Johns Hopkins University Press, 1992); William Christian, *Local Religion in Sixteenth-Century Spain* (Princeton, NJ: Princeton University Press, 1981); Simon Ditchfield, *Liturgy, Sanctity and History in Tridentine Italy* (Cambridge, UK, and New York: Cambridge University Press, 1995).

[33] For these calculations of district size, see Contreras and Dedieu, "Estructuras geográficas," 10.

[34] This can also be seen in anxieties around imposture. Javier Villa-Flores, "Wandering Swindlers: Imposture, Style, and the Inquisition's Pedagogy of Fear in Colonial Mexico," *Colonial Latin American Review* 17 (2008): 251–72.

[35] I refer here to the case of Bartolomé Carranza, about which see Chapters 1 and 2.

Spain.[36] Inquisitors frequently bumped into the jurisdiction of civil judges, the most important of whom sat in the two Chanceries, located after 1505 in Valladolid and Granada. In their education, their career trajectories, and in the law that they drew upon and elaborated, inquisitors shared much with both the civil judiciary and the canonists.[37] The *Suprema*, moreover, formed part of the growing conciliar structure of the Habsburg monarchy and jockeyed with other councils for authority. For instance, when Spanish inquisitors and Spanish viceroys came into conflict in Sicily, the *Suprema* and the Council of Italy (itself reorganized in the mid-sixteenth century) were integral players in the ensuing negotiations.

The funding of the Spanish Inquisition was a similarly complicated affair. Like seemingly all early modern institutions, each of its organs perpetually proclaimed financial shortfalls. Its monies came from the crown, from accumulated rents and properties, from the goods confiscated in heresy trials, and from cathedral prebends reserved as inquisitorial income.[38]

When a heresy trial was conducted, guilt was presumed; confession was the most authoritative proof and the desired means of provoking a penitential reconciliation to the body of the Church. There were guidelines for judicial procedure. Inquisitors proclaimed edicts that announced heretical crimes; these often inaugurated a grace period when those who confessed would receive a light penalty. Those tried either denounced themselves or were denounced by others. When a critical mass of proof had been obtained, inquisitors might vote to initiate a trial and imprison the accused, who would remain in custody for the rest of his or her trial; the accused's goods would be inventoried and confiscated. Witness testimony was ratified and rendered secret, the eliding of witnesses' names justified by the likelihood of reprisals against them. In a series of audiences, the accused

---

[36] On the complicated relationships between bishops and inquisitors and disputes over confessional practices, see Pastore, *Il Vangelo e la Spada*. For earlier efforts to distinguish sacramental confession from confession in heresy trials, see Ames, *Righteous Persecution*, 179. For negotiations between a monastic order and the Inquisition about jurisdiction over investigations within the order, see Starr-LeBeau, *In the Shadow of the Virgin*. Multiple courts sometimes claimed the right to judge crimes like sodomy or witchcraft; for a detailed examination of the latter, see María Tausiet, *Ponzoña en los ojos: brujería y superstición en Aragón en el siglo XVI* (Madrid: Turner, 2004).

[37] On legal culture and legal institutions, see Richard L. Kagan, *Lawsuits and Litigants in Castile, 1500–1700* (Chapel Hill: The University of North Carolina Press, 1981).

[38] For an overview, see J. Martínez Millán, "Estructura de la hacienda de la Inquisición," *HIEA* 2:885–1075; B. Escandell Bonet, "Estructuras económicas de la Inquisición indiana," *HIEA* 2:1077–1105.

was admonished to confess and questioned by the inquisitors; the prosecutor published the charges and made his case; the defendant responded orally – sometimes also in writing, sometimes with the aid of legal counsel – and might seek to guess at and disqualify witnesses or call other witnesses for the defense. Notaries recorded the proceedings and the records were archived, with few allowed access. A representative of the local bishop – given his authority as an ordinary inquisitor – was often present during trial proceedings or consultations. The judges conferred on the case and might appeal to the *Suprema* for direction, search their archives, or write to other tribunals for information; they sometimes called in consultants to assess difficult theological or legal issues.[39] When they had what they deemed to be strong half-proofs (witness testimony that did not precisely coincide, for instance), they might vote that the accused be tortured. Three methods seem to have been used: water torture that simulated drowning (*toca*), a pulley (*garrucha*), and the rack (*potro*). Torture was argued to have an interrogative purpose, to elicit confession, the "queen of proofs." Inquisitors were dubious about confessions obtained under torture and required later ratification of the testimony obtained by that means.[40] The length of trials varied widely as did the resolution; there were occasionally exonerations and some defendants were not found guilty of their supposed crimes and were released, with their trials "suspended." Although often effectively an acquittal, suspension of a case also left open the possibility that it could be resumed at some later date.

Like civil trials, they concluded with an *auto* – a judicial act – sometimes conducted privately within the tribunal; alternatively, this developed into the infamous *auto de fe*, a public ceremony of varying scale that put on display the convicted heretics – dressed in penitential garb (the *sanbenito*) – their crimes, and the punishments.[41] Light abjurations and penances were assigned for some crimes; more serious sentences included exile (usually for a fixed term), flogging, galley service, reclusion to a monastery, and perpetual prison, which, despite the name, tended not to extend beyond three years or so. There was also capital punishment that, although termed

---

[39] From the mid-sixteenth century, this became the primary site of involvement by theologians (as versus jurists), often members of the regular orders. A similar process of deliberation and consultation developed to censor books.

[40] Edward Peters, *Torture* (Philadelphia: University of Pennsylvania Press, 1996).

[41] Bethencourt, *The Inquisition*; Alejandro Cañeque, "Theater of Power: Writing and Representing the Auto de Fe in Colonial Mexico," *The Americas* 52 (1996): 321–43; Maureen Flynn, "Mimesis of the Last Judgment: The Spanish *Auto de fe*," *Sixteenth Century Journal* 22 (1991): 281–97.

and practiced as "relaxation to the secular arm," in keeping with the clerical ban on bloodshed, was essentially an outcome of the inquisitorial process and perceived as such. Those sentenced to death, by burning at the stake, were generally relapsed heretics, that is, those who had been once reconciled for their transgressions and re-offended. Documentation – and the survival of what was written – was much lower in the first forty years than it would be later; the rates of execution and torture among those tried then seem to have been quite high. Examining the subsequent period, historians have discovered that the total trial rate was low, and the number tortured or executed even smaller. Henningsen and Jaime Contreras drew upon the summaries of cases sent to the *Suprema* to calculate that about 45,000 trials were held in Spain between 1540 and 1700, that of those tried 1.8 percent were executed, another 1.7 percent were burnt in effigy, and less than 5 percent were subjected to torture.[42]

Following its first decades, in which intense persecution focused on *conversos* charged as Judaizers, the courts turned their attention to other targets. Dedieu sketched out four phases of inquisitorial activity, based upon his research in the archive of Toledo's tribunal. The second of these, from around 1525 through the first quarter of the seventeenth century, centered on Protestants (generally lumped together as "Lutherans"), *moriscos*, and increasingly so-called Old Christians for offenses ranging from blasphemy to bigamy to false witness; charges were brought against priests who solicited in the confessional and those who pretended to be priests. Part and parcel of these changing emphases was the increasing involvement of the Inquisition in book censorship; it began issuing indices of prohibited books in the 1550s, and the lists dramatically expanded in the 1580s.[43] These were the years of the Inquisition's greatest institutional

---

[42] This approach tends to minimize more violent outbreaks of persecution. Similarly, due to insufficient evidence, the first six decades of the Inquisition – probably its bloodiest – are exempted. Jaime Contreras and Gustav Henningsen, "Cases of the Spanish Inquisition (1540–1700): Analysis of a Historical Data Bank," in *The Inquisition in Early Modern Europe: Studies on Sources and Methods*, ed. Henningsen and John Tedeschi (DeKalb: Northern Illinois University Press, 1986), 100–29. Cf. the estimate that around 30 percent of those tried in Guadalupe in 1485 were executed and nearly all those tried in the town of Belalcazar in that epoch, Starr-LeBeau, *In the Shadow of the Virgin*. Perhaps as many as 2,000 people were executed and 15,000 reconciled from 1480 to 1530, Rawlings, *The Spanish Inquisition*.

[43] There is much debate about whether such initiatives began a kind of intellectual closing of Spain from the middle of the sixteenth century. For this thesis, see Marcel Bataillon, *Erasme et l'Espagne*, ed. Daniel Devoto and Charles Amiel, 3 vols. (1937; Geneva: Droz, 1991). For a response to Bataillon, see Lu Ann Homza, *Religious Authority in the Spanish Renaissance* (Baltimore, MD, and London: The Johns Hopkins University Press,

force, and the focus of trials varied over time and place. William Monter has shown, for example, the use of the Inquisition to try sodomy cases and the greater propensity to impose sentences of galley service in the crown of Aragon's tribunals. The third epoch – the remainder of the seventeenth century and opening years of the eighteenth – saw diminishing activity overall, coupled with a renewed emphasis on Judaizing trials against *conversos*, particularly those of Portuguese origin. In the final era, the number of cases was low, and Enlightenment ideas were an object of concern.[44] Nevertheless, the implications in the life of the individual tried were never insubstantial. Aside from the duration and hardship of the trial, the tribunal also became a site that deauthorized (or, through not censuring, implicitly authorized) an individual with a reputation for sanctity.[45] As even the Inquisition's 1498 instructions reflected, the material consequences extended not only to the individual, but also to family members, who stood to lose property and honor, have their marriage and career prospects compromised, and risked establishing an archival record of their suspicious nature, available to be consulted in the future. In the face of this, there is evidence of significant legal strategizing by Inquisition defendants.[46]

2000). On censorship, see Virgilio Pinto Crespo, *Inquisición y control ideológico en la España del siglo XVI* (Madrid: Taurus Ediciones, 1983); recently, Nesvig, *Ideology and Inquisition*. See also the evidence of a persisting range of debate and thought across Spanish society in Kamen, *The Spanish Inquisition*; Stuart Schwartz, *All Can Be Saved: Religious Tolerance and Salvation in the Iberian Atlantic World* (New Haven, CT: Yale University Press, 2008).

[44] Dedieu, *L'Administration de la foi*; Monter, *Frontiers of Heresy*. Still, throughout the seventeenth and well into the eighteenth centuries, some of the most severe instances of inquisitorial persecution targeted Judaizers.

[45] For example, in the later sixteenth century, Inquisition trials halted the prophetic careers of Lucrecia de León and Miguel de Piedrola, Kagan, *Lucrecia's Dreams*; Kagan and Abigail Dyer, eds. and trans., *Inquisitorial Inquiries. Brief Lives of Secret Jews and Other Heretics* (Baltimore, MD, and London: The Johns Hopkins University Press, 2004), chap. 3. For further consideration of inquisitorial courts as sites that sought to arbitrate sanctity see Anne Jacobson Schutte, *Aspiring Saints: Pretense of Holiness, Inquisition, and Gender in the Republic of Venice, 1618–1750* (Baltimore, MD, and London: The Johns Hopkins University Press, 2001); Andrew Keitt, *Inventing the Sacred: Imposture, Inquisition, and the Boundaries of the Supernatural in Golden Age Spain* (Leiden and Boston: Brill, 2005).

[46] Nathan Wachtel has argued, in studying the Portuguese Inquisition, that defensive strategies were transmitted across generations of crypto-Jewish families; see *La logique des bûchers* (Paris: Seuil, 2009). Reports of prison collaboration and strategizing were not uncommon; see, for instance, Starr-LeBeau, *In the Shadow of the Virgin*; Homza, *Religious Authority*, chap. 1.

THE DEVELOPMENT OF AN OFFICE

In the local tribunals, the inquisitors were the senior officials. They judged cases and oversaw the administration of their court and its district. The recommendation was that there be at least two inquisitors in every tribunal. Between the mid-sixteenth and mid-seventeenth centuries, the evidence I have seen suggests that the number of inquisitors active at the same time was as high as four. It was also not infrequent for there to be only one inquisitor for some periods, especially following the death of a colleague; moreover, inquisitors were sometimes away from the tribunal because of illness or while pursuing business in the district or serving other official charges. Most of the year, the inquisitors held audiences in the morning and in the afternoon, with a break at midday. At least the senior inquisitor tended to live in the tribunal building. As administrators, they oversaw a large staff, the court's finances, and its secret archives; they corresponded about judicial and administrative matters with the *Suprema* and the Inquisitor General and directed preparations for *autos de fe*. They also had a mandate – much like that of bishops – to visit the tribunal district. On these visitations, inquisitors traveled with a notary in tow, soliciting denunciations and often assigning penances, collecting fines, and reconciling those who confessed to them on the spot. The conditions on visitations could be difficult for a variety of reasons. The Toledo inquisitors, for example, found the summer heat grueling and their visitations decreased markedly in the later sixteenth century; the Palermo inquisitors reported great difficulty finding a suitable house in which to lodge in Messina.[47]

The general shape of tribunal staffing – aside from the inquisitors nearly all laypeople – remained fairly constant between the mid-sixteenth and mid-seventeenth centuries. In addition to the inquisitors, there was a prosecutor, the *fiscal*, who in some circumstances also exercised considerable influence in a tribunal, and other lawyers, assigned to the prisoners' defense or acting as additional legal officers. Notaries and secretaries recorded the trial proceedings and had their hands in correspondence and the maintenance of the archives; an accounting staff dealt with the confiscated goods. In most cases, the tribunal maintained its own prison – in which those on trial were housed – and so also a prison staff of a warden and associates. There was also a medical doctor. On an ad hoc basis, the Inquisition called theological consultants to weigh testimony and the

---

[47] See Chapters 1 and 3. Cf. Nalle, "Inquisitors, Priests, and the People."

contents of books. The inquisitors occasionally left the tribunal in the care of a temporary deputy; out in the districts, they appointed standing commissaries to serve in their stead, surrogates with a limited array of powers. The tribunals also appointed lay assistants, known as familiars, who gave at least a nominal presence in more remote places. The benefits of such appointments could be substantial: just as an inquisitorial prosecution could mar a family's honor, having inquisitorial officials in the family could be used as proof of honorable lineage. It was also a jurisdictional boon, as familiars and other officials could have their civil and criminal affairs tried before the inquisitors. Thus, the judges dealt with more than trials of faith.

The *Suprema* maintained a similar staff. In each of the years between 1555 and 1565, annual salaries were listed for the Inquisitor General, between four and seven councillors, two to three secretaries of varying degrees of importance, a *fiscal*, a reporter (*relator*) who prepared information for the council, a constable (*alguacil mayor*), a medical doctor, a nuncio, two porters, and an official who was both the receiver and accountant. The salaries held fairly steady over this period, with the Inquisitor General allotted 400,000 *maravedís*; the councillors 150,000 each (or occasionally 100,000); and the porters, the lowest paid, 25,000 each. After 1561, most of the members' salaries doubled to 300,000, whereas the Inquisitor General's increased to 600,000 in 1568.[48] By comparison, during the sixteenth century, inquisitors in Córdoba's tribunal drew between 100,000 and 150,000 *maravedís* annually in regular salary and extra disbursements. Judges in the royal courts of appeal earned the same. Such salaries put them many orders of magnitude below the expenditures of the wealthier nobility, but at annual incomes roughly ten times that of a middling family in a Castilian town. Pay seems to have continued rising in the early seventeenth century. At times of crisis, however, revenues might dry up entirely; in the 1640s, many inquisitorial judges and officials found themselves without royal salaries.[49]

---

[48] AHN, Inq., lib. 248, fols. 71, 72v-73r, 75v-76r, 78, 90v-91r, 94v-95r, 101v-102r, 106r, 118r-19r, 143r, 148v-49r, 181v. These sources also have been used extensively in Sánchez Rivilla, "Inquisidores," and Martínez Millán, "Estructura de la hacienda."

[49] Fernand Braudel, drawing on Noël Salomon's research from the *relaciones geográficas*, estimated such family income at around 15,522 maravedís per year in the later 1570s; see *The Mediterranean and the Mediterranean World in the Age of Philip II*, trans. Siân Reynolds (New York: Harper and Row, 1972), 1:456. See also Martínez Millán, "Estructura de la hacienda," 978–79; López Vela, "Sociología de los Cuadros Inquisitoriales," *HIEA* 2:758–59; Kagan, *Lawsuits and Litigants*.

In the daily discharge of their office, inquisitors negotiated their authority over other inquisitorial officials, the accused, and the local population of the tribunal's district. They vied and collaborated with municipal officials; other clerics, regular and secular; and royal judges. They also contended with one another, even as they were ranked by seniority (that was also sometimes disputed) and voted in the tribunal and on the *Suprema* in that order. Their actions were also circumscribed: they might exercise wide judicial discretion but they worked in a court subject to both king and pope, and they were often checked by higher royal and ecclesiastical authorities or by visitations, the primary mode of inspection and auditing. They were notable both as recipients and distributors of patronage. In the time under consideration here – from mid-century to mid-century – although inquisitors in Spain tended to have a common profile, there were no detailed regulations on the criteria for appointment. Mostly jurists and secular clerics, they were unlike many of their medieval predecessors and the majority of late-fifteenth-century Spanish inquisitors, who were Dominicans, often with degrees in theology. By the later sixteenth century, theologians engaged more in the work of consultation than of judgment, and there were few regular clerics among the judges. In the earlier eighteenth century, the Society of Jesus would have a presence among the inquisitors. In Portugal's Inquisition, there was a strong preference toward those with degrees in canon law; in Italy's tribunals, however, inquisitors tended to be drawn from the mendicant orders, initially often Franciscans, more usually Dominicans after the mid-sixteenth century. In each of the early modern inquisitions, promotion from inquisitor to bishop was a fairly common pattern.[50]

Predictably, the *Suprema's* councillors tended to be better connected and more accomplished than their provincial counterparts. About two-thirds of the 158 appointees to the council between 1541 and 1664 had previous experience of some kind in an Inquisition tribunal, usually as inquisitors, a pattern that intensified markedly after 1566. Several were married laymen. All those nominated Inquisitor General between 1539 and 1596 were members of the *Suprema*, though most had not previously served in a regional tribunal. In the first half of the seventeenth century, the cumulative profile remained roughly the same, but there were signal appointments of theologians, members of the higher nobility, and Dominican friars who had also held high office in their order. Although

---

[50] For a comparative summary of inquisitorial profiles, see Bethencourt, *The Inquisition*, 135–45.

the Inquisitors General tended to hold that office – often at the same time as other elite charges – until their deaths, seats on the *Suprema* were ideally stepping-stones to bishoprics, archbishoprics, and presidencies of royal councils.[51]

Basing their work on close readings of tribunal records, historians have suggested a range of inquisitorial practice. The ebb and flow of activity in the district courts has been attributed to initiatives from above and to the inclinations, health, and commitment of the inquisitors; inquisitors and tribunal officials sometimes sued one another and slung accusations of negligence, laxity, incompetence, partisan dealings, excessive zeal, greed, and graft. Sara Nalle has shown the experience and knowledge of defendants that judges could acquire, as long-serving inquisitors in Cuenca were baffled for years over the case of a self-proclaimed messiah who kept turning up in court, eventually tabling proceedings against him on grounds of insanity. She has also observed the complexities of distinguishing religious authority in early modern Spain, as the commissaries who were the face of the Inquisition in remote areas were also often parish priests.[52] Other historians have emphasized the inquisitors' remove from those they tried. Bartolomé Bennassar stressed the inquisitors' exercise of a pedagogy of fear, framed as in the interest of the public good. Studying Valencia, Ricardo García Cárcel found the judges as, in one sense, agents of Castilian power, using trials to quash members of a "counterculture." Assessing the tribunal in Santiago de Compostela, Contreras observed that the power and efficiency of the inquisitor lay in freedom from local ties. At the same time, he saw a tremendous gap between rhetoric and realities on the ground; many inquisitors neglected the tribunal's business, and particularly in distant locales, the rigor and intensity of practice tended to depend on the work ethic of the judges. Carlo Ginzburg turned the question another way, reading the gap between inquisitors and the populace they encountered as akin to that between anthropologists and their subjects. Thus, he described them as observers of an alien culture, foreigners and

[51] To offer these observations, I have drawn on the invaluable data assembled by Sánchez Rivilla in "Inquisidores." There were 17 appointments made to the post of Inquisitor General between 1539 and 1664. Of those elevated to the *Suprema*, it seems that 91 had been tribunal inquisitors, 13 had some other previous Inquisition experience, while 54 did not. There was a marked shift to promoting from within the hierarchy after 1566. Between 1541 and 1566, 17 of the 23 councillors appointed had no prior inquisitorial experience. See also Martínez Millán, "Las elites de poder durante el reinado de Carlos V a través de los miembros del Consejo de Inquisición (1516–1558)," *Hispania* XLVIII/168 (1988): 103–67.

[52] Nalle, *Mad for God*; also "Inquisitors, Priests and the People."

outsiders, like other religious authorities, vis-à-vis the unlearned populace. When inquisitors reinterpreted the testimonies their notaries had recorded, they changed the content in fundamental ways, imposing universalizing learned categories on particular narratives.[53]

BUILDING A THEORY OF OFFICE

The office of inquisitor was forged in polemic. In 1498, a set of instructions for the Spanish Inquisition stipulated the requirements for its judges, enjoining that each tribunal have two inquisitors, by training either a theologian and a jurist or two jurists, and that they be "good people, of knowledge and conscience."[54] Published in the name of the institution's first Inquisitor General – the Dominican friar Tomás de Torquemada, the prior of Santa Cruz – the opening paragraph continued, then, to insist that the two must collaborate in the gravest matters before them (the decision to imprison, to initiate interrogative torture, the authorizing of witness testimony), whereas they might act independently to expedite lesser charges and to enable them to go out into the surrounding dioceses to conduct inquisitorial business. In the fifteen points that followed, the requirements for holding the office were sketched out more fully: to be virtuous in action and living, including in the manner of dress and ornament; to act in judicial business with brevity and diligence; to pursue penalties and cases with circumspection; and to show judicial restraint and consult with superiors in signal matters. These subsequent paragraphs dealt not only with the inquisitors themselves, but also with an array of institutional concerns, from the mandate to establish separate jails for men and women, to the hardships that arose when open cases against the deceased dragged on inconclusively, to the prohibition on relatives of inquisitors holding office in the same tribunal.[55]

[53] Bartolomé Bennassar, "Modelos de la Mentalidad Inquisitorial: Métodos de su 'Pedagogía del Miedo,'" in *Inquisición Española y Mentalidad Inquisitorial,* ed. Ángel Alcalá (Barcelona: Editorial Ariel, 1984), 174–81; García Cárcel, *Herejía y Sociedad,* 317–41; Contreras, *El Santo Oficio,* 12, 188. Carlo Ginzburg, "The Inquisitor as Anthropologist," in Ginzburg, *Clues, Myths, and the Historical Method,* trans. John and Anne C. Tedeschi (Baltimore, MD: The Johns Hopkins University Press, 1989), 156–64. See also the argument advanced in Silvana Seidel Menchi, "The Inquisitor as Mediator," trans. John Jeffries Martin, in *Heresy, Culture, and Religion in Early Modern Italy: Contexts and Contestations,* ed. Ronald K. Delph, Michelle M. Fontaine, and John Jeffries Martin (Kirksville, MO: Truman State University Press, 2006), 173–92.

[54] "buenas personas, y de ciencia y conciencia," Jiménez Monteserín, *Introducción,* 116.

[55] Ibid., 116–21.

Drafted after the now infamous Torquemada's attempted retirement from the post of Inquisitor General, and not long before his death, such a document suggests one manner of approach to the Inquisition's long history. The practices and theories of inquisitorial office were not static; inquisitors drew upon a circulating body of procedural guidelines and in turn sought to revise these in the face of a range of experiences in the world. This process, moreover, served to constitute both a growing legal institution and the careers of its officials. The 1498 instructions were not a comprehensive guide to the legal procedure to be used in trials of faith, but rather a supplement to earlier directives. A document issued only two decades after the Spanish Inquisition's establishment, it depicted a certain permanence, "having been so much time that the Inquisition is in these kingdoms."[56] In the face of resistance, it drew an agenda of reform – elevating conformity to the law, decrying official greed, promoting the secrecy and quality of testimony, directing inquisitors when to consult with their superiors on the *Suprema* or the Inquisitor General – that would legitimate and solidify the Inquisition's place in Spanish society. The instructions that inquisitors penned expose a continuing attempt to build an institution and its practices, in contests both internal and external to the court.

Although the 1498 instructions were the last issued during Torquemada's term, they were merely another installment in the drafting of regulations that had begun with his appointment in 1483.[57] Circulated in the Castilian vernacular, in manuscript and in print, the writing of regulations was bound up with the founding of tribunals and the creation of Spain's inquisitorial office from its very beginnings. Even then, the inquisitors turned to an earlier body of opinions, citing the writings of those like the fourteenth-century Italian expert in canon law Giovanni Andrea.[58] They also drew upon a tradition – already well established by thirteenth-century inquisitors – of composing Latin legal tracts about heresy inquisitions, in the vein of the Dominican friar Nicolau Eymeric's manual for inquisitors. Active as an inquisitor in Aragon and Catalonia in the second half of the fourteenth century, still a century before the Spanish Inquisition's creation as a discrete entity, Eymeric had also enumerated qualities an inquisitor should possess: prudence, virtue, religious

---

[56] "habiendo tanto tiempo que la Inquisición está en estos Reinos ..." ibid., 119.

[57] Meseguer Fernández, "El Período Fundacional (1478–1517)," *HIEA* 1:312–22; Sánchez Rivilla, "Inquisidores," 276.

[58] For example, Jiménez Monteserín, *Introducción*, 93.

learning.[59] Such a seemingly bland and formulaic list masks the drama that informed its composition.

In the early hours of September 15, 1485, the inquisitor Pedro Arbués was attacked in Zaragoza's cathedral. He died from his wounds two days later. Arbués, a canon of the cathedral and a master of theology, was one of two inquisitors who had been appointed to establish a new tribunal of the Spanish Inquisition in that city a mere year earlier. His murder was an act of symbolic violence, designed to prevent the growth of inquisitorial roots in Aragonese soil. As such, it exposed religious and political divisions among the city's elites and between Ferdinand and Isabel's recently united kingdoms. Amid controversies that could reach such a pitch, to begin the Inquisition's 1498 instructions with directives aimed at the qualifications and conduct of the tribunals' inquisitors was itself a dramatic act. Even in their phrasing, which persistently echoed with a set of judicial ideals, the instructions defended both the system of judging heresy in courts of a hybrid royal-papal mandate and the rectitude and lawfulness of the tribunals in practice against a range of opponents. They pointed to the push and pull of inquisitors within the institution, whose ability to correct and overrule one another was under debate, from the Inquisitor General to the councillors of the *Suprema*, to the judges in the increasing numbers of regional tribunals.

Equally telling were the ways in which later instructions were crafted. Issued in the name of another much remarked Inquisitor General, Fernando de Valdés y Salas, those published in 1561 were a wholesale recodification of procedure. Formulated as a clear sequence of steps that any inquisitorial proceeding ought to follow, they took the standardization of inquisitorial practice as a point of departure.[60] Although the actions inquisitors should take were mentioned in nearly every point, the characteristics and authority of the inquisitors were taken for granted. By the mid-sixteenth century, Spain's inquisitors were mostly jurists by education and secular clerics, and for the most part not friars (like Torquemada) or theologians (like Arbués). The 1561 instructions established one of the possibilities left open in 1498 as the new status quo. They specified when theologians should be called for consultation, writing them out of habitual presence as judges of the tribunal. They also further wrote inquisitors into

---

[59] Nicolau Eymeric and Francisco Peña, *El manual de los inquisidores*, ed. and trans. Luis Sala-Molins (Barcelona: Muchnik, 1996); A. Borromeo, "Eymerich, Nicolau," *DSI* 2:568–70. Cf. Ames, *Righteous Persecution*, chap. 4.

[60] For a modern edition, see Jiménez Monteserín, *Introducción*, 198–240.

the work of religious correction and inspection that had once been principally the province of bishops. To respond to the dissent that continued to
surround and infuse the routine work of the Inquisition, the institution's
elite offered a regularized set of norms for inquisitorial business. Revised to
fit a changing world, the rules of 1561 became the touchstone for how
inquisitors organized and argued about their office over the century that
followed. Later referred to as the "Madrid Instructions," they coincided
with King Philip II's fixing of the capital in that city the same year.
Published a decade before the establishing of the first inquisitorial tribunals
in the Americas, they were among the building blocks of colonial administration shipped across the Atlantic. That process, how individual Spanish
inquisitors worked to shape and reshape their office over a crucial century
of institutional growth, territorial expansion, and administrative elabora-
tion, is one of the subjects of this book.

From Voltaire to Dostoevsky, from Monty Python to Mel Brooks, the
figure of the inquisitor – and especially the Spanish inquisitor – is ubiq-
uitous. It is shorthand for intolerance, for zealous interrogation, for the
abuse of rights and the law; it is a type that, upon even passing mention,
tends to raise a shudder, a gesture of repugnance, or a vague sense of dread.
These images of the inquisitor have a longer history, however, than such
common associations might suggest. The office of inquisitor and its mythology developed in tandem. One of the most powerful currents of the
inquisitor's iconography derived from those acclaimed as inquisitors martyred for their work. The Dominican friar Peter of Verona (1202–52) was
murdered on the road to Milan while on an official papal charge to pursue
heresy inquisitions there. Canonized less than a year later, the second
papally recognized saint of his order, he and his cult became central to
inquisitorial authority.[61] One account of the saint's life, compiled in the
1260s – but widely circulated in subsequent centuries – depicted him as a
man who "applied himself diligently to his work as inquisitor and sought
out the heretics wherever they were, giving them neither rest nor
quarter."[62]

---

[61] Ames posits the thirteenth-century contests over Peter of Verona's cult as part of a process
of sacralizing heresy inquisitions, and so the work of inquisitors, in part by aligning them
with the motifs of the *imitatio Christi*, see *Righteous Persecution*, chap. 2.

[62] Jacobus de Voragine, *The Golden Legend: Readings on the Saints*, trans. William
Granger Ryan (Princeton, NJ: Princeton University Press, 1993), 1:257. For one of the
multitude of early modern editions, see *Legenda, ut Vocant, Sanctorum* (Lyon: Eustache
Barricat, 1554), fol. 51v. The copy consulted belonged to Granada's Jesuit College and is

From the later sixteenth century, the cult of Saint Peter Martyr – as he was called – became increasingly important to the Spanish Inquisition. In 1604, the *Suprema* moved to regularize a confraternity dedicated to him; its membership across the Catholic Monarchy swelled with the Inquisition's officials and familiars, and even wives of these lay associates. One 1607 edition of the brotherhood's rules proclaimed its direction "in honor and praise" of the saint, the "protector and defender of the holy Catholic faith, as a true soldier in the standard of the faith, who we take as our principal advocate and patron."[63] Such corporate affiliation with the figure of an inquisitor-saint and his feast day mirrored – and was intertwined with – similar devotions and associations in the lands under the jurisdiction of the Roman Inquisition, and with the growth across the seventeenth century of a similar confraternity in the Portuguese Inquisition's orbit, from Lisbon to Goa to Brazil.[64]

Among the signal proponents of these initiatives were the inquisitors themselves. They reworked idealized precedents for inquisitorial action to fit changing circumstances, transporting this historical baggage across time and space. Thus, Páramo's voluminous history of the Inquisition, published in Madrid in 1598, featured scores of holy inquisitors, each depicted as acting in a model of divine initiation begun when God questioned Adam. The inquisitorial activities of some thirteenth-century Dominicans were made a crucial stage in the transmission of the work of inquisition across the theological ages. Saint Dominic became the "first Inquisitor General," noted as Spanish in his origins; sixteenth-century inquisitorial confraternities were linked to their thirteenth-century counterparts; Saint Peter Martyr was commemorated and listed in a chapter on "the many" inquisitors from the Order of Preachers, beginning with Dominic and stretching through Eymeric (also made an Inquisitor General) and into

now in the University of Granada and available at http://adrastea.ugr.es/tmp/_webpac2_1098166.102951.

[63] "honra y alabanza," "Protector y Defensor de la Santa Fe Católica como verdadero soldado en el estandarte de la fe de quien tomamos por nuestro principal Abogado y Patron," AHN, Inq., lib. 500, fol. 106r.

[64] See Francisco Bethencourt, *L'Inquisition à l'époque moderne: Espagne, Portugal, Italie XVe-XIXe siècle* (Paris: Fayard, 1995), 85–115; Richard Greenleaf, "The Inquisition Brotherhood: Cofradía de San Pedro Mártir of Colonial Mexico," *The Americas* 40.2 (1983): 171–207; Wadsworth, *Agents of Orthodoxy*, 162–71; Elena Sánchez de Madariaga, "Familiares de la Inquisición e Integración Social: la Cofradía de San Pedro Mártir de Madrid en el Siglo XVII," in *Integrazione ed Emarginazione. Circuiti e Modelli: Italia e Spagna nei Secoli XV–XVIII*, ed. Laura Barletta (Naples: Istituto Suor Orsola Benincasa, 2002), 53–89.

the fifteenth century.[65] For his own age, Páramo cataloged inquisitions geographically, dedicating significant space to Arbués when he came to the kingdoms of Aragon and Catalonia. There, he advanced a case for the murdered inquisitor's sanctity and created a kind of lineage of inquisitor-martyrs in those realms that reached back to three Dominicans killed in the county of Urgell in the thirteenth century. Already venerated by the later fifteenth century, Páramo noted ongoing lobbying for Arbués's canonization; he was ultimately beatified in 1664.[66]

That year, Diego García de Trasmiera's hagiography of Arbués was reissued in Madrid with the papal brief of beatification appended. First published in Sicily, García de Trasmiera described the book as "the life of a learned, prudent, zealous, and merciful inquisitor," qualities that purportedly mirrored those of the Inquisitor General to whom the 1647 dedication was addressed.[67] The work sought to transmit both the virtues of the inquisitor and the perfidy of his killers. So Pedro Arbués was linked to two other signal Peters, to the apostle and his papal authority and to the earlier sainted inquisitor-martyr of the same name, Peter of Verona. The *conversos* involved in the Aragonese resistance of 1485 and the inquisitor's killing also acquired a lineage, as García de Trasmiera wrote them into an anti-Jewish discourse that stretched from condemnation for the betrayal of Christ to praise for the 1492 expulsion.[68] In this fashion, the account might be read as shaped to increase the resonance of Arbués's martyrdom with Christ's passion, the fundamental template for the Christian holy death.[69] Such books deployed a historical vision ready-made to apply to current events: suspected seventeenth-century Judaizers might be collapsed into a long history of criminality, inquisitors and their proponents aligned with the fundamental work of Christian societies. The writing of inquisitorial histories in the sixteenth and seventeenth centuries

---

[65] Luis de Páramo, *De Origine et progressu officii Sanctae Inquisitionis* (Madrid: Juan Flandro, 1598), 95–102, 107–11. On early depictions of Dominic as inquisitor, though he did not conduct that work during his life, see Ames, *Righteous Persecution*, 94–134.

[66] On the thirteenth-century veneration within the order of these three (never canonized) – Pons de Blanes (d. 1242), Bernard de Traversa (d. 1260), Peter de la Cadireta (d. 1277) – see Ames, *Righteous Persecution*, 65. Páramo lists all three but qualifies only the latter two as "sanctus," *De Origine*, 175–84. Arbués was canonized in 1867. See also Bethencourt, *L'Inquisition*, 23, 102–5.

[67] "la vida de vn Inquisidor docto, prudente, zelante, y benigno," Diego García de Trasmiera, *Epitome de la Santa Vida, y Relacion de la Gloriosa Muerte del Venerable Pedro de Arbves, Inquisidor Apostolico de Aragon* (Madrid: Diego Díaz de la Carrera, 1664), dedication.

[68] Ibid., 7–8, 37–45. Or, as the title page framed this dichotomy, it was the tale of one "A qvien la obstinacion Hebrea diò muerte temporal y la liberalidad Divina, vida eterna."

[69] Cf. Ames, *Righteous Persecution*, 72–75.

was intertwined with the general increase in both sacred and profane history writing. As polemicists sought to authorize the work of inquisitors (as practiced in a particular moment) and justify the primary targets of inquisitions (as they changed over time and place), they engaged in a propaganda war of sorts. Intending to articulate authority in multiple ways, they drew upon and created a complex field of institutional memory, binding individual cases and adaptable practices to venerable and universal precedents.

If inquisitors often described their work in the idealized language of diligence, justice, and mercy, it was precisely this idiom of Christian virtue that dissent turned against them. In print and in manuscript, in speech and in symbolically charged action, a range of figures across the social spectrum, within and outside Iberia, contested the virtue of individual inquisitors and their affiliates, the merits of particular procedures and trials, and the Spanish Inquisition's legitimacy itself.[70] The high profile trials of elite Spanish "Lutherans" – and their very public condemnation in an *auto de fe* in Valladolid in May, 1559 – resulted in a flurry of manuscript reports, quickly sent to Protestant audiences abroad and further disseminated in printed accounts in Italian, Dutch, and German that appeared within the year.[71] Inquisitors acquired a more distinctive set of characterizations in the pamphlet skirmishes that surrounded the Dutch Revolt; from 1550, rumors about plans to impose the Spanish Inquisition in the Habsburg-ruled Low Countries fueled arguments about the monarchy's abusive nature.[72] One 1571 leaflet asserted Spanish inquisitors' proclivity toward "the most false slanders and other corrupt crafty means." They became the source of corruption in Habsburg realms, creating disorder under the pretence of defending the republic, subjecting the populace to their "most cruel yoke."[73] The most famous sixteenth-century exposé of the

[70] On the circulation of news and polemic in the Iberian world, see Fernando Bouza, *Corre manuscrito. Una historia cultural del Siglo de Oro* (Madrid: Marcial Pons Historia, 2001); Michele Olivari, *Entre el trono y la opinión: la vida política castellana en los siglos XVI y XVII*, prologue by Ricardo García Cárcel, trans. Jesús Villanueva (Valladolid: Junta de Castilla y León, 2004). Cf. Filippo de Vivo, *Information and Communication in Venice: Rethinking Early Modern Politics* (Oxford, UK, and New York: Oxford University Press, 2007).

[71] Among many manuscript accounts in Spanish, see BNE, MSS 721, 883, 6176. At least twelve editions in these three languages appeared in print in 1559; Emil van der Vekene, *Bibliotheca Bibliographica Historiae Sanctae Inquisitionis* (Vaduz: Topos Verlag, 1982–92), 1:191–93, 3:36–37. See also Monter, *Judging the French Reformation*, chap. 2; Elias Amezaga, *Auto de Fe en Valladolid* (Buenos Aires: Gráficas Ellacuría, 1966).

[72] See especially Duke, *Dissident Identities*, chaps. 4–5.

[73] *A Defence and True Declaration of the Things Lately Done in the Low Country* (London: John Day, 1571), in *The Dutch Revolt*, ed. and trans. Martin van Gelderen (Cambridge,

Inquisition's practices, an insider's view of the court (and principally of the tribunal in Seville) that posed as an account of the experiences of a Protestant victim, took a similar point of departure and came complete with an appended list of other such martyrs. Inquisitors, it insisted, "were altogether as bad" as that persecutor of early Christians, the Roman Emperor Julian the Apostate, had ever been; they too were "making but a jest of the laws of true religion."[74] Rapidly translated and widely disseminated, tracts like these enshrined inquisitors as enemies of both true Christianity and the just administration of law.

Crystallized in Catholic-Protestant conflict, such representations of inquisitors became a core element of polemics about Spain's evils.[75] Other writings suggested that inquisitors and their ilk had compromised their humanity. João (Moseh) Pinto Delgado, a seventeenth-century poet, hinted that inquisitorial office was alien to the realm of the human heart and to the Christian mercy it pretended to offer. Of Portuguese extraction and born in the 1580s, he resided among a prominent community of *conversos* with Iberian origins in Rouen and had passed time in Lisbon as well. He eventually moved to Amsterdam, where he lived as an authority in the Jewish community from the 1630s until his death in 1653.

The *conversos* of Rouen, who included merchants active in the French city's trading relationships, became a focal point of the Spanish Inquisition's investigations of suspected Portuguese Judaizing networks in the early 1630s. In the years that followed, Pinto Delgado would use the institution's very name to formulate his opposition to it: "Hard marble

UK: Cambridge University Press, 1993), 7. This tract was a translation of one issued in Latin the previous year.

[74] Reginaldus Gonsalvius Montanus, *A Discovery and playne Declaration of sundry subtill practises of the Holy Inquisition of Spayne* (London: John Day, 1568), fol. 31v. Published under a pseudonym, first in Latin in Heidelberg in 1567, this treatise circulated widely; one theory holds that its author was the Spanish evangelical theologian and former Hieronymite monk Antonio del Corro, a relative of the Antonio del Corro who had been an inquisitor in Seville in the first half of the century. See Peters, *Inquisition*, chaps. 5–6; B. A. Vermaseren, "Who Was Reginaldus Gonsalvius Montanus?" *Bibliothèque d'Humanisme et Renaissance* 47.1 (1985): 47–77. On Corro's dramatic conversion and mobile career, see Paul J. Hauben, *Three Spanish Heretics and the Reformation: Antonio del Corro, Cassiodoro de Reina, Cypriano de Valera* (Geneva: Librairie Droz, 1967). Another theory is that it was a collaboration primarily between two authors, Corro and Reina; see Nicolás Castrillo Benito, *El "Reginaldo Montano": Primer Libro Polémico contra la Inquisición Española* (Madrid: CSIC, Centro de Estudios Inquisitoriales, 1991), 117–27.

[75] There is an extensive literature on the Black Legend; for an introduction to the subject, see J. N. Hillgarth, *The Mirror of Spain, 1500–1700: The Formation of a Myth* (Ann Arbor: University of Michigan Press, 2000).

would soften at the cry, / And with it the fierce breast hardens, / O hard *Office*, who calls you *Holy*?" The poet's verses were informed by the observation of inquisitorial activity in his own community; significantly, he composed his poems in Spanish.[76] He, too, cast inquisitors in the trappings of tyranny, although adopting a particularly emotive language to number them among the agents of worldly suffering. He implied that inquisitors were part of a divine logic operating in mundane affairs, but not at all in the ways they presumed.

Spurred by a set of specific circumstances, Pinto Delgado picked up already long-standing refrains and used them to formulate a critique. If inquisitors could be isolated from their society and painted as the deviants, their actions and their institution might be combated; in a series of implicit appeals for intervention, authorities might be persuaded to dismiss rather than empower the inquisitors and their methods. Writings designed to build and to undermine inquisitorial authority were thus part of a field of strategic publications. Their authors evidenced diverse aims and opinions, while also constructing a recognizable universe of attributes and events associated with the figure of the Spanish inquisitor. Those dynamics – of how Spanish inquisitors participated in the polemics that surrounded their office – are another of the subjects of this book.

Particular circumstances profoundly informed these collective images. Both Páramo (author of the Inquisition history and the subject of Chapter 3) and García de Trasmiera (author of the holy life of Arbués), for example, wrote while serving as inquisitors in Palermo, attempting to call royal and papal attention to affairs of the Spanish Inquisition in Sicily

---

[76] "Al duro marmol enternece el llanto, / y con el se endurece el fiero pecho, / o duro *Officio*, quien te llama *Santo*?"; Révah, "Autobiographie," 128. Even earlier he published a collection of poetry, also in Spanish, that grappled with similar themes; João Pinto Delgado, *Poema de la Reina Ester. Lamentaciones del profeta Jeremiás. Historia de Rut y varias poesías*, ed. Révah (Rouen: David du Petit Val, 1627; repr. Lisbon: Institut Français au Portugal, 1954). See also "En Alabanza del Señor: In Praise of the Lord," in Pinto Delgado, *The Poem of Queen Esther*, trans. David R. Slavitt (New York and Oxford, UK: Oxford University Press, 1999), 3–9. On the Portuguese "nation" and perceptions of religious identity, see especially Daviken Studnicki-Gizbert, *A Nation Upon the Ocean Sea: Portugal's Atlantic Diaspora and the Crisis of the Spanish Empire, 1492–1640* (Oxford, UK, and New York: Oxford University Press, 2007). On Iberian merchants in Rouen and the Spanish Inquisition, see Gayle K. Brunelle, "Migration and Religious Identity: The Portuguese of Seventeenth-Century Rouen," *Journal of Early Modern History* 7.3–4 (2003): 283–311; C. Roth, "Les Marranes à Rouen. Un chapitre ignoré de l'histoire des Juifs de France," *Revue des études juives* 88 (1929): 113–55. See also Miriam Bodian, *Hebrews of the Portuguese Nation: Conversos and Community in Early Modern Amsterdam* (Bloomington: Indiana University Press, 1997), 143.

and to their own merits.[77] It is in following the individuals – those tried and their judges – that the ambiguities of the institution emerge: the vagaries of inquisitorial action, the negotiations involved in all inquisitorial business, and the impracticability of many theories of reform in the early modern world. Breaches of the Inquisition's much vaunted secrecy (sometimes orchestrated by prisoners and their associates, sometimes calculated releases of information by inquisitors) were commonplace. It is in just this messy landscape that inquisitors developed and deployed what Adriano Prosperi has so elegantly termed their "arsenal," the literature designed to aid, regulate, and authorize their office.[78]

In print, Simancas (the subject of Chapter 2) was a principal stockpiler of Spain's inquisitorial arsenal. In 1552, with some experience as a legal consultant to Valladolid's Inquisition tribunal under his belt, he published his first manual of inquisitorial law. When he came to the chapter on inquisitors, he asserted that inquisitors must be worthy of the dignity, gravity, and complexity of their office and that they should be prudent legal minds and zealous Catholics ready to combat the threat heresy posed not only to individual souls, but also to the social fabric of the republic. He sought simultaneously to reform the office and to advertise its virtues.[79] In one sense, such volumes were a gloss to the Spanish Inquisition's instructions, which were much slimmer documents, circulated in Spanish, and meant as more succinct directions for procedure. Signal redactions appeared in 1484, 1485, 1488, 1498, 1500, 1514, 1521, and 1561. Afterward, they continued to be printed and reissued in a variety of formats and locales. As with the more compendious Latin manuals of legal theory, the reissue of older instructions was itself a means to revive or claim a spirit of reform. Promoting or editing such publications also had careerist motivations. For example, Gaspar Isidro de Argüello, the secretary to the *Suprema*, republished the Spanish Inquisition's collected

---

[77] García de Trasmiera (1604–61) had been an inquisitor in Valencia and in Aragon before Sicily; he was later promoted to the *Suprema*; Sánchez Rivilla, "Inquisidores," 344.

[78] Eliseo Masini entitled his seventeenth-century manual for inquisitors a "holy arsenal." See, in particular, the approaches offered in Adriano Prosperi, *L'Inquisizione Romana: Letture e Richerche* (Rome: Edizioni di Storia e Letteratura, 2003). Scholars of thirteenth- and fourteenth-century inquisitors have also evaluated them as those who "organisée, composée et professionalisé." Albaret, *Les Inquisiteurs*, 10. See also Ames, *Righteous Persecution*.

[79] See the initial paragraph of chap. 34, "De Inquisitoribus," Simancas, *Institutiones Catholicae* (1552), fol. 120v.

instructions in 1627 and 1630, in a tidy edition for which he prepared an alphabetized index to aid consultation.[80]

The manuals – like those of Simancas – summarized procedure but also, in the long tradition of legal commentaries, explored troubled points of law, weighed in on juridical debates, and delineated jurisdiction. For instance, chapters on the confiscation of goods or torture tended to be among the lengthier ones. They drew upon the varied corpus of canon and civil law, among a range of other sources; the instructions were also part of this body of authoritative legal precedent. The manuals gestured to a history of inquisitorial practice, both implicitly and explicitly, in the citations they included and in the occasional insertion of recent cases. Inquisitors justified their decisions, especially when they wrote to their superiors on the *Suprema*, through the opinions enshrined in the manuals. These reference books, on the other hand, drew authority from their close connection to current judicial practice.

This theoretical literature followed two principal tracks, which were to some extent interwoven, but might also be decoupled. One was geared toward legal and procedural reference; the other cataloged an array of heresies, often fitting them into categories established in the early Church. Both strands circulated in print and in manuscript, with a variety of intended audiences. Edicts warning against specific heresies were often printed and proclaimed aloud to a gathered public. Inquisitorial archives also contained procedural instructions and legal references copied out in manuscript, as well as guides to heretical behavior drawn from the experience of trials.[81] The writings of Alfonso de Castro (1495–1558), a Franciscan and a theologian, demonstrated the sense of interconnection between genres; among other works he published, in Latin, a catalog of heresies, a compendium of anti-heretical law, and a more general treatise on criminal law.[82]

---

[80] *Instrucciones del Santo Oficio de la Inquisición, sumariamente, antiguas, y nueuas* (Madrid: Imprenta Real, 1630). The editing and indexing work of Argüello also stemmed from the expertise he acquired in overhauling the organization of the council's archives. Martínez Millán, "Las fuentes impresas," *HIEA* 1:141–49.

[81] For a consideration of the ethnographic aspects of some such documents, see James Amelang, "Ethnographies of Error," in *L'Europa divisa e i nuovi mondi. Per Adriano Prosperi*, ed. Massimo Donattini, Giuseppe Marcocci, and Stefania Pastore (Pisa: Edizioni della Normale, 2011), 2:105–15.

[82] Each saw multiple early modern editions: Alfonso de Castro, O.F.M., *Aduersus omnes haereses Libri XIII*; *De iusta haereticorum punitione libri tres*; and *De potestate legis poenalis libri duo*.

Virgilio Pinto Crespo has noted the spike in such publishing in the middle and later sixteenth century. This was the literature that underpinned the rapid growth of inquisitorial practice, not only the Spanish Inquisition but also civil courts, bishops, and Italian tribunals drew upon these books. Andrea Errera has reasoned that after initial production for use in Spain's tribunals, the 1542 bull establishing the Roman Inquisition guaranteed a market in both Spain and Italy. Some of the most prominent compilers – like Simancas or Juan de Rojas (d. 1578) – held office in the Spanish Inquisition. Others, like Castro, the fifteenth-century canonist and auditor of the Rota Gonsalvo García de Villadiego, or Francisco Peña (c. 1540–1612) – another Iberian dispatched to the Rota in Rome and the most famous inquisitorial authority of the sixteenth century – did not. After 1578, Peña's new edition of Eymeric's fourteenth-century manual became the most important source for inquisitorial jurisprudence.[83] Edward Peters deftly summarized the utility of such works: Peña's commentary "made available to any inquisitor a one-volume library of inquisitorial history, theology, authority, procedure, and bibliographical and documentary citations."[84] Many of the manuals were printed and reprinted not only in Italy, but also in the Low Countries, Lyon, and Paris. As with the tremendously successful Eymeric edition, there was a boom in printing earlier medieval manuals at the same time as sixteenth- and seventeenth-century jurists were compiling new ones. Peña edited and reissued other works. Simancas had engaged in similar activity, publishing his annotations on Zanchino Ugolini's fourteenth-century legal commentary, which had recently been reprinted and glossed by Cardinal Camillo Campeggi, a prominent figure in the Roman Inquisition of Simancas's day.[85]

---

[83] Virgilio Pinto Crespo, "La Justificación Doctrinal del Santo Oficio," *HIEA* 1:880–86; Andrea Errera, *Processus in Causa Fidei: L'Evoluzione dei Manuali Inquisitoriali nei Secoli XVI–XVIII e il Manuale Inedito di un Inquisitore Perugino* (Bologna: Monduzzi, 2000), 83–153; "Manuali per inquisitori" and "*Repertorium inquisitorum,*" *DSI* 2:975–81, 3:1313; Prosperi, *L'Inquisizione Romana*; V. Lavenia, "Albert, Arnau (Arnaldo Albertini)," and "Peña, Francisco de," *DSI* 1:26, 3:1186–89; Tedeschi, "Rojas, Juan de," *DSI* 3:1337; J. Wickersham, "Castro, Alfonso de," *DSI* 1:301–2.

[84] Edward Peters, "Editing Inquisitors' Manuals in the Sixteenth Century: Francisco Peña and the *Directorium Inquisitorum* of Nicholas Eymeric," *The Library Chronicle* 40 (1974): 101. See also the approaches in Eymeric and Peña, *El manual de los inquisidores*; Kenneth Stow, *Catholic Thought and Papal Jewry Policy, 1555–1593* (New York: Jewish Theological Seminary of America, 1977).

[85] Simancas, *Adnotationes in Zanchinum*, published as an appendix in editions of his shorter manual. See also Peter Diehl, "An Inquisitor in Manuscript and in Print: The *Tractatus super materia haereticorum* of Zanchino Ugolini," in *The Book Unbound: Editing and Reading Medieval Manuscripts and Texts*, ed. Siân Echard and Stephen Partridge (Toronto: University of Toronto Press, 2004), 58–77; Prosperi, "Campeggi, Camillo," *DSI* 1:252–53. Alastair Duke noted that Campeggi, as a papal legate to the Diet of

The making of this legal literature, more and less speculative, by inquisitors and their canonist and civil lawyer colleagues served both to bind together early modern inquisitorial regimes with a shared jurisprudence and to articulate their differences. In print, inquisitors sought alternately to limit and to expand their institution's jurisdiction. They enshrined their own experiences as precedent, potentially available to shape the judicial decisions of others. The manuals also point to the wider legal, administrative, and religious arenas in which inquisitors functioned, embedding polemic within seemingly dispassionate legal disputation. Alongside a set of procedures and practices, commentators appropriated a corpus of ideals.[86] This projection of authority found its way into other sorts of writing. Thus Sebastián de Covarrubias Orozco's 1611 dictionary reflected that long-standing association between the verb "to inquire" (*inquirir*) and diligence in seeking out the truth of a matter. The definition's last variant identified inquisitors as the Holy Office's "most upright judges." The entry repeated the virtues that inquisitorial theorists sought to claim for their office and to use as spurs to reform their erring or negligent colleagues. Covarrubias gestured to an ideal archetype of the judge, the man in whom nothing was lacking, just, unbreakable, and not swayed by "hate, love, or interest."[87]

THE INQUISITOR'S WORLDS

Beyond their institutional context, Spanish inquisitors traversed a host of worlds, physical and intellectual, over the course of their lives. As sons of the gentry, they often knew smaller Castilian towns or provincial cities in their childhoods. They were part of family negotiations about inheritance, navigating the Castilian custom of partition among heirs and the changes in that body of law over the sixteenth and seventeenth centuries. They

Augsburg in 1530, recommended for the Holy Roman Empire "una inquisitione como se [sic] usa in Spagna contra li Marrani," quoted in *Dissident Identities*, 104, n. 15.

[86] On such issues, see Pastore, *Il Vangelo e la Spada*; José Ignacio Tellechea Idígoras, "Inquisición española e Inquisición romana, ¿dos estilos?" in *Perfiles jurídicos de la Inquisición Española*, ed. José Antonio Escudero (Madrid: Instituto de la Historia de la Inquisición, 1988), 17–48. Doris Moreno has identified, following Antonio Márquez, a category of "inquisitor-writers," associates of the institution whom she frames as having created a self-legitimating literature ("un rosario de tratados jurídico-teológicos"), works characterized by "una mirada narcisista y beligerante." *La Invención*, 193–94.

[87] "5. Inquisidores sus integérrimos jueces." "Integer" was defined as "la cosa que no le falta nada. Hombre entero, hombre cabal, justo, que no se dobla ni tuerce, por odio, amor o interés." Sebastián de Covarrubias Orozco, *Tesoro de la lengua castellana o española*, ed. Felipe C. R. Maldonado (Madrid: Editorial Castalia, 1995), 479, 670.

drew on their parents' networks of associations and the patronage of their uncles, corresponded with their kin, and later contributed to dowries and aided in arranging offices and marriages for their nieces and nephews. They left charitable bequests from place to place across their careers. For such young men, leaving the family home meant departing for Spain's booming universities, where they furthered their study of Latin, and proceeded to that of laws, canon and civil, and occasionally theology as well, most often at the premier institutions in Salamanca or Valladolid. In addition to the Latin and the licentiates or doctorates that they acquired in long years of study, they also met contemporaries with whom they would cross paths again and again in their ascent through royal and ecclesiastical offices; the elite *colegios mayores* of the universities, of which Salamanca's San Bartolomé was the most prestigious, formed the cohorts of young men who dominated Habsburg administration.

The rate of university education, and especially of the production of law degrees, increased rapidly in Spain during the sixteenth century. Those inquisitors who were educated in the first decades of the century were shaped by one of the most dynamic academic climates in Europe. The School of Salamanca – propelled by intellectuals like Francisco de Vitoria and Domingo de Soto – was renowned for its legal, political, economic, and religious theory and for its revival of Thomas Aquinas's thought. Future inquisitors like Valtodano and Simancas were still university students when the focus of inquisitorial investigations began to extend beyond suspected Judaizers; the heated disputes of the 1520s over the writings of Erasmus, the heresies of Luther, and the religious beliefs of the so-called *alumbrados* (judged to be proponents of illuminist heresies) occurred during the years of their intellectual formation. Those with legal degrees were increasingly channeled into positions in the royal administration. They were appointed to positions in *audiencias* – royal courts with regional administrative functions – in Chanceries, and in Inquisition tribunals.

The growing Habsburg world was governed as a composite monarchy; the crowns of Aragon and Castile, among other royal possessions, preserved varied jurisdictional and administrative relationships vis-à-vis their monarch. Parallel to what occurred with the organization of the Spanish Inquisition, a conciliar system was established and adapted over time to govern the far-flung Catholic Monarchy. Oriented toward a capital fixed in Madrid after 1561 (with the exception of a few years in Valladolid in the early seventeenth century), councillors of the *Suprema* were, on one level, courtiers much like those who populated the Councils of State, Italy, or the Indies. Inspections and audits, generally termed visitations, were a central component of this administrative culture, and inquisitors – like other jurists, councillors, and judges – were frequently commissioned as visitors. The Spanish crown had also developed a particular relationship to the Church in its domains, exercising what was known as the *Patronato Real* – primarily royal oversight of ecclesiastical revenues and episcopal appointment – through papal concession. Thus both crown and Church offices were acquired through royal patronage, benefices in cathedrals sometimes functioning to supply income to absent clerics working in other institutions and bishoprics often used to reward service to the king. In each of the offices they held over their careers, inquisitors navigated an administrative landscape that was, at one and the same time, oriented toward a centralizing conciliar system and fragmented by regional structures of authority and jurisdictional competition. The legal, political, and religious culture in which they lived was marked by persistent tensions between the local and the universal.

Jockeying among a multiplicity of overlapping religious authorities was, similarly, a hallmark of the political culture of Catholicism in sixteenth- and seventeenth-century Spain. Historians have shown how, in France, ecclesiastical power tended to reside increasingly in bishops, while in Habsburg Spain, conversely, religious orders, cathedral chapters, the episcopacy, and inquisitors all could command significant authority.[88] There was no simple pattern to allegiances among these groups. For example, since the early church, bishops had been charged to correct heterodoxy in their diocese; from the late fifteenth century, this important episcopal duty – then construed as the powers of inquisition – became contested terrain. The apostolic inquisitors who staffed the Spanish Inquisition's tribunals came into conflict with bishops who still claimed to be the primary inquisitors in their diocese, even as the court delineated a place for bishops in its workings, requiring the presence of the so-called ordinary inquisitor – or his deputy – in particularly important deliberations. Such procedural regulations demonstrated an inquisitorial theory that knitted together episcopal and inquisitorial spheres while seeking to establish the supremacy of apostolic inquisitors in trials of

---

[88] Joseph Bergin made this comparison in order to put in perspective the rapid reconstitution of the French episcopate – and simultaneous failure of the cathedral chapters to retain their authority – following the sixteenth-century religious wars; *The Making of the French Episcopate 1589–1661* (New Haven, CT, and London: Yale University Press, 1996), 547–55.

faith by regularizing the presence of the bishop's representative in their institutional setting.

As judges of the Holy Office and in their appointments as cathedral canons or bishops, inquisitors worked with canon law and ecclesiastical courts. They were subject to papal decrees and rulings of the Rota in Rome. The debates and initiatives of Catholic reform were, moreover, one of the most important shaping forces of their careers. Culminating in the Council of Trent (1545–63), they lived in an era of potent disputes over what ought to constitute Catholic reform and how best to enact it, including contests about the characteristics of an ideal bishop and the merits of a jurist's or a theologian's expertise in the pastoral, administrative, and judicial work of bishops. The council marked a sea change in what was considered exemplary or even permissible clerical behavior. Tridentine reforms insisted on the importance of episcopal residence and emphasized the dangers of corruption in the management of ecclesiastical revenues or appointments.[89] Inquisitors' work was implicated in deliberations about how to prevent and correct heresy; how best to educate and persuade the flock; and when to employ fraternal correction, the confessional, or judicial denunciation to correct error. When they assessed issues surrounding conversion and confession, inquisitors entered some of the most important theological terrain, that touching the sacraments of baptism and penance.

For Spanish inquisitors in the sixteenth and early seventeenth centuries, their judicial work and their religious objectives were bound up with a variety of other concerns. Among them was the perception that many heretics were part of vast conspiracies, often with political dimensions, agents of Muslim or Jewish plots against a Catholic *res publica.* Inquisitorial actions were inflected by the observation of religious warfare – by looking toward battles in northern Europe – and the stance that the Spanish Inquisition's trials were part of a conflict against Protestants of global dimensions. They were conditioned by debates about what served the common good, whether religious toleration degraded the body politic, and to what extent – especially in the context of seventeenth-century peace treaties – it was permissible to establish diplomatic and economic relationships with heretics. There were no rigid boundaries between the political, the religious, and the economic. Ideas about heresy also infused debates about what kinds of commerce were beneficial to the crown, about

---

[89] For an approach to this subject, see Barbara McClung Hallman, *Italian Cardinals, Reform, and the Church as Property* (Berkeley, Los Angeles, and London: University of California Press, 1985).

whether trade should be filtered through the metropole, what harm might come from dispersing the monarchy's gold and silver, and what scale of threat smuggled contraband posed. Inquisitors encountered these debates from their official positions, from broader responsibilities as royal councillors and Catholic authorities, and also as part of families who sought to conserve status or manage social ascent through avenues like officeholding, lawsuits to establish noble status, or admission to the military orders.

The social world of inquisitors was built on a host of evolving ideals. The most suitable education for courtiers was a subject of discussion, as skill in arms was increasingly viewed as incomplete without skill in letters, and the duties of royal councillors revolved more and more around paperwork, and around knowing what was advisable to preserve in writing, to circulate anonymously, or to reserve for personal communication. The men who became inquisitors were reared in a society with a remarkable legal savvy, as early modern Spaniards made their way through the courts, obligations, and benefits of an array of jurisdictions – seigneurial, municipal, royal, inquisitorial, and ecclesiastical. With university study (often followed by a stint of teaching) and junior officeholding or consultation in a range of legal and religious institutions before their acquisition of higher posts, they became expert navigators of jurisdictions, among the most important ordering forces of their society. They learned to build a case, weigh evidence, assess proofs, and collect witness testimony, skills used in their courtroom practice and in their written opinions. They also began to populate their mental worlds with the host of revered authorities of the ancient world and of earlier Christian thought, and with later jurists, theologians, and chroniclers, a process they continued as they read, built libraries, and corresponded with educated contemporaries throughout their careers. Inquisitors oversaw archives in an age that saw a surge in history writing and compiled treatises that drew on legal, political, theological, and historical evidence.

In the sixteenth and seventeenth centuries, initiatives of moral and political reform were broadcast through public displays, religious space was demarcated, and hierarchies were advertised. Models of what to imitate and what to avoid were offered in processions and celebrations, the built environment and its ornamentation, and in the images and words circulated in a range of printed forms. These were arenas in which relationships of patronage and clientage were exhibited. They were also arenas in which inquisitors sought to defend the faith, and in which they also perceived heretics as operating, spreading their deceptions in speech and in print. Aristotle's *Politics* – a text they revered – explained: "the real difference between man and other animals is that humans alone have perception of good and evil, just and unjust, etc. It is the sharing of a common view in *these* matters that makes a household and a state."[90] The chapters that follow are about the politics of Spanish inquisitors in this very broad sense. They are about the strategies inquisitors pursued to carve out a role in their society as experts in discerning good from evil; to persuade others of the truth of their judgments; and, so they believed, to save souls and maintain the social and political order of their Christian republic in the process.

FIVE INQUISITORIAL LIVES

Caro Baroja remarked that "An 'inquisitor,' a 'tyrant', a 'knight', a 'poet,' an 'artist' are words that already predispose us to judge a man."[91] The challenge is to attempt to distinguish the interplay between the individual and the office, especially in light of the profoundly corporate ways in which early modern people tended to express their identities.[92] The inquisitors under consideration here were often born into families with multiple connections to the Spanish Inquisition, they frequently lodged within the tribunal buildings, and their contemporaries regularly referred them to as inquisitors. The nature of the sources available to study inquisitors – primarily the Inquisition's own archives and the official correspondence of other royal and ecclesiastical bodies – further complicates any attempt to untangle the official from his office. To try to capture the complexities of how an individual was shaped by his office and, alternately, what room he had to shape it, the chapters that follow examine how inquisitors theorized about and approached the administration of their office, their attempts to acquire and exercise authority, and the stances they adopted. Each seeks to explore an inquisitor's early influences, to track the experience he accumulated, and to see how he applied his education and experience over his career. Even in their arbitrative work as judges, inquisitors inhabited a

---

[90] Aristotle, *The Politics*, ed. Trevor J. Saunders, trans. T. A. Sinclair (London: Penguin, 1992), 1.1253a7, p. 60, emphasis in original. This distinguishing characteristic of man is also linked to speech. Simancas's *De Republica Libri IX*, for instance, is littered with references to the *Politics*. See also Louis Sala-Molins, "Utilisation d'Aristote en droit inquisitorial," in *Platon et Aristote à la Renaissance* (Paris: Librairie Philosophique J. Vrin, 1976), 191–99.

[91] "Un 'inquisidor', un 'tirano', un 'caballero', un 'poeta', un 'artista' son vocablos que nos predisponen ya para enjuiciar a un hombre." Caro Baroja, *El Señor Inquisidor*, 12.

[92] Cf. John Jeffries Martin, *Myths of Renaissance Individualism* (Houndmills, Basingstoke, Hampshire, UK, and New York: Palgrave Macmillan, 2004).

delicate set of tensions surrounding the relationship between individuals and society. They sought to discern the crimes of individuals, to spur the accused into a penitent reconciliation to the Church, and they understood their work as seeking the salvation of individual souls; at the same time, inquisitorial processes were framed as protection of the community against the scourge of heresies, often thought to be transmitted through families and networks of associates. They were indebted to an Aristotelian notion of politics that they understood as prioritizing the whole over the part, the state over the household and the individual, and to a theory of Christian society that valued both individual salvation and the protection of the Church as a community.

Chapters 1 and 2 examine figures involved in the expansion of inquisitorial authority and activity that occurred between the 1540s and 1570s: Cristóbal Fernández de Valtodano (c. 1500–72) and Diego de Simancas (1513–83). Their careers were profoundly influenced by the deliberations at the Council of Trent and the first years of Tridentine reforms, as well as by the politics of the early years of the reign of Philip II (r. 1556–98). Colleagues on the *Suprema* and both bishops, in the early 1560s they worked together as judges in the sensational seventeen-year trial of Bartolomé Carranza, the archbishop of Toledo, accused of promoting Lutheran heresies; meanwhile, they revised the Inquisition's procedures under the patronage of the Inquisitor General Fernando de Valdés. The first chapter argues that Valtodano sought to take a pastoral approach to his inquisitorial work and examines how he construed inquisitors as an essential part of Catholic reform. The next chapter analyzes Simancas – made famous to modern historians thanks to his autobiography and Caro Baroja's essay – whose career was dominated by the time he spent in Rome during the later stages of the Carranza case and his experience of the Roman Inquisition's operations under Pius V (1566–72) and Gregory XIII (1572–85). It examines how he turned increasingly to compiling and publishing commentaries, becoming a principal architect of inquisitorial law.

The action of the third chapter takes place during the waning years of Philip II's reign and the opening ones of the young Philip III's (r. 1598–1621), years of shifting political priorities. In general, inquisitors were able to exercise less influence on royal policy in this era, a trend augmented by a succession of short-serving Inquisitors General between 1595 and 1608. With the negotiated peaces of the early seventeenth century also came more viable consideration of measures of religious toleration, along with substantive opposition to the purity of blood statutes. Chapter 3 profiles

Luis de Páramo (c. 1545–1608), who spent the bulk of his career as a judge in the Spanish Inquisition's tribunal in Sicily, with an interlude lobbying at Court in Madrid. It analyzes the strategies that an inquisitor in a peripheral tribunal adopted to attract attention to his service and to shore up the diminishing authority of his office, engaging in jurisdictional battles, carefully crafting his correspondence, and writing histories.

Chapters 4 and 5 examine inquisitors who propelled the investigations of those they tarred as Judaizing Portuguese conspirators. These trials – first termed the "Great Complicity" in Lima and pursued on both sides of the Atlantic – led to an interconnected series of prosecutions in the 1630s and 1640s. They were part and parcel of the political and military crises of the era, as the favorite of Philip IV (r. 1621–65), the count-duke of Olivares, fell from power in 1643, taking down the long-serving Inquisitor General, Antonio de Sotomayor, with him. They were bound up with court factions as well as with combat with France, revolts in Catalonia and Portugal, and a broader panorama of financial crisis and competing ideas about proper economic policy. The fourth chapter uses the dramatic rise and fall of Juan Adam de la Parra (c. 1596–1644) to examine the roles available to an inquisitor at Court. It examines how he sought to cast himself as persistently unmasking dangerous impostors – that is, as an expert in inquisitorial discernment – in his jurisdictional combat with a bishop, in his pursuit of those he supposed to be false saints and Judaizers, in his poetic skirmishes, and in his political propaganda. The life of Juan de Mañozca y Zamora (c. 1577–1650), from his long experience as an inquisitor to his term as archbishop of Mexico, forms the basis for the fifth chapter. It analyzes how Mañozca learned to navigate the long distances of the monarchy, adeptly framing reports, exercising strategic patronage, and staging dramatic public celebrations. Whereas the first five chapters exhibit a degree of variety among the Inquisition's judges, Chapter 6 offers an account of how inquisitors built a shared argumentative culture during the sixteenth and seventeenth centuries and examines how they persuaded their contemporaries of their authority and the importance of their office.

CHAPTER I

Visiting the Flock

The Pastoral Agenda of Cristóbal Fernández de Valtodano

The shepherd's excuse will not be accepted if the wolf devours the sheep and he knows it not.[1]

Late in the spring of 1561, an extraordinary set of legal proceedings began in Valladolid. There, two judges – Lic. Cristóbal Fernández de Valtodano and his junior colleague, Dr. Diego de Simancas – presided over the Spanish Inquisition's trial of the archbishop of Toledo, Bartolomé Carranza, suspected of Lutheran inclinations and charged with heresy. Valladolid was one of Castile's chief cities, having often hosted the royal Court; possessing a significant university; and serving as the permanent seat of both a local tribunal of the Inquisition and a Chancery, the kingdom's most important institution of royal justice. The city's elite, however, had been shaken by the identification of Protestant heretics in their midst a few years before, from whose trials had grown much of the evidence against Carranza. It had taken two years of wrangling to create the archbishop's courtroom. During that time, the prelate had managed to have three potential judges disqualified. When the pair of delegated inquisitors finally began their audiences that summer, their aim was to show their impeccable adherence to inquisitorial procedure while also adapting it to the unprecedented affair at hand. For business as delicate as trying the head of the Spanish Church, the judges lodged in Valladolid, removed from the routine work of the *Suprema*, on which both were councillors; they sought

---

[1] *Canons and Decrees of the Council of Trent*, trans. Rev. H. J. Schroeder, O.P. (Rockford, IL: Tan Books and Publishers, Inc., 1978), 47.

47

to insulate the proceedings, conducting them in a private house that also served as Carranza's jail.

Valtodano had been instrumental in creating this judicial environment. Born at the turn of the century, he was an inquisitor in Toledo's tribunal for eleven years before his appointment to the *Suprema*. On that council, he supplied the crucial link between the Valladolid Lutheran trials and the initiation of the Carranza case, his intimate knowledge of the former causing him to push for the archbishop's prosecution. By 1561, Valtodano knew he was embroiled in a complicated affair. Still, he could have anticipated that the Carranza case would move expeditiously toward a conclusion in his courtroom. With his legal knowledge, his wide judicial experience, the reams of evidence already assembled, and the involvement of a cadre of esteemed religious authorities, he seemed to have a mandate to proceed definitively. It looked as if the apparent Lutheran contamination of high-ranking Spanish clergy could be brought to an end with the Valladolid trial of the archbishop. In years when the Council of Trent was suspended and Philip II had only recently returned to Spain, this was judicial work that many perceived to be on the vanguard of both Catholic reform and the defense of the Habsburg monarchy. Valtodano could have expected that his actions would serve the spiritual well-being of the kingdom while also bringing him recognition and rewards.

As it turned out, Valtodano did not live to see the end of the Carranza case, although it did bring him notable royal attention and approval. Made the bishop of nearby Palencia in 1561, when he died in 1572, he was archbishop of Santiago de Compostela, one of the most important ecclesiastical offices in Spain. Yet while Valtodano, Simancas, and Carranza sat in a house in Valladolid, their world changed dramatically. The Council of Trent reconvened and concluded; from the start of 1564, Spanish prelates were expected to throw themselves into the work of implementing the Tridentine reforms. The experience of serving as the senior delegated judge in Carranza's trial seems also to have changed Valtodano. He had become the orchestrator of a scenario that left the archdiocese of Toledo headless – not to mention two other bishops absent their cathedral cities – in the years just after Trent's close. Increasingly, he sought to direct his energies to episcopal rather than inquisitorial work, writing many letters to this end and spurring the publication of liturgical tracts.

Valtodano has been largely ignored in modern scholarship. Studies of institutions he served – the *Suprema*, his dioceses, the Toledo tribunal – mention him. His name crops up in passing in José Ignacio Tellechea Idígoras's prolific publication on the Carranza case, but he is not a focus of analysis and is treated as one among many creatures of the Inquisitor General Fernando de Valdés. The most sensitive work on Valtodano appears in Jean-Pierre Dedieu's investigation of the Inquisition in Toledo, where he is identified as an inquisitor who visited the tribunal's district with exceptional diligence in the early 1550s.[2]

In response, this chapter uses Valtodano's life to illuminate how a Spanish inquisitor could pursue a pastoral approach to his work, as he sought to align himself with the shifting ideals for both episcopal and inquisitorial office in the era of Trent. Shaped by a climate of religious and judicial reform, Valtodano returned to the same tools – visitations and diligent letter writing chief among them – throughout his career as an inquisitor and as a bishop. He met with the most professional success of the five inquisitors I have considered, in long service in an important Inquisition tribunal and on the *Suprema* and in attaining, with his archbishopric, a more prestigious post than any of the others. His self-effacing judicial personality, coupled with his shows of personal diligence, was likely key to his achievements. Ultimately, his experience led him to turn from an inquisitorial career in which he had enjoyed considerable success and toward the work of a reforming bishop, seeming, by the mid-1560s, to see that as the greatest hope for combating heresy.

INQUISITOR ORDINARY, INQUISITOR EXTRAORDINARY

Cristóbal Fernández de Valtodano was born in the town of Fontiveros, in the diocese of Ávila, around 1500, the son of Diego de Valtodano and María Suárez.[3] He had at least two siblings, Diego Fernández Valtodano and María Velázquez. An uncle of his mother's, don Alonso Suárez de Fuente el Saúz, was a prominent ecclesiastic and inquisitor and, from 1500 to 1520, an especially construction-oriented bishop of Jaén. He also built the family fortunes, instituting an entail that Valtodano's brother was the first to hold and that subsequent generations litigated at the turn of the seventeenth century.[4] Valtodano lent further credit to the family. He was

---

[2] Jean-Pierre Dedieu, *L'administration de la foi: L'Inquisition de Tolède (XVIe-XVIIIe siècle)* (Madrid: Bibliothèque de la Casa de Velázquez, 1989); Dedieu, "Les inquisiteurs de Tolède et la visite du district. La sédentarisation d'un tribunal (1550–1630)," *Mélanges de la Casa de Velázquez* 13 (1977): 235–56.

[3] I follow his practice in shortening his name to Valtodano. His mother also appears with the surname Sánchez.

[4] Suárez was bishop of Mondoñedo and then of Lugo before his appointment to Jaén on February 7, 1500, where he held a diocesan synod and was known as the "builder," using his own funds to finance a bridge over the Guadalquivir. He died November 5, 1520. He

recorded in the mid-seventeenth-century family tree of one niece, Olaya de Valtodano of Fontiveros, in order to augment her honor. Olaya's children and grandchildren acquired numerous royal and ecclesiastical offices, and it is even likely that Valtodano assisted her son, Lic. Benito Rodríguez Valtodano, in an impressive ascent akin to his own: from the *colegio mayor* of San Bartolomé to the civil judiciary (as an *oidor*) and legal consultation for the Inquisition in Seville, to the royal Councils of the Indies and the *Cruzada*.[5] Valtodano's origins were typical of the Spanish administrative class in his era, but his career trajectory suggested particular skill in navigating the treacherous political waters.

Not so far from his native town, Valtodano pursued his education at the preeminent Spanish legal faculty of his day, making his choice of profession in the early 1530s. He took orders and, in 1533, entered the University of Salamanca's most prestigious *colegio mayor*, San Bartolomé, eventually earning a licentiate in both canon and civil law and so entering a network of well-connected jurists. He received his first significant clerical appointment in early 1537, when the bishop of Badajoz, Jerónimo Suárez Maldonado, appointed him vicar general (*provisor*) in that cathedral; he was made a doctoral canon there in 1546.[6] Although the opening session

was also a sub-delegated Inquisitor General, *DHEE* 2:1222; *HC* 2:159, 181, 193; 3:219; Teresa Sánchez Rivilla, "Inquisidores Generales y Consejeros de la Suprema: documentación biográfica," *HIEA* 3:354. On the entailed estate (*mayorazgo*), seemingly created to benefit his niece's family, see two printed accounts relating to its litigation in 1601 and 1602, RB, MS II/2334, fol. 45r and fol. 59r. Valtodano's maternal grandfather was Toribio Sánchez, brother of Bishop Suárez. Valtodano's sister died without children, while his brother had at least three surviving children: Toribio, María, and Catalina Baltodano. The lawsuit was between descendants of Valtodano's nephew Toribio (in whose favor the court in Andújar ruled) and those of Valtodano's mother's brother, who was apparently an *alcalde*. Valtodano may have had another relative in Ávila's ecclesiastical hierarchy; a document dated May 4, 1536, mentioned "el Reuerendo senor bachiller Juan Fran[cis]co hernandez de valtodano teniente de provisor entodo el obispado de avila," AFZ, Altamira 453, doc. 12.

[5] Her precise relationship to Valtodano is unclear. She married Jerónimo Rodríguez of Fontiveros. Benito married, first, in Valladolid, doña Luisa del Aguila y Montoya (daughter of Dr. Belliza and doña María de Montoya) and, second, Inés Carrillo de Guzmán. Further descendants held other notable offices: Bishop of Nicaragua, Chaplain of the New Kings in Toledo, Archdeacon of Santa Gemma in Pamplona, and Abbot of Sesma. RAH 9/302, fol. 73r.

[6] There are biographical notes in Luis de Páramo, *De Origine et progressu officii Sanctae Inquisitionis* (Madrid: Juan Flandro, 1598), 172; Gil González Dávila, *Teatro Eclesiástico de España* (Madrid: Francisco Martínez, 1645), 1:95, 2:183; Antonio Alvarez Reyero, *Crónicas Episcopales Palentinas* (Palencia: Abundo Z. Menéndez, 1898), 262ff.; Manuel R. Pazos, O.F.M., *Episcopado Gallego* (Madrid: CSIC and Instituto Jerónimo Zurita, 1946), 1:35–50; José Martínez Millán, "Las elites de poder durante el reinado de Carlos

of the Council of Trent did not convene until December 1545, talk of Catholic reform permeated Valtodano's environment. Spanish religious authorities – including many of those associated with Salamanca – debated the most effective approaches to conversion, how to renovate the clergy, what constituted the ideal bishop, and the appropriate governance of the Church, among many other topics. They disputed when and whether to employ judicial punishment of heresy, as opposed to milder forms of persuasion, fraternal correction, or absolution in the confessional. Part of a growing legal class, Valtodano was among the jurists increasingly nominated to ecclesiastical and inquisitorial posts in the first decades of the sixteenth century, displacing theologians, a circumstance that some reformers criticized as compromising pastoral care.

Many commentators identified clerical absenteeism as among the principal forces of disorder in Catholic religious life, reasoning that a bishop's capacity to protect the souls under his care depended upon his physical presence. In 1516, Gasparo Contarini, a prominent figure in reform-minded circles and eventually a cardinal, had termed it "the calamity of our age." At the same time, he explained that the pope might sometimes need his bishops elsewhere, having "the welfare of all Christendom in mind." At a bare minimum, he emphasized that bishops ought to preside in their cathedrals during Holy Week.[7] Contarini encapsulated the tensions around residency. Central to any project of religious renewal or education, it was also a mandate that could clash with other work perceived as critical to the Church. Another prevalent line of reasoning held that the Spanish Inquisition was of such importance precisely because bishops had failed in their duty to prevent the spread of heresy; as a result, both bishops and inquisitors, the argument went, were needed to revitalize the Church. During the sixteenth century, inquisitors moved increasingly into arenas that had been the preserve of bishops. Possessing the authority to act as ordinary inquisitors in their dioceses, bishops or their

V a través de los miembros del Consejo de Inquisición (1516–1558)," *Hispania* 168 (1988): 155, n. 188; Sánchez Rivilla, "Inquisidores," 354. González Dávila recorded that he took his habit November 11, 1533, Alvarez Reyero that he took his *beca* in San Bartolomé November 11, 1531, and competed for two university chairs after graduation; Martínez Millán and Sánchez Rivilla give his entrance into San Bartolomé as November 11, 1535, and September 11, 1533, respectively.

[7] "Chapter VII. "Contarini's *De officio episcopi*, 1516" in *The Catholic Reformation. Savonarola to Ignatius Loyola,* John C. Olin (New York: Fordham University Press, 1992), 94–95. On bishops and reform, see José Ignacio Tellechea Idígoras, *El Obispo ideal en el siglo de la Reforma* (Rome: Iglesia Nacional Española, 1963); Lu Ann Homza, *Religious Authority in the Spanish Renaissance* (Baltimore, MD, and London: The Johns Hopkins University Press, 2000), chap. 4.

representatives were given a place in Inquisition tribunals – whose mandate was technically of an extraordinary quality – when particularly serious affairs were under consideration. While bishops and inquisitors often came into jurisdictional conflict, it was also fairly common for a Spanish cleric to move from one office to the other or even, occasionally, to hold the two offices simultaneously. Regarding the frequent promotion of inquisitors to bishoprics, the historian José Martínez Millán has argued that the populating of the Spanish episcopate with prelates who had prior inquisitorial experience vastly increased the Inquisition's influence on society.[8] In sum, Valtodano began to build his career in an era when there was complicated cross-pollination between Spanish ecclesiastical offices, when relationships between inquisitorial and episcopal authority were especially contested, and when the practices and formations of bishops and inquisitors were a particular focus of reforming efforts.

VISITING THE DISTRICT, VISITING THE DIOCESE

The professional culture in which Valtodano was formed elevated diligence as one of its highest ideals. The word itself was a persistent refrain, along with its opposite, negligence; sixteenth-century officials sought to depict themselves as embodying the former and reviling the latter. Even administrative tasks, particularly in the conduct of legal business, were often called *diligencias*. From 1543 to 1554, Valtodano was an inquisitor in Toledo's tribunal, even as he retained his appointment in the cathedral of Badajoz; he grappled with the competing claims of his offices. In 1552, he tried and failed to obtain a prebend in Toledo's cathedral, while sometime before 1561 he acquired a benefice in Ávila, perhaps as a nonresident source of income, as was increasingly common practice among inquisitors.[9] Toledo's court was then in the midst of a period of transition, turning to new targets in the middle of the sixteenth century. After a flurry of

---

[8] Promotion was also sometimes a way to remove members of rival factions from Court, Martínez Millán, "Las elites," 167. For thoughtful analyses of the relationships between bishops and inquisitors, see Adriano Prosperi, *Tribunali della coscienza: Inquisitori, confessori, missionari* (Turin: G. Einaudi, 1996); Prosperi, *L'Inquisizione Romana: Letture e Richerche* (Rome: Edizioni di Storia e Letteratura, 2003); Stefania Pastore, *Il Vangelo e la Spada. L'Inquisizione di Castiglia e i Suoi Critici (1460–1598)* (Rome: Edizioni di Storia e Letteratura, 2003).

[9] He lost the competition to a client of the archbishop, then Cardinal Martínez Silíceo; Martínez Millán, "Las elites," 155 n. 188. In the late 1540s, he sought partial remissions from residency in Badajoz. Later, Inquisitor General Valdés intervened with the chapter on his behalf, according to the mid-seventeenth-century history of Juan Solano de Figueroa y

morisco trials in the 1540s trailed off, the tribunal mostly investigated so-called Old Christians for relatively minor heretical offenses. Although infrequently encountered, inquisitors continued to consider Protestant and Judaizing heresies particularly threatening. In the heart of Castile and as the seat of Spain's primate, Toledo's religious environment was a particular focus of new initiatives. District inspections were a cornerstone of the reforming agenda of Inquisitor General Valdés – who took office in 1547 – because a tribunal was not meant to confine its investigations to the city in which it sat. As a result, Valtodano participated in the most systematic and intense period of inquisitorial visitation, which Dedieu located at its peak in Toledo between 1548 and 1558. Dedieu read these tours as acts of self-perpetuation, aiming to find more heretics to justify the Holy Office's continued existence and scale. They also suggested a certain faith in procedural form and in a system of administration that enshrined perpetual investigation and correction as a means to combat abuses and errors. As Dedieu elegantly concluded, "one visited for the purpose of visiting, and the visitation found in itself its own logic."[10]

Royal and ecclesiastical administrators throughout the Catholic Monarchy voiced the ideal of diligent visitation. Diligence was understood to be closely related to zeal, and both terms recurred in sixteenth-century descriptions of clerical virtue. Defining the word in the early seventeenth century, Sebastián de Covarrubias implied that diligence could be judged by the care devoted to a charge; it was an indication that something had been done with love. If diligence was thus envisioned as a bridge from religious ideals to the practical realm of administration, it was also a key to mundane successes; one proverb reportedly held that "diligence is the mother of good fortune."[11] The more men like Valtodano inscribed themselves within the ideal of diligence, the more they could argue that they pursued a particular vision of pastoral care. This model rested upon the physical presence of officials, upon the personal knowledge of a given situation and the individuals involved in it, and upon the expeditious dispatch of business; its primary tools were a multitude of forms of inspection and correction of other administrators, institutions, and the populace.

Altamirano, *Historia Eclesiástica de la Ciudad y Obispado de Badajoz* (Badajoz: Imprenta del Hospicio provincial, 1929), 3:267–73.

[10] "on visite pour visiter et la visite trouve en elle-même sa propre logique." Dedieu, *L'administration de la foi*, 187.

[11] "La diligencia es madre de la buena ventura." Sebastián de Covarrubias Orozco, *Tesoro de la Lengua Castellana o Española*, ed. Felipe C. R. Maldonado (Madrid: Editorial Castalia, 1995), 428. For "negligencia," 775.

Valtodano's 1543 elevation directly to the office of inquisitor in the important Toledo court was already a mark of professional success. Over the next decade there, he actively engaged in the standard official duties, deliberating with his colleagues and presiding over trials and *autos de fe*. He assisted in the court's administration, corresponding about its cases, personnel, and finances with the *Suprema*. In the early 1550s – an era from which extensive correspondence survives – the Toledo tribunal had two inquisitors. Even with only this minimum number of judges, the tribunal members adhered to an annual round of visitations, such that they often entrusted the tribunal to a temporary delegate.[12] At the same time, Valtodano continued to request periodic leave to travel to the Badajoz cathedral. As was common practice, Toledo's inquisitors used the accounts of *autos de fe* that they sent to the *Suprema* as demonstrations of their diligence over the previous year, and as petitions for funds to cover the court's expenses. Thus, in January 1552, Dr. Alonso Pérez (then the senior inquisitor) and Valtodano reported of the most recent *auto de fe*: "we have worked as we should, for our part, and in all justice has been administered with equity, that Our Lord might be served from it, as it is done in defense of His holy Catholic faith." They stressed the tribunal's particular financial need given the shortage of goods in Toledo that year, yet they assured their superiors that "each one does not cease to work as he is obligated in his office."[13] They had not held an *auto* in 1551 and reported processing an astonishing 230 cases since the last public *auto* of March 25, 1550.

Of these, fifteen figured in the January 1552 *auto*. It displayed nine *penitenciados* (those convicted and given penances): two women for bigamy and seven men for offenses ranging from multiple marriages to blasphemy to meddling with the Inquisition's trials. One penitent had apparently burned the doors of the house of someone he suspected of giving a deposition against him to the Inquisition. In addition, it exhibited another six *reconciliados* (those reconciled to the Church, a graver judgment). One man from Burgos was convicted of professing Islam, practicing

---

[12] On the Toledo tribunal, see Dedieu, *L'administration de la foi*. For their correspondence to the *Suprema* between 1551 and 1555, AHN, Inq., leg. 3067, unnumbered exp., nos. 1–91. For a fairly typical investigation and mild penancing for "deshonestidad" – Alonso de Córdoba of Agudo had fornicated and denied it was a sin – from 1546, involving Lic. Beltrán de Guevara and Valtodano as inquisitors, AHN, Inq., leg. 69, exp. 31.

[13] "de n[uest]ra p[ar]te se a trabajado como deuemos y en todo se a administrado justicia con eq[ui]dad. plega a n[uest]ro s[eñ]or se sirua dello pues se haze en defensa de su s[an]ta fe catholica." "no cesan de trabajar cada uno como es obligado en su officio." Pérez and Valtodano, January 17, 1552, AHN, Inq., leg. 3067, no. 5.

its ceremonies, and marrying five times. A friar from Oran, Jerónimo de Vargas, was prosecuted for administering the sacraments without being an ordained priest, and even then without the proper solemnity; for breaking out of the tribunal's prison with a Lutheran in tow; and for returning to his previous errors before his recapture. Finally, two *moriscos* and a *morisca* were found guilty of engaging in Islamic practices, and a *converso* of having Judaized. All of the serious offenders were categorized as coming from places outside the city of Toledo. The penalties included penitence, abjurations of error, whipping, and brief terms of exile; the *moriscos* and the *converso* were assigned penitential incarceration. None received capital sentences (relaxation to the secular arm in inquisitorial parlance), but three were condemned for multiple marriages and the *reconciliados* from Burgos and Oran were sentenced to terms of galley service.[14] It was Vargas's case and the saga of the prison break that continued to preoccupy the inquisitors. They found it such a serious matter for several reasons: Vargas relapsed, he flaunted inquisitorial authority with his escape, and he aided a perfidious Lutheran. As a friar, he compromised clerical dignity; moreover, his initial crime had severe implications, as he had placed souls in peril by performing sacraments illegitimately. A month later, Pérez (sick and confined to his bed) and Valtodano appealed to the *Suprema* to review the Vargas trial, especially because the ordinary had not voted on how to proceed in that matter. They deliberated about what additional penalty Vargas – as among three of the five prisoners recaptured – should receive for his escape. The case required consultation because, aside from sentencing him to be whipped (like the two others) for the offense of jail breaking, the inquisitors had also voted to relax him to the secular arm as an impenitent heretic. In any case, the two inquisitors stressed the need to finish this affair, pleading for brevity in the council's review, "so that it remains dispatched before we leave on the visitation." In response, the ministers of the *Suprema* asked to see the warden's testimony about the escape.[15]

Framed by assertions of diligent activity, the correspondence betrayed a host of administrative problems. On February 22, 1552, Valtodano wrote

[14] The sentencing to terms of galley service is noteworthy, given that it has been identified as a practice more of Aragonese inquisitorial courts than Castilian ones; see William Monter, *The Frontiers of Heresy: The Spanish Inquisition from the Basque Lands to Sicily* (Cambridge, UK: Cambridge University Press, 1990).

[15] "porq[ue] quede despachado antes q[ue] salgamos a la bisita." Pérez and Valtodano, February 10, 1552, AHN, Inq., leg. 3067, no. 12; Valtodano, February 16, 1552, ibid., no. 11. I have not found a resolution to this case.

that Pérez had died that morning, having fallen ill rapidly, and that "we are trying to take him for burial, for which his power of attorney did not leave money."[16] The tribunal staff had quarreled about where to direct his last salary payment and awaited permission – which soon arrived – to give it to his sister. Valtodano, now the senior – and sole – inquisitor, rushed to conclude other business so that he could proceed with the scheduled visitation of the tribunal's district. He negotiated with Toledo's councilmen about the prisoners bound for galley service, resolving that he would hand them over to the royal jail until their transport. Four days after Pérez's death, he detailed his plan for the tribunal's interim administration:

I will leave within four or five days, with God's blessing, to visit those places which I have written to Your Lordships, and I will leave the commissary informed about what he should do during my absence, with which it is settled that he will come to this Holy Office every morning one hour, and the three days a week that they have council he will come another hour, and the other days he will see to whatever else is necessary.[17]

He answered the *Suprema*'s requests for information, describing the condition of the jails (under scrutiny following the escape), and responding to the council's inquiry into the genealogy of an inquisitor in Murcia. He reported that a strong witness – the mother of another inquisitor – claimed that the Murcian inquisitor was descended from someone called "the boasting Jewish woman." Valtodano followed this piece of information into the tribunal archives: "and proceeding to look at the books and writings that are necessary to take for the visitation, I found that among many other condemned people, citizens of Ciudad Real and Campo de Calatrava, is the boasting woman. I am sending testimony of it, in case it happens to be necessary there."[18] He sought to prove himself useful to the council in a matter infringing on the Inquisition's authority, revealing dramatic conflict between inquisitors and even involving their families.

---

[16] "estamos tractando dele lleuar ala sepultura pa[ra] lo qual en su poder no se hallo dinero." Valtodano, February 22, 1552, ibid., no. 13.

[17] "yo me partire dentro de 4 o 5 dias media[n]te dios a visitar por los lugares q[ue] a v[uestra] s[eñorí]a tengo escrito y dexare informado al comisario delo q[ue] deve hazer durante mi absençia conel qualesta conçertado q[ue] venia aeste s[an]to offi[ci]o todas las mañanas vna hora y las tres dias dela semana q[ue] tienen con[sej]o ala tarde venia otra hora y los otros dias vera todo lo q[ue] fuere menester." Valtodano, February 26, 1552, ibid.

[18] "la judia baladrona"; "y andando yo mirando los libros y escripturas que son menester llevar parala visita halle q[ue] entre /otras muchas personas condepnadas v[ezin]os de çiudad real y canpo de calatraua: esta la baladrona / enbio testimonio dello para si acaesçiere ser alla menester." Ibid.

In March, Valtodano wrote from the town of Siruela, where he had been since the start of Lent. He arrived in Almadén at the beginning of Holy Week. Meanwhile, the deputy in Toledo attempted to arrange a residence for Valtodano in the tribunal building, as he was now the senior inquisitor, choosing the room in which he had left his belongings upon departing the city. In September, the inquisitors – by then Valtodano and his junior associate Lic. Francisco Horozco de Arce – urged the *Suprema* to send their approval for the lodgings quickly, as winter approached (the resolution arrived the same day).[19]

In 1552 and 1553, the inquisitors' correspondence frequently revolved around their absences from Toledo, although not from the duties of the tribunal. In January 1553, Valtodano again sought a deputy, a cleric of suitable health and faculties to manage the tribunal in the absence of the two inquisitors. Just before departing, he selected a canon of the cathedral. As a secondary plan, he also left authorization with two Dominican friars who had long been consultants of the Inquisition there. None of the three clerics Valtodano nominated was keen to accept responsibility for the tribunal. The canon, Lic. Baltasar de Salazar, was trained in jurisprudence but protested poor health; even when he did appear, the *fiscal* reported that he spent a mere two hours in the tribunal each afternoon. The Dominicans, on the other hand, "would not come to pursue proceedings in a case because they were theologians and that was not of their profession and if they were to hear [a case] there could be something lacking in it." Valtodano had delegated theologians to pursue judicial business, but – indicative of changing institutional norms – they had declined, wary of the consequences.[20]

Valtodano also continued to follow the pursuit of the two remaining fugitive prisoners. He received word that one of them, Juan Pérez Osorio, had been imprisoned in Tudela in Navarre. There, again, he had attempted to escape out a window, hurting himself. The *Suprema* then had to decide whether to have Valtodano send the trial record to the inquisitors in Calahorra or remit Pérez Osorio back to Toledo; the council transferred the case to Calahorra, on the face of it to avoid additional costs, although the fear of further escapes and the lack of an inquisitor in Toledo may

---

[19] Valtodano, April 26, 1552; Lic. Valdivieso, June 2, 1552; Valtodano and Horozco, September 14, 1552, ibid., nos. 17, 21, 33.

[20] "no vendrian pa[ra] cosa de substanciar processo porq[ue] eran teologos y aquello no era de su profession y q[ue] si ello sentendiessen en ello podria aver alguans faltas." January 1553, ibid., no. 47; Valtodano, January 18, 1553; Lic. Ortíz de Funes, February 9, 1553, ibid., nos. 45, 75.

certainly have played a role. In the mid-August heat, which others used as an excuse for absence, Valtodano returned to the tribunal.[21]

Valtodano and Horozco kept a grueling schedule in these years. In January 1554, Horozco – worried about the tribunal's inadequacies, a vacancy in the office of constable just the most recent trouble – was overseeing the court so that Valtodano could go to the cathedral in Badajoz before embarking on the annual visitations.[22] Each inquisitor negotiated a thicket of competing claims: in mid-February, upon his return to Toledo, Valtodano again wrote to the *Suprema*, reminding it – in a defensive tone – that the Inquisitor General had granted him a license in December for the trip to Badajoz. On arrival in Toledo, a royal provision was waiting, charging him to inspect the important Chapel of the Old Kings in Toledo's cathedral. He requested permission to fulfill this order, pledging "all possible brevity" and seeking the assistance of one of the inquisitorial notaries. The Inquisitor General refused and the *Suprema* insisted that Valtodano first finish the inquisitorial visitation, and so he left the city on the day after Easter.[23]

After Valtodano's era, inquisitors increasingly protested the time spent away from Toledo; while the inspections remained in form for many years, they declined precipitously in content. Before the end of the century, they were no longer a predictable annual event, and the practice had been virtually abandoned by the mid-seventeenth century. Dedieu chronicled Valtodano's series of visitations in the southern region of Toledo's district in four successive years: 1551, 1552, 1553, and 1554. In sum, he spent nearly twenty-three months of those four years out on visitations, and Dedieu emphasized the intensity, efficiency, and regulated routine of Valtodano's final inspection, counting more than 400 interviews conducted in six places over three and half months. The inquisitor faced significant pressure from his superiors to uncover further crimes and criminals; in 1553, he protested that he and his colleagues had thoroughly investigated the whole of the district and found no substantial heretical threats.[24]

---

[21] Salazar, February 25, 1553, ibid., no. 52. See also nos. 65, 66.

[22] Inquisitor Horozco also spent most of 1553 on visitations, including to Pastrana and Alcalá, ibid., nos. 55, 73. In 1555, he was commissioned to inspect Palermo's Inquisition tribunal; Manuel Rivero Rodríguez, "La Inquisición Española en Sicilia," *HIEA* 3:1213.

[23] "yo trabajare co[n]cluirlo co[n] la breuedad posible." Valtodano, holograph, February 17, 1554, AHN, Inq., leg. 3067, no. 76; Horozco, April 5, 1554, ibid., no. 77.

[24] Dedieu noted that Valtodano spent eight months on the visitation in 1551, four in 1552, and seven in 1553. He noted his precise movements between March and July 1554: Aldea

Valtodano's visitations showed – as scholars like Adriano Prosperi have argued in other contexts – how inquisitors could work in overtly pastoral ways.[25] Both in their tribunal city and in the district, they used *autos de fe* and edicts to visibly and viscerally condemn error and advertise repentance. They engaged even more directly with the local populace, however, during visitations. Then, they functioned, in part, as itinerant confessors. They prioritized places less recently visited. In hundreds of individual interviews, they received confessions, granted absolution and reconciliation, and assigned penances on the spot; they generated additional activity for their tribunal and levied fines to cover some of their costs. They also aggregated authority to the court, publicizing both orthodox doctrine and their role in regulating it. The timing of the visits was significant. On one level, the spring and early summer were the most practical times to travel: the weather was milder and a wider range of provincial accommodations might be considered habitable. On another level, it reinforced the pastoral function of these tours, bringing vetted religious authority to smaller towns in the season before and after Easter, during Lent, and through such signal feasts of the early modern Catholic liturgical year as Pentecost and Corpus Christi.

Such inspections also generated records stored in the inquisitorial archives. In Valtodano's case, notaries traveled with him, compiling a register, as did a constable. The entries for 1553 and 1554 included brief accounts of those who confessed or whom Valtodano investigated. They noted where edicts of grace were sent ahead of the inquisitor's arrival, notifying those in surrounding villages when he would be in the nearby town.[26] In Ciudad Real, a young man of that city presented himself and reported that in his mother's home, he had heard a gentleman's son proclaim that he did not believe in God.[27] The same day another deponent, a native of Villarubia, came to the inquisitor. He reported that working in his employer's house, he took to swearing at the mules, blaspheming in front of others. Hearing this confession of blasphemy, Valtodano

del Rey, La Calzada, Santa Cruz de Mudela, El Viso, Valdepeñas, Moral, and Manzanares. Dedieu cites AHN, Inq., leg. 496, exp. 3, fols. 69v-164v and Valtodano, August 29, 1553, AHN, Inq., leg. 3067, exp. 2. Dedieu, *L'administration de la foi*, 185; Dedieu, "Les inquisiteurs de Tolède et la visite du district."

[25] Prosperi, *Tribunali della coscienza.*

[26] The visitation book begins with an alphabetized index of individuals penanced and investigated, AHN, Inq., leg. 496, exp. 3, fols. 1–169. In 1553, Valtodano arrived in Ciudad Real on April 21 and came to Almagro on June 15; in each case, after publishing edicts, he conducted interviews nearly every day of the week, from April 24 to June 14 and from June 18 to August 2, respectively, ibid., fols. 1–68r.

[27] Gonzalo de Mena, May 2, 1553, ibid., fol. 6r.

questioned him further. He asked the man "if he has believed ... at any time that the devil was worth more than God." The man denied such a belief, responded that he had confessed and communicated, and said the Ave Maria and the Pater Noster well. He erred slightly in the Credo and did not know the Salve. At the end, Valtodano ordered a light penance, telling the man to pray in penitence, attend a mass that week, and pay a fine to cover the Holy Office's expenses and admonished him to refrain from such outbursts. Valtodano then absolved him. The inquisitor assigned similar penances for blasphemy in numerous cases. Other times, he warned that the offense was one that he ought "to punish gravely," reprimanding the confessant to adhere to the terms of the penance and avoid such errors in the future.[28]

In some instances, Valtodano noted genealogies; in others, he probed witnesses for more details. One woman in Almagro appeared before him and denounced a neighbor after a disagreement over the proper way to fast. Valtodano questioned her further to establish exactly what heresy she was accusing her neighbor of committing. He "asked if the said Ynes de Santa Cruz said that the good fast was to not eat until the stars had come out." The witness replied that this was so, and that hearing this from a woman who made the appearances of a good Christian had scandalized her.[29] She denied bearing ill will against Ynes. The results of this conversation, if any, were unclear; sometimes the information was simply recorded for future reference.

In June 1554, Valtodano was notified of his promotion to the *Suprema* while in the countryside; after the letter's arrival, he continued his visitation in Manzanares for another month before leaving for Valladolid.[30] Thus, he passed from itinerant inspections directly to the Inquisition's governing council, bringing with him a decade of inquisitorial experience and an insider's knowledge of the Toledo tribunal. The subsequent correspondence hints at the personal dynamics that inflected the conduct of inquisitorial business. Toledo's officials showed a certain expectation of sympathy from their former senior inquisitor. The Toledo physician, for instance, petitioned the *Suprema* on the grounds that – contravening the

---

[28] "sy a creydo ... en algun t[iem]po q[ue] el diablo vale mas q[ue] dios"; "castigar grabemente," June 8, 1554, ibid., fol. 124v. For similar examples, see also fols. 126v, 160v, 164r.

[29] "preguntada si dixo la dicha ynes de santa cruz que el buen ayuno era no comer hasta salida la estrella," Mari López, June 19, 1553, ibid., fol. 36v. Ynes was presumably suspected of inclining toward Muslim practices.

[30] Ibid., fol. 168v. See also Dedieu, *L'administration de la foi*, 185.

tribunal's customary practice – he alone among the staff had been passed over in the distribution of mourning alms after Queen Juana's recent death. Valtodano testified to the veracity of his account.[31] Valtodano even supervised the visitations he had so lately executed: October 1556 saw the *Suprema* praising the effectiveness of inquisitor Ramírez's recent inspection and ordering inquisitor Reinoso to leave soon to continue the circuit of the district.[32]

The *Suprema* was particularly concerned with clerical status. In 1555, the council – then Valtodano and two more senior colleagues – urged the tribunal to be cautious in proceeding against the abbot of Toledo's Cistercian monastery of San Bernardo. Inquisitor Reinoso claimed precedent for bringing charges against the abbot (accused of blasphemies) in their court's famous trial of the Franciscan friar Francisco Ortíz (1529–32) as well as concessions – later disputed – made by the Augustinians that inquisitors might try a member of their order if they had a representative present. Yet the *Suprema* advised the inquisitors to pay "attention to the quality of the witnesses because they tell us that there has been much passion between the religious of that monastery where he is abbot, [and be] mindful of that and that the [heretical] propositions result from conversations between them ... in order that he does not receive offence." Furthermore, the *Suprema* ordered that any future investigations of suspect friars be referred first to it before proceeding with capture and imprisonment. The council explained that it did not dispute the local inquisitors' jurisdiction in the matter. On the contrary, it argued that more inquisitorial eyes should decide business that implicated distinguished suspects and had repercussions for the reputation of the entire monastic order.[33] Such rulings aimed to increase the authority of the *Suprema* vis-à-vis the tribunals, proposing layers of judicial review as an essential component of good legal practice. The case also revealed the difficult position of the Inquisition with respect to potentially erring clerics, who had grounds to refute

---

[31] Lic. Pedro de Oseguera, July 12, 1555, AHN, Inq., leg. 3067, no. 86.

[32] *Suprema* (de los Cobos, Otalora, Valtodano, Pérez) to Toledo, October 1, 1556, ibid., no. 101.

[33] "atençion ala qualidad de los t[estig]os porque nos dizen q[ue] a abido mucha pasion entre los religiosos deese monest[eri]o adonde es abbad atento lo qual y q[ue] las proposiciones resultan de platicas q[ue] an pasado entre ellos ... para q[ue] no reçiba agrauio." Reinoso, July 2, 1555; *Suprema* (Tavera, de los Cobos, Valtodano), July 7, 1555, ibid., nos. 87–88. On Ortíz: Lu Ann Homza, "How to Harass an Inquisitor-General: The Polyphonic Law of Friar Francisco Ortíz" in *A Renaissance of Conflicts: Visions and Revisions of Law and Society in Italy and Spain,* eds. John A. Marino and Thomas Kuehn (Toronto: Centre for Reformation and Renaissance Studies, 2004), 299–336.

inquisitorial jurisdiction. Judging heretical clergy, whose heresies could cause immense harm as a result of their office, was understood to be among the most important work of inquisitors; at the same time, trials of clerics were likely to cause scandal, which also hurt the Church and jeopardized religious authority.

The *Suprema*'s opinions may also have been colored by Valtodano's personal knowledge of Toledo's religious landscape. Later that year, the council reprimanded the tribunal. It harshly critiqued the Toledo court's failure to obtain sufficient and coincident witness testimonies in a set of bigamy cases before ordering the imprisonment of the suspects. In addition, it rebuked the two inquisitors for separately writing conflicting accounts to the *Suprema*. Instead, "they should not write each one for himself, but together in things of the Holy Office, as it is accustomed to do."[34] Valtodano and his three colleagues elevated a model of judicial practice that privileged consensus in tribunals and insisted that accord should be reached before drafting correspondence. In this ideal, the good judge was self-effacing; when individual judges vanished into their corporate identities, as they so often did in correspondence, they did so by design.

As they did with the Toledo tribunal, the *Suprema* supervised the workings, personnel, and trials of the regional courts with varying degrees of scrutiny and circulated reforming measures – edicts, instructions, and indices – to the districts. Throughout the 1550s, the *Suprema* generally met in Valladolid and paid particular attention to that city's religious affairs.[35] There, Valtodano gained an acquaintance with a royal Court in flux. Charles V abdicated in 1556, while his heir, Philip II, was absent from Spain from the middle of 1554 until the autumn of 1559. In the spring of 1558, Valtodano and his colleagues conferred with the regent, Philip II's sister, Princess Juana, about the status of *moriscos*. They published an edict calling for *moriscos* to confess their sins and be absolved; they depicted the move as one away from excessive "rigor," aiming to prevent *moriscos* from emigrating and to avoid alienating those in error from the Church "for fear of punishment."[36] The religious environment in which

---

34 "no deban de escreuyr cada uno por si, sino juntos en cosas del s[an]to off[ici]o como se acostumbra hazer." *Suprema* (de los Cobos, Galarza, Valtodano, Pérez) to Toledo, December 23, 1555, AHN, Inq., leg. 3067, no. 102.

35 For one appeal from the Valladolid tribunal involving Valtodano – the 1555–56 case of Ana Bravo de Lagunas of Soria, accused of "words offensive to God" – see AHN, Inq., leg. 2124, exp. 4.

36 "por temor de la pena," Inquisitor General, de los Cobos, Córdoba, Valtodano, Pérez, April 10, 1558, AHN, Inq., lib. 248, fol. 80.

Valtodano worked in those years was also one of uncertainty. The Council of Trent, with its imperative to strengthen and renovate the Church, particularly in the face of Protestant challenges, had opened in December 1545 but ground to a halt again in 1547. Beset by difficulties and political conflict, it met again in 1551 and 1552, only to be suspended – it would eventually turn out – for an entire decade. In those first phases, there were major debates and decisions on such theological questions as scriptural authority as related to tradition, justification, and the sacraments. The delegates raised issues of papal versus conciliar authority and of preaching, visitations, clerical officeholding, and residency. The Catholic hierarchy was consumed by the need to reform and to combat heresy, yet it lacked clear direction for those efforts.

Valtodano made his inquisitorial career under Inquisitor General Fernando de Valdés y Salas (1483–1568). Valdés's licentiate in canon law was also a product of Salamanca's San Bartolomé, and, along with other episcopal and conciliar experience, he had served on the *Suprema* for twenty-three years before becoming Inquisitor General in 1547 (just after being made archbishop of Seville).[37] At the head of the Inquisition, Valdés was particularly attuned to codifying procedure, combating heretical print, and reworking the institution's finances (seeking to shift costs more toward the local tribunals and generate income from dedicated ecclesiastical benefices). During the turbulent 1550s, he managed to appoint an entirely new *Suprema*; Valtodano's elevation to the council was the fifth of seven such nominations. Only one of Valtodano's new colleagues in 1554 – Diego Tavera – predated Valdés's tenure, and he left for the bishopric of Jaén the next year. There were common patterns of experience among Valdés's selections: Dr. Diego de los Cobos y Molina (1548), Dr. Diego Fernández de Córdoba (1550), Lic. Sancho López de Otalora (1553), Lic. Beltrán de Galarza (1553), Valtodano, Dr. Andrés Pérez (1555), and Simancas (1559). Most were products of Salamanca's university, though the last two hailed from Valladolid's. Most were jurists by discipline, though de los Cobos had, additionally, a doctorate in theology and Pérez was solely a theologian. They had experience in visitations. Some were formed by the civil judiciary – de los Cobos, Galarza, and Simancas had been judges in Valladolid's Chancery. Only Córdoba had

---

[37] José Luis González Novalín, *El Inquisidor General Fernando de Valdés (1483–1568): Su vida y su obra* (Oviedo: Universidad de Oviedo, 1968); Martínez Millán, "Grupos de Poder en la Corte Durante el Reinado de Felipe II: La Facción Ebolista, 1554–1573," in *Instituciones y Elites de Poder en la Monarquía Hispana Durante el Siglo XVI*, ed. Martínez Millán (Madrid: Ediciones de la Universidad Autónoma, 1992), 137–97.

also been a tribunal inquisitor, in Llerena and in Córdoba. Otalora and Galarza had other kinds of conciliar experience, and the latter was not a cleric; all but these two would eventually be promoted to the episcopate. Pérez's appointment was indicative of both the wider awareness that change was afoot in the *Suprema* and of resistance to it, as it was seemingly made against Valdés's inclinations, in an effort to temper the concentration of jurists with a theologian.[38] Thus, Valtodano had relatively unique expertise among the courtiers at the head of the Inquisition. He was more familiar with the daily work of tribunal inquisitors. In his years of intensive district visitations, moreover, he had been asked to behave in a manner akin to a bishop visiting his diocese, learning how to apply inquisitorial procedure in multiple environments.

JUDGING CARRANZA

Between 1557 and 1559, the Inquisitor General and the *Suprema* repeatedly declared their pursuit of Protestant heresies, depicting Lutheran doctrine as on the advance and inflicting ever-greater harm with each passing day.[39] They announced their particular intent, that "these kingdoms be free of similar errors ... [and that the Inquisition] place all diligence in this and use the necessary remedies for the augmentation and conservation of the faith, investigating and punishing exemplarily those that still separate themselves [from the Church], in such a dangerous time as the present."[40] They charged Spanish authorities, clerical and lay, to monitor their

---

[38] Pérez had accompanied Prince Philip's entourage to England as a chaplain. Valtodano officially took possession of the office September 6, 1554. AHN, Inq., lib. 1232, fols. 174v, 176r; González Novalín, *El Inquisidor General*, 2:227–28. Sánchez Rivilla, "Inquisidores," *HIEA* 3:278–79, 325, 338, 342, 354, 364, 390; Henar Pizarro Llorente, "Las Relaciones de Patronazgo a través de los inquisidores de Valladolid durante el siglo XVI," in *Instituciones y Elites de Poder en la Monarquía Hispana Durante el Siglo XVI*, ed. Martínez Millán, 223–52; Martínez Millán, "Las elites," 155–56.

[39] See Werner Thomas, *La represión del protestantismo en España, 1517–1648* (Leuven: Leuven University Press, 2001); Jesús Alonso Burgos, *El Luteranismo en Castilla Durante el S. XVI. Autos de fe de Valladolid de 21 de mayo y de 8 de octubre de 1559* (San Lorenzo de El Escorial: Editorial Swan, 1983); Elias Amezaga, *Auto de Fe en Valladolid* (Buenos Aires: Gráficas Ellacuría, 1966).

[40] "estos rreyons esten libres de semejantes errores ... y aunque el santo officio dela inquisicion cerca desto pone toda diligencia y usa delos rremedios necesarios para abmento y conservaçion dela fee inquiriendo y castigando exemplarmente los que della se apartan toda via conuiene en tienpo tan peligroso como el presente," October 9, 1558, Valladolid, AHN, Inq., lib. 248, fol. 86. Cf. ibid., fols. 87–88, 90.

jurisdictions for suspicious doctrines and books and emphasized the need for all clerics to understand and teach the Church's doctrine well. The importance of their work soon appeared to be proven, as they began to uncover and investigate a network of "Lutheran" notables within the Court, many of them clerics. Philip II and his confessor, friar Bernardo de Fresneda, writing from the Low Countries, praised their efforts. Fresneda found that "the affair is such as to give great feeling even to the stones" and noted the king's particular sorrow at the "loss of those miserable religious."[41] He painted the events onto a much broader canvas, characterizing the king as a divine instrument sent to bring England back to the faith and depicting events in Castile as evidence of demonic conspiracy; reputedly, heretics in Germany were joyfully "preaching ... publicly great congratulations about the new church that Satan had given them in our Spain."[42]

Valtodano became one of the principal figures in the affair. The *Suprema* was stretched thin as it intensified its prosecutorial activity, especially with two councillors ill and one having recently died, circumstances that Valdés emphasized in his correspondence to the king. As a result, he decided to split the council in half. De los Cobos and Pérez pursued the ordinary administration of the Inquisition. Valtodano was assigned, with Córdoba (who was unwell and would die in 1558), to investigate the supposed Lutherans, directing a succession of audiences with the prisoners in Valladolid. Valdés thus maneuvered Valtodano – experienced as a tribunal judge – into the oversight of these extraordinary cases.[43] On May 21, 1559, Valtodano and his colleagues flanked the Inquisitor General at one of the most famous *autos de fe*, where those they had convicted as a cell of Protestant heretics were displayed to the city of Valladolid. There was an unusually high rate of capital punishment; between that *auto* and the second held in the city in October, a dramatic twenty-six convicted heretics were relaxed in person (i.e., publicly burned

---

[41] "el neg[oci]o es para dar gran sentimi[ent]o aun a las piedras ... doliole mucho mas que a todos la perdida de aquellos miserables religiosos." Fresneda to *Suprema*, March 1, 1558, Brussels, received April 28, 1558, Valladolid; see also Philip II to *Suprema*, June 5, 1558, Antwerp, AHN, Inq., leg. 100, fols. 102r, 105r.

[42] "predicando ... publicamente grande congratulaçion dela nueua yglesia que sathanas les hauia dado en nuestra españa." Fresneda to *Suprema*, August 26, 1558, ibid., fol. 109r.

[43] Martínez Millán, "Las elites," 158; González Novalín, *El Inquisidor General*, 2:191; Diego de Simancas, "Vida y Cosas Notables," in *Autobiografías y Memorias*, ed. Manuel Serrano y Sanz (Madrid: Bailly, Bailliére, S. B., 1905), 154.

at the stake). These events would mark the culmination of Valtodano's inquisitorial career.

Thereafter, the *Suprema* was briefly reunified in its conduct of business, meeting in Aranjuez, Toledo, and Madrid, apparently following Philip II's Court.[44] The Valladolid trials had opened the possibility that a circle of esteemed religious authorities might be found to be secret Lutherans, corrupting the Church from within. They allowed the Spanish Inquisition to claim a place on the vanguard of the fight against heresy. At the same time, there remained substantive theological differences and intense political competition among the Castilian religious elite.

It was in this ferment that the *Suprema*, Valtodano among them, voted in the middle of 1559 to initiate trial proceedings against Bartolomé Carranza, the newly appointed archbishop of Toledo. Carranza was of the same generation as Valtodano but had made a far more impressive ascent. He had become a key figure in Catholic reform, publishing a treatise on episcopal residency in 1547, serving in posts at the helm of the Dominican order, and twice attending sessions of the Council of Trent as an imperial theologian. In England, in Philip II's retinue, he had constructed himself as a combatant against heresy; from Flanders, before his return to Castile in October 1558, he had reported on his anti-heretical actions in letters to the *Suprema* and Valdés. Yet some theologians began to align him, instead, with the heretics, arguing that heretical propositions littered the archbishop's recently published vernacular *Commentaries on the Christian Catechism* (1558). These consultants' opinions underpinned the prosecutor's first accusation, which would charge Carranza with thirty-one counts of being a "heretic and Lutheran dogmatizer."[45] Nevertheless, charging an archbishop was no uncomplicated feat. The

---

[44] See consultations of October 1559 to April 1561. In 1561, Valtodano was often the senior signatory, AHN, Inq., lib. 248, fols. 94r-102v.

[45] Quoted in Tellechea Idígoras, "El Proceso del Arzobispo Carranza," *HIEA*, 1:571. Tellechea Idígoras has described the wider persecution of Carranza's circle and shown how the affair stemmed from the climate around Emperor Charles V's deathbed at Yuste, becoming a lightning rod for fears about the Church's loss of northern Europe; see especially his *Fray Bartolomé Carranza, documentos históricos*, 7 vols. (Madrid: Real Academia de la Historia, 1962–94); Tellechea Idígoras, *El Arzobispo Carranza, "Tiempos Recios,"* 4 vols. (Salamanca: Publicaciones Universidad Pontificia, Fundación Universitaria Española, 2003–7), which includes a helpful bibliography of his voluminous publications on the subject, 1:495–506. Stefania Pastore has argued that the Carranza affair exposed key tensions of Catholic reform, including when to favor fraternal correction or judicial discipline, *Il Vangelo e la Spada*, 349–404. Martínez Millán sorted the participants into ideological camps, "intellectualists" (Cano, Valdés, Simancas, Friar Alonso de la Fuente, most Dominicans) versus "mystics" (Carranza, Luis de Granada,

Spanish Inquisition's jurisdiction over a prelate's presumed heresy was not clear-cut; such a case was arguably reserved to the papacy. It was also understood that the trial of an archbishop, poorly conducted, would further endanger the Church, not to mention imperil the Spanish Inquisition's own future.

In these circumstances, it was Valtodano who heard some of the most damaging depositions against Carranza and then wrote a report, in his own hand, which seems to be a recommendation to the Inquisitor General – made, he noted, with the agreement of the rest of the *Suprema* – to undertake the trial of the archbishop.[46] Valtodano made the two purposes of his brief clear. He summarized the mounting evidence against Carranza and considered what order of procedure would be appropriate in such a case.[47] There were various sources of proof: witnesses both imprisoned and those "that are not imprisoned or guilty," and Carranza's own books and writings "in which are noted many erroneous and offensive heretical propositions." After addressing the kinds of evidence, Valtodano moved to its substance. One imprisoned witness had declared that purgatory did not exist; the archbishop reportedly concurred. Another heard him speak "about the justification from which heretics deduce this error and on other things that do not seem catholic." Another reported hearing him say, "that now there is no sin and that everything is paid." To this, Valtodano added, "this same conclusion is deduced from his book." Many other witnesses "say they have stopped praying the Pater Noster and Ave Maria to the saints to whom they had devotion, by the accused's persuasion and for having read it in his

Juan de Ávila, Ignatius Loyola, Francisco de Borja, most initial members of the Society of Jesus); see his "Grupos de Poder." In English, see John Edwards and Ronald Truman, eds., *Reforming Catholicism in the England of Mary Tudor. The Achievement of Friar Bartolomé Carranza* (Aldershot, UK, and Burlington, VT: Ashgate, 2005); Henry Kamen, *The Spanish Inquisition: A Historical Revision* (New Haven, CT, and London: Yale University Press, 1997), 160–63; Lu Ann Homza, ed. and trans., *The Spanish Inquisition 1478–1614. An Anthology of Sources* (Indianapolis, IN, and Cambridge, UK: Hackett Publishing Company, Inc., 2006), 176–211.

[46] For example, the voluntary denunciation (spurred by Valdés) of the Hieronymite friar Juan de Regla was given before Valtodano in Valladolid, December 9, 1558. Tellechea Idígoras, *Tiempos Recios* 1:32ff.

[47] I have not seen this letter analyzed elsewhere. I think it dates from 1559 and was part of the deliberation preceding Carranza's arrest. It predates June 1561, as after that point, Valtodano changed his signature to reflect his election as bishop. It is indexed as "Arzobispo Carranza 1565 [sup.] carta del lic. Valtodano sobre la causa." Valtodano to Valdés, holograph, n.d., AFZ, Altamira 219, doc. 68.

book."[48] Valtodano found that the prisoners' testimony confirmed the errors discerned in Carranza's *Catechism*. He suspected that the archbishop had begun to promote a doctrine of grace akin to that of Lutherans.

It has long been understood that Carranza's trial grew out of those of the so-called Lutheran heretics in Valladolid. Valtodano's memorandum demonstrates, however, how he functioned as the bridge from the earlier trials to that of the archbishop, making the case against Carranza using his extensive knowledge of the Valladolid proceedings. The testimony of imprisoned witnesses shaped his first impressions of the Carranza case. He noted that some of those on trial had expected Carranza's arrival back in Spain to reverse their fortunes. One prisoner even predicted that ultimately Carranza would stay archbishop of Toledo and Valtodano would be found to be a heretic. Damagingly, to the inquisitor's eye, when Carranza did arrive in Valladolid, he did not testify against associates who were in the midst of being tried for heresy. Valtodano looked at this evidence and saw conspiracy. There were discrepancies between imprisoned witnesses' accounts that the judge suspected stemmed from their collusion to protect themselves through the omission of relevant details. He saw their camaraderie in the same light, noting "the great friendship and familiarity that the majority of these prisoners had with the accused [Carranza], especially the most prominent among them, because they are his disciples or very old sons of penitence."[49] Valtodano sorted the individuals involved into categories and weighed their opinions accordingly. He took the sheer number of imprisoned witnesses, presumed heretics themselves, as evidence of Carranza's error. On the other end of the spectrum, he noted that honorable men – learned theologians – had found "erroneous and ill-sounding" material in Carranza's *Catechism*.

Valtodano reasoned that heretics betrayed themselves through their choice of language. Thus, Carranza's writings, as "his own confession and [made] with great deliberation," were especially telling evidence. The inquisitor argued: "It does much against the accused that the language and manner of

---

[48] "q[ue] no estan p[re]sos ni son culpados"; "en q[ue] esta[n] notadas muchas p[ro] posiçiones hereticas herroneas y malsona[n]tes"; "dela justificacion de do[n]de los hereges deduze[n] este herror y en otras cosas q[ue] no pareçe[n] catolicas"; "q[ue] ya no ay pecado y q[ue] todo esta pagado"; "esta mesma co[n]clusio[n] se deduze de su libro"; "dize[n] aver dexado de rezar el p[ate]r noster y ave maria a los sa[n]tos q[ue] tenian devocio[n] por p[er] suasion del reo y por aver lo leido en su libro," ibid.

[49] "la gra[n]de amistad y familiaridad q[ue] los mas de estos p[re]sos tenia[n] co[n] este reo señaladame[n]te los mas prinçipales porq[ue] son diçipulos suyos o hijos de penite[n]cia muy a[n]tiguos," ibid.

speaking of his writings is the same as that of the heretics that are imprisoned in these jails, as it seems by the propositions that have been taken out of them, and much more clearly by the original trials, so much that it seems to be all of one school."[50] Similarity of language suggested similarity of belief. With such logic, Carranza became a teacher of heretics, a heresiarch. Looking northward, it would have been reasonable to surmise that if Spain was going to have its Luther, he would come in the form of a renegade prelate or revered religious, someone akin to the distinguished Italian bishop Pier Paolo Vergerio, who had defected only a decade before, in the midst of his trial by the Venetian Inquisition.[51] When Valtodano considered the situation, he saw coherence among the accused and thus the risk of a rival church in the making within Castile.

The judge was sufficiently convinced of Carranza's culpability to paint a dire picture, echoing Fresneda. He construed the archbishop as a source of grave danger, both to his own soul, "and of what it will sound for all Christianity, which can cause scandal among the people and fear in the judges, and even boldness and impudence in the heretics outside of these kingdoms." Valtodano railed against him for his errors, but even more for his refusal to confess his opinions as error. He warned of "the harm that could result from this dissimulation, that could be the cause of the total destruction of these kingdoms, if under the authority and in the name of religion these errors were gaining ground shielded by the shadow of such a principal prelate."[52] He expected any serious challenge to Catholicism to come from elites with access to the corridors of power and ideas too near the border with heresy. The defense he proposed was judicial discipline, the rigorous application of proper inquisitorial procedure.

To forestall suspicions of inquisitorial misconduct, Valtodano noted that it might be wise to have prelates from the Council of Castile in

---

[50] "porq[ue] es p[ro]pia co[n]fesion y co[n] gra[n] deliberacion"; "haze mucho co[n]tra el reo q[ue] el lenguaje y manera de hablar delos escriptos del es el memso q[ue] el de los hereges q[ue] estan p[re]sos en estas carceles como pareçe porlas p[ro]posiçiones q[ue] de ellos sea[n] sacado y mucho mas claro por los p[ro]cesos originales ta[n]to q[ue] pareçe ser todo de una escuela," ibid.

[51] On Vergerio, Anne Jacobson Schutte, *Pier Paolo Vergerio: The Making of an Italian Reformer* (Geneva: Droz, 1977); John Jeffries Martin, *Venice's Hidden Enemies: Italian Heretics in a Renaissance City* (Baltimore, MD, and London: The Johns Hopkins University Press, 2004).

[52] "y de lo q[ue] sonara por toda la cristia[n]dad q[ue] puede causar esca[n]dalo e[n] las ge[n]tes y temor en los juezes y au[n] atrevimie[n]to y desvergue[n]ça e[n] los hereges de fuera destos reynos"; "el daño q[ue] de esta disimulacio[n] podria resultar q[ue] podria ser causa de la total destruçio[n] de estos reynos. Si debaxo de autoridad y con no[m]bre de religio[n] fuese[n] gana[n]do tierra estos herrores a[m]parados ala so[m]bra de ta[n] pri[n]cipal p[re]lado," AFZ, Altamira 219, doc. 68.

attendance at the proceedings. Carranza's archiepiscopal dignity merited significant concern, but he quickly dismissed any claim that this was sufficient cause to alter inquisitorial practice. "On the contrary," he reasoned, "it seems that all the times that the affairs of the Holy Office have been tried outside the order and secrecy which in it are taken as the style, it has been in great harm to the trials and persons and consciences of the accused." Implicitly, the trial might also serve to publicize well-ordered inquisitorial procedure, while making a powerful and public example of the erring archbishop. Framed as his personal opinion, Valtodano offered one caveat: he advised that Carranza be isolated from other prisoners and outside communication. He recommended incarceration in a private house rather than a monastery, "because there will be better guard and greater secrecy." He worked from experience – knowing that inquisitorial secrecy often existed more in theory than in practice – as an inquisitor who had presided in Toledo during a jailbreak and who suspected communication among the prisoners in Valladolid.[53]

Thus, Valtodano argued that there were sufficient bases and adequate procedural tools available to try Carranza. In doing so, he served the agenda of others, Valdés chief among them, and sought to increase the authority and powers of his office, thereby also allowing the crown a significant role in ecclesiastical affairs. He identified himself with prevalent currents of thought that held the Inquisition as a necessary tool to combat heresy, fraternal correction as sometimes an insufficient measure, and a corrupted clergy as an existential threat to religion and the kingdom. The very construction of his memorandum modeled good inquisitorial procedure: he compared the quality and variety of proofs and witnesses, he recommended practices both fitted to the case at hand and conforming to institutional norms, and he drew upon his judicial experience to respond to a situation without clear precedent. And Valtodano was gaining a reputation. In the wake of the Valladolid trials, Valdés – searching for the conditions that had allowed a network of heretics to grow – ordered a visitation of Valladolid's Inquisition. During the inspection, one man reported having come all the way from Cuenca to the Valladolid tribunal because Valtodano had put it in such good order.[54]

---

[53] "por el co[n]trario se e[n]tre de q[ue] todas las vezes q[ue] se a[n] tratado los negoçios de este sa[n]to offiçio fuera de la orden y secreto q[ue] en el se tiene de estilo asido en gra[n] daño de las causas y p[er]sonas y co[n]çie[n]çias delos reos"; "porq[ue] aura mejor guarda y mayor secreto," ibid.

[54] May 1560, AHN, Inq., leg. 2136, exp. 2, fol. 11r.

The archbishop was taken into custody in a dramatic nighttime ambush, on August 22, 1559. It was Valtodano and Simancas who first appeared – as representatives of the *Suprema* and the Inquisitor General – before the prisoner in Valladolid a week later, to notify him that he might select two servants to attend him during his trial.[55] Carranza, demonstrating remarkable legal savvy, quickly initiated proceedings to recuse Valdés from his case, largely on the basis of personal enmity. The recusal process demonstrated the myriad interconnections between those involved in the trial. One deponent mentioned how he had once substituted for Valtodano in the entourage of the late bishop of Badajoz. Another offered insight into the inquisitorial rumor mill, recounting a conversation at the university in Valladolid, in which friar Melchor Cano (one of Carranza's chief opponents) reported hearing from the inquisitors – and, in particular, from Valtodano, just before Carranza's return to Spain – that they planned to ban the *Catechism*: "He said that, among other things in the book that scandalized the inquisitors, was that those that were to be bishops, had to know themselves how to preach and teach the Gospel of Jesus Christ."[56] This seemingly absurd objection perhaps indicates how, in a highly charged environment, some read the *Catechism* as favoring Lutheran ideas about pastoral care.

A pair of specially appointed judges found in Carranza's favor in February 1560; Valtodano and Simancas were with Valdés when he was notified that he had been recused. Carranza also successfully excluded two other members of the *Suprema*: Pérez and de los Cobos. In March, Pope Pius IV conceded the power to Philip II to appoint a replacement judge, and the king named the archbishop of Santiago de Compostela, Gaspar de Zúñiga y Avellaneda. Zúñiga, then, subdelegated the judicial work to Valtodano and Simancas on May 2, 1561, and the pair opened the proceedings in Valladolid on May 22. Carranza continued to protest and appeal to Rome. The trial of Spain's primate had been placed under the daily oversight not of the pope, nor even of another archbishop, but merely a pair of sub-delegated jurist-clerics, royal councillors who gained their

---

[55] Tellechea Idígoras, "El Proceso del Arzobispo Carranza," *HIEA* 1:566.

[56] "entre otras cosas que dezía en el libro que se escandalizavan los inquisidores, hera que los que avían de ser obispos, avían de saber por sus personas predicar y enseñar el Evangelio de Ihesu Christo," testimony of Dr. Martín Malo, December 29, 1559, Alcalá; on Badajoz, testimony of Lic. Céspedes, December 29, 1559, Toledo; Tellechea Idígoras, *Documentos Históricos*, 1:213, 228.

bishop's mitres only while they judged Carranza.[57] Meanwhile, in a round of extrajudicial politicking, Spanish agents in Rome advocated for the suitability of these judges. They successfully lobbied Pius IV, contending that Carranza would not be satisfied with any judge, and asserting the archbishop of Santiago's impeccable character and the "goodness and integrity" of Valtodano and Simancas, "beyond their learning."[58] The stage finally set, Tellechea Idígoras has sketched Archbishop Zúñiga as flummoxed by how to proceed with the trial, striving to adhere to customary procedure in a legal situation without precedent.

The start of Carranza's trial has usually been told in that fashion, as a contest among the highest elites: Carranza, Cano, Valdés, Zúñiga, Philip II, Pius IV. Mid-level judges like Valtodano and Simancas have often been rendered collectively, as zealous, cynical, and inhumane slaves of procedure.[59] Yet to a significant extent, Valtodano had designed the legal environment in which Carranza's trial would begin. His actions were indeed circumscribed by legal procedure, by his institutional context, and by the directives of higher authorities. At the same time, it was individual judges like him who gave specific shape to a trial even as important as Carranza's, who sifted the evidence, gauged the heretical threat of the accused, proposed a means of proceeding, persuaded their colleagues, and implemented it. The initiation of the Carranza case can serve as a useful reminder to attend not only to the actions, experience, aspirations, loyalties, and ideological commitments of those at the helm of institutions, but also to those below them. The Carranza trial, moreover, grew out of contests over the directions religious reform would take in the Spanish Church. Regarding the range and vibrancy of Catholic thought in the early sixteenth century, modern scholars have seen those who brought about Carranza's downfall as narrow-minded, retrograde opponents of blossoming reform. Many of their contemporaries thought likewise. Still, it is worth remembering that inquisitors like Valtodano also perceived themselves as reformers. For them, efforts to rework and strengthen inquisitorial procedure were, in part, attempts to renovate ecclesiastical justice and with it, the Church.

---

[57] Tellechea Idígoras, *Documentos Históricos*,1:6, see also 4:12–14. The pair had already worked together on another special commission in 1560; for their initial audience with Carranza, including their suspicions about correspondence being sent to him, see Valtodano and Simancas to Zúñiga, May 23, 1561, RAH 9/1810, fols. 100r-101r.

[58] "è bondad, è integridad dellos, ultra dela doctrina," Francisco de Vargas, June 28, 1561, AHN, Inq., leg. 100, fol. 136r. This letter is partly in cipher; for the decoded text and analysis, see Tellechea Idígoras, "Documentación cifrada y diplomacia inquisitorial," *HIEA* 3:41–56.

[59] For example, Tellechea Idígoras, "El Proceso del Arzobispo Carranza," *HIEA* 1:570, 576.

RESIDENCE AND REFORM

Carranza's trial would dominate the next five and a half years of Valtodano's life. The pair of sub-delegated judges ceased to participate in the regular work of the *Suprema* after the middle of May 1561; in June, Valtodano became the bishop of Palencia, the promotion making his judgment of Carranza more legitimate. After 1562, Valtodano's income came from his diocese instead of from the *Suprema*, yet he remained principally in Valladolid, presiding over the case – in correspondence with Zúñiga – and orchestrating the roles of other participants in it, witnesses, consultants, attorneys, servants, a physician, and other officials.[60] By the Lenten season of 1563, the Council of Trent was on the cusp of its final sessions, and Valtodano faced a dilemma familiar to sixteenth-century prelates: he could not be in three places at the same time. His inquisitorial office and special delegation continued to require his presence in Carranza's courtroom in Valladolid, while his episcopal office implied other priorities. As bishop of Palencia, he sought to visit his diocese (of which Valladolid was, admittedly, a part) in anticipation of celebrating Easter in his cathedral city. As a bishop, his presence in Trent could also have given him and his diocese a vote in the great council; instead, he had sent a younger Franciscan friar there.

At the same time, those convened at Trent railed against absenteeism. In 1547, they had renewed earlier decrees on the subject; the penalties began with partial forfeiture of income after six months of absence. They rebuked such negligent clerics:

Like hirelings they desert the flocks committed to them and do not attend to the guardianship of their sheep, whose blood will be required at their hands by the supreme judge; since it is most certain that the shepherd's excuse will not be accepted if the wolf devours the sheep and he knows it not.[61]

---

[60] After May 1561, the *Suprema* was usually in Madrid. AHN, Inq., lib. 248, fols. 103r, 106rff. For his elevation to Palencia (June 2, 1561) and to Santiago de Compostela (February 20, 1570), *HC* 3:189, 285; *DHEE*, 3:1870, 4:2201; *EE*, 71. On the *Suprema*'s salaries (Valtodano's had been 150,000 maravedís; it leapt, as all did, to 300,000 in his final payment of March 8, 1561), AHN, Inq., lib. 248, fols. 63vff. Cf. AHN, Inq., lib. 500, fols. 370v–76r. For letters from Valtodano and Simancas to Zúñiga, at least one a month, from May 1561 through the end of 1563, see RAH 9/1810, fols. 87rff. Correspondence decreased in 1564. In an exceptional case, Valdés asked them to cast their opinions when the *Suprema* was in disagreement over a trial in January 1563, AHN, Inq., lib. 575, fol. 152r.

[61] Council of Trent, January 13, 1547, sess. 6, decree concerning reform, chap. 1, *Canons and Decrees*, 47. On uses of the biblical imagery here (related to Matt 7:15), cf. Christine

Exceptions remained for prelates called to special duties (for which the Carranza trial could arguably qualify). When the delegates met again at Trent in the summer of 1563, they addressed the problem of episcopal residence more emphatically, if still ambiguously, continuing to recognize some absences as legitimate and necessary. They enjoined clerics to examine their own consciences on the subject and then stressed "that unless their episcopal duties call them elsewhere in their diocese," they were to be in their cathedral church in signal periods of the liturgical year, "on which days especially the sheep ought to be refreshed and to rejoice in the Lord at the presence of the shepherd."[62]

In his letters from Valladolid – to Archbishop Zúñiga and to the cathedral chapter in Palencia – Valtodano grappled with these mandates and the imperative to be diligent as both inquisitor and bishop. He repeatedly expressed his desire both to visit and reside in his cathedral and to acquaint himself with the canons "by sight and by word." He lamented missing his first Easter season as a bishop in 1562, but "that the affairs which I treat here will not allow it, nor do I have license to leave them even for an hour." In subsequent years, he negotiated temporary absences from the trial in order to go to Palencia for Holy Week. Even during those interludes – as he had done as an inquisitor in Toledo years earlier – he remained in frequent communication. Zúñiga sent dispatches directly to Valtodano in Palencia; Valtodano and Simancas corresponded, often with only a day's lag time; and Simancas assured Zúñiga that their business would resume as soon as Easter had passed.[63]

Before long, Valtodano was seeking to extricate himself from his inquisitorial work. He depicted his contribution to the lengthening Carranza case as minimal, proposed that Simancas could easily handle it alone, and stressed "[his] extreme inconvenience as much to [his] estate as the affairs of [his] church" at the current arrangement.[64] The issue of residency preoccupied Valtodano, although there are multiple ways to interpret his behavior. The trial had more or less stalled, and questions were again

---

Caldwell Ames, *Righteous Persecution: Inquisition, Dominicans and Christianity in the Middle Ages* (Philadelphia: University of Pennsylvania Press, 2009), chap. 1.

[62] Council of Trent, July 15, 1563, sess. 23, decree concerning reform, chap. 1, *Canons and Decrees*, 165.

[63] "por vista y por palabra"; "q[ue] los neg[oci]os q[ue] aqui tracto no dan lugar a ello ni tengo lic[enci]a para dexarlos ni por vna ora." Valtodano to chapter, December 15, 1561, holograph, ACP, Armario XIV, caja 3A, no. 1. Cf. letter there of December 19, 1564; RAH 9/1810, fols. 212r, 297r, 299v, 305, 306r-7v, 309r-10r, 311, 408.

[64] "muy gra[n]de incomodidad mia asi de mi hazienda como de los negocios de mi iglesia." Valtodano to Zúñiga, February, 23, 1563, holograph, RAH 9/1810, fol. 286r; cf. fol. 207.

coming from Rome. With the publication of the Tridentine decrees, a plan for reform had been clarified; for Valtodano, it pointed to residence in his cathedral and directing his energies to implementing the new directives as a bishop. The experience he acquired in Valladolid may well have changed his perceptions. Maybe, as the prosecution dragged on (or as his knowledge of the case and the accused grew), his support for the endeavor waned. The inventory of his more than two-hundred-volume library, made after his death, would list not only numerous proceedings of church councils, among them copies of the Tridentine decrees, but also works on residency; it even included Carranza's 1547 tract in favor of episcopal residence.[65]

Changing political winds were also in the air. The tension only increased as the archbishop's trial hung in limbo throughout 1566. The inquisitors reasoned that justice required them to convene at least one audience a month with Carranza, even as the process had ground to a halt, awaiting negotiations between Madrid and Rome. Valdés fell from favor that year – largely a result of his pursuit of Carranza – and was forced out of the office of Inquisitor General and into retirement (and residence) in his archiepiscopal city of Seville. If Valtodano likely contemplated a weak papacy and stalled conciliar reform when he advocated opening Carranza's case in 1559, by 1566, he saw a vibrant reforming pope and a crown invested in promoting Trent's new mandates.[66] That year, the newly elected Pius V – involved in the dicey renegotiation of the Carranza affair, and himself a former inquisitor – sent a pastoral letter to Valtodano (in his capacity as bishop of Palencia). The pope summoned him to the work of Tridentine reform as the sole remaining remedy for an embattled Church and reminded him to act with an eye to eternal judgment, as mortal life was fleeting. He urged his bishop to model pastoral ideals, persuading and educating his subordinates to do the same, while also to "take care and great vigilance to divert your sheep from the artifices of the heretics as from wolves, butchers, and highwaymen, and … if there is a sheep that is

---

[65] José García Oro and María José Portela Silva, "El arzobispo Valtodano (1570–1572). Un recuento de su Testamentaría" *Compostellanum* 50 (2005): 725. This work of Carranza's, published in Latin, was not condemned. For a modern edition, see Bartolomé Carranza de Miranda, *Controversia sobre la necesaria residencia personal de los obispos y de los otros pastores inferiores*, ed. José Ignacio Tellechea Idígoras (Madrid: Fundación Universitaria Española, Universidad Pontificia de Salamanca, 1993).

[66] Both judges attempted to depart for their provincial councils in July 1565; Zúñiga released Valtodano before Simancas, see RAH 9/1810, fol. 410. On the "religious dynamism" of the 1560s, see Ignasi Fernández Terricabras, *Philippe II et la Contre-Réforme: L'Église Espagnole à l'Heure du Concile de Trente* (Paris: Éditions Publisud, 2001), 51.

touched by this evil illness of heresy, do not grant it a place to infect the others with its contagious pestilence."[67]

At the end of the year, the Valladolid phase of the trial ended as Carranza's case was revoked to Rome. With that courtroom's close, Valtodano turned toward episcopal work for the remainder of his career, while his colleague Simancas would take a decidedly different route. From that vantage point, Valtodano could have seen Carranza's inquisitorial process as a failure on multiple counts. It had brought no judicial resolution to serious heretical charges; in a poignant irony, in the name of reform, it had caused the principal archdiocese of Spain to be lacking a prelate at a crucial reforming juncture in the Church's history.

Although there was nothing unusual in the promotion of an inquisitor to the episcopate, Valtodano made his choice of a new path increasingly clear. In 1564, Philip II had nominated him to the presidency of Valladolid's Chancery; Valtodano declined the appointment as incompatible with his pastoral duties in Palencia. Other options were available to him, as his successor in Palencia held the two offices simultaneously, and other Spanish prelates occupied important royal offices even after Trent.[68] Nor was his focus on Palencia an effort to decrease his activity. He still took short-term commissions in the region, continuing his career-long regime of frequent official travel. In the summer of 1565, he returned to Salamanca to inspect his own *colegio mayor* of San Bartolomé; in 1567, he conducted the visitation of the *colegio mayor* of Santa Cruz at the University of Valladolid.[69] Subordinate councils followed Trent's conclusion, and so Valtodano traveled to Toledo to attend his provincial council.

Toledo's cathedral chapter protested that the council should await the end of the archbishop's trial. When it nevertheless began in February 1566, Valtodano was selected (with the council's president Cristóbal de Rojas y Sandoval, the bishop of Córdoba) to inspect the interim governance of the

---

[67] "...ten cuidado y vigilancia grandissima de desuiar de tus ouejas las asechanzas delos herejes como de lobos carnizeros y salteadores, Y ... si ay alguna oueja, queesté tocada de esta maluada enfermedad de heregia, no tenga lugar de inficionar a las otras, con su contagiosa pestilencia." Pius V to Valtodano, February 1, 1566, BL, Add. 16176, fol. 101r.

[68] González Dávila, *Teatro*, 1:97; Richard L. Kagan, *Lawsuits and Litigants in Castile, 1500–1700* (Chapel Hill: The University of North Carolina Press, 1981), chap. 5.

[69] Valtodano, holograph, August 2, 1565, AGS, PR 22, doc. 21; February 25, 1566, ibid., doc. 35. Although an account of the latter is indexed in the pencil catalogs of the BNE, I was unable to locate the document. González Dávila, *Teatro*, 1:97; García Oro and Portela Silva, "La visita de Cristóbal de Valtodano y el proceso de codificación académica," *Liceo Franciscano* 55 (2003): 71–80.

archdiocese. The pair drafted a list of questions to put to witnesses. First, they asked about diligent administration, inquiring whether the governor, don Gómez Tello Girón, had inspected the cathedral building and its chapter and whether he had personally visited the diocese. Then, they probed for evidence of misconduct: irregularities in practice, failure to receive all petitioners and supplicants, poor administration of goods and rents. They made the application of the two-year-old Tridentine decrees the benchmark and concluded with stinging criticism of the governor, who was soon replaced. They enumerated his failures. He had not held a synod nor repartitioned the cathedral prebends according to the terms of the council. He had not compelled residence, nor punished absent canons, nor applied the Tridentine ban on absences longer than ninety days. He had failed to keep the convents properly cloistered and belatedly published the new ruling on clandestine marriages. The bishops found the governor not merely negligent, but deliberately fraudulent, abusing the Tridentine decrees – particularly in matters of appointments and patronage – right under the provincial council's nose.[70] In this fashion, Valtodano could be seen to construct himself as an expert in the application of Trent. For Carranza's judge to root out abuses in Toledo had added effect; it could reflect back on the inquisitorial proceedings, suggesting that the trial was more about a coherent plan to defend orthodoxy and improve the Church, and less about the rivalries and enmities that also animated the archbishop's prosecution.

Next, Valtodano turned to Palencia. In April 1566, he convened a diocesan synod. In the years that followed, he began construction of a new episcopal palace, tackled monastic reforms in Valladolid, and carried out a visitation of the diocese. He ordered an updated inventory of the cathedral's relics and collected revenue to build a "house of studies." He directed his accumulated experience to implementing reforms in the diocese. He had the ordinary types of conflicts with the cathedral chapter, clashing on elements of the new Tridentine decrees and negotiating the funneling of a deceased canon's alms to the city's prominent hospital of San Antolín. The chapter protested Valtodano's decision to conduct a

---

[70] On the investigation: AFZ, Altamira 149, doc. 12. On the council: IVDJ, Envío 89, caja 1, nos. 268–303; AGS, Estado, legs. 148, 153; Valtodano, January 7, 1566, ACP, Armario XIV, caja 3A, no. 1. See also Fernández Terricabras, *Philippe II et la Contre-Réforme*, 183–217. For one sense of the many other approaches to reform, see Gillian Ahlgren, "Francisca de los Apóstoles: A Visionary Voice for Reform in Sixteenth-Century Toledo," in *Women in the Inquisition*, ed. Mary E. Giles (Baltimore, MD: The Johns Hopkins University Press, 1999), 119–33.

visitation of the cathedral, complaining it was a violation of its statutes and privileges; each side appealed to the Rota in Rome, and the struggle continued even after the bishop's departure from Palencia.[71] Throughout, Valtodano continued to focus on clerical dignity and malpractice. When he wrote to Palencia's cathedral chapter about scandals that implicated canons, he urged good comportment, reasoning that "being all one body, we participate in the good or bad outcome of our affairs."[72] In his first months as a bishop, when faced with a contest over the conditions of imprisonment of a canon charged with various crimes, he explained: "I want so much to excuse inconveniences that what I would most like is that no one of that, our holy church, arrive at similar situations, which would be done through God's grace if we were all very determined to not offend Him and we respected very much the ecclesiastical state and habit which we profess." He also offered a theory of correction and judgment to his new colleagues in Palencia: "To err once, although it may be in disrespect of his superior, seems that it could in some manner be tolerated and concealed, but to add one mistake to another is to give an opportunity so that the judges lose patience."[73] Thus, Valtodano rebuked the chapter, urging its members to temper accusations of judicial excess with recognition of the canon's failure to reform his ways. Still, he advocated on the erring canon's behalf, matching the rebuke with care for his new flock. As he sat in judgment over Carranza, he grappled with how a bishop could prevent further scandals among the clergy, balancing fraternal and judicial modes of correction.

As a bishop, Valtodano's attitude toward the Inquisition was mixed. He commissioned an inquisitor to undertake a visitation in his diocese; against

---

[71] This is the palace still standing in Palencia. González Dávila, *Teatro*, 1:97; Alvarez Reyero, *Crónicas*; Jesús María Parrado del Olmo, "Datos Inéditos de Entalladores Palentinos del Siglo XVI," *Publicaciones de la Institución Tello Téllez de Meneses* 54 (1986): 264–65; Valtodano, August 22 and December 11, 1562, January 17, 1564, ACP, Armario XIV, caja 3A, no. 1; ACP, Armario IV, leg. 1, estatutos, no. 2 and leg. 8, nos. 7–8; ACP, Armario I, leg. 1, doc. 15; Valtodano, January 20, 1569, AGS, PR 23, doc. 127.

[72] "siendo todos un cuerpo participamos enel bueno o malo suçeso de n[uest]ros negoçios." Valtodano, January 17, 1564, ACP, Armario XIV, caja 3A, no. 1.

[73] "Desseo ta[n]to escusar ynconuenie[n]tes quelo q[ue] yo mas querria es q[ue] ning[un]a persona de essa n[uest]ra s[an]ta yglesia viniese a semejantes occasiones lo qual se haria mediante la gra[cia] de Dios si estuuiesemos todos muy determinados a no le offender y respectasemos mucho el estado y habito ecclesiastico q[ue] professamos"; "errar una vez aunq[ue] sea en desacato de su superior, parece q[ue] se puede en alguna manera tolerar y dissimular, pero añadir un yerro a otro es dar occasion aque los Juezes pierdan el sufrimie[n]to." The case was of Master Torres, first jailed in his brother's house. Valtodano, December 15, 1561, ibid.

the wishes of the cathedral chapter, he attempted to appoint the same inquisitor of Valladolid's tribunal to an empty prebend, and so to provide funding for the tribunal.[74] Yet he also resisted jurisdictional encroachment. In 1568, Valladolid's inquisitors sought to obtain the permanent delegation of the powers of local bishops, as the ordinary inquisitors in their dioceses; Valtodano was the lone holdout. The inquisitors complained to the *Suprema*, "that by two letters we have entreated His Lordship and he has responded that he will not give [his] power to another." They termed the bishop's refusal "negligence" and insisted on their right to determine the cases in question without his involvement. Valtodano offered a rather different account. When the inquisitors had asked him to send authorization for them to decide any matters that concerned his bishopric, he implied malpractice, explaining that "in that inquisition they are in the habit of not treating with the ordinary as they do in other inquisitions, and in order to prevent innovations," he would grant his power only on a case-by-case basis. He too appealed to the Inquisitor General and the *Suprema*. He summoned his reputation as an inquisitor to make his refusal even more resounding: "I have a more particular obligation than any other to write to the Holy Office for the reason that is notorious to everyone and also I have to watch the authority of my [episcopal] dignity."[75] Valtodano used his knowledge of inquisitorial procedure and his influence to seek to maintain equilibrium between bishops and inquisitors in combating heresy, and to defend the potential role for bishops in inquisition tribunals.

In November 1569, Philip II nominated Valtodano to succeed Zúñiga, his former superior in the Carranza case, as archbishop of Santiago de Compostela. Such high promotion had evaded most of his former colleagues. When he arrived in Santiago nearly a year later, he was suffering

---

[74] The *visita* was of Valladolid's Carmelites. When the canon Francisco Zapata died in August 1568, the chapter approved Lic. Merida (who promptly took possession), while Valtodano nominated inquisitor Dr. Guijano de Mercado (who appealed to the Chancery). Guijano de Mercado to Inquisitor General, July 25 and October 5, 1568, AHN, Inq., leg. 3189, nos. 76, 98.

[75] "q[ue] por dos cartas lo emos supplicado a su s[eñorí]a y ha respondido q[ue] no dara poder a otro," Valladolid inquisitors to *Suprema*, July 17, 1568. And: "en essa inq[uisici]on estan en stilo deno hazer conel ordina[ri]o lo q[ue] en otras inquisiçiones/ y para escusar novedades me apresçio dar el poder a v[uestra] m[erced] Insolid., elqual renovare todas las vezes q[ue] conel se satisfiziere[n]." And: "obligacio[n] tengo yo mas particular q[ue] otro ninguno de [scr]uir al s[an]to off[ici]o por la razo[n] q[ue] a todos es notoria y tan bien la tengo a mirar por la auctoridad de mi dignidad," Valtodano to Valladolid inquisitors, copy, June 14, 1568, AHN, Inq., leg. 3189, no. 74. The senior member of the tribunal was inquisitor Guigelmo and the case in question was of Leonor de Cisneros.

from an illness that had delayed him for months in Valladolid; he left scant written traces of his two years as archbishop. Even in poor health, however, Valtodano maintained his pose as a reformer, seeking to demonstrate his persisting diligence, particularly in applying Tridentine reforms.[76] He promoted monastic orders as potential agents of reform. Noting the lack of a Hieronymite house in Galicia, he proposed ejecting – with compensation – the current occupants of the priory of Santa María de Sar on the city's edge, regular canons "although they live[d] without a rule." His aim was "so those clerics would leave there and the Hieronymite order come to this land, to give some doctrine, politeness, and Religion to the people that are so barbarous." He may have been particularly inclined to that order, as he owned a Hieronymite missal. Rendering the region a peripheral zone in need of imported examples, his initiative paralleled inquisitorial developments – in which there is no evidence of the archbishop's involvement – as a tribunal was founded in the city in 1574, after more than a decade of false starts. Nor did Valtodano neglect his place of origin and its sacred geography; in his later years, he donated funds sufficient to found an Augustinian monastery in Fontiveros.[77]

Valtodano returned to a tool of governance he had used throughout his career, embarking on a visitation of Santiago's hospitals in October 1571, authorized by a papal brief and spurred by royal suspicion of negligence; as institutions at the heart of urban life, hospitals were a focus of reforming directives issued in both Madrid and Rome in the 1560s and 1570s. Over the next several months, Valtodano investigated the administration of all the city's hospitals and made some notes on the works, wealth, and

[76] Consecrated May 21, he took possession by proxy June 2, and attended the chapter meeting September 22, 1570, ACS, IG 516, fols. 494r-96v; IG 517, fol. 21r; AGS, PR 57, docs. 23, 27, 28, 89. For a lawsuit from 1572, see AHDS, no. 298 antiguo, exp. 6, Cabildo de Santiago. See also Pazos, *Episcopado Gallego*, 1:35–50; D. Antonio López Ferreiro, *Historia de la Santa A. M. Iglesia de Santiago de Compostela* (Santiago de Compostela: Seminario Conciliar Central, 1905), 8:237–49; notes from June 1887 for an episcopologio, Biblioteca Universitaria, Santiago, RSE Espino, Foll. 3–21; Ángel Rodríguez González, "Notas al Episcopologio Compostelano: Relaciones del Arzobispo D. Cristóbal Fernández Valtodano con la Ciudad de Santiago," *Compostellanum* 14 (1969): 671–82.

[77] "aunq[ue] ellos biuen sin regla"; "como aq[ue]llos clerigos saliesen, de alli y la orden de sanct Jer[oni]mo viniese, a esta tierra, a dar siquiera doctrina, de policia, y de Religion a la gente, q[ue] esta tan barbara," Valtodano to Cardinal of Sigüenza, February 26, 1572, BL, Add. 28336, doc. 89, fol. 177. García Oro and Portela Silva, "El arzobispo Valtodano," 719; González Dávila, *Teatro*, 1:97. On the tribunal, see Jaime Contreras, *El Santo Oficio de la Inquisición de Galicia, 1560-1700: poder, sociedad y cultura* (Madrid: Akal, 1982).

membership of the city's confraternities. He inquired into compliance with the terms of foundation, financial solvency, the quality of hospitality, and the performance of pious works.[78] He had attended to similar reforms as Palencia's bishop, corresponding in 1562 about that city's principal hospital of San Antolín; in a lean year, he had proposed, if no other monies could be found, to divert funds allocated for building a library to the hospital, in order to mitigate the suffering of the poor.[79] There was particular demand on Santiago's charitable foundations in these years. Aside from the regular traffic of pilgrims, recurring waves of plague struck Galicia between 1567 and 1570, causing some eight thousand deaths in the city alone, and disease continued to ravage the region well into the 1580s. This would be the final visitation of a long career, and even though its completion would be left for later prelates, it was the demonstration of a perpetual concern for reform that was most important.[80]

MISSIVES, MISSALS, EXORCISMS

A career like Valtodano's often dealt in paper; in letters, edicts and trial records; in recorded councils and inspections. Yet the kinds of writings Valtodano produced – and, equally, did not produce – reflected a particular sort of pastoral approach to his work. They may also offer a clue to his record of successful promotion. He did not devote his energies to writing for print; rather, he was honored in printed books written by others. He did write a notable amount of substantial official letters in his own hand (usually quite a bit longer than those of his colleague Simancas, for example), using his handwriting to more palpably offer his presence to places from which he was absent. Thus, he protected his opinions from a broader public view, while using his substantive missives to demonstrate his diligence in serving his offices.[81]

Valtodano patronized the careers of younger theologians. They, in turn, exalted him in print, commemorating him as a defender of the Church and

---

[78] AHDS, visita pastoral, 1.52.2 (old no. 1262), fols. 141–71r.

[79] Valtodano, August 17, 1562, ACP, Armario XIV, caja 3A, no. 1.

[80] The visitation ultimately concluded in 1586. On such initiatives, see García Oro and Portela Silva, *Las Reformas Hospitalarias del Renacimiento en la Corona de Castilla: Del Gran Hospital de Santiago a los Hospitales Generales* (Santiago de Compostela: Editorial del Eco Franciscano, 2005), 54–71, 83–86, 229–30.

[81] There is a cache of more than twenty holograph letters from Valtodano to the cathedral chapter in ACP, Armario XIV, caja 3A, no. 1. Among the others from across his career are those in the Carranza proceedings, including many from 1566: RAH 9/1812, fols. 237r-66v, 349, 353, 463r-64v.

elevating themselves by association. The most famous of his clients was Benito Arias Montano (1527–98), famous as one of the foremost Spanish humanists and biblical translators.[82] One of Arias Montano's earliest printed works – a treatise on rhetoric, drafted in León in 1561 and published by the Plantin Press in Antwerp in 1569 – placed Valtodano in a cohort of virtuous clerics.[83] Composed when Valtodano was both Palencia's bishop and Carranza's judge, Arias Montano depicted the diocese as blessed with an exemplary pastor for troubled times, using reason to persuade and teach his flock. He praised Valtodano's "service as severe judge and pious father" and cast him as a victorious military commander, wishing him a long career continuing to foil any who brought Luther's deceptions "to our shores."[84] Friar Francisco de Orantes y Villena (1516–84) was another recipient of Valtodano's patronage, sent to Trent in his stead. Orantes lauded Valtodano's service to the faith in the dedications of both the printed version of a sermon he delivered at the council and in his hefty refutation of Jean Calvin's *Institutes*. Valtodano seems to have owned a copy of the latter, Orantes's *Locorum Catholicorum*.[85]

Valtodano's name also circulated in connection with his official duties. He was listed in the publication of a censorship edict in Toledo and in accounts of the May 1559 *auto de fe* in Valladolid.[86] He appeared in the

[82] In the same treatise, Arias Montano termed Valtodano "my refuge since childhood and after the death of my father." Born in the environs of Badajoz, the son of an Inquisition notary, Valtodano provided him financial support, aided his education (in theology at Alcalá), ordination, and acquisition of a prebend and likely helped him secure the position of royal chaplain in 1559. Guy Lazure, "To Dare Fame: Constructing a Cultural Elite in Sixteenth-Century Seville" (PhD diss., The Johns Hopkins University, 2003), 138–39, 154; *DHEE* 1:90–92.

[83] María Violeta Pérez Custodio, ed. and trans., Los *Rhetoricorum Libri Qvattvor* de Benito Arias Montano (Badajoz-Cádiz: Diputación Provincial de Badajoz-Universidad de Cádiz, 1995), IV, ll. 1000–36, 305–7.

[84] "tu servicio de severo juez y piadoso padre"; "nuestras riberas," ibid., 306–7.

[85] Orantes, an Observant Franciscan, had been associated with the universities of Alcalá de Henares, Salamanca, and Valladolid, and he studied with another prominent Franciscan anti-heretical writer, Alfonso de Castro. Later, he would become don Juan de Austria's confessor and, in the early 1580s, bishop of Oviedo. C. Gutiérrez, S.J., *Españoles en Trento* (Valladolid: CSIC, Instituto Jerónimo Zurita, 1951), 426–31. Francisco de Orantes, *Oratio Francisci Orantii Hispani* ... (Venice: Giordano Ziletti, 1563); de Orantes, *Locorum Catholicorum* ... *Libri Septem* (Venice: Giordano Ziletti, 1564). I think the "Locorum catholice sacre escripture" listed in the inventory refers to this book, which also had two Paris editions by 1566; García Oro and Portela Silva, "El arzobispo Valtodano," 730. For a report of Orantes's travel expenses, see RAH 9/1813, fols. 274–76, 283r.

[86] For example, the edict of Pérez and Valtodano, October 24, 1551, *Catalogvs librorvm reprobatorvm* ... (Toledo: Juan de Ayala, 1551; facsimile repr., New York: De Vinne Press, 1896), [30–32].

constitutions of his diocesan synod, printed in Palencia in 1567. Organized to aid in identifying what had changed or been reconfirmed with the recent Tridentine decrees, they gave particular care to the liturgy, working out the practical applications of changes to the liturgical calendar, and seeking to standardize Palencian worship.[87] As a reform-minded bishop, Valtodano was persistently attuned to the liturgy. Essential to the spiritual health of a diocese, its performance was one of the most public gauges of the Church's relative order or disorder.[88] When Palencia's canons sent rich ornaments and vestments for his consecration, he kept the crosier for use on feast days but quickly returned the rest to the cathedral. He urged his chapter to go further than requested by a royal decree and put special care into composing cycles of prayers. In Santiago, he ordered the choir to pray according to the new Compostellan breviary. After Valtodano's death, the canons remembered his concern for the use of proper forms and his creative solution to the problem of lengthy feast day offices, spacing out the preaching and the celebration of the solemn liturgy so that neither would be compromised.[89]

Valtodano's turn toward episcopal reform entailed sponsoring the publication of four liturgical tracts.[90] Such projects provided opportunities to dispense patronage, and two presbyters of Palencia's cathedral – Dr. Arze and Tomás Paz – became Valtodano's principal collaborators. Though Valtodano was already urging rapid completion of a Palencian breviary and missal in 1562, judging abridgement preferable to further delay, the missal only appeared in 1567, with a revised edition following the next

---

[87] *Constituciones synodales del Obispado de Palencia* ... (Palencia: Sebastián Martínez, 1567), fol. 10v. There are copies in ACP, Armario IV, leg. 5 (lacking fol. 15) and ADP, no. 3555. The synod concluded with the reading of the constitutions on June 29, 1566, in Palencia's cathedral. See also José Antonio Fuentes Caballero, *Concilios y Sínodos en la Diócesis de Palencia* (Palencia: Imprenta Provincial, 1980), 52–57.

[88] Simon Ditchfield has cautioned: "Scholars of Early Modern Catholicism ignore at their peril the significance that the correct performance of liturgy had as a basis for a reformed priesthood." Ditchfield, *Liturgy, Sanctity and History in Tridentine Italy* (Cambridge, UK: Cambridge University Press, 1995), 11–12.

[89] Valtodano, October 15, 1561, and March 14, 1565, ACP, Armario XIV, caja 3A, no. 1; October 15, 1571, and January 9, 1573, ACS, IG 517, fols. 71r, 136v-37r.

[90] *Methodus consecrationis sacri Chrismatis* ... (Valladolid: Sebastián Martínez, 1563); *Missale Pallantinum* ... (Palencia: Sebastián Martínez, 1567); *Missale Pallantinvm* ... (Palencia: Sebastián Martínez, 1568). A final work survives only in seventeenth-century editions: *Exorcismi sive adivrationes ad usum Palentinae Diocesis* ... [Valladolid?]: s.n., [1628?]. Two copies, seemingly of 1628, belonged to Palencian parishes (much of the episcopal archive was destroyed in the Napoleonic era), ADP, nos. 161, 162. There are listings of other Valladolid editions of 1651 and 1667. See also Alvarez Reyero, *Crónicas*, 264.

year, its dedication stressing the diligence of the diocese despite its great poverty.[91] Paz also composed a prescriptive treatise on the consecration of the chrism – an exercise fundamental to the performance of the sacraments and tied to the liturgy of Holy Week – published in Valladolid in 1563 and advertised by Valtodano "as a very beneficial and necessary thing for the metropolitan churches and cathedrals of these kingdoms."[92] These works emphasized correct performance of ceremonies, and each sought to balance the order of the Roman Church with Spanish ecclesiastical customs and local devotions, all the while defending the liturgy with a range of precedents from scripture and authorized tradition.[93] The canons, meanwhile, wrote Valtodano into a genealogy of virtuous practice and sought to shape his course of action. Arze, for instance, depicted him as continuing the work begun by his predecessor in the see, Pedro de la Gasca (who had also been a councillor of the *Suprema*), and following in apostolic footsteps: "It will be of your labors, best pastor, to diligently take care that these [missals] are distributed properly, and edited in the most suitable order, just as Paul advises that it be accomplished in the Church of God."[94] This project included offering orthodox remedies to combat superstitions. Thus, the Palencian synod categorized sorcery as a false remedy, and Valtodano commissioned a manual for exorcisms, licensed for reprinting in the 1620s. Like some of the prayers in the missal, it responded to the routine catastrophes of early modern life, providing authorized means for clerics to cure all manner of ills, from storm clouds to people possessed by demons to the devastation of fertile land by insects. Such work aimed to bring common practices under clerical supervision, consolidate the social

---

[91] Valtodano to Arze and Paz, January 12, 1562, ACP, Armario XIV, Caja 3A, no. 1; *Missale Pallantinum* (1568), fol. 1v.

[92] *Methodus consecrationis*, fol. [ii]r. Cf. Valtodano's dedicatory letter, *Missale Pallantinum* (1567), fol. [ii]r. At his death, Valtodano mourned Arze as an exemplary canon, June 3, 1564, ACP, Armario XIV, Caja 3A, no. 1.

[93] See, for example, the liturgy for the mass for Palencia's patron, *Missale Pallantinum* (1567), fol. 343; Valtodano also owned a manuscript book of the martyrology according to Palencian custom; García Oro and Portela Silva, "El arzobispo Valtodano," 728; cf. letters regarding Philip II's promotion of universal breviaries and missals, AGS, Estado, leg. 153, docs. 10, 26. On these issues, see especially Ditchfield, *Liturgy, Sanctity and History*; William Christian, *Local Religion in Sixteenth-Century Spain* (Princeton, NJ: Princeton University Press, 1981); Sara T. Nalle, *God in La Mancha: Religious Reform and the People of Cuenca, 1500–1650* (Baltimore, MD: The Johns Hopkins University Press, 1992).

[94] "Tuarum erit partium, pastor optime, curare sedulo, vt quae apte digesta sunt, et in conuenientissimum redacta ordinem, prout Paulus monet, in ecclesia Dei peragantur." The marginalia noted 1 Cor 14. *Missale Pallantinum* (1567). Paz offered similar praise in his dedication of December 15, 1562, *Methodus consecrationis*, fol. [ii]v.

roles of the secular clergy, and improve clerical behavior. These were among the sort of books that Valtodano himself owned: conciliar decrees, reforming polemics, liturgical manuals, and tracts against witchcraft and superstition. He not only spurred their publication, but also distributed them across his networks of affiliation, giving twelve copies of Paz's work on consecration to the Badajoz cathedral, where he had once served. Valtodano might have expected that such work would be his principal legacy, with his name recorded in the kinds of books he understood as essential to reforms.

His cathedrals did seek to lay claim to his memory and to his estate. After Valtodano's death, the Santiago chapter sent a piece of his silver to Palencia as a remembrance; Paz, still a canon in Palencia, in turn pursued an even division of the late archbishop's pontifical goods between the two churches.[95] Valtodano was buried between the Santiago cathedral's two choirs, and his epitaph – inscribed on a bronze plaque – identified him by his birthplace, his status as a jurist, and his two episcopal offices and praised him for his broad learning and as "a zealous champion of the Catholic faith."[96]

Two later accounts of the Carranza trial also sought to lay claim to Valtodano. Several years after the archbishop's death, Simancas remembered him for his pivotal role in the 1559 Lutheran trials and depicted him as a model of juridical learning and prudence.[97] If Simancas invoked Valtodano's virtues to justify the Carranza affair, in the 1580s, Pedro Salazar de Mendoza, a jurist and canon of Toledo's cathedral, summoned him in a bid to rehabilitate the reputations of both Carranza and the Spanish Inquisition in the trial's wake. Salazar offered a vivid depiction of that Valladolid courtroom, noticeably omitting Simancas, and describing how, early in his trial, Carranza "was accustomed to say to the bishop of Palencia, Valtodano, his judge, whose conversation he greatly enjoyed: that if God removed him from prison, he would build in la Vega de Toledo a sumptuous hospital, receiving in it some of the city's humblest folk, that being uncared for, created filth and were a great detriment to the general

---

[95] Paz, October 27, 1573, ACS, Espolios, IG 174. See also November 29, 1572, ACS, IG 517, fol. 131r.

[96] "catholicae fidei acerrimus propvgnator;" González Dávila attributed it to the canon Dr. Alonso Bravo de la Cabaña; *Teatro*, 1:97–98. Miguel Taín Guzmán, *Dibujos históricos, epigráficos, y heráldicos del archivo de la catedral de Santiago* (A Coruña: Editorial Diputación Provincial, 2002), 187–88.

[97] Simancas, *Vida*, 157.

health."[98] Salazar drew together judge and accused in shared spiritual conversation about plans for charitable works. He offered Valtodano as the humane face of an Inquisition that was compatible with Tridentine reforms.

Valtodano left a last glimpse of himself in a letter. In February 1572, he wrote to Diego de Espinosa – then president of the Council of Castile, cardinal of Sigüenza, and Inquisitor General – petitioning for a license to return from Galicia to Castile. He described a disintegrating body:

I am in bed since the month of October [1571], although sometimes I get up as one who leaves, sent from jail, in order to return. Then, the other day, I did not have feet to walk or hands to write, nor to do any other thing, and many times, even, I cannot eat with my own hands. Last summer I had written to Your Lordship that I was thinking of leaving for Castile, to spend the winter, and I did not do it to take more experience [here] and it has been very much to my harm.[99]

By the end of the year both men – and even the pope, Pius V – would be dead. Valtodano never returned to Castile, dying in Santiago de Compostela on November 14, 1572.

Valtodano's plea – folded into a series of updates on official business – revealed the contingent nature of early modern institutions, reliant on such fragile bodies to administer them. It emphasized qualities that made a valuable servant of Crown, Church, or Inquisition: skill in persuasion and a pursuit of diligent administration to the point of self-neglect. Once imprisoned in his incapacity, however, Valtodano evoked the specter of negligence – what good was a prelate who could neither circulate among his flock nor write instructions to his subordinates and reports to his superiors? In sum, the letter offers a key to his career. He strived to embody two ideals of his day: the jurist serving justice with his expertise and the

[98] "Solia decir al Obispo de Palencia, Baltodano su Juez, de cuia conbersacion gustaba mucho: Que si Dios, lesacaba dela Prision, hauia de labrar enla Uega de Toledo un Hospital muy sumtuoso, reciuiendo ael algunos muy pequenos dela ciudad, que por estar desacomodados causaban inmundicia, y hera de gran detrimento ala salud en General." Pedro Salazar de Mendoza, *Vida, causa, y sucesos, prósperos, y adversos del Ilustrísimo y Reverendísimo Señor Don Fray Bartolomé de Carranza, y Miranda*, chap. 23, Spanish History MSS, Lilly Library, Indiana University.

[99] "estoi desdel mes de octubre, [en]la cama Aunq[ue] algunas vezes me levanto como quien sale, [en]viado de la carcel, para boluer, luego otro dia, ni tengo pies para andar ni manos para escreuir, ni para hazer otra cosa, y aun muchas vezes no puedo comer con mis propias manos. El verano pasado auia escripto a V[uestra] S[eñorí]a q[ue] pensaua yrme a castilla, a pasar el inuierno, nolo hize por tomar mas expiriencia y a sido mucho a mi daño." Valtodano to Cardinal of Sigüenza, February 26, 1572, BL, Add. 28336, doc. 89, fols. 177r-78v.

pastor attending to the spiritual health of the populace through diligent inspection and correction. The fervor with which he seemed to pursue the opening of the Carranza trial can be partly explained through these aims: pastoral care included correction, tailored to the scale of the threat at hand. The energy with which he later turned to ecclesiastical reforms, as a bishop, echoed his earlier patterns of behavior and ideological commitments. At the same time, it suggested his ability to adapt to a changing climate, marked by the confirmation of the Tridentine decrees and the double failure of the early phases of the Carranza affair, which had left Toledo without a prelate and had shown the Spanish Inquisition unable to successfully prosecute the archbishop. In an era of wide-ranging interpretations of reform and vehement disputes among Catholic authorities, he could reason that he was improving another line of the Church's defenses through diocesan reforms, liturgical revitalization, and the guarding of the powers of bishops even in heresy inquisitions. Throughout, he preserved the ability to dissolve into his corporate and official identities when it was useful to do so. Decisions like these enabled Valtodano to navigate the treacherous waters of royal and ecclesiastical politics without apparent misstep, his inquisitorial career serving as a vehicle to one of the highest offices in the Spanish Church, while he attempted in each post to promote his vision of what constituted reform.

CHAPTER 2

Writing the Inquisition

The Trials of Diego de Simancas

He who writes premeditates.[1]

For Castilians in the second half of the sixteenth century, Rome was a place where careers could be made. Although outside Philip II's domains, the papal city drew a steady traffic of Habsburg subjects, pursuing diplomatic affairs and charges related to the administration of Spanish Sicily and Naples. Spanish clerics could become influential papal courtiers, whereas some went there to make appeals, as agents of cathedral chapters, or on the business of monastic orders; others were appointed to the Rota, the pope's appellate court. Their conduct in Rome – including the patronage they extended, the households they built, and the relationships they forged there – could lead to increased honor, repute, and position back in Castile or elsewhere in the Habsburg monarchy. Spaniards in Rome navigated a complicated set of political dynamics, and this was even truer for those who landed there as a result of the Carranza trial. In 1567, nearly eight years after the archbishop of Toledo's imprisonment, Pius V revoked the case to his court; Carranza was transferred from his ad hoc inquisitorial jail in Valladolid to a less restrictive imprisonment in the Castel Sant'Angelo. Among those who

---

[1] From an anonymous polemic appended to Diego de Simancas, "Vida y Cosas Notables del Señor Obispo de Zamora Don Diego de Simancas," in *Autobiografías y Memorias*, ed. Manuel Serrano y Sanz, vol. 2 of *Nueva Biblioteca de Autores Españoles*, ed. Marcelino Menéndez y Pelayo (Madrid: Bailly, Bailliére, S. B., 1905), 208; all subsequent citations of the *Vida* are to this edition.

arrived in Rome with him was Diego de Simancas, sent as a representative of the Spanish Inquisition.[2]

Simancas's appointment to the Carranza case and, even more so, his assignment to Rome would fundamentally reshape inquisitorial law. Born in 1513, by 1567 Simancas was an experienced judge, having spent years on Valladolid's Chancery before his appointment first to the *Suprema* and then to Carranza's trial; he had recently been made a bishop. Toward the end of his life, Simancas claimed never to have had the desire to go to Rome. Nonetheless, the prospect might have seemed quite different in 1567. Although the Carranza case had already grown long and problematic, Simancas could have hoped for a fresh start in Rome. With the fall from favor of the Inquisitor General Valdés – to which Simancas may have owed his Roman exile – it was also an opportune moment to be away from the Spanish Court. A papal conviction would vindicate the actions of the Spanish Inquisition and elevate Simancas's work in Valladolid and service in Rome as indispensable to the fight against heresy. Simancas could reasonably have anticipated that after a spell in Rome, he could make a bid for more influence in Castile. At the end of the 1560s, the city offered even further possibilities. A bishop temporarily posted there gained a chance to be at the nerve center of Tridentine reform. For an inquisitor particularly interested in legal theory, it promised a chance to observe – and perhaps influence – other judicial environments.

Any such expectations were largely disappointed. Pius V died without concluding the case, and when Gregory XIII finally passed judgment in the spring of 1576, he left no party fully satisfied. He pronounced Carranza strongly suspicious of heresy; Carranza then abjured sixteen heretical propositions on April 14, fulfilling the papal judgment, and died in Rome, reconciled to the Church, a mere two and a half weeks later. After nine years in Rome, Simancas lived to return to his native Castile, where he would die in 1583. Still, his career had stalled. His subsequent promotions were more or less lateral moves and not the rewards he persistently sought. The experience of judging Carranza propelled Simancas in a decidedly different direction than it had his senior colleague in the early years of the case, Cristóbal Fernández de Valtodano. The Carranza case turned Simancas into a theorist. He began to publish on a host of subjects during

---

[2] For approaches to the Carranza trial, see Chapter 1, n. 45. On Spanish experiences in Rome, see Thomas James Dandelet, *Spanish Rome, 1500–1700* (New Haven, CT, and London: Yale University Press, 2001); Michael Levin, *Agents of Empire: Spanish Ambassadors in Sixteenth-Century Italy* (Ithaca, NY: Cornell University Press, 2005).

the years of the trial, printing tracts in Latin on political theory, inquisitorial jurisprudence, purity of blood statutes, the dignity of bishops, and
even inheritance law. He also put the trial at the center of his written life, a
Vida narrated in the first person that he began writing in 1577.

It is this autobiographical document, more than anything else, that has
attracted scholars to Simancas. Many historians have plucked juicy mor-
sels from the *Vida*, without analyzing in systematic fashion how it figured
in Simancas's career or how it intersected with his other writings. A
seemingly more personal glimpse into the world of the inquisitors, the
Vida – coupled with Simancas's prominence as a commentator on inquisitorial law – has allowed him to be depicted as the typical Spanish inquisitor. In a seminal essay of 1968, for example, Julio Caro Baroja argued that
Simancas was the quintessential jurist-inquisitor, an apt model for characterizing the inquisitors of his age.[3] In many ways, Simancas's face is a
deceptive one to pin on Spanish inquisitors as a group. His career was a
peculiar one. He was never an inquisitor in a local tribunal and arrived on
the *Suprema* from the civil judiciary and occasional legal consultation to
Valladolid's inquisitorial court, joining the council just months before
Carranza's imprisonment. Thus, the bulk of Simancas's judicial experience
in the Inquisition was confined to the Carranza trial, and much of that,
even, was in Rome.

This chapter, instead, approaches Simancas as a theorist who sought to
more firmly ground the role of the inquisitor in his society. His writings –
both his *Vida* and those in print – constitute a coherent body of thought.
His theorizing, moreover, was deeply intertwined with the particular
experiences of his career. In the midst of service to higher temporal authorities, he made his writings a means by which to knit his multiplicity of
official appointments and temporary charges into a more coherent whole.
In so doing, he sought to depict himself as a reformer of contemporary
institutions. Like Valtodano, he was simultaneously a bishop, a courtier,
and a judge in the later 1560s, yet he focused on different remedies for

---

[3] "puede servir de *modelo* en la caracterización de los inquisidores de esta época," Julio
Caro Baroja, *El Señor Inquisidor y otras vidas por oficio* (Madrid: Alianza Editorial, 1968),
34. The two other essential approaches to his thought are Stefania Pastore, *Il Vangelo e la
Spada. L'Inquisizione di Castiglia e i Suoi Critici (1460–1598)* (Rome: Edizioni di Storia e
Letteratura, 2003), 210–14, 242–53; José Ignacio Tellechea Idígoras, "Cartas inéditas de
un inquisidor por oficio. El Dr. Simancas y el proceso romano de Carranza," in *Homenaje a
Julio Caro Baroja*, ed. Antonio Carreira, Jesús Antonio Cid, Manuel Gutiérrez Esteve, and
Rogelio Rubio (Madrid: Centro de Investigaciones Sociológicas, 1978), 965–99. See also
Pastore, "Simancas, Diego de," *DSI* 3:1430–31.

society's ills, turning to print and stressing the centrality of law and legal reform more than such tools as personally conducted visitation.

Even as Simancas attracted the attention of influential audiences, his career did not advance as far as he had hoped. Despite his failure to be promoted to council presidencies or beyond middling bishoprics, he did much to shape later inquisitorial practice. In the years after 1567, his books began to be published by important presses outside of Spain and he became one of the signal theorists of inquisitorial law in both Spain and Italy.[4] He also modeled a particular way of being an inquisitor that was largely uncharted in his day, that is, a judge who intertwined theorizing with practice, who sought to build his career through strategic publication and to use his writings to influence the cases in which he was embroiled.

SON OF CÓRDOBA, JUDGE, AND BISHOP

If Diego de Simancas's life often turned around Rome, his heart was never far from Córdoba, where he was born in January 1513 into a privileged, noble, Old Christian family with strong ties to the city's cathedral. The "fourth of this name," he was the son of Lic. Diego de Simancas Bretón and doña María de Simancas, one of at least six children.[5] At the time of Simancas's birth, his family was establishing itself in Córdoba, having relocated from its namesake town in northern Castile. When his parents moved, they joined his mother's uncle, Francisco de Simancas, who was the archdeacon there. This uncle and his father seem to have served the Inquisition.[6] Simancas was groomed to follow them in just such legal and

---

[4] On the influence of his manuals in Spain: Virgilio Pinto Crespo, "La justificación doctrinal del Santo Oficio," *HIEA* 1:880–86; Pastore, *Il Vangelo e la Spada*; Doris Moreno, *La Invención de la Inquisición* (Madrid: Marcial Pons Historia, 2004); for evidence of him as a "revered authority" in Italian practice and manuals, as early as 1573: John Tedeschi, *The Prosecution of Heresy: Collected Studies on the Inquisition in Early Modern Italy* (Binghamton, NY: Medieval and Renaissance Texts and Studies, 1991), 10, 20, 72–73.

[5] His birthdate is given as January 26 and 29, respectively, in Mariano Alcocer and Saturnino Rivera, *Historia de la Universidad de Valladolid: Bio-Bibliografías de Juristas Notables* (Valladolid: Imprenta de la Casa Social Católica, 1924), 38; Teresa Sánchez Rivilla, "Inquisidores Generales y Consejeros de la Suprema: documentación biográfica," *HIEA* 3:417. See also Nicolás Antonio, *Bibliotheca Hispana Nova*, ed. Mario Ruffini (Turin: Bottega d'Erasmo, 1963), 1:316–17. "Quarto deste nombre," Gil González Dávila, *Teatro Eclesiástico de España* (Madrid: Francisco Martínez, 1645), 2:417.

[6] The Inquisitor General Diego de Deza appointed a Francisco de Simancas – of the correct generation – to conduct a general visitation of all the Inquisition tribunals in the early sixteenth century. José Martínez Millán, "Las elites de poder durante el reinado de Carlos V a través de los miembros del Consejo de Inquisición (1516–1558)," *Hispania* XLVIII/168

religious work, first gaining the basics of an education – reading, writing, grammar, and Latin – at home and in Valladolid.

When he gave a literary shape to his life, Simancas credited his mother for his education: she sent him away from his native Córdoba because it would have weighed on her conscience if this boy did not study and "become a great doctor." In beginning his tale, he suggested a promising destiny as a jurist and the difficulties of a wandering life; he classified himself as inclined to juridical learning by disposition and familial expectation. In 1527, their parents sent Diego and his brother Juan together to Valladolid to study Latin and law. After a year in that city, Diego left for Salamanca. Juan proceeded to the *colegio mayor* of San Clemente at the University of Bologna. Simancas arrived at the University of Salamanca at age sixteen, his nine-year tenure there in the 1530s coinciding with the university's apogee. He then gained admission to the *colegio mayor* of Santa Cruz, at the University of Valladolid, a place just a shade less prestigious than Salamanca's San Bartolomé. There, after three more years of study, he earned the degrees of licentiate and doctor in both laws, canon and civil; he won the post of rector of the university and a prominent lectureship.[7]

In 1545, just after completing his legal training, and while still part of the University of Valladolid's legal faculty, the Inquisition tribunal in that city first called Simancas to serve as a *consultor*, or legal advisor. While in his mid-thirties, he also began to practice civil law. Simancas's first royal appointment was to serve as an *oidor*, or judge, in Valladolid's Chancery – one of the two royal courts of appeal – an office he held from 1548 to 1559.[8] Simancas later hinged his professional ascent on these years: he recounted that the famous jurist Diego de Covarrubias served as a "godfather" to him early in his career, when he went to conduct some business

(1988): 120. In 1511, a Diego de Simancas was a judge of confiscated goods in the Córdoba tribunal. Rafael Gracia Boix, *Colección de Documentos para la Historia de la Inquisición de Córdoba* (Córdoba: Publicaciones del Monte de Piedad y Caja de Ahorros de Córdoba, 1982).

[7] This was the *cátedra de vísperas de leyes*. *Vida*, 151. During this era of his life, he may have begun compiling a catalog of notable graduates, BUS, MS 1925, fols. 122r-32v. See, inter alia, Richard L. Kagan, "La Salamanca del Siglo de Oro," in *Salamanca en la Edad de Oro*, ed. Conrad Kent (Salamanca and Delaware, OH: Ohio Wesleyan University and Librería Cervantes, 1993), 287-305; Kagan, *Students and Society in Early Modern Spain* (Baltimore, MD, and London: The Johns Hopkins University Press, 1974).

[8] *Vida*, 151-55. Charles V nominated him as *oidor* on November 6, 1548. Sánchez Rivilla, "Inquisidores," 417; Alcocer and Rivera, *Historia de la Universidad de Valladolid*, 38-39. See also Richard L. Kagan, *Lawsuits and Litigants in Castile, 1500–1700* (Chapel Hill: The University of North Carolina Press, 1981).

in Granada's Chancery. He also described how he had composed his first inquisitorial manual; when Valladolid's tribunal called him as a consultant, he had been dissatisfied with the available law books in that subject and so drafted a new one. Even before he became an inquisitor, Simancas had begun to arrange his thoughts by writing treatises and to approach legal problems by looking for appropriate reference books. He even credited his move from manuscript to print to Covarrubias, who "persuaded me that I should publish the book of my *Institutiones Católicas*, because he had seen my draft." Simancas thus established for himself a kind of spiritual kinship of jurists, a kinship of professional expertise. When he gained his first episcopal appointment in 1564, it was even to succeed Covarrubias as bishop of Ciudad Rodrigo. Simancas indicated a relationship, moreover, that was deeply felt, recording the condolences he received when Covarrubias died in 1577. In connecting himself to Covarrubias, a renowned legal commentator, he summoned the exemplary jurist of his age. When Simancas published this first manual of inquisitorial law in 1552, while still at a post in the civil judiciary, he could have understood it as carrying the codifying work of those like Covarrubias into another legal sphere.[9]

By the time he was in his mid-forties, Simancas had to his credit important connections, a legal publication, and a decade-long record of judicial experience in the king's service. And he cast himself in precisely such fashion – as a judge – asserting that he never had the "inclination of spirit" to be a lawyer, and so claiming for his office a substantial moral component. He was not a legal mind ready to serve any faction; instead, as a judge, he reasoned, his work was predicated on conscience; it was work of discernment and not simply of argument for hire. Moreover, he depicted himself as conserving the judiciary: he pointed to his very few recusals, his objections to the sale of Chancery offices, and an astonishing record of case completion. In 1558, he and his colleagues pronounced 432 definitive sentences and presided over innumerable *autos* in a mere twenty-seven days.[10] The approach he would bring to his work as inquisitor, councillor,

---

9 "padrino," "me persuadió que imprimiese el libro de mis *Instituciones Católicas* porque había visto el borrador mío," *Vida*, 152, 197. See Katherine Elliot van Liere, "Diego de Covarrubias y Leyva," in *Encyclopedia of the Renaissance*, ed. Paul F. Grendler et al. (New York: Charles Scribner's Sons, 1999), 2:96–97.

10 *Vida*, 162. Cf. the Florentine Francesco Guicciardini's comment on contemporary Spanish courts: "Little justice is done, and civil cases are dealt with very slowly." Quoted in Clive Griffin, *The Crombergers of Seville: The History of a Printing and Merchant Dynasty* (Oxford, UK: Clarendon Press, 1988), 62.

and bishop was inflected by his close family ties, his sense of professional kinship, and his long years of not only judicial but also academic experience, where he had formed habits of study and writing and begun to show an inclination toward theorizing.

FRAMING THE REPUBLIC AND BUILDING A CAREER: THE ARCHITECT OF A SPANISH STYLE

Simancas's inquisitorial career grew out of his service as a legal consultant. In that capacity, he participated in the Inquisition trials of suspected Protestants and caught the eye of Valdés, who was responsible for his appointment to the *Suprema* on April 20, 1559.[11] Although he had not been a local inquisitor, his formation was similar to that of the other courtiers the Inquisitor General chose. In his first six months as a councillor, he stepped immediately into high-profile work, as the *Suprema* presided over Valladolid's two infamous *autos de fe* showcasing supposed Lutherans and the initiation of Carranza's trial. Simancas was well prepared to draft initiatives of the style Valdés proposed. When he and Valtodano were paired as the judges sub-delegated to Carranza's case in 1561, Simancas brought the expertise of a legal consultant – learned in civil, canon, and inquisitorial law – to inform Valtodano's years of practical experience as an inquisitor. The controversies of that affair pushed Simancas even more into the work of elaborating legal justification. Yet he pursued that course not only in his official functions. When he was appointed to the *Suprema*, he had only one printed book to his name; he produced at least fifteen more editions from 1565 – when the pace of the case began to slow – to the end of his life.

Valdés's tenure as Inquisitor General saw a redefinition of inquisitorial procedures and a growth of inquisitorial powers. Substantiating such developments, Simancas depicted the Inquisition's judicial work as especially significant and required to maintain a Christian republic assaulted by heretics. His description of his first years on the *Suprema* was triumphant, claiming that they had proceeded with brevity, diligence, and lack of passion and

---

[11] He took possession April 22. AHN, Inq., lib. 1232, fols. 175r, 176v. Henar Pizarro Llorente, "Las relaciones de patronazgo a través de los inquisidores de Valladolid durante el siglo XVI," in *Instituciones y Elites de Poder en la Monarquía Hispana Durante el Siglo XVI*, ed. Martínez Millán (Madrid: Ediciones de la Universidad Autónoma, 1992), 231. José Luis González Novalín, *El Inquisidor General Fernando de Valdés (1483–1568): Su vida y su obra* (Oviedo: Universidad de Oviedo, 1968); González Novalín, "Reorganización valdesiana de la Inquisición española," *HIEA* 1:613–48.

emphasizing the solemnity and sheer scale of the *auto de fe* of May 1559. He amplified the sense of danger: "In the meantime," he wrote, "in Murcia a great Synagogue was discovered, in which at night a guardian of Saint Francis was preaching Mosaic Law."[12] He portrayed inquisitors' essential service as using true knowledge to correct false belief and, like Valtodano, saw corrupted clerics as their most dangerous opponents. As a result of Luther's wicked twisting of sacred learning, he "was chief [among heretics], an infamous and pertinacious man." Simancas opined, moreover, that "pride makes a heretic, not ignorance," and that heresies both "perverted doctrines and ensnared souls."[13] He claimed that he and Valtodano had drafted one of Valdés's most notable reforms, the Inquisition's new 1561 instructions, although they were printed in the Inquisitor General's name. They mandated

that in all the Inquisitions should be held and kept a same style of proceeding and that in this they should conform: in some Inquisitions it has not been kept, or not kept as it should be. And in order to provide for this, that from here onwards there will not be discrepancy in the said order of proceeding, practiced and conferred various times in the Council of the general Inquisition, it was agreed that in all the Inquisitions the following order should be kept.[14]

Simancas described them as "ninety-one chapters of the order that Inquisitors should observe in proceeding."[15]

---

[12] "Entretanto se descubrió en Murcia una gran Sinagoga, en la cual de noche predicaba la ley de Moisén un guardián de San Francisco." *Vida*, 154. On the *Suprema* in these years, see AHN, Inq., lib. 575; for Valdés's May 18, 1560, commissioning of Valtodano and Simancas to review, with the Toledo inquisitors, cases tried in Murcia, see fol. 99v. For the 1559 *autos de fe*, AGS, Estado, leg. 137, nos. 5–11. For analysis of the Murcia affair, see Jaime Contreras, *Sotos contra Riquelmes: regidores, inquisidores, y criptojudíos* (Madrid: Anaya and M. Muchnik, 1992).

[13] "Quorum princeps fuit Lutherus, homo scelestus, & procax"; "Quia superbia facit haereticum, non ignorantia"; "dogmata peruersitatis, animas illaqueantia," Simancas, *Institutiones Catholicae* (Valladolid: Egidio de Colomies, 1552), fols. 106r, 107v, 113r.

[14] "que en todas las Inquisiciones se tenga, y guarde un mismo estilo de proceder, y quen esto sean conformes: en algunas Inquisiciones no se ha guardado, ni guarda como conuenia. y para proueer, que de aqui adelante no aya discrepancia en la dicha orden de proceder; practicado, y conferido diuersas vezes en el Consejo de la general Inquisicion, se acordò, que en todas las Inquisiciones se deue guardar la orden siguiente." Reprinted in *Instrucciones del Santo Oficio de la Inquisición, sumariamente, antiguas, y nueuas* (Madrid: Imprenta Real, 1630), fol. 27. For a modern edition, see Miguel Jiménez Monteserín, *Introducción a la Inquisición española* (Madrid: Editoria Nacional, 1980), 198–240.

[15] "noventa y un capítulos del orden que debían guardar en proceder los Inquisidores," *Vida*, 158. González Novalín depicted them as a collaborative effort, "Reorganización Valdesiana," 641.

The Spanish Inquisition had been issuing procedural guidelines in the vernacular since its inception, at the level of the local tribunal and the royal council; those of 1561, however, were dramatically expanded and of a different quality. They sought to delineate a uniform style of procedure in order to reform localized and variegated practice. They served as a parallel, arguably, to the work of Trent: the Inquisition, too, presented itself as producing – from a process of deliberation within the *Suprema* – universal guidelines to apply in individual tribunals. In so doing, they increased – implicitly and explicitly – the weight of the *Suprema* and the Inquisitor General, as administrators charged to supervise and reform and as a locus of appeal. Simancas often attended to procedural details in his *Vida*. He elevated the *Suprema*'s mode of deliberation in judging the infamous cases of 1559, noting their adherence to the correct hierarchical order for offering opinions, their moderation, and their more than sufficient evidence and proofs. The 1561 instructions thus enshrined the authority of inquisitorial practice in a particular moment, and of practitioners then at work. They sought to decide debated aspects of practice. For instance, when the instructions repeated the need to call theologians as consultants in knotty cases, they assumed a preponderance of jurists as inquisitors, a transition not yet definitively effected in the Spanish Inquisition's operations by 1561. The clear inclination toward an Inquisition run by jurists might even be seen as a snub to those of like mind with Carranza, who not long before had lobbied to have another theologian added to the *Suprema*.[16]

The 1561 instructions were, moreover, spurred by the Carranza trial. The institution made a show of reviewing and codifying its practices even while they were the objects of significant dispute; in the process, the inquisitors directly overseeing the archbishop's case were identified as the Inquisition's experts in proper procedure. In that same year, Valdés directed Simancas to inspect the inquisitors and other officials in the Valladolid Inquisition tribunal. In 1563, he was charged to research legal precedents applicable to the proposed revocation of Carranza's case to Rome.[17] Even before commissioning the instructions, Valdés had asked Valtodano and Simancas to prepare a summary of the Inquisition's procedures:

In that time [around 1559], the king of France, hearing that his kingdom was full of heretics, sent a request to our king, his brother-in-law, that he might send him an

---

[16] *Vida*, 154. On the polemic between jurists and theologians, see also Pastore, *Il Vangelo e la Spada*.

[17] AHN, Inq., leg. 2136, exp. 3; Simancas to Zúñiga, holograph, May 19, [1563], RAH 9/1810, fol. 334r.

account and instruction about the method that they had in Spain for proceeding against heretics. The king told this to the Inquisitor General, and he charged it to us – to Valtodano and to me – and we made it and sent it to him; and he began through the hand of the bishops, ordinary inquisitors, to proceed against those heretics, and some were imprisoned; but they were so many and so well-protected, that that which would suit the purpose was not carried out, from where they have come to the perdition in which they now are.[18]

The consolidation of Spanish power against the French with the 1559 treaty of Cateau-Cambrésis was nowhere in evidence here. Rather, the purported exchange of fraternal counsel was suggested to be part of the universal Christian work of maintaining orthodoxy. The anecdote favorably compared the Spanish Inquisition to a deficient French episcopate and a French judiciary destabilized in the wake of its attempts to combat heresy.[19] Recounting this incident in the late 1570s, Simancas construed himself as particularly able to summarize the tenets of inquisitorial practice, the Spanish Inquisition as especially suited to fight heretics, and the health of any republic as judged by whether or not its powerful heretics avoided punishment. According to Simancas, France was lost when it failed to follow the Spanish model.

In the instructions and in his printed theory, Simancas depicted the codification of inquisitorial procedure as a response to extraordinary threats; such guidelines were subsequently converted into ordinary precedent. Hence, Simancas constructed his reputation in inquisitorial jurisprudence in a twofold manner: he fought the Carranza case on the ground, while simultaneously seeking to become an inquisitorial authority in print. His experiences pushed him to become a theorist. He sought to show that this inclination was merely a logical outgrowth of his early successes, reporting the approval of Prince Philip – to whom the book was dedicated – for his first inquisitorial manual, the 1552 *Institutiones Catholicae*, or *Catholic Institutes*, that he "received it graciously and caused that for nine nights they read to him from it an hour each night, and he ordered it brought to his bedchamber when he went for a little while to the *Cortes*

---

[18] "En aquel tiempo, entendiendo el Rey de Francia que su reino estaba lleno de herejes, envió a pedir á nuestro Rey, su cuñado, que le enviase una relación é información de la forma que se tenía en España de proceder contra los herejes. Díjolo el Rey al Inquisidor general, y él nos lo encargó á Valtodano y á mi, y la hicimos y se le envió; y comenzó por mano de los Obispos, Inquisidores ordinarios, á proceder contra aquellos herejes, y fueron algunos presos; mas ellos eran tantos y tan favorecidos, que no se ejecutó lo que convenía, por donde han venido al perdimiento en que ahora están." *Vida*, 157.

[19] See William Monter, *Judging the French Reformation: Heresy Trials by Sixteenth-Century Parlements* (Cambridge, MA: Harvard University Press, 1999).

at Monzón."[20] Legal commentaries were an established category of writing, and medieval inquisitors had written theory, but much of that was not accessible and very little was specifically fitted to the Spanish Inquisition when Simancas began his project.[21] His title carried multiple resonances. Most significantly, it echoed Justinian's *Institutes*, one of the core texts of Roman law (and part of the corpus of civil law), and so implied that Simancas had assembled a definitive textbook for a new branch of jurisprudence. The title was commonly used for other educational literature, and so might also have played upon, to take one example, the humanist revival of Quintilian's *Institutes*. Perhaps he even sought to combat a heresiarch in the print marketplace, parodying the title of Jean Calvin's *Institutes of the Christian Religion* (*Institutio Christianae Religionis*), first issued in Latin in 1536 and dedicated to King Francis I of France.

Simancas defined a Spanish style of religious justice not only in opposition to the failings of France, but also to the practices of Italian Inquisitions. Throughout his Roman years – from 1567 to 1576 – he turned his attentions even more to drafting, revising, and publishing treatises. Given the glacial pace of the Carranza trial, he wrote additions to his manuals, he said, in order to "pass the time in public usefulness." The pope wanted to hear the whole case himself; however, he could devote only a day each week to it. As an early riser, Simancas claimed that his assignment in Rome left him with a surplus of time, despite the sights to see there; he thus composed a new manual in just fifty days. In 1568, his first full year in the city, and the year of Valdés's death, he issued the first edition of his *Enchiridion*, or *Judicial Handbook*, printed in Venice. It was a condensed guide for how to identify and prosecute heretics that he intended primarily for Italian inquisitors. Further editions of the *Enchiridion* followed in Venice in 1569 and in both that city and Antwerp in 1573, whereas he revised and reissued the *Institutiones* in Alcalá in 1569 and again in Rome in 1575.[22] He designed a legal idiom

---

[20] The *Cortes* was a sort of parliamentary assembly: "Lo recibió graciosamente y hizo que nueve noches le leyeran dél una hora cada noche, y lo mandó llevar en su recámara cuando fué de ahí á poco tiempo á las Cortes de Monzón." *Vida*, 153.

[21] The recent Spanish anti-heretical theorists then in print included the late fifteenth-century appointee to the Rota, Gonzalo de Villadiego, and, of the generation before Simancas, Arnaldo Albertini – inquisitor in Mallorca, Valencia, and Sicily – and Alfonso de Castro, Franciscan, theologian, and courtier.

[22] "pasar el tiempo en utilidad pública," *Vida*, 160, 170, 180, 187. The two later editions of the initial volume: *De catholicis institutionibus* (Alcalá de Henares: Andrea de Angulo, 1569); *De catholicis institutionibus* (Rome: in aedibus Populi Romani, 1575). The shorter handbook: *Praxis haereseos siue Enchiridion iudicum violatae religionis* (Venice:

for export, a tool to build his authority in the immediate context of the opening of the Roman phase of the Carranza case.

Simancas reworked and added to his arguments over time, while retaining the same general shape and function. Similar to contemporary manuals for confessors, these compendiums were reference works for diagnosing and treating a scourge among the faithful. Instead of aiding in identifying and remitting sins in the confessional, they instructed in the detection of heresy and the proper conduct of inquisitorial proceedings to correct it.[23] Simancas classified the new German heretics – Luther first among them – as the greatest threat to Christianity. He listed many causes of heresy: fragile intellects, malice, negligence, pride, and conscious conversion to sin and error. He weighed jurisdictional claims, professing uncertainty about whether divination and some witchcraft (*sortilegia*) were really heresies; given their ambiguous status, he advised inquisitors not to pursue those crimes.[24] He also opposed jurists who had argued that inquisitorial tribunals might extend their jurisdiction to professing Jews, in addition to baptized Christians suspected of Judaizing, although this was in no way evidence of an inclination toward policies of toleration.[25] He treated a wide variety of procedural questions. He maintained – following the Spanish Inquisition's custom – that accused heretics be allowed to mount

Giordano Ziletti, 1568), rev. eds. 1569, 1573; *Enchiridion Ivdicvm violatae religionis, ad extirpandas haeredes* [sic], *theoricen & praxim* (Antwerp: Christophe Plantin, 1573).

[23] On confessors' manuals, see Lu Ann Homza, *Religious Authority in the Spanish Renaissance* (Baltimore, MD, and London: The Johns Hopkins University Press, 2000). I am grateful to Thomas M. Izbicki for sharing with me his "When the Judge Is Not a Judge: Nicholas Eymeric on the Office of the Inquisitor," unpublished conference paper, Newberry Library, 1985.

[24] *Institutiones* (1552), fols. 107v, 112r, 113r; *De Catholicis institutionibus* (1575), 281–83. His stances on witchcraft are treated (via the 1575 manual) in Giovanni Romeo, *Inquisitori, esorcisti e streghe nell'Italia della Controriforma* (Florence: Sansoni, 1990). This was one of the many problems Simancas revised his thinking about over time; through it, he speculated about the boundaries between jurisdictions and the relative value of different kinds of proof, addressing the difficulty of testimony in such cases, and of distinguishing the roles of secular and inquisitorial judges. In his 1575 treatment of witchcraft, for instance, he discussed infanticide, asserting that it had nothing to do with trials of faith (and was a criminal affair), but maintaining inquisitorial jurisdiction over what could be securely deemed heresy or apostasy. Editors could also alter the quality of such arguments. Simancas appeared in a later collection of treatises on witchcraft, dedicated to the Inquisitor General Everard Nithard. There, however, only portions of his work were published, which had the effect of dramatically diminishing their deliberative quality. Heinrich Institoris and Jakob Sprenger, *Malleus Maleficarum, Maleficas et Earum haeresim frameâ conterens, ex variis auctoribus compilatus, & in quatuor Tomos iustè distributus* (Lyon: Claude Bourgeat, 1669), vol. 2, pt. 2, 186–87.

[25] *Enchiridion* (1568), fols. 16v-17r.

a defense, "in order that innocents may not be accidentally condemned."[26] Still, he was caught up in the tensions of protecting the corporate before the individual. The 1552 manual left space to define what a "legitimate defense" was, and the 1561 instructions insisted on inquisitorial supervision of consultations between those on trial and their defense attorneys (thus supporting the judges' controversial practices in trying Carranza). Simancas also appended other short treatises – such as his defense of episcopal dignity – to later editions of his manuals. In one, he explored whether a child of heretics should denounce his or her parents, weighing religious injunctions against heretics with those in favor of filial devotion and obedience.[27]

One of the principal complexities of Carranza's case – and a primary justification for its revocation to Rome – was his status as an archbishop; an ample body of canon law suggested that bishops should be judged only by the pope or other prelates. Philip II allowed the remission of the trial to Rome only under protest and had his ambassador in Rome, Juan de Zúñiga, keep him informed on developments in the trial. As a result, the inquisitors sent to Rome often found themselves as proxies for the Spanish king in a power struggle between the crown and the papacy. José Ignacio Tellechea Idígoras aptly noted the "phenomenal" level of juridical confusion that all this occasioned, and that the trial spurred a polemical contest between inquisitorial styles: "The Roman Inquisition believed it kept better to the exigencies of the law and considered the Spanish Inquisition excessively harsh. On the contrary, the Spanish Inquisition believed itself more perfect and efficient and considered the Roman Inquisition pliant and feeble."[28] In such fashion, Simancas filled his writings with observations about the insufficiencies of Italian practice. He recounted how he had successfully declined a position on the Roman Rota in 1554, boldly asserting that "neither is Rome for me, nor I for

---

[26] "ne forte innocentes damnentur." *Institutiones* (1552), fol. 87v.

[27] *De Patre Haeretico* was printed in the 1569 and 1573 Venice editions of the *Enchiridion*.

[28] Tellechea Idígoras, *Documentos Históricos*, 2:346–47. "La Inquisición romana creía guardar mejor las exigencias del derecho y consideraba excesivamente dura a la Inquisición española. Por el contrario la Inquisición española se creía más perfecta y eficaz, y consideraba blanda y floja a la Inquisición romana." Tellechea Idígoras, "Inquisición española e Inquisición romana, ¿dos estilos?" in *Perfiles jurídicos de la Inquisición Española*, ed. José Antonio Escudero (Madrid: Instituto de la Historia de la Inquisición, 1988), 48. He also suggested that the Carranza trial had probably spurred Simancas to revise his inquisitorial manuals over time. See also Antonio Domínguez Ortiz, "Regalismo y Relaciones Iglesia-Estado en el Siglo XVII," in *Historia de la Iglesia de España*, ed. Ricardo García-Villoslada (Madrid: Biblioteca de Autores Cristianos, 1979–82), 4:73–121.

Rome." Once in the city, he petitioned to leave on a wide variety of grounds, even claiming: "I am so hated by those who are here awaiting the release of the prisoner and by all those who dislike the Spanish Inquisition that I believe that they would not hesitate to rough me up if they could." He expressed surprise that the tribunals there could not prosecute sodomy. He claimed that the Romans treated Spaniards with "indecency"; the Italian advisors "said the most disgraceful things."[29] In Rome, Simancas depicted his identity as supplied by his inquisitorial affiliation. Decades later, another courtier serving there remembered the Spanish pun Simancas had used to poke fun at the city: he would joke that a mule owed its less honorable half to Rome.[30]

Seeking to promote his evolving vision of inquisitorial reform, Simancas described his abridged manual, the *Enchiridion*, as composed at Pope Pius V's request, dedicating it to him and tailoring the book for use in Italian tribunals. He presented a copy of the Spanish Inquisition's 1561 instructions to Pope Gregory XIII, and later dedicated the final version of the *Institutiones* to him. Ambassador Zúñiga reported the Italian cardinals' dislike of Simancas, as he "has noted so many errors in their mode of proceeding, that I suspect that someday he will write some work against the style of the tribunals of Rome."[31] Simancas also commented on the administration of Spanish Italy. The king and the ambassador nominated him, more than once, to engage in deliberations on reform in Naples. Simancas was disinclined to take on such charges, painting the people of Naples – who did not have a district tribunal of the Spanish Inquisition – as "resolved to lose themselves [in vice], before suffering the Inquisition." Ultimately, Simancas arrived in Naples with a different mandate: he spent two weeks as the interim viceroy of the city in May 1572, substituting for Cardinal Granvelle, who was attending the papal conclave that would elect Gregory XIII (see Figure 1). Simancas had little to report about the

---

[29] "Ni Roma es para mí ni yo para Roma." *Vida*, 153, see also 151, 152, 166, 169–71. "Estoi tan odiado de los que están aquí esperando la soltura del preso y por todos los que quieren mal la Inquisición de España, que creo no dudarían de tosciarme si pudiesen," October 15, 1571, Tellechea Idígoras, "Cartas," 992–93, cf. a similar letter, June 30, 1571, ibid., 990.

[30] "acuerdome, que el d[oct]or Simancas, ob[is]po de Çamora solia dezir en essa misma ciudad, que del roma digo (q[ue] es el vocablo Hespañol puro deste trabajo) tiene la mitad Roma." A "roma" is a hinny, or a mule bred from a horse and a female ass. Francisco de Vera y Aragón to the duke of Sessa and Baena, Spanish ambassador in Rome, January 25, 1603, Venice, AFZ, Altamira, 39, GD 15, doc. 80.

[31] "les tiene notados tantos yerros en su modo de proceder, que sospecho que ha de escribir algún día alguna obra contra el estilo de los tribunales de Roma," minuta de carta, Zúñiga to the king, June 19, 1573, *CODOIN*, vol. 102, 167–70.

FIGURE 1. Engraving of Diego de Simancas as interim viceroy that appeared in a seventeenth-century showcase of the viceroys of Naples, Domenico Antonio Parrino, *Teatro Eroico, e Politico De'Governi de'Vicere del Regno di Napoli dal tempo del Re Ferdinando el Cattolico fino al Presente* (Naples: Nuova Stampa del Parrino, e del Mutti, 1692), 301–2, from the collection of Spain's National Library. © Biblioteca Nacional de España.

city; he did not find Neapolitan justice so weak, although he did note an epidemic of false witnesses who went unpunished. Back in Rome, the Spanish ambassador pushed for a papal commission to review ecclesiastical justice in Naples; he proposed Simancas as an ideal candidate for the task, mentioning his learning, his expertise in Spanish tribunals, and his discontent with the curia's style, although he noted that his manner in negotiations was rather curt. Simancas never joined such a junta, but Zúñiga's proposal gives a sense of the inquisitor's reputation and of the politics of judicial reforms.[32]

Simancas's service in the Carranza affair brought him ecclesiastical offices. Appointed bishop of Ciudad Rodrigo in 1564, he was promoted to the bishopric of Badajoz while in Rome, holding that office from 1569 to 1578. He thus spent his Roman years as a bishop absent from first one diocese, then another. Back in Castile, his final promotion was to the diocese of Zamora.[33] This end, however, signaled a series of disappointments, as he had observed his colleagues, Valtodano among them, ascend to higher offices. The two Inquisitors General who followed Valdés in office – Diego de Espinosa (1566–72) and Gaspar de Quiroga (1572–94) – were contemporaries of Simancas. Their career trajectories had moved in parallel, though Espinosa and Quiroga surpassed Simancas while he was marooned in Rome, acquiring higher crown office and elevated as cardinals.

Espinosa, trained in both theology and law, had risen to the head of the Spanish Inquisition when Valdés's involvement in the Carranza affair eroded his power at Court. Although Valdés had been accused of coveting Carranza's appointment to Toledo, the Inquisitor General in office at the end of the trial, Quiroga, received precisely that dignity, serving simultaneously as Spain's primate and as Inquisitor General for many years. In his *Vida*, Simancas often drew comparisons to Quiroga, who likewise was

---

[32] "que está resuelto en perderse, antes que sufrir Inquisición." Tellechea Idígoras, "Cartas," 992–93. For the 1573 recommendation of Simancas, *CODOIN*, vol. 102, 167–70. See also Zúñiga to the king, copy, October 28, 1571, IVDJ, Envío 111, doc. 186; Zúñiga to the king, March 29 and May 24, 1572; Simancas to the king, holograph, May 26, 1572; and Lic. Temiño to the king, June 8, 1572, AGS, Estado, leg. 918, nos. 1, 166, 313, 325; minuta de carta, Zúñiga to don Pedro Manuel, March 27, 1573, *CODOIN*, vol. 102, 62–63; Tellechea Idígoras, "Cartas," 994; Simancas was even included in a history of Naples's viceroys: Domenico Antonio Parrino, *Teatro Eroico, e Politico De' Governi de' Vicere del Regno di Napoli dal tempo del Re Ferdinando el Cattolico fino al Presente* (Naples: Nuova Stampa del Parrino, e del Mutti, 1692), 301–2. For an account of conflicts over heresy trials in Naples in those years, Peter Mazur, "Negotiating with the Inquisition. *Conversos*, the Holy Office, and the Viceroy of Naples, 1569–1582," *Archivio Italiano per la storia della pietà* 20 (2007): 39–54. On Simancas's tenure in Naples and his likely reasons for accepting the commission, Macarena Moralejo, "El Obispo Diego de Simancas y su Papel como Virrey en Nápoles," *Librosdelacorte.es* 4 (2012): 141–53.

[33] He was promoted December 15, 1564, and consecrated April 1, 1565, in Valladolid, *Vida*, 159–60; HC 3:168, 266, 339; DHEE 4:2480; EE, 71. He did not mention his ordination in his *Vida*, but in 1564 he was already a coadjutor of Córdoba's archdeaconry.

trained in both laws; he had assumed the place on the Rota that Simancas declined in 1554 and had proved able to use an interlude in Rome to his advantage in a way that eluded Simancas.[34]

Thus, when Simancas supplied himself with an illustrious history as a jurist, he did so in part as a way to rival such contemporaries; at the same time, he supplied the office of inquisitor with a genealogy reaching back to classical antiquity. To seek to become the principal architect of Spanish inquisitorial practice was also to distinguish himself from other authorities. If not only Valdés, Espinosa, and Quiroga, but also Pius V and Gregory XIII had all been involved in inquisitorial affairs, only Simancas had paired that work with the composition of such an extensive theoretical corpus. His writings intertwined theorizing and practice, as he based the authority of his judicial practice on the breadth of his legal knowledge and rooted the authority of his legal theory in the extent of his judicial experience. At the same time, he supplied the office of inquisitor with a genealogy reaching back to classical antiquity.[35]

Of a piece with these aims was Simancas's work on his *Collectaneorum de Republica*. First published in 1565, it had as many editions as the inquisitorial manuals and also received his revising and expanding attentions in Rome. There, in the vein of much contemporary political thought, he compiled nine books of Latin quotations, plucked from works ancient and more recent, and offered them as a guide to good government.[36] He again sought to shape perceptions of Spanish practices, touting the conciliar organization of the Habsburg monarchy and emphasizing the importance of legal order and a strong magisterial culture – like the Spanish monarchy's – for any Christian republic. Unsurprisingly, Simancas praised the virtues of Ferdinand and Isabel, Charles V, and Philip II; he rendered Spain exemplary

---

[34] Quiroga went to Rome as an auditor in 1555 and returned to Spain in 1564; Gregory XIII made him a cardinal in 1578. Espinosa was also a professor of theology in Valladolid; Pius V made him a cardinal in 1568. Sánchez Rivilla, "Inquisidores," 246–47, 264–66. On Valdés's fall and the rise of the *ebolista* faction at Court, see Pizarro Llorente, "Las Relaciones de Patronazgo"; Martínez Millán, "Grupos de Poder en la Corte Durante el Reinado de Felipe II: La Facción Ebolista, 1554–1573," in *Instituciones y Elites de Poder*, 137–97.

[35] *Vida*, 189; Kimberly Lynn Hossain, "Was Adam the First Heretic? Luis de Páramo, Diego de Simancas, and the Origins of Inquisitorial Practice," *Archive for Reformation History* 97 (2006): 185–211.

[36] *Collectaneorum de Republica Libri nouem* (Valladolid: Adrian Ghemart, 1565); *De Repvblica Libri IX* (Venice: Bolognino Zaltieri, 1569); *Collectaneorvm de Repvblica Libri IX* (Antwerp: Plantin, 1574). The nine books were De Urbe, Civitate & Cive; De Rebus publicis; De Monarchia & Rege; De Legibus; De Magistratibus, & eorum virtutibus; De His, quae vitanda sunt à Magistratibus; De Republica Hispaniae; De Praefectis Urbium; De Regni Gubernatione.

in matters of religion and government, often using the family as a metaphor for the kingdom. He repeatedly relied upon aphorisms from Aristotle and Plato to indicate that laws – and their correct administration – were the bedrock of a healthy polity and drew from the Roman law codes to extol judicial diligence. Whereas there were innumerable books on republics, he claimed to bring a fundamentally important perspective by approaching the subject from the art of jurisprudence.[37] Simancas suggested that his books would help encourage prudent administration and application of laws. In this way, he made his *Collectaneorum de Republica* and *Institutiones Catholicae* part of the same project of governmental reform and religious renewal, filling both with praise for judges.

The books themselves could function as a kind of currency in the world Simancas sought to navigate in Rome. He gave copies of his books as tokens of esteem and bids for favor and as part of lobbying efforts. Books he designed to reform the administration of the *res publica* – the mundane political order – also mapped his view of which writers and which books belonged in a Christian republic.[38] In his writings, Simancas disputed with other jurists; he praised his friends and mentors and critiqued his opponents. The practice of censorship can be read, in part, as another way in which the boundaries of republics – in the sense both of political and intellectual communities – were drawn. While in Rome, Simancas sat on a junta mediating between the king and the pope about how to treat a recently published book on free will. In autumn 1567, Philip II alerted Spanish authorities in Rome to a volume published in Louvain, censured by the universities of Salamanca and Alcalá. Luis de Requesens then summoned Cardinal Granvelle, Simancas, and the General of the Benedictine order, showing them the censures and the king's letter.[39] The cardinal reported that he had already discussed the book with Pius V more than four months before, but the pope had refused to issue a censure.

Requesens then arranged a papal audience, arguing for a condemnation of the opinions in the book, a prohibition on its printing, and the

---

[37] For example, *Collectaneorum de Republica* (1565), fol. 3r.

[38] On correspondence, books, intellectual affinities, and lettered relationships, see Constance Furey, *Erasmus, Contarini, and the Religious Republic of Letters* (New York and Cambridge, UK: Cambridge University Press, 2006).

[39] They referred to the book as "libro de libero hominis arbitrio et eius potestate," Requesens to the king, September 13, 1567, AHN, Inq., leg. 4436, no. 2. I thank Violet Soen for alerting me that the author was probably Michael Baius, on whom see her *Geen pardon zonder Paus!: studie over de complementariteit van het koninkrijk en pauselijk generaal pardon (1570–1574) en over inquisiteur-generaal Michael Baius (1560–1576)* (Brussels: Paleis der Academiën, 2007).

confiscation of copies already in print. The pope agreed to further consideration and sent his confessor, a high-ranking Dominican, along with three other representatives to the next meetings, held first in Simancas's house, then in Cardinal Granvelle's.[40] The junta concluded that the pope should dispatch two briefs. One would condemn the heretical propositions in the book, with the moderation that Philip II had requested. The other would provide for a private correction of the author, in an effort to avoid scandal. They determined that the author should have a chance to repent and submit his ideas to correction; otherwise, Spanish authorities would pursue him as a heretic. These relatively discreet censures aimed to squelch heretical ideas and to avoid inflaming Louvain. Even as the Carranza trial continued, Simancas supported a range of methods for combating heresies, more and less public.

Such interactions were part of Simancas's official duties and his participation in lettered networks of clientage and patronage that traversed the Habsburg world. In 1568, he assisted other prelates involved in the Carranza trial in the consecration of a bishop in the Sistine Chapel. He found a willing patron in Zúñiga, and the ambassador wrote letters on his behalf even after Simancas left Rome. He also joined the circle of Antoine Perrenot de Granvelle (1517–86), cardinal and influential courtier during the reigns of both Charles V and Philip II, who had been driven out of the Council of State in the Low Countries by the well-aimed propaganda of rebels there and who spent his later years serving the crown in Italy. Granvelle and Zúñiga helped Simancas attract both royal and papal attention. Simancas likewise supported a circle of clients, including younger members of his family. The painter and humanist Pablo de Céspedes benefited from his patronage in both Córdoba and Rome. Simancas established a close friendship with Lic. Pedro Fernández Temiño, another Castilian inquisitor – originally of the Calahorra tribunal – in Rome for Carranza's case. He arranged for Temiño to travel to Naples with him and facilitated the junior judge's ascent to the *Suprema* in June 1572, although Temiño could not assume his seat until 1576, after the trial's end.[41]

---

[40] The Master of the Sacred Palace and the bishop of Santa Agata dei Goti (the future Sixtus V) were also there, with the General of the Benedictines. AHN, Inq., leg. 4436, no. 2. On the process of book censorship, see Virgilio Pinto Crespo, *Inquisición y control ideológico en la España del siglo XVI* (Madrid: Taurus, 1983).

[41] The new bishop of Patti (who was promoted in 1582 to Córdoba) was consecrated December 8, 1568, *EE*, 79. Zúñiga also discussed affairs in Flanders with Simancas, minuta de carta, Zúñiga to the king, November 30, 1573, *CODOIN*, vol. 102, 409–10.

The famed Spanish humanist Benito Arias Montano's time in Rome also overlapped with Simancas's; he departed that city for Flanders in October 1572. Subsequently, Arias Montano – a client of Valtodano's earlier in his life – facilitated Simancas's connection with Christophe Plantin's prestigious Antwerp press. He wrote the approbations for the books Simancas published there, partly self-financed, in the next few years. After meeting again at the Spanish Court in the late 1570s, Arias Montano credited Simancas with spurring him to write his commentary on Joshua, a book that appeared in print in 1583, the year of Simancas's death. He closed that theological work – framed as counsel for the sustenance of the republic, a subject near Simancas's heart – with a reference to Simancas's persuasive influence.[42]

From Rome, Simancas also exchanged a wide range of news with the second interim governor of Toledo, Lic. Busto de Villegas.[43] They commented on the affairs of the delegation and the archdiocese, the progress of the trial, the health of its participants, and even the weather. Busto de Villegas assisted Simancas with his affairs in Spain, including negotiating with a printer in Alcalá de Henares to arrange the publication of the second edition of the *Institutiones*. Simancas thanked him profusely; he had feared he might have to print it in Rome instead. On this possibility, he commented: "I never wanted to print it there because all the ordinary Inquisitors of Italy are theologians and in the council of the Inquisition are two theologians, besides His Holiness, and I defend the party of Jurists by art; I believe that it will not appeal to the Theologians." He explained his decision to print both his *Enchiridion* and his *Collectaneorum de Republica* in Venice and took stock of his competitors. One friar had recently published a book on the Inquisition that seemed worthless to him. Another Dominican had just issued a gloss on an earlier manual;

See also Zúñiga to the king, May 1, 1572, Rome, AGS, Estado, leg. 918, no. 194 and leg. 158, no. 39; *Vida*, 166; Sánchez Rivilla, "Inquisidores," 339–40.

[42] Zúñiga to the king, October 13, 1572, AGS, Estado, leg. 919, no. 28; Benito Arias Montano, *De Optimo Imperio Sive In Lib. Iosvae Commentarium* (Antwerp: Christophe Plantin, 1583), 713; Leon Voet, *The Plantin Press (1555–1589): A Bibliography of the Works Printed and Published by Christopher Plantin at Antwerp and Leiden*, 6 vols. (Amsterdam: Van Hoeve, 1980), 1:170–72, 5:2090–94. Plantin was favored by the king in the 1570s and cornered the monopoly contract on the new Tridentine missals. See Griffin, *The Crombergers of Seville*; Fernando Bouza Alvárez, *Del Escribano a la Biblioteca* (Madrid: Síntesis, 1992).

[43] For their correspondence see RAH 9/1811, fols. 155r-69r. For another cache of twenty-odd letters sent by Simancas from Rome, see Tellechea Idígoras, "Cartas" (and for the originals, RAH 9/1809, fols. 228–54).

this friar made some useful points, "but," Simancas contended, "my book will not be superfluous as a result of that."[44]

Both Simancas's writings and his correspondence revealed a careful calculus of isolating opponents and favoring allies. When he chose whom to praise and to cite, he populated his own imagined virtuous republic. He sought, moreover, to write himself into a community of letters through recounting the praise he had received from learned contemporaries. Simancas filled his *Vida* with such testimonies. He noted that he debated "in front of many doctors" even as a student at Salamanca, including the great Dominican theologian Domingo de Soto and members of the royal councils.[45] He recorded that the Inquisitor General of Venice – notably, the zone of Italy least susceptible to Spanish influence – had lauded the usefulness of his *Enchiridion*. He disseminated the printer Plantin's remark that his *Collectaneorum de Republica* "would not perish for many centuries."[46] Another contemporary – a lawyer and courtier – reportedly gushed over his defense of jurists: "Having read it three times, it is the best thing that I have seen in my life ... and I believe that Saint Thomas [Aquinas] and Duns Scotus would not deny that."[47]

Moreover, as he did in connecting himself to the most famous of scholastic theologians, Simancas drew on the simultaneous fixity and fluidity of disciplinary boundaries in advertising his own erudition. He categorized his collection of sources in the *Collectaneorum de Republica* to such effect: illustrious theologians, legislators, jurists, physicians, philosophers, poets, historians, and other experts in good arts. He claimed to have read an "infinite number" of books both in law and in the other faculties. This range, he claimed, distinguished him from other jurists. Others also recognized both disciplinary boundaries and the virtue of transcending them. Thus, the humanist Juan de Verzosa praised Simancas as worthy of admiration, "both when you correctly place the ecclesiastical canons, the laws, and the jurisprudence, as when you deliver to us in your agreeable

---

[44] "yo nunca tuue gana de inprimirlo aca por que todos los Inquisidores ordinarios de Italia son theologos y en el consejo dela Inqui[sici]on estauan dos theologos y mas su s[antida]d y yo bueluo por el partido de los Juristas de arte que creo que no les sabra bien a los Theologos," Simancas to Busto de Villegas, April 28, [1568], RAH 9/1811, fol. 159r; "pero no por eso sera mi libro superfluo," [July 21, 1568], ibid., fol. 167r.

[45] "delante de muchos doctores," *Vida*, 151.

[46] "aquel libro no perecería en muchos siglos," *Vida*, 180, 182.

[47] "Es la mejor cosa que he visto en mi vida ... y creo que Santo Tomás y Escoto no lo negarán ellos, leídos [estos papeles] tres veces." *Vida*, 162. The courtier, Andrés Ponce Caballero, served on the Royal Council and Council of State and had held major offices in Milan and Naples.

conversation philosophical opinions, and your wisdom makes us firm in the midst of our doubts."[48] The very inclusion of Simancas in Verzosa's book of Latin letters, moreover, located him in Rome's lettered elite. The 1569 Venice edition of Simancas's *Collectaneorum de Republica* was, in turn, prefaced by Verzosa's laudatory epistle.

Simancas operated in an argumentative culture that revered citation and the repetition of tradition and precedent. In print, he revealed his intellectual affinities through strategic inclusion and occasional praise, associating himself with those he cited. Thus, Simancas frequently invoked Covarrubias and Alfonso de Castro, author of important anti-heretical tracts; he appropriated the latter to Spain as "our" Castro. He filled his texts with learned references, adducing legal precedents, biblical texts (with an unsurprising partiality for the Pauline epistles), and the patristics. In his *Institutiones*, for example, he simultaneously marshaled Augustine, Plato, Plutarch, Aristotle, and Pliny's *Natural History* to claim that Lutheran theories of scriptural interpretation were leading all of Germany directly into Satan's hands.[49] Glossing a medieval inquisitorial manual, he invoked a bit of classical poetry. He legitimized the punishment of heresy through Greek and Roman writings, using an epigram of the poet Martial to observe that it was ancient practice to reject false knowledge and heretics not only among Christians, but even among those peoples for whom "There are no gods: heaven is empty."[50]

To compile his *Collectaneorum de Republica* was to construct his own republic of letters. Simancas implicitly located himself in conversation with the ancients and with more recent humanists, whose efforts to supply ancient precedents to reform the contemporary political landscape he imitated. He used his years of study to attempt to supply a civic language to his contemporaries. In blatant and subtler ways, he sought to cast Spain as a model republic, possessing authorities ancient and modern: he used

---

[48] *Vida*, 151. "Seu Canones sacros legesque et iura reponis, / Seu miti sophiae tradis praecepta beatae / Eloquio et tua nos uarios sapientia firmat." Juan de Verzosa, *Epístolas*, ed. and trans. Eduardo del Pino González (Alcañiz and Madrid: CSIC, Centro de Estudios Humanísticos, 2006), 3:860.

[49] *Institutiones* (1552), fol. 114r.

[50] "Nullos esse deos, inane caelum," Martial, *Epigrams*, trans. Walter C. A. Ker (London and New York: William Heinemann and G. P. Putnam's Sons, 1919), bk. IV.XXI, p. 244. Simancas cited it simply as book four of Martial in his *Adnotationes ad Zanchinum*, in *Enchiridion* (Antwerp 1573), 378. On the medieval manual see Peter Diehl, "An Inquisitor in Manuscript and in Print: The *Tractatus super materia haereticorum* of Zanchino Ugolini," in *The Book Unbound: Editing and Reading Medieval Manuscripts and Texts*, ed. Siân Echard and Stephen Partridge (Toronto: University of Toronto Press, 2004), 58–77.

possessives to address Seneca and Juan Ginés de Sepúlveda, sometimes calling each "my fellow citizen."[51] He revered Cicero. He drew extensively from Marco Girolamo Vida's writings on the dignity of the republic – thus invoking as a model an Italian bishop who wrote in the era of Trent – and quoted repeatedly from Petrarch, Thomas More, and Juan Luis Vives; he enlisted Marsilio Ficino and Andrea Alciato.

Simancas's use of Vives provides an especially interesting case of his willingness to constitute his republic even through potentially dubious figures. Vives, who had died in 1540, was the child of parents burned for Judaizing by the Inquisition in Valencia, one in person, the other post-humously, although it is not clear whether Simancas knew of the family's encounters with the Inquisition. By the end of the sixteenth century, Vives's works – among them his commentaries on Augustine's *City of God* – had fallen under increasing suspicion, some appearing on Quiroga's indices of prohibited books (although that index was issued the year of Simancas's death).[52] Yet Simancas drew on several of Vives's writings – preferring his deliberative works on wisdom and on the soul – in preparing his books on the republic. He also disputed Vives in a noteworthy section of his inquis-itorial manuals.

Vives was well known for the rejection of torture that he had folded into his commentary on Augustine's *City of God*. In the chapter on interrog-ative torture in his 1552 *Institutiones*, Simancas directly refuted Vives, and he expanded the rebuttal in the 1575 edition. This was no less than a debate about the nature of justice in Christian society, centered on Augustine's ideas about the insufficiency of human judgment. In response to Vives, Simancas asserted the antiquity of the custom of judicial torture of those vehemently suspected of crime. He maintained that this judicial usage had passed into the Christian republic from the customs of wise men and prudent legislators; he insisted that it was not barbarous. Simancas contended that the complete prohibition of interrogative torture – the removal of a judicial armament – would be even more intolerable than its use. He described those who attempted to hide their sins as living in fear, their souls as tormented by guilt at their crimes; in this way, he framed carefully administered judicial torture as spiritual medicine. Simancas argued that Augustine did not prohibit torture, that he urged judicial

---

[51] Elsewhere he also emphasized the connection to Córdoba ("municeps meus") he had in common with Seneca, *Institutiones* (1552), fol. 5r.

[52] On Vives and inquisitorial censorship, see J. Martínez Bujanda, "Índices de libros prohib-idos del siglo XVI," *HIEA* 3:773–828; Ángel Alcalá, "El control inquisitorial de intelec-tuales en el Siglo de Oro. De Nebrija al 'Índice' de Sotomayor de 1640," *HIEA* 3:829–958.

restraint, not that criminals should go unpunished. Restricting his critique to the interpretation of Augustine on that point, Simancas termed Vives "not otherwise unlearned."[53] Even this slim praise – or restrained collegial critique – might seem remarkable: Simancas addressed the then-deceased Vives as a distinguished colleague with whom he differed on a point of law. Simancas found it more useful to imagine himself as part of Vives's humanist republic of letters than to exclude him from his universe of authorities.

AN INQUISITOR'S DEFENSE: INTERTWINING THEORY AND PRACTICE

Simancas's experience of the Carranza case shaped not only his drafting of inquisitorial reference books but also the written version of his life. After the archbishop's reconciliation to the Church and the conclusion of the seventeen-year trial – in which Simancas had worked from start to finish – Simancas used his *Vida* to publicize his version of the trial's history. Divided into three books, the *Vida* began with Simancas's youth, but the bulk of it was consumed by the years of the trial. He stressed the length of the hardship posting to which the king had assigned him, not only reporting his hesitance to go to Rome, but marking his eventual return to Castile pointedly: "I say that I was there nine years and four days."[54] In such ways, he strategically shaped his account to serve a multiplicity of ends. Each detail that Simancas narrated in his *Vida* emphasized his devotion to the crown and to his inquisitorial duties and highlighted the personal sacrifices required by his service. At the same time, he made his retelling of the Carranza case a gloss on inquisitorial practices in Spain and Italy.

In April 1567, Simancas – then both the bishop of Ciudad Rodrigo and a councillor of the Inquisition – had found himself in mortal danger. En

[53] At issue was Augustine's bk. XIX, chap. 6. In his initial opposition to Vives, Simancas recounted Augustine's questions about the "miserable and deplorable" nature of "those judgments passed by men upon their fellow-men." He cited Ulpian and Cicero's *De partitione oratoria*, which were among the classic precedents for justifying interrogative torture. *Institutiones* (1552), fols. 220v-21r and *De catholicis institutionibus* (1575), 494–96. Vives's stance was also opposed in Diego de Covarrubias y Leyva, *Opera Omnia* (Venice: heirs of Girolamo Scoto, 1597), 520. See *Ioannis Lodovici Vivis, Valentini, Commentarii ad Divi Avrelii Avgvstini de Civitate Dei*, ed. F. Jorge Pérez Dvrà and José María Estellés González (Valencia: Vniversitat de València, 2004), 5:277; Augustine, *The City of God Against the Pagans*, ed. R. W. Dyson (Cambridge, UK: Cambridge University Press, 1998), 926–28; Edward Peters, *Torture* (Philadelphia: University of Pennsylvania Press, 1996), 20–22.

[54] "digo que yo estuve allí nueve años y cuatro días," *Vida*, 189.

route to Italy, his galley encountered a storm in the gulf of Valencia; even the sailors worried the contrary winds would scatter the fleet. Fearing for his life, he enjoined his companions to help him remind God of their plight. Just two years before, Lic. Buenaventura had not (despite his name) been fortunate: that delegate from the *Suprema* to Rome had drowned at sea on his return, lost with all of his negotiated dispatches. And so they recited the litany and other prayers. Simancas made the sign of the cross. Then, he ordered one of his fellow clerics to climb the ship's poop and throw a piece of the host into the waves. Miraculously, the storm subsided, though the "sea delayed a bit in calming itself."[55] Simancas and his companions continued their journey toward Rome.

Or so Simancas recounted this episode in the *Vida*, more fully entitled an account of his "Life and Notable Things," which he began writing back in Spain in 1577. In hindsight, he rendered the crossing an ominous prelude to the turning of his own fortunes in Rome, using a storm at sea to introduce his turbulent years there. He signaled that he had traveled not only as a judicial expert pursuing a trial at the king's behest, but also as a prelate trusting in divine protection, promoting Eucharistic piety among the flock, even aboard ship. Upon their arrival, he portrayed himself as the leader of the Spanish delegation:

We went to kiss the pope's foot, and it fell to me to speak to him, as bishop and the most senior; they had been telling me that it would suffice to speak to him in romance, and later they warned me that he did not understand it well, nor did any of the cardinals that would be present.[56]

Foreshadowing his discomfort during the Roman proceedings, he depicted himself as wrong-footed and deceived there from the start. He continued,

We were waiting with four cardinals of the Inquisition, and I told him in my Latin what I was going to tell him in romance, which was the following: King Philip, as the Catholic that he is, conforming himself with Your Holiness' will, has sent us with the person and trial of the archbishop of Toledo, and although we have encountered work and danger in the journey, we take it as well worth it, in kissing

---

[55] "la mar tardó algo en sosegarse," *Vida*, 160, 165. Lic. Buenaventura de Guzmán (buenaventura translates to fortune) died when his ship sank at the end of October 1563, along with another inquisitor Juan de Becerra (of the Sicilian tribunal), delegated to the same embassy; Sánchez Rivilla, "Inquisidores," 352.

[56] "fuimos á besar el pie á el Papa, y cúpome á mí hablarle, como á Obispo y más antiguo; habíanme dicho que bastaba hablarle en romance, y después me avisaron que no lo entendía bien, ni algunos de los Cardenales que habían de estar presentes." *Vida*, 165–66.

the feet of Your Holiness and seeing your most blessed person, and coming to do in this and in the rest that which you might be served to order us.[57]

He persisted in casting their arrival as providential, while also showing his ability to improvise on the ground, to assess the politics of a court and react strategically to new circumstances. He implied the potential conflict inherent in serving both Spanish king and Roman pontiff and so sought to establish his negotiating ability, of courts and of languages. Each detail served to stress the authority of his account, and of his capacity to serve as the definitive interpreter of the trial.

This vignette closed with an indication of Pius V's particular interest: after each member of the delegation had kissed the pope's foot, he called Simancas again. Then, the pope asked him where they had encountered danger in their voyage: "I answered him that [it was] in the gulf of Valencia; and as he did not ask more, I told him that I had been in that affair [Carranza's trial] since the beginning and had been [there] in initiating the trial; that if he wanted to know anything about those, I would recount it to him." Pius V responded to this new information: "He said that he would give me an individual audience whenever I would like. I told him that there was nothing I wanted to say in private, but rather in public, that the affair touched His Holiness more than me, and with this we left."[58] In such fashion, Simancas sought not only to establish his rectitude at a signal moment, but also to remind his audience of the extensive experience that he had accumulated by the time he began writing his *Vida*, ten years after this initial papal audience.

The *Vida* demonstrated elements of what was understood as good judicial practice. Simancas constructed his written life in a manner akin to the accumulating of proofs and tracking of evidence in an inquisitorial investigation. He assembled defense witnesses, enumerating famous

---

[57] "Estúvonos esperando con cuatro Cardenales de la Inquisición, y yo le dije por mi latín lo que había de decir en romance que fué lo siguiente: El Rey Felipe, como católico que es, conformándose con la voluntad de Vuestra Santidad, nos ha enviado con la persona y proceso del Arzobispo de Toledo, y aunque habemos pasado trabajo y peligro en el camino, lo damos por bien empleado por besar los pies de Vuestra Santidad y ver su beatísima persona, y venir á hacer en esto y en lo demás lo que fuere servido de mandarnos." Ibid., 166.

[58] "Respondíle que en el golfo de Valencia; y como no preguntó más, le dije que yo había estado en aquel negocio desde el principio y había sido en hacer el proceso; que si alguna cosa quisiese saber de aquéllas, yo le daría cuenta della." "Dijo que él me daba audiencia particular todas las veces que yo quisiese. Díjele yo que ninguna cosa quería decir en particular, sino en público, que aquel negocio más tocaba á Su Santidad que á mi, y con esto nos fuimos." Ibid., 166. For a very similar description, Simancas to Busto de Villegas, May 31, 1567, RAH 9/1811, fols. 155r–56r.

contemporaries who praised his learning and his virtues as judge and bishop. He nested himself in good networks of affiliation, emphasizing his associations with renowned figures and the honor of his family. Likewise, he rebutted rumors of his misconduct. He sought to disqualify his presumed opponents and compiled a litany of promotions and honors missed and often snatched by those he depicted as less deserving. He crafted a tale of prudent fighters of heresy pitted against blind defenders of error; one friar who fell from grace for the opinions he offered in the Carranza trial even became "the Danaüs of that tragedy."[59] As evidence, Simancas charted conversations and correspondence, referring to letters and anecdotes stretching over nearly a half century. He wrote his life's story as a defensive case, justifying his version of the most famous case of his day as one rooted in personal experience and eyewitness observation coupled with the legal and religious expertise necessary to discern the truth of the matter.

At several junctures during the Roman phase of the trial, Simancas reported thinking that the pope was on the verge of issuing a sentence. Fearing that "the affair would never finish," he portrayed himself and his colleagues as captives of its interminable vacillations. He laid the blame for this partly with Carranza: "The criminal was so particular and confused and slow in resolving himself and so suspicious in everything, that he gave us great fatigue." In Simancas's telling, not only was he certainly guilty, he slowed the trial process; papal inefficiency was nearly as vexing. He complained about an audience with Pius V that lasted two hours, but where "a few pertinent things were touched upon many times ... in such a manner that it was impossible to remember what they were reading, until at the end summaries and memoranda of their subjects were made, which if it had been done when I said it, would have greatly shortened the trial."[60] He repeatedly emphasized the failings of the Roman Inquisition, often invoking the polemical contest between jurists and theologians; he aligned the virtue of brevity with the former and the failing of prolixity with the

---

[59] "el cual fué el Danao de aquella tragedia," *Vida*, 169. He referred to fray Tomás Manrique, providing an allegory about reverses in fortune and a warning about the eternal payment for sins that awaited Manrique (and the complicit Italian inquisitors) for their treachery.

[60] "nunca el negocio se acabaría;" "Era el reo tan prolijo y confuso y tardo en resolverse y tan sospechoso en todo, que nos daba mucho fastidio." "en dos horas se tocaban muchas veces pocas cosas pertenecientes ... de manera que era imposible retenerse en la memoria lo que se iba leyendo, hasta que al fin se hicieron sumarios y memoriales por sus materias, lo cual si se hiciera cuando yo lo dije, se abreviara mucho la causa." Ibid., 157, 159, 166.

latter. In this way, he argued in favor of the transition well under way in Spain, in which jurists were assuming the principal work of the Inquisition.

In the *Vida*, Simancas turned his official life into a portrait of a model inquisitor. Acknowledging that inquisitors were susceptible to outside influences, he insisted that "My opinions were always free, without human considerations, but very obliging and not obstinate; all of which is very well-known." In one encounter in Rome, he reported exclaiming: "Leave me alone! That neither the pope nor the king will think that I have voted in this affair to their liking, but rather conforming to my conscience." Despite such conduct, his argument went, when he returned to Castile from his "exile," he did not receive the honors he had anticipated, asserting that "I have given all my labors toward being well employed, although in this life they have not been rewarded." He theorized that his "secret enemies" had influenced Philip II to turn against him, as he reported leaving Rome with favored status. Gregory XIII had granted him several privileges: permission to establish a family chapel in Córdoba, a plenary indulgence, license to return to Spain with relics he had collected, and authorization to break the secrecy of the Carranza proceedings.[61] Thus the *Vida*'s very existence – filled as it was with privileged knowledge – was to be read as evidence of papal favor.

Unlike his theoretical print, which was all in Latin, the *Vida* was composed in Spanish and has survived in manuscripts. Simancas seemingly had a keen sense of what language and mode of circulation were appropriate for different kinds of writings. Yet there is evidence that the *Vida* once circulated in print; in 1643, members of the *Suprema* referred to a printed copy of it while deliberating about another signal Inquisition case. They took the *Vida* as an authoritative account of the Carranza trial that gave precedents for the recusal of an Inquisitor General and members of the *Suprema*. A 1685 copyist of the *Vida* understood it to have been a petition for honors and rewards. That scribe took the liberty of appending a pair of polemical letters to the life, uniting them to suggest a method of evaluative reading to his seventeenth-century audience, or perhaps

---

[61] "Siempre fueron mis votos libres, sin respetos humanos, pero muy comedidos y no porfiados; lo cual todo es muy notorio." "Dejadme, que no han de pensar el Papa ni el Rey que yo he de votar en este negocio á su gusto, sino conforme á mi conciencia." (This referred to the proceedings in 1568.) "He dado por bien empleados todos mis trabajos, aunque en esta vida no se me agradeciesen"; "enemigos secretos;" "destierro," ibid., 168, 178, 184, 189, 196, 202. Cf. Tellechea Idígoras, "Cartas," 991, 996. Simancas implied that Pius V's "inclinación del ábito" había made him overly sympathetic to Carranza; both were Dominicans.

suspecting Simancas was the author of one of the letters.[62] Like Simancas's *Vida*, they were part of the vibrant publicity war that surrounded Carranza's case. One purported to be a posthumous vindication of Carranza by his defense attorney, Dr. Martín de Azpilcueta (1492–1586), the other, a rebuttal – reasserting Carranza's multiplicity of heresies – from an anonymous "friend" (perhaps Simancas).[63] Praising the pope's sentence and diminishing the inquisitors in the same breath, the letter circulated in Azpilcueta's name commented that "no lesser judge could use [the same mercy]." After the end of the case, Azpilcueta cited Carranza favorably in his manual for confession.[64] Despite Simancas's theoretical support for defense attorneys, he used scornful terms in his *Vida* to describe Azpilcueta. He first introduced him as "the criminal's lawyer, [who acted] with infinite passion, that he always had in this affair."[65] He cast the famous Azpilcueta – who had studied and taught theology and canon law at the universities in Alcalá de Henares, Toulouse, Cahors, Salamanca, and Coimbra – as one who undermined the law. After Carranza's reconciliation to the Church and precipitous death, pamphlets praising his sanctity quickly began to circulate; some lives of Pius V included sympathetic depictions of Carranza.[66]

One life of Carranza, begun in 1586, insisted that the trial's initiation had been "pure calumny." The biographer Pedro Salazar de Mendoza –

---

[62] The 1643 deliberation related to the trial of Jerónimo de Villanueva, AHN, Inq., lib. 1231, fol. 292r. The surviving 1685 copy is "La <u>Vida</u> y cossas notables del s[eñ]or obispo de Zamora D[o]n Diego de Simancas Cordubense, y colegial Vallesoletano, escripta desu mano, cuio trasumpto es este," BCS, MS 84–6–29, Microfiche 58–5–23. The copyist reported obtaining the letters from a different source. Ibid., fols. 1r-2v, 83r, 84v, 93v.

[63] He was popularly known, for his place of birth, as Dr. Navarro. *Vida*, 206–10. Ronald Truman refers to a seemingly similar pair of letters, with the rebuttal purportedly from Azpilcueta's "nephew," a "Vespers Professor" at Salamanca; see his "Pedro Salazar de Mendoza and the first biography of Carranza," in *Reforming Catholicism in the England of Mary Tudor. The Achievement of Friar Bartolomé Carranza*, ed. John Edwards and Truman (Aldershot, UK, and Burlington, VT: Ashgate, 2005), 181. Marcel Bataillon read the letters as evidence of Azpilcueta's singular courageousness, see his *Érasme et l'Espagne: en trois volumes* (Geneva: Droz, 1991), 1:757–58.

[64] "de la cual [misericordia] ningún juez podía usar," *Vida*, 207; for example, Azpilcueta, *Enchiridion sive Manvale Confessariorvm, et Paenitentivm* (Venice: heirs of Francesco Ziletti, 1589), 887, 910.

[65] "Abogado del reo, con infinita pasión, que siempre tuvo en esto negocio;" *Vida*, 159. There is similar material – "á ojos ciegos las defendía todas" – in the anonymous letter, ibid., 207.

[66] Joannes Antonius Gabutius, *De Vita et Rebus Gestis Pii V. Pont. Max. Libri Sex* (Rome: Aloisius Zannetti, 1605), 91–93; Girolamo Catena, *Vita del Gloriosissimo Papa Pio Quinto* (Rome: Vincenzo Accolti, 1586), 97–98; Antonio de Fuenmayor, *Vida y Hechos de Pío Quinto Pontífice Romano* (Madrid: widow of Juan Sánchez, 1639), fol. 103.

jurist, canon of Toledo's cathedral, and Quiroga's client – adopted argumentative strategies markedly similar to those of the *Vida*. He too stressed the length of the trial, but in order to show Carranza's virtue in the face of hardship during so many years of confinement. Salazar (who made hardly any mention of Simancas) also gauged the conduct of the trial through the nature of the voyage to Rome, recounting how Carranza's lawyer had "issued a requirement to the bishop of Ciudad Rodrigo [Simancas], that the archbishop be taken in the poop, and not in the escort of the galley in which he would endanger his person and his life." He reported that at nightfall on the first day of Pentecost, the archbishop, his companion, and his servant embarked in one of the galleys and were accommodated in the stern's cabin. Their arrival augured even better. They landed and progressed toward Rome on the eve of Corpus Christi, the archbishop in a litter and his companions mounted on mules. The conditions in papal custody were better than those in Valladolid. Carranza was allotted more opportunities to confess, if, following procedure, he was still denied communion and hearing mass; following a serious bout of illness in Castile, his bodily health improved markedly in Rome.[67]

When Simancas and his interlocutors reargued Carranza's trial in extrajudicial form, they employed language redolent of the Catholic liturgy and spiritual medicine. The health of the participants became a barometer of the relative justice of the proceedings. If Carranza reputedly regained his strength in Rome, Simancas reported that his own health failed there. Salazar – supporting his patron Quiroga, Inquisitor General and Archbishop of Toledo – sought to rehabilitate the Spanish Inquisition by rendering the Carranza case an aberration, whereas Simancas sought to show its justice and to counter the rehabilitation of Carranza's reputation seemingly under way. As in the exchange he recalled with Pius V, Simancas implied that the case could serve as instruction and would better be aired publicly rather than confined to private conversation. Following his experience of the Carranza proceedings – as Stefania Pastore has recently argued – Simancas became increasingly skeptical of fraternal correction

---

[67] "hizo un requerim[ien]to al Ob[is]po de Ciudad Rodrigo, para que lleuase al Arzob[is]po en la Popa, y no en la escolta de la Galera, deque corria peligro su Persona, y vida." Pedro Salazar de Mendoza, *Vida, causa, y sucesos, prósperos, y adversos del Ilustrísimo y Reverendísimo Señor Don Fray Bartolomé de Carranza, y Miranda*, chap. 25, in Spanish History MSS, Lilly Library, Indiana University; see especially chaps. 22–26. On Salazar, see Truman, "Pedro Salazar de Mendoza and the first biography of Carranza"; Richard G. Mann, *El Greco and His Patrons. Three Major Projects* (Cambridge, UK: Cambridge University Press, 1986), 111–46.

and more strongly supportive of inquisitorial denunciation, especially in affairs so serious for the Church.[68] Much like his colleague Valtodano, he found Carranza's diffusion of his errors in vernacular print especially offensive, "because," as the anonymous commentator reasoned, "he who writes premeditates, and premeditation argues for bad and pertinacious intention."[69] Simancas's writings reflected an inquisitorial culture that was increasingly sensitive to the manipulation of language as the terrain on which operated both esteemed preachers and denounced heretics, both judges and the accused. These stances might also illuminate the logic of Simancas's career. In such reasoning, to write was to intentionally create and advance a system of thought, one that might reform or might mislead. The official components of an inquisitorial process could be bound up with a series of related skirmishes in manuscript and in print. Even the writing of an individual life, then, could be read as an attempted act of persuasion, a lesson about justice and a contribution to ongoing debates about the place of papal versus royal authority and about how to approach religious reform in the wake of the Council of Trent, particularly in such signal institutions as the Toledan archdiocese and the Spanish Inquisition. To write this kind of self-defense was also to argue for a particular vision of how to conserve the *res publica*.

CONSERVING THE REPUBLIC: KIN, CATHEDRALS, COURTS

In Simancas's vision, a republic was distinguished by the virtue of its families. He had at least two brothers, Francisco and Juan, and three sisters, Isabel, María, and Catalina. Their great-uncle, the archdeacon of Córdoba's cathedral, was one of their principal benefactors; he made the younger Francisco a coadjutor of his office, seemingly to ensure that it would stay in the family. He left the "principal houses that he built, that are the best of Córdoba" to his niece, and they were later arranged to pass to the family of Diego's sister Isabel. The family founded an entail (*mayorazgo*), which María's family inherited. Isabel, María, and Catalina allied with prominent Cordobans, marrying Gonzalo de Hoces, Juan de Venegas, and Luis de Venegas, respectively. Isabel's grandson, Luis de

---

[68] Pastore, *Il Vangelo e la Spada*, 227–31. Simancas derided a friar who preferred the fraternal correction model in Carranza's case as holding "falsa doctrina." *Vida*, 170.

[69] "porque el que escribe premedita, y la premeditación arguye mal ánimo y pertinaz;" *Vida*, 208.

Acevedo, obtained a post in the Córdoba Inquisition tribunal.[70] In short, over the course of the sixteenth century, the Simancas family consolidated its position in its adopted city: marrying into the Cordoban elite, strengthening its connections with local religious institutions, and passing both wealth and ecclesiastical positions from one generation to the next.

Diego de Simancas aided this endeavor, taking the same strategies he used in his judicial career to the business of his family and of his dioceses. He wrote a treatise on entail, published in 1566 and reissued in 1575. With that book, he added to a growing body of legal scholarship on inheritance practices, a topic popular with Spanish commentators since the 1505 Laws of Toro, which had promoted the practice of primogeniture. Simancas's treatise was more an account of the legal reasoning behind Spanish property laws than a manual for navigating the regulations. He dedicated the book to Prince Carlos, suggesting that it would aid his education in Spain's laws, and so lobbying for his cause. As was his customary style, Simancas began with an exploration of the origins of Spanish inheritance practices. Ultimately, he advocated the division of property among heirs, adamantly asserting that primogeniture was a humanmade institution and did not stem from divine law.[71] In defending partible inheritance practices, he sought to conserve an older order and to combat a set of reforming currents. His stances also related to his family's fortunes: the scion of a family whose three brothers all became clerics, he advocated strategies that would keep the lineage intact through female lines.

He wove his family into his writings in other ways. He expressed concern for their well-being when he was away from Córdoba, intertwining his attachment to his kin with that to his city. He used his influence in Rome to serve family interests, helping secure a papal dispensation for his niece and nephew, first cousins, to marry; this honor was explicitly framed as part of the

---

[70] "las casas principales que él edificó, que son de las mejores de Córdoba," *Vida*, 151. Isabel's daughter doña Isabel de Hoces married don Pedro de Acevedo (a knight of the order of Santiago). Their daughter, doña Catalina de Acevedo, married don Alonso de Argote in Córdoba in 1578. *Vida*, 203. For their son Luis's 1593 genealogical investigation (for the office of *alguacil mayor*), AHN, Inq., leg. 512, exp. 17. A 1572 document details the mayorazgo de la Huerta de Pantoja, possession of which passed to María's oldest daughter, doña Catalina de Venegas, RAH 9/826, fols. 129–30. In 1577, Simancas arranged for the dispensation for two of Catalina's grandchildren, don Diego de los Ríos and doña Catalina de Venegas, to marry each other. *Vida*, 195.

[71] *Vida*, 162; *De primogenitis Hispaniae libri quinque* (Salamanca: Juan María de Terranova, 1566), 94–95; *Liber Disceptationvm* (Antwerp: Christophe Plantin, 1575). See Bartolomé Clavero, *Mayorazgo: Propiedad Feudal en Castilla (1369–1836)* (Madrid: Siglo Veintiuno Editores, 1974), 140–41.

conservation of goods in a lineage. He recounted his good works toward other relatives, offering dowries, arranging marriages, and placing a poor relative as a nun in the convent of Santa Cruz.[72] Moreover, all three Simancas brothers assisted one another with various aspects of their ecclesiastical careers. Juan became a bishop first, elevated to the see of Cartagena de Indias, on the Caribbean coast, in 1561; not consecrated until 1564, in 1571, he resigned his office and returned to Castile.[73] Back in Spain, he acquired the posts of canon and archdeacon in Córdoba's cathedral. The archdeaconry passed not only from their great-uncle to each of the three brothers (Diego had also once been coadjutor), but also to their nephews. Juan helped Diego administer the diocese of Badajoz – while the latter was in Rome – and, later, frequently visited him in Zamora. Juan also lobbied his courtier friends in order to help Diego seek promotions. Diego, on the other hand, provided Juan with an alternate channel to the papal court; when Córdoba's cathedral chapter discussed its compliance with Tridentine decrees in the early 1570s, Juan supplied it with new information. He understood from his brother's letters that the pope had recently voiced new opinions about how to fill vacant prebends. The chapter replied that it had not yet received any news to that effect from its agents in Rome.

From Italy, Diego involved himself in other Cordoban affairs. He participated in the settlement of his brother Francisco's estate in 1570. Luis de Simancas, his nephew, traveled to Rome in 1571 as an agent (*procurador*) of the cathedral chapter and died there later that year.[74] In 1573, when Diego petitioned the king and the Inquisitor General to allow him to return to Castile, he used his health – attacks of gout, among other maladies – and his family's troubles as grounds for the request. Not only did his church in Badajoz and his recently orphaned nieces in Córdoba require his supervision and a return to "my land," his household in Rome had plunged into

---

[72] *Vida*, 151, 195–96.

[73] First a beneficed priest in Palencia, he was promoted December 5, 1561, and consecrated as bishop in Bogotá in April 1564. An alternate account puts his promotion in 1557, and one source mistakenly places his death in 1570. He became archdeacon and canon on November 14, 1571, and served actively there through 1579. *EE*, 74; *Vida*, 151; González Dávila, *Teatro Eclesiástico de la Primitiva Iglesia de Indias Occidentales* (Madrid: Diego Díaz de la Carrera, 1655), 2:71r; Manuel Nieto Cumplido, *La Catedral de Córdoba* (Córdoba: Publicaciones de la Obra Social y Cultural de Cajasur, 1998), 405–6.

[74] For the Simancas family as exemplifying how ecclesiastical benefices were often converted into family dynasties, see Ignasi Fernández Terricabras, *Philippe II et la Contre-réforme: l'église espagnole à l'heure du concile de Trente* (Paris: Éditions Publisud, 2001), 425. For some of their activities: *Vida*, 153, 196; ACC, Actas Capitulares, 20, fols. 64r, 65r, 68v, 124r, 144r, 145r, 173v, 211, 229r, 233v, 251v, and Actas Capitulares, 21, fols. 234r–35v.

mourning: "my two nephews that I had in the house, and treated and entertained them, both died, and that quit me of interest in those entertainments that are customary after eating, of which I was never fond."[75] He presided over a household that linked Córdoba to Rome, overlapping obligations to his relations with those to his diocese, the crown, and the Inquisition. He even framed his travels to and from Rome with accounts of his progress through Córdoba. Before he left in 1567, the city's bishop had solemnly accompanied him in procession through the principal streets and to his house. On his return, he recounted how Juan – his last surviving sibling – met him on the road six leagues out of Córdoba.[76]

In his *Collectaneorum de Republica*, Simancas drew heavily upon Aristotle's *Politics* – with Cicero and Plato in tow – to construe the civic order and the magistrates who upheld it as central components of any healthy republic. It rested on the order of its families and the physical order of its cities, from water supplies to the upkeep of private buildings. He pulled from a range of authorities, from philosophers to Roman law codes and imperial edicts to the architectural works of Vitruvius, to emphasize the role of building projects in the edification of the *res publica*. He traced a series of precedents about sacred architecture – from a mandate in the Book of Kings to build a temple to a recent decree of the Council of Trent – even as he sponsored religious construction in his native city.[77] In September 1568, Francisco de Simancas, acting as his brother Diego's proxy, introduced a petition to the chapter to found a family chapel in Córdoba's cathedral. The chapter quickly granted a site, and together the three brothers built a chapel dedicated to the Holy Spirit to house their family's remains; previously, Francisco had obtained permission to bury their parents in the royal chapel. Diego recorded that he alone spent nine thousand ducats on the project, and, as the date 1574 was etched near the altar, it was probably completed quickly.[78] As part of building the chapel, the brothers left monies for its upkeep and endowed chaplaincies and alms for the poor to be

[75] "mi tierra;" "dos sobrinos míos que tenía en casa, y los convidaban y entretenían, ambos murieron, y me quitaron la gana de aquellos entretenimientos que suele haber después de comer, de los cuales nunca fuí amigo"; *Vida*, 165, 186. See similar accounts in ibid., 177; Tellechea Idígoras, "Cartas," 992–93; Zúñiga to the king, copy, October 28, 1571, IVDJ, Envío 111, doc. 186.

[76] *Vida*, 165, 190.

[77] *De Republica* (Venice, 1569), 22; there are, for example, chapters regarding public and private buildings.

[78] ACC, Actas Capitulares, 20, fols. 144r, 227v, 229; *Vida*, 187. On the chapel's construction, Nieto Cumplido, *La Catedral*, 405–6.

administered as part of the foundation. The family was also present in its iconography. The gate still bears its arms and it houses two sixteenth-century oil paintings; one is a depiction of the baptism of Jesus; the other is of Christ crucified with Diego, Francisco, and Juan de Simancas surrounding the base of the crucifix (see Figures 2, 3, 4, and 5). These

FIGURE 2. Chapel of the Holy Spirit, Cathedral, Córdoba, founded by the Simancas family and constructed c. 1569–74. The gate still bears the family arms: a gold castle in a red field, with a star above it and a border of seven hands. Photograph by Dr. Fernando Marías.

FIGURE 3. The interior of the chapel, showing the two late sixteenth-century paintings commissioned by the chapel's founders. The painting of the Holy Spirit at the top dates from the nineteenth century. Photograph by Dr. Fernando Marías.

may be the work of Céspedes, a learned cleric who was educated at the University of Alcalá and a longtime associate of the family; he had traveled to Rome, likely with Diego, in 1567, painted commissions for nobles there, and returned to Córdoba and acquired a prebend in the cathedral in 1576. It is easy to imagine that the two had much to converse

FIGURE 4. Possibly the work of Pablo de Céspedes, the figures surrounding the base of the crucifix are the three Simancas brothers. Photograph by Dr. Fernando Marías.

about, as Céspedes also wrote on a range of topics, including the history of their cathedral, and showed a preference for Seneca.[79]

[79] The gate has been attributed to Fernando de Valencia, and the sculpture to Hernán Ruiz II (Hernán Ruiz III likely completed the work). See Fernando Marías, *El Largo Siglo XVI: los usos artísticos del renacimiento español* (Madrid: Taurus, 1989); Alfredo J. Morales, *Hernán Ruiz "el Joven"* (Madrid: Akal, 1996); María Angeles Raya Raya, *El retablo barroco cordobés* (Córdoba: Publicaciones del Monte de Piedad y Caja de Ahorros de Córdoba, 1987); Raya Raya, *Catálogo de las pinturas de la Catedral de Córdoba* (Córdoba: Publicaciones del Monte de Piedad y Caja de Ahorros de Córdoba, 1988); Jesús Rubio Lapaz, *Pablo de Céspedes y su Círculo. Humanismo y Contrarreforma en la Cultura Andaluza del Renacimiento al Barroco* (Granada: Universidad de Granada, 1993).

FIGURE 5. Possibly the work of Pablo de Céspedes, this painting depicts the baptism of Jesus. Photograph by Dr. Fernando Marías.

The bishops Simancas, Juan and Diego, gave liberally in Córdoba. Nor did Diego forget his family's origins: he donated money to the town of Simancas for a public granary, to their poor, and to endow two dowries for poor girls there each year. He followed familiar patterns of charitable acts, his gifts simultaneously reinforcing pious ideals, the authority of his office, and the power and wealth of his Cordoban family. While remaining rooted in his native city, he also distributed charity in each of the cities where he served. In his *Vida*, he recounted these good works in part to rebut accusations of greed and that he was more concerned with temporal matters than spiritual ones. He emphasized that he also gave money to his servants' children and, when he had provided for his orphaned nieces, that "none of these things exceeded what a bishop should do."[80]

Simancas confronted multiple impediments to framing himself as an ideal sixteenth-century bishop. He was more often than not absent from his dioceses. The shape of his career contravened the emphasis on residency that many Catholic reformers – Carranza among them – had championed. Appointed to Ciudad Rodrigo in December 1564, Simancas's episcopal career began just as the Council of Trent concluded. Still assigned to Carranza's Valladolid courtroom, he absented himself from his inquisitorial work to attend the Compostellan provincial council (to which his diocese was subject) in Salamanca in the fall of 1565 and spring of 1566. Part of the process of disseminating Trent, its decrees contained a predictable emphasis on episcopal diligence in combating heresy and preaching doctrine well.[81] In his *Vida*, Simancas recounted his impatience with the council and concluded it was a tiresome affair, more inconvenient than useful. In so doing, he again tapped into a rhetoric that elevated brevity over prolixity. He made the prelates' conflicts over precedence seem trivial but painted himself as a facilitator of ecclesiastical harmony, reporting a quip the king's representative had made "that it could not be denied that I was the Angel of Peace."[82]

Simancas then attempted to turn his attentions to his new diocese, later noting his activities in his *Vida*. He arrived in Ciudad Rodrigo in May 1566. Much, he claimed, to his annoyance, the king ordered him to inspect the University of Salamanca just days later; he noted having had time only to confirm about a thousand of the city's residents. His account of the visitation reemphasized his experience in Valladolid's legal faculty and painted Salamanca as in decline. In short order, he was back to the work of his diocese, in a flurry of pastoral activity and Tridentine reforms. He helped the city council compel a Franciscan tertiary convent to move from the countryside into the city, presided over the cathedral chapter a few times, called local clerics to a synod, and disputed with municipal officials

---

[80] "ninguna cosa de éstas se excedió de lo que un Obispo debía hacer," *Vida*, 196. At the end of his life, he made bequests to Córdoba's Minorites of San Francisco de Paula and the hospital of San Lázaro and left additional funds for the city's poor. González Dávila, *Teatro*, 2:417–18; *Vida*, 186, 197. For his works in Badajoz, see the seventeenth-century Juan Solano de Figueroa y Altamirano, *Historia Eclesiástica de la Ciudad y Obispado de Badajoz* (Badajoz: Imprenta del Hospicio provincial, 1929), 3:347ff.

[81] For example, *Concilium Prouinciale Compostellanum* (Salamanca: Andrea Portonari, 1566), fol. 85r; see also Fernández Terricabras, *Philippe II et La Contre-Réforme*, 184–99; González Dávila, *Teatro*, 1:96.

[82] "que no se podía negar que yo no fuese Angel de Paz." *Vida*, 161–62.

who wanted seats in that council. He inspected five of the city's churches, ordering building repairs and consecrating altars.[83] Simancas even had time to absolve a French journeyman-printer, Pierre de Ribera, for his flirtation with Protestant heresy; apparently, he then found secret reconciliation via the confessional (as opposed to inquisitorial investigation) appropriate in some cases.[84] Yet this phase was short-lived. He took official leave of the chapter on January 23, 1567, in preparation for his departure for Rome. Still, he continued to climb the ladder of episcopal appointments. Promoted to the bishopric of Badajoz not long into his Roman sojourn, he delegated the same agent he had employed in Ciudad Rodrigo to take possession of his new diocese and govern it in his stead. Then, before June 1571, Juan de Simancas arrived in Badajoz – fresh from the resignation of his post as bishop of Cartagena de Indias – and served as its governor for nearly five years. Juan administered the sacraments and visited the diocese; his first order of business was to suggest a more practical arrangement of the Corpus Christi feast day celebrations.[85]

Although he spent only a small fraction of his career as a resident bishop, Simancas strived to identify himself with episcopal ideals. He enumerated the pastoral obligations he completed on the occasional returns to his dioceses. More consequential, however, was how he described his daily routine in Rome: he rose early, then prayed and celebrated mass. He studied and wrote until his first meal; he spent the *siesta*

---

[83] The convent of *Sancti-Spíritus* was transferred from Valdárrago, its new urban convent and church blessed on the last Sunday of June 1566. Michele Olivari mentions the Salamanca visitation in his *Entre el trono y la opinión: la vida política castellana en los siglos XVI y XVII*, trans. Jesús Villanueva (Valladolid: Junta de Castilla y León, 2004). Mateo Hernández Vegas, *Ciudad Rodrigo: La Catedral y La Ciudad* (Ciudad Rodrigo: Excmo. Cabildo de la Catedral de Ciudad Rodrigo, 1982), 2:68–72; *Vida*, 162–63.

[84] "un frayle con quien se confeso en salamanca le confeso y dixo q[ue] no le podia absolver y este [i.e. Ribera] se queria yr A Roma y el frayle busco orden para absoluelle y lo comunico conel dotor Simancas ob[is]po y le absoluio," trial of Pierre de Ribera, AHN, Inq, leg. 112, exp. 8 [olim 60], fol. [12]r. Friar Francisco de Alcocer was the intermediary. I am very grateful to Clive Griffin for sharing with me his transcription. See his detailed study of such printers, *Journeymen-Printers, Heresy, and the Inquisition in Sixteenth-Century Spain* (Oxford, UK, and New York: Oxford University Press, 2005).

[85] The agent was Lic. Luis Picado, previously of Palencia and eventually canon and archdeacon in Jerez. Ciudad Rodrigo's chapter corresponded some with Simancas in Rome; in those years, the abbot of its Praemonstratensian friars arrived there with all their assets liquidated, after his monastery had rioted against the reforms. Hernández Vargas, *Ciudad Rodrigo*, 2:69–70; *procurador* to Ambassador Zúñiga, September 24, 1567, BL, Add. 28403, doc. 24. The bull presenting Simancas for Badajoz was dispatched December 3, 1568, and he took possession March 25, 1569. Solano de Figueroa, *Historia Eclesiástica*, 3:348, 356–57; *EE*, 76; AGS, PR, caja 62, docs. 94, 95.

"without sleeping, with some good entertainment, until the hour to pray vespers." He received visitors and visited others, although not to excess. He supervised his household well, promoting beneficial activity. He even bragged that "in my house there was no sport, rather only chess at appropriate hours."[86] He construed himself as moderate in his actions and constantly occupied in profitable enterprises. In short, he described a routine appropriate to a model Tridentine bishop, uniting prayer, good works, and sober living. He sought to prove that even as an inquisitor and courtier absent from his diocese, he continued to behave like a bishop. As the years passed, Simancas and his colleagues directly referred to the Tridentine requirements of residency in their entreaties to return to Castile, invoking the danger to their churches and to their own consciences from such absenteeism.[87] Nevertheless, Philip II did not permit Simancas to leave Rome and Simancas did not resign his office; instead, he reverted to using his brother as his proxy. The brother who had chosen to forsake his episcopal office and return from an American outpost to Castile supported the attempts of the other to ascend the ladders of Inquisition, Church, and Crown.

Simancas also involved himself in Toledo's affairs while Carranza was disabled from doing so, though in a different manner than Valtodano had done. He depicted his battles with Carranza's partisans as intertwined with his support for the Toledo cathedral's purity of blood statutes, which had been promulgated in 1556 by Carranza's predecessor, Archbishop Juan Martínez de Silíceo. In the 1570s, the Discalced Franciscan friar Alonso de Lobo attracted attention by preaching against the statutes in Rome. Lobo's opponents – Simancas among them – used a range of tools to halt him: the Roman Inquisition, Latin print, and vernacular manuscripts.[88] Inflamed by Lobo's sermons, Simancas reputedly pressured Gregory XIII and other

---

[86] "sin dormir con algún entretenimiento bueno, hasta hora de rezar vísperas;" "en mi casa no había juego, sino de solo ajedrez á horas pertinentes." *Vida*, 187. He expressed revulsion at some clerical abuses, as in his inclusion of clerical marriage in his inquisitorial manuals, *Institutiones* (1552), fols. 113–14.

[87] *Vida*, 160; Tellechea Idígoras, "Cartas," 987, 997. On disputes over such issues, see Dandelet, *Spanish Rome*, 69.

[88] *Vida*, 172, 176, 187–88, 190, 196, 202. On the Lobo affair see Pastore, *Il vangelo e la spada*, 414–15; Albert A. Sicroff, *Les Controverses des Statuts de 'Pureté de Sang' en Espagne du XVe au XVIIe Siècle* (Paris: Didier, 1960), 157–67, 170–79. The Rota issued a judgment against the statute in the early seventeenth century. I thank Robert A. Maryks for sharing with me his work in progress, now published as *The Jesuit Order as a Synagogue of Jews: Jesuits of Jewish Ancestry and Purity-of-Blood Laws in the Early Society of Jesus* (Leiden: Brill, 2009), chap. 1.

high-ranking prelates to pursue Lobo, himself a *converso*, on charges of heresy. The Roman Inquisition compelled the friar to abjure his errors on November 11, 1572. As governor of the archdiocese, Busto de Villegas closely followed Lobo's actions in Rome. He reported to the king that

a foreigner named Henri Mauroy, years ago, printed an apology against the statute of this church, about which discoursed Lobo, discalced friar, in Rome's pulpits (which Your Majesty knows). The one and the other have moved the bishop of Badajoz [Simancas] to write and print that small book (that he sent to Your Majesty) in defense of the said statute.[89]

The governor painted Simancas as a champion of the Toledo cathedral: "to the bishop is owed much in this part for having resisted Lobo."[90] Simancas had once again transmuted his experiences into a printed tract. He manipulated the modes of writing available to him, publishing the treatise in Antwerp, in Latin, in 1575. He employed a pseudonym – thus circumventing a royal ban on treating the purity of blood statutes in print – although the author's identity was no mystery, as the trail of correspondence and manuscript copies, some of which circulated in the vernacular, attest.[91] Simancas's defense of the statutes recited the tropes of such literature, drawing on an arsenal of anti-Jewish slurs. To wit, he lauded the virtue of biblical Jews while harshly condemning their latter-day coreligionists. He trotted out stereotypes of perfidy and venality. He accused Toledo's Jews of betraying the city to Muslim invaders during the Reconquest. Thus, he offered pointed praise to Carranza's predecessor in office; he constructed a justification of Silíceo's actions that included a polemical history designed to resonate with sixteenth-century ideas about religious threats.

When he treated the statutes, Simancas articulated a tenet that underpinned his legal theory more generally. He argued that the common good

---

[89] "vn estrangero q[ue] se llama Henrrico Mauroy ymprimio los años passados vna apologia contra el statuto desta ygl[es]ia sobre el qual Discanto lobo frayle descalco en los pulpitos de Roma (lo q[ue] v[uestra] m[agestad] sabe). Lo uno y lo otro a mouido al o[bis]po de Badajoz a escriuir y ymprimir esse librico (q[ue] a v[uestra]m[agestad] embio) en defensa del d[ic]ho statuto." This correspondence indicates that Simancas first printed his treatise in Rome. Busto de Villegas to the king, October 22, 1573, RAH 9/1811, fol. 25r.

[90] "Al o[bis]po se le deue mucho en esta parte por aver Resisitido al lobo," ibid. Cf. Busto de Villegas to the king, February 9, 1574, ibid., fol. 26r; Zúñiga to the king, November 12, 1572, IVDJ, Envío 111, doc. 317.

[91] Didacus Velásquez, *Defensio statuti Toletani a Sede Apostolica saepe confirmati, pro his, qui bono et incontaminato genere nati sunt* (Antwerp: Christophe Plantin, 1575). On Lobo, see pp. 123–24. Simancas and Busto de Villegas obtained the pope's permission to discuss the topic. The tract was later circulated in manuscript and translated into Spanish; see copy of August 1592, BNE, MS 2592. Manuscripts of Lobo's sentence and abjuration also circulated, BNE, MS 6035, fols. 101–3.

trumped the protection of individuals. He recognized that some *conversos*, sincere Christians, would be unjustly excluded. Still, Simancas contended that laws should be based upon general circumstances, and not individual exceptions. He portrayed the barring of *conversos* from some offices as analogous to the exclusion of natural children of clerics or of the children of unmarried parents.[92] He accepted, and even lauded, such hierarchies and exclusions as an inherent cost of good laws.

In these same years, Simancas launched defenses in print of jurist-bishops and of the dignity of bishops. Invoking a genealogy of episcopal authority that stretched from the Tridentine decrees back to antiquity, he paid particular attention to medieval Spanish exempla. This theorizing about bishops connected to reforming currents, both by elevating the status of bishops and by persuading them to prove themselves worthy of their offices. At the same time, he aimed to refute the charge that Carranza's case showed the Spanish crown's lack of deference toward its prelates, arguing instead that Spanish kings had a long and uninterrupted history of revering and relying upon their bishops. Implicitly, Simancas also defended himself against allegations of episcopal negligence and of excessive subservience to the crown.[93] When he argued for the advantages of appointing jurists as bishops, he opposed prominent friars – the Dominican Domingo de Soto, the Franciscan Miguel de Medina – who had deprecated jurist-bishops. Soto had reportedly quipped that he'd lobby for a shoemaker to be made a bishop before a jurist. Defending his discipline, Simancas insisted that jurists had administrative skills far superior to those of theologians.[94] He argued that his own cohort, adepts in law inclined toward administration, was most suited to be champions of reform.

It was not until Carranza's trial concluded that Simancas had the license to attempt to put this theory into practice. He finally arrived in Badajoz on November 18, 1576. With Gregory XIII's permission, he carried with him two relics – arms of the martyr-saints Stephen and Lawrence – from Rome to the cathedral. He brought other gifts: six silver cruets for holy oils and a

---

[92] Simancas advocated a two-generation term of restrictions in "De poenitentibus and conuersis," *Institutiones* (1552).

[93] For example, *De Dignitate Episcoporum Summarium* (Antwerp: Christophe Plantin, 1575), 31; *De episcoporum dignitate, scriptorum veterum auctoritates* (Rome: Bartolomeo Bonfadino, 1592); for Trent, *De dignitate Episcoporum*, in *Enchiridion* (Antwerp, 1573), 386, 393–94, 412; cf. *Canons and Decrees of the Council of Trent*, trans. Henry Joseph Schroeder (St. Louis, MO, and London: B. Herder Book Co., 1960), 250.

[94] *De Episcopis iuris peritis, opusculum* (Antwerp: Christophe Plantin, 1574); *Vida*, 151–53, 162, 181, 200.

blue velvet canopy adorned with his own and the church's devices.[95] He later recounted how he traveled directly to his diocese instead of first to Madrid, despite much advice to the contrary. Thus, he repeatedly sought to demonstrate that his absences from his sees were by necessity rather than inclination, that he did not seek the Court when he might serve his flock. He also implied a critique of those who surpassed him in promotions, advancing their interests in Madrid rather than attempting to serve their offices diligently. Meanwhile, Simancas publicized his desire to obtain an office nearer to Córdoba. These were hard years in Badajoz, with drought and bread shortages. Just a month after his return, Simancas formally received a royal visitor, when Portugal's King Sebastian passed through on his way to Guadalupe to meet with Philip II. Soon the bishopric of Jaén fell empty. Simancas petitioned for it and convinced three of his friends to write on his behalf, to no effect. Still, his time in Badajoz was brief, as Philip II proposed him for Zamora in 1578. Simancas accepted the nomination, eventually moving even farther from his city. But first he traveled to Court, presiding over the burial of Prince Fernando in the Escorial in October. It was a commonly held theory that kings should remove inquisitors, bishops, and other officials from their native lands, where they had competing claims on their loyalties. Even though Córdoba fell vacant in 1582, Simancas remained in his Zamoran post.[96]

Simancas's four-year term in Zamora turned out to be the final act of his career. His writing activities tapered off in those years as a resident prelate. He left only two treatises that identified him in his role of bishop of Zamora: the *Vida* and the fourth edition of his *Collectaneorum de Republica*, whose title page advertised that it had grown from the previous edition and now contained nearly thirty-six hundred opinions. The administration of his diocese in those few years was filled with conflicts, both jurisdictional and ideological. The quarrels began even before Simancas's

---

[95] González Dávila, *Teatro*, 2:417. Apparently the canopy was still used during Advent and Lent in the mid-seventeenth century; Solano de Figueroa, *Historia Eclesiástica*, 3:360.

[96] Probably while at Court, he assisted the bishop of Piacenza and the nuncio, Filippo Sega, in consecrating Francisco Trujillo García as bishop of León. Elevated to Zamora June 13, 1578, Solano de Figueroa reported that Simancas left Badajoz with considerable wealth, perhaps 100,000 ducats; *Historia Eclesiástica*, 3:360–61, 367–68; *EE*, 76, 89; González Dávila, *Teatro*, 4:67–68; AGS, PR, caja 62, docs. 127–28, 147; *Vida*, 191–95, 198; IVDJ, Envío 89, caja 2, doc. 329; Simancas to the king, January 7, 1578, BL, Add. 28371, fol. 162, for his persisting contact with Rome; Zúñiga to Simancas, March 17, 1577, Add. 28410, fol. 143 and November 10, 1579, Add. 28412, fol. 55.

arrival, when local authorities claimed that his agent did not have sufficient documentation to act in the bishop's place.[97]

By Simancas's account, Zamora's government was far less serene than that of Badajoz. One scandal involving three convents pitted local elites against one another. Starting in 1573, religious authorities had attempted to cloister Zamora's tertiary religious, an especially contentious aspect of Tridentine reform.[98] Stepping into this scene, Simancas soon drew fire. In 1581, complaints reached the king that the new bishop had failed to correct the dissolute behavior of Franciscan tertiaries in the three convents. Simancas was accused of negligence and compared unfavorably to his predecessor, who was described as more reform minded. The nuns had reputedly displayed shocking behavior, hosting inappropriate visitors and leaving their cloister too frequently and in improper garb. The youngest nuns had dressed as boys and danced with young men during Carnival; they had hosted a "profane" comedy put on by traveling Italians without putting up a curtain to shield the host. Simancas's critics charged not only that he had allowed the tertiaries to flout the reforms, but also that he had caused scandal by allowing his clients to run amok. His servant Fulano Tablares, archdeacon of Ávila, was reviled. Rumors flew that his *provisor*, don Diego de Orozco, had gotten one of the tertiaries pregnant. Moreover, Orozco was reported to be of insufficient age and learning to hold his office.[99] Adding insult to injury, Simancas – his opponents charged – had failed to investigate fully or to discipline his

---

[97] *Collectaneorum de Republica libri IX* … (Salamanca: heirs of Matías Gast, 1582). While still at the royal Court in Madrid, on December 29, 1578, he delegated his powers to Lic. Rodrigo Arias González, who then attended Zamora's cathedral chapter January 13, 1579. Simancas was in Zamora by March 6, 1581, AGS, PR 8, doc. 61; Actos de posesión, ACZ, leg. 152(1)/exp. 4.

[98] As a result of a fire in 1591, Zamora's cathedral archive retains few documents from this era. There was resistance to initial attempts to impose the reforms (e.g., conflict between the chapter and bishops over appointments to prebends); the synod was finally convened in 1584. Cesáreo Fernández Duro, *Memorias Históricas de la Ciudad de Zamora: su provincia y obispado* (Madrid: Establecimiento tipográfico de los sucesores de Rivadeneyra, 1882–83), 328–29; Armando Cotarelo Valledor, *El Cardinal Don Rodrigo de Castro y su fundación en Monforte de Lemos* (Madrid: Imprenta de Editorial Magisterio Español, 1945), 1:101–3; *CODOIN*, vol. 102, 62–63. For an approach to the Tridentine reform of convents, see Elizabeth Lehfeldt, *Religious Women in Golden Age Spain: The Permeable Cloister* (Aldershot, UK, and Burlington, VT: Ashgate, 2005); Fernández Terricabras, *Philippe II et La Contre-Réforme*, 580–81.

[99] The houses included Santa Marina and Santa Marta; see reports of 1581 in AGS, Estado, leg. 161, nos. 53, 54. See also F. J. Lorenzo Pinar, "Monjas disidentes. Las resistencias a la clausura en Zamora tras el Concilio de Trento," in *Disidencias y exilios en la España Moderna*, ed. A. Mestre Sanchís and E. Giménez López (Alicante: Caja de Ahorros del Mediterráneo, Universidad de Alicante, AEHM, 1997), 71–80.

household. The petitions indicated a city divided into factions: Simancas's critics recommended that the king avoid involving the local Dominicans in any investigation, as their prior was very friendly with Simancas.

Other authorities claimed that Simancas governed the three tertiary convents in Zamora – and another in Toro – very well, and several noblemen and municipal officials vouched for him. The cathedral chapter reported its dismay at hearing that the city's chief magistrate (*corregidor*) – a "person with such little fear of God and conscience" – had denounced Simancas to the king. They sought to protect themselves and their bishop, urging the king to use restraint in punishing any canons whom he might find guilty of misconduct.[100] Defending Simancas in the customary language of merit, the canons found him "so lettered, so good, and such an example" to Spain's other prelates. They praised "the care with which he exercises everything that pertains to his pastoral office, and the paternal love, and charity with which he treats his sheep."[101] One canon composed a particularly detailed account of how Simancas's good governance proved him the most "honorable" bishop in the region in many years, exemplary in his alms, "public and secret," and in his hospitality. He enumerated his reforms: attending to the liturgy, executing the services on feast days correctly, and celebrating Holy Week without skipping any of the divine offices. He praised him for remedying gross neglect in the saying of perpetual masses that the deceased had endowed in their wills and for governing the chapter and the ecclesiastical courts well. The bishop and his ministers had visited nearly the whole diocese, a feat not accomplished in more than a decade. Among other good works, he provided funds for the cathedral's music and gave dowries to two orphan girls.[102]

The papal nuncio also intervened in the affair; he weighed the tertiaries' protests that their status exempted them from strict cloistration, compiled reports of abuses, and recommended reforms. Together, the king and the nuncio requested two papal briefs: one to order prosecution of those who had committed crimes and one to reform the cloistering of the monasteries.

---

[100] "persona con tan poco temor de dios y de conciencia," chapter (Arcediano Delgadillo, Lic. A[ntoni]o López de Mella, Lic. don Miguel Ordóñez) to royal secretary Vázquez, January 1, 1582, BL, Add. 28343, doc. 60, fol. 169r; "El estado de caballeros hijos-dalgo," January 23, 1582 and "el comun de la ciudad de Zamora" (16 signatories), n.d., ibid., doc. 97, fols. 190r-91v and doc. 98, fol. 192r.
[101] "ser tan letrado, tam bueno, y tan exemplar"; "el cuydado conque exerce todo lo que incumbe a su officio pastoral, y al amor paternal, y charidad con que trata a sus ouejas," BL, Add. 28343, doc. 60, fol. 169r.
[102] Canon Martín de Vivar to Vázquez, January 23, 1582, ibid., doc. 84, fol. 188.

Yet shortly thereafter, the nuncio became involved in graver disputes in Guadix and then fell ill, and the situation in Zamora remained unsettled.[103] Such half-finished reforms were not uncommon, hanging on as persisting battles between authorities; waged in letters, in print, in censures pecuniary and judicial; and in honors granted and promotions withheld. Without clear resolution to conflicts, the public display of good reputation took on even greater importance, and the distinction between the conduct of the individual and the authority of an office was blurry. Any hope of effecting episcopal, inquisitorial, or judicial reforms required establishing the political capital with which to do so. In this light, writing a remonstrance and bestowing charity were not unrelated actions. Thus, Simancas aligned himself with clerical and magisterial ideals in writing while making large bequests in Zamora. He donated wheat to the needy and monies to the jail. He funded the completion of the Discalced Franciscan monastery of Saint John the Baptist and gave to the city's convents, hospitals, and churches. As a codicil to his will, he left four thousand ducats to Zamora's poor, from which to provide them alms of two or four ducats each year on Saint John's Day and Christmas. Even in this act, he fit himself into a lineage of charitable prelates and showed his attention to administrative reform. His gift was meant to supplement an earlier bishop's foundation, which Simancas claimed no longer served the city's great need.[104]

OBSERVING OTHER REPUBLICS

In the slow years of his official work, Simancas developed a practice of writing, leaving behind tracts that were intimately intertwined with one another and with the vicissitudes of his career. Together, they proposed a set of ideals. In his *Collectaneorum de Republica*, he reflected on the social fabric to which his *Vida* and his inquisitorial law books belonged: an organic whole of the family, city streets, churches, magistrates, law courts, and the crown. Offering Spain as a model, he sought to write his career and inquisitorial office into the larger universe of the Christian republic. He

---

[103] Report from the nuncio to Secretary Zayas, AGS, Estado, leg. 161, nos. 134–35.

[104] For the codicil, see ACZ 19/1 bis, and, with paperwork relating to the administration of the pious foundation, ADPZ, orden 1776, leg. 86, exp. 1; see also ACZ, orden no. 1427, leg. 19, no. 1. These are indexed in A. Matilla Tascón, *Guía-inventario delos Archivos de Zamora y su Provincia* (Madrid: Dirección General de Archivos y Bibliotecas, Diputación Provincial de Zamora, Ayuntamiento de Zamora, 1964), 181. See also González Dávila, *Teatro*, 2:417; Fernández Duro, *Memorias*, 327; Solano de Figueroa, *Historia Eclesiástica*, 3:368.

revealed the intellectual culture upon which he drew and which he aspired to join in the range of disciplines, authorities, and precedents he marshaled, stemming from the ancients and extending to sixteenth-century humanists.

It was not only the delays in the Carranza trial that led Simancas to pick up his pen so often. This activity also revealed a particular ideal that Simancas pursued, informed by his early years in Salamanca and Valladolid: the lettered doctor using his accumulated knowledge to comment on the world around him, and, ideally, to persuade its elites of much needed reforms. Other peers behaved similarly. On the other side of the case, Azpilcueta also turned his academic background toward print, folding his experience of the Carranza case into his collections of legal opinions and treatises on prayer and confession; he, like Simancas, positioned himself as fighting heresy, but with different emphases and persuasive tools. If the experience of Carranza's case led Simancas to warn against preferring fraternal correction to public denunciation, it led Azpilcueta in precisely the opposite direction.[105]

The observation of other judicial regimes and other republics seemingly spurred the reforming and writing impulses, leading to the codification of Spanish practices formulated in comparison to those of other realms. Although a certain inquisitorial logic tended to equate mobility with heretical threats, it was also travelers, but those in official capacities, like Simancas, who did much of the work of elaborating inquisitorial theory. Heretics and their books crossed borders and infiltrated Christian republics, and circulation could frequently be equated to contagion. But mobile careers also turned learned clerics toward revising procedures and practices as they were confronted with novel environments that sometimes offered them an opening to pitch their practices to wider European audiences. Perhaps the three most famous sixteenth-century "Spanish" anti-heretical writers composed their treatises, in large part, while out of Spain: Simancas, Castro, and Francisco Peña. Simancas's theory proliferated as he was marooned in Rome; Castro's mushroomed as he traveled with the imperial Court in the middle of the century, often in northern Europe; and Peña compiled his reeditions and glosses while sitting on the Rota in Rome at the century's close.[106]

---

[105] See prefatory material and consilia on heresy in Azpilcueta, *Opera Omnia* (Venice: Domenico Nicolini, 1601).

[106] Neither Castro nor Peña were inquisitors. Cf. Edward Peters, "Editing Inquisitors' Manuals in the Sixteenth Century: Francisco Peña and the *Directorium Inquisitorum* of Nicolas Eymeric," *The Library Chronicle* 40 (1974): 95–107.

Shaped by legal study and consultation and by experience in the civil judiciary, and lacking a background as a tribunal inquisitor, Simancas's career developed in a manner relatively unlike those of his contemporaries in the Spanish Inquisition. Few others had seen the workings of the Italian inquisitions firsthand, much less spent nearly a decade in Rome. His legal expertise made him an excellent candidate for the most juridically complicated work of his generation – that of the Carranza case – but that initially prestigious selection eventually estranged him further from his peers. His theorizing across so many arenas of law, politics, and ecclesiastical governance showed his virtuosity and built his reputation in lettered circles, even as its immediate results were limited, vis-à-vis both his career advancement and the Carranza trial. There were, perhaps, political costs to the strategies Simancas adopted. He held to his opposition to Carranza even when the climate of opinion changed and very nearly to the point of challenging papal judgment; in so often choosing to print and to print in Latin, he circulated his opinions broadly, with his name and office prominently attached to them.

When Simancas died in the autumn of 1583, still mere bishop of Zamora, he was buried in the chapel of the Holy Spirit in Córdoba's cathedral, which he and his brothers had built.[107] That spring, just months before his death, he had signed the conditions for the chapel's governance in his episcopal palace in Zamora. Seemingly each of the three brothers was interred there: Francisco in 1570 and both of the bishops Simancas, Diego and Juan, in 1583.

In assessing Simancas's career, we have tended to read his complaints and see his stymied promotions as evidence of professional stagnation and, ultimately, failure. Perhaps, however, we have been reading his *Vida* too instrumentally and too literally. The *Vida* was certainly an apologetic text. A remonstrance that listed the services Simancas had rendered, the defeats and disappointments he had suffered, and seemed to ask for recompense, it often followed the form common in petitions for royal patronage. It was definitely an attempt to assert his view of Carranza's guilt, the justice of the Spanish Inquisition in trying the archbishop, and the generalized chaos and mismanagement of the affair. Nevertheless, by the time Simancas began to

---

[107] I think Simancas died in Zamora in November: a pious bequest states that he made and signed a codicil to his will before witnesses in the episcopal palace, November 7, 1583; see the copy dated November 28, 1589, ACZ 19/1bis. For the claims that he died in Madrid or October 16 in Córdoba, see González Dávila, *Teatro*, 2:417; *EE*, 76.

write his *Vida*, he may have had a far different time horizon in mind than his own career.

It is quite possible that Simancas came to an alternative understanding of his work, its prospects, and its meaning as he began to turn increasingly toward writing and publication in the middle of the 1560s. He was then in his mid-fifties and had not been able to make an advantageous exit from his inquisitorial work on the Carranza case. His actions in those years can be read as also about leaving a legacy, via patronage, charity, the promotion of his family, and inquisitorial and more broadly ecclesiastical reforms. Perhaps, as he churned out at least fifteen printed editions and the *Vida* in the space of not much more than fifteen years, he had decided to pursue a longer course. As he signaled in the *Vida*, he had come to not expect justice – as he understood it – in the mortal life. As befitted a cleric, he claimed to look beyond the physical life and human justice. From that perspective, his writings sought to shape the life of the Church and Christian society beyond the lifetime of a single bishop. In part, they made his experiences a cautionary tale and offered them to others as a means by which to acquire experience – that commodity so important to the judge's essential work of discernment – through reading. His actions in the years after 1567 also suggested another form of communion. Modeling himself on the ancients, like Cicero, who were touchstones of his writings, Simancas also left traces of himself in monumental architecture, in the records of his republic, and in his books. He put his case before posterity as much as before his contemporaries.

Even in his lifetime, Simancas succeeded in converting himself into precedent. From early in his inquisitorial career, his opponents – from a friar suspected of Lutheran heresy to the esteemed Azpilcueta – cited him in their arguments.[108] Later sixteenth-century treatises invoked him, and his

---

[108] In 1559, Simancas held an inconclusive audience with friar Luis de la Cruz, one of the many accused of Lutheranism and consorting with Carranza. Two years later, the friar justified a particular opinion on the role of the saints by reasoning that Simancas had promoted the very same interpretation in his *Institutiones*. Tellechea Idígoras, *Tiempos Recios: Inquisición y Heterodoxias* (Salamanca: Ediciones Sígueme, 1977), 171, 188. In May 1566, Azpilcueta cited Simancas (*Institutiones*, chap. 29) in a memorandum; he took up the case of a man who, as a child of heretics, had been deprived of goods and the ability to occupy some offices. He argued for a distinction between the children of reconciled heretics and those of relapsed heretics who had died impenitent, and that the former should be free of any restrictions. He noted that in this question, Simancas followed the opinion of the fourteenth-century canonist Giovanni Andrea, and so ruled that – born before the parental sin – even the children of relapsed, and burnt, heretics "should be free of that penalty of infamy." Azpilcueta located his opinion as more conservative than the one Simancas held, who he explained had cited the *Siete Partidas* (the Spanish law code)

works quickly became authoritative in each field of jurisprudence: inquisitorial, civil, ecclesiastical. By the century's end, officials in many of the
Spanish Inquisition's tribunals cited his manuals. Even his *Vida* became a
source of institutional memory, referred to during the *Suprema*'s deliberations in 1643. Simancas infiltrated seventeenth-century libraries in similar
ways. His *Collectaneorum de Republica* saw new editions in northern
Europe and made its way even to the shelves of a Protestant book collec-
tor.[109] Protestant polemic further solidified his place in the canon of
inquisitorial literature, as his manuals figured prominently in Philipp van
Limborch's late seventeenth-century *History of the Inquisition*.[110] In the
Catholic world, the 1561 instructions continued to be reissued, and
Gregory XIII's 1584 recompilation of canon law commentaries gave
Simancas's writings a place in the volume on inquisitorial jurisprudence.
Later Catholic jurists used Simancas to attempt to advance their own
careers, as the printing of his *Opera* in Ferrara in 1692 attests. Even the
economy of praise in which Simancas participated was perpetuated in the
next century. Nicolás Antonio – the late seventeenth-century Spanish
bibliographer – used the compliments that Simancas and his contemporaries paid one another as a kind of bibliographical map. As Antonio
cataloged a Spanish community of letters, he justified his inclusion of
Simancas with praise for him culled from the legal commentaries of
Covarrubias and Francisco Sarmiento.[111]

---

to the effect that children born before the father sinned should not be punished or suffer
his lack of honor. AHN, Inq., lib. 1231, fols. 753r–58v. See also Truman, *Spanish
Treatises on Government, Society and Religion in the Time of Philip II: The 'de regimine
principum' and Associated Traditions* (Leiden: Brill, 1999), 287, 331.

[109] There were at least four posthumous editions: *Collectaneorum de Republica libri IX …*
(Salamanca: Diego de Cusio, expensis Ioannis Pulmani bibliopolae, 1598 and 1600); *De
Republica recte instituenda, conservanda, et amplificanda libri IX* (Cologne: Lazare
Zetzner, 1609); *Promptuarium Politicum ad Regulas Prudentiae formatum* (Strasburg:
Georg Andreas Dolhopff; Johann Eberhard Zetzner, 1664). Three editions (1574, 1609,
1664) made their way into the Duke August call numbers of the German HAB, and two of
them bear marks that some owner of the book devoted special attention to it. In the front
matter of the 1609 edition, one hand noted that there was also a 1664 Strasburg edition
published without the author's name and another hand copied out Verzosa's letter in
praise of Simancas, which had been printed in the 1569 edition. There is even a hint that
the book was given as a gift between learned friends, as Latin lines about absent friends,
seemingly written in 1673, appear on the initial sheets of the 1574 Plantin edition.

[110] Philipp van Limborch, *Historia Inquisitionis* (Amsterdam: Henricus Wetstenius, 1692).

[111] For Simancas as "vir omnium consensu doctissimus," praised also in the writings of
Jacobo Stephano, see Antonio, *Bibliotheca Hispana Nova*, 1:316–17. *De catholicis
institutionibus* and *Adnotationes in Zanchinum cum animaduersionibus in Campegium*
appear in the *Tractatus Universi Iuris*, vol. 11, pt. 2, among 68 tracts under the heading

As Simancas's legal opinions and reference books entered the universe of authoritative precedent, they also modeled a way of writing about the Inquisition. Part of an increasing tide of polemical literature, they implied that inquisitors could expand the campaign – against the Carranzas and the Calvins and those they had corrupted – from the tribunal room to the field of print. They suggested that competing visions of Catholic reform – like the preference for fraternal correction or the inquisitorial style that predominated in Rome – also deserved to be publicly challenged. Although the trajectory of Simancas's working life was uncommon among Spanish inquisitors, his writings contained a common vocabulary of Spanish inquisitorial ideals. Simancas used that idiom to align inquisitors more closely with other kinds of judges, both sacralizing the work of the latter and contending that jurists made the best arbiters of faith; he made conscience a refrain, and so put the primary value of inquisitors' work in their capacity to discern. With his emphasis on conscience, on procedure, and on theory, he proposed a model of practice in which it was essential for inquisitors to turn to books, to attend to the written as well as the spoken word, in investigating possible heretics and in informing their judgments and deliberations. A century into the Spanish Inquisition's existence, he supplied arguably the most ample theory to date for how to be an inquisitor and what service that office rendered to the Spanish monarchy. It was not so much his own life that was a portrait of the sixteenth-century inquisitor, but the written version of himself that captured a certain vision of the inquisitor that Simancas sought to propagate. With his pen, Simancas made himself an architect of the office.

"De iudiciis criminalibus S. Inquisitionis." See Gaetano Colli, *Per Una Bibliografia dei Trattati Giuridici Pubblicati nel XVI Secolo: Indici dei Tractatus Universi Iuris* (Milan: Giuffrè Editore, 1994), 110–11; Izbicki, "Problems of Attribution in the *Tractatus Universi Iuris* (Venice 1584)," in *Friars and Jurists: Selected Studies*, ed. Izbicki (Goldbach: Keip Verlag, 1997), 413–27. Also, *Opera Jacobi Simancae* (Ferrara: Bernardino Pomatelli, 1692).

CHAPTER 3

Courting the King, Courting the Pope

Luis de Páramo between Spain and Italy

A doorman from Modica is worth more than the inquisitors.[1]

Toward the end of 1586, Luis de Páramo Rincón arrived in Palermo, newly appointed as an inquisitor and posted to the Spanish Inquisition's tribunal there. Perched on the edge of the Tyrrhenian Sea, the city then had a population of around seventy thousand and competed with Messina to be the principal city of Spanish Sicily. The island had come under the control of the Aragonese crown early in the fifteenth century and, under Habsburg rule in the later sixteenth century, was governed by a viceroy and overseen by the Council of Italy in Madrid. Claiming a grant of authority known as the *Monarchia*, Spanish kings had extensive ecclesiastical powers in Sicily, including the right to appoint bishops. The highest Sicilian civil authority was an appellate body called the *Gran Corte*, made up primarily of local nobility. The Inquisition was also one of the poles of Spanish authority in Sicily, where it sought to carve out space in a complicated religious and judicial environment; by one inquisitorial count, the island had a dizzying fifty-four separate secular, ecclesiastical, and baronial jurisdictions.[2]

A Spanish inquisitor sent to Palermo thus had a challenging landscape to learn to navigate. Born in mid-century, a Castilian trained as a jurist, Páramo entered the Inquisition in his early forties. At his arrival, he could

---

[1] AHN, Inq., lib. 882, fol. 318r.

[2] For the population estimate of 1570, see H. G. Koenigsberger, *The Practice of Empire* (Ithaca, NY: Cornell University Press, 1969), 74. For the tally of jurisdictions, see Maria Sofia Messana, *Inquisitori, negromanti e streghe nella Sicilia moderna, 1500–1782* (Palermo: Sellerio, 2007), 203–5.

have expected judicial and linguistic complexity in his work, amplified by the island's connections to the Italian mainland. He could have anticipated that his office would require political finesse. The tribunal's conflicts with the viceroy were well known, and it sought to maintain both a larger number of familiars than was customary and the unusual privilege of appointing nobles as familiars. Sicily was in many ways a frontier zone in the Spanish world; facing Italy and the Muslim Mediterranean, it was considered strategically important. An inquisitor who served there could expect both to acquire special expertise and to be able to depict his work as uniquely valuable for the defense of the faith. Páramo could plausibly have seen his new post as one that would allow him to offer particular service to the Church, which might give him skills he could parlay into promotions within the Inquisition or at Court in Madrid, and was very likely to gain him a nomination to a Sicilian bishopric.

Páramo met with more than he had bargained for. On the last day of 1589, he had a brush with catastrophe. Although he had arrived in Palermo a scant three years before, he had rapidly shifted from being the most junior of three inquisitors to the senior of only two. Following common practice, he lodged in the court's headquarters; unlike in other places, however, the Inquisition did not have its own building but was located inside Palermo's castle, the domain of the viceroy. There (the inquisitors would report a few days later), in the middle of the night, "out of the window of a room that is below those that we inhabit, where the archive of the trials is . . . burst much smoke and flames."[3] Páramo and other officials rushed into the secret archives to save their files. The tribunal sustained significant damage and only a change in the wind saved Páramo's quarters. The next time, the inquisitor had less luck. On August 19, 1593, there was another fire: reportedly, enemies of the Inquisition exploded a store of gunpowder in the castle, destroying many records and much of the tribunal's facilities. This time, Páramo's lodgings were damaged and he was seriously injured in the explosion, even taking a blow to the head. The inquisitors wrote that their survival was a "miracle" and that some three hundred had died in the explosion.[4] Confronted with this state of affairs, Páramo turned to a series of interconnected strategies to defend his authority, his office, and his court. He tailored his letters to

---

[3] "por una bentana de un aposento que esta debaxo delos que hauitamos donde esta el Archibo delos procesos . . . salia mucho humo con llamas de fuego," Páramo and Barahona, January 10, 1590, AHN, Inq., lib. 880, fol. 246r; see also fols. 248–55.

[4] Olloquí and Llanes, December 9, 1596 (copy of December 2), AHN, Inq., lib. 881, fol. 336.

the circumstances at hand and went to Madrid to lobby in person; once there, not unlike Simancas, Páramo turned to print, publishing opinions on contentious jurisdictional problems and edging into the increasingly fashionable field of historiography. Still, Páramo's career stagnated. Mired in political skirmishes, he died in Palermo in 1608, still no more than the tribunal's senior inquisitor.

Páramo has gained fame as the author of the first history of the Inquisition.[5] He has also drawn the attention of scholars, if to a lesser degree, for his role in the series of dramatic conflicts between the viceroy and the Inquisition around the turn of the seventeenth century. With waning royal support – particularly after the accession of Philip III in 1598 – Páramo's struggles to conserve inquisitorial authority in Sicily demonstrate how inquisitors could act as colonial administrators.[6] Far less attention has been paid, however, to how Páramo's seemingly universal history of the Inquisition was profoundly tied to the particular experiences of his career in Sicily and to his lobbying for that tribunal's authority.

Tracing Páramo's inquisitorial career in Sicily, this chapter examines how his theory and his practice developed in tandem, drawing from each other. Jurisdictional contests were a central component of his work. In his published tracts, Páramo melded theological and juridical arguments with an array of historical precedents and stepped into the growing field of

---

[5] Páramo, *De Origine et progressu officii Sanctae Inquisitionis* (Madrid: Typographia Regia, Juan Flandro, 1598). For polemical uses of Páramo's history, see Philipp van Limborch, *Historia Inquisitionis* (Amsterdam: Henricus Wetstenius, 1692); Nicolau Eymeric, *Le manuel des inquisiteurs, à l'usage des inquisitions d'Espagne & de Portugal...*, ed. André Morellet (Lisbon [Paris?], 1762). See especially the approaches in Adriano Prosperi, *L'Inquisizione Romana: Letture e Richerche* (Rome: Edizioni di Storia e Letteratura, 2003), 70–75 (which contains a particularly sensitive analysis of Páramo's use of biblical time); Doris Moreno Martínez, *La Invención de la Inquisición* (Madrid: Marcial Pons Historia, 2004), 202–7; Edward Peters, *Inquisition* (Berkeley and Los Angeles: University of California Press, 1989), 266–72. It is drawn upon frequently, if not explicitly analyzed, in Henry Charles Lea, *A History of the Inquisition of Spain* (New York: The Macmillian Company, 1906–7). See also my "Was Adam the First Heretic? Luis de Páramo, Diego de Simancas, and the Origins of Inquisitorial Practice," *Archive for Reformation History* 97 (2006): 185–211.

[6] See, inter alia, Koenigsberger, *Practice of Empire*; William Monter, *Frontiers of Heresy: The Spanish Inquisition from the Basque Lands to Sicily* (Cambridge and New York: Cambridge University Press, 1990); Manuel Rivero Rodríguez, "La Inquisición Española en Sicilia," *HIEA* 3:1031–222; Carlo Alberto Garufi, *Fatti e personaggi dell'Inquisizione in Sicilia* (1917; repr., Palermo: Sellerio, 1978); Vito La Mantia, *Origine e vicende dell'Inquisizione in Sicilia* (1886; repr., Palermo: Sellerio, 1977); Francesco Renda, *L'Inquisizione in Sicilia: I fatti. le persone* (Palermo: Sellerio, 1997); Messana, *Inquisitori, negromanti e streghe.*

polemic about sacred history. When he presented the merits of the tribunal in official correspondence, he depicted its approach as pastoral and its diligent administration of justice as far superior to that in other Sicilian courts. The immediate results of all this argumentative effort were modest; it did not translate into promotions for Páramo and, at best, barely held back the tide of opposition against the Palermo tribunal. Nevertheless, Páramo's career affords a window onto some key elements of inquisitorial work. Páramo and his colleagues, like other Spanish inquisitors posted in places considered peripheral, sought to use their marginalized position to their advantage, developing a rhetoric of affliction in their correspondence while also depicting themselves as gaining specialized knowledge as intermediaries. Páramo's actions indicate how inquisitorial work was, in part, rhetorical work. The successful justification of actions in the field to authorities at the royal Court required a range of persuasive tools. Faced with this challenge, Páramo responded by developing a particular kind of historical thinking, which would inscribe both the office of inquisitor and his own work into a long and venerable genealogy.

THE ROAD TO SICILY

In a sense, Luis de Páramo Rincón hailed from the center of the Spanish monarchy. A native of the small agricultural towns at Castile's geographical heart, like many inquisitorial judges, he was born into the class that often construed itself as the core of Castilian society, and acted to maintain its place there. The son of Hernán Gutiérrez Páramo, a propertied *hidalgo*, and Mari Fernández del Rincón, citizens of Borox, Luis was born in that town around 1545. He had four brothers and a sister and a broad network of relatives in the surrounding region. His parents, grandparents, and at least some of his great-grandparents were natives and residents of places at a distance of about a day's journey from one another: the village of Lominchar and the towns of Casarrubios del Monte, Borox, and Sesña.[7] Localities in Toledo's archdiocese and inquisitorial district, they were roughly equidistant to Toledo and Madrid, although the latter was not yet the capital during Páramo's youth.

Like many of their contemporaries, Páramo's family members made use of the courts and offices of the Habsburg monarchy to solidify and

---

[7] On the agricultural, municipal, and judicial organization of such zones of Castile, see Helen Nader, *Liberty in Absolutist Spain: The Habsburg Sale of Towns, 1516–1700* (Baltimore, MD: The Johns Hopkins University Press, 1990).

publicize their social station, leaving traces in the archives of their efforts. Páramo became an inquisitor after the practice of investigating the genealogies of applicants to inquisitorial office had been regularized. Thus, officials from Toledo's tribunal inquired into Páramo's background over two weeks in the fall of 1585. Thirteen years later, a similar process permitted his entrance into one of Spain's prestigious military orders.[8] In each instance, the investigators collected marks of good repute. Those interviewed voiced no doubts about the family's status as Old Christians. In 1535, Páramo's paternal grandfather had litigated in Valladolid's Chancery to secure a writ of nobility.[9] Residents of Borox recalled this and that the family had long lived with the privileges of the gentry and tallied the honors Páramo's father accrued: he had served several times as a local judge; one son, Gabriel Gutiérrez, had also held offices reserved for esteemed *hidalgos*; and two of his sons had become inquisitors.[10] They referred to other relatives who held regional offices. A cousin of Páramo's on his father's side – Diego Iañez de Páramo – was a familiar of the Inquisition in Casarrubios del Monte, his mother's brother – Andrés Martín del Rincón – a familiar in Borox, and one of his mother's uncles – Alonso Lorencío – a curate in Villaseca de la Sagra. Deponents reported distinctions that conferred special civil status, rooting the reputation of a family in its recourse to other jurisdictions and exemptions from taxation; they mentioned those who had marked their status through investigations, lawsuits, and the acquisition of documentary proof.[11]

---

[8] The inquiries were initiated September 5, 1585, they involved four towns, and he was deemed eligible for office in Madrid, May 17, 1586; AHN, Inq., leg. 1306, exp. 14. The second investigation was ordered January 14, 1599; AHN, OM, Religiosos, Alcántara, exp. 315. For biographical information, see also Rivero Rodríguez, "Inquisición"; and "Páramo, Luis de," *DSI* 3:1170–71; Monter, *Frontiers of Heresy*, 62–63, 179–85; Garufi, *Fatti e personaggi*; Renda, *L'Inquisizione*; Nicolás Antonio, *Biblioteca Hispana Nueva*, trans. Miguel Matilla Martínez (1788; Madrid: Fundación Universitaria Española, 1999), 2:67.

[9] Obtained January 26, 1535, Borox's council confirmed the writ January 11, 1536. I have not consulted them, but records of lawsuits (*pleitos de hidalguía*) seem to survive in Valladolid's Chancery for Páramo's grandfather Rodrigo Gutiérrez del Páramo of Borox (1534), and one of his father's two brothers, Alonso Gutiérrez del Páramo of Lominchar (1562), and other likely relatives, http://pares.mcu.es/. Alonso married a daughter of Domingo Fernández of Toledo, and one of their (four?) children became a captain. On such litigation, see Richard L. Kagan, *Lawsuits and Litigants in Castile, 1500–1700* (Chapel Hill: The University of North Carolina Press, 1981).

[10] "alcalde de la ermandad del estado delos hijosdalgo," AHN, OM, Religiosos, Alcántara, exp. 315, fol. 5.

[11] His father was native to Casarrubios del Monte, as were his paternal grandparents, Rodrigo Gutiérrez Páramo (some said he was from Lominchar) and Juana Hernández

Páramo had a model in his older brother, Rodrigo Gutiérrez Páramo, who had ascended to another level of the Castilian elite. Rodrigo, who died sometime before 1598, was admitted to the military order of Calatrava as a religious, holding the office of prior of Coronada.[12] A licentiate, he was an inquisitor in Llerena and in Seville, and a consultant for Córdoba's tribunal, before becoming an inquisitor in Toledo in the 1570s. Luis eulogized his brother (and identified him as such) in his history of the Inquisition, praising him as a "man famous everywhere in letters, prudence, and religion."[13] Royal and ecclesiastical service extended the family's geographical horizons. One of those interviewed in the 1599 inquiry knew – because news had made its way back to Castile and because someone had come to make inquiries about his noble status – that one of their cousins had gone to fight in Italy or in Flanders and died a captain. Similarly, some in Borox reported that Luis had graduated as a doctor in canon law, that he was very learned, and that he had gone to Rome in the 1560s.[14]

I have found little other evidence to sketch the contours of Páramo's early life or his preparation for the office of inquisitor. His epitaph would

Heredera (possibly of Galician origin, the daughter of Martín Fernández el Viejo, also of Casarrubios, and sister of Martín Hernández Heredero and Hernán Gallego). After Juana's death, Rodrigo remarried but had no more children. Páramo's mother was native to Borox, and her parents, Andrés Martín del Rincón and Mari Hernández Lorenzo (daughter of an Esteban Lorenzo or Andrés Lorencío, native of Seseña and reputedly of one of its oldest families), were natives of Borox and Seseña, respectively. Her siblings were Blas or Juan, Andrés, Esteban, Alonso (the curate), and a sister who married Diego de San Juan. Andrés Martín del Rincón had first married Estefanía Martín, from Morata, lived in Borox, and produced two children; in his second marriage, he had a daughter Mari (Páramo's mother) and sons. It is likely that some of Páramo's maternal relations from Borox entered a convent in Toledo affiliated with the order of Santiago, as Juana del Rincón y Cortés and Eugenia de Rincón y Cortés were received as nuns into the order's Convent of Santa Fe in Toledo in 1580 and 1590, respectively; the nuns' genealogical information mentions inquisitor relatives, although not by name. AHN, OM, Religiosas, Santiago, exps. 577–78.

[12] On the social capital supplied by inquisitorial office or the religious orders, see James E. Wadsworth, *Agents of Orthodoxy: Honor, Status and the Inquisition in Colonial Pernambuco, Brazil* (Lanham, MD: Rowman and Littlefield, 2007); Elena Postigo Castellanos, *Honor y Privilegio en la Corona de Castilla. El Consejo de las Ordenes y los Caballeros de Hábito en el s. XVII* (Almazán, Soria: Junta de Castilla y León, Consejería de Cultura y Bienestar Social, 1988), 133–36.

[13] "vir vndique literis, prudentia, & religione clarus," *De Origine*, 174. He is mentioned in Jean-Pierre Dedieu, *L'administration de la foi: L'Inquisition de Tolède (XVIe–XVIIIe siècle)* (Madrid: Casa de Velázquez, 1989), 162.

[14] For example: "sabe que esta graduado de doctor en canones y que es un gran letrado y como atal le dieron la inquisicion," Alonso Correa of Borox, AHN, OM, Religiosos, Alcántara, exp. 315.

label him an illustrious jurist, a doctor of both laws.[15] He seems to have had a religious vocation and may also have studied theology. Apparently already a cleric, he was a canon and archdeacon of León's cathedral at the time of his appointment, although the extent of his residence in that city is unclear.[16] He entered the Inquisition's hierarchy with his appointment to the Palermo tribunal; his genealogy approved, he received the title of inquisitor on May 21, 1586. Shaped by his upbringing in the shadow of Toledo and his legal education, Páramo may also have brought experience in a cathedral chapter and perhaps knowledge of Rome and an interest in Italian affairs to his new office. Departing relatively quickly for his new post, he took ship for Sicily and was signing inquisitorial business in Palermo before the end of the year.[17]

He arrived to a tribunal in flux. In 1583, the inquisitor Diego de Haedo gained the Sicilian bishopric of Agrigento and promptly resigned his inquisitorial office; he remained a player in the Sicilian scene for many years, soon becoming the archbishop of Palermo, where he stayed until his death in 1608. The *fiscal*, whom the two remaining inquisitors – Juan de la Peña and Juan Correonero – lobbied to have promoted, died in 1585. Instead, the *Suprema* sent them Juan Aymar, previously an inquisitor in Barcelona, with whom Peña was soon locked in conflict. Purportedly, Aymar undermined the dignity of the Inquisition, allowing his henchmen to don its regalia and involving himself in a counterfeiting scandal; he was even accused of necromancy. All this happened against the backdrop of conflict with a viceroy who sought to influence the composition of the tribunal, claiming that if Aymar left Sicily, "it would be to break the thread in the direction of affairs and the execution of justice."[18] He petitioned Philip II to appoint a new inquisitor more amenable to the viceregal administration, citing Aymar's rectitude and temperance as a model, and even proposing that the other two inquisitors be replaced. They, meanwhile, petitioned the *Suprema* for extra consideration, claiming to be under siege; Páramo's appointment was the result. The first business that Páramo signed in Palermo related to the censure of Aymar; although that

---

[15] Renda, *L'Inquisizione*, 210–11. Renda notes that it reflected the increasing prestige of jurists.

[16] In 1585, several informants reported his status as archdeacon and used the titles "doctor" and "sacerdote"; AHN, Inq., leg. 1306, exp. 14 and lib. 881, fol. 231; *De Origine*, 216.

[17] Peña, Correonero, and Páramo, December 26, 1586, AHN, Inq., lib. 879, fol. 80v. For the tribunal's correspondence during Páramo's era, see libs. 879–84.

[18] "seria romper el hilo a la direction, de los negocios, y execucion de la Justicia." Alba de Liste to the king, September 10, 1585, IVDJ, Envío 80, caja 106, doc. 677.

inquisitor was soon ejected, he was still pursuing business related to the scandal more than a decade later. To the viceroy's displeasure, Aymar left, Peña and Correonero remained in office, and Páramo began to follow their example.[19]

THE ISLAND AND THE INQUISITION

In the letters they sent to Castile, Palermo's inquisitors insisted on the liminality of their post: "so separated from the eyes of your Majesty, and so surrounded by enemies."[20] Such language – fairly common in the administrative correspondence of a composite monarchy – was designed to draw royal attention and to highlight the dangers of neglecting a Mediterranean outpost so susceptible to heretics and infidels. Sicily's religious and political landscape was unique. The kingdom had been definitively incorporated into the crown of Aragon in 1409, from which it became part of the Habsburg inheritance. In theory, the Spanish Inquisition had been in Sicily for nearly a century before Páramo's arrival. If its foundation there dated to 1487, it did not establish an active judicial practice until 1500, and even then its privileges were frequently contested, and occasionally suspended, throughout the first half of the sixteenth century.

According to H. G. Koenigsberger, the island was relatively less exploited: "It was commonly said in Sicily the Spaniards nibbled, in Naples they ate, and in Milan they devoured."[21] With Sardinia, these zones held a key place in Philip II's military thinking – a Mediterranean line of defense against the Ottoman Turks. Throughout the 1560s and 1570s, fortifications and garrisons there received substantial royal attention, even though the importance of Sicily as a military staging ground contracted somewhat thereafter. Sicily was also significant for its grain, becoming a breadbasket for Philip II's other kingdoms. The prevailing

---

[19] Peña and Correonero, May 11, 1583, February 13, and October 8, 1585, AHN, Inq., lib. 878, fol. 445r, lib. 879, fols. 226r, 297r; Peña, Correonero, and Páramo, December 26, 1586, and Peña, August 20, 1587, lib. 879, fols. 80v, 104r, 129r; Alba de Liste to the king, January 1586, AGS, Estado, leg. 1155, doc. 85. The conflicts long predated Páramo's arrival, and Peña, a model for his junior colleague, had written copiously against the viceroy's infractions; see the memorandum in AHN, Inq., lib. 878, fol. 205r, and the analysis of Peña's arguments in Rivero Rodríguez, "Inquisición," 1084–120. See also n. 67.

[20] "tan apartado delos ojos de su M[agesta]d y tan rodeado de enemigos." RB, MS II/265, fol. 94v.

[21] Koenigsberger, *Practice of Empire*, 96.

theory of governance held all of the Catholic Monarchy as organically intertwined, thus the defense of one region was connected to that of others, physically and spiritually. The practical implications of this were predictably complicated. A multiplicity of channels of communication proliferated between Spain and Sicily and a variety of lay and ecclesiastical Spanish authorities on the ground negotiated with Sicilian barons. What, precisely, it meant to serve the crown thus became one of the chief idioms in disputes among officials, as a host of players claimed to be pursuing the common good rather than particular interests.[22]

The chief authority in Sicily was the viceroy, a tangible proxy for the king. This did not, however, forestall conflict with him; rather, Philip II and Philip III – governing from Castile via missives, councils, and secretaries – often promoted ambiguity and conflict among their ministers to prevent any one party's consolidation of power, even to the detriment of administrative efficiency. Sicily's viceroys were noblemen, generally from grandee families; each served for a few years, overseeing royal administration and military defense.[23] The appellate court for civil and criminal cases was the *Gran Corte*, which also functioned as an assembly of Sicilian elites. The next site of appeal was to the king's councils. The Council of Italy – after its cleavage from the Council of Aragon in 1555 – oversaw Sicily's government and reviewed jurisdictional disputes.[24] Sicilian nobles wielded substantial local power but were largely excluded from royal administration. Philip II preferred to employ crown servants – moved frequently between posts – tied more to his patronage than to the region's populace.

[22] Monter, *Frontiers of Heresy*, 164–85; Rivero Rodríguez, "Inquisición," 1035–44; Koenigsberger, *Practice of Empire*; J. H. Elliott, "A Europe of Composite Monarchies," *Past and Present* 137 (1992): 48–71. See also Rivero Rodríguez, *Felipe II y el Gobierno de Italia* (Madrid: Sociedad Estatal para la Conmemoración de los Centenarios de Felipe II y Carlos V, 1998); Geoffrey Parker, *The Grand Strategy of Philip II* (New Haven, CT: Yale University Press, 1998), 77–109; Thomas James Dandelet and John A. Marino, eds., *Spain in Italy: Politics, Society and Religion 1500–1700* (Leiden and Boston: Brill, 2007); Mireille Peytavin, *Visite et gouvernement dans le royaume de Naples, XVIe–XVIIe siècles* (Madrid: Casa de Velázquez, 2003).

[23] The viceroys during Páramo's term, not counting interim appointments, were Marcantonio Colonna, Prince of Paliano (1577–84); Diego Enríquez de Guzmán, Count of Alba de Liste (1585–92); Enrique de Guzmán, Count of Olivares (1592–95); Bernardino de Cárdenas y Portugal, Duke of Maqueda (1598–1601); Lorenzo Suárez de Figueroa y Córdoba, Duke of Feria (1602–6); and Juan Fernández Pacheco, Duke of Escalona (1607–10).

[24] Castilians came to dominate the most important positions on the new council, although the financial arm remained with the Council of Aragon. Koenigsberger, *Practice of Empire*, 21–23.

Adding further jurisdictional complication, Sicily was a locus of conflict between the Spanish crown and the papacy. The *Monarchia Sicula,* a claim to juridical authority, allowed Spanish kings the right of ecclesiastical appointment and the privilege of royal approval of any papal bull or brief to be published there; moreover, the residence of a papal nuncio was barred. Most of the Sicilian bishops appointed under Philip II were Spanish, and often former inquisitors. At times, the papacy tried to curb the crown's rights or revoke these privileges, but it also abandoned such wrangling in the face of more immediate challenges, and trade from Sicily was important to Rome. The presence of the Spanish Inquisition in the kingdom only complicated the picture. Inquisitors could petition the Council of Italy or attempt to trump it, approaching the king through the *Suprema* or the Inquisitor General instead. Its precise practical relationship to Rome was also ambiguous, and some Sicilians seem to have perceived the papal court as a locus of inquisitorial appeal. On the other hand, viceroys and inquisitors – so often at odds – united to defend the *Monarchia.* Páramo would later argue that it aided clerical discipline: "because if the clerics were free and only the ordinary [ecclesiastical courts] were to know their crimes, without fear of the temporal prince, they would perturb the peace and quiet, and each day would commit great and atrocious crimes, which now they do not commit so frequently more for fear of punishment than love of virtue."[25] He justified his tribunal's service to the faith in similar ways and asserted its legitimacy by giving it a distinguished lineage, stretching back to thirteenth-century papal and imperial concessions of authority and augmented by its status under the Spanish Inquisition.

At the same time, the inquisitors needed at least a modicum of local cooperation to be able to conduct their work and to obtain testimony. They had to learn to handle more negotiations directly with Rome and correspondence with inquisitors in Italian tribunals than confronted their peers in peninsular Spain. Illustrating the importance of policing the faith in such a crossroads in the Mediterranean, they took Naples as a counter-example, suggesting that its resistance to a tribunal had made Calabria into a springboard for Lutherans to invade the island. They claimed that superstitious behavior was rampant among the Sicilian populace and the local

---

[25] "porque si los clerigos fuesen libres y sus delictos se huuiesen de conoçer por solos los ordinarios sin temor del Principe temporal, perturbarian la paz y quietud, y cada dia cometerian grandes y atroces delictos los quales agora no tan frequentemente cometen mas por temor dela pena, que amor dela virtud." BNE, MS 8851, fol. 197r.

priesthood insufficient, such that inquisitorial visitations – mobilizations of pastoral care and heretical investigation – were particularly necessary; they frequently prosecuted clerics who blasphemed, flirted with heresy, or were married. Their reports of *autos de fe* drew on a repertoire of common refrains. Designed to argue for the value of their work, for special royal protection, or at least for funds sufficient to cover their operating expenses, they described the people as particularly given to "novelties" and the island as vulnerable to "bad neighbors," eyed by Turks and Protestant corsairs as a stepping-stone to Spain.[26]

The tribunal did net a peculiar mix of suspects. It brought charges of witchcraft and superstitious practices far more frequently than its counterparts on the Iberian Peninsula. Shortly after Páramo arrived, the judges uncovered what they deemed a conventicle of heretics practicing witchcraft and necromancy; the supposed ringleaders appealed to Rome, opening negotiations between Palermo and the papacy over their custody.[27] As they made bids to increase the tribunal's personnel, the inquisitors expressed particular concern about apostates to Islam. They described their strategy in such cases: persuasion and accommodation of those who confessed their errors freely coupled with harsh treatment of those who refused to do so. In 1589, preparing for an *auto* and bemoaning a lack of secretaries, they lamented "that we have not been able to attend to the renegades that are in the Barbary Coast."[28] During Páramo's tenure – from the second half of 1586 through 1608 – the tribunal frequently brought charges of bigamy, blasphemy, and bearing false witness, often in combination; accusations of Judaizing were relatively rare. In addition to the trials of faith, they dedicated significant time to the civil and criminal cases of their familiars and other officials. They held an *auto de fe* in

[26] For example, Páramo and Llanes, March 18, 1605, and September 24, 1606, AGS, Estado, leg. 1161, doc. 169 and leg. 1162, doc. 101.

[27] In this instance, the Sicilian tribunal cooperated with the Roman Inquisition. Don Joan and don Francisco de Moncada – the ringleaders – went from Sicily to Rome to appeal. In 1587, the pope sent Joan and his case back to Sicily, while Francisco remained imprisoned in Rome. See letters from 1586–88, AHN, Inq., lib. 879, fols. 92r, 106r, 117r. See also Garufi, *Fatto e personaggi*, 59; Messana, *Inquisitori, negromanti e streghe*.

[28] "no emos podido atendera los delos Renegados queestan en berbería," Páramo and Barahona, October 19, 1589, AHN, Inq., lib. 880, fol. 26. See also Correonero, Páramo, and Barahona, May 12, 1589, fol. 94. On renegades, see L. P. Harvey, *Muslims in Spain, 1500 to 1614* (Chicago: University of Chicago Press, 2005); Bruce Taylor, "The Enemy Within and Without: An Anatomy of Fear on the Spanish Mediterranean Littoral" in *Fear in Early Modern Society*, ed. W. G. Naphy and P. Roberts (Manchester, UK, and New York: Manchester University Press, 1997), 78–99; Anita González-Raymond, *La croix et le croissant: les inquisiteurs des îles face à l'islam, 1550–1700* (Paris: CNRS, 1993).

Palermo about once a year – a regular public projection of the court's authority – usually displaying twenty to thirty of those recently convicted and reported an additional forty to sixty trials of faith conducted per year. This made them a quite active tribunal, their persistent complaints about inadequate staffing notwithstanding.[29] During these years, the court meted out a death sentence – relaxation to the secular arm – to one man, Jacobo Bruto, in person, and two more in effigy.[30]

The tribunal's staffing was particularly fragile in these years. When Páramo arrived, Peña and the viceroy were embroiled in conflict, the judge repeatedly alleging that his life was in danger. He died on April 11, 1588 (seemingly of natural causes), and so Páramo lost his initial mentor while away in Messina on his first visitation of the tribunal's district; before long, Correonero obtained the Sicilian bishopric of Catania, as well as permission to reside there and resign his inquisitorial office. In less than three years – by May 1589 – Páramo had become the senior inquisitor.[31] He described a neglected outpost that had lost its most experienced personnel and where even correspondence failed to arrive. He compared his diligent administration to the negligence of other Spanish officials. Yet, as in the Aymar affair, the rectitude and authority of the Inquisition were repeatedly called into question, and an individual official's fortunes could rise or fall rapidly. In autumn 1590, the *Suprema* stripped the *fiscal* of his office, revoking Alonso Peña's title and recalling him to Spain. At the same time, rumors circulated that don Lope de Barahona, the junior inquisitor, had abused his office. The tribunal

---

[29] According to Garufi, 38 people were condemned in the *auto* of March 19, 1587. Others followed on August 14, 1588; July 25, 1589 (29); October 18, 1589; September 30, 1594 (31); February 11, 1596; June 29, 1597 (31); November 22, 1598 (18); February 25, 1600; May 5, 1602 (32); November 17, 1602 (8); December 14, 1603 (21); June 13, 1604 (23); March 13, 1605; September 21, 1606 (25); December 13, 1607 (40). *Fatto e personaggi*, 142. For October 1589, AHN, Inq., lib. 880, fols. 6r-11 and leg. 100, fol. 678r; for an account of an *auto* on September 28, 1591, lib. 880, fol. 384r; for 1597, lib. 882, fols. 60–61, the judges reported finishing an additional 28 trials (including 6 reconciliations) since the 1596 *auto*; for 1605, lib. 883, fol. 195; for 1606, AGS, Estado, leg. 1162, docs. 101–2, where they reported 23 in the public *auto* and another 61 cases over the year; for 1607, AGS, Estado, leg. 1162, docs. 223–24, they reported 45 cases and another 40 over the year.

[30] Relaxed in effigy were Giacomo Traper (from Siracusa, condemned as a fugitive Judaizer), on February 22, 1591, and Sozamo Cannata of Modica (died in prison impenitent, condemned as both a Muslim and a Lutheran, his goods were also confiscated), on December 13, 1607. La Mantia listed 458 people "relaxed" from 1487–1732, *Origine e vicende*, 194.

[31] AHN, Inq., lib. 880, fol. 42r. For lists of the inquisitors, see *De Origine*, 216–17; Rivero Rodríguez, "Inquisición," 1214–17; La Mantia, *Origine e vicende*, 220–22.

portrayed these reverses as evidence of viceregal treachery, reprisals for their zealous defense of the Holy Office.[32]

Páramo's sense of isolation only increased. In October 1590, Barahona died while his colleague was away on visitation, again receiving word of the loss in Messina. When Páramo sent the news to the *Suprema*, he recounted a model death: Barahona's illness had lasted ten days, during which time he had prepared his soul well, writing a will and receiving the sacraments. He lamented that "for me, it has left me much grief for having lost a good inquisitor and companion." Páramo then pleaded to hurry the new inquisitor's arrival, reasoning that constant jurisdictional conflicts, combined with the business of prosecuting heresy, offered too much work for a single judge.[33] In these same months, one of the most sympathetic of Sicily's secular officials died, replaced by an "enemy" of the Inquisition. Later that year, the tribunal's long-serving treasurer reported with concern that Páramo had been very ill when he returned to Palermo from Messina; just eight days after writing this letter, the treasurer, too, was dead.[34] From October 1590 until March 1591 (when Dr. don Martín de Olloquí arrived), Páramo would be the sole inquisitor. The conflicts between authorities had both institutional and individual dimensions; thus, setting the right tone with a new appointee became quite important. In one more successful parlay, Páramo and Olloquí had retired to their lodgings in the tribunal following the midday meal, when two royal judges appeared, sent by the new viceroy, the count of Olivares, who had just arrived from a term as ambassador in Rome. They negotiated a compromise about how the viceroy would take an obligatory oath without harming his or the tribunal's reputation.[35] When things went awry, however, the skirmishes could

[32] Peña, October 22, 1590; Barahona, October 12, 1590; and Páramo, January 4, 1591; AHN, Inq., lib. 880, fols. 208, 219, 341–42. Páramo protested that Barahona was "uno delos mas virtuosos, limpios y honrrados hombres," and "es muy circunspecto en todas sus actiones y viue religiosissimamente con grande assistençia y desseo de açertar en su officio." He suggested that the baron who denounced him merited punishment. Páramo, July 18, 1590, fol. 211. For the two inquisitors' August 1590 possession of the spiritual and temporal jurisdiction of the abbey of St. Michael in Troina (as proxies for don Fernando de Vega y Fonseca of the Council of the Indies), AFZ, Altamira, 9, doc. 23.

[33] "ami me ha dexado mucha pena por hauer perdido un buen Inquisidor y compañero," Páramo to *Suprema*, and to Inquisitor General, October 28, 1590, AHN, Inq., lib. 880, fols. 306–7, 321.

[34] Joan de Pinedo (*contador*), December 7, 1590, ibid., fol. 308.

[35] Audience of October 3, 1592, ibid., fol. 365. The count had experience in Italy: ambassador in Rome (1582–91), viceroy of Sicily (1591–95), then of Naples (1595–99). Parker, *Grand Strategy*, 39.

impact material conditions: the next year, the inquisitors claimed that the viceroy had deliberately interrupted their regular supply of meat.[36]

Some of the most contentious trials in Palermo were those of English Protestants. In these investigations, the politics of trade, diplomacy, and heresy collided. Páramo first presided over the condemnation of English sailors at an *auto de fe* on August 24, 1588, the close of the same month that had opened with the catastrophic loss of the Spanish Armada. It is difficult to know how much news – if any – of these events had reached Sicily, but the judges certainly acted in the climate of confrontation that had led up to the Armada's departure, a ferment that produced accounts of Spanish Catholics martyred in England, histories of the "schism" of the English Church, and exhortations to physical and spiritual combat. The *auto* displayed twenty penanced Englishmen, the crew of a ship en route to Venice, taken prisoner in Messina. According to the inquisitors' memorandum, six Catholic witnesses described how they read prayers used in England and ministers of Calvin's sect preached in the vernacular. They read and responded from the "psalms of Geneva" and refused to praise the saints or abstain from meat on fast days. Their penalties were linked to the degree of apostasy. Only three – who had lived as Catholics – were sent to the galleys for "having had much knowledge of the faith." The others they sentenced "to two and three years of reclusion to better instruct them in the faith, and partly in punishment, and so that they do not escape and lose their souls." The *auto* was apparently a persuasive success: the inquisitors convinced the viceroy that they were zealously saving souls, and he relented in his demands that all the Englishmen be sentenced to the galleys. The account was well calibrated for the year of the Armada, including ammunition about the state of the faith: "[the sailors] have declared, as well, that in England there are many Catholics among the old men, and even named some that pay the queen a great quantity of money, because she lets them live Catholically in secret, because in public she does not permit it."[37]

---

[36] They claimed they had been denied the customary meat provisions for eight months, under the pretext of a kingdom-wide shortage; Páramo, Olloquí, and Llanes, November 5, 1593, AHN, Inq., lib. 881, fols. 98–99. In 1605 and 1606, a poor grain harvest exacerbated long-standing conflicts; the viceroy petitioned Philip III and the Inquisitor General to prevent the inquisitors from meddling in the wheat trade; AGS, Estado, leg. 1162, doc. 128. A letter likely from the 1590s shows the inquisitors attempting to gain jurisdiction over – and assert the innocence of – a familiar accused of interfering with the wheat supply; AHN, Inq., lib. 1252, fol. 377r-80r. In 1604, they again defended familiars on charges of hoarding wheat and disobeying royal grain regulations; RB, MS II/265, fol. 91v.

[37] "aber tenido mucha noticia dela fee"; "a dos y tres Años de Reclusion para mejor ynstruyrse la fee, y parte en pena y para que no se huyan y se pierdan estas almas"; "An declarado ansi mismo que en Inglaterra ay delos hombres viejos muy muchos catholicos, y

Sentencing was a frequent point of contention between the inquisitors and the viceroy. Such disputes allowed authorities to argue the relative merits of their administrations, while also opening substantial conflicts about the purpose of penalties: whether they should be rehabilitative, penitential, or punitive and how they should serve the needs of the state. In their correspondence about the Englishmen, the inquisitors outlined the range of debate, lambasting both the viceregal prisons and the galleys:

To put them in the public jails would be to die of hunger, to condemn them in the galleys would not attain the end that is solicited of instructing them and saving their souls, as there they do not learn anything but blasphemies and vices and evils and no good thing. To put them in monasteries or hospitals is represented as less inconvenient, although there is fear of escape.[38]

The inquisitors appealed for funds to build penitential prison cells in the tribunal. Although the accused were customarily imprisoned in the Inquisition's facilities during their trials, the court did not administer the incarceration that could follow sentencing. There was particular pressure in sixteenth-century Sicily to punish those convicted of crimes of faith with galley service. The number of galleys supported by Philip II's Mediterranean possessions leapt from 55 in 1562 to 155 in 1574. As military commanders, viceroys depended upon courts to provide their galleys with free labor. The inquisitors, on the other hand, construed excessive recourse to the galleys as undermining both their spiritual mission and their institutional authority. The lack of prison space combined with viceregal demand resulted in pressure to send reconciled heretics to the galleys rather than to penitential jails, and so – according to Páramo and Barahona – to lose cases and souls, further debasing rather than rehabilitating those who went to the oars.[39]

aun nombrado algunos y que pagan a la Reyna gran cantidad de dinero, Porque les dexe viuir Catholicam[en]te en secreto, porque en publico no lo permitte." Correonero, Páramo, and Barahona, August 25, 1588, AHN, Inq., lib. 879, fol. 12. The 1588 *auto* also included two blasphemers, three bigamists, one *hechicero*, five false witnesses, two *renegados*, one married priest, two Lutherans, four *moros*, and one *bruja*. Páramo and Barahona to the king, August 25, 1588, IVDJ, Envío 80, caja 106, doc. 745.

38 "Poner los a las [carceles] Publicas seria morirse de hambre, condenarlos en Galeras nose consiguiria elfin que se pretende de ynstuyrles, y saluar les sus animas, pues alli nose aprenden sino blasfemias y vizios y males y ninguna cosa buena. Ponerlos en monasterios o hospitales se representa por menos inconueni[en]te aunq[ue] ay temor dela fuga." AHN, Inq., lib. 879, fol. 12.

39 Páramo and Barahona, June 29, 1590, AHN, Inq., lib. 880, fols. 180–81. See also their account of the October 1589 *auto*, fol. 4r. Aragonese Inquisition tribunals imposed sentences of galley servitude with particular frequency; Monter, *Frontiers of Heresy*. On Philip II's galleys, see Parker, *Grand Strategy*, 84. For the view that reforms of jail facilities

These pressures often forced the inquisitors into a defensive stance: in 1589, they felt the need to justify why two men found guilty of bearing false witness were not sentenced to the galleys. One they deemed too old; the other, also unsuitable, they exiled and ordered to a period of reclusion in a hospital. In the same *auto*, they reconciled a *morisco* slave who had escaped to the Barbary Coast and lived as a Muslim there. They reported that they had remanded him to a monastery for instruction, rather than to the galleys, because of his youth.[40] The galleys were also at the heart of two of the most serious cases that the tribunal addressed during Páramo's first years in Sicily. Inquisitors first penanced Vincenzo Lupo, a Palermo priest, in the May 1586 *auto de fe*. He abjured *de vehementi* for worshipping the devil. The judges condemned him to the galleys; after a brief stint there, he relapsed and reappeared in the tribunal in 1589. They summarized, "he turned to invoke and adore him, fasting for him seven Sundays, at the end of which the devil appeared to him and told him that he should abnegate his baptism and he would free him from the galley, and in the same instant, he was totally covered in leprosy and so he spontaneously came to denounce himself."[41] In 1590, the inquisitors voted to relax Lupo to the secular arm as a relapsed heretic. Following procedure, they sent the *Suprema* a copy of their proceedings for approval. They then spent months conferring with the council in Madrid, which requested a full copy of the trial. By 1592, the inquisitors were petitioning the *Suprema* to cease its deliberations, noting the excessive length of Lupo's imprisonment and its cost to the tribunal. Lupo's persistent self-denunciation also presented the inquisitors in Palermo and Madrid with a quandary. Lupo was "saying he would prefer that they burn him, to finish it at one time, and not to suffer the galley again."[42] Still, on the *Suprema*'s orders, Lupo returned to the galleys. He continued to write to the tribunal, claiming to be a Lutheran;

were a means to increase the scope and size of the institution, see Harvey, *Muslims in Spain,* chap. 6.

[40] Páramo and Barahona, October 19, 1589, AHN, Inq., lib. 880, fols. 6r, 10v.

[41] "le torno aymbocar y adorar ayunandole siete domingos al cabo delos quales sele apareçio el demonio y le dixo que renegase el baptismo y le libraria de galera y enel propio ystante secobrio todo de lepra y ansi se uino espontaneamente a denunçiar." AHN, Inq., lib. 880, fol. 8v.

[42] "diziendo quisiera mas que le quemaran por acabar de una vez y no ir a padezer de nueuo a galera." Páramo and Olloquí, August 13, 1592, AHN, Inq., lib. 880, fol. 358. Páramo, January 31 and February 28, 1591, and Páramo and Olloquí, May 24, 1591, fols. 336–37, 345; Páramo and Olloquí, May 22, 1592, BNE, MS 2827, fol. 55.

the judges reported his missives and even forwarded one of them to the
Suprema, but to no effect.[43]

In these same years – ones in which Páramo was sometimes sole inquisitor – the torments of galley service were again central to the case of Jacobo
Bruto, a Piedmontese cleric who had traveled all over Europe and landed in
Palermo teaching Latin. In 1589, he was tried for many Lutheran and
Calvinist heresies, reconciled, and sentenced to ten years in the galleys,
followed by "perpetual reclusion" (which usually meant a year or two, in
practice). In the first year, Bruto wrote a letter to the tribunal in his own
hand, revoking his abjuration of heresy. As a result, the inquisitors voted to
relax him to the secular arm and sent a notification of their intent to the
Suprema. His case moved quickly: he was burned as a heretic on October
28, 1591, the only victim to meet this fate during Páramo's twenty years on
Sicily's court.[44] The similarities between Bruto's and Lupo's cases were
powerful. Both clerics, they voluntarily, and aggressively, notified the
inquisitors of their relapse into heresy, seemingly seeking a heretic's
death (and maybe months or years in the tribunal jail during a new trial)
as preferable to years, and likely an effective death sentence, suffering in
the galleys. For the inquisitors, this behavior – particularly from priests –
highlighted the incompatibility of galleys and the reformation of
consciences. Galleys were synonymous with evil living and an insufficient
institutional structure caused the loss of salvageable souls. Páramo and
Olloquí made this connection explicit: "they easily begin to despair and
lose their souls as has been seen these last years in Jacobo Bruto who was
relaxed and Vincenzo Lupo who at present is in the galleys by order of
Your Lordships."[45] As a remedy, the inquisitors announced their intention
to use a confiscated house within sight of the castle as additional jail space.

---

43 Páramo and Olloquí, October 8, 1592, AHN, Inq., lib. 880, fol. 363, duplicate lib. 881,
    fol. 72. The inquisitors also sent a Spanish translation of Lupo's letter to the *Suprema*; it
    described how he had sent many letters declaring that he was a Lutheran and would live as
    such, slurred inquisitorial justice for not prosecuting him as a relapsed heretic, and
    threatened writing to the viceroy about the Inquisition's failure to see justice done to
    him, lib. 880, fol. 366. Cf. Miriam Bodian's account of those who martyred themselves
    in inquisitorial processes, *Dying in the Law of Moses: Crypto-Jewish Martyrdom in the
    Iberian World* (Bloomington: Indiana University Press, 2007).
44 Páramo, January 26, January 31, and February 28, 1591; AHN, Inq., lib. 880, fols. 336–
    38. Garufi categorized Bruto's death as an instance of Protestant martyrdom, *Fatto e
    personaggi*, 141; La Mantia, *Origine e vicende*, 194.
45 "facilm[en]te se vienen a desesperar y perder las Almas como se ha visto estos años atras en
    Jacobo bruto que fue Relaxado y Viçinçio Lupo que al press[en]te esta en galera por orden
    de V[uestra] S[eñoría]." Páramo and Olloquí, October 8, 1592, AHN, Inq., lib. 880, fol.
    363; also, January 28, 1593, lib. 881, fol. 70.

If such negotiations demonstrated the limits of the inquisitors' powers –
as well as their strategies to circumvent limitations – so too did other
petitions they sent to the *Suprema*. Residing in Palermo, they visited
other parts of the district nearly every year, corresponding, unsurprisingly,
about the inconvenience, labors, and expense of sending two inquisitors
out for six months or more each year, even more so in a "kingdom [where]
no one will leave his house without a company of people for his security."[46] As an alternative, they suggested increasing the number of
Inquisition officials in regions where they rarely, or never, ventured or
establishing a permanent inquisitorial presence in Messina. Páramo often
spent a third of the year there. Near the mainland, it was a potential point
of heretical contamination. As the viceroy was often there, it was also a
place where authorities might either project the dignity of their office or fail
to do so. At the very least, the inquisitors wanted the tribunal to keep a
house in that city. They complained that "to be always looking for houses
to rent is dishonorable to the office," and, worse, when the viceregal court
was in residence, the best houses were already taken.[47]

PETITIONING FROM THE MARGINS

Seeking to turn their difficulties to some advantage, Páramo and his
colleagues constructed their letters carefully. When he became the senior
inquisitor in the later 1580s, one of Páramo's principal charges was to
create authority for himself and, by extension, his court. Petitions to the
Suprema were one means by which to negotiate an official culture tied to
Castile, a cadre of local Sicilian elites, and a religious environment linked
more closely to Italian networks and to Rome than to Spain. Páramo's
missives give the impression of careful composition; they suggest, simultaneously, the contingency of inquisitorial power and the potential utility of
depicting a tribunal as perpetually embattled and in need of immediate aid.

---

[46] "en este Reyno no saldra ninguno de su casa sin compañía de gente para su seguridad,"
Páramo and Olloquí, May 22, 1592, BNE, MS 2827, fol. 59, also fol. 55.

[47] After negotiations with Páramo, the count of Olivares agreed to appear – and did – at the
publication of an edict of faith in Messina, although he balked at processing in the *autos de
fe* in Palermo, protesting it was against custom. Olivares, July 19, 1592, AHN, Inq, lib.
880, fol. 398. Also "andar sienpre buscando casas de alquiler es desrreputacion del
Officio," Correonero and Barahona, May 6, 1588, lib. 879, fol. 30r. On the visitations,
especially in Messina, the Valleys of Mazara and of Noto, lib. 879, fol. 16r; lib. 880, fols.
176r-78v, 195, 198–207, 347, 402; lib. 881, fols. 28, 31–32; lib. 883, fol. 311; BNE, MS
2827, fol. 55.

In differentiating their experience, the inquisitors sought to demonstrate its particular value and to earn permission for oddities in practice. Unlike other Spanish tribunals, the Sicilian one did not customarily employ its own theological consultants. Instead, it shared the one who aided the ordinary ecclesiastical courts, usually a Dominican friar, thus tying the tribunal to Palermo's archiepiscopal justice.[48] There was a constant shortage of qualified secretaries – the inquisitors preferred to have at least four – because, "as Your Lordships know that in Italy everything is done in Latin, and when rescripted papers or other acts are brought here or are done in the tribunal according to that style, if some notary was not Latinate, he would suffer greatly."[49] As a result of the difficulty of the terrain and expense of tracking families outside Sicily – and from regions outside the inquisitors' epistolary networks – the tribunal investigated the genealogies of its familiars and officials less stringently than the instructions prescribed.[50] In another departure from Castilian practices, it did not display *sanbenitos* in local churches, and the inquisitors feared a backlash if they attempted to alter the custom.[51]

The inquisitors made their anxieties plausible. They gestured to earlier resistance in Sicily and to the powerful and proximate counterexample of the kingdom of Naples, where the Spanish Inquisition had been repulsed.[52] Their dynamics with the papacy were complicated, and the viceroy had been known to appeal to the pope when sparring with the inquisitors. Accused heretics sometimes fled to the jurisdiction of the Roman Inquisition.[53] And the

---

[48] Olloquí and Llanes, January 24, 1597, AHN, Inq., lib. 882, fol. 3.

[49] "que algunos delos notarios del sean latinos, pues como V[uestra] S[eñoría] sabe en Italia todo se actua en latin, y quando aqui se traen papeles rescriptos o otros actos o se hazen enel tribunal segun estilo, si algun notario no fuese latino se padeceria mucho." Correonero and Páramo, December 16, 1588, AHN, Inq., lib. 879, fol. 1r.

[50] This was a consistent point of contention, the inquisitors protesting that so many there had origins in Milan, Venice, Pisa, Genoa, Florence, Siena, or other parts of Italy. People who came from the Levant also stayed and married in Sicily, further complicating investigations. In 1606, the *Suprema* overturned a 1575 ruling that had prohibited foreigners from becoming familiars without the permission of the *Suprema* and Inquisitor General. *Suprema* (Quiñones, Zamora, Alava), July 15, 1606, and Páramo and Llanes, July 22, 1603, May 5 and July 28, 1606, BNE, MS 2827, fols. 21r, 28r, 31r, 32–33.

[51] Llanes and Hoyo, June 30, 1600, AHN, Inq., lib. 882, fol. 364.

[52] Páramo, June 4, 1590, AHN, Inq., lib. 880, fols. 176r-78v.

[53] Alba de Liste to the pope, copy, and Correonero, Páramo, Barahona, May 12, 1589, ibid., fols. 137–39. In 1590, Jacob Lamana (just condemned by the Sicilian court to the galleys for three years as a bigamist and suborner of false witnesses) escaped to Rome, presented himself at the Congregation of the Inquisition, and pleaded for a pardon or a commuting of his penance. The inquisitors warned Rome of the dangers of rewarding such actions and asked for a decision "con beneficio universal dela Republica Christiana." July 13 and July 20, 1590,

tribunal could be caught between Rome and Madrid: if an order arrived from the papacy, it first consulted with the *Suprema* about it, or that, at least, is what the *Suprema* was told. Rome also watched events in Sicily. In one instance, a cardinal reprimanded the Sicilian tribunal for allowing Machiavelli's discourses – banned by the Roman index – to be printed in Palermo.[54] Even the fate of their correspondence became fodder for petitions. Proper inquisitorial procedure depended – at least in theory – upon communication between the *Suprema* and the tribunals; every dispatch that failed to arrive meant secretarial labor in producing new copies as well as an added layer of uncertainty in whatever matter was at hand. Usually, letters took around three months to travel between Madrid and Palermo. The judges commented on periods of silence, sometimes learning that their correspondence had gone missing. In 1591, they heard that the French had stolen their mail. In 1596, it was lost in the Gulf of Lyon. Papers and people could both face delays in trying to find space for passage in the galleys. The coup de grâce, of course, was that the viceroy had been known to meddle in the tribunal's mail, even opening its dispatches in 1593.[55]

The court reached a complement of three inquisitors again when Dr. Domingo Llanes arrived on August 1, 1593. By then, Páramo had weathered one attack on the tribunal's chambers; the next crisis occurred only weeks after Llanes's arrival. Although one contemporary account hinted that the explosion began in a fire near the Inquisition's kitchens, the inquisitors depicted it, definitively, as a premeditated assault on their court.[56] Framing their reports with particular care, the inquisitors suggested a pattern of episodic violence stretching back to the century's start. They sent an initial volley of outraged letters, reporting their injuries and their efforts to save the tribunal and its records. The assault would become a fundamental component of Páramo's subsequent narratives of service. The letters demonstrated that despite severe injuries (including to his head), Páramo returned to work a mere six days later; he petitioned for a license to travel to Madrid, to give evidence "from the mouth" about what

ibid., fols. 191–93. For similar concerns, also expressed by the viceroy, January 16, 1588, AHN, Inq., leg. 100, fol. 478.

[54] Páramo and Barahona, June 22, 1589, AHN, Inq., lib. 880, fols. 158–59. In 1597, the inquisitors, acting on the special order of the pope, tried a friar for distributing false indulgences and stamping medals under the rubrics of His Holiness and Gregory X, lib. 882, fols. 60v–61r. See the approach in James S. Amelang, "Exchanges between Italy and Spain: Culture and Religion," in *Spain in Italy*, 433–55.

[55] For example, Páramo, February 28, 1591; Llanes, August 5, 1593; Páramo, Olloquí, and Llanes, December 3, 1593; Olloquí and Llanes, November 1, 1596; AHN, Inq., lib. 880, fol. 336r; lib. 881, fols. 1, 17r, 321.

[56] Monter, *Frontiers of Heresy*, 63, 179–80.

had happened. Events seemed to prove that the Sicilian barons would rather destroy the tribunal than allow their inferiors to enjoy the use of its jurisdiction, if the king denied it to them; even news of a royal resolution to "quit the titled men and barons" had begun to erode inquisitorial authority. Thus, the mounting opposition to the appointment of nobles as familiars was termed "diabolical."[57]

The three inquisitors sought to seize the opportunity offered them. They rather quickly translated the events into a coherent report and a systematically argued program of action: the explosion occurred on August 19; on September 16, they petitioned the *Suprema* for more suitable facilities. They explained that the attack had only worsened an already untenable situation: "all these inconveniences represented themselves to us when the house and jails were standing, but now after the fire and ruin of the castle happened, we are completely deprived of the ability to exercise the office there." Royal orders as far as back as 1553 had planned to relocate the tribunal, but to no effect. They compiled "reasons" why "it was not suitable in any manner" for the Inquisition to be located in Palermo's castle, a situation that compromised inquisitorial procedure and, consequently, justice.[58] They broke their argument into a series of interrelated grievances, contending "that the particular most needed to conserve the Inquisition is secrecy." They sought to show that this was simply impossible in Palermo's castle. Their location inside the city's principal military installation undermined not only the court, but also the defense of the island, and so should be viewed as a "matter of state." They urged the *Suprema* "to consider that in the case of revolution, or if [the populace] wanted to effect what they attempted in the past, they could do it very easily and without any resistance, taking possession of the castle a day of

---

[57] "aquitar Titulados y Barones." Olloquí gave harrowing accounts: Páramo's dwelling was completely demolished when the munitions and gunpowder exploded, although he did manage to save the tribunal's paperwork. Olloquí, August 19 and August 24, 1593; Páramo to Inquisitor General, August 24, 1593; Páramo, Olloquí, and Llanes to Inquisitor General, December 31, 1593; AHN, Inq., lib. 881, fols. 89, 94r, 97r, 111r.

[58] "Todos estos inconuenientes se nos representauan quando las casa y carceres [sic] estauan en pie, pero aora despues que succedio el incendio y ruina del Castillo totalmente estamos priuados de poder exercer alli el Off[ici]o" and "no conuenga en ninguna manera." Páramo, Olloquí, and Llanes, Sepember 16, 1593; AHN, Inq., lib. 881, fols. 11–12 (another undated copy, fols. 19–21). When he arrived in 1591, Olloquí brought orders to move locations; they negotiated with the viceroy in 1592 but found no suitable alternative location. Correonero and Páramo, October 21, 1588, and Páramo and Olloquí, March 29, 1591, AHN, Inq., lib. 880, fols. 29v–30v, 335.

an *auto de fe* or an [inquisitorial] edict."[59] Two thousand people often entered the facility on those days, with a guard of only eighty soldiers. Moreover, they amplified Palermo's particular vulnerability, under constant threat of siege from the Turks or "whichever corsair." In the event of an attack, the inquisitors would need to evacuate the prisoners. They reasoned that a freestanding Inquisition house would be strong enough to avert minor threats and that they were, evidently, no safer in the castle.

The mixing of space muddled authority and jurisdiction. Beyond the confusion that resulted from a variety of legal institutions and jails operating within the same confines, an institution's physical space and its reputation were intertwined. The judges asserted that "the Inquisition is not so respected for seeing it in the house of another and subject to it, as in the end it is, and its ministers [subject] to the castellans and castle's guards." The castle was open only from sunrise until the *Ave Maria* was sung, and – quite reasonably for a military installation – "a person cannot or should not enter covered without first being examined by the soldier and guards." Inquisitors could not have their prisoners brought in at night, as they preferred; every entrance and exit occurred during daylight hours, exposing prisoners, officials, and potential witnesses to public scrutiny.[60] They argued that this was significantly to blame for the lack of denunciations they received. Gesturing to the ongoing debate about how to combat heresy, they lamented, "if sometimes they reveal [heresies] it is through the confessors." They claimed that no honorable woman would submit herself to the soldiers' examination. Anyone who entered the castle depended upon the vice-castellan, a viceregal official, for his or her release from the facility; reputedly, many knights and nobles would not present themselves for fear of having their debts called. The accused or their friends could also "easily take notice of a witness, seeing him enter the castle as we have seen in infinite instances."[61] This was even more obvious after the explosion, when both the viceroy and the inquisitors sequestered suspects

---

[59] "que el mas necessario particular para conseruarse la Inqui[sici]on es el secreto;" "considerar que en caso de reuolucion, O que quisiessen poner en execucion lo que en tiempos passados tentaron, muy facilmente y sin ninguna contradicion lo podrian hazer apoderandose del Castillo un dia de aucto de fee O edicto," AHN, Inq., lib. 881, fols. 11r, 12r.

[60] "la Inqui[sici]on no es tan respectada por verla en casa de otro y subgeta como al fin lo esta ella y sus ministros alos Castellanos y guardias del Castillo"; "[no] puede ni deue ninguna persona entrar tapada sin ser primero reconocida de los soldados y guardias"; ibid., fol. 11r.

[61] "si alguna vez reuelan es por medio delos confessores" and "con facilidad pueden tener noticia del testigo viendole entrar en el Castillo como hauemos visto infinitas vezes." Ibid., fol. 11r.

in the (presumably still damaged) castle, enabling those under investigation to observe everyone who testified.

The tribunal did not have its own jail or space to build one and so all kinds of prisoners were often kept together. Eighteen prisoners might share one small cell. This situation quickly became dangerous "especially in the summer, and there is danger that so many people could break a jail, or kill the warden, as has been done this year, when two of them wanted to kill the jailer and they escaped, leaving him for dead with three or four head wounds." Even without jailbreaks, when the accused were confined together, they conferred about their trials. As a result, some revoked their statements; others decided not to confess or invented confessions. Beyond the overcrowding, the inquisitors asserted that the viceroy's jails were unhealthy both physically – being "very low and almost over the sea" – as well as spiritually, as the accused gained pernicious new ideas there.[62] Moreover, they were quartered cheek by jowl with the fort's operations: the women were housed in the warden's house, and the castle's busy butcher adjoined the existing cells. The traffic opened innumerable possibilities for spying on the inquisitorial process, and the room where audiences were held was especially vulnerable. On one side, the windows were so low that a tall person, standing in the castle's courtyard, could clearly hear and even glimpse trial proceedings. On the other side, the windows overlooking the sea were such that the accused could watch passing boats and even chat with the people in them; prisoners' relatives and friends managed to transmit warnings to them this way.

It was common enough to have breaches in secrecy, prisoner collaboration, or escapes, but Palermo's inquisitors insisted that the situation was much worse than might be imagined in Castile. They described a tribunal in jeopardy, one in which inquisitorial practices were quickly becoming a farce. They had found the right moment to make their case. Even before the attack, the *Suprema* had been scrutinizing the Palermo court, deliberating about whether to order a visitation.[63] Instead, it had just commissioned a jurist – who had been in Sicily for ten months on other business – to investigate. Resoundingly supportive of the inquisitors, the informant

---

[62] "particularm[en]te en verano y se esta a peligro que tanta gente pueda romper una carcel, O matar al Alcayde como se ha hecho este año que dos dellos quisieron matar al carcelero y se huyeron dexandole por muerto con tres o quatro heridas en la cabeça"; "muy baxas y casi sobre la mar"; ibid., fol. 11v.

[63] By spring 1593, the inquisitors were already expressing disappointment in the new viceroy, Páramo and Olloquí, November 6, 1592 and July 17, 1593 (copy of May 21), AHN, Inq., lib. 880, fol. 401; lib. 881, fol. 2.

praised Olloquí's piety and considered Páramo learned, well liked, and well intentioned; he found no obvious transgressions on their part and painted them as the viceroy's prisoners, trapped in the castle and subjected to corrupt officials.[64] His report gave weight to the inquisitors' alarming claims, as the Inquisition treated even its internal correspondence like evidence to be weighed, questioned, and verified. By October, the *Suprema* recommended to the king that he grant both funds for the construction of a separate tribunal and a license for Páramo to travel to Madrid as a special envoy.[65] It suddenly seemed that the judges might soon find their situation improved.

BATTLING FOR JURISDICTION

Páramo set sail on May 15, 1594, while Llanes and Olloquí manned the Palermo court. In Madrid, he acted as a kind of extraordinary advocate – in the Council of Italy and the *Suprema* – for the Inquisition's tribunal in Sicily. The inquisitors reported, rather hopefully, that those who harassed them grew nervous as Páramo's departure approached. He was accompanied by an official who would assist with paperwork; later, one of his servants was sent from Sicily to join him at Court, bringing updated news of the tribunal. As Páramo was a client of Gaspar de Quiroga, when the long-serving Inquisitor General died at the end of the year, his colleagues back in Palermo worried openly "about the harm received from the death."[66] Many of the power struggles in which the tribunal was involved took shape in jurisdictional conflicts. These were most acute around the issue of the familiars. Authorities argued at length over who could be appointed to the Inquisition's lay offices; how many familiars it was permissible to have; what privileges those officials could enjoy; and, especially, when the Inquisition could claim jurisdiction over civil and criminal cases involving familiars. These battles were waged in a variety of arenas: from courtrooms to royal councils, from legal tracts to hastily circulated

---

[64] Lic. Domínguez to *Suprema*, July 26, 1593, AHN, Inq., lib. 881, fols. 5–9r.

[65] Páramo had also petitioned Quiroga directly, invoking his losses in the explosion and stressing his particular aptitude for the task and his desire to attend to affairs in Spain, September 9, 1593; ibid., fols. 36, 93.

[66] "del daño receuido de la muerte," Olloquí and Llanes, December 1, 1595 (copy of November 3); ibid., fol. 311. Quiroga was Inquisitor General from April 1573 until his death in November 1594. Páramo's *criado* left Sicily to join him in October 1598. Páramo, Olloquí, and Llanes, December 31, 1593 and April 21, 1594; Olloquí and Llanes, May 19, 1594; Llanes and Hoyo, December 26, 1598; fols. 118v, 137r, 144; lib. 882, fols. 198, 375v–76r.

pamphlets, from processions to confrontations laden with symbolism. Officials claimed that even the knowledge, in Sicily, of Páramo's presence at Court and that negotiations were underway gave the Inquisition greater local currency. It was in that environment that Páramo turned increasingly to writing in support of his causes, choosing between letters, manuscript books, and print to fit the matter at hand.

The strategic appointment of familiars was one of the principal ways in which the Spanish Inquisition sought to carve out a place in Sicilian society. In contrast to peninsular tribunals, Palermo inquisitors appointed local nobles. The jurisdictional benefits were a primary attraction of the office: familiars could step outside the purview of customary civil and criminal jurisdiction and, simultaneously, establish a special relationship to the inquisitorial court. In a jurisdictional environment as complicated as Sicily's, local elites were presumably already skilled at sizing up the relative merits of the courts that surrounded them; inquisitors, likewise, were well aware of the competition. Secular officials, conversely, denounced the presence of an "army of familiars" and sought to reserve trials of some crimes to their courts. Despite the ways in which Spanish authorities depicted all this as a set of peculiarly Sicilian problems, it may not have been so foreign to men like Páramo.[67] He, too, had been raised among a gentry that negotiated a patchwork of courts and jurisdictions, racking up petty offices. His relatives included *hidalgos*, clerics, inquisitors, and familiars; presumably they made use of their jurisdictional assets. There is evidence that Páramo – like many inquisitors – was involved in civil suits tried in inquisitorial courts. A certain Alonso Gutiérrez de Páramo, a familiar in Yuncos (near Toledo), underwent criminal proceedings in Toledo's Inquisition tribunal in 1592 on charges of usury, seemingly in an agricultural scam of buying carob, lentils, and vegetables and then reselling them to the initial owners at an inflated price. Although it seems likely that he was related to the inquisitor, he was not among the relatives mentioned to those who investigated Páramo's genealogy in 1586 and 1599.[68]

---

[67] Francesco Benigno has observed the tendency of historiography on Spanish Sicily to replicate the polemical categories of early modern stakeholders; see his "Integration and Conflict in Spanish Sicily," in *Spain in Italy*, 23–44. On the jurisdictional complexities in Sicily, see also Koenigsberger, *Practice of Empire*, 163; Lina Scalisi, *Il controllo del sacro. Poteri e istituzioni concorrenti nella Palermo del Cinque e Seicento* (Rome: Viella, 2004); Valentina Vigiano, *L'esercizio della politica. La città di Palermo nel Cinquecento* (Rome: Viella, 2004).

[68] Páramo was named in two civil suits, one in 1597–98 relating to the payment of services used in composing a book about the Holy Office, another of 1599–1600

The Sicilian Inquisition tribunal had reached the peak of its authority in the 1570s; one barometer of this was the number of its trials and of its familiars. The latter seem to have tripled during the 1560s and 1570s, surpassing 1,500, even if the numbers were frequently exaggerated for polemical purposes. Around a hundred familiars were in Palermo itself. A concordat that placed restrictions on the court had been negotiated in 1580; throughout Páramo's term, the prosecutorial activity of the tribunal was already markedly declining. Thus, Páramo's position in Palermo and in Madrid was essentially one of conservation. Nowhere is this more evident than in the rhetoric of jurisdiction that he developed. One of the most common charges against the tribunal was that its delinquent familiars dishonored the Holy Office. As William Monter noted, a census of the jail shows that nearly 500 familiars underwent criminal trials between 1595 and 1634; they were charged with bearing false witness, civil unrest, counterfeiting, murder, and homosexuality, though many prominent figures tried on the last count had their cases remitted to Rome.[69] This evidence can point to inquisitors' collaboration with dissolute figures to shore up their authority, admitting familiars who thought they had found a jurisdictional umbrella under which to pursue crimes with less fear of prosecution. Páramo, however, framed it another way. He argued that the Inquisition's criminal trials of its associates were proof of the seriousness with which the inquisitors pursued justice.

An ongoing polemic concerned which courts – inquisitorial or secular – were more honorable and more just. The president of the *Gran Corte*, the regent Modesto Gambacorta, typified an anti-inquisitorial stance. Gambacorta complained that inquisitors made far too frequent recourse to excommunication and repeatedly undercut the honor of secular officials, insulting them and treating them like heretics. Moreover, he found sentencing restrictions compromised the Inquisition's capacity to administer justice well; in cases of murder, he reasoned, only capital punishment

regarding a Barcelona merchant and debts from the sale of Aymar's books; AHN, Inq., leg. 2039, exp. 19 and leg. 1578, exp. 1. For the criminal case of the Yuncos familiar, leg. 55, exp. 28, I have not consulted these three files, but they are indexed suggestively at http://pares.mcu.es/.

[69] Monter identifies the apex as the 1575 report of 1,572 familiars. Renda recorded that the network of familiars and officials rose from 439 in 1561 to 1,721 in 1577. Monter, *Frontiers of Heresy*, 63–64, 180; Renda *L'Inquisizione*, 98–104; Koenigsberger, *Practice of Empire*, 74, 163; Rivero Rodríguez, "Inquisición," 1096–1115. On the polemics about the familiars in the 1570s, see La Mantia, *Origine e vicende*, 62. By way of comparison, there were 144 appointments to familiatures in Mexico City between 1577 and 1646; Solange Alberro, *Inquisition et Société au Mexique, 1571–1700* (Mexico City: Centre d'Études Mexicaines et Centramericaines, 1988), 340–43.

could adequately serve the right to justice of the surviving family.[70] Páramo, on the other hand, reasoned thus: "although in criminal [cases], capital punishment is not given in the Holy Office, it is certain that the crimes remain more punished and castigated than in the *Gran Corte*." He asserted that the Inquisition's associates were better disciplined than the viceroy's. He alleged that the barons disdained the secular tribunals because the greedy magistrates who staffed them were not motivated "by charity or zeal that they have for the republic and its justice," thus implying that the inquisitors were. His appraisal of the procedure in secular courts was scathing. He charged that they admitted many false witnesses and that they "proceed to put [the accused] to torture, without giving them a copy or excerpt of the witnesses or any other thing ... [which is] so against natural and divine law, as against positive [law], and this is the reason why the noblemen and lords want to be in the jurisdiction of the Holy Office, and not in order to commit crimes."[71]

Despite the arrival in Madrid of an inquisitor experienced in the Sicilian scene, there were no rapid resolutions to the long-standing conflicts. Páramo offered his opinions in the councils, lobbied the Inquisitor General directly, and circulated his arguments in manuscript. He also turned to print for the first time, publishing a tract on the Sicilian jurisdictional situation in Madrid in 1594. By these means, he advanced a wide range of particular grievances, skirmishes in the larger campaign. He sought funding for more prisoners' lawyers to handle the civil cases that fell under inquisitorial jurisdiction. Stressing the piety of the cause and the particular danger to the cases of poor defendants, he gained a favorable viewing from the Inquisitor General.[72] At the same time, the inquisitors still in Sicily pointedly reminded the *Suprema* that they had a particular advocate at Court, with whom they were in close correspondence. Nevertheless, they sensed an impending loss. By the end of 1596, they were petitioning to keep Páramo in Madrid until the issues had been fully treated; they wondered why the provisions for their new buildings had not been forthcoming, despite their and Páramo's inquiries. Páramo also

---

[70] RB, MS II/265, fol. 72r.

[71] "aunque enlas criminales nose da pena de sangre enel santo off[ici]o, es çierto que los delictos quedan mas punidos y castigados que en la gran Corte" and "por charidad ni çelo que tengan dela Republica y just[ici]a deella"; also "se proçede sindarles copia ni traslado de los Testigos ni de otra cosa los ponen al tormento ... tan contra el derecho natural y diuino, como contra el positiuo y esta es la causa porque los titulados y señores desean ser deel foro deel santo off[ici]o, y no para cometer delictos"; BL, Eg. 1508, fol. 369.

[72] Páramo, May 11 and May 13, 1595, AHN, Inq., lib. 881, fol. 282.

expressed his frustration that the junta's meetings had ended without agreement on any of the major conflicts. He complained of ill health and wrote that he would retire to "my land" – his native region not far to Madrid's south – until the election of the new Inquisitor General, who he correctly assumed would be don Pedro Portocarrero.[73]

In 1597, a new agreement was reached, but it decreased the Inquisition's powers in Sicily. Back in Palermo, Inquisitor Olloquí fell ill and died on July 16, 1597, and some of the secretaries also took sick. Llanes thus gained sole charge of the tribunal, obligated both to continue cases that Páramo had initiated years before and, per the *Suprema*'s directive, to implement the new reforms that the councils were sending from Madrid. Still in Castile, Páramo sought to make this an opening for procedural reform. He recalled the difficulties he had experienced as a sole inquisitor and petitioned the *Suprema* to grant single inquisitors the power to close any type of open case or to delegate their authority. He compiled supporting legal citations, arguing that each inquisitor possessed discrete jurisdictional and administrative authority and should be able to act individually in case of necessity, that the authority of the whole tribunal would inhere in the inquisitor who remained living or resident. There was no evidence of new policy and the vacancy was quickly filled: on April 1, 1598, a new inquisitor, Pedro de Hoyo, and a new viceroy, the duke of Maqueda, arrived in the same galley fleet.[74]

Páramo persisted in trying to turn circumstances to his advantage. He printed a second defense of the Sicilian tribunal's practices in Madrid in 1599 and published his magnum opus – a history of the Inquisition – there in 1598. He may have looked after assets near Toledo, and he gained admission to the elite military order of Alcántara in 1599, securing a further proof of nobility, but he was unable to translate his six years at Court into a permanent appointment to the Council of Italy or the *Suprema* or any similar promotion.[75] In part, he was unlucky in his timing. These were years of political reshuffling, as Philip II died and Philip III

<hr>

[73] Páramo, January 27, 1596, AHN, Inq., lib. 1252, fol. 389; Olloquí and Llanes, February 28, July 15, and August 13, 1594, and January 27 and April 21, 1595, and June 14 and November 1, 1596, lib. 881, fols. 121, 128r, 225r, 259r, 288–89, 307, 321.

[74] RB, MS II/265, fols. 85r-86r; Llanes, July 18, September, and December 27, 1597; Hoyo, April 9, 1598; Llanes and Hoyo, December 26, 1598, AHN, Inq., lib. 882, fols. 50, 72, 104, 116, 198, 220.

[75] Páramo's file was viewed and approved in the Council of the Orders in Madrid, March 24, 1599; he was given the habit of a friar of the order in the convent of San Benito de Alcántara. AHN, OM, Religiosos, Alcántara, exp. 315.

came to the throne in 1598. Portocarrero was a short-lived Inquisitor General, as were his successors; that office changed hands five times between 1595 and 1603.[76] In the months before his return to Sicily, Páramo wrote to the king and to the Inquisitor General from Casarrubios del Monte – his father's native town – still seeking to justify the contested appointments of familiars. He revived well-known arguments for new audiences, stressing the exceptionality of the Sicilian scene: the distance "from the eyes" of both king and Inquisitor General required "a much heavier hand and authority" to defend the faith than in Castile, where the Inquisition's roots were firmer. He claimed that the familiars served the "common good" or the "the universal good of that kingdom" and predicted that the barons would sabotage the Inquisition if not co-opted into it.[77]

Still, royal agreements of 1606 and 1607 continued the trend of 1597, further diminishing inquisitorial powers.[78] These decisions reverberated not only at the level of institutions and their jurisdictions, but also at that of individuals and their experiences and ambitions. Even before Páramo left Madrid, his colleagues bemoaned the degradation of their office. They reported the appearance of pamphlets insulting the Inquisition, one "saying that already they did not have to pay attention to the Holy Office and that they could burn it and the inquisitors and eat meat on prohibited days and other lewd words." In the city of Modica, several men were loitering in the cemetery of the church of St. Peter; one remarked: "you already know that the Holy Office isn't worth anything now, because our King Philip took away its power, now they can burn it together with the two clerics,

---

[76] Only a year later, Portocarrero resigned; compelled by papal mandate and the drive of Philip III's favorite, the duke of Lerma, to remove rivals from Court, he went to reside in his diocese of Cuenca and died not long after. Sánchez Rivilla, "Inquisidores," 263; Rivero Rodríguez, "Inquisición," 1139–46. On the fundamental political shifts of this era and afterward, see Francesco Benigno, *La sombra del rey: Validos y lucha política en la España del siglo XVII*, trans. Esther Benítez (Madrid: Alianza Editorial, 1994).

[77] "mucha mas mano y autoridad," Páramo to Inquisitor General and Páramo to the king, March 9, 1600, BL, Eg. 1508, fols. 367r-70v. See also Páramo and Olloquí, August 13, 1592, AHN, Inq., lib. 880, fols. 353–57. Rivero Rodríguez transcribed similar documents, like a mid-seventeenth century copy of a letter of Páramo's, in his "El Consejo de Italia y el gobierno de los dominios italianos de la monarquía hispana durante el reinado de Felipe II (1556–1598)," (PhD diss., Universidad Autónoma, Madrid, 1992), 475–76.

[78] Rivero Rodríguez described how the disputes reached a new intensity in the early 1580s, as the tribunal lobbied Philip II; their loss of power under Philip III, in turn, he attributed to the king's desire to increase viceregal authority; "Inquisición," 1084–1155; cf. Garufi, *Fatto e personaggi*, 154, 175–77; La Mantia, *Origine e vicende*, 57–58.

meaning with the two inquisitors." They joked that "a doorman from Modica is worth more than the inquisitors."[79] The inquisitors thus offered evidence of how jurisdictional debates translated on the ground, showing their authority under full attack.

Páramo was back in Palermo by December 1600, with Llanes providing some continuity with the court he had left. Their plans had failed to come to fruition. The viceroy reputedly deprived them of funds to the point that they moved the tribunal "to one of our lodgings, where now we are with much work and discomfort and without hope that the jails might be made (as we still have them in the castle), or that he will give money in order that the building begun for the secret archive might be completed."[80] Viceroy Maqueda and the inquisitors revisited old conflicts. The judges composed litanies of harm caused by the new concordat and the polemical tone only escalated with Maqueda's death in 1601 and his successor's arrival. Lorenzo Suárez de Figueroa y Córdoba (1559–1607), the second duke of Feria, would become one of Páramo's most formidable opponents. Born in the Low Countries – the son of a prominent courtier who accompanied Philip II to England and Jane Dormer, a lady-in-waiting to Mary I – he arrived in Sicily with substantial experience. Ambassador first in Rome, then in France in the early 1590s – where he led the losing Spanish faction in the negotiations that preceded the accession of Henry of Navarre to the throne – he had most recently been viceroy in Catalonia.

Apparently, Páramo failed spectacularly in his efforts to win over the new viceroy. When Feria arrived, the inquisitor sent him some carafes of wine and copies of his books about inquisitorial jurisdiction, a thinly veiled way to put his case before a new appointee. The tone, however, was soon set: Llanes likened inquisitorial office in those years to martyrdom. Feria, he claimed, arrived in Sicily with his impressions already formed, with hatred for the Inquisition.[81] Feria, on the other hand, would later assert his

---

[79] "diziendo que ya no ay que hazer caso del s[an]to officio y que pueden quemar ael y alos Inquisidores y comer carne en dias prohibidos y otras palabras deshonestas" and "ya sabeis queel santo offico no vale ya nada, porque n[uest]ro Rey Philippo le quito la potestad, aora le pueden quemar juntamente con los dos clerigos, entendiendo conlos dos Inq[uisido]res"; also "vale mas un portero de Modica que los Inq[uisido]res." Llanes and Hoyo, April 16, 1599 (copy made April 30), AHN, Inq., lib. 882, fols. 317–18.

[80] "a uno de nuestros aposentos, adonde aora estamos con mucho trauajo y descomodidad y sin esperança de que aya de hazer las carceres (que aun las tenemos enel castillo), ni dar dinero para quese acaue la fabrica començada para el Archivo de Secreto." Páramo, Llanes, and Hoyo, November 9, 1601, AHN, Inq., lib. 883, fol. 2; see also lib. 882, fol. 394.

[81] Feria to Inquisitor General, July 8, 1602, and Llanes, August 13, 1602, AHN, Inq., lib. 883, fols. 14, 17–18, 22–23. See also Rivero Rodríguez, "Inquisición," 1154.

good intentions, that he changed his mind only after he witnessed the inquisitors' corruption and partisan dealings. In his letters, the duke simultaneously sought to prove his status as a good Christian, his faith in the Holy Office in general, and the failings of Sicily's particular tribunal. He wrote that "from holy theologians and wise men I have heard it said that works of charity are the oil with which the faith is sustained, and when these are absent, that the time is coming to darken the heavens' light, and especially when under the name of religion are treated affairs of the world or of tyranny."[82] With such language, Feria condemned the inquisitors and made the conduct of the familiars – carrying arms, in flagrant violation of the 1597 concordat – an example of their abuse of both viceregal justice and their apostolic authority.[83]

In August 1602, the conflicts escalated into open combat. The duke imprisoned messengers who had recently delivered inquisitorial writs against secular authorities and viceregal troops surrounded the tribunal. As the soldiers battered the doors, the inquisitors made an incredible show of their authority. They declared all the troops excommunicate, rang the bells, and waved the standard used in *autos de fe* – displaying a crucifix and the arms of both pope and king – out the window. Eventually, the archbishop (Haedo, the former inquisitor) managed to negotiate a decrease in open hostilities, and Páramo issued a mass absolution out of the window of the tribunal to the excommunicated soldiers kneeling below. The scope of the symbolic vocabulary involved would have not been lost on anyone present. The drama of these conflicts has attracted many retellings, and Monter eloquently observed that they might be termed a "comic-opera war."[84] They illuminated the circumscribed range of actions available to inquisitors as well as the surprising resilience of the system, even when assaulted. Such experiences also became part of the baggage that officials took with them when they moved around the Habsburg world, informing their writings and their dealings with one another.

The personal dynamics of administration took on clear importance. Llanes's ribs had been broken in the 1593 explosion, just weeks after his

---

[82] "a theologos sanctos y sabios he oido dezir que el açeite conque se sustenta la fee son las obras de charidad, y quando esta faltan viene andando el t[ie]mpo a apagarse la luz del cielo, y esto principalmente quando de baxo de nombre de Religion tratan neg[oci]os de mundo o de tirania." Feria to the king, December 19, 1603, AGS, Estado, leg. 1160, doc. 230.

[83] AGS, Estado, leg. 1161, doc. 80.

[84] For a more complete account and analysis of this episode, see Monter, *Frontiers of Heresy*, 63. See also Páramo, Llanes, and Hoyo, August 9, 1602, BNE, MS 9393, fols. 35r-39v.

arrival at his new inquisitorial post; it is hard to imagine this would not have colored his view of future situations. The *Gran Corte*'s regent Gambacorta also had a long history with the Inquisition; he had even once belonged to its jurisdiction, counted as a member of the St. Peter Martyr confraternity in 1577. He dated the rupture between viceroys and inquisitors to the 1580s, blaming the latter for acting imperiously and publicly shaming royal officials and faulting their hunger for power to pervert the government of Sicily, as "there should not be two heads in one kingdom, but rather only one, that is the viceroy."[85] In response, the inquisitors attacked Gambacorta's credibility as a Calabrian naturalized in Sicily, neither Spaniard nor Sicilian. Supposing he sought promotion to a marquisate – and beyond that his charges resulted either from enmity or senility – they flatly denied that they sought dominion equal to that of the viceroy, the undisputed "head," and were, with other magistrates, mere "coadjutors and executors."[86]

Feria and Páramo developed an even more particular enmity. Even before his troops encircled the tribunal, the duke had attacked, writing to the Inquisitor General while Páramo was away from Palermo, urging him to order a visitation of the tribunal. With a barrage of letters, Feria and Páramo hurled accusations at each other. Feria positioned himself as a defender of royal justice, exposing scandals that the inquisitors had carefully hidden, and singling out Páramo:

without misgivings about deceiving myself, I can say that everything proceeds from the head, which is the inquisitor Páramo, who, although he has income in Castile and takes out a lot of money from his office of inquisitor, it is him who conceals and favors how much evil there is in this kingdom's familiars, [and he] is such a great spender and is so encumbered in debts, entwining himself in new evils and looking for remedies at the cost of the exercise of the office, that it is all extortions and means to avail himself of them.[87]

---

[85] "no aya de auer en un reyno dos cabezas, sino una sola q[ue] es el Virrey," Gambacorta, May 26, 1603 and March 4, 1604, RB, MS II/265, fols. 70r-74r, here fol. 71. See also Renda, *L'Inquisizione*, 100, 131.

[86] "coadjutores y executores," Páramo and Llanes to Gambacorta, September 24, 1604, RB, MS II/265, fol. 92r. See also unsigned letter to Inquisitor General, defending the inquisitors, July 28, 1606, fols. 74v-75v; Páramo, n.d., fols. 85r-86v.

[87] "sin recelo de engañarme puedo decir que viene todo de la cabeça que es el Inquisidor Páramo, el qual aunque tiene renta en Castilla y saca mucho dinero de su officio de Inquisidor, por ser el que encubre y fauorece quanto mal ay en los familiares deste Reyno, es tan grande gastador y esta tan cargado de deudas. enlaçandose en nueuos males y buscando remedios A costa del exercicio del officio que todo es estorsiones y medios como aprouecharse," Feria to Inquisitor General, July 8, 1602, AHN, Inq., lib. 883, fols. 17-18, 22-23. See also fol. 283.

They had met in Catalonia two years before, as the inquisitor was returning to Palermo. There, the viceroy reported, he was traveling with a suspicious woman whom he called a relative, who accompanied him to Sicily. During his current illness, he was convalescing where she lived outside the city. The duke implied that Páramo not only lived in vice, he accused him of encouraging it in others. As further proof, Feria told how Páramo had sheltered a fugitive and granted a license to dance the sarabande to a woman from Barcelona and her daughters. In short, he tapped into a powerful set of archetypes: the venal inquisitor, the magistrate who perverts the body politic in pursuit of power, the lascivious cleric. He cast Páramo in terms often used to characterize heretical conspiracies and their masterminds; he made usurpations of royal jurisdiction the least of his sins, as a cleric behaving in such fashion profaned his office.

Feria's missive had effect. The *Suprema* began to question Páramo's actions, and so the inquisitor – writing to the council and to the king from Trapani – compiled a case in self-defense. Although he chose a far more abbreviated form, Páramo's method of arguing for the worth of his career had much in common with the strategies Simancas had pursued in his *Vida*. He first sought to prove his honor and good repute as a loyal crown servant, recalling his seventeen years of service and his injury in the 1593 explosion; he emphasized his defense of the Inquisition's jurisdiction against the "ill will" of many viceroys, at such great personal cost. He construed himself as measured and pious, humbly fulfilling his office, his only prize a loss of his wealth and health.

Páramo coupled an account of his merits with an attack on Feria, beginning with the charge of enmity. He saw Feria as sowing calumnies in order to eliminate any opposition. Though conveniently dead, he called the previous viceroy as a character witness and painted them as opposites: Maqueda had been a prudent Christian knight, learned in government; Feria was an opportunist, waiting until Páramo had dutifully left on visitation to attack. He returned the accusations of greed, abuse of office, and dishonorable conduct, claiming to expose Feria's transgressions, both public and secret, and so to disqualify his accuser. He alleged that the duke favored certain lady singers from Barcelona and that he went out at night in disguise to drink, "not without great danger to his life and even greater to his reputation and office." He sold the king's agricultural goods and the goods of deceased prelates on the side, for profit. He made fun of ecclesiastical censures and publicly insulted the inquisitors. Worse, he administered justice "with great inequality aggrieving some and dissembling with others." Moreover, he used official correspondence to advance personal aims, as he had done in libeling Páramo. Such charges had worked in the past: in the 1570s and 1580s, Philip II had reprimanded Feria for gambling and attempted to intervene when he promised marriage to more than one noblewoman. Perhaps Páramo was using more than stock charges, seeking to tap into a history of gossip about moral and sexual impropriety that he either recalled from previous decades or had heard from others.[88]

These conflicts extended into the trials of faith. If seventeen years earlier, in the summer of 1588, the Spanish crown had welcomed reports of English sailors publicly condemned at a Palermo *auto de fe*, the situation was quite different by 1605. Agents of Philip III were engaged in negotiating peace with former enemies. On October 27, 1604, the English ship *St. Peter Bonaventure* docked in Palermo, carrying twenty Englishmen and a French merchant. The royal ministers, knowing it "to be from such infected parts," put the vessel and its goods under embargo and called the Inquisition to investigate the crew. The judges found them "from their own confessions, to be Protestant Christian Englishmen of the religion that is kept in that kingdom." With such clear cause, they initiated trials.[89] Páramo – now disappointed in his fortunes and experienced in both the tribunal's business and the politics of the royal Court – oversaw these cases. Wary because he knew Sicily could expect news of a treaty with England's James I any day, he noted his extensive consultation with the most knowledgeable jurists and theologians. Fulfilling Páramo's fears, Feria ordered the inquisitors to free the Englishmen and their goods. Lacking precedent for such a situation, and, arguably, stalling for time, the inquisitors wrote to the *Suprema* for an additional ruling. They framed their actions as in full compliance with earlier decisions; they reported adhering to a 1603 decree that those from Holland and Flanders – even heretics – could trade and travel in Sicily with licenses but noted that the *Suprema* had not issued a definitive ruling on the English. They reasoned that although the current royal will was not clear,

[88] "no sin mucho peligro dela uida y con mayor de su reputacion y officio;" "con gran desygualdad agrauiando aunos y disimulando conotros." Páramo, December 22, 1602, ibid., fols. 47, 49. For other complaints against Feria, from 1602 to 1605, fols. 55, 61–62, 80, 112. On Feria's past, see Geoffrey Parker, *Philip II* (Chicago: Open Court, 2002), 57; Henry Kamen, *Philip of Spain* (New Haven, CT: Yale University Press, 1997), 173, 198, 231.

[89] "ser de partes tan Infectas" and "de sus propias confesiones ser Ingleses cristianos Protestantes dela Religion que se guarda en aquel Reyno." AHN, Inq., lib. 883, fols. 333–48. On the peace, Paul Allen, *Philip III and the Pax Hispanica, 1598–1621: The Failure of Grand Strategy* (New Haven, CT: Yale University Press, 2000); Werner Thomas, *La represión del protestantismo en España, 1517–1648* (Leuven: Leuven University Press, 2001), 301–20.

the status of the sailors as heretics was. When "called here [to the tribunal], they confess to be of the sect of the Protestants and Puritans of that kingdom." Flouting the viceroy, the inquisitors sentenced them to two years of instruction in the Catholic faith and processed the new penitents in an *auto de fe* held March 14, 1605.[90]

Feria – bombarded with petitions from the Englishmen – protested that they were already under the security of the peace treaty when they arrived in Sicily. He incensed the inquisitors by publicly criticizing their trials. Despite promises to do so, Páramo avoided meeting with Feria; as this was a religious matter, the viceroy hesitated to take further action.[91] The inquisitors looked to strengthen their claims, arguing that the prisoners were not only heretics but also corsairs, taken captive after raiding the coast. Thus, when Feria defended them, he implicitly condoned the robbery and murder of the king's Sicilian subjects. The lynchpin of their argument was that the Englishmen had been imprisoned before the conclusion of the treaty. They also pointed to the harm that the viceroy's actions might already have caused, as other Englishmen in Sicily were behaving scandalously. One merchant openly proclaimed the superiority of the Protestant sect, rattling off stock arguments. Contradicting fasts, he said "that which entered by the mouth could not harm the soul." He asserted that confession should be made only to God and not to a confessor and talked about how the king of England was pope and head of the church in his lands. Despite the peace treaty, the inquisitors began a trial against him, claiming that his offenses were not specifically protected.[92]

When it responded, the *Suprema* addressed some of the inquisitors' concerns, while allowing each side a way to depict its authority as still intact. The councillors ruled that the inquisitors could engage only with foreigners who made a spontaneous confession and asked to return to the faith. Those they should gently examine, instruct, and reconcile secretly (i.e., not in an *auto de fe*); they could not confiscate their goods. Presumably, this remedy was intended to avoid public scandal and

---

[90] "llamados aqui confiesan ser de la setta delos protestantes y puritanos de aquel Reyno." Páramo and Llanes, October 22, 1604, AHN, Inq., lib. 883, fol. 101. See also Páramo and Llanes, December 17, 1604, and March 4, 1605, fols. 87, 198; Páramo and Llanes to the king, March 18, 1605, AGS, Estado, leg. 1161, doc. 169.

[91] Páramo, Llanes, and Hoyo, May 1, 1605, AHN, Inq., lib. 883, fol. 197; Feria to the king, November 7, 1604, and June 18, 1605, and *consulta*, Council of State, September 1605, AGS, Estado, leg. 1161, docs. 214–16, 281, 304.

[92] "quelo que entraua por la boca no hazia daño al alma." Páramo and Llanes, April 8, 1605, AHN, Inq., lib. 883, fol. 88.

promote conversion without breaking the peace or hampering commerce. Soon thereafter, the *Suprema* would stipulate that such heretics should confess their errors to confessors, bypassing the inquisitorial court. They also ordered Páramo and his associates to reform their conduct of the cases at hand, to commute the Englishmen's penances to merely spiritual ones and fasts, to remove their *sanbenitos*, and to allow them to move freely. The inquisitors' reply indicated that the conflict had reached an even more dramatic pitch while they had awaited a response: many of the Englishmen had already escaped from the monasteries and shed their *sanbenitos*. After recapturing these men, the judges began trials against them as relapsed heretics (and so with the threat of execution). Yet they agreed to concede these cases so as not to jeopardize the peace, although they noted pointedly that the *Suprema* had thereby ordered them to release unpunished, impenitent heretics.[93] Even as the inquisitors' work was downgraded in significance, they sought to demonstrate their diligence. They assiduously tracked supposed networks of English Protestants for future use, recording their ships' cargoes and the ports they had visited. They used the occasion to write once again about the tribunal's need for its own penitential cells.

By the early years of the seventeenth century, the arguments that had once brought Páramo success no longer did. He intensified his diatribes against Feria, claiming that his actions contravened papal bulls and undermined the sacred contract between king and pope to protect the Inquisition. Páramo also counter-maneuvered with the legal tools available to him, initiating Inquisition proceedings against those who jeered at him and his fellow inquisitors; he even collected evidence against one of the *Gran Corte*'s prosecutors and used his jurisdictional powers to protect associates from the duke. Nevertheless, his accusations failed to have an effect, although the repercussions to Páramo's career were clear. Páramo and Llanes both ended up in the unusual situation of serving more than twenty years in their posts, marooned on an island and in a political climate in which promotion grew increasingly less likely.[94]

---

[93] Páramo, Llanes, and Hoyo, July 1, September 23, and October 21, 1605; Páramo and Llanes, January 13, 1606, ibid., fols. 153, 155, 193, 264. These were not the only new mandates. In April 1605, the inquisitors also noted receipt – in this case without protest – of Pope Clement VIII's general pardon of all *converso* descendants of Portuguese Jews, excepting only cases of relapsed heresy. They explained that "en este Reyno no ay ningun portugues que este proseguido y silo fuere de aqui adelante alguno guardaremos el orden"; Páramo, Llanes, and Hoyo, September 23, 1605, fol. 156.

[94] Several historians have noted this, inter alia, Renda, *L'Inquisizione*, 212–13. See also Páramo and Llanes, May 10 and July 28, 1606; and Páramo's audiences of April and May 1605, AHN, Inq., lib. 883, fols. 171–90, 224, 241–43.

Promotion – or lack of promotion – was read as a gauge of royal favor. The *Suprema*, for its part, might have had reasons to keep experienced judges in the court; such figures, arguably, allowed the *Suprema* to capitulate in negotiations with a certain confidence that sufficient inquisitorial power would be maintained in the kingdom. Páramo and Llanes knew their careers broke with recent precedent. When Haedo was promoted in 1583, his junior colleagues – Peña and Correonero, each soon to gain similar appointments – framed it as a "prize for his efforts, but also in increase of this Inquisition especially in a time so overworked by the viceroy."[95] Throughout the 1590s, whenever a diocese fell vacant, Páramo and his colleagues petitioned for his appointment to it, emphasizing his years of experience and knowledge of local customs and language. With each disappointment, they reminded the *Suprema* that such neglect caused the tribunal's local authority to decline. As time passed, they tailored the arguments even more closely. They noted Páramo's particular suitability for a vacancy in Messina; they claimed a year in Sicily was like two in another tribunal, a hardship posting. They were on the losing side of royal policy, petitioning for bishoprics to at least go to Spaniards – if not inquisitors – rather than to locals. Páramo's colleagues professed shock to see him return from Court with "empty hands." Perhaps even more clearly than the 1597 concordat, Páramo's failure to acquire an ecclesiastical benefice signaled a loss of standing, which the inquisitors sought to attribute to the viceroy's machinations or even a plot against them in the Council of Italy.[96] His promotions had, seemingly, been negotiated away to advance other careers and models of governance.

---

[95] "premio de sus trauajos pero tambien en augmento de esta ynquisicion mayormente en t[ienpo] q[ue] tan trauajada esta del Virrey." Peña and Correonero, May 11, 1583, AHN, Inq., lib. 878, fol. 445r. By 1587, the king chose Peña for Messina and Correonero for Catania, lib. 879, fol. 129r.

[96] On a vacancy in Cefalù, Olloquí and Llanes, February 24, 1595, AHN, Inq., lib. 881, fol. 257v. For similar refrains, Olloquí and Llanes, January 27, September 16, November 3, and November 4, 1595, and March 22 (copy of February 21) and April 18, 1597, lib. 881, fols. 267–69, 292–93; lib. 882, fols. 9, 21; Páramo, lib. 1252, fol. 389r; Llanes, August 13, 1602, lib. 883, fol. 14. They wrote with increasing despair after they were passed over for posts in Zaragoza, Mazara, and Catania; Páramo, Llanes, and Hoyo, March 29, 1602, and May 7, 1604, fols. 8, 79, also fols. 83, 98. Many of these letters were earmarked at Court for consultation, and the inquisitors were pleased to read in summer 1604 that the Inquisitor General had interceded with the king; Páramo, Llanes, and Hoyo, February 13 and August 27, 1604, fols. 94–95. Páramo and Llanes then sent an agent to Court to advocate for them, July 1605, fol. 160. In 1605, Hoyo – who curried favor with Feria – did earn a promotion to inquisitor in Barcelona's tribunal, fols. 111, 120. The others noted that virtually all the bishoprics, abbacies, and priorates in Sicily had come vacant and been

By 1602, Páramo asked instead to return to Castile on the basis of his service, merits, and poor health. In November, in the Valley of Mazara on a visitation, he received word that the *Suprema* had licensed him to return to Castile to recuperate. Within a month, a second notice arrived, revoking the license, presumably as a result of Feria's report. The viceroy's forces again assaulted the tribunal in 1606. The *Suprema* chided the inquisitors for noncompliance with the 1606 and 1607 reforms, admonishing them to follow all the Inquisition's laws and instructions and to consult that body before removing anyone from the galleys or commuting punishments. It advised restraint in dealing with the viceroy, and especially not to over-shadow him on public occasions.[97] Páramo tried other tacks. He wrote in defense of the *Monarchia* and dedicated a final treatise – an attack on Venetian abuses of ecclesiastical immunity – to Pope Paul V and printed it in Palermo in 1606.

In Páramo's last years, the inquisitors adopted an even more intense rhetoric of affliction: their friends deserted them; their enemies increased their attacks. Late in 1606, Páramo called himself "unfavored and forgot-ten" and asked for a pension of sorts, a reward "with which he could retire to a corner" for the remainder of his days.[98] Ignored again, he had a new plan by the summer of 1607: he went to Messina on the customary visitation with the intention of continuing to Rome, reputedly licensed to do so by the Inquisitor General. He would look, in a sense, for a better jurisdiction and seek his fortune in the Roman court of Paul V, returning to a city he had likely visited decades earlier. He was not away from Palermo long, as he was back in time to help complete trials for the December 13, 1607, *auto de fe*. His colleagues reported that he was never well after his return; after several days confined to his bed with a severe illness – liver disease, retained urine, aches and pains – he died on November 13, 1608.

denied them over the past twenty years; Páramo, Llanes, and Matienzo, October 19, 1607, fol. 304.

[97] Páramo's 1602 visitation was an unusually long four months, eleven days (August 1602 to January 1, 1603). Páramo, Llanes, and Hoyo, March 9, 1602, and Páramo, December 22, 1602, AHN, Inq., lib. 883, fols. 7, 47, see also fols. 31, 53–54, 64. Later, see Páramo and Llanes, July 28, 1606, fol. 243r; RB, MS II/265, fol. 75; *Suprema* (Quiñones, Zamora, Tassis, Márquez de Prado), October 13, 1606, and December 22, 1607, BNE, MS 2827, fols. 160, 161v; Páramo, Llanes, and Matienzo, April 4 and September 19, 1608, AHN, Inq., lib. 884, fols. 11–14, 26, 42.

[98] It was perhaps a pun on his second surname (Rincón): "conque pueda recogerme aun rincon," Páramo, November 18, 1606; cf. Páramo, Llanes, and Hoyo, June 4, 1604, AHN, Inq., lib. 883, fols. 82, 248.

Páramo was buried in Palermo's Jesuit church, then undergoing elaborate renovations, where the city's colonial elite worshipped.[99]

THE INQUISITOR AS HISTORIAN

Páramo came to be known as the Inquisition's initial historian. Unusual among Spanish inquisitors in the volume of his printed writings, Páramo, like Simancas, turned increasingly to theorizing to make his claims intelligible when he found himself operating in a new environment. There was much common ground among Páramo's treatises: they blended theological and juridical proofs; they drew on his tribunal experience; they argued via historical precedents. Scholars have considered, in particular, how Italian inquisitors developed patterns of reasoning and official practices that drew from, overlapped with, and ultimately played a role in shaping other kinds of work and modes of argumentation. Carlo Ginzburg illustrated how inquisitors might be assessed as anthropologists; Adriano Prosperi showed how they moved into the spheres of confessors and missionaries. Such polyvalence was also evident in their writings, as Simon Ditchfield described how a Dominican inquisitor of Piacenza, Umberto Locati (1503–87), both chronicled the city's history and compiled an inquisitorial manual.[100]

Inquisitors like Páramo had many reasons to develop their historical thinking. They created sources meant to enable specific types of inquiry into the past; they oversaw the work of notaries and the organization of inquisitorial archives, increasingly developed in the sixteenth century to extend institutional memory beyond that of transient individuals. They kept correspondence, instructions and procedural directives, financial registers, records of visitations, genealogical inquiries, and trial dossiers. When he rushed into the burning archives, Páramo protected the fruits of his labor, tools to combat heresy, and a repository like those preserving records of his own family's honor in Toledo's tribunal and Valladolid's

---

[99] Páramo, January 9, 1608; Llanes and Matienzo, August 23, 1607 and November 14, 1608; Lic. Villegas (*fiscal*), November 14, 1608, ibid., fol. 303 and lib. 884, fols. 2, 23, 32; Rivero Rodríguez gives the date as November 2, "Inquisición," 1216. For Páramo's epitaph in S. Maria di Gesù, see Garufi, *Fatti e personaggi*, 280.

[100] Carlo Ginzburg, "The Inquisitor as Anthropologist," in his *Clues, Myths, and the Historical Method*, trans. John and Anne C. Tedeschi (Baltimore, MD: The Johns Hopkins University Press, 1989), 156–64; Prosperi, *Tribunali della coscienza: Inquisitori, confessori, missionari* (Turin: G. Einaudi, 1996); Simon Ditchfield, "Umberto Locati, O. P. (1503–1587): Inquisitore, Vescovo e Storico – un profilo bio-bibliografico," *Bollettino Storico Piacentino* 84 (1989): 205–21. See also *L'Italia dell'Inquisitore: storia e geografia dell'Italia del Cinquecento nella Descrittione di Leandro Alberti*, ed. Massimo Donattini (Bologna: Bononia University Press, 2007).

Chancery. Shaped by the administration of an archive and the judicial investigation of the histories of individuals and families, he also lived during a sort of boom in history writing. Educational theorists argued that reading history was a means to acquire experience; kingdoms, cities, and families sought to demonstrate their virtue by proving the quality of their historical origins. Sacred history was an increasingly favored form of Catholic polemic in the years following the Council of Trent. The Spanish crown also patronized the writing of histories. Among many examples that might have encouraged Páramo, Philip II so appreciated the Jesuit Juan de Mariana's triumphalist history of Spain, first published in Latin in 1592, that he sponsored its translation into Spanish.[101]

Historical exempla were, moreover, useful tools. In Páramo's correspondence and in his treatises, he intertwined them with citations of conciliar deliberations, legal precedents, and papal and royal writs. They served to make accusations of corruption resonate by aligning contemporary actors with older templates for action. Thus, when Feria attributed venal motives to the inquisitors in their choices for appointments to the office of familiar, he called them Pharisees and so made them embody the inverse of the apostolic authority they claimed. The inquisitors fought back with their own storehouse of historical figures. The *Suprema* wrote "that he does not seem a viceroy who has come to Sicily, but rather an envoy of the emperor Diocletian." The tribunal likewise emphasized how poorly Feria's behavior reflected on the king by likening him "to those that have humiliated Theodosius, Arcadius, and infinite other emperors and kings." A providential logic of history also appeared in the letters of Páramo and Llanes. When they received news of Feria's death in Naples early in 1607, they suggested it should be interpreted as evidence of divine judgment; recompense for the scandals, hunger, and poverty the duke had inflicted on Sicily; and so as a lesson for future viceroys.[102]

[101] Among the wealth of scholarship on these subjects, see especially David Nirenberg, "Mass Conversion and Genealogical Mentalities: Jews and Christians in Fifteenth-Century Spain," *Past and Present* 174 (2002): 3–41; Ditchfield, *Liturgy, Sanctity and History in Tridentine Italy* (Cambridge, UK, and New York: Cambridge University Press, 1995), pt. III; Kagan, *Clio and the Crown: The Politics of History in Medieval and Early Modern Spain* (Baltimore, MD: The Johns Hopkins University Press, 2009), 117–23, 150; A. Katie Harris, *From Muslim to Christian Granada: Inventing a City's Past in Early Modern Spain* (Baltimore, MD: The Johns Hopkins University Press, 2007).

[102] "queno parece Virrey el que a venido a Sicilia sino legado del Emperador Diocleciano," *Suprema* to the king, January 16, 1603, BNE, MS 9393, fol. 39r; "a las que han humilado Theodosio, Arcadio y otros infinitos emperadores y Reyes..."; Páramo and Llanes, February 9, 1607, AHN, Inq., lib. 883, fol. 242v.

Páramo's career in print began in the 1590s, during his years at Court.[103] His first treatise, printed in Madrid in 1594, gave a series of legal opinions defending the jurisdiction of the Holy Office in Sicily. An opening salvo in his negotiations in the Council of Italy, he dedicated it to the *Suprema*. He described a hasty process, protesting that there had not been enough time for more formality, given the importance of the case and the need to respond rapidly to his adversaries' opinions.[104] He posed the problem as one of definition; he would delineate what properly belonged to inquisitorial jurisdiction. He asserted that the truth of his arguments would make them persuasive. His approach evidenced a certain historical thinking, as he first sought to establish the source of the Inquisition's temporal powers. Páramo published a companion piece in Madrid in 1599 that functioned as a coda to the negotiations, adding arguments developed while lobbying at Court. These volumes supplied a tailored history of an administrative problem, informed by experience in the field and designed to persuade courtiers to base their policies on the repertoire of precedents Páramo offered them. His correspondence offered a clue to his research methods, as he had long drawn up arguments after consulting "many letters which we have registered in this [Inquisition] archive."[105]

After his return to Sicily, Páramo took up another jurisdictional cause, joining a famous contest in Catholic historiography. In 1604, Cardinal Cesare Baronio (1538–1607) published the eleventh of twelve volumes of his monumental *Annales Ecclesiastici* (1588–1607), which chronicled the Church's history through the year 1198. That volume delegitimized claims that the papacy had delegated ecclesiastical supremacy to the Norman rulers of Naples and Sicily in the eleventh century. In so doing, Baronio undermined the administration of the Spanish Habsburgs, who justified privileges in those kingdoms via their Norman inheritance. When Baronio presented the *Monarchia* as a stumbling block to reform in the Church –

---

[103] He published four Latin treatises: *Responsvm ... pro defensione jurisdictionis Sancti Officii...* (Madrid: Luis Sánchez, 1594); the *De Origine* (1598); *Responsum ... adversus obiectiones secundo loco ...* (Madrid: Pedro Madrigal, 1599); *Ad Sanctissimvm D.N.D Pavlvm V. Pontficem Max. Confutationes decretorum ...* (Palermo: Gio. Antonio de Franciscis, 1606). See also Cristóbal Pérez Pastor, *Bibliografía Madrileña, o descripción de las obras impresas en Madrid* (1891; repr. Pamplona: Analecta, 2000), 1:227, 339.

[104] Dedication, *Responsum* (1594). For similar material, AHN, Inq., lib. 1252, fols. 373r-75v, 381r-83r; lib. 880, fol. 24; Páramo, Llanes, and Hoyo, August 9, 1602, BNE, MS 9393, fols. 35r-39v. See also Garufi, *Fatto e personaggi*, 177.

[105] Páramo, June 4, 1590, AHN, Inq., lib. 880, fols. 176r-78v; he also described his research efforts (tracking down privileges, old writings, authoritative opinions) in BNE, MS 8851, fol. 187r.

one of the abusive usurpations of religious authority by polities such as Spain and Venice – he tapped into an already live debate. Pope Pius V had tried to renegotiate the issue in 1571. Baronio, moreover, had already incurred Spanish displeasure in earlier volumes, questioning the veracity of the legend of Santiago, Spain's patron saint, and supporting negotiations that had reconciled Henry of Navarre to the Church and so brought him to the French throne.[106] Páramo quickly joined the latest opposition to Baronio, packaging his rebuttal in two forms: a book-length Latin manuscript of 1605 and a vernacular letter addressed to Philip III.[107]

Páramo depicted himself as the true defender of the faith, painting Baronio's decision to print – thus so broadly disseminating his criticism – as scandalizing the public. He constructed parallel arguments. He, too, attended to the origin of the word. He maintained that the papal delegation had been made in perpetuity and coupled legal precedents – canon law and customary – with detailed historical justifications to make a competing chronological account. Including numerous transcriptions of proof texts and adorning his manuscript with genealogical trees, he charted the *Monarchia*'s exercise over more than five centuries. The Norman Count Roger was the invariable starting point of arguments, as the eleventh-century Christian conqueror of an island then under Muslim rule. It was to him that Pope Urban II (r. 1088–99) had supposedly made the concessions. For Páramo, proving that Baronio was "deceived" meant arguing that Urban II's bull was not a forgery and that "the true successors of Count Roger" – up to Philip III – had used their authority well. Páramo was also clearly commenting on contemporary politics. He noted that the

---

[106] A supposed proof letter for the donation of the *Monarchia* had been unearthed and circulated in 1513. See Cyriac K. Pullapilly, *Caesar Baronius: Counter-Reformation Historian* (Notre Dame, IN, and London: University of Notre Dame Press, 1975), 14–17, 103–107; Stefano Zen, *Baronio storico: Controriforma e crisi del metodo umanistico* (Naples: Vivarium, 1994), 177; Koenigsberger, *Practice of Empire*, 144–45; Ditchfield, *Liturgy, Sanctity and History*, 273–85. On Baronio and Santiago, Erin K. Rowe, *Saint and Nation: Santiago, Teresa of Ávila, and Plural Identities in Early Modern Spain* (University Park: Pennsylvania State University Press, 2011).

[107] There are multiple manuscript copies of each; the letters suggest that Páramo revised and amplified these arguments from the 1590s onward: September 8, 1598, BNE, MS 8851, fols. 187r-99; MS 1332, fols. 55–68; MS 2612, fols. 50–76; MS 2666, fols. 405v-11; August 31, 1605, MS 2668, fols. 197–222. Cf. another letter in defense of the *Monarchia*, written under Feria's auspices, by Monsignor Manzanedo, auditor of the Rota, MS 1332, fol. 70r. For the Latin treatise: *Apologeticon Aduersus Baronii S[an]tae Romanae Ecclesiae Cardinalis amplissimi obiecta Contra Monarchia Regni Siciliae*, BNE, MSS 1555, 2667, 2792; *Tractatus de monarchia regni Siciliae*, BL, Add. 19319 (prefaced by the letter to Philip III, translated into Latin). Páramo's manuscripts were still being copied and circulated in the 1620s and beyond, see BNE, MS 2668, fols. 223–24.

tyrannical French kings might covet Sicily but possessed no legitimate
claim; he explained that the papal concessions were earned by freeing
Sicily from Muslim rule and solidifying the island's return to the Church,
"building many chapels, founding many churches." Thus, Páramo rendered Roger a model for princely defense of Catholicism, and Roger's
reconquest a tale of partnership between a good Catholic prince and an
appreciative pope.[108] In this manner, as well as through blood, he sought
to show Philip III as Roger's heir and to make the narrative resonate with
later events. Páramo also drew on his judicial experience to argue for the
arrangement's practical utility. It limited litigation, forestalling appeals to
Rome in clerical matters – in which, Páramo asserted, the wealthier or
more powerful party always won, often at the expense of justice – though
the king could still send exceptional cases there.

Baronio protested to the Spanish crown that his treatment of the
Monarchia was utterly ordinary given the chronological organization of
his *Annales* and insisted his intention was not "to destroy the two kingdoms, but rather to confirm and to fortify that which in them is declining."
He aligned himself with the reforming spirit of the recently deceased Pope
Clement VIII, who had hoped "that they may remove the Sicilian
Monarchia, that as poorly instituted and founded against the rights of
the Church, they knew that it could not remain." Spanish courtiers found
little merit in such arguments, casting Baronio as aligned with Spain's
enemies and a source of great harm. Some advocated banning the book
outright – they did so in the kingdoms of Naples and Sicily – whereas many
suggested that they should take action "with the least noise possible." In
Sicily, Feria – who had opposed Baronio before, as an envoy in France –
sponsored numerous refutations. He expressed indignation at the insult to
Philip III's royal predecessors and at the decision to circulate such arguments in Latin (thus inviting public consideration); he pointedly noted that
Pius V's approach had been preferable to Clement VIII's.[109] In this affair,

---

[108] BNE, MS 2667, 536; BNE, MS 2666, fols. 405v-6r. Even an account of Palermo's
municipal privileges began with concessions of authority from Roger ("rex") to the
archbishop of that city: *Antiche Consuetudini delle Città di Sicilia*, ed. Vito la Mantia
(Palermo: Alberto Reber, 1900), 225. The political claims on which the *Monarchia* rested
had been contested from the outset; see David Abulafia, *The Western Mediterranean
Kingdoms 1200–1500: The Struggle for Domination* (London and New York: Longman,
1997), 3–15.

[109] "destruyr los dos Rey[n]os … sino para confirmar y forticiar lo que en ellos se va
cayendo"; "quitassen la Monarchia de sicilia que como mal Instituyda y fundada contra
los derechos dela Iglesia sabian que no podia permanecser"; "con el menos ruido que se
pudiere." *Consulta*, Council of State, August 1605; Feria to the king, September 1 and

Feria and Páramo collaborated, even as they battled on other fronts. The duke sent a copy of Páramo's manuscript book to the royal Court. There, in the spring of 1606, courtiers praised its "good parts and the zeal with which the author has made it." One wrote to Páramo: "The liberty with which the cardinal treats the king is so great, that he deserves the style and rigor with which Your Lordship sometimes advises him of the truth." Páramo cast such writing as part of his official work, done "to discharge the obligation of my profession."[110]

Simultaneously, Páramo courted the new pope. He printed his *Confutationes decretorum* – advertised from its title as refuting decrees of the Venetian doge that violated ecclesiastical immunity – in Palermo in 1606 and dedicated it to Paul V (r. 1605–21). It was both a bid for papal attention and, still, a defense of Spanish practices in Sicily; to attack Venice as abusing the Church was also, implicitly, to distance other delegations of apostolic authority from those that supposedly harmed the faith. Páramo intervened in the controversy at its most heated moment, during the papal interdict of Venice in 1606 and 1607, joining a furious outpouring of publicity on both sides.[111] Papers supporting the Venetians had even been reported in Sicily, and the inquisitors in Palermo received orders to track down and remove such offensive materials from circulation.[112]

The treatise showed continuities across Páramo's career. It again dealt with questions of jurisdiction and appeal, in this case, putting in doubt the legitimacy of Venice's prohibition on its subjects litigating outside Venetian domains. The book was presented as a tool to bring the schismatic Venetians back into the fold and was divided into seven articles, each designed to emphasize the supremacy of religious laws. He defended ecclesiastical control of churches, offered a catalog of the manifold and

---

September 22, 1605; *Consulta*, Februrary 16, 1606, AGS, Estado, leg. 1161, docs. 251, 260, 302 and leg. 1162, docs. 110–11. See also Pullapilly, *Baronius*, 107–8.

[110] "buenas partes y zelo conque lo hà hecho su auctor"; "La libertad conque trata el Card[ena]l al Rey, es tan grande, q[ue] mereçe el estilo y rigor conque V[uestra] S[eñoría] alg[una]s vezes le advierte dela verdad." Regent Quintana Dueñas, BNE, MS 2667, fols. 1, 2; "por cumplir ala obligacion de mi profession," MS 2666, fol. 405v.

[111] Baronio also opposed Venice, whose most famous defender was the Servite friar Paolo Sarpi (1552–1623). A. D. Wright characterized the papacy's battles with Spain and Venice between 1584 and 1610 as of central importance to the redefining of Catholic authority, *Federico Borromeo and Baronius: A Turning-Point in the Development of the Counter-Reformation Church* (Reading, UK: University of Reading, 1974), 20. On the Venetian polemics (Páramo's is not mentioned), see Filippo de Vivo, *Information and Communication in Venice: Rethinking Early Modern Politics* (Oxford, UK, and New York: Oxford University Press, 2007).

[112] Páramo and Llanes, December 23, 1606, AHN, Inq., lib. 883, fol. 237.

obstinate errors of the Venetian doge, and argued for the inviolate nature
of ecclesiastical honors. The tract supported the dignity of the ecclesiastical
class, to which Páramo had long aggregated inquisitors. After two decades
of struggling with viceroys, Páramo composed arguments that spoke not
only to papal conflicts with Venice, but also to Sicily's politico-religious
landscape. He contended that religious authorities had a duty to correct
erring princes.[113] He crafted a history of the rights of God's ministers,
progressing through theological ages. He recalled that after Jesus' death,
Tiberius and his successors had usurped the Church's authority. When he
failed to recognize the authority of Peter, Emperor Tiberius became an
archetypal tyrant. The implications for Venice – and any other usurpers of
ecclesiastical authority – were clear. Still, Páramo signaled that reform was
always possible; the prince had only to consult his conscience – make what
was construed as the only virtuous choice – and return penitently to the
fold. As support, he cited apostolic models for humble conversion and the
examples of Emperors Constantine and Justinian, who had sinned in
idolatry and heresy before they, too, had converted to find fame as devout
Christians.[114]

Páramo had already developed this vein of historical thinking in his
masterwork: *De Origine et Progressu Sanctae Inquisitionis* – that is, "On
the Origin and Progress of the Holy Inquisition" – published in Madrid in
1598.[115] As the title indicated, the book both advanced sacred foundations
for inquisitorial work and described the development of current practice,
all while claiming historical continuity in heresy inquisitions. Páramo's
opening has received the most attention. There, he argued that the
Inquisition's origins were coeval with those of humankind: the practice
of inquisition began with God's questioning of Adam and Eve and their
expulsion from the Garden of Eden. With such a precedent, he construed
the inquisitorial process as the essential mode of religious discipline in the
postlapsarian world. Páramo then traced the exercise of the office through
six theological ages, sketching a continuous succession of inquisitors and
acts of inquisition throughout the Old Testament, New Testament, and
into the early Church. This comprised the first part of the treatise; then, he

---

[113] *Confutationes decretorum*, 8, 10.

[114] Ibid., 56–57, 90–91. For another use of Tiberius in seventeenth-century political invective, see María José del Río Barredo, *Madrid, Urbs Regia: La capital ceremonial de la
Monarquía Católica* (Madrid: Marcial Pons Historia, 2000), 200.

[115] La Mantia called it "la più estesa esposizione di notizie e privilegi del S. Officio." He, like
many others, used it as a point of departure for his own history of the Inquisition, *Origine
e vicende*, 5.

devoted the second portion to the current age (mostly the preceding four centuries), in which chronological accounts of inquisitorial action were divided up geographically. Here, he took an approach distinct from Simancas's; Páramo argued for the legitimacy of the Spanish Inquisition more by making all inquisitions of a piece than by distinguishing one from another. He devoted chapters to inquisitions in particular kingdoms or regions, thus writing each locality into a parallel, organic progression. He cataloged the customs and the achievements of a unified Inquisition. Still, Páramo's composition might be understood as a kind of hybrid. Weighing in at nearly nine hundred pages, his pretensions to offer a definitive statement of the Inquisition's universality and to justify its exercise by connection to unimpeachable origins were clear. But the book was also partly in the form of earlier manuals of inquisitorial law. The third and final section was primarily a compendium of inquisitorial procedure, coupled with an exploration of contentious legal issues.

Despite its universal posture, Páramo's history was also profoundly local in its concerns. It was firmly part of what Ditchfield has so aptly termed the "parallel processes of universalizing the particular and particularizing the universal," that characterized the climate of reforms after Trent.[116] The *De Origine* shared much with Páramo's other writings. It offered ways to make sense of contemporary developments by aligning them to past precedents, thus creating a system of events specific to inquisitorial history. Páramo chose to write in Latin, demonstrating his learning, while also aiming at an international audience of elites. He included proof texts – papal bulls and royal decrees – and thus the bull condemning Martin Luther, classified as an act of inquisition, became a precedent for inquisitorial trials of Lutherans. Like so much of the sacred history writing of Catholics and Protestants, it was an outgrowth of polemic. As in each jurisdictional dispute he engaged, the *De Origine* defended a concession of apostolic authority to a secular ruler that had gained unintended permanence; it sought to render the Inquisition part of an unbroken sweep of Christian history, its modern practices consonant with those of biblical and apostolic time.[117] The history drew heavily from

---

[116] Ditchfield, *Liturgy, Sanctity, and History*, 357.

[117] Not so dissimilar to the debates about the *Monarchia*, contemporary critics of the Spanish Inquisition disputed that Pope Sixtus IV intended the birth of a new institution when he granted the bull authorizing the delegation of inquisitorial authority to Ferdinand and Isabel. Stefania Pastore, *Il Vangelo e la Spada: L'Inquisizione di Castiglia e i Suoi Crtici* (Rome: Edizioni di Storia e Letteratura, 2003), 62–132; Koenigsberger, *Practice of Empire*, 146.

Páramo's experiences in Sicily and functioned, in part, as one of his lobbying efforts in Madrid.

The *De Origine* sought to grant legitimacy to the practices of the Spanish Inquisition by giving them long histories. The *sanbenito*, for instance, became simply an imitation of the garb Adam and Eve donned when they were cast out of Eden after the fall, penitents in the first *auto de fe*. Inquisitors General proliferated across Páramo's pages, authorizing a specific institutional organization as it had evolved by the late sixteenth century. Toledo's court, to which members of his family were connected, was made into a template for others; in its chapter, he listed each official position a tribunal should have. Páramo detailed everything from the standards used in processions to the form of edicts to the intricacies of the papal delegation of inquisitorial jurisdiction. His treatise displayed the intermediary knowledge he had gained in Sicily and argued, repeatedly, for the worth of inquisitors' particular actions and privileges there.[118] He gave the treatment of papal jurisdiction a prominent location (opening book 3), referenced the *crucesignati*, Italian lay associates of the Inquisition, and attended to the place of the cross in inquisitorial regalia. He sketched resistance in Naples in terms reminiscent of the attacks on the Sicilian tribunal. By implication, he justified how the Sicilian court argued for its legal authority, projected its mandate in public, and invited secular participation.

Páramo began the chapter on Sicily – one of the longer regional sections – with his experience in the negotiations at Court, in which he was involved as he wrote the *De Origine*.[119] He named and praised the councillors involved in the junta: two from the *Suprema*, two from the Council of Italy. As an implicit spur to Portocarrero and future Inquisitors General, he recounted how Quiroga had ordered and financed his presence there so that the tribunal would have just representation. He gestured to the competition between Palermo and Messina, defending the tribunal's location in the former, as the kingdom's historical capital; he reprised his jurisdictional arguments, dwelling on the privilege of appointing Sicilian barons as Inquisition familiars. He also deployed recent events to present them as indispensable to the tribunal's ability to function. He recalled how six

---

[118] Monter termed the court "between Aragón and Rome," *Frontiers of Heresy*, 181. Cf. the analysis of captives as cultural intermediaries in Lisa Voigt, *Writing Captivity in the Early Modern Atlantic: Circulations of Knowledge and Authority in the Iberian and English Imperial Worlds* (Chapel Hill: Omohundro Institute, University of North Carolina Press, 2009).

[119] *De Origine*, 195–217.

years earlier Jacobo Bruto left Geneva – "which is the most filthy strong-
hold of heretical iniquity" – to spread false doctrine in Sicily. The inquisitors, Páramo continued, called together their associates among the barons
and nobles of Sicily, who were especially skilled in pursuing religious
impostors. They delivered Bruto to the tribunal, where the inquisitors
reconciled him, although he soon relapsed into heresy.[120] Páramo wrote
the Bruto case for public consumption in such a fashion as to make the
special privileges of the tribunal essential to its struggle against Protestant
evangelizing, the most serious threat the souls on the island faced. Even the
index called attention to the affair: the letter "I" began with an entry
pointing readers to the account of the burning of Bruto as an impenitent
and relapsed heretic that would follow.

Páramo not only provided instructions for legal procedure, he also
supplied ways to make sense of human action. From biblical text through
events observed over the course of his own judicial career, he assembled a
repertoire of good judges, watershed cases, and infamous criminals –
templates for inquisitorial action – that might be used to underpin a host
of arguments, as a set of symbolic reference points. He advanced a mythology for inquisitors, codifying and promoting arguments already in circulation; the index and the first section stressed that they followed in the
line of Old Testament prophets, apostles, and the more recent blessed such
as St. Dominic or St. Peter Martyr. The figures Páramo appropriated as
inquisitors struggled against great odds, opposing their zeal to the continuous onslaught of insidious heresies. Thus, he crafted a historical framework that could serve current debates: critics might be less apt to slur an
institution with an unimpeachable divine mandate as a worldly tool of the
Spanish king or corrupt inquisitors.[121] He listed famous men associated
with the Inquisition and recounted praise for it from a range of figures,
from Charles V to Luis de Granada.[122] Páramo suggested that, on the one
hand, the institution was ancient, authoritative, and universal; on the
other, it could accommodate local variations in practice. His accounts of
regional tribunals were replete with detail, each beginning with an initial
instance of inquisitorial procedure and identifying a first Inquisitor

---

[120] On the junta, ibid., 196. Two subsections – 27 and 28 – treated the issue of the familiars
specifically; they were indexed as "Nobilium Familiarium diligentia in rebus fidei" and
"Incommoda, quae sequuntur, si nobiles prohibea[n]tur esse Familiares S. Officii," ibid.,
199; "qu[a]e spurcissima est iniquitatis haereticae arx," ibid., 214.

[121] On Páramo as one of the chief elaborators of a self-justifying inquisitorial rhetoric, see
Moreno, *La invención*, 193ff.

[122] *De Origine*, 273.

General, thus fabricating conformity. He noted a tribunal's most common heretical charges or described a particularly famous trial. For instance, he lumped polygamy, witchcraft, and Judaizing together as crimes the Inquisition in Mexico had frequently tried.[123] Even as he sat on a tribunal that brought relatively few charges of Judaizing, he treated at some length the Mexican trials of those accused of relapsing into the practice of Judaism; he repeated such rote slurs as accusations that *conversos* had engaged in host desecration and turned the infamous case of the *converso* Luis de Carvajal into a particular achievement of that tribunal. Similarly, he framed the discovery of Lutherans in Valladolid in 1558 – and the subsequent uncovering of Archbishop Carranza's heresies – as one of the greatest examples of inquisitorial "diligence."[124] He defended the Spanish Inquisition's model both to an external audience and to competing authorities within the Spanish monarchy.

Frequently read as a testament to the Spanish Inquisition's power, the paradox of the *De Origine*'s composition is that it was compiled as part of a relatively unsuccessful attempt to advocate for embattled inquisitorial privileges in Sicily and to advance a stalled judicial career.[125] Some of Páramo's citations may have been tailored for potential patrons. He drew from the histories of Jerónimo de Zurita (1511–80), once a secretary of the Inquisition; Zurita's *Anales* – a chronologically ordered history of Spain from 711 – had won him the admiration and patronage of Philip II. He dedicated significant paragraphs of praise to both Quiroga and Portocarrero, as model Inquisitors General. But the king died just two weeks before Páramo dated the dedication to his *De Origine* in Madrid, and Portocarrero – to whom it was dedicated – was edged out in the transition.[126] Páramo also listed the inquisitors who had staffed some of the tribunals. He used their qualities to buttress the authority of the institution, describing them as distinguished and accomplished men. He also spoke to his own career. Looking at the catalog of Sicilian inquisitors, it was apparent that up until his day, they had almost all been promoted

---

[123] Ibid., 239.

[124] Agustín Cazalla – burned in 1559 – also received considerable attention. Ibid., 242, 299–301.

[125] Rivero Rodríguez has made similar observations about Páramo's writings; see his "Inquisición," 1150–51.

[126] *De Origine*, 161–62; dedication, October 1, 1598. Páramo's use of Zurita is mentioned in José Antonio Escudero, *Los orígenes del "Consejo de la Suprema Inquisición,"* in *Inquisición Española y Mentalidad Inquisitorial*, ed. Ángel Alcalá (Barcelona: Editorial Ariel, 1984), 81–122. On Zurita, Kagan, *Clio and the Crown*, 102–6.

into the episcopate. He noted that Haedo was still Palermo's archbishop. He referred favorably to Sicily's one-time *fiscal* Alonso Peña, giving him honor in print as eventually an inquisitor in Sardinia. Conflicts were silenced, as the entry for Aymar was merely dry, not critical. Páramo also praised those who theorized about the Inquisition, emphasizing the brief service in the Sicilian court of Juan de Rojas and the renown of his writings on inquisitorial law. He noted how the editorial efforts of Francisco Peña in Rome had revived the memory of many works of medieval inquisitors. Páramo's attention to these details was strategic, but it also commemorated his intimates, offering them lasting fame. He eulogized his brother in the section for Toledo's tribunal and praised his two colleagues working in Sicily while he wrote in Madrid. Olloquí and Llanes were distinguished, he claimed, by their erudition, virtue, and prudence; he credited them with keeping Sicily free from heresy.[127]

The complexity of the enterprise that Páramo undertook in the *De Origine* was on display in its final chapter.[128] There, he treated the incitement to libidinous acts in the confessional, crafting a history of the crime. He termed it the tenth *quaestio*, aligning it simultaneously with theological and juridical modes of arguing; moreover, this might be seen to mimic the structure of Nicolau Eymeric's manual, recently reissued and glossed by Peña, which was fast becoming the preeminent guide for inquisitors. The particular shape of Páramo's judicial experience likely underpinned the chapter, given his frequent concern with clerical behavior. His varied erudition was also in evidence, as he plucked from a range of legal authorities, several inquisitorial theorists (Peña, Simancas, and Rojas among them), as well as classical sources, folding in bits of Virgil and Terence, among others. He proposed a significant extension of inquisitorial jurisdiction, which also allowed a glimpse of his thinking about the psychology of sin. Páramo argued that not only clerics should be criminally responsible for the offense of solicitation; when female confessants had also behaved lustfully, they too should be tried on suspicion of heresy. Here, he echoed the initial sections of the *De Origine* and their biblical exempla, offering young Daniel, once again, as a model inquisitor. He recalled how Daniel had used his good judgment to correctly discern Susanna's chastity and the falseness of the accusations against her; latter-day inquisitors were to perform the same act of sorting. He thus offered examples to simultaneously defend, elevate, and reform the practice of his contemporaries. He

---

[127] *De Origine*, 216–17, 223, 259.
[128] Ibid., 838–87.

depicted the worth of inquisitorial work as resting both on skill and good intentions; elsewhere, Páramo had asserted that inquisitors did not desire men's and women's perdition but rather their correction.[129]

A product of the Castilian gentry and his legal education, Páramo's ecclesiastical career was shaped by the jurisdictional circumstances of the Sicilian Inquisition tribunal. His twenty-two-year posting to a court seen as peripheral led him to develop his techniques as a writer of letters and of treatises. He constructed himself as the quintessential reformer, telling a story of decadence and of a purified, historical institution whose procedural integrity and jurisdictional authority would correct the body politic. Though they won him praise, Páramo's books had few tangible effects in his lifetime. He attached himself too visibly to policies that were falling out of favor and did not tack his stances well to the political winds. The history of the Inquisition that Páramo left behind enshrined a mode of historical thinking fitted to the needs and experiences of his career. He offered patterns and precedents through which inquisitors might give sense to events and so provided ways for later judges to frame their experiences, to connect the cases they tried to earlier crimes, and themselves to a genealogy of inquisitors in which Páramo had firmly fixed himself.

[129] Ibid., 363, 376, 886. Lea asserted that Páramo was the first to treat female culpability in solicitation cases, *History of the Inquisition*, 2:111. In the 1530s, Francisco Ortíz invoked the example of Daniel and Susanna in his defense before the Inquisition in Toledo; see Lu Ann Homza, "How to Harass an Inquisitor-General: The Polyphonic Law of Friar Francisco Ortíz" in *A Renaissance of Conflicts: Visions and Revisions of Law and Society in Italy and Spain*, ed. John A. Marino and Thomas Kuehn (Toronto: Centre for Reformation and Renaissance Studies, 2004), 299–336.

CHAPTER 4

Falling from Grace

The Disenchantments of Juan Adam de la Parra

The pen is the tongue of the soul.[1]

By the initial years of Philip IV's reign (1621–65), promotion through the ranks of the Spanish Inquisition had become an established avenue to approach the royal Court in Madrid. Still, the exercise of inquisitorial authority there was ill defined. The town fell under the jurisdiction of Toledo's tribunal; yet from the time Philip II first made it his capital in 1561, the specific form of the Inquisition's presence at Court became, unsurprisingly, a contentious subject. Oversight by commissaries was followed by the creation of a post of inquisitor of Toledo with attendance in Madrid. Despite several attempts to make a new tribunal there, it was ultimately the last one to be founded, not taking definitive shape until the 1660s. Meanwhile, the presence of the *Suprema* and a string of strong Inquisitors General brought further scrutiny. From special juntas to the *Suprema*'s direct involvement in local affairs, the presence of several kinds of inquisitorial activity in Madrid fitted the city's status as the heart of the Catholic Monarchy, arguably in need of additional defenses. In the 1620s and 1630s, inquisitorial action was inflected by the reforming climate of the young king's government and the initiatives of the royal favorite, the count-duke of Olivares, as officials debated purity of blood statutes and investigated claims to sanctity and the orthodoxy of Portuguese *conversos*. Courtiers pursued reforms through judicial and conciliar action, and also through a flood of writings; *arbitristas*, so called, lobbied the crown, and

---

[1] Miguel de Cervantes Saavedra, *Don Quixote*, trans. Edith Grossman (New York: Ecco, 2003), 557.

191

pamphlets, poetry, and polemics of many stripes proliferated.[2] It was in this environment that Juan Adam de la Parra set out to make his career.

In 1634, Adam de la Parra was just shy of forty – considered by some the suitable minimum age for inquisitors – and in pursuit of a promotion.[3] Educated in law and shaped by his early experiences as an attorney in Seville's courts, he was then the *fiscal* – or prosecuting attorney – of the Inquisition tribunal in Murcia. He sought to demonstrate what he could offer at Court, making a show of his diligence, competence in jurisdictional disputes, and expertise in signal religious questions. He displayed his potential utility as a polemicist, writing a diatribe against France and sending copies to Olivares and the Inquisitor General. Adam de la Parra anticipated – correctly – that an inquisitor in Madrid would be poised between the roles of courtier and judge. When he arrived at Court in 1635 and was soon made an inquisitor, he seemingly hoped to gain further rewards and increase his intimacy with the power brokers there. Positioned at the center of the Habsburg world, he might have seen an opportunity to be involved in the most important anti-heretical work of his day. He could have expected that the office would allow him to pursue cases he perceived as important, to promote the Inquisition's authority in Madrid, and to use his influence to unveil deceptions of a religious nature.

For a few years, Adam de la Parra appeared to be realizing such ambitions. He joined exclusive circles and was tapped for juntas; he used his new position to open cases and advance stalled investigations. He adapted his writing to the exigencies of the Court. Having already published a Latin treatise on purity of blood statutes, he turned increasingly to vernacular propaganda inflected with historical exempla, becoming one of a cadre of royal pamphleteers. He failed, however, to navigate the shifting tides at Court in the early 1640s, and a scurrilous verse attributed to him led to his dramatic fall. Imprisoned in the autumn of 1642 and released in

---

[2] On the Inquisition in Madrid, see María del Pilar Domínguez Salgado, "Inquisidores y fiscales de la Inquisición de Corte (1580–1700)," *Revista de la Inquisición* 4 (1995): 205–48; Jaime Contreras and Jean-Pierre Dedieu, "Estructuras Geográficas del Santo Oficio en España," *HIEA* 2:17–21; Joaquín Pérez Villanueva, "Felipe IV y su política," *HIEA* 1:1036–37. On the seventeenth-century Court and its shaping of Madrid, see especially J. H. Elliott, *The Count-Duke of Olivares: The Statesman in an Age of Decline* (New Haven, CT, and London: Yale University Press, 1986); María José del Río Barredo, *Madrid, Urbs Regia: La capital ceremonial de la Monarquía Católica* (Madrid: Marcial Pons Historia, 2000), 173–233.

[3] On long-standing disputes over whether thirty was instead sufficient, see Henry Charles Lea, *A History of the Inquisition of Spain* (New York: The Macmillian Company, 1906–7), 2:233–37.

the aftermath of Olivares's dismissal from Court, the inquisitor, too, was sent away from Madrid. He died precipitously, in a kind of exile – if, technically, transferred rather than demoted – early in 1644. The politics around writing – which subjects might be treated in which manner and at which moment – had both facilitated his ascent and abruptly halted his career.

It is this scandal that has attracted significant interest from historians. The coincidence in timing between the inquisitor's imprisonment and that of the famous writer Francisco de Quevedo, both in León, fuelled speculation about the connection between them. Much of this has been dismissed as John Elliott has shown the source of Adam de la Parra's disgrace – distinct from Quevedo's – to be his crossing of a powerful family of Portuguese *conversos* at Court and his impolitic publicizing of his criticisms. The inquisitor was also long associated with a collection of letters, now deemed apocryphal, that purported to be correspondence between him and Quevedo. Likewise, very little poetry is now securely attributed to him. What remains is Adam de la Parra's reputation as a poet, similarities between his arguments and those of Quevedo, and some evidence of familiarity between the two men. Additionally, recent scholarship has shown more fully how the inquisitor participated in the historiographical projects of Olivares and Philip IV.[4] In sum, the portrait of Adam de la Parra has been one of a courtier immersed in the politics of the Olivares era and in the genres of political writing that flourished then, both in support of and critiquing the regime. Long treated as an exceptional case, Henry Charles Lea, the famous early twentieth-century historian of the Inquisition, commented that Adam de la Parra, "though an inquisitor, was a poet and a man of culture."[5] Yet his work as an

---

[4] For example, Richard L. Kagan, *Clio and the Crown: The Politics of History in Medieval and Early Modern Spain* (Baltimore, MD: The Johns Hopkins University Press, 2009), 214–23.

[5] Lea, *Inquisition*, 3:291. See Joaquín de Entrambasaguas, "El Inquisidor Juan Adam de la Parra," in *Estudios y Ensayos*, ed. Entrambasaguas (Madrid: CSIC, 1973); Entrambasaguas, "Prólogo," in Adam de la Parra, *Conspiración Herético-Cristianísima*, trans. Angeles Roda Aguirre (Madrid: CSIC, 1943), vii–lii; and *Varios Datos Referentes al Inquisidor Juan Adam de la Parra* (Madrid: Tipografía de Archivos, 1930); Eduardo Juliá Martínez, *La Amistad Entre Quevedo y Adam de la Parra* (Madrid: Anales de la Universidad de Madrid, 1932); J. H. Elliott, "Nueva luz sobre la prisión de Quevedo y Adam de la Parra," *Boletín de la Real Academia de la Historia* 169 (1972): 171–82; James O. Crosby, ed., *Nuevas Cartas de la Última Prisión de Quevedo* (Woodbridge, Suffolk, and Rochester, NY: Tamesis, 2005), 111–13; María Soledad Arredondo, *Literatura y Propaganda en Tiempo de Quevedo: Guerras y Plumas Contra Francia, Cataluña y Portugal* (Frankfurt and Madrid: Iberoamericana Vervuert, 2011).

inquisitor was never incidental to his other activities. He perceived himself – and was depicted by his contemporaries – as aligned with and committed to that office.

This chapter demonstrates how Adam de la Parra pursued the same causes over two decades. He persistently sought to build up inquisitorial authority and to try those he discerned to be pretenders: false saints and false converts. In this way, his life allows an examination of both the strictures on inquisitorial action and the motivations behind it, as Adam de la Parra's socially mobile career points to a potent combination of ideological commitment, politics, and ambition underlying the decisions of the Inquisition's judges. His fall might be read as mere miscalculation or an accident of timing; alternately, it could be seen as showing his dedication to particular stances on economic and religious policy, even when they had become less popular. His writings, like Diego de Simancas's or Luis de Páramo's, demonstrate how inquisitors sought to carve out space for themselves in a lettered elite and for their institution in the political arena, depicting the Inquisition as the defender of religion and opposing policies of alliances, trade, and toleration, which they claimed jeopardized the religious health of the monarchy. His career, moreover, exemplifies how inquisitors construed themselves as essential to their society for their ability to unmask harmful ruses, to use their knowledge and experience to puncture dangerous illusions in the world around them.

APPROACHING THE COURT

Juan Adam de la Parra was born around 1596 in the town of Soto en Cameros, in the mountainous region within a day's journey to the south of the city of Logroño, to whose inquisitorial district it belonged. His parents and grandparents had also been natives of the town, part of the diocese of Calahorra. The son of Juan Adam y Soto and Cecilia de la Parra y Martínez, he was orphaned at an early age. Evidence suggests that from about 1600, his uncle Francisco Adam – a beneficed priest in Soto's church and the local commissary of the Inquisition – raised Juan, his brother Francisco, and his sister Anastasia. Juan's siblings would marry and have children in the same environs. His maternal grandfather and a great-grandfather had been municipal judges (*alcaldes ordinarios*) in Soto, and there are no indications that the family had held more than local offices. Perhaps as a result of efforts made either by Juan or his uncle in the early seventeenth century, several relatives – the husband of a cousin, his brother-in-law, two nephews – were familiars of the Inquisition.[6]

Adam de la Parra trained as a jurist, first at Salamanca's university, where he earned a bachelor's degree in civil and canon law in 1613, then at the university in Seville, where he received his licentiate in laws in 1620.[7] He then began to work up through the legal ranks, obtaining his first post the same year as a lawyer in Seville's royal court (*audiencia*). In 1624, he acquired an additional position, officially entering the Inquisition's hierarchy as a prisoners' attorney (*abogado de presos*) in Seville's tribunal, though he had worked with that court even before the appointment; his primary function was to assist those on trial. As he began to build his career in Seville, he also kept ties to Soto – where his uncle remained the Inquisition commissary until 1630 – and seems to have been in Madrid rather frequently. Perhaps working to forge connections at Court, he was there at least briefly in early 1624 to nominate a new secretary for the town of Soto; Seville was likewise a hub of administrative activity.[8] It is provocative to wonder how much Adam de la Parra was aware of the workings of the Logroño Inquisition tribunal in his youth, as the years when he began his legal education were the same ones that saw the famous Zugarramurdi witch trials come before that court. More than a decade later, the Spanish inquisitor who has become perhaps the most famous to modern historians, Lic. Alonso de Salazar Frías (c. 1564–1636), known for

---

[6] His contemporaries sometimes also wrote "Adán." His sister, born in Treguajantes and baptized there December 14, 1599, married Juan Sancho Verciño, born in Cabezón de Cameros and resident in Laguna where he was a familiar; their son, Juan Sancho Adam, would become a familiar in Hornillos. His brother married María Calvo, of Soto, in 1622, and had three children: Margarita, Juan, and Francisco (who became an Inquisition official in his youth). His brother was recorded as selling a slave – described as a *moro* youth of the kingdom of Fez, age 20 – for 950 reales in Logroño, January 30, 1624. A maternal aunt, María, married Francisco Zalabardo in 1620; her daughter, Francisca, married another familiar, Juan Lerdo. His paternal grandparents were Nicolás Adam and María de Soto. His maternal grandparents were Prudencio de la Parra (*alcalde*, son of Felipe de la Parra of Soto) and María Saénz Martínez (daughter of Felipe Martínez of Trevijano). AHN, Inq., leg. 1258, exp. 1; "Relacion delos Inquisidores" (Seville), leg. 2960; José María Lope Toledo, "Un Hermano del Célebre Inquisidor Riojano Juan Adam de la Parra," *Berceo* 33 (1954): 473–74; Entrambasaguas, "El Inquisidor," doc. II. I thank Conchi Redondo Moreno for sharing her work with me: "Adam de la Parra, el inquisidor indomable," in *Hijos Ilustres del Camero Viejo*, ed. R. Calvo Torre and C. Redondo Moreno (Soto en Cameros: A.R.C.E. S., 2005), 20–27.

[7] "Relacion delos Inquisidores" (Murcia), 1632, AHN, Inq., leg. 2809 and leg. 1258, exp. 1. Entrambasaguas also noted his epistolary relationship with the humanist Lorenzo Ramírez de Prado, a graduate of Salamanca, *Varios datos*, 172–73.

[8] AHPM, protc. 3.823 de Diego de Escobar, March 2, 1624, fol. 175. This notarial document is cited in Pablo Jaraulde Pou, *Francisco de Quevedo (1580–1645)* (Madrid: Editorial Castalia, 1998), 480.

questioning the evidence against the witches, signed a piece of very routine tribunal business: the Logroño court's order of February 6, 1626, to investigate Adam de la Parra's genealogy.[9]

Approved by the *Suprema* in Madrid on February 23, those inquiries provided Adam de la Parra the credential necessary to pursue a career in the Inquisition. The informants – twelve in Soto and eight in the nearby hamlet of Trevijano, where his great-grandfather was born – testified to his purity of blood and to his virtue. They were also aware of the young lawyer's movements: several reported hearing he was in Madrid or, even more precisely, that he was an *abogado* in Seville and presently in Madrid.[10] Raised by a local religious authority, both priest and representative of the Inquisition, like so many of his contemporaries, Adam de la Parra used juridical degrees and offices to seek to move beyond the world of his parents and grandparents, further afield than the regional networks of the Rioja.

The acquisition of sufficient reputation and patronage to rise in the inquisitorial hierarchy took some time and a few failed attempts. In 1628, the *Suprema* advanced Adam de la Parra as a candidate for *fiscal* in Córdoba and for inquisitor in the Canaries. Both times, however, Inquisitor General Antonio Zapata Cisneros y Mendoza chose another candidate.[11] Still in his mid-thirties, Adam de la Parra seems to have turned to publication to aid his bids for promotion. His first printed work – *Pro Cautione Christiana*, advertised from its title as advocating Christian caution – was issued in Madrid in February 1630, a choice of clear importance for a young official seeking to influence royal policy and to be noticed at Court. The work was a treatise in favor of purity of blood ordinances, and Adam de la Parra dedicated it to Cardinal-Prince Ferdinand of Austria – the archbishop of Toledo from 1618 to 1641 and the brother of Philip IV – whose cathedral's infamous statutes Simancas had also once defended.[12]

---

[9] AHN, leg. 1258, exp.1. Salazar later became the *Suprema*'s *fiscal* (1628), then councillor (1631), Teresa Sánchez Rivilla, "Inquisidores Generales y Consejeros de la Suprema: Documentación Biográfica," *HIEA* 3:408; Gustav Henningsen, *The Witches' Advocate: Basque Witchcraft and the Spanish Inquisition (1609–1614)* (Reno: University of Nevada Press, 1980).

[10] *Suprema* (Cifuentes, Gaviria, Chacón, Pacheco), AHN, leg. 1258, exp. 1, fol. 29v; see also fol. 3r.

[11] "Relacion de los Inquisidores," 1632, AHN, Inq., leg. 2809.

[12] Adam de la Parra, *Pro Cautione Christiana in supremis Senatibus sanctae Inquisitionis, & Ordinum, Ecclesia Toletana* (Madrid, 1630). See also the analysis in Antonio Domínguez Ortiz, "Una obra desconocida del Inquisidor Adam de la Parra" *Revista Bibliográfica y Documental* 5 (1951): 97–114; Lea, *History of the Inquisition*, 3:291–92. The copy in BNE, MS 6157, fols. 141rff. is heavily annotated, almost obfuscating the printed text in some places. I think that the marginalia are in Adam de la Parra's hand; it

By 1630, Adam de la Parra had amassed experience in Seville in the administration of justice and had gained a rather close acquaintance with some of those on trial before the Inquisition. In the 1620s, that court was particularly concerned with the cases of several religious who had gained reputations for holiness but were suspected of feigning sanctity and of being *alumbrados*, as well as with the alleged Judaizing of those labeled as Portuguese. The union between the Spanish and Portuguese crowns, which lasted from 1580 to 1640, increasingly brought subjects of the latter before Spanish Inquisition tribunals. Stemming in part from the varied histories of forced conversion, expulsion, and inquisitions across the Iberian Peninsula, a widespread association was made connecting the Portuguese with *converso* identity and the suspicion of Judaizing, an association often deployed in the context of refigured dynamics of rivalry for prized royal offices and for access to Court in Madrid.

The exigencies of governing a composite monarchy, increasingly global networks of trade, and the crown's financial crises made financiers and merchants with Portuguese origins into power brokers in Madrid and Seville. As Portuguese with *converso* origins gained influence at Court, accusations of suspect religious allegiance took on a new cast. In this set of circumstances, there were pronouncements against inquisitorial prosecution of the Portuguese – such as the one Páramo and his colleagues acknowledged receiving in Palermo early in the century – and intensified debates about the validity and practicality of the purity of blood statutes. The 1620s saw inquisitors arguing vehemently on both sides of that question. Henry Kamen has suggested that even toleration of an openly practicing Jewish population within Spain – in essence, a reversal of the 1492 expulsion – was discussed in these years. The first Inquisitor General of Philip IV's reign – Andrés Pacheco (1622–26) – advocated institutional reforms; he and the *Suprema* debated loosening the proofs required for inquisitorial office. It was for such inclinations that Olivares had backed Pacheco's candidacy, as he then supported reforming genealogical investigations, and the young king granted concessions and protection from the Inquisition to those *conversos* who offered him financial support.[13]

suggests that he was continuing to assemble citations and refine his arguments, perhaps with an eye toward preparing a revised second edition.

[13] Henry Kamen, "A Crisis of Conscience in Golden Age Spain: The Inquisition against limpieza de sangre," in *Crisis and Change in Early Modern Europe* (Aldershot, UK, and Brookfield, VT: Variorum 1993), 1–27. There were also *conversos* nominated for appointment to the *Suprema*. The Spanish and Portuguese Inquisitions remained discrete legal entities. See Elliott, *The Count-Duke of Olivares*, 117; and Domínguez Ortiz, "Las Presuntas 'Razones' de la Inquisición," *HIEA* 3:57–82; Patrick Williams, "A Jewish

In sum, Adam de la Parra's career began during an era of potent disputes about religious toleration and liberty of conscience, in which polemics about heresy and pollution were bound up with theological debates about charity and conversion, contests about the virtue of mercantile economics, and anxieties about pretense and deceit.

The *Pro Cautione* showed the development of the jurist's thinking, as he formulated both political strategies and stances on controversial policies. Not yet in favor with Inquisitor General Zapata (1627–32), he was learning to seek out powerful patrons and to exploit fissures in the relationship between the *Suprema* and the Inquisitor General. He made himself part of the vocal backlash against the Pacheco era; in this, he joined a chorus in which Quevedo featured prominently. He began to develop arguments that he would continue to hone throughout his career, drawing on common refrains in praising the paradigmatic statutes of Toledo's cathedral, insisting on the use of such regulations in the Inquisition, and mapping the language of political fidelity onto questions of genealogy. Starting from the title, he adamantly asserted that Christian society was in imminent danger and required defense. He warned about a crisis of imposture, arguing that it was imperative to sort Christians from those who falsely passed themselves off under that name and appearance.[14] He gave his claims a historical undergirding; even the dedication to Cardinal-Prince Ferdinand likened him to his ancestor (and presumed namesake) the Catholic King, who Adam de la Parra praised as author of the 1492 expulsion.

The treatise fanned fears of international conspiracies and fifth columns.[15] It cast the purity of blood statutes not only as a method of preventing fraud, but also as a form of instruction, rendering them the

Councillor of Inquisition? Luis de Mercado, the Statutes of *limpieza de sangre* and the Politics of Vendetta (1598–1601)," *Bulletin of Hispanic Studies* 67 (1990): 253–64; Albert A. Sicroff, *Les Controverses des Statuts de 'Pureté de Sang' en Espagne du XVe au XVIIe Siècle* (Paris: Didier, 1960); Mercedes García-Arenal and Gerard Albert Wiegers, *A Man of Three Worlds: Samuel Pallache, a Moroccan Jew in Catholic and Protestant Europe*, trans. Martin Beagles (Baltimore, MD: The Johns Hopkins University Press, 2003), chap. 1.

[14] Domínguez Ortiz identified the reforms of 1623 as the context for the treatise and termed it a lengthy exercise in "casuistry"; "Una obra desconocida," 102–13. See also Bernardo J. López Belinchón, "Olivares contra los portugueses. Inquisición, conversos y guerra económica," *HIEA* 3:511; Daviken Studnicki-Gizbert, *A Nation Upon the Ocean Sea: Portugal's Atlantic Diaspora and the Crisis of the Spanish Empire, 1492–1640* (Oxford, UK, and New York: Oxford University Press, 2007), chap. 6.

[15] For example, *Pro Cautione*, fol. 3r.

regulatory equivalent of *sanbenitos*, the Inquisition's penitential robes for convicted heretics, which remained on display in churches for decades after a reconciliation; it claimed that both the *sanbenitos* and the statutes reminded the populace of the dangers that Jews and Muslims had posed – and could still pose – to the Christian community. Thus Adam de la Parra opposed halting either practice and, in numerous such ways, tied an apology for the Spanish Inquisition into his arguments. He reported that some critics "murmured" against Spain's Inquisition, objecting that Italy had remained in the orthodox fold without anything approaching it in scale. In retort, Adam de la Parra countered that the presence of the head of the Church might sustain Italy but that France and Germany fell to heretics because they lacked an equivalent institution. He asserted that *conversos* masked the real cause of their hatred of the Inquisition, which – according to him – was that its officials possessed the truth about corrupted genealogies. After building his case for why such "truth" needed to be preserved in the inquisitorial archives, the lawyer then dedicated about half his treatise to outlining the specific methods that should be followed in investigating genealogies. He rearticulated inquisitorial procedures for a new generation of officials and social conflicts, fitting genealogical investigations into a discourse of reform that claimed to maintain justice and procedural integrity.[16] He condemned accusations of impurity that lacked sufficient proofs; he defended a range of expedient judicial practices, for instance, advocating the use of secret testimonies to facilitate inquiry into sensitive cases. Yet he did not confine himself to the Inquisition's practices; he warned the cardinal to carefully examine his priests, lest the Church begin to become secretly Jewish, that "little by little under the appearance of Christ it may be reformed toward Moses."[17] He slung accusations of rampant fraud. Rich *conversos*, he maintained, bribed officials to have their genealogies faked, while some venal courtiers sought affluent *conversos* to promote in lieu of poorer Old Christians. In such fashion, the treatise also exposed tensions around social mobility in Adam de la Parra's generation.

The young official displayed his learning, even as he glossed his choice of Latin another way: it was necessary to limit the readership for such

---

[16] This might be compared to how, the same year, Gaspar Isidro Argüello, a secretary of the *Suprema*, reissued the Inquisition's instructions and supplied an alphabetized index to aid his book's use as a reference tool; *Instrucciones del Santo Oficio de la Inquisición, sumariamente, antiguas, y nueuas* (Madrid: Imprenta Real, 1630).

[17] "vt paulatim sub specie Christi ad Moysem reformetur," *Pro Cautione*, fol. 7v.

delicate subjects to a select and educated group. He critiqued any vernacular treatment of the purity of blood statutes, including in sermons, on the grounds that even to publicize the contests about them in Spanish was to cause scandal; he reminded his audience that this had been Philip II's view. To the Court of a young king who particularly admired his royal grandfather, Adam de la Parra offered an interpretation of sixteenth-century policies tailored to the concerns of the 1620s.[18] The experience taught him that he might be able to publish his way into the elite.

Beginning in 1630, Adam de la Parra worked as an attorney not only for Seville's tribunal but also for the *Suprema* in Madrid. A mere six months after his treatise's publication, the *Suprema* commissioned him to inquire into disputes – touching on purity of blood investigations – among canons in Ávila, sending him there with a notary in September. Two canons of the cathedral chapter had brought suit against each other. As one of them – Dr. Rodrigo Gómez – was a consultant of the Inquisition, he appealed to the *Suprema* to claim jurisdiction; the council responded by sending Adam de la Parra to assess the situation. The case hinged on certain injurious words exchanged between the canons. Allegedly, Gómez had called his colleague Antonio Ciaño y Arias a "rogue friar" and a "dirty Jew," among other slurs. Gómez maintained his innocence and claimed that Ciaño continually sought "to disconcert" him. Adam de la Parra read the dossier and deposed those involved. He took the opportunity to show his diligence, scrawling marginalia around the notary's report, addressing points of procedure, and calling attention to the prime facets of the case, in order to inform the *Suprema*'s deliberations. The council ordered Gómez imprisoned in a monastery and kept there under threat of excommunication and substantial fines. When Gómez finally gave a confession in October, he still denied the slurs but rationalized that he had been concerned that when Ciaño was appointed to his prebend, the investigations into his genealogy and purity of blood had not been properly executed. The case dragged on into 1631, although Adam de la Parra's involvement did not.[19] Instead, he was finally granted a promotion, becoming the Murcia tribunal's *fiscal*.

---

[18] *Pro Cautione Christiana*, fol. 48v. On Philip IV's admiration for Philip II, and the reflection of this in treatises of his era, see Kagan, *Clio and the Crown*, chap. 6.

[19] "pícaro fraile," "sucio judío," "descomponer," AHN, Inq., leg. 2120, caja 2, exp. 5. He was back in Madrid in October.

THE POWER TO DISCERN: INQUISITORS, COURTIERS, AND CHARLATANS

As a *fiscal*, Adam de la Parra promoted a specific role for the Inquisition in his society: the institution most suited for the work of discernment. For inquisitors, this meant the judicial attempt to sort truth from falsehood, orthodoxy from heresy. From the fifteenth century, an ample religious literature had treated the problem of distinguishing experiences of the divine from those of the demonic from those with more mundane causes; by the sixteenth century, inquisitors had established their right to bid for jurisdiction over cases of pretense to holiness. For Adam de la Parra and his colleagues, this charge resonated with other contemporary trends: the writing of histories, which had blossomed in sixteenth-century Spain, was framed as the pursuit of truth; the literary flourishing of the day hinged on the motifs of *engaño* and *desengaño*, of deceiving and undeceiving. A high-profile scandal over spiritual imposture was underway in Madrid just as Adam de la Parra took up his post in Murcia. In 1628, the start of contentious trials of nuns of the Benedictine convent of San Plácido – following an outbreak of demonic possession and raising issues of religious prophecy, divination, *alumbradismo*, and false sanctity – gave renewed force to arguments for fixing an inquisitorial presence in Madrid. To seek to establish inquisitors as experts in the theological problem of "discernment of spirits" was both an attempt to sway public perceptions of the holy and, simultaneously, to advance a contentious jurisdictional claim that such judgment belonged more properly to their courts than to other mechanisms of religious discipline.[20]

The question of who was qualified to engage in the work of religious justice was at issue for the *fiscal* in other ways. In 1632, Adam de la Parra was not yet a priest. And his recent promotion was in jeopardy, as the Inquisitor General had issued an order that all *fiscales* had to be ordained within six months of taking office. Nevertheless, he was attempting to obtain a benefice in Soto's church (which was under the bishop of Calahorra's jurisdiction), perhaps seeking to succeed his uncle in office.

---

[20] For a particularly lucid explanation of discernment of spirits, see Anne Jacobson Schutte, *Aspiring Saints: Pretense of Holiness, Inquisition, and Gender in the Republic of Venice, 1618–1750* (Baltimore, MD, and London: The Johns Hopkins University Press, 2001). For an approach to the concepts of *engaño* and *desengaño*, see Margaret R. Greer and Elizabeth Rhodes, "Volume Editors' Introduction" and "A Note on the Translations," in María de Zayas y Sotomayor, *Exemplary Tales of Love and Tales of Disillusion*, ed. and trans. Greer and Rhodes (Chicago: University of Chicago Press, 2009), 41.

Claiming to have been approved as the first candidate and then cheated out of both the office and its income, he sought to initiate a lawsuit through inquisitorial channels. In April 1633, he still had not taken orders, and he protested that this was because he did not have the title to ecclesiastical rents that would support him.[21] He requested a year – and was granted six months – to continue pursuing a benefice in the diocese of Calahorra and to complete his examination for ordination.

In Murcia, Adam de la Parra became the tribunal's chief combatant in a jurisdictional competition that pitted the Inquisition against the bishop of Cartagena. At stake were both the local exercise of religious authority and the broader contest over how best to correct error. As I have noted in earlier chapters, persistent tensions existed between bishops and inquisitors over the authority to inquire into, preach against, and absolve heresy. In this case, the bishop was Antonio Trejo de Sande, who had been in office since 1618, and the quarrel had begun before the *fiscal's* appointment. Nevertheless, Adam de la Parra intensified the conflict, composing numerous refutations of the bishop's arguments between 1632 and 1634 and arguing for the jurisdictional preeminence of the tribunal in any matters involving suspected heresy. As he had done in his defense of the purity of blood statutes, he sought to construe an open and disputed issue as one that had long been settled. To this end, he argued that the roles of bishop and inquisitor were long fixed: as soon as the papacy delegated authority to the Spanish Inquisition, Spain's bishops could no longer be identified as inquisitors. He asserted that the continued abundance of heretics throughout the Christian world proved that the "correction and vigilance" of bishops had failed; framing this failure as collective and permanent cast inquisitors' work as all the more essential and legitimate.[22]

To the supreme aggravation of the tribunal, Trejo apparently published edicts in which he called himself both "bishop" and "inquisitor," publicizing his authority as the ordinary inquisitor in his diocese. In one manuscript brief – addressed to the Inquisitor General – Adam de la Parra took a

---

[21] He was also attempting to improve his accommodations in Murcia, seeking to move to one of the Inquisition's lodgings so as not to be housed in the midst of the noise of the marketplace; May 15, July 7, and July 8, 1632, holograph, AHN, Inq., leg. 2809.

[22] There is a cache of documentation about the conflict (in which he figures prominently) in BNE, MS 6157, fols. 1r-94r, here fol. 43v. See also María Luisa de Miguel González, "El Problema de los Conflictos Jurisdiccionales (Memorial de Antonio Trejo a Felipe IV)," in *La Inquisición Española: Nueva visión, nuevos horizontes*, ed. J. Pérez Villanueva (Madrid: Siglo Veintiuno, 1980), 83–88. On the larger debate, Stefania Pastore, *Il Vangelo e la Spada. L'Inquisizione di Castiglia e i Suoi Critici (1461–1598)* (Rome: Edizioni di Storia e Letteratura, 2003), 349–404.

striking selection from 1 Kings 15 for the epigraph: "Because it is like the sin of witchcraft, to rebel: and like the crime of idolatry, to refuse to obey."[23] With his choice of scriptural text, he dressed the bishop in the trappings of heresy and linked the prelate's supposed crime – overstepping the boundaries of his episcopal office – to a whole vocabulary of transgression and inversion, conjuring up the demonic and the treasonous. He made the issue one of pretense: "the truth of this case was that this criminal (*reo*) put the said title [of inquisitor] in emulation of the inquisitor's voice, so that giving the bishops as sharing the name, he might decrease [the name] of inquisitor and increase [the name] of bishop."[24] Opposing the claims of the bishop's *fiscal*, he contended that the inquisitors were not required either to consult with the bishop before promulgating edicts or sentences or obtain his permission to publish censures; he cited papal bulls as justification. He added that the bishop's opinion was also irrelevant because, with three inquisitors in Murcia's tribunal, they already had the ability to break a tied vote.[25]

The conflict touched on the order of procedure and of public functions and divided local authorities. The bishop (who was a prominent Franciscan) managed to persuade the majority of the religious orders – with the exception of the Jesuits – to his cause, while Murcia's cathedral chapter and city council aligned with the tribunal.[26] Adam de la Parra described the bishop's actions as calculated to sabotage the court and anyone associated with it, even accusing him of fomenting hatred among the regular clergy, who "he has rewarded as enemies of the Inquisition." The *fiscal* painted himself as the portrait of impartial diligence, a "minister who is greatly pained by this rivalry."[27] Murcia's council expressed its desire to see him rewarded, while the chapter praised his "good relations"

[23] "Quasi peccatum est ariolandi repugnare, et quasi scelus idolatriae nolle acquiescere. 1 Kings 15[:23]." BNE, MS 6157, fols. 30r–38r. I have used the customary English, if "ariolandi" inclines more specifically toward divination.

[24] "la verdadeste caso fue que este reo puso dicho titulo en emulacion de la voz inq[uisid]or para que dandole participes a los obispos del nonbre descaeciese el de Inq[uisid]or y creciese el de obispo." Ibid., fol. 41r.

[25] Ibid., fol. 8r.

[26] Adam de la Parra to Inquisitor General, March 13, 1634, AHN, Inq., leg. 2810; Entrambasaguas, *Varios Datos*, doc. XVIII; see also BNE, MS 6157, fol. 30r. Cf. the perceptive analysis of how – in later sixteenth-century Murcia – trials divided local elites, in Jaime Contreras, *Sotos contra Riquelmes: regidores, inquisidores, y criptojudíos* (Madrid: Anaya and M. Muchnik, 1992).

[27] "ha premiado por enemigos de la Inquisicion" and "ministro a quien tanto duele esta emulación," August 2, 1634, AHN, Inq., leg. 2810; Entrambasaguas, "El Inquisidor," doc. XXVII.

with other authorities as well as "his studies, good learning, and upright manner of proceeding."[28] The tribunal's own secretaries, however, told a different story, that of a *fiscal* who

has had many encounters and troubles with the Lord Inquisitors and with all of us and other gentlemen and principal people of this city, putting us in danger of going astray, for being by nature hotheaded and rash, if he were to come to this Inquisition [as an inquisitor], it is certain he would be the cause of great unrest and some misfortune could occur.[29]

Adam de la Parra's opposition to Trejo had even further dimensions; he saw the bishop as inclined toward suspicious religious figures. The Seville Inquisition tribunal had given Adam de la Parra an education in the pursuit of "false saints." There, in his first year as an attorney, he encountered "Brother Juan," the subject of an inquisitorial investigation. That man had gained a reputation for holiness based, in part, on letters that a certain Mother Luisa had written to him and he reported both personal and spiritual communication with the *beata*. In 1623, the tribunal issued edicts targeting *alumbrado* sects, and Adam de la Parra reported his opinion that Brother Juan was a fake, and so it seemed to follow that "if M[other] Luisa was holy and her revelations true, it cannot be believed that God would permit her to deceive herself in supporting the said false and feigned sanctity."[30] He suspected her by association. Brother Juan de Jesús María – a tertiary of unspecified religious order – appeared in the *auto de fe* of November 1624, found guilty of having deprecated saints and images; used and solicited alms improperly; and claimed that food, drink, and embracing women facilitated prayer and spiritual union. By then an attorney for the tribunal, Adam de la Parra was likely well acquainted with many of the prisoners and the details of their trials, experience that would

[28] "buena correspondencia"; "sus estudios, buenas letras y recto proceder." January 3 and 9, 1634, AHN, Inq., leg. 2810; Entrambasaguas, "El Inquisidor," docs. XV(a) and XV(b).

[29] "ha tenido muchos enquentros y disgustos con los Señores Inquisidores y con todos nosotros y otros caballeros y jente principal desta ciudad poniéndonos en ocasión de perdernos, por ser de natural collérico y arroxado y si viniesse a esta Inquisición, es cierto sería causa de mucha inquietud y podrían suceder algunas desgracias." September 26, 1634, AHN, Inq., leg. 2810; Entrambasaguas, "El Inquisidor," doc. XXVIII(b).

[30] "si la M. Luisa fuera santa y sus revelaciones ciertas, no se puede creer que permitiera Dios que se engañara en apoyar dicha santidad falsa y fingida." Quoted in Patrocinio García Barriuso, O.F.M., "El Milagrismo. Sor Luisa de la Ascensión, La Monja de Carrión. Fr. Froilán Díaz y el Inquisidor Mendoza," *HIEA* 1:1097. García Barriuso wrongly terms Adam de la Parra an inquisitor in 1620, when he was still merely an *abogado* of the tribunal. Seville's inquisitors wrote to the *Suprema* that they had been totally occupied with Hermano Juan's case, September 25, 1623, AHN, Inq., leg. 2960.

inform his approach to affairs in Murcia.[31] The Mother Luisa in question
was a well-known figure in seventeenth-century Spain: Sor Luisa de la
Ascensión (c. 1565–1636) – Luisa de Colmenares Cabezón before her
profession – was a nun, and eventually an abbess, in the Franciscan
convent of Santa Clara in Carrión de los Condes, a town to the north of
Palencia, on the pilgrimage route to Santiago de Compostela. She had
gained popular fame as a holy woman and significant interest from the
royal Court.[32] In 1633, the majority of Murcia's Inquisition cases dealt
with charges of minor witchcraft, a few with renegades. Nevertheless, in
1634, another matter caught the eye of the *fiscal*: Valencia's tribunal
mentioned the circulation of "some small manuscript books touching on
the wonders (*maravillas*) of Mother Luisa de Carrión."[33]

Not only had Adam de la Parra been suspicious of Mother Luisa for
more than a decade, Bishop Trejo was also associated with the *beata*'s
growing cult. Trejo cut an imposing figure: the son of the counts of Oliva,
prominent in the Franciscan order. Made secretary-general in 1609, and
from 1610 to 1613 commissary general of the Indies, he had advocated for
the order's role in missionary activity and the canonization of Franciscan
martyrs. It was as vicar general – an office he held from 1613 to 1618 – that
he became involved with Mother Luisa. She had already been receiving
patronage from the counts of Lemos – close relatives of Philip III's favorite,
the duke of Lerma – before their departure for Naples in 1610. Because she
was a Franciscan nun, it fell to Trejo to investigate, and so in 1614, he went
personally to question her about her seemingly miraculous fasting and
visions.[34] In Adam de la Parra's reasoning, then, Trejo had tacitly licensed
the *beata* when he chose not to publicly censure her.

Trejo and Mother Luisa shared other spiritual affinities, as both were
devotees of the cult of the Immaculate Conception – the doctrine that Mary

[31] *Memorias de Sevilla (1600–1678)*, ed. Francisco Morales Padrón (Córdoba: Publicaciones
de Monte de Piedad y Caja de Ahorros de Córdoba, 1981), 33–35, 41–48. On the
seventeenth-century trials of *beatas*, see also Mary Elizabeth Perry, *Gender and Disorder
in Early Modern Seville* (Princeton, NJ: Princeton University Press, 1990), chap. 5.

[32] On Madre Luisa, see García Barriuso, "El Milagrismo. Sor Luisa," *HIEA* 1:1093–1103.

[33] "unos librillos manuscritos tocantes a las maravillas dela Madre Luysa de carrion," June 4,
1634, AHN, Inq., leg. 2810.

[34] García Barriuso, *La Monja de Carrión*, 184–85; *EE*, 136, 163. In 1612, he prepared a brief
supporting the canonization of Peter Baptist (martyred with twenty-five others in Japan in
1597); it was presented to Paul V by the Spanish ambassador and Francisco Peña, the
famous inquisitorial commentator and longtime auditor of the Rota (the martyr was
beatified in 1627 by Urban VIII). Lázaro Lamadrid, O.F.M., ed., "Report on the
Missions by the Franciscan Commissary General of the Indies (1612)," *The Americas*
2.4 (1946): 489–97.

was conceived free from original sin – which gained the crown's support but bitterly divided the religious orders in the early seventeenth century.[35] Both Philip III and Philip IV seem to have sent Trejo to Rome to lobby for the doctrine and the universal celebration of its attendant feast; as a bishop, he energetically promoted the cause in his diocese, building a chapel devoted to *la Purísima* in Cartagena's cathedral, where he would be buried in December 1635, and having her proclaimed patroness of the cathedral and the city in 1624. Trejo's consecration as bishop had taken place in 1618 in the prominent convent of the *Descalzas Reales* in Madrid, before members of Philip III's Court. His brother, moreover, had initially found a prized place in the administration of the new king; Gabriel Trejo y Paniagua (1562–1630), a cardinal influential in both Madrid and Rome, had once been a member of the *Suprema* and was made president of the Council of Castile in 1627. Olivares, however, soon perceived Cardinal Trejo to be opposed to his reforming program, and in November 1629 he was dismissed from Court; he died en route to his diocese of Málaga. Bishop Trejo had thus likely lost much of his political capital by the 1630s, while Mother Luisa was perhaps also perceived as a critic of Olivares.[36] In

35 On the cult at Court, see del Río Barredo, *Madrid, Urbs Regia*, 186–87; on the theological stakes, see Thomas M. Izbicki, "The Immaculate Conception and Ecclesiastical Politics from the Council of Basel to the Council of Trent: The Dominicans and Their Foes," *Archive for Reformation History* 96 (2005): 145–70. For M. Luisa's stance, see García Barriuso, *La Monja de Carrión*, 134. I have not seen evidence indicating Adam de la Parra's position. His friend Francisco de Rioja wrote in favor of the doctrine in 1621, drawing upon the purported Dextro chronicles, but did a *volte face* and joined the anti-Dextro faction within a few years; see Kagan, *Clio and the Crown*, 260–61.

36 Bishop Trejo seems to have been an extraordinary ambassador to Rome in 1618–20 and 1627–30; *Legatio Philippi III et IV ... De definiendâ Controuersiâ Immacullatae Conceptionis B. Virginis Mariae* (Louvain: Henricus Hastenius, 1624); Antonio Palau y Dulcet, *Manual del librero hispano-americano* (Barcelona: A. Palau, 1948–77), 24:93. For more on the Trejos and on his first embassy to Rome, see Silvano Giordano, ed., *Istruzioni di Filippo III ai suoi ambasciatori a Roma, 1598–1621* (Rome: Ministero per i beni e le attività culturali, 2006), LXXVII–LXXIX, 128–32. On his career in Cartagena, see Javier Nadal Iniesta, "Fray Antonio de Trejo: El Primer Príncipe Contrarreformista de la Diócesis de Cartagena," in *Congreso Internacional Imagen Apariencia. Noviembre 19, 2008–Noviembre 21, 2008* (Murcia: Universidad de Murcia, 2009); María Trinidad López García, "El auge del dogma de la Inmaculada Concepción auspiciado por el franciscano fray Antonio de Trejo, obispo de Cartagena, y la implicación del concejo de Murcia, a principios del siglo XVII," in *La Inmaculada Concepción en España: religiosidad, historia y arte: actas del simposium, 1/4-IX-2005*, ed. Francisco Javier Campos y Fernández de Sevilla (San Lorenzo de El Escorial: Ediciones Escurialenses, Real Centro Universitario Escorial-María Cristina, 2005), 1:119–38, both available at http://dialnet.unirioja.es/. On Cardinal Trejo, see Elliott, *The Count-Duke of Olivares*, 305–6, 393–94; José López de Toro, "Respuesta del cardenal Trejo a una carta de Tomás Campanella,"

this new constellation of forces, Adam de la Parra had an opening to pursue both his jurisdictional disputes with Trejo and his suspicions about Mother Luisa.

And so when the *fiscal* saw the news from Valencia in 1634, he wrote to the *Suprema*, urging it to direct that tribunal's inquisitors to more fully investigate not only the distribution of manuscripts about Mother Luisa, but also the claims contained in them. Then, he drafted another report, informing the Inquisitor General that he had reviewed some of the materials in question and had found that "in them were some things worthy of revision, that in a less applauded person than this nun would have sufficed to become a demonstration [of suspicious beliefs]."[37] Adam de la Parra – long dubious about her orthodoxy, much less her sanctity – became one of the primary engines behind the initiation of an Inquisition trial against Mother Luisa in 1635. Trejo's death at the end of that year likely diminished resistance to the prosecution, yet the *fiscal* persisted in seeking a connection between the *beata* and the bishop. He reported finding – and so, by implication, having searched for – evidence of devotion to Mother Luisa in the deceased prelate's personal effects. He continued his involvement in the case after his arrival at Court, at least through the spring of 1637, although the nun had died in 1636. He suspected her of involvement with sects of *alumbrados* in Seville, and was particularly disturbed by crosses bearing her name or that of Mary or Jesus that she made and gave to her admirers.[38] Ultimately, Mother Luisa's trial lasted fourteen years, well beyond Adam de la Parra's death as well; as a result of her being suspected of feigning sanctity and of being an *alumbrada*, the Inquisition prohibited any veneration of her and destroyed most of the images and accounts of her holy life.

By 1634, moreover, there was a new Inquisitor General and Adam de la Parra was working to gain his notice. Antonio de Sotomayor (1557–1648) had assumed the office in the summer of 1632, after holding significant

Revista de Estudios Políticos 122 (1962): 161–78; Sánchez Rivilla, "Inquisidores," 425; on Mother Luisa, see Entrambasaguas, *Varios Datos*, 73.

[37] "en ellos hubo algunas cosas dignas de repaso, que en persona menos aplaudida que esta religiosa bastaban para hacerse demostración," Adam de la Parra, July 10, 1634, holograph, AHN, Inq., leg. 2810; Entrambasaguas, "El Inquisidor," doc. XXIV. On the case, see AHN, Inq. leg. 3708, caja 1, nos. 1–2; leg. 3704, caja 1, no. 1.

[38] AHN, Inq., leg. 3704, caja 1, no. 1, fol. 335v; no. 3, fol. 162r. According to García Barriuso, on December 3, 1636, he signed a seventy-seven folio response to the opinion of two Franciscan consultants of the Inquisition and was also mentioned in the trial papers in March 1637, "El Milagrismo. Sor Luisa," 1093–1103; García Barriuso, *La Monja de Carrión. Sor Luisa de la Ascensión Colmenares Cabezón* (Madrid and Zamora: Ediciones Monte Casino, 1986), 280–85.

posts in the Dominican order and, most recently, serving as the king's confessor.[39] The *fiscal*'s activities in Murcia not only drew from his own experience but were also calibrated to an audience at Court. He cast local affairs as having far-reaching implications. In positioning himself as correcting the negligence of a neighboring tribunal – which had failed to investigate the growing cult around a holy woman with a reputation for miracles – he suggested a broader approach to the problem of false sanctity, as he understood it. In Adam de la Parra's thinking, if the Inquisition decided not to investigate such figures and writings, if it chose not to initiate trials or to suspend open proceedings, it could be read in the public arena as tacit approval. He opposed a model of religious discipline – exemplified by Trejo – that privileged fraternal correction, whereby bishops and religious examined their subordinates and associates and persuaded them away from error. And he pursued a concerted strategy of publicizing his opinions and activities. He sent a variety of letters and briefs through the Inquisition's institutional channels, and he seems also to have turned to print in the Trejo affair; Murcia's two inquisitors asked that he be reimbursed for the costs of printing a brief in defense of the tribunal and praised the erudition, style, and legal knowledge evident in it, claiming it not only aided them but also held "great importance for the rest of the tribunals."[40]

At the end of the spring of 1634, the *fiscal* also advertised his role in the assertion of jurisdiction over the capital trial of two familiars. He apprised the Inquisitor General of the situation and prepared a brief publicizing the Inquisition's side of the case. The pair were brothers, don Diego and don Jorge Bernal, who had been involved in a heated ball game that escalated into a brawl, leaving don Pedro Celdran dead. Murcia's royal judges claimed the right to try the case, taking control of the persons and goods of the brothers Bernal and accusing them of premeditated murder. In their defense, the *fiscal* argued that the witness testimony was insufficient, implied that the murder had been committed in self-defense, and stressed the obligations of the fraternal bond. He claimed to have printed his brief

---

[39] On Sotomayor's long career – Provincial of the Dominicans in Castile (1615–19), a theologian and consultant for the Inquisition, member of the *Suprema* (1622), royal confessor, and Inquisitor General (1632–43) – see Sánchez Rivilla, "Inquisidores," 272–73. For an approach to theological currents at Court, Orietta Filippini, *La coscienza del re: Juan de Santo Tomás, confessore di Filippo IV di Spagna, 1643–1644* (Florence: Olschki, 2006).

[40] "mucha importancia para los demas tribunales." May 15, 1634, AHN, Inq., leg. 2810. See also leg. 2809 and Entrambasaguas, *Varios Datos*, 66–74.

because the issue was "so serious," elevating the broader jurisdictional questions in the affair.[41] In Murcia, Adam de la Parra increased his skill as a publicist, defending inquisitorial prerogatives.

One motivation for all this activity was the hope of promotion, for which the *Suprema* was considering him at the start of 1634. In a flurry of correspondence that divided the local elite, Murcia's inquisitors took perhaps the most politic course: they recommended his appointment as an inquisitor, but in another tribunal.[42] At the same time, Adam de la Parra was trying another tack. He had written a second Latin treatise. Entitled the *Conspiratio Haeretico-Christianissima* (the *Heretical-Most Christian Conspiracy*), it was a foreign policy diatribe against the French, filled with the language of anti-heretical combat, as its name suggested. He was also in pursuit of greater quarry: the notice of the royal favorite. Seeking to show his talent as a polemicist, that spring he sent copies of his manuscript to Olivares and to Sotomayor, identifying himself on the title page as both Murcia's *fiscal* and an *abogado* for the *Suprema*. To Sotomayor, he explained: "since there is little to do in this Inquisition, I have busied myself in writing."[43] Thus, Adam de la Parra simultaneously marked himself as energetic, efficient, and diligent – able to battle for jurisdiction with bishops and royal judges, search out heretical threats, and compose treatises at the same time – and distinguished himself from the Murcia tribunal, which he hinted was lethargically administered. He received permission to publish the book in Murcia; by October, the count-duke was praising the treatise in conciliar deliberations.

Olivares proposed creating a special junta of historians to engage a propaganda war with France, an imperative that only gained urgency after the French declaration of war on April 1, 1635. By the end of that month, as Richard Kagan has shown, Adam de la Parra was in Madrid, a

<hr>

[41] "tam grave," June 23, June 30, 1634, and Adam de la Parra, holograph, May 30, 1634, AHN, Inq., leg. 2810; see also May 15 and August 2, 1634, AHN, Inq., leg. 2810; Entrambasaguas, "El Inquisidor," doc. XXVII; for the printed materials, BNE, MS 6157, fols. 47r-51v, 85r-96r. I have not consulted a similar case in which he seems to have been involved, of a secretary of Toledo's tribunal also accused of murder, 1636–37, AHN, leg. 2098, exp. 5, indexed at http://pares.mcu.es/.

[42] September 26, October 16, and October 17, 1634, AHN, Inq., leg. 2810; Entrambasaguas, "El Inquisidor," docs. XXVIII(a), XXIX.

[43] "Como en esta Inquisición hay poco que hazer, me he occupado en escrebir." Adam de la Parra, holograph, May 23, 1634, AHN, Inq., leg. 2810; Entrambasaguas, "El Inquisidor," doc. XIX. It was printed as Adam de la Parra, *Conspiratio Haeretico-Christianissima in Religionem Imperivm, Hispanvm Austriacos & fiduciales eorum Iure sacro, Oeconomico Politico Canonico Ciuili, & à temporum euentibus damnata* (Murcia: Luis Berós, 1634).

participant in the newly created committee.[44] It was again a Latin polemic that had moved his career forward, as he catapulted from being a second-tier Inquisition official in a peripheral city to part of the talent assembled around Olivares. Still, he did not dispense with his inquisitorial career. He was made an inquisitor in 1636: attached to the Toledo tribunal, but with attendance at Court in Madrid. That same year, the archbishop of Toledo – to whom he had dedicated the *Pro Cautione* six years before – awarded him a prebend in the cathedral whose revenues he could enjoy in Madrid, and which his nephew would even be able to inherit in 1645. He seems to have secured further income – again without residence – from Málaga's cathedral.[45] It was a promising arrival at Court.

A WORLD OF CONSPIRACIES

Adam de la Parra imbibed and disseminated a logic of conspiracy. Although the specters of collusion and deception had haunted his *Pro Cautione*, he developed these themes even more explicitly in the *Conspiratio*. He continually emphasized the scope of threat, declaring that Spain and Catholicism were under attack from all sides. When he presented his motivations for writing to Olivares, he claimed that "these times, and the tempests in which one sees the Church, moved me to take up my pen." In this climate, he explained that he had chosen to write "in Latin because I speak with all the princes of Europe, putting the interests of each one before his eyes, in case he may let himself be taken in by the vague and false promises of the French."[46] The book's orientation was clear from its title, as a "heretical-most Christian conspiracy" suggested nefarious alliances between heretics and the "Most Christian King," the French crown's honorific. He alleged that France conspired with the Low Countries, undermining Spain's territorial and economic security, even pulling the

---

[44] Kagan, *Clio and the Crown*, 214–23. Elliott analyzed this via the nuncio's report of April 1, 1635, and a *consulta* of the Council of State, October 17, 1634, "El Conde Duque y Quevedo," in *Memoriales y Cartas del Conde Duque de Olivares*, ed. J. H. Elliott and José F. de la Peña (Madrid: Ediciones Alfaguara, 1978–80), doc. XV, 2:185.

[45] Entrambasaguas, "El Inquisidor," 190–91; Juliá Martínez, *La Amistad*, 9–13; Crosby, ed., *Nuevas Cartas*, 111.

[46] "los tiempos y tempestades en que se ve la Iglesia me movieron a tomar la pluma," and "en latín porque hablo con todos los principes de Europa poniéndole a cada uno su mina delante los ojos en caso que se deje llevar de las promesas tam vaga e inciertas de franceses." May 23, 1634, AHN, Inq., leg. 2810.

papacy into its schemes, and proposed building a new alliance with the Holy Roman Empire to defend Habsburg interests and the Church.[47]

With the *Conspiratio*, Adam de la Parra established himself as part of the current of thought, now referred to as Catholic reason of state, inspired, in part, by Giovanni Botero, whose *Della Ragione di Stato (On the Reason of State)*, first published in Italian in 1589 and soon incorporated into Spanish theorizing, was among the most famous rebuttals to Machiavelli's view of political life. He shared tenets of Botero's thought, such as an acute sense of the dangers of scandal, against which even the most prudent of rulers must guard vigilantly, or that divine providence moved events and moral failings drove the downfall of states and princes. Yet he also differed from Botero. The Piedmontese theorist had critiqued Spain's expulsion of its Jewish population in 1492, suggesting that it had caused economic harm, whereas Adam de la Parra rendered it central to his narratives of Spanish royal virtue and Catholic governance.[48]

Adam de la Parra marshaled the customary authorities – biblical references, Church fathers, canon law, exempla from classical antiquity – in order to tell a history of decline: when heretics triumphed within France, sedition and corruption began to blemish even the highest levels of society. And so he painted Cardinal Richelieu, Louis XIII's favorite, as a perversion of the priesthood, "audacious in war, unable to bear peace."[49] He contended that a tyranny of ambitions, particular interests, and corrupt clergy had led the pious French king astray. He used the language of pastoral care and of heretical combat to amplify the dangers of such a state of affairs. Princes became either "shepherds" or "wolves"; tyranny, heresy, and sedition were aligned with plague and contagion. He judged France fickle and inconstant. Again, fears of imposture came to the fore. He claimed that the French covered their heretical conspiracy with a "mask painted in false colors," and that their claims to virtuous action were but "feigned and empty pretexts" and "invidious deceptions" (*engaños*). Despite

---

[47] Cf. arguments of Philip III's era for a broader policy of Habsburg alliances, described in Magdalena Sánchez, "Spain, Austria, and the Bohemian and Hungarian Successions," *Sixteenth Century Journal* 25 (1994): 887–903.

[48] For example, "for licentiousness drove the kings and the decemvirs from Rome, introduced the Moors into Spain and lost Sicily for the French." Giovanni Botero, *The Reason of State*, trans. P. J. and D. P. Waley (New Haven, CT: Yale University Press, 1956), chaps. 1.4, 5.9, pp. 5, 111. On such political thought, see Kagan, *Clio and the Crown*, chap. 6; Robert Bireley, *The Counter-Reformation Prince. Anti-Machiavellianism or Catholic Statecraft in Early Modern Europe* (Chapel Hill and London: The University of North Carolina Press, 1990), 45–71.

[49] "audaz en la guerra, sin poder soportar la paz," *Conspiración*, trans. Roda Aguirre, 19.

appearances, he argued that military and diplomatic machinations had destabilized France, for "nothing is steadfast in the conspiracy."[50]

He summoned Roman history to his side, invoking the examples of the emperors Constantine and Jovinian to argue that it was useless to attempt to negotiate with heretics or to seek to correct them with clemency, that compromise would bring only ruin, and that his audience should "know for the future that tigers are not tamed outside of the cave nor do old foxes forget their cunning."[51] He expressed deep skepticism about the sincerity of conversions and about the wisdom of toleration or alliances that crossed religious boundaries. Thus, Spain became the true defender of Catholicism and a more desirable ally, elevated both by good works and by comparison to the failings of France.

In a brief dedication from the author to his *librito*, or little book, Adam de la Parra personified the *Conspiratio* as his champion, about to enter battle, warning him that the ire of Gaul would seek to burn him. He assumed the language of military honor, equated writing to combat, and evoked images of both book banning and martyrdom, all the while making his aspirations clear, as he charged his manuscript to "Go, then, and grow more than a small name and make a great house for your master."[52] The post to which Adam de la Parra was appointed in June 1636 – inquisitor of Toledo's tribunal with attendance at Court – was the most recent permutation of the Inquisition's official presence in Madrid, first framed that way in the titles conferred in 1633. For the new inquisitor, the prospects must have seemed promising: two incumbents had just been promoted directly to the *Suprema*, after only three years of service. Adam de la Parra and his new senior colleague made an unsuccessful bid that year to establish an independent tribunal; by the 1650s and 1660s, the practices of a separate court would be mostly in place, even though the official letter of foundation was not issued until 1752. As María del Pilar Domínguez Salgado has explained, the Inquisition in Madrid – town and Court – was subject to a kind of "double" positioning: tied to Toledo but also under the sway of the

---

[50] More fully: "Así retiren estos fingidos y vacíos pretextos y arranquemos a los envidiosos engaños franceses la máscara pintada de falsos colores y aparecerán no sólo diferentes, sino aun opuestas a aquellas que alegan. . ." And: "nada es firme en la conspiración," ibid., 43, 59.

[51] "conozca para el porvenir que no se amansan los tigres fuera de la cueva ni las viejas zorras olvidan su astucia," ibid., 244. The "zorra" here is a female fox, an image that carried with it a strong connotation of sexual decadence.

[52] "Vete, pues, y crece más de un pequeño nombre y haz gran descendencia de tu señor." Ibid., 7.

Suprema. There was a predictable hum of jurisdictional contests, and inquisitorial officials there enjoyed a status higher than their nominal rank.[53] Toledo's judges, the council, and the Inquisitor General all had significant, and often competing, interests in Madrid's inquisitorial business. Adam de la Parra had thus acquired a contested but potentially powerful office.

Once a judge, he continued to work on cases similar to those that had occupied him earlier in his career. He stepped into a series of trials already underway in Madrid and Toledo, of a range of individuals – most but not all of them women, as there was even a mat maker who hosted impromptu theater in his home – who had cultivated vibrant reputations for holiness.[54] The behavior of the judges in these trials pointed to contestation over what an inquisitorial verdict meant in the public arena, struggles given greater urgency by the proximity to Court. From the inquisitors' perspective, when they penanced someone for false sanctity, they had completed an act of spiritual discernment and exercised their judicial discretion. If people continued to venerate those whom the inquisitors had sentenced or even were known to be investigating – valuing their own powers of discernment over those of the tribunal – it was an implicit insult to inquisitorial dignity and, according to Adam de la Parra, a failure to establish authority. Such trials were part of ongoing conflicts about which model of correction – confessional or courtroom, private or public reconciliation and penance – was more appropriate for which religious errors.

In Adam de la Parra's courtroom, some of the accused sought to use these tensions to make a viable defense. One of the Madrid *beatas*, María Bautista, heard – and recorded – inner voices while in the Inquisition's

---

[53] They were also drawn from a higher social profile. The two inquisitors appointed in 1633 and promoted in 1636 were Juan Ortiz de Zárate and Dr. Astiria; the other inquisitor in 1636 was Juan de Sosa, who died by year's end. Here I follow Domínguez Salgado, "Inquisidores y fiscales"; Contreras and Dedieu, "Estructuras Geográficas."

[54] On these trials, see Andrew W. Keitt, *Inventing the Sacred: Imposture, Inquisition, and the Boundaries of the Supernatural in Golden Age Spain* (Leiden and Boston: Brill, 2005); Lara Mary Diefenderfer, "Making and Unmaking Saints in Seventeenth-Century Madrid" (PhD diss., University of Virginia, 2003); María José del Río Barredo, "Representaciones Dramáticas en Casa de un Artesano del Madrid de Principios del Siglo XVII," in *Teatros y Vida Teatral en el Siglo de Oro a través de las Fuentes Documentales*, ed. Luciano García Lorenzo and J. E. Varey (London: Tamesis Books Limited, 1991): 245–58. On similar concerns about how political prophecies both captured popular attention and swayed royal opinion, see Richard L. Kagan, *Lucrecia's Dreams: Politics and Prophecy in Sixteenth-Century Spain* (Berkeley, Los Angeles, and Oxford, UK: University of California Press, 1990).

prison, which she claimed instructed her to seek Adam de la Parra and Olivares as spiritual directors and persuade them to treat her as fathers rather than as judges. She sought to shift the equation, to create a relationship that would make her a pious penitent rather than a presumed criminal. At the same time, she emphasized her reverence for inquisitorial authority and her disdain for charlatans, striking a stance of humility and submission to correction, to distance herself both from other presumed heretics and from the appearance of *vanitas* – the vain pursuit of her own fame.[55] Thus, she wrote to Adam de la Parra: "My Lord Inquisitor, since I saw you when I came to tell you how wrong the errors of that woman of San Gil seemed to me I have seen you as a spiritual father, and I cannot cease calling you father."[56] María Bautista's plea also gave a flattering account of Adam de la Parra's status in Madrid, associating him with Olivares and hinting that he was gaining a reputation for his work.

Adam de la Parra fashioned himself as an inquisitor dedicated to the renewal of his office and so sought to align with reforming currents at Court. In the late 1620s, Olivares had enumerated the corrupted administration of justice – reduced to such a condition that the powerful avoided prosecution and public sins were ignored – as among the existential threats to the kingdom.[57] Throughout his career – as attorney, *fiscal*, and finally inquisitor – Adam de la Parra subscribed to an ideal of diligence, corresponding in his own hand and annotating the margins of depositions, trial records, and correspondence to an unusual degree. He returned again and again to charges of dissimulation against those reputed to be holy women and to allegations of Judaizing. By the late 1630s, special juntas had become a hallmark of the political order, the crown was at war with France, and the situation in both Portugal and Catalonia was precarious. A substantial backlash against earlier reforms had occurred, and Adam de la Parra had become particularly involved in investigating merchants and financiers of Portuguese origin. In 1637, he had a hand in the sequestration

---

[55] On these kinds of dynamics, see Alison Weber, *Teresa of Ávila and the Rhetoric of Femininity* (Princeton, NJ: Princeton University Press, 1990); Jodi Bilinkoff, *Related Lives: Confessors and Their Female Penitents, 1450–1750* (Ithaca, NY: Cornell University Press, 2005); Kagan, *Lucrecia's Dreams*.

[56] This is Keitt's transcription and translation – from what he identifies as her autobiography – in "'Inventing the Sacred': Religious Enthusiasm and Imposture in Mid-Seventeenth Century Madrid" (PhD diss., University of California, Berkeley, 1998), 261. Diefenderfer also uses this letter as evidence that popular support for a *beata* could persist and even grow in the face of official condemnation.

[57] Here I follow Elliott's description of the reforming program of 1629, in *The Count-Duke of Olivares*, 382.

of the goods of the Lisbon banker Jorge de Paz, in part an attempt to force a
subsidy to the crown. In 1639, Olivares and Sotomayor convened a junta –
meeting in the Inquisitor General's house – to probe those with trading
contacts with France or other "rebel provinces." The committee included
Adam de la Parra and José González, a close associate of both the count-
duke and influential Portuguese.[58]

The inquisitor used his investigative experience to inform his political
writings, while simultaneously using his treatises to argue for the necessity
of the Spanish Inquisition. He continued to develop the ideological stances
exposed in the *Pro Cautione* and the *Conspiratio* and in his memoranda
against Trejo and Mother Luisa. His *Comercio Impedido (Trade
Forbidden)* – a pamphlet dated in Madrid, January 30, 1640 – indicated
his increasing knowledge of French politics and opposed trade with the
crown's enemies, especially in wartime.[59] The pamphlet sought to shape
debates about economic policy, while following the stylistic conventions of
a sensitive communiqué; he printed it anonymously and noted that he had
not named the individuals involved in the cases to which he would refer.
He hinted at the authority, expertise, and privileged knowledge he drew
from Inquisition trials. He asserted the truth of his arguments and the
purity of his intentions, even calling God as witness that he had refrained
from including any news or political concerns tangential to the question at
hand and that he was moved only by the public good, by the desire to
protect the Catholic religion and serve the crown and its good and loyal
vassals (in contradistinction to its hidden enemies within the realm), and
not by enmity, envy, or desire for vengeance.[60]

Adam de la Parra broke the *Comercio Impedido* into four sections –
charting who conducted such business, what types of trade were involved,
how the commerce had developed, and what crimes had already been

---

[58] López Belinchón, "Olivares contra los portugueses," 516; and *Honra, Libertad y
Hacienda (Hombres de Negocios y Judíos Sefardíes)* (Alcalá de Henares: Instituto
Internacional de Estudios Sefardíes y Andalusíes, Universidad de Alcalá, 2001), 312;
Lea, *History of the Inquisition*, 3:280.

[59] I attribute it to him, following Schaub's judgment and my observation of the inquisitor's
signature on the copy in the BL; for copies of the pamphlet, BNF, MS 4-OC-427; BL Eg.
339, fols. 321–39. The latter is signed on the final page, in what I think is the inquisitor's
hand. See also Jean-Frédéric Schaub, *Le Portugal au temps du Comte-Duc d'Olivares,
1621–1640: le conflit de juridictions comme exercice de la politique* (Madrid: Casa de
Velázquez, 2001), 78, 288. Daviken Studnicki-Gizbert has recently treated the pamphlet as
the work of José Pellicer, *A Nation Upon the Ocean Sea*, 167. On Pellicer, and his tendency
to inflate his own bibliography (for instance, in claiming to have written Adam de la Parra's
Conspiratio), see Kagan, *Clio and the Crown*, 235–44.

[60] *Comercio impedido*, fols. 2r, [19]r.

proved – all to persuade against commercial relations with France, Holland, and their associates, and to criminalize those who engaged in such trade. His economic arguments were dressed in language long associated with polemics against usury and heresy. Imported luxury goods were like "drugs"; the trade of manufactured goods for gold and silver (rather than for other goods) was inherently perverse as healthy commerce rested on trade in kind; the import of finished goods and export of raw materials were destroying the artisanal knowledge of Spain; such trade, releasing the monarchy's gold and silver, was akin to bloodletting (he used the verb *desangrar* repeatedly). He wrote a narrative of decline. Robust kingdoms had turned against themselves to such extent that even the heart was infected: Madrid's silversmiths now "pervert their office, and are not occupied in making vases, but rather in unmaking chains, plates, jewels, and making doubloons to deliver to the merchants," who in turn took the coin to France.[61] The final metaphor of his treatise was especially vivid. He likened the monarchy to Tantalus – condemned to the eternal torment of reaching for something just beyond his grasp – letting gold and silver slip through its fingers and failing to profit from the commerce it licensed; encoded in this was the further indictment that Spain too suffered divine punishment.[62]

All this, he argued, was facilitated by insidious dissimulation. Gold and silver were smuggled out by subterfuge. Worse, he contended, the agents of this illegitimate transfer of Spanish wealth to Dutch and French hands masqueraded as loyal subjects of the crown, all the while maintaining ties in enemy territory and so profiting regardless of the monarchy's fortunes, equally from piracy as from licensed trade. Thus, Adam de la Parra located a conspiracy at the heart of Spain's economic and military woes. The key to finding a remedy, he reasoned, was to search for deceivers, for those who seemed to be one thing but were of another nature entirely. He regarded with suspicion the commercial balancing acts of merchants from Lisbon to Rouen and beyond, judging their economic dealings to be evidence of malicious plotting. He depicted the Portuguese men of commerce as the worst threat, as they found it "more useful to conduct business with a mask," a practice in which – he claimed – they were masters, even teaching the Dutch to behave in similarly dishonorable ways. He classified them as of another order than the Genoese, who had also siphoned wealth from the

---

[61] "preuierta[n] su oficio, y no se ocupe[n] en hazer vasos, sino en deshazer cadenas, tejos, joyas, y hazer doblones para entregar a los mercaderes," ibid., fol. 7v.
[62] Ibid., fol. [19]r.

crown, but at least had done so as allies and had funded pious Catholic works with some of their treasure.[63]

Adam de la Parra then offered a second act of undeceiving: he found the Portuguese men of affairs to be conspirators in both trade and religion. He described them as systematic Judaizers who lived openly as Jews – with other names, contracting marriages, attending and building synagogues, funding dowries in Jewish communities – among their relatives in Amsterdam, Venice, and other locations that he repeatedly enumerated, but who dissimulated when in Spain's kingdoms. He assaulted them with a barrage of anti-Jewish rhetoric, construing them as the antithesis of loyal vassals. He provoked fear, casting commerce as a mere pretext and the true motivations of the Portuguese as hatred of Christians and the desire to erect synagogues throughout the Catholic world. In this logic, the use of ciphers in business letters, the lack of distinguishing dress, and any concern with the safety of material fortunes became sinister. In the world of Adam de la Parra's pamphlet, the Portuguese merchants were diabolically ambitious and astonishingly successful, already "the lords of the sea."

These arguments were draped on a historical frame. The destination of the profit extracted from the Indies was made a gauge of the health of the body politic and the actions of Philip IV's forebears were held up as both example and warning. Adam de la Parra constructed his case around two signal dates: 1492 and 1628. The first he made into a model, advancing a causal relationship between Ferdinand and Isabel's expulsion of the Jews and the economic boom that had come from access to the Indies. The latter date marked the start of the current crisis, when Portuguese merchants were granted freedom of movement in the crowns of Castile and Aragon. Adam de la Parra insisted that Philip II had apprehended the growing danger to his kingdoms but not its gravity, or he would have acted. He argued that the trade with Protestants permitted in the treaties of 1604 – the very policy that had torpedoed Páramo's prosecution of Englishmen in Palermo – had been a crucial error.[64] He cast the

---

[63] "... teniendo por mas vtil negociar con mascara ..." ibid., fol. 9v; see also fol. 15v. For one analysis of how merchants in France shifted between Protestant and Catholic identities – including members of a prominent family of *converso* origin who maintained their ties to Spanish relatives – and used a variety of methods (from false documents to working through Iberian intermediaries) to pursue trade in Spain and the Spanish Americas, see Gayle K. Brunelle, *The New World Merchants of Rouen 1559–1630* (Kirksville, MO: Sixteenth Century Journal Publishers, 1991), 42–48, 85–86, 150, 158.

[64] "dueños de la mar," *Comercio impedido*, fol. 14v. See also fols. 3r, 5r, 9v, 10v, 15v, 16r, 17r. On the negotiations of this era, see Juan Ignacio Pulido Serrano, "La expulsión frustrada. Proyectos para la erradicación de la herejía judaica en la Monarquía Hispana," in *La Declinación de la Monarquía Hispánica en el Siglo XVII*, ed. Francisco

decree of 1628 as tragically ironic, as it coincided with a royal prohibition on trade with the crown's enemies; intending to exclude them, the king had instead invited them into the fold.

As a result, what 1492 meant – at a century and a half's distance – became a focal point of the pamphlet. Adam de la Parra painted it as inaugurating a flourishing age, in which divine favor created trade beneficial to the crown and its vassals. He explained that commerce in the Indies was then allowed only to Castilians and Aragonese, because of the reciprocity of the union of their crowns, in which the latter had also admitted the former to Naples and Sicily. Nevertheless, the seeds of the crisis were already planted in the 1490s; he perpetuated rumors that the expulsion was incomplete, that those who had dissimulated in their baptism remained, along with their property. He mentioned that some considered this the cause of the crown prince's death and attributed the death of Portugal's Prince Alonso to the permission his father had given to Jews fleeing to Africa to halt there briefly. There were also notable silences: Granada was nowhere in evidence, neither was Islam much of a factor, nor was there much history before 1492, save a vague gesture to the refrains of anti-Jewish polemic used to justify the expulsion.[65] Thus, Adam de la Parra sought to assemble evidence of a providential logic behind events – that divine wrath or pleasure promptly followed from royal actions.

He rejected outright the kind of religious toleration practiced elsewhere but argued that the current status of the Portuguese in Spain was even more intolerable: "to secretly cloak them with the certainty that they are Judaizers, and that they deceive Christians with the dress and external appearances that they do today, is more fatal than admitting them in the dress of Jews."[66] He proposed that ultimately their trade should be blocked and their commercial networks in Spanish lands dismantled; he opined that pardons should not be granted. He offered the Spanish Inquisition as an antidote, an institution designed to discover deceptions, unmasking the Portuguese and carefully assembling evidence of merchants' connections to enemy lands; Portuguese inquisitors, on the other hand, he classified as part of the problem, if perhaps unintentionally so.[67]

José Aranda Pérez (Cuenca: Ediciones de la Universidad de Castilla-La Mancha, 2004), 891–904.

[65] Ibid., fol. 2r-v. He also emphasized the transience of worldly affairs, for example, fol. 3v.

[66] "Dissimularlos en secreto con certeza de que son Iudaiçantes, y que engañan a los Christianos con el trage, y exterioridades en que oy estan, es mas fatal que admitirlos en trage de Iudios." Ibid., fol. 17r.

[67] When they gave sentences of exile to Angola or Brazil, they had, Adam de la Parra claimed, helped entrench a global mercantile network of Judaizing Portuguese. Ibid., fol. 10v.

The pamphlet also publicized and justified the recent actions of some inquisitors, pointing to an exceptional *auto de fe* held by the tribunal in Lima the year before. On January 23, 1639, inquisitors in that city had put on display seventy-three men and women, sixty-three of them convicted as Judaizers, of whom eleven were burned at the stake. The judges referred to them as part of the "Great Complicity," the term itself indicating their claim to have found a hidden network of Portuguese Jews, merchant conspirators with treasonous ambitions.[68] Adam de la Parra raised the specter of a fifth column, asserting that "what was revealed" in Peru was a warning that Portuguese factors of the Dutch and French were preparing footholds there as they had done in Brazil. He made inquisitors seem central to the health of the monarchy.

Even as the *Comercio Impedido* had much in common with other contemporary writings, it was shaped by individual experience. Adam de la Parra was not merely reporting – and disseminating – news that circulated at Court; rather, he was intimately involved in handling trials of Portuguese there. The investigations that grew into the "Great Complicity" had begun in Lima in April 1635, the same month Adam de la Parra arrived in Madrid. Over the next two decades, the persecution spiraled into other tribunals: Cartagena de Indias, Mexico, Seville, Toledo. Just weeks before the pamphlet's printing, on January 14, 1640, Adam de la Parra and his colleague Francisco Salgado Taboada wrote to the Inquisitor General, informing him that they had just reviewed testimonies received from Lima.[69] The evidence, they asserted, showed networks linking Lima, Valladolid, Bordeaux, and the Court, among other locales. When they looked at the associations between trading partners, the pair of inquisitors saw proof of a company

[68] "Gran Complicidad" is often translated as the "Great Conspiracy." I have chosen "complicity" as it preserves better, I find, the resonances with the language of the law. Seventeenth-century Spanish Inquisition documents made frequent reference to *complices*, accomplices, as in a letter that reviewed the procedures used in one of the Lima trials; Isidoro de San Vicente, September 15 [July 10], 1642, AHN, Inq., leg. 1648, exp. 4. For recent approaches to these events, see Studnicki-Gizbert, *A Nation Upon the Ocean Sea*; Irene Silverblatt, *Modern Inquisitions: Peru and the Colonial Origins of the Civilized World* (Durham, NC: Duke University Press, 2004); Miriam Bodian, *Dying in the Law of Moses: Crypto-Jewish Martyrdom in the Iberian World* (Bloomington: Indiana University Press, 2007); Nathan Wachtel, *La Foi du souvenir. Labyrinthes marranes* (Paris: Seuil, 2001). See also my Chap. 5.

[69] Educated at Salamanca, Salgado had been a minor official with the *Suprema* in the mid-1610s, then an inquisitor in Cuenca and Valladolid; formally receiving the title of inquisitor with attendance at Court in July 1640, he was promoted to the *Suprema* in 1643 (first nominated the council's *fiscal* in July 1642), and died February 16, 1644. Sánchez Rivilla, "Inquisidores," 410; Domínguez Salgado, "Inquisidores y fiscales," 244.

of heretics. Lima's inquisitors, they reported, had charted individual lives back six or eight years and concluded that the merchants were in "continuous movement." As a result, Adam de la Parra and Salgado argued that these accomplices posed a potentially explosive threat to the Church and requested that all related letters from the tribunals be funneled through them in order to better monitor suspicious persons, especially those fleeing from enemy countries.[70] With this letter and the subsequent pamphlet, Adam de la Parra sought to position himself as an architect of the Inquisition's pursuit of the Portuguese.

He quickly gained a reputation for these efforts. In a diary entry for January 17, José Pellicer de Ossau y Tovar – an associate of Adam de la Parra's – noted:

The Inquisitions of Lima and Cartagena, in the Indies, have written to His Majesty how, in the *autos* they have executed, they have discovered that many Judaizing Portuguese had not only transgressed against our holy Catholic faith, but also had significant connections with the synagogues of Holland and the Levant, aiding them against Spain and Christianity with warnings and monies. As his [Inquisition] tribunal had already punished that which touched on the Catholic [religion], His Majesty should take care to put a remedy for the future in political matters. From here resulted the order that, that same day in Spain, the parcels of letters of all those Portuguese who had [such] connections be opened, [which] have verified not only [the affair] of the Indies, but also uncovered a certain cipher with which they communicate with the synagogues of Holland ... The verification of this has been committed to the Inquisitors Adam de la Parra and Villoslada.[71]

Pellicer circulated an image of Adam de la Parra toiling to defeat well-organized conspirators. By 1642, another observer at Court would

---

[70] Adam de la Parra and Salgado to Inquisitor General, January 14, 1640, AHN, Inq., lib. 1041, fol. 448r (it was filed by the *Suprema* in the materials related to Lima's tribunal).

[71] "Las Inquisiciones de Lima i Cartagena de las Indias han Escrito a Su Magestad cómo, en los Autos que han celebrado, han descubierto que muchos Portugueses Judaiçantes no sólo delinquían contra nuestra Santa Fe Católica, pero que tenían grandes Correspondencias con las Sinagogas de Olanda i de Levante, asistiéndolas contra España i la Cristianidad con avisos i Dineros. Que ya su Tribunal havía castigado lo que le tocava en lo Católico; que Su Magestad cuidasse de poner la Emienda para lo de adelante en lo político. De aquí resultó mandar que se les abriesen en vn mismo día en España los Pliegos a todos los Portugueses que tenían Correspondencia. Han hallado verificado no sólo lo de las Indias, pero descubierto cierta Cifra con que se entiended con las Sinagogas de Olanda; ... La averiguación desto se ha cometido a los Inquisidores Adán de la Parra i Villoslada." José Pellicer de Tovar, *Avisos: 17 de Mayo de 1639 – 29 de Noviembre de 1644*, ed. Jean-Claude Chevalier and Lucien Clare (Paris: Éditions Hispaniques, 2003), 1:81–82. I have not been able to identify "Villoslada." If Pellicer was in error, he might very well have been referring here to Salgado Taboada; alternately, it seems plausible that he might have meant Juan Bautista de Villadiego, also involved in the inquisitorial pursuit of the Portuguese.

identify him as behind the pursuit of the businessmen (*hombres de nego-cios*).[72] The inquisitor, meanwhile, had set about reviewing earlier cases, requesting that numerous files housed in Toledo's Inquisition archives be copied and sent to him in Madrid, sometimes specifying that they were "necessary for the complicity."[73] His extensive marginalia on the Inquisition's criminal trial of two Portuguese merchants in 1639 and 1640 suggest an attempt to track the itineraries and associates of the accused. The legal proceedings – like the polemics – intertwined economic, political, and religious concerns, as the merchants were tried on charges of contraband and smuggling rather than heresy.[74]

Significant resistance to Adam de la Parra's actions came from several quarters. In March 1640, Sotomayor received a petition from Portuguese men of affairs, claiming that the judge had done them grave injury and offense: "in every occasion offered and that he could procure, he has shown aversion and capital hatred to their nation, and continuing the ill will he holds toward them, he has tried to discredit their faith and loy-alty."[75] The inquisitor was described as a liability for the crown, his enmity – phrased so as to make it a disqualifying offense – leading to losses of revenue and affronting the honor of good subjects. There was an attempt to recuse him from the contraband cases, and the Inquisitor General or members of the *Suprema* seem to have intervened to suspend these trials. By October, Adam de la Parra's activities had stalled in the face of opposing pressures. Apparently rebuked by Sotomayor, he sent a sharp retort: "in this state Your Illustriousness reprimands me that I do not work, and I, although I come each morning … most of the time I am idle, well against my nature, and if I work in the trials of the Portuguese, nothing will happen, and if in those of the *beatas* there will be outcries," followed – he contended – by a reversal of the sentence, thus leading the people to venerate them even more.[76] He marveled that despite discrediting by the

---

[72] "el que hizo tomar las cartas alos h[omb]res de negocios." Luis Antonio Morales, November 4, 1642, RAH 9/3663, exp. 124, fol. 742r.

[73] "le a menester para la conplicidad." November 14, 1639, AHN, Inq., leg. 3109. There was similar phrasing in April 30, 1641, AHN, Inq., leg. 3110.

[74] Criminal trial of Vasco Fernandez Diaz and Geronimo Lopez de Salcedo, AHN, Inq., leg. 54, exp. 10.

[75] "todas las ocasiones que se han ofreçido y ha podido procurar, ha mostrado auersion y odio capital a su naçion, y continuando la mala voluntad que les tiene ha yntentado desacreditarlos en la fee y lealtad …" March 7, 1640, AHN, Inq., leg. 3110.

[76] "en este estado me reprehende su il[ustrísim]a de que no trabajo y yo aunque vengo todas las mañanas … lo mas del tiempo estoi ocioso bien contra mi natural, y si obrare en causas de Portugueses abra nulidad, si en las de beatas clamores." Adam de la Parra, holograph,

Inquisition, the people of Madrid still flocked to those who had been judged spiritual impostors; when the account of yet another *beata*'s miracles circulated, he even hesitated to denounce it publicly, fearing that this would only grant her greater popular renown.[77] Depicting his judicial practice as altered by local resistance, like many polemicists of his day, he suggested a breakdown in the systems of governance; 1640 was a catastrophic year for the Habsburg monarchy. Just weeks before the publication of the *Comercio Impedido*, in mid-January, a joint Spanish-Portuguese naval force had failed to dislodge the Dutch in Brazil (where they had established a foothold in 1630), although the news of that debacle would not yet have reached Madrid. With Spain at war with France, over the course of the year, the economic structure, centered on trade with the Americas filtered through Seville, showed signs of disintegration: it was the first year that no silver fleet arrived. Revolt in Catalonia amplified the conflict with France, and dissent in Portugal culminated in a coup d'état on December 1.[78]

Against this backdrop, there was also evidence of friction between Adam de la Parra and his colleagues. To wit, on April 30, 1641, the three inquisitors in Toledo petitioned Sotomayor to slow Adam de la Parra's and Salgado's zealous reopening of cases and repeated requests to make copies of proceedings that the Toledo tribunal had suspended. They reported that Salgado had requested a trial that they had decided to halt not out of negligence, but because of the "effort and care" that they devoted to trials of faith. They asked that the inquisitors in Madrid be required to obtain the express permission of the Inquisitor General before ordering any further papers or trial records from the tribunal archives.[79] On the surface, this conflict over institutional powers was a tug-of-war over which inquisitors had the authority to proceed in an open case; the Toledo inquisitors cleverly implied that Sotomayor could not possibly have authorized such breaches of procedure and hierarchy. Other components of this conflict can be conjectured. The judges in Toledo might have wanted to slow particular cases or prevent the initiation of others because

October 22, 1640, AHN, Inq., leg. 3110. This letter is cited by both Keitt and Diefenderfer and excerpted and translated in Keitt, "Inventing the Sacred" (1998), 74–75.

[77] Here he referred to Ana Maria del Carpio; October 22, 1640, AHN, Inq., leg. 3110.

[78] On the events of 1640, see J. H. Elliott, *Imperial Spain, 1469–1716* (New York: St. Martin's Press, 1964), 341–49.

[79] "el desbalo y cuydado," Lic. Pedro Díaz de Cienfuego, Dr. Martín Real, and Dr. don Baltasar de Oyanguron to Inquisitor General, April 30, 1641, AHN, Inq., leg. 3111, [fol. 229r].

they had grown skeptical of the methods being used to pursue false sanctity trials or cases against the Portuguese, whether as Judaizers or as smugglers.

Evidence suggests the divisions between inquisitors in this era. One of the Toledo inquisitors, Martín Real, had nearly two decades of experience by the time he signed the letter to Sotomayor in 1641. In the 1620s, Real had spent four years as Inquisitor General Pacheco's secretary and had served as the commissary at Court. Pacheco made Real an inquisitor in Sicily, and he advocated for the powers and jurisdiction of that tribunal, returning to Madrid to lobby for it much as Páramo had done three decades before. A seasoned inquisitor, Real had been aligned with different currents of thought within the Inquisition than had Adam de la Parra, and he associated with those who questioned the purity of blood regulations. Promoted to the *Suprema* in January 1643, he was commissioned in March to conduct a visitation of the tribunals in Lima and Cartagena de Indias, and so in effect to conduct an internal review of the Great Complicity trials. Real tangled not only with Adam de la Parra and Salgado, but also with other associates of theirs. Juan Bautista de Villadiego, for example, had investigated Portuguese merchant communities as early as 1633, when Sotomayor sent him into France as a specially commissioned inquisitorial agent, leading to his brief imprisonment in Rouen. In Madrid, he had worked with Adam de la Parra in 1639 as the *fiscal* in María Bautista's trial. Made an inquisitor of Cartagena de Indias in 1641, he was appointed at the height of the fears of Portuguese conspiracy. Moreover, Villadiego seemingly engineered the revocation of Real's commission in 1644; the visitor left the Caribbean port while Villadiego remained.[80]

The politics of the Portuguese question were complicated. By late 1640, the revolt simultaneously made conspiratorial arguments more persuasive and soon diminished their importance, as the union of crowns dissolved.

---

[80] Real returned to Madrid where he died in 1647. Villadiego had begun as the Inquisition secretary in Llerena in 1610, before becoming a notary in Seville in 1617, where he likely met Adam de la Parra. The two seem to have arrived in Madrid at the same time, as Villadiego was made a secretary of Toledo's tribunal, with residence at Court, in 1634, and then a *fiscal* there in October 1638. From Cartagena de Indias, he was transferred back to Spain, to Cuenca, and granted a retirement on March 31, 1650. Domínguez Salgado, "Inquisidores y fiscales," 228, 246–47; Sánchez Rivilla, "Inquisidores," 3:400; Manuel Rivero Rodríguez, "La Inquisición Española en Sicilia," *HIEA* 3:1217; Keitt, *Inventing the Sacred*, 130–31; Gayle K. Brunelle, "Migration and Religious Identity: The Portuguese of Seventeenth-Century Rouen," *Journal of Early Modern History* 7.3–4 (2003): 283–311; C. Roth, "Les Marranes à Rouen. Un chapitre ignoré de l'histoire des Juifs de France," *Revue des études juives* 88 (1929): 113–55.

As Olivares's influence waned and opposition to his policies mounted, some Portuguese *conversos* managed to consolidate positions of privilege as crown financiers, whereas others became scapegoats in trade wars with northern Europe.[81] Pellicer sought to make pursuit of the Portuguese into a mark of honor. In late May 1641, the diarist, like the inquisitor, argued that there was a dangerous and growing *converso* faction at Court. He reported that the Portuguese pretender, the duke of Braganza, was in business with Portuguese Jews, having offered them forty years of "liberty of conscience," and that the bishop of Málaga had been dispatched as a special ambassador to Rome to oppose these negotiations. He claimed that those "of the Nation" (i.e., the Portuguese) in Madrid were busily attempting to leverage the situation to their advantage to gain concessions in Spain, proposing "extravagant conditions" and to "moderate the severity of the Inquisition." He advertised Adam de la Parra's combat against the Portuguese, noting that the inquisitor had written a "well-learned memorandum" on the subject, perhaps referring to the *Comercio Impedido* of the previous year.[82]

THE HIRED PEN: POLEMICIST, PROPAGANDIST, POET

Court life changed some aspects of Adam de la Parra's writings. Whereas his first two printed works had been issued in Latin and with his full name, the three later treatises that can be attributed to him were somewhat different; each was in the vernacular and none printed his name. In 1640, his *Comercio Impedido* and his *Súplica de Tortosa* – Tortosa's plea, so called, meant to undermine the ideological bases of the Catalan revolt – appeared anonymously, and a 1642 polemic against the

---

[81] See Elliott, *The Count-Duke of Olivares,* 117–19, 303–4, 449–50. For a detailed analysis of anti-*converso* arguments and persecution during this era, see López Belinchón, "Olivares Contra Los Portugueses"; and *Honra, Libertad y Hacienda*; Pulido Serrano, *Injurias a Cristo. Religión, política y antijudaísmo en el siglo XVII. Análisis de las corrientes antijudías durante la Edad Moderna* (Alcalá de Henares: Instituto Internacional de Estudios Sefardíes y Andalucíes, Universidad de Alcalá, 2002); Studnicki-Gizbert, *A Nation Upon the Ocean Sea,* chap. 6; Jonathan I. Israel, *Empires and Entrepots: The Dutch, The Spanish Monarchy and the Jews, 1585–1713* (London and Ronceverte: The Hambledon Press, 1990), especially chap. 14; see also his *European Jewry in the Age of Mercantilism 1550–1750* (Oxford, UK, and Portland, OR: The Littman Library of Jewish Civilization, 1998).

[82] "condiciones extravagantes," "templar la severidad de la Inquisición," and "bien docto memorial," Pellicer, *Avisos,* 1:239.

Portuguese rebels bore only his initials.[83] Olivares surrounded himself with a circle of lettered men who could act as polemicists, seeing their treatises as useful weapons against the crown's enemies. When Adam de la Parra joined the newly formed junta of historians in 1635, he went to work alongside the royal secretary Francisco de Calatayud, Alonso Guillén de la Carrera, Jusepe de Nápoles, and Juan de Palafox y Mendoza. The young man from Soto had perhaps taken such men as models. Calatayud was a poet and had first attracted Olivares's gaze in Seville. Guillén de la Carrera was also a jurist, and Olivares had spotted the Aragonese Palafox quite early in the latter's career. Although the *Conspiratio* moved Adam de la Parra into such favored company, the count-duke soon recalled all copies for further revisions, and there is no evidence that Adam de la Parra produced a second edition or a vernacular translation. John Elliott suggested that Olivares rethought the wisdom of disseminating such arguments in Latin, explicitly seeking an international audience. Nevertheless, after 1635, Adam de la Parra's inquisitorial career was intertwined with his activities as what the seventeenth-century Jesuit writer Baltasar de Gracián called a "hired pen," to borrow Richard Kagan's category for such propagandists at the court of Philip IV.[84]

Writing in an era of expanding publicity wars, these hired pens defended royal policy in print and sought to make their own careers as courtiers on the strength of their skill at such polemical combat. Dropping his public claim to authorship reflected Adam de la Parra's experiences in Madrid; he no longer needed to try to attract attention from elite courtiers, and there was a collaborative element to this kind of writing, as all three of his vernacular publications originated in juntas convened to address signal threats to the monarchy. At Court, it was known what he had written and he was protected from the royal prohibition on anonymous publication; also, propaganda was perhaps more effective if not so immediately associated with an individual author and his particular passions and motivations.

The junta of 1635 was charged to build an arsenal of arguments against the French and drew upon Adam de la Parra's *Conspiratio* in doing so.

---

[83] *Súplica de la muy noble y muy leal ciudad de Tortosa* (Tortosa: Pedro Martorell, 1640); *Apologetico contra el Tirano y Rebelde Verganza, y Conivrados Arzobispo de Lisboa, y sus Parciales* (Zaragoza: Diego Dormer, 1642).

[84] Elliott, *The Count Duke of Olivares*, 449, 489; Kagan, *Clio and the Crown*, chap. 6. See also José María Jover, *1635: Historia de una Polémica y Semblanza de una Generación* (Madrid: CSIC, Instituto Jerónimo Zurita, 1949); and, now, Arredondo, *Literatura y Propaganda en Tiempo de Quevedo*.

That work was further reflected in the *Comercio Impedido*, which was likely an outcome, in part, of the junta Sotomayor convened in 1639 to investigate enemy trade. The *Súplica* resulted from yet another junta, as Olivares charged Adam de la Parra, Pellicer, and Francisco de Rioja to rebut the Catalan rebels' claims. All three did so in short order, but the inquisitor's contribution, published in Tortosa in December 1640 and noted in Pellicer's *Avisos* in late November, was the first one printed. Adam de la Parra's final published work, *Apologético contra el Tirano y Rebelde Verganza* – opposing Braganza as a "tyrant and rebel" – was once again a response to a royal call to (written) arms, to delegitimize Portugal's revolt. Published in Zaragoza in February 1642 and dedicated to Olivares, it was perhaps also an attempt to recuperate his standing at Court in the wake of the conflict over his investigations of Portuguese merchants.[85] Rivalry and collaboration were comingled in these endeavors. Adam de la Parra has been described as the "only and best friend" of Rioja, Olivares's client and librarian. Likewise an inquisitor, Rioja was less active in that work; although promoted to the *Suprema*, he never participated in the business of the council, instead accompanying Olivares into exile in 1643.[86] Although Pellicer warmly praised Adam de la Parra in his *Avisos*, he also tried to appropriate some of the inquisitor's writings, claiming to be their true author.

Like many of his contemporaries in the era of the *arbitristas*, Adam de la Parra urged that a wide variety of social, economic, and religious ills be remedied. He developed his writing in the realm of political history, marrying positions about the exigencies of the state to an anti-heretical vocabulary. There was a tension between artifice and the act of undeceiving in these writings. His pamphlets claimed to draw aside the masks worn in politics and diplomacy. Yet the *Comercio impedido* maintained that the delicacy of affairs and the protection of reputations required the elision of specific names and references, and the *Súplica* feigned to be something other than what it was, posing as a plea for royal pardon composed on behalf of the loyal citizens of the city of Tortosa, which had fallen to the

---

[85] Pellicer, *Avisos*, 1:239. The dedicatory letter was dated in Zaragoza, February 28. On Spanish propaganda in the Portuguese revolt, see Schaub, *Le Portugal au temps du Comte-Duc d'Olivares, 1621–1640*; Fernando Bouza Álvarez, *Imagen y propaganda. Capítulos de Historia Cultural del Reinado de Felipe II* (Madrid: Akal Ediciones, 1998). The inquisitor appears only in the former.

[86] "único y mayor amigo," Elliott, "El Conde Duque y Quevedo," 2:185; Kagan, *Clio and the Crown*, 238–40. Sánchez Rivilla, "Inquisidores," 401–2.

rebels in July.[87] In that work, Adam de la Parra engaged in another kind of discernment: sorting true history from false, and, with it, political legitimacy from false pretensions to authority. The *Súplica* was a rejoinder to a Catalan declaration of liberty, published as the "Catholic Proclamation," the confiscation of which Olivares simultaneously directed Adam de la Parra to supervise.

It marked a more historical turn for the inquisitor, as each side made the ninth-century taking of Barcelona the origin of the current order. In their account of the city's 801 Christian reconquest, the rebels presented their traditional privileges as gained in that moment of victory, when they accomplished an act of "self-liberation" from the Muslims. A whole political logic flowed from this view, as their acceptance of a king became an issue of election rather than conquest. To salvage the place of Catalonia in the Catholic Monarchy, Adam de la Parra located the true source of the troubles once again in conspiracy, depicting the rebels as fed by the false arguments of the French historian Jacques Cassan.[88] He used evidence similar to what Páramo had presented to justify the Sicilian *Monarchia*, offering a litany of marriages, treaties, and conquests. He concluded that the Reconquest had made the Catalans into vassals, their many privileges stemming from the generosity of the king; he thus made Philip IV the source of Catalan liberties rather than a tyrant who had usurped them. He alleged that the Catalans' great mistake lay in succumbing to innovations (*novedades*), which had led them into the trap of sedition. He accused their leaders of rampant corruption: feigning divine approval for their cause, falsifying geography and royal privileges, committing sacrilege in their churches. Even daring to call their rebellious manifesto a "Catholic Proclamation" became a mark of perversion. The inquisitor allowed that they had indeed had their moment of splendor when Count Raymond

---

[87] For the attribution of the *Súplica*, see María Soledad Arredondo, "Noticia de la *Súplica de Tortosa* (1640), atribuida al Inquisidor Juan Adam de la Parra" *Cuadernos de Historia Moderna* 22 (1999): 139–56. Pellicer listed Adam de la Parra among those writing against the Catalans, November 27, 1640, *Avisos*, 1:167. For a detailed examination of both sides of this polemic, see Jesús Villanueva López, *Política y Discurso Histórico en la España del Siglo XVII. Las polémicas sobre los orígenes medievales de Cataluña* (Alicante: Universidad de Alicante, 2004). See also J. H. Elliott, *The Revolt of the Catalans: A Study in the Decline of Spain, 1598–1643* (Cambridge, UK: Cambridge University Press, 1963); and *The Count-Duke of Olivares*; Arredondo, "Armas de Papel: Quevedo y sus contemporáneos ante la guerra de Cataluña," *La Perinola: Revista de investigación quevediana* (1998): 117–54.

[88] On Cassan, the similarity of the rhetoric to François Hotman's *Francogallia*, and the use of history to argue for political legitimacy, see Villanueva López, *Política y Discurso Histórico*, 11–12, 136.

Berenguer threw off the "Moorish yoke," but that their virtues then grew dormant, and they had neglected the lessons of history, which demonstrated the "alterations and conversions of Empires." He asked: "These memories, what do they serve the Greeks, Arabs and Goths today, commanded by other peoples ... They should have been to serve only as breath, in order that the valor concealed in their descendants be stirred to similar deeds."[89] Adam de la Parra used the memory of the Reconquest to indict the revolt; he claimed that the Catalans had betrayed their Catholic history and ignorantly fallen prey to French wiles, trading away the fidelity, loyalty, and constancy of good vassals for sedition, heresy, and treason.

He had an argumentative framework at the ready for the next revolt. The *Apologético* turned the vocabularies of tyranny, dissimulation, and Judaizing against the Portuguese rebels, again implicating the meddling French.[90] Once more, he took aim at a specific treatise: the manifesto of the Portuguese friar Mascareñas. He sought to brand Braganza as a tyrant, repeatedly alleging that he manipulated religion to his own ends and that heretics and rebels were the only ones served by not exposing his abuses. Botero had observed that "Aristotle advises the tyrant to do his utmost to be thought pious ... It is, however, extremely difficult for one who is not truly religious to be thought so, for nothing lasts so short a time as pretence."[91] The inquisitor asserted Philip II – and by extension his grandson – as the true heir of imperial virtue and attributed his acquisition of Portugal to divine providence; the king became the "restorer of Portugal, as Charlemagne was of Italy," its liberator as Augustus purportedly was of Rome. This was paired with an ambivalent justification of tyrannicide. Citing Deuteronomy 23, Adam de la Parra claimed it was worse to offend religion than to kill a king who failed to defend the faith or actively conspired against it. He quoted Pope Honorius's commentary on Psalm 5 to the effect that murder was not a sin when done in the service of God's people, as in David's killing of Goliath or Judith's of Holofernes.[92]

He borrowed from Augustine to assert that "Braganza [had] defected from the general pact of human society with his inobedience" to God,

---

89 "mudanças y conversiones de Imperios"; "Estas memorias, de que sirven oy a Griegos, Arabes y Godos imperados de otras gentes? ... Deuieran seruir solo de aliento, para que el valor supresso en los decendientes concitasse a hechos semejantes." *Súplica*, fol. 8v.

90 The metaphor of storms and a darkened sky (or heavens) also underscored the threat to religion, for example, *Apologético*, fol. 4v.

91 Botero, *Reason of State*, chap. 2.15, p. 63.

92 "Restaurador de Portugal, como Carlo Magno de Italia." Adam de la Parra, *Apologético*, fols. 10v, 23r, 47v.

forfeiting any obedience due to him.[93] He repeated Mascareñas's reasoning why Braganza's rule was legitimate: he had been generally acclaimed as a ruler, possessed a hereditary right, and was favored by God, as signs and celestial oracles showed. This, Adam de la Parra retorted, was an invitation to tyranny that smacked of the Calvinists' argument that all unjust kings should be obeyed if they were popularly acclaimed. He countered with an example taken from Suetonius, explaining that even if Caesar's rule was later perpetuated by tyranny, and even if he had taken the helm of Rome by force, he had been chosen to rule spontaneously and his claims had been judged legitimate by the prudent men present and so his murder was unjust.[94] He entered complicated argumentative terrain as he sought to distinguish Philip II's legitimate claim to the Portuguese throne from Braganza's, which he termed all illusion and conspiracies; the popular support and the celestial signs were hoaxes that masked all manner of dealings with heretics. He made Braganza resemble a heresiarch who abused religion and "vomited" irreverence at every turn.

In print, the inquisitor made himself a judge of recent events, exposing the triumphal entry of Braganza into Villaviciosa on December 1, 1640 – to calls of "long live the king don Juan" – as staged. The rebels, he maintained, self-consciously imitated biblical time, seeking to reenact David's entry into Hebron. He drew again from Augustine to insist that their intentions had not been pure, that they had not been motivated by a "good spirit or peaceful heart," and that in Villaviciosa – unlike in Hebron – the events had not been the work of providence.[95] He alleged that the cheering crowd had been paid and the archbishop of Lisbon had "conjured" omens, rigging a seeming miracle to mislead the populace, arranging it so that in the middle of the procession the right arm of a statute of Christ on the cross would fall at just the right moment and point to Braganza as Portugal's rightful king. He depicted the archbishop, whose ruses struck "at the innermost heart of the faithful Portuguese," as a source of corruption and the populace – much as he had characterized the Catalan people – as led astray by poor leaders.[96] He revived the vision articulated in

[93] Citing Augustine, *Confessions*, bk. 3, chap. 8, he invoked a passage about irreligiosity, about the vacancy of things that do not contain Jesus: "auiendo faltado Verg[ança] al pacto general de la sociedad humana, con la inobediencia," ibid., fol. 48r.

[94] Ibid., fols. 31r, 35. Here, he suggested an engagement with resistance theory, perhaps attempting to undermine Protestant political thought then in circulation.

[95] "buen animo y coraçon pacifico;" his citation was to "S. August. de correct. et grat. cap. 14." Ibid., fol. 32v.

[96] "à lo intimo del coraçon de los fieles Portugueses." Ibid., fol. 19r.

the *Pro Cautione* years before, continuing to argue that Portugal was already a weakened republic because of its especially obstinate Judaizing *converso* population and that the commercial plots of the New Christians accelerated the naturally corrupting influence of the Portuguese colonies. Nevertheless, he claimed that divine intervention had turned the hearts of the Portuguese Inquisitor General and the archbishop of Braga back toward truth. He patterned the clerics who resisted Braganza after the righteous prophets of the Old Testament. In so doing, he returned to arguments akin to those he had used against Trejo, relying heavily on proof texts from the Hebrew Bible and aligning rebellion with the demonic. It was exceedingly common for early modern Catholics to turn to Old Testament exempla when writing about kingship. Yet Adam de la Parra's frequent use of such material in his *Apologético* took on an added layer of meaning after his years of persecuting Portuguese merchants who he had depicted as Judaizing conspirators; he assigned the Portuguese rebels a pejorative latent Jewishness while simultaneously appropriating biblical Jewish history to serve the cause of the Catholic king.

To emphasize the existential nature of threats to the Catholic Monarchy, Adam de la Parra turned to the motif of the shipwreck, which knitted together biblical imagery and contemporary experience. He may have drawn scriptural inspiration from Paul, who had instructed: "This charge I commit unto thee, son Timothy, according to the prophecies which went before on thee, that thou by them mightest war a good warfare; Holding faith, and a good conscience; which some having put away concerning faith have made shipwreck." Although the inquisitor had a Pauline model, he also wrote in the era after the loss of Spain's Armada, when to invoke a shipwreck was to raise the dangers both of naval defeat and of fleets gone awry.[97] In the *Pro Cautione*, he proposed that one

---

[97] 1 Tim 1:18–19. On the Armada as a seventeenth-century literary motif, cf. Elizabeth Wright, *Pilgrimage to Patronage: Lope de Vega and the court of Philip III, 1598–1621* (Lewisburg, PA: Bucknell University Press, 2001). Christine Caldwell Ames noted how Peter of Verona had referred to "various theological 'shipwrecks'" in railing against heresy; she also observed that medieval accounts of miracles often referenced the salvation of a sinking ship, *Righteous Persecution: Inquisition, Dominicans and Christianity in the Middle Ages* (Philadelphia: University of Pennsylvania Press, 2009), 29, 43, 88. Diego de Simancas also placed the image at the opening of his inquisitorial manual, *De catholicis institutionibus* (Rome: in aedibus Populi Romani, 1575), 2. For Miguel de Piedrola's sixteenth-century use (as precedent for his prophetic speech) of Jonah's casting into the sea during a storm to assuage divine wrath, Richard Kagan and Abigail Dyer, eds. and trans., *Inquisitorial Inquiries. Brief Lives of Secret Jews and Other Heretics* (Baltimore, MD, and London: The Johns Hopkins University Press, 2004), 69; Jon 1:11,12.

successful attack on Catholicism in its staunchest adherent would destroy the Church: "for if its severity, unexhausted thus far, is crippled here, here religion will waver, and if here it will be shipwrecked, it will sink everywhere."[98] In the *Conspiratio*, he judged that "France was being inundated by the immoderate waves and contrary winds of the heretics, as if, abandoned in the shipwreck, it was beaten by internal evils."[99] The *Súplica*, meanwhile, proposed that the Catalans "shipwreck in the ambitious spirit of some of their leaders, that attending to their own interests . . . all regard for both divine and human has been forgotten."[100] Braganza became a threatening storm, who had "caused such squalls, that the hurricanes of the North penetrated later to Angola, and to the Malaccas, disordering that which was ordered by the Catholic Kings so much that by derivation from this evil the globe's most faithful provinces shipwreck and Portugal will lose the empire."[101] He used the vivid imagery of a world economically dependent on the seas to cast those polities not bound to the defense of Catholicism as rudderless in dangerous waters; as a hired pen, he supplied such written arms to the crown, advocating, as he did so, for the worth of inquisitorial work.

INQUISITORIAL AMBITIONS

The tools that Adam de la Parra used with skill were the same implements used to engineer his disgrace. He wrote both prose and verse. In the years when he was studying in Seville, the second part of Miguel de Cervantes's *Don Quixote* appeared in print. In one chapter, Don Quixote counsels a gentleman whose son, a talented student, has professed his desire to become a poet: "Your grace should reprimand your son if he writes satires that damage other people's honor; you should punish him and tear up the poems." At the same time, he praises Horace's *Satires* as model poetry that attacks vice without naming and so dishonoring individuals. He relates the

---

[98] "nam si eius seueritas intrita adhuc, debilitetur hìc, hìc fluctuabit Religio, dum naufraga hìc fuerit, vbique submergetur." *Pro Cautione*, fol. 2r.

[99] "estaba Francia inundada por los inmoderados oleajes y contrarios vientos de los herejes, como si, abandonada en el naufragio, fuese batida por males intestinos." *Conspiración*, 17.

[100] "que naufraga en el ambicioso espiritu de algunas cabeças, que atendiendo a sus propios intereses . . . se han olvidado a todo respecto divino y humano," *Súplica*, fol. 5r.

[101] "mouido tales borrascas, que los vracanes del Norte penetraron luego a Angola, y à Malaca, desquicidando lo que estaua compuesto por Reyes Catolicos, tanto, que por deriuacion deste mal naufragan las Prouincias mas fieles del Orbe, y Portugal perdera el imperio." *Apologético*, fol. 48r.

poet's character to the morality of his poetry, claiming that if a poet were chaste in habits, he would also be so in his verses, for "the pen is the tongue of the soul."[102] Thus, Cervantes exposed some of the tensions around poetic composition. Potentially a salutary tool of critique, it was also dangerous, as politically charged poetry was all too likely to injure reputations. Poetic combat was part of seventeenth-century Court life; whereas the ideal courtier was skilled in both arms and letters, those like Adam de la Parra, jurists proficient only in the latter, often turned their words into weapons. Although the inquisitor was known to write poetry, there is no poetic oeuvre definitively attributed to him. The anonymous polemical poem *La cueva de Meliso* (*Meliso's Cave*) was once thought to be his, but the literary scholar Joaquín de Entrambasaguas disputed that identification in the early twentieth century.[103] In general, verse afforded a way to make a show of wit and to air grievances too controversial for print.

The poem most clearly attributed to Adam de la Parra was the one that triggered his downfall. A *décima*, it attacked the honor of several influential courtiers and so, by extension, that of their families and networks of associates:

> For the nun the triumph
> the *Justicia Mayor* went out
> with Contreras. What valor
> worthy of a *morisco* scoundrel!
> One and the other a Jew
> purged with this action.
> It isn't so grand, the great miracle,
> since with golden potions
> they have purged the Cortijos
> in the holy Inquisition.

Elliott identified the likely targets of the first lines as don Antonio de Contreras, a member of the Council of Castile, and Agustín de Villanueva, the *justicia* of Aragon and brother of the *protonotario* Jerónimo de Villanueva, a close associate of Olivares later suspect for his

<hr>

[102] Cervantes, *Don Quixote*, trans. Grossman, 557. This is drawn from pt. 2, chap. 16, published in 1615; also raised was the risk of exile that unwise poets ran. See also Cervantes, *Don Quijote de la Mancha. Edición del Instituto Cervantes 1605–2005*, dir. Francisco Rico (Barcelona: Galaxia Gutenberg, 2004), 1:827–28. Cf. the analysis of a "rhetoric of honor," as part of a range of symbolic social action, in Scott K. Taylor, *Honor and Violence in Golden Age Spain* (New Haven, CT, and London: Yale University Press, 2008), 9, 14.

[103] For the attempt to establish his literary corpus, Entrambasaguas, "El Inquisidor"; and *Varios Datos*.

affinity for the nuns of San Plácido. The second half seemingly took aim at Manuel Cortizos de Villasante and his family, influential Portuguese financiers at Court. The scandal broke at the end of September 1642, when the satirical *décima* began to circulate in Madrid and was assumed to be the inquisitor's handiwork. The poem claimed to pull the mask of honor away from the dishonorable and mocked the society that had played along with the pretense. It hinged on the ease with which elites skirted purity of blood restrictions, buying what should not be sold, as Adam de la Parra suggested in his reference to the "golden potion" that had produced a pure genealogy, an insult that echoed with the refrains of anti-Jewish polemic. He also attacked an Inquisition so corrupted as to supply pure genealogies for a price – rather than uncovering and exposing the truth – and so portrayed himself as a reformer who would correct and restore his institution.[104]

The inquisitor's accusations were serious ones, and his opponents responded strategically. They likely circulated copies of the poem, and so – given the importance of the figures involved – elevated it to the level of public scandal. By October, Olivares decided Adam de la Parra needed to be removed from Court; with members of the *Suprema* – themselves implicated in the poem's insults – he orchestrated the inquisitor's imprisonment in León. Court observers took note of the dramatic turn of events. Jesuits remarked on it in their correspondence, recording rumors that the inquisitor might even be exiled to the Canaries, and gossip that he had received his due: "Everyone says that it had God's permission and was His judgment for the extortions" that Adam de la Parra had committed at Court. Another letter reported that he was denied pen and ink in his imprisonment, because of the offense he had given to a courtier who "in the proofs for his office of familiar, being so well known and a gentleman, [was shown] one of the greatest vassals that the King has." One responding *décima* began with a clever play on words, observing that Adam had been cast out of Eden. Word of Adam de la Parra's disgrace reached Quevedo –

---

[104] "Por la monja el desafío / salió el Justicia Mayor / con Contreras. ¡Qué valor / digno de un morisco brío! / Uno y otro lo judío / purgaron con esta acción. / No es muy grande el milagrón, / pues con áureos bebedizos / han purgado los Cortijos / en la sancta Inquisiçión." The *décima* is a type of Spanish stanza of ten verses, each with eight syllables. Elliott, "Nueva luz"; *The Count-Duke of Olivares*, 303; and "El Conde Duque y Quevedo." Jaraulde Pou, *Francisco de Quevedo*, 779, 803–4, 814; Studnicki-Gizbert, *A Nation Upon the Ocean Sea*, 151–52. Cf. the analysis of polemic and insult in poetry in David Nirenberg, "Figures of Thought and Figures of Flesh: Jews and Judaism in Late-Medieval Spanish Poetry and Politics," *Speculum* 81 (2006): 398–426.

who had been jailed in León since 1639 – who, in a similar epistolary punning on that other Adam of Genesis, conveyed a certain familiarity with the inquisitor.[105]

Although Adam de la Parra had risen rapidly by showing his skill as a publicist, publicity was also at the root of his fall. He had circulated letters, memoranda, and print in the service of his chosen causes, even as he sought to silence writings he deemed dangerous, such as the accounts of *beatas*'s marvels. On September 9, 1642 – just weeks before his imprisonment – Pellicer recorded that an "evil pamphlet," damaging to the reputations of both Philip IV and his ancestors, had fallen into his hands, and so "he notified" Adam de la Parra, "in order that the tribunal of the Holy Office could proceed against those who had it without showing it."[106] The two pamphleteers collaborated both to produce print and to suppress it. Likewise, circulation made his poem into a scandalous matter, costing him the support of Olivares, who, in a letter to the king, made it clear that the inquisitor's "imprudence" had been his crucial miscalculation.[107] Although the count-duke hesitated to recommend permanent exile from Court, the inquisitor had become a liability. Incarcerated in November in the monastery of San Isidro in León, he was denied writing materials by the *Suprema* and ordered not to correspond with patrons at Court.

The Toledo tribunal took up his cause, indignantly petitioning for his release and complaining about the breach of ecclesiastical prerogatives: it seems he had been taken into custody by the secular arm of justice. By the next year, the inquisitor – apparently once more in possession of pen and ink – was again sending appeals, protesting the disregard for customary procedures.[108] Not long into the inquisitor's incarceration, Olivares fell from power, leaving Court in January 1643 and exiled farther afield in

---

[105] "Todos diçen a sido permision de dios y juicio suio por las extorsiones …" And, "en las pruebas de su familiatura siendo tan conosido y cavall[er]o y uno de los mayores basallos q[ue] el Rey tiene." These two letters from Court observers to authorities in the Society of Jesus confirm Elliott's analysis and gloss the affair further. I am grateful to Katrina Olds for directing me to them. Luis Antonio Morales, November 4, 1642, and Sebastián González, November 12, 1642, RAH 9/3663, exp. 124, fols. 742rff. See also Quevedo to Juan Antonio Velázquez, S.J., Provincial of Castile, November 25 and December 4, 1642, Crosby, ed., *Nuevas Cartas*, 111–13.

[106] "el malvado Papel" (*Anti Pelargesis ibero*), and "dio quenta … para que proceda el Tribunal del Santo Oficio contra los que le tuvieren sin manifestarle." Pellicer, *Avisos*, 1:405.

[107] Olivares to the king, October 19, 1642, cited in Elliott, "El Conde Duque y Quevedo," 189–90.

[108] Entrambasaguas, *Varios datos*, docs. XXXI, XXXV, XXXVI.

June, and Sotomayor was also dismissed.[109] By the year's end, a new Inquisitor General, Diego de Arce y Reinoso, was charged to carry a new banner of reforms and to counteract what was corrupted in the Olivares years. He strove to show himself as reversing Sotomayor's aggregation of authority to the office, working in greater concert with the *Suprema*. He initially blocked the foundation of a tribunal at Court, but it was ultimately during his tenure that one began to take definitive shape. Moreover, he attempted to tighten the procedures for investigating the purity of blood of inquisitorial officials and functionaries.[110] He advanced some of the initiatives that Adam de la Parra had so doggedly promoted.

In a letter he sent from León in October 1643, Adam de la Parra claimed that his imprisonment was by no means appropriate "penitence," that it defied historical precedent and was "without example in the tribunals of Christian republics," and that it harmed the Inquisition's "holy and pious conscience" and the reputation of the Inquisitor General.[111] Jailed for just less than year, after he was freed, the *Suprema* appointed him as an inquisitor in Logroño's tribunal and promptly filled his former post at Court, despite his protests. By November 1643, his career's itinerary had come nearly full circle: he was headed north toward Logroño and away from Court. According to Pellicer, the common wisdom was that the inquisitor would someday have returned to Madrid and resumed his former position. Whether this was likely or simply the stuff of eulogy remains uncertain; Adam de la Parra died not long after his release, in Logroño in April 1644.[112]

In his *Conspiratio*, Adam de la Parra had opined that "it will appear more clear than the light at noon that this lamentable heretical-most

---

[109] Roberto López Vela deemed Sotomayor "the most regalist Inquisitor General of the century"; see his "Estructuras administrativas del Santo Oficio," *HIEA* 2:116. Yet he also could be swayed by papal nuncios; Elliott, *The Count-Duke of Olivares*, 373, 668. While Adam de la Parra was imprisoned, Sotomayor appointed Rioja and Salgado to the *Suprema*; even though the former went into exile with Olivares and the latter died in February 1644, perhaps they helped facilitate Adam de la Parra's release, Sánchez Rivilla, "Inquisidores," 289, 401–2, 410.

[110] He also sought to suppress the practices both of selling offices and of awarding supernumerary posts on the council, given primarily to members of the orders earlier in the century. Sánchez Rivilla, "Inquisidores," 239–40; Lea, *History of the Inquisition*, 1:545–46; López Vela, "Sociología de los Cuadros Inquisitoriales," *HIEA* 2:714–15. Lea argued that with the scandal of the nuns of San Plácido, the trials of Portuguese merchants spurred the creation of the tribunal at Court.

[111] Adam de la Parra, October 13, 1643, AHN, Inq., leg. 3112; Entrambasaguas, *Varios datos*, doc. XXXI.

[112] July 14, 1643, and April 26, 1644, Pellicer, *Avisos*, 1:411, 505.

Christian conspiracy is directed by a double, but adjacent, passion (that is to say, by ambition and by hatred of religion)."[113] Earlier, he had noted: "Such is, in effect, the nature of ambition, that once insinuated, it always attempts, by all means, to arrive at the greatest power."[114] Even as he sought access to the corridors of power, Adam de la Parra wrote ambivalently on the topic, construing ambitiousness as "characteristic of man's nature," but a tyrannical force there, and malicious in government, where it led men away from true religion and the public good in favor of particular passions and interests.[115]

Caught in the tensions of ambition, Adam de la Parra's life offers an apt case to consider what drove inquisitorial careers. A law degree and the Inquisition's ladder of promotions offered the orphan from the Rioja an entrance to life at Court. He calculated well that displaying his talent at writing polemics and at managing the publicity that surrounded the Inquisition's affairs could be a means to gain the support of the Inquisitor General and to rise in a political world mediated by Olivares. He acquired experience in some of the signal religious controversies of the day – about purity of blood statutes, false sanctity cases, and the alleged Judaizing of Portuguese merchants – and strategically showed his expertise. Once in Madrid, he increased his standing by his work as a pamphleteer. Through writings of varied kinds, he cast himself as a champion of reforms, combating the corruption of religious justice and the multiplication of frauds and illusions. In a climate that rewarded calls for reform, he argued persistently that the Inquisition was the institution most suited to arbitrate religious disputes and to correct error.

Adam de la Parra offered an inquisitorial response to the concerns of seventeenth-century Spanish reformers, who sought to stave off imperial decline in arenas from the moral to the economic. He summoned earlier eras – of Ferdinand and Isabel and of Philip II – to provide examples of the defense of the faith and proposed that the failings of bishops and inquisitorial negligence allowed impostors to infiltrate the Catholic Monarchy and claim its resources. He painted a society littered with deceptions and offered a renovated Inquisition as a remedy, tailored to the work of

---

[113] "... aparecerá más claro que la misma luz del medio día que esta funesta conspiración herético-cristianísima es dirigida por una pasión doble, pero afín; (es decir, la ambición y el odio a la Religión)." *Conspiración*, 43.

[114] "Tal es, en efecto, la naturaleza de la ambición, que, una vez insinuada, pretende siempre, por todos los medios, llegar al mayor poder." Ibid., 24–25.

[115] "propio de la naturaleza de los hombres." Ibid., 115. Cf. the analysis of the tension between *fama* and *vanitas* in history writing in Kagan, *Clio and the Crown*.

undeceiving and so of social reform. As an inquisitor at Court, he was at once more and less powerful than other inquisitors, perhaps more able to influence the monarchy's policies and acquire important patrons, but also at dangerous proximity to those whose temporal authority was far greater than that of a junior tribunal judge. All of this might be attributed to careerism, to savvy tracking of the political winds. Still, Adam de la Parra's repeated pursuit of particular causes over more than two decades seems more than purely instrumental; it seems to suggest how he created his own synthesis of widely circulating ideas about political reform in the midst of fears of decline, about the corruption of religious and moral life, about the judicial defense of religious authority, about the particularly insidious nature of some deceptions, about individual and communal salvation, about vesting some elements of society while violently divesting others. He subscribed to a line of reasoning that held that extraordinary means were needed to address abuses; to combat pretense and hypocrisy; and to dislodge entrenched interests that had become, in essence, above the law. Adam de la Parra's fall from favor might be reassessed in this light. Perhaps he simply made a political miscalculation, publicizing a critique that had served him well in other circumstances at the wrong moment, his career a victim of poor timing. Yet from another perspective, the poem that sent him into exile was a refusal to silence his critiques or to negotiate on his ideological stances, even when they became politically inconvenient. It was perhaps the consistency and insistence of his commitments that both made his career and ended it prematurely.

CHAPTER 5

Negotiating the Catholic Monarchy

The Transatlantic Maneuvering of Juan de Mañozca y Zamora

In my long age and experiences I had not seen nor heard that any vassal would have imagined meddling in such a sovereign subject.[1]

On the feast day of the holy cross in September 1648, the archbishop of Mexico staged a procession celebrating the installation of a monumental stone cross in front of his cathedral. Juan de Mañozca y Zamora was then not only the viceroyalty's chief prelate, but also a councillor of the *Suprema* and a visitor delegated to inspect Mexico's Inquisition tribunal, and so one of the highest officials in the bustling viceregal capital. By the middle of the seventeenth century, Mexico City had some 100,000 inhabitants, and civic life was punctuated by such festive displays, from the cycles of the Catholic liturgy to the ceremonial entrances of new viceroys to more local events; by one estimate, there were around a hundred public celebrations each year.[2] Yet the 1640s were also a decade of notable hardship in the viceroyalty. These were years of economic contraction and political strife across the Habsburg world, with wars on several fronts and a reshuffling at Court following Olivares's fall, beyond the recurring hardships wrought by floods, earthquakes, and disease. Authorities in

---

[1] Mañozca, July 15, 1650, RB, MS II/1992, fol. 43r.

[2] Here I follow Linda A. Curcio-Nagy, *The Great Festivals of Colonial Mexico City: Performing Power and Identity* (Albuquerque: University of New Mexico Press, 2004), 2–10. See also Alejandro Cañeque, *The King's Living Image: The Culture and Politics of Viceregal Power in Colonial Mexico* (London and New York: Routledge, 2004). Mexico's entire estimated population was 200,000 whites (Creoles, *peninsulares*, other Europeans), 30,000 blacks, 20,000 mulattos, 150,000 *mestizos*, and 3.5 million *indios*, Fabio Troncarelli, *El mito del 'Zorro' y la Inquisición en México. La aventura de Guillén Lombardo (1615–1659)*, trans. Pau Oliva (Lleida: Editorial Milenio, 2003), 20.

New Spain, meanwhile, had been embroiled in conflict with one another, as Juan de Palafox y Mendoza (1600–59) – then the bishop of Puebla de los Angeles – the viceroy, the *audiencia* (which functioned as both appellate court and governing council), the Inquisition tribunal, the secular clergy, and the religious orders in the province (the Jesuits in particular) sparred with one another.[3] In this complicated religious and political geography, Mañozca skillfully defended his authority as an inquisitor and projected an aura of clerical reform.

Often described as Basque – or, more specifically, Vizcayan – Mañozca was in his late sixties by the time he arrived in Mexico as an archbishop. Trained as a jurist, with a network of family and associates in his native province and in Mexico, he had crossed the Atlantic at least seven times. He had held office in Cartagena de Indias, Lima, Quito, Granada, and Madrid and had nearly forty years of inquisitorial experience behind him. In Mexico, he knew more or less what to expect. He had returned to a city he had known in his youth, where his younger cousin was already serving in the Inquisition tribunal. A long career had taught him strategies to negotiate the life of an administrator in the Catholic Monarchy, how to frame petitions, conduct inspections, and manage relationships with patrons and clients. He could have anticipated that his multiple offices would allow him significant latitude in managing religious affairs in the viceroyalty. This was influence he could turn toward increasing his family's fortunes and securing places for longtime companions. In years when the crown was particularly interested in stabilizing its kingdoms, Mañozca may also have approached his return to Mexico as an opportunity to promote his vision of religious and political reforms, to stimulate inquisitorial activity, and to advance the application of Tridentine decrees.

To do so, he resorted to techniques he had developed over his career, adapting them for the environment at hand. Mañozca had coordinated other religious spectacles before orchestrating the relocation of the stone cross to the cathedral from Tepeapulco, a few days' journey northeast of the viceregal capital. Tepeapulco was not just any town. On the road from Veracruz to Mexico City, it had appeared in accounts of Cortés's expedition and was the site of an early and well-known Franciscan foundation, where, in the middle of the sixteenth century, friar Bernardino de Sahagún

---

[3] On the political situation, see Cayetana Álvarez de Toledo, *Politics and Reform in Spain and Viceregal Mexico: The Life and Thought of Juan de Palafox 1600–1659* (Oxford, UK: Clarendon Press, 2004), 159–240; Jonathan I. Israel, *Race, Class and Politics in Colonial Mexico, 1610–1670* (London: Oxford University Press, 1975).

had begun to compile his famous history, drawing on the reports of Nahuatl informants.[4] Mañozca both presided over the celebrations and sponsored a published account, the narrative emphasizing his dedication to his archdiocese.[5] Reportedly, he "was visiting ... the extended flock with untiring love," when he arrived in Tepeapulco and encountered a town that had been sumptuous and opulent in antiquity, but with changing times had almost been destroyed; where there had once been sixty thousand citizens, there were a mere twenty inhabitants.[6] While surveying the area, he discovered a beautiful stone cross, nearly "drowned" in the cemetery's vegetation. Wanting to carry it to his cathedral, the archbishop first asked the permission of the local Indians, who reputedly gave their consent and told him how the town had once prized the now forgotten cross. The ensuing procession – and the pamphlet that recorded it – presented a parable about true religion threatened and reclaimed: neglect nearly allowed weeds to choke out adoration of the cross, but diligent pastoral care arrived as a remedy. The cross was offered as a balm for both the plague that had set upon the city and for the monarchy's ills more generally. The episode bound the surrounding district and its spiritual geography to the city and its cathedral, the indigenous populace to the viceregal elite, and the sixteenth-century history of evangelization by mendicant friars to contemporary religious reforms. Through Mañozca, the authority of the Inquisition was intertwined with that of the archbishop, associating each office with Tridentine ideals of pastoral virtue, of visiting the flock, combating heresy, and investigating and correcting the state of religion in the district.[7] These years were the final act of a long

---

4 The convent was founded as early as 1527, and Sahagún was there between 1559 and 1561. Miguel León-Portilla, *Bernardino de Sahagún, First Anthropologist*, trans. Mauricio J. Mixco (Norman: University of Oklahoma Press, 2002), 140–46. For the town's depopulation over the later sixteenth and seventeenth centuries (the district was estimated at 143 in 1643), see Peter Gerhard, *A Guide to the Historical Geography of New Spain Revised Edition* (Norman: University of Oklahoma Press, 1993), 52–54.

5 *Relación de la Pompa Festiva, y Solemne colocación de una santa, y hermosa cruz de piedra* (Mexico City: Hipolyto de Ribera, 1648; repr. Mexico City: widow of D. Joseph Bernardo de Hogal, 1748), copy in ACM, lib. 16, Fábrica Material, fols. 277–84.

6 "Visitaba ... con incansable amor el rebaño estendido," *Relación de la Pompa Festiva*, 2. Tepeapulco was described as twelve leagues from Mexico City, that is, a bit more than 80 kilometers.

7 There were unmistakable resonances with anti-heretical language that likened heretics to weeds. Christine Caldwell Ames noted the many uses of the parable of the wheat and the tares (Matt 13:24–30) in the imagery used to authorize and to contest medieval heresy inquisitions; *Righteous Persecution: Inquisition, Dominicans and Christianity in the Middle Ages* (Philadelphia: University of Pennsylvania Press, 2009), chap. 1.

career, as Mañozca would die in Mexico at the end of 1650. And the festivities of 1648 marked a culmination of strategies learned through experience. They both served a pastoral function and were part of the combat and competition among local authorities, while the print Mañozca sponsored broadcast his activities to audiences near and far.

The image of Mañozca that has appeared in the historiography, however, has been a particularly menacing one. He has been offered as a face for the Spanish Inquisition in the Americas, where he and his cousin have become emblems of severity, corruption, and colonial abuse. The prolific nineteenth-century historian José Toribio Medina commented on their "almost conspiratorial" connection to each other. Medina condemned Mañozca as notable for his "maliciousness"; he characterized him as "perhaps the cruelest" inquisitor and as "one of the most perverse men" ever seen in the Americas.[8] The inquisitor also figured prominently in John Leddy Phelan's perceptive study of Spanish imperial bureaucracy, in which he emerged as a rigorous visitor and judge, an unusually persistent administrator frequently embroiled in controversies. Other historians have deemed Mañozca particularly concerned with investigating cases of witchcraft and found him to be an orchestrator of the "Great Complicity" trials, that is, of the pursuit of Portuguese merchants in the viceroyalties of Peru and New Spain on charges of Judaizing. In her reading of those persecutions, Irene Silverblatt made him emblematic of the imperial bureaucrat informed by "ambition, self-interest, and self-righteousness."[9]

This chapter examines how Mañozca navigated the politics and institutions of the Catholic Monarchy with such skill, sustaining an inquisitorial career of more than forty years' duration and acquiring further promotions as councillor of the *Suprema*, president of the Granada Chancery and archbishop of Mexico. By such measures, he was one of

---

[8] Manuel Ballesteros Gaibrois quoted Medina's use of "malvada" and referred to "su actuación casi conspiratoria apoyando a su primo carnal," in his "La Instalación del Tribunal del Santo Oficio en Cartagena de Indias. Nuevas Noticias," *HIEA*, 3:1026. "Uno de los hombres más perverso," José Toribio Medina, *Historia del Tribunal del Santo Oficio de la Inquisición en Cartagena de Indias* (Santiago de Chile: Imprenta Elzeviriana, 1899), 100–101; "acaso el más cruel," and *Biblioteca Hispano-Americana, 1493–1810* (Santiago de Chile: Fondo Histórico y Bibliográfico José Toribio Medina, 1958), 2:423–24.

[9] John Leddy Phelan, *The Kingdom of Quito in the Seventeenth Century; Bureaucratic Politics in the Spanish Empire* (Madison: University of Wisconsin Press, 1967); Irene Silverblatt, *Modern Inquisitions: Peru and the Colonial Origins of the Civilized World* (Durham, NC, and London: Duke University Press, 2004), 57–58; Alfonso Quiroz Norris, "La expropiación inquisitorial de cristianos nuevos portugueses en Los Reyes, Cartagena y México, 1635–1649," *Histórica* 10.2 (1986): 237–303.

the most successful of the inquisitors I have considered here, his trajectory comparable to Cristóbal Fernández de Valtodano's nearly a century before, even if culminating in the somewhat less prestigious offices of the Americas. He distinguished himself by his deft responses to controversy, from carefully composed missives to arranging spectacles such as that of September 1648. Like Valtodano, he did not work as a theorist in print. Rather, he too appeared in published writings primarily as a patron, the object of dedications and praise. Each prelate was elevated simultaneously by his distance from the craft of writing and his visibility in laudatory print. Mañozca also orchestrated some of the most elaborately publicized inquisitorial affairs of the seventeenth century, advertising the Inquisition's uncovering of the "Great Complicity" much as he did the translation of the stone cross, the reforms of the Dominicans, and the jubilees of the Society of Jesus, in which he also had a hand. His exceptional career demonstrates how, in the right constellation of circumstances, an inquisitor could accrue substantial authority to his office and to his person. The history of the monument from Tepeapulco – which came to be known as the "cross of Mañozca" – shows how he sought to shape the religious practice of his contemporaries and to memorialize his own actions as a defender of the faith, to leave a physical trace of them in monuments and in print accounts that might circulate in other parts of the monarchy or be left for posterity. In a world often understood as a theater, Mañozca cast himself as using artifice in order to instruct and to persuade, to promote truth rather than to lead astray.

CRISSCROSSING THE ATLANTIC

Juan de Zamora Mañozca was born about 1577 in Marquina, a town in a mountainous region in the northeast of the Basque province of Vizcaya, not far inland from the Bay of Biscay.[10] Located in Logroño's inquisitorial district, the tribunal there was still providing genealogical information about members of the family well into the 1640s. The son of Domingo de Zamora, a Castilian, and Catalina Mañozca, a Basque, he began to use Mañozca as his principal surname as a young man – now Juan de Mañozca y Zamora – thus associating himself more immediately with Vizcaya and

---

[10] The town is now Markina-Xemein and is located just over 10 kilometers from the coast. I have used the spelling of the seventeenth-century records, as also with the Castilian Vizcaya (instead of Bizkaia).

his maternal kin.[11] And it was his mother's brother who apparently offered the youth a route out of his hometown. In 1593, his uncle, Pedro Sáenz de Mañozca, likewise a native of Marquina, had already been affiliated with the Inquisition for nearly two decades. An official in the service of the *Suprema*'s secretary, that year he was nominated to the secretarial staff of Mexico City's tribunal. The uncle and nephew both seem to have departed for Mexico City in February 1594. Juan was licensed for passage to the Americas as part of the entourage of the newly appointed Inquisition *fiscal*, Dr. Gonzalo Martos de Bohórquez, who, like Juan's uncle, was setting out for his post in New Spain.[12]

Through his late teens and early twenties, Mañozca lived in his uncle's household in Mexico City. A few years after his arrival, don Pedro Sáenz de Mañozca married doña Catalina Murillo, the daughter of a familiar, thus strengthening his ties to his adopted city; both Catalina and her mother had been born in New Spain, whereas each of her parents' families hailed from Andalusia.[13] Sáenz de Mañozca would remain the tribunal's secretary from 1594 until his death in 1618. Even twenty years afterward, Mañozca and his colleagues in Lima would praise his uncle's long service in the Holy Office and assert that in Mexico the secretary's work continued

<hr>

[11] For biographical information, see Phelan, *Kingdom of Quito*, 244–45, 311–19; Solange Alberro, *Inquisition et Société au Mexique, 1571–1700* (Mexico City: Centre d'Études Mexicaines et Centramericaines, 1988); Teresa Sánchez Rivilla, "Inquisidores Generales y Consejeros de la Suprema: Documentación Biográfica," *HIEA* 3:367–68. He was listed as age 57 in "Relación delos inquisidores y oficiales," May 1, 1634, AHN, Inq., lib. 1040, fol. 329.

[12] Licenses of May 5, 1593, AGI, Contratación, 5243, no. 2, r. 60; of February 7, 1594, AGI, Pasajeros, lib. 7, exp. 3344 and Contratación, 5247, no. 2, r. 79. For a study of how the region was shaped by emigration, see Juan Javier Pescador, *The New World Inside a Basque Village: The Oiartzun Valley and Its Atlantic Emigrants, 1550–1800* (Reno: University of Nevada Press, 2004).

[13] Inquiries into her genealogy began in 1599, before her marriage; a June 1600 letter referred to her as contracted to marry Pedro, a June 1601 letter, as his wife, AGN, Inq., vol. 204, exp. 6. Her parents were Juan López Murillo (sometimes Morillo) and Petronila de Pedraza. Her widowed maternal great-grandmother, grandmother, and great-uncle arrived from Málaga around 1545. Granada's tribunal turned up reports of their honorable repute there, as well as recollections of the family's origins in Medina de Ríoseco and in Azpeiteia, which they placed in Vizcaya. Her father – whose line Córdoba's tribunal investigated – was a native of the town of Belalcázar (in Mexico, they were unsure if it was that district's or Llerena's; Córdoba affirmed jurisdiction). He was made a familiar December 16, 1592, and Solange Alberro classified him as a merchant; cf. her genealogical table of the Sáenz de Mañozca and related families (in which Juan de Mañozca is not included), *Inquisition et Société*, 340, 364.

to be "esteemed and respected."[14] There, Mañozca began his education. At the University of Mexico – which had been founded in 1553 – he gained admission to the *colegio* of San Ildefonso and graduated as a bachelor in arts in 1596. He began to establish ties in Mexico to administrators arriving from the peninsula, like his uncle, and to Creoles, like his uncle's wife and her family. He also must have gained an acquaintance with the work of the Inquisition in these years, watching the activities of a tribunal founded just twenty-odd years before.

Mañozca observed inquisitorial officials at close range, as his uncle and Martos de Bohórquez took up their new positions. The *fiscal* – who appears to have been a Creole, born in Santa Fe de Bogotá, in the kingdom of New Granada – was eventually made an inquisitor in Mexico, holding that post from 1609 until his death in 1611.[15] Mañozca's first sojourn in Mexico also coincided with a famous inquisitorial case. The first of the Inquisition's prosecutions of the Carvajal family as Judaizers had concluded in 1590 and quickly garnered fame in inquisitorial quarters; in his 1598 history of the Inquisition, Luis de Páramo concluded his treatment of New Spain's tribunal with a reference to the family's trials. Mañozca was in Mexico City when the tribunal arrested Luis de Carvajal the younger – who would come to be known for his prolific writings and visionary experiences – for the second time, in February 1595, along with other members of his family. During this second trial, Pedro Sáenz de Mañozca was present to record nearly every act, and Martos de Bohórquez was the *fiscal*. A quarter century after its foundation, on December 8, 1596,

---

[14] They recounted that the *Suprema* employed him for more than eighteen years and that he served more than twenty-eight as Mexico's secretary (which does not quite match the records), Lima tribunal to Inquisitor General, May 19, 1637, AHN, Inq., lib. 1041, fols. 326–27. The *comisario* in Puebla de los Angeles wrote to the Mexican tribunal lamenting his death, January 28, 1618, AGN, Inq., vol. 318, exp. 8G, fol. 418. The *Suprema* noted that he had served it very well for years as an official under its secretary Alonso de Doriga, December 23, 1593, AGN, Inq., vol. 223, exp. 28, fol. 128r; nomination, September 4, 1593, AGI, Contratación, 5788, lib. 1, fols. 257v-58; for his salary, fol. 258; for his license, September 22, 1593, Contratación, 5243, no. 2, r. 54, 61; February 7, 1594, Pasajeros, lib. 7, exp. 3348. He was the son of Pedro Sáenz de Mañozca and Graciana de Orozco, who were presumably Mañozca's maternal grandparents. He was seemingly the secret courier to Puebla in 1598, during the first notable case of *alumbradismo* tried in Mexico's court, A. Huerga, "El Tribunal de Mexico en la Época de Felipe II," *HIEA* 1:951; and "El Tribunal de Mexico en la Época de Felipe III," *HIEA* 1:973–74.

[15] Luis de Páramo also noted both the *fiscal* and the secretary as among the current office-holders in Mexico in his *De Origine et progressu officii Sanctae Inquisitionis* (Madrid: Juan Flandro, 1598), 243. See also Martin Austin Nesvig, *Ideology and Inquisition: The World of the Censors in Early Mexico* (New Haven, CT, and London: Yale University Press, 2009), 168–70, 274–75; Alberro, *Inquisition et Société*, 333.

Mexico's tribunal held its first large *auto de fe* in the city's Plaza Mayor. Among the convicted heretics displayed and executed that day was Carvajal, who was relaxed as a relapsed Judaizer alongside his mother, three of his sisters, and another three men and a woman.[16]

It is tempting to wonder how that watershed *auto de fe* – at which Mañozca was very likely present – might have shaped his later actions. He soon crossed the Atlantic again, returning to Castile and taking up a place in the most prestigious Spanish *colegio mayor*, that of San Bartolomé at the University of Salamanca. There, he graduated as a bachelor in laws in 1600 and as a licentiate in canon law in December 1608. He would remember it in his testament, leaving sufficient monies to rebuild one of San Bartolomé's edifices.[17] By the start of 1609, he had established sufficient credentials as a jurist to seek an office.

NEW INQUISITOR, NEW INQUISITION: FOUNDING THE TRIBUNAL IN CARTAGENA DE INDIAS

The new licentiate soon found a post: in June 1609, Philip III nominated him as one of the two founding inquisitors of the Inquisition tribunal in Cartagena de Indias. It was a precocious start for a career. Mañozca became an inquisitor closer to the age of thirty than to the often-preferred forty and was elevated directly to the rank of judge. His appointment indicated that he already had effective patrons within the Inquisition, or elsewhere at Court, and that he was beginning to distinguish himself by a combination of political savvy, juridical ability, and vocation. He seems to have taken orders before departing for Cartagena and to have acquired an ecclesiastical income in short order; by 1619, he described himself as a subdeacon.

[16] There is quite a bit of scholarly work on the Carvajal family. For one approach to the literature, see Miriam Bodian, *Dying in the Law of Moses: Crypto-Jewish Martyrdom in the Iberian World* (Bloomington: Indiana University Press, 2007), chap. 3. See also Páramo, *De Origine et progressu*, 242. Alberro counts that *auto* as the thirteenth held (the first in 1574), *Inquisition et Société*, 270, 362. Curcio-Nagy estimated that public celebrations in the Plaza Mayor (or Zócalo) could accommodate a crowd of around 40,000, *The Great Festivals of Colonial Mexico City*. See also Luis González Obregón, ed., *Procesos de Luis de Carvajal (el Mozo)* (Mexico City: Talleres Gráficos de la Nación, 1935).

[17] He started at Salamanca in 1600, entered San Bartolomé on October 6, 1607, graduated with his licentiate December 16, and willed monies to the "Casa de Texares"; Sánchez Rivilla, "Inquisidores," 368; Medina, *Cartagena de Indias*, 114. On the connections between the universities in Salamanca and Mexico and the role of faculty and students as censors in Mexico's Inquisition tribunal, see Nesvig, *Ideology and Inquisition*.

On paper, Philip III established the new tribunal in 1609, although the *Suprema* and the Inquisitor General – then Bernardo de Sandoval y Rojas, archbishop of Toledo and cardinal of Santa Balbina – decided its jurisdiction in February 1610. Philip II had instituted two tribunals of the Spanish Inquisition in the Americas in 1569, supplanting earlier inquisitions conducted by mendicant friars and under the authority of bishops; the new foundations in Lima and Mexico City began to operate in 1570 and 1571, respectively, and expressly excluded the Indians, so called, from their jurisdiction. The new court's instructions followed the same model. The need for a third tribunal was justified by the vastness of Lima's inquisitorial district, even as the Mexican court's territorial reach was also unwieldy, stretching across the Pacific to the Philippines. The decision rested even more on the perception of vulnerability. A rather unsatisfactory peace was negotiated with the Dutch United Provinces in 1609 and Cartagena de Indias was an important port. Located on the Caribbean rather than the Pacific, the city was far more accessible to communications than Lima, and thus theoretically more nimble in matters of appeal and correspondence with the king and his councils in Spain.[18] Aside from considerations of judicial expediency, ports, with their traffic of commodities and people, licensed and illicit, were feared to be easy points of entry for foreign heretics and their heresies, both in the flesh and in print. And this port was known as "the key to all the Indies."[19]

There Mañozca would learn how to work as an inquisitor. Before taking ship, he served the Inquisition in Seville for several months while he and his new colleagues waited for passage. The officials essential to the operation of an inquisitorial court left Spain on June 29, 1610, sailing from the port of Cádiz: the two inquisitors, Lic. don Pedro Mathe de Salcedo and Mañozca; the *fiscal*, Francisco de Bazán; and the secretary, Luis Blanco de Salcedo. They made a stop in Santo Domingo (which had been

---

[18] See Fermina Álvarez Alonso, *La Inquisición en Cartagena de Indias durante el siglo XVII* (Madrid: Fundación Universitaria Española, 1999); Ballesteros Gaibrois, "La Instalación del Tribunal," *HIEA* 3:1025–29; Tejado Fernández, "La Ampliación del Dispositivo: Fundación del Tribunal de Cartagena de Indias," *HIEA* 1:984–95; "El Tribunal de Cartagena de Indias. La Primera Mitad del Siglo XVII (1621–1650)," *HIEA* 1:1141–45; and "Las Modificaciones Estructurales en Cartagena de Indias," *HIEA* 1:1189–95. For the tribunal's correspondence to the *Suprema* during Mañozca's term, see AHN, Inq., libs. 1008, 1009. See also Anna Maria Splendiani, *Cincuenta Años de Inquisición en el Tribunal de Cartagena de Indias, 1610–1660* (Bogotá: Centro Editorial Javeriano, Instituto Colombiano de Cultura Hispánica, 1997).

[19] "la llave de todas las Yndias," quoted in Ballesteros Gaibrois, "La Instalación del Tribunal," 1026.

considered as a location for the new tribunal), where they read an edict of faith in the cathedral, announcing heresies against which the populace should guard itself. Thus, they began the exercise of their office even before arriving in Cartagena in September, where they established the new tribunal, announcing its foundation and, two months later, reading an edict of faith in the city's cathedral.[20] Both inquisitors would occupy their new posts for little more than a decade. Salcedo would die there in December 1621 and Mañozca would leave in 1623. The new court was not equipped with judicial experience, as neither man had been an inquisitor before his appointment. Instead, Salcedo, the senior inquisitor, had previously been the *fiscal* in Zaragoza's tribunal.

The city in which Mañozca arrived in the fall of 1610 had been founded in 1533. Cartagena de Indias (so called to distinguish it from the port of Cartagena on Spain's southeastern coast) was primarily a military outpost of strategic importance, a theme that dominated the inquisitors' early correspondence back to Madrid. They noted that only 500 Spanish citizens (*vezinos*) were there and described the place as the "bridge" and "passage" to the Americas.[21] Other early seventeenth-century estimates counted fifteen hundred Spaniards in the city or estimated three hundred Spanish citizens, and from that two thousand Spaniards in total, along with two hundred soldiers in the military garrison and somewhere between three thousand and four thousand slaves of African origin. There were also persons of various European origins, mestizos, mulattos, and free people of African descent. Not only military but also commercial traffic passed through the city, and it was a magnet for piracy, assaulted in 1544 by the French, razed by the English in 1580, and attacked by Sir Francis Drake in 1586. It was both a way station for transatlantic vessels and a key stop in intra-Caribbean itineraries. It was also the principal Spanish American port into which enslaved Africans were brought; one estimate puts the number of slaves in transit through the port between 1595 and 1640 at 135,000. Some were sent to the kingdom's gold mines, others were among those who plumbed the Caribbean waters for pearls, and many enslaved port inhabitants worked in trades and domestic service. Cartagena was under the authority of a governor – the principal military and political authority – and, as part of the kingdom of New Granada, subject to the

---

[20] Nomination, November 7, 1609, AGI, Contratación, 5793, lib. 1, fols. 26v-27; AHN, Inq., lib. 1009, fol. 6v; Tejado Fernández, "Las Modificaciones Estructurales," 1189–90; and "La Ampliación del Dispositivo," 995.

[21] "puente," "paso," Salcedo and Mañozca, December 18, 1610, AHN, Inq., lib. 1008, fol. 1v.

audiencia in Santa Fe de Bogotá, a difficult journey inland that took near forty days in good conditions. The inquisitors were but two among many religious authorities, as the city's elite included members of several regular orders, the cathedral chapter, and the bishop. The Society of Jesus was also planting new foundations in these years, establishing a province in New Granada in 1596 and arriving in Cartagena in 1604. Two fathers who began their careers in the port gained renown for their missionary work among the slaves there; Alonso de Sandoval (1577–1652) – who would write a treatise on the subject – and Pedro Claver (1581–1654) – beatified and canonized in the nineteenth century – arrived in 1605 and 1610, respectively.[22]

Still, the inquisitors described the populace as unconcerned with religion, at best. Their first proclamation of an edict of faith was disastrous: "Sunday, day of the publication, as it was already being read with the solemnity possible, the church went into an uproar, the governor and the master of the galleys going out, and many others with them, to pacify a quarrel that was the cause of the riot between the soldiers of the garrison and those of the galleys."[23] That initial edict had an encyclopedic quality to it, alerting the assembled (if inattentive) populace to heresies associated with, as they phrased it, the law of Moses, the sects of Mohammed, of Luther, and of *alumbrados*, as well as to an assortment of heresies from

---

[22] Another 135,000 slaves were estimated to have transited through the other ports combined – Veracruz, Havana, Santo Domingo, Puerto Rico, Santa María (Venezuela), and Buenos Aires. Another reckoning set the city's population at about 3,000 whites and 7,000 "negros de servicio," with about 25,000 *indios* in the surrounding district (that is even more difficult to estimate); Enriqueta Vila Vilar, "Introducción," in Alonso de Sandoval, *Un tratado sobre la esclavitud*, ed. and trans. Vila Vilar (Madrid: Alianza Editorial, 1987), 18, 20. See also Nicolás del Castillo Mathieu, *La Llave de las Indias* (Bogotá: Ediciones El Tiempo, 1981); María Cristina Navarrete, *Historia Social del Negro en la Colonia Cartagena, siglo XVII* (Santiago de Cali: Universidad del Valle, 1995), 23–25; Molly A. Warsh, "Enslaved Pearl Divers in the Sixteenth-Century Caribbean," *Slavery and Abolition* 31.3 (2010): 345–62; Nicole von Germeten, "Introduction" in Alonso de Sandoval, S.J., *Treatise on Slavery. Selections from De instauranda Aethiopum salute*, ed. and trans. von Germeten (Indianapolis, IN and Cambridge, UK: Hackett Publishing Co., 2008), x–xiii. A survey of foreign residents in the 1620s counted 154 Portuguese (or about 10 percent of the European population); Jonathan Israel, *Empires and Entrepots: The Dutch, the Spanish Monarchy and the Jews, 1585–1713* (London and Ronceverte, WV: The Hambledon Press, 1990), 277.

[23] "conla solemnidad posible, el domingo dia de la publicacion estandose ya leyendo se alboroto la iglesia saliendose della el Gobernador y Cabo delas galeras y otros muchos conellos a apaciguar una pendencia que fue causa del alboroto entre los soldados del presidio y los delas Galeras." Salcedo and Mañozca, December 18, 1610, AHN, Inq., lib. 1008, fol. 2r.

heterodox opinions to blasphemy to witchcraft and demonic pacts, the administering of the sacraments by the unordained, clerical marriage, soliciting in the confessional, a catalog of prohibited divination practices, and love magic, among others; they warned against harmful books and announced their special authority to absolve the cases listed, reserved to them via papal delegation.[24] The tribunal held few trials in its first years, although its initial decades would be its most active period; Manuel Tejado Fernández counted eighty-one trials between 1610 and 1621. The inquisitors staged their first *auto de fe* in February 1614 and a smaller one in July 1618. In the first appeared nineteen souls penanced, primarily for blasphemy and witchcraft, and in the second, just four criminals: two bigamists, a married friar, and a Portuguese *converso* convicted of Judaizing. The tribunal put a particular emphasis on cases of witchcraft, most of them focused on women of African origin in Cartagena, Tolú, and Zaragoza. A decade after Mañozca's departure, the particularly dramatic *auto de fe* of 1632 – in which several women from Tolú were relaxed as witches – provoked the *Suprema*'s intervention; it demanded that any capital sentence be sent to it for review and annulled several such sentences.[25]

Inquisitors' work required persistent negotiation with other authorities and with local conditions and populations, a circumstance even more true when carving out space for a new tribunal. Not unlike Páramo and his colleagues in Sicily, Salcedo and Mañozca strove to show both the

---

[24] Diana Luz Ceballos Gómez, *Hechicería, brujería, e Inquisición en el Nuevo Reino de Granada. Un duelo de imaginarios* (Bogotá: Editorial Universidad Nacional, 1995), 214–19; Medina, *Cartagena de Indias*, 128–41.

[25] Up until 1621, the tribunal received denunciations of a group of one hundred witches, although they could only capture and try four. Of the eighty-one trials, Tejado categorized them as nineteen for blasphemy, ten for witchcraft (*brujería*), seven for less serious witchcraft (*hechicería*), ten for generalized heresies, five for heretical propositions, three for Judaizing, three for solicitation in the confessional, five for bigamy, one for celebrating sacraments without ordination, five for renegades, and thirteen as miscellaneous; "La Ampliación del Dispositivo," 989, 992–94; and "Las Modificaciones Estructurales," 1191–93; see also Medina, *Cartagena de Indias*, 43–46. Ceballos Gómez suggests the witchcraft trials were an instrument of ideological acculturation and deculturation aimed at *indios* and *negros*, and she characterized Mañozca as "un poco obsesionado con las fantasías demonológicas" and the author of the first witch hunts in Cartagena, *Hechicería, brujería, e Inquisición*, 54–55, 93, 95. The most colorful case in these years was that of Lorenza de Acereto; accused of minor witchcraft, she appealed to the *Suprema*, which inclined toward absolving her. At issue was the inquisitorial investigation of sins already expunged in the confessional, conflict between inquisitors and other ecclesiastics, and Mañozca's reputed capital enmity toward her lover, Francisco de Santander, the *Sargento Mayor*; Tejado Fernández, *Aspectos de la Vida Social en Cartagena de Indias durante el Seiscientos* (Seville: Escuela de Estudios Hispano-Americanos, 1954), 45–79.

difficulties of the place where they had been posted and their ability to establish authority and follow procedure even in unusual conditions. They painted themselves as guardians of orthodoxy on the edge of the Indies and expressed doubts about whether the prelates in the region were sufficient for the task at hand, declaring that "we lament the miserable state that religion has [here]." A district ringed with ports was one where heretical poison always lurked nearby. To further emphasize the liminality of the region, they described how the populace engaged in incestuous relationships, barely noticing kinship in their liaisons. A city composed of soldiers, they explained, made for an unstable society. Making it seem an even less respectable place, they noted that the majority of the cases of heresy related to women involved in witchcraft and other superstitious behavior. Honorable men or women were in short supply. Like their peers in other tribunals, they made these observations the basis for petitions for extra funds and for proposals to modify inquisitorial practice for their environment. They did not see any reason why a candidate for familiar – of known purity of blood, they noted – should be barred from office for his marriage to a *mestiza*. From their first year in Cartagena, they lobbied for funds to build a new facility, making the hot climate their primary rationale.[26]

The pair of inquisitors enumerated other difficulties. They consistently lacked the necessary officials and familiars to staff their tribunal in the manner usually done in Spain. Lacking a proper jail, they converted the *corral* at the center of the Inquisition's house into impromptu cells. Unsurprisingly, they also wrote to Madrid about matters of jurisdiction. For example, it was apparently uncertain to which inquisitorial court the diocese of Nicaragua belonged. Salcedo and Mañozca advanced their claim, citing its great distance from either Mexico City or Lima.[27] Even as they debated their district's scope – competing with other Inquisition tribunals – their judicial activities had a distinctly urban flavor. When the tribunal acted farther afield, it tended to do so through deputies and correspondence, the district's geography providing an impediment to the peninsular model of visitation.

Clashes occurred between the judges and other local elites. Reminiscent of conflicts elsewhere, irregularities in the appointment and conduct of

---

[26] "lloramos el miserable estado que la religion tiene," Salcedo and Mañozca to Inquisitor General, July 14, 1612, AHN, Inq., lib. 1008, fols. 34r, 35r; Ballesteros Gaibrois, "La Instalación del Tribunal," 1026.

[27] Tejado Fernández, "Las modificaciones estructurales," 1189; and "La Ampliación del Dispositivo," 993; Ballesteros Gaibrois, "La Instalación del Tribunal," 1026–28.

officials were consistent refrains of complaints against the Holy Office. Perhaps because of the lack of familiars, the inquisitors seem to have used their African slaves as their primary lay officials, a practice that other royal authorities anxiously reported to Madrid. From the sixteenth century, escaped slaves had established fortified communities, known as *palenques*, in the regions around Cartagena, and a host of colonial regulations sought to curtail escapes and to respond to fears of revolt. Local magistrates complained that the slaves who acted as the inquisitors' stewards were "so free and impudent that they do not fear the ordinary justices."[28] The tensions boiled over into open conflict. When one of Mañozca's slaves was found armed and out at night, the secular justices punished him with one hundred lashes. Mañozca retaliated: he used his judicial authority to arrest the officials who had carried out the punishment, sentenced them to an equal physical punishment, and banned them from the city.[29] By 1613, complaints about Mañozca had already begun to reach Madrid. The inquisitors allegedly meddled with and undermined the jurisdiction of the secular courts, causing them to suffer a loss of reputation. The governor protested that the inquisitors did not show him sufficient deference in Cartagena's cathedral and that they set a dangerous example, wishing "with their shows of distinction, to annihilate those of this government." Their behavior had reputedly spurred the cathedral chapter to act in similar ways.[30] In sum, Mañozca's formative experiences as an inquisitor occurred in an environment that required improvization, where institutional structures were less firmly in place, and where authority was established and contested in the public arena even more than usual.

FRAMING CASES, BUILDING NETWORKS

One of the most intricate cases that Mañozca assembled during his years in Cartagena de Indias was that of his own defense against accusations of malpractice. From Cartagena and Santa Fe, appeals against the inquisitor were routed to the *Suprema* and to the Council of the Indies. The Inquisition tribunal's foundation was only one element of the port's shifting political landscape. The fleets also brought many other officials and religious initiatives. Jesuits continued to set sail for Cartagena, another twenty departing

---

[28] "son tan libres y desconpuestos que no temen las justicias hordinarias," Diego Fernández Alvo, *Procurador General*, February 25, 1622, AGI, Santa Fe, 63, no. 34.

[29] This incident is recounted in Phelan, *Kingdom of Quito*, 245.

[30] "aniquilar con sus preheminençias las deeste gouierno," Diego Fernández de Velasco, July 8, 1613, AGI, Santa Fe, 38, r. 4, no. 120.

the peninsula in 1620 and suffering an attack from Muslim pirates en route. The viceroy of Peru, passing through in 1615, launched an investigation into contraband, centering on the slave trade. He quickly sent dispatches on the subject back to Spain, and in 1618, especially serious charges were levied against a certain Manuel Bautista Pérez – whom Mañozca would eventually try for heresy in Lima years later – for bribing the governor and royal officials of Cartagena with slaves and silver in order to allow him to transport twice the number of slaves he had registered with the crown. In 1615, proponents of the Immaculate Conception – a disputed doctrine that divided the orders – had sought to rally support for their cause with public celebrations in Seville, particularly focused on the black and mulatto inhabitants of that city; that December, the controversy arrived in Cartagena. By the summer of 1616, secular authorities complained that the Dominicans – long opposed to the doctrine – made scandalous displays against the devotions to the Immaculate Conception. Augustinian, Franciscan, Jesuit, and Mercaderian friars allied against the Dominicans. Increasing the unrest, the governor reported, the bishop of Cartagena joined forces with the Dominicans, shouted at the processing populace and friars, and even instructed his servants to pelt them with stones. Each side began a campaign of sermons against the other, and the governor claimed that there was so much commotion that he feared that recent converts to Christianity would lose their faith. The Inquisition attempted to intervene in the conflict and ran afoul of some of the city's elites as a result.[31]

One of the fathers posted to the Jesuit college, Baltasar Mas Burgués, proved to be among Mañozca's staunchest allies. In July 1616, he wrote to the *Suprema*, praising the inquisitor – whose lodgings were near the college – as the epitome of the good magistrate:

I have always discovered in him a great prudence in directing affairs, not only his own, but also others', for there are many that owe him for asking his counsel and direction, no less providence in discovering and preventing future [disturbances], an admirable comprehension in business, and dexterity in everything to which he puts his hand.[32]

---

[31] The bribes were estimated as worth 6,170 pesos, and Pérez seems to have been related to "at least two of the Madrid Portuguese bankers"; Israel, *Empires and Entrepots*, 278; Castillo Mathieu, *Llave de las Indias*, 67, 229–30; see also Medina, *Cartagena de Indias*, 100–14; Diego de Acuna, August 22, 1616, AGI, Santa Fe, 38, r. 5, no. 140; Linda A. Newson and Susie Minchin, *From Capture to Sale: The Portuguese Slave Trade to Spanish South America in the Early Seventeenth Century* (Leiden and Boston: Brill, 2007).

[32] "Siempre he descubierto en el una gran prudencia en dirigir las cosas, no solamente suyas, sino tambien agenas, por ser muchos los que deuden a pedir su consejo y direccion: la prouidencia no menor en descubrir y preuenir lo uenidero: una admirable comprehension

He proceeded to describe Mañozca as very learned and showing "great fidelity and vigilance in his office." Mas Burgués claimed that the inquisitor's force of character rendered him a powerful asset, as he had greater authority "alone, than all the others who govern them, put together."[33] The letter sketched Mañozca as an administrator with the talents necessary to operate far from his superiors as a worthy representative of the crown.

For Mañozca, matters came to a head in 1620. A cascade of letters about him was sent to the peninsular councils, and he gained a license to return to Castile to defend himself in person before the Inquisitor General. His supporters and opponents shared a common language of administrative virtue and of corruption. On the one hand, Mañozca's accusers claimed that he abused his authority as an inquisitor, living loosely, extorting funds, and engaging in inappropriate relationships with local women. They suggested that he overstepped the Inquisition's jurisdiction, interfering in royal governance or the work of the religious orders. When Mañozca penned his defense, he sought to guess who his accusers were and discredit them; his reasoning had much in common with the process of recusation in an inquisitorial trial. He supposed that his recent difficulties stemmed from his conflict with a lieutenant. He also claimed that everyone related to the collection of the *alcabala* – one of the primary taxes – disliked him, as he had questioned their keeping of accounts. He depicted those aligned against him as a faction whose motivations were personal, all associates, debtors, or relatives of those whom Mañozca had charged with crimes or whose administrative actions he had questioned. In short,

---

enlos negocios, y destreza en todo lo que pone mano." Mas Burgués, July 6, 1616, AHN, Inq., lib. 1009, fol. 188. Mas Burgués (1568–1642) was born in Alcira, Valencia, and educated at Valencia's Jesuit college of San Pablo; he taught in the province of Aragon several years, first crossing the Atlantic in 1612. Briefly sent to the *colegio* in Panama, he was soon made rector of Cartagena's new college (1613–15 and 1617–20). In 1621, he was sent to be rector in Bogotá (1621–28) and was involved in founding the Universidad Javeriana there in 1623. In the late 1620s, he was made a *procurador* to Madrid and Rome, where he advocated for the Society in New Granada. Returning to the Americas in 1631, he was sent to various charges in Quito (heading the Universidad Gregoriana there, 1631–32), back to Madrid as an advocate once again in 1635, and finally to the *colegio* in Bogotá in 1639, where he remained until his death August 3, 1642. José del Rey Fajardo, S. J., *Los Jesuitas en Cartagena de Indias 1604–1767* (Bogotá: Centro Editorial Javeriano (Pontificia Universidad Javeriana), 2004), 206–9. Mas Burgués (then rector in Bogotá) wrote an approbation for Sandoval's *De instauranda Aethiopum Salute*, December 10, 1623. The rector in Cartagena then, Antonio Agustín, described himself as *calificador* of the Inquisition. Sandoval, *Un tratado sobre la esclavitud*, ed. Vila Vilar, 49–51.

33 "gran fidelidad y vigilancia en su officio." And: "solo, que todos los demas que los gouiernan, juntos," Mas Burgués, July 6, 1616, AHN, Inq., lib. 1009, fol. 188.

he dismissed the opposition to him as stemming from particular passions and enmity.[34]

Mañozca also assembled character witnesses to vouch for him, soliciting letters of support. That correspondence praised the inquisitor's judicial ability or his pious works as a "father of orphans, crutch of the poor, defender of the Religions."[35] The quality of his referees was also notable: many were members of the regular clergy and officials in their orders. The second prong of this defense was for the sympathetic witnesses to also discredit Mañozca's enemies. An Augustinian friar drew on his knowledge of both the place and the workings of the tribunal to support the inquisitor, "sinister informations having been divulged to be the cause of his departure, and I, knowing the scant truth in them as a resident here and as the minister [who examines heretical propositions] in the tribunal." Instead, he emphasized Mañozca's honorable behavior, his chastity, and the breadth of his learning, testifying that "his pastimes are not games ... but rather the books not only of his faculty, but of the rest, [of which] he has many and in all of them he studies, because he is eminent not only in canon and civil law but also in arts, theology, history, and Latin, that which is most lofty."[36] As he had done four years earlier, Mas Burgués – by then the rector of Cartagena's Jesuit college – gave further evidence of the honor Mañozca conferred on the tribunal. He maintained that all of the inquisitor's opponents were "liars and troublesome men," who sought to sabotage his reputation. He supported his assertions with verifiable proof: the *audiencia* had condemned one of the accusers for bearing false titles, exiling him from the Indies. Mas Burgués reserved even harsher terms for friars who spoke against the inquisitor, explaining that "some religious fomented similar inventions ... unworthy of Christians."[37] One was a Jesuit who had since been evicted from the order; another he characterized

---

[34] See letters, primarily from summer 1620, AHN, Inq., lib. 1009, fols. 64–108, also fols. 241–44; AGI, Santa Fe, 243, the latter also contains letters in support of a cleric of Cartagena's cathedral who was an ally of the Inquisition.

[35] "padre de huerfanos arrimo de pobres, deffensor delas Relijiones" (i.e., defender of the orders), numerous signatories, June 6, 1620, AHN, Inq., lib. 1009, fol. 190.

[36] "auiendose diuulgado ser la causa de su ida informaciones siniestras y sabiendo yo la poca verdad dellas como asistente aqui y ministro calificador del tribunal." And: "sus pasatiempos son no juegos ... sino los libros q[ue] no solo de su facultad sino de las demas tiene muchissimos y entodos ellos estudia porque no solo en sus canones y leyes es eminente sino en artes Theologia historia y latinidad la que es eminentissimo." Gaspar de Herrero, July 7, 1620, AHN, Inq., lib. 1009, fol. 193.

[37] "hombres inquietos y embusteros," and "fomentaro[n] semeja[n]tes inue[n]ciones ... algunos religiosos, siendo indignas de Christianos." Mas Burgués, July 24, 1620, AHN, Inq., lib. 1009, fol. 220r.

as a Franciscan who preached scandalous sermons; a third, a Dominican, had also been expelled from his order.

The rector further recounted how the people of Cartagena had persecuted several friars who, in his telling, had made public defenses of religion. He added Mañozca to that good company. He described how a former Jesuit rector who attempted to impose greater morality had found himself viciously attacked, "as much for telling truths in his sermons, as for having concluded serious affairs in the service of God, and [for the] good of his Religion." To discredit this friar, his enemies contrived "to feign false letters from the councillors of the Royal Council of the Indies, and if the said inquisitor had not discovered and undone their falsehood and lies, they would have been a stumbling block and a cause of deception for many."[38] While characterizing Mañozca as the embodiment of the good inquisitor, exercising his powers of discernment for public benefit, he also called attention to his order's virtuous works. Mas Burgués recalled attacks made on the Company of Jesus, about whom "they said such infamous things, as they could say about a company of thieves or highwaymen." His fellows had drawn particular ire, he noted, "for having preached against games, which were used here with insolence, and without any restraint, without respect to Lent nor to holy days and weeks." The immorality had reached such height that "a friar preached publicly one day in Lent in defense of [games], with such scandal, that many of the people said that that was to preach liberty of conscience, as if we were in Geneva." The gaming houses maintained they had royal licenses to operate, even during Lent, while the rector retorted that this was a lie. Instead, he announced that Mañozca, as a champion of the faith, "undid all these frauds."[39] In response to the litany of vices of which the inquisitor had been accused, his defenders submitted affidavits of his virtues, painting him as the true victim of persecution.

Mañozca sailed for Spain in late July, and by the end of 1620, he was in Madrid in order to make his appearance before the *Suprema*. The

[38] "assi por dezir verdades en sus sermones, como por hauer concluido negocios graues en seruicio de Dios, y bien de su Religion," and "fingir cartas falsas de consejeros del Real Consejo de Indias que si el dicho Inquisidor no deescubriera y deshizera su falsedad y mentira, fuera[n] tropieço y engaño de muchos," ibid., fol. 220v.

[39] "dixero[n] cosas tan infames, como pudieran dezir de una Comp[añí]a de ladrones, o, salteadores," and "por hauer predicado contra el juego, que se usaua aqui con insolencia, y sin freno alguno; sin respecto a quaresmas, ni a semanas y dias sanctos;" also "un frayle predicasse publicam[en]te un dia de quaresma en defensa del, con tanto escandalo, que muchos del pueblo dixeron, que aquello era predicar libertad de conciencia, como si estuuieramos en Geneua," and "Todos estos embustes deshizo," ibid., fol. 220v.

Inquisitor General – the Dominican friar Luis de Aliaga Martínez – seemingly put stock in the inquisitor's account. He not only retained his post, receiving his license to sail again for Cartagena de Indias in April 1621, just weeks after the death of Philip III, but was also nominated to the more prestigious tribunal in Lima; an intimate of Mañozca's later ascribed the promotion to Aliaga's favor. Not for the last time, Mañozca weathered significant sea changes at Court. Aliaga, whose tenure as Inquisitor General had been short, was one of those to be dismissed from his post in the first weeks of Philip IV's reign that same April.[40] In September, Mañozca received a commission from the Council of the Indies to travel to Quito as the visitor of that city's royal *audiencia*, although he was soon instructed to delay his departure for several months.[41] With Salcedo's death at the end of 1621, Mañozca became the sole and senior inquisitor of the Cartagena tribunal, and he marked his return to the city with a show of authority and judicial diligence, presiding over an *auto de fe* on March 13, 1622. He related his activities to his superiors in Castile, taking a defensive tone; he protested that despite presenting only eight completed cases, the *auto* had provided powerful examples to instruct the populace and proclaimed that he had produced an *auto de fe* of equal caliber to those held in Spain. Witchcraft again featured prominently, and Mañozca emphasized that it had even included a capital sentence, for a Protestant Englishman who had refused to admit his errors.[42] The judge was building the experience he would rely upon to navigate through future conflicts.

Having parlayed controversy into promotion, Mañozca left Cartagena with a large retinue of servants and associates in September 1623, after his replacement had arrived and recovered from an illness.[43] The journey from Cartagena to Lima took six long months, and he described it as

<hr>

[40] AHN, Inq., lib. 1040, fol. 96; J. H. Elliott, *The Count-Duke of Olivares: The Statesman in an Age of Decline* (New Haven, CT, and London: Yale University Press, 1986), 101–2. Dispatches addressed him as an inquisitor of Lima's tribunal as early as 1622.

[41] *Consulta*, September 29, 1621, AGI, Indiferente, leg. 754. Indexed in Antonio Heredia Herrera, dir., *Catálogo de Consultas de Consejo de Indias* (Seville: Diputación Provincial, 1988), vol. 4, no. 1293. See also April 21, 1622, AGI, Quito, 209, lib. 2, fol. 12.

[42] Six women were also convicted of witchcraft (four *brujas*, two *hechiceras*), and a Spanish man of bigamy, Tejado Fernández, "La Primera Mitad," 1141. Tejado – similar to other historians – judged Mañozca zealous and ambitious and saw in the correspondence resentment at being junior inquisitor and attempts to bypass his senior colleague whenever possible; "La Ampliación del Dispositivo," 994–95; Medina, *Cartagena de Indias*, 148–49.

[43] José Toribio Medina, *Historia del Tribunal del Santo Oficio de la Inquisición en Lima, 1569–1820* (Santiago de Chile: Fondo Histórico y Bibliográfico J. T. Medina, 1956), 2:14. Phelan, *Kingdom of Quito*, 285.

exceptionally difficult, the hardships duly finding their way into a report. Heat, illnesses, swollen rivers, rough seas, and depopulated swaths of terrain caused his party to lose men along the way. The ship's mast even snapped en route from Panama to Callao, Lima's port. The sights that greeted him upon his arrival in March – or so he promptly wrote to the *Suprema* – were disappointing; he immediately noted the "general complacency" of Lima's tribunal. As the new senior inquisitor, he took possession of the tribunal's buildings and encountered disrepair:

The house is falling down, and uninhabitable, and each day will be more so, of the whole only one room is serviceable, and this is open as [the houses are in] Granada, the inside is not prepared for me, it offends greatly to see how badly arranged everything is: the ministers are few and mainly discontented, today, that we have the salaries embargoed.[44]

He deemed each aspect of the tribunal, from the officials' morals to its judicial efficiency, to be in equivalent disorder.

Between March and August 1624, Mañozca professed indignation that the orders of the king's councils went unheeded and construed himself as the tribunal's much-needed reformer. The senior inquisitor had left in 1623 when he was made a bishop, in order to reside in his highland Peruvian diocese. That left one inquisitor, Lic. Juan Andrés Gaitán in Lima, first awaiting his new colleague, then again alone at the helm of the court when Mañozca soon departed. But six months was enough to embroil the two in conflict.[45] Mañozca quickly established that he would become the senior inquisitor; at the same time, he wrote to the *Suprema* about Gaitán's misconduct, accusing him of treating the tribunal's resources and its personnel as his personal treasury and simultaneously neglecting the business of the Inquisition. Yet Lima's new inquisitor soon set off again to take up his commission as Visitor General of Quito's *audiencia*. It

[44] "complacencia Gen[er]al," and "la cassa se esta caiendo, e inhabitable, y cada dia lo estara mas, de toda ella solo un quarto sirue, y este esta abierto como Granada, no esta me preparado lo de alladentro, lastima grandem[en]te el ver quan mal acondicionado esta todo: los ministros son pocos y descontentos y maiorm[en]te, hoy que tenemos los salarios embargados," Mañozca, April 27, 1624, AHN, Inq., lib. 1039, fols. 16–17.

[45] The inquisitor Dr. Francisco Verdugo y Cabrera became bishop of Huamanga. María del Pilar Pérez Canto, "Tribunal de Lima," *HIEA* 1:1133–34. For the Lima tribunal during these years, see AHN, Inq., libs. 1038–41; René Millar Carvacho, *Inquisición y sociedad en el virreinato peruano: Estudios sobre el tribunal de Lima* (Lima: Instituto Riva-Agüero, Pontificia Universidad Católica del Perú, 1988); Paulino Castañeda Delgado y Pilar Hernández Aparicio, *La Inquisición de Lima* (Madrid: Editorial Deimos, 1989); Teodoro Hampe Martínez, *Santo Oficio e Historia Colonial* (Lima: Ediciones del Congreso del Perú, 1998).

took Mañozca about two months to travel from low-lying Lima to the highland city, the presence of the Dutch fleet in the Pacific adding threat and delays to his journey from Callao to the port of Guayaquil, as the former was under siege and the latter had been raided.[46] When Mañozca reached Quito at the end of October, he was presented with another new urban scenario: a city of maybe ten thousand inhabitants around the turn of the century, half indigenous, with perhaps another twenty-five thousand native Andeans in the surrounding region.[47] As an inquisitor still within Lima's district, Mañozca introduced a new element into Quito's religious geography, which already included a bishop and a significant number of regular clergy.

Although the nature of visitations, designed to draw up charges of misconduct, was inherently contentious, this one soon became especially combative. In theory, the purpose of official inspections was to investigate whether a royal institution was free of corruption and judicial abuses and honest in its finances, and whether its magistrates and other officials were following proper procedures; these were the sorts of yardsticks to which sixteenth- and seventeenth-century administrators were trained to be attuned. Mañozca was quickly at odds with many of Quito's authorities, and he became locked in dispute with the president of the *audiencia*, Dr. Antonio de Morga (1559–1636), exchanging charges and countercharges. Morga also had one Basque parent, although he had been born in Seville, and he too had studied law in Salamanca. He had begun his career in Manila in 1593 – building a legal reputation, acquiring the experience he later used to publish an account of events in the Philippines, and enriching himself in part through contraband trade – before gaining a middling appointment in the *audiencia* of Mexico in 1603; made head of that of Quito in 1615, he remained there until his death. Not only Morga and Mañozca, but also their factions in Quito slandered and assaulted each other, both sides appealing to the royal councils for a favorable resolution.[48]

The decision to order inspections of several American *audiencias* was part of the reforming spirit of Philip IV's early administration; throughout Mañozca's term in Quito as Visitor General, the king – through the Council of the Indies – continued to revise his instructions. In one instance,

---

[46] I draw here from the beginning of Phelan's chapter on Mañozca, based on his letter to the king of April 10, 1625, *Kingdom of Quito*, 243.

[47] Kris Lane, *Quito 1599. City and Colony in Transition* (Albuquerque: University of New Mexico Press, 2002), 1.

[48] On Mañozca's role in the visitation, see especially Phelan, *Kingdom of Quito*, 243–319.

the inquisitor received orders to reinterview witnesses about the scandalous life and procedural incompetence of one of the *audiencia*'s judges. In another, he was commanded to also investigate the treasurer of the port of Guayaquil and his handling of revenues. As Quito fell under his court's jurisdiction, Mañozca decided to use his inquisitorial authority there as well; with the *Suprema*'s permission, he erected an Inquisition tribunal that he operated for the duration of the visitation.[49] This choice proved especially contentious, his opponents repeatedly accusing him of using inquisitorial jurisdiction as a personal weapon, citing his investigations of those in opposing factions, particularly Augustinians.

In 1626, friar Leonardo de Araujo, the provincial of the Augustinian order in Quito, slipped out of the city and crossed the Atlantic. Once he reached Court that fall, he appealed for Mañozca's dismissal, printing a report of the scandal the inquisitor had caused. Araujo described a city pitted against itself: the Dominicans and Augustinians allied and facing off against Mañozca's party, depicted as made up mainly of local Inquisition agents. The provincial turned the language of instruction against Mañozca, claiming that the conflict he had caused among the religious hierarchy offered a poor example for the populace and so undermined the orders' central project of conversion.[50] He accused Mañozca of orchestrating a faction of sometimes armed supporters to bully his opponents and enforce his jurisdiction (including establishing a makeshift jail to house those he tried). Araujo made the Inquisition's rules the grounds for his complaint, noting that the Holy Office had stringent standards of practice, but that Mañozca had flaunted inquisitorial procedures with improper imprisonments and interrogations.[51] The friar attracted the attention of Olivares, and his grievances, along with others arriving from Quito, were reviewed in the Council of the Indies. Mañozca wrote a rebuttal to Araujo, sent missives to Madrid explaining his actions and lambasting his

---

[49] Council of the Indies to Mañozca, March 29 and October 20, 1625, AGI, Quito, 209, lib. 2, fols. 14v, 15; *consulta*, February 11, 1628, AGI, Lima, 5, doc. 113/2. It was later noted (in 1634) that Mañozca had gone to Quito with three thousand pesos in royal salary and another two thousand as an *ayuda de costa*, AHN, Inq., lib. 1040, fol. 329.

[50] Leonardo de Araujo, *Relacion de las cosas que svcedieron en la civdad de Quito … con las Ordenes de Santo Domingo, y san Agustin, por mano del Licenciado Iuan de Mañosca …* [1627?], BNE, R/17270(47), fol. 324v; for dating, see P. Gregorio de Santiago Vela, *Ensayo de una Biblioteca Ibero-Americana de la Orden de San Agustín* (Madrid: Imprenta del Asilo de Huérfanos del S. C. de Jesús, 1913), 1:193–94. The Council of the Indies considered both Araujo's account and a report from Mañozca, July 8, 1631, AGI, Lima, 5; Heredia Herrera, dir., *Catálogo de Consultas*, 6:61.

[51] Araujo, *Relacion*, fol. 340r.

opponents, and even employed an advocate at Court. Nevertheless, the king acted on the council's censure of Mañozca, deciding in March 1627 to deprive him of his authority as Visitor General; the order arrived in Quito in September, even though a replacement inspector would not come from Lima until February 1630, and royal announcements about the affair were still being made in the viceregal capital in August 1630.[52]

The council especially disapproved of Mañozca having proceeded in areas outside his specific jurisdiction and of his interference in the Dominicans' affairs, intervening in a contested election. They chastised him for his haste and excessive zeal in judicial matters, and for suspending the *audiencia*'s judges, which had thrown the administration of the kingdom into chaos. When news of the censure arrived in Quito, some friars reputedly behaved jubilantly. Morga remained president of the *audiencia*, and Mañozca returned as senior inquisitor to Lima, the two jurists taking their leave of each other with displays of courtesy, about which each was careful to leave a written record. The visitation demonstrated a certain tension between administrative dynamism and torpor. Mañozca had invigorated legal processes in Quito that had languished before his arrival and that quickly ground to a halt when his authority was stripped. The council acted fairly rapidly on the evidence against Mañozca, even as it reprimanded his actions as a visitor as hasty. At the same time, some elements of the affair never really concluded. The new inspector did not submit his report until 1635, the king and council waited another two years to judge the charges, and the second visitor was even fined for unknown cause in 1639.[53] The inquisitors in Lima, moreover, were still writing to the *Suprema* about Araujo's "deceits" in the spring of 1635.[54]

After returning to Lima, the secretary Juan de Ybarra Lizaranzo – who had been vilified by Mañozca's opponents in Quito – petitioned the *Suprema* to continue to reward the inquisitor's service to the king. Seeking to rehabilitate both Mañozca's reputation and his own, he defended the judge's conduct in Quito, decried the "calumnies" against him and those that tried to damage his "reputation and good credit," and emphasized his good work there in the ordinary business of the Inquisition. Ybarra gave a history of Mañozca's career, describing his achievements in the foundation of Cartagena's tribunal, "in whose execution, as a new

---

[52] Juan Antonio Suardo, *Diario de Lima de Juan Antonio Suardo (1629–1639)*, ed. Ruben Vargas Ugarte S.J. (Lima: Universidad Católica del Perú, Instituto de Investigaciones Históricas, 1936), 1:93–94.

[53] Phelan, *Kingdom of Quito*, 282–85, 294–95.

[54] "embustes," May 31, 1635, AHN, Inq., lib. 1040, fols. 432–35.

plantation, and in such remote land, and to where the faith, in some parts of its district, was not known to the Indians, he put special work, and in setting up its privileges and exemptions [was] poorly received by some of the royal ministers." When the *Suprema* read this letter in January 1631, it noted that it would confer with the Council of the Indies on Mañozca's behalf.[55]

As shown in these exchanges of letters, Mañozca's career left evidence of the human ties that he sustained for decades, building networks of clients that spanned the Atlantic. Ybarra, for one, seems to have spent many years with Mañozca. They likely met in Lima in 1624, where Ybarra had arrived in exile from Quito, his earlier experiences in that kingdom perhaps coloring Mañozca's impressions during the visitation. Together in Quito, Ybarra returned with the inquisitor to Lima, traveling with him later to Madrid and possibly even to Mexico.[56] When Mañozca was dismissed from his charge in Quito, he received the news in advance of the royal order, thanks to a message sent from Tomás de Larraspuru, the commander of the fleet in Cartagena de Indias and an associate of the inquisitor's from his time there; their correspondence later allowed Mañozca to apprise Lima of the latest military news.[57] Moreover, on each of Mañozca's voyages across the Atlantic, he included retainers in his license for passage, as Martos de Bohórquez had once done for him. In 1620 and 1621, Matías de Mañosca, a man described as a free black – and given his surname perhaps a slave the inquisitor had manumitted – traveled with him between Cartagena and Castile. There were often natives of Marquina and the surrounding region in his retinue, as on his first voyage to Cartagena in 1610.[58]

---

[55] "en cuya execucion como planta nueua y entierra tan remota y a donde la fe en algunas partes de su distrito no hera conocida de los yndios pusso particular trauajo, y en entablar sus priuilegios y exsenciones mal reciuidos de algunos delos ministros Reales," Juan de Ybarra, AHN, Inq., lib. 1040, fol. 96.

[56] Phelan described him as Mañozca's "principal lieutenant" and remarked: "To the critics of Lic. Mañozca, Juan de Ibarra was the evil genius of the visita general." *Kingdom of Quito*, 257.

[57] Suardo, *Diario*, 1:15, 117, 153.

[58] The initial license to Cartagena included four unmarried *criados*: Nicolas Esteban, of Corrales; Francisco de Orozco, of Marquina (likely a relative); Martín de Fullaondo, of the district (*anteiglesia*) of Maruri; and Domingo de Atecayllona, of Mundaca, June 8, 1610, AGI, Pasajeros, lib. 9, exps. 1944–47, 1971; Contratación, 5320, nos. 32–36. See also the license including the *criados* Diego de Otanla and Matias de Mañosca, April 14 and 15, 1621, AGI, Pasajeros, lib. 10, exps. 2794, 2796; Contratación, 5379, no. 17.

THE POWER OF PUBLICITY, THE POWER OF SECRECY

At fifty, the inquisitor who arrived back in Lima was one of formidable capacities.[59] In Quito, Mañozca had added to his trove of experience and managed another political survival. Affirming his place as senior inquisitor – and once again dislocating Gaitán – he began to reshape a tribunal that had been minimally active and noticeably short staffed. At the same time, he had to adapt to a city of another caliber from those in which he had held office. Whereas Cartagena was of substantial strategic and commercial importance, Lima was one of the two chief Spanish cities in the Americas. Like Mexico City, it was the seat of a viceroy, an *audiencia*, and an archbishop. It was the site of a flourishing legal culture and of the University of San Marcos, founded in the mid-sixteenth century, that had been turning out law degrees since the 1570s. Although it was the region's administrative nerve center, its early seventeenth-century population of around 25,000 inhabitants was dwarfed by that of the mining city of Potosí, which exceeded 160,000.[60] The lag in correspondence with Madrid, which was more than six months in Lima's case, hampered the quick notification of authorities in Castile about anything. On the other hand, the exceptional mobility of figures such as Mañozca and their multiple channels of communication, official and familial, meant that those who passed through the monarchy's urban centers often encountered familiar faces or those with whom they shared acquaintances. A third inquisitor, Dr. don Juan Gutiérrez Flores, had come on the scene in 1625. Briefly the *fiscal* in Palermo's tribunal in the first years of the century, he had proceeded to become an inquisitor in Mallorca, and then in Mexico, reaching New Spain's tribunal in 1612. He had been the inquisitor sent as a replacement when Mañozca's early patron Martos de Bohórquez died, and so Mañozca returned from Quito to a new colleague who had also worked with his uncle – Mexico's tribunal secretary – until his death.[61]

Gutiérrez Flores – who would die in Lima in 1631 – had made charges similar to Mañozca's against Gaitán, likely inclining the *Suprema* toward

---

[59] Phelan also emphasized Mañozca's accumulation of bureaucratic experience, *Kingdom of Quito*.

[60] I am grateful to Renzo Honores for sharing his work in progress with me. For Lima's scale and insights into the region's legal culture, see his "*Pleytos*, letrados y cultura legal en Lima y en Potosí, 1540–1640" (paper presented at Instituto Riva-Agüero, Lima, July 15, 2008); and "Caciques as Legal Benefactors: Cacical Legal Offensive in the Andes, 1550–1572" (paper presented at AHA/ CLAH, New York, January 2–5, 2009).

[61] Alberro, *Inquisition et Société*, 333; Nesvig, *Ideology and Inquisition*, 274–75.

confirming Mañozca as the senior judge after his return to Lima in late 1627.[62] Picking up his mantle of would-be reformer, Mañozca spurred repairs to the tribunal's buildings. He wrote to the king, seeking additional sources of revenue and claiming that the Holy Office had been unable to pay its salaries. Seemingly, it was the favorable hearing of Mañozca's petitions by the president of the Council of the Indies, the count of Castrillo, that secured royal permission for the Lima court to enjoy the rents of several vacant prebends in Peruvian churches. Once obtained, Mañozca zealously guarded these concessions.[63]

He built favorable relations not only with the count of Castrillo but also with the viceroy, the count of Chinchón, with whom he negotiated the boundaries between royal and inquisitorial jurisdiction.[64] He ensconced himself in the city's elite through his appearance at ceremonial events, attending funerals, welcoming new officials, and celebrating the marriage of a close associate of the viceroy; in July 1633, he hosted a lavish dinner in his house for his colleagues and the bishop of Tucumán, sent dishes to the vicereine, and put on a comedy for the religious authorities of the viceregal court.[65] Although the number of cases tried in Lima's Inquisition was never great compared to those tried in many peninsular courts, its activities peaked in the 1630s. Between 1621 and 1700, only four public *autos de fe* were held in Lima's central plaza and seven more in churches or the tribunal chapel, a significant proportion between 1625 and 1641; charges of Judaizing, witchcraft, and bigamy were a persistent focus of this judicial activity.[66] The tribunal proclaimed its authority in other ways; in 1634, for example, it publicly reprimanded the chief magistrate of La Paz for

---

[62] He was buried in the Inquisition's chapel and reputedly died very indebted. Suardo, *Diario*, 1:185–86.

[63] They received permission to a repair a room that had collapsed thirty years before; the work began in 1630 and it was made Gaitán's dwelling, June 12, 1632, AHN, Inq., lib. 1040, fol. 158. On the rents: Mañozca to Castrillo, May 18, 1636, AHN, Inq., leg. 4797, exp. 1; March 30, 1636 and May 24, 25, and 28, 1637, AHN, Inq., lib. 1041, fols. 275, 278–81, 313–14.

[64] See, for instance, their correspondence about a new *concordia*, April 10, 1636, AGI, Lima, 47, no. 41.

[65] Suardo, *Diario*, 1:108,109, 161, 224, 280.

[66] Here I follow the work of Pérez Canto, "Tribunal de Lima," 1136–37. She found public *autos* in 1625 (23 cases), 1631 (17), 1639 (79), and probably 1664 (23). She listed other *autos* in 1635 (12), 1641 (16), 1666 (7), two in 1667 (3, 8), 1693 (13), and 1694 (4). Of 395 cases, she counted 137 tried as Judaizers, 6 as Lutherans, 31 for heretical propositions, 90 for bigamy, 8 for solicitation in the confessional, 77 for witchcraft, 16 for contempt of the Inquisition, and 30 miscellaneous; she found 322 sentences, including 13 relaxed in person and 3 in effigy, 186 abjurations, 94 reconciliations, 5 absolutions, and 46 suspended cases.

denying that it was necessary for Christians to believe in God, a Lima diarist noting the elegance and effectiveness of the three-quarters of an hour discourse Mañozca delivered on that occasion.[67]

In Lima, Mañozca's life changed in another material way. He was joined there by Juan Sáenz de Mañozca y Murillo (c. 1606–75), the son of his uncle Pedro and his wife, born in Mexico City while Mañozca was a student in Salamanca. Following common practice, he began to guide his younger cousin, who entered Lima's university, eventually earning his bachelor, licentiate, and doctor in laws degrees there. In 1635, Sáenz de Mañozca entered the Inquisition's hierarchy at the same level Juan Adam de la Parra had a decade before, as an attorney for the tribunal, charged with the defense of prisoners and fiscal affairs (*abogado de fisco y presos*). The judges attempted to propel his career further, as two years later – with Mañozca as chief signatory – they petitioned the Inquisitor General to help him secure a doctoral prebend in Lima's cathedral, praising the young jurist's intellectual merits and work in the tribunal and recalling his family's long service to the Holy Office.[68] Mañozca not only sponsored his cousin; over time, the two would come to collaborate quite closely in the Inquisition's business.

During the 1630s, Lima would become the site of one of the most famous inquisitorial affairs of the day. Mañozca and his colleagues declared that they had uncovered a conspiracy of global dimensions and termed it the "Great Complicity." It began with a series of arrests in the summer of 1635. The perpetrators they identified were primarily merchants of Portuguese origin, tried as Judaizers.[69] The trials gained

---

[67] The *corregidor*'s crime was to be publicized then in La Paz and in Seville. Suardo, *Diario*, 2:47–48.

[68] Mañozca, Gaitán, and Castro to Inquisitor General, May 19, 1637, AHN, Inq., lib. 1041, fols. 326–27. See also September 20, 1644, AHN, Inq., lib. 1054, fols. 223–26. Suardo, *Diario*, 2:160.

[69] There has been significant work on the Great Complicity trials, including Quiroz Norris, "La expropiación inquisitorial"; Silverblatt, *Modern Inquisitions*; Bodian, *Dying in the Law*; Seymour Liebman, "The Great Conspiracy in Peru," *The Americas* 28 (1971): 176–90; Stuart Schwartz, "Panic in the Indies: The Portuguese Threat to the Spanish Empire, 1640–50," *Colonial Latin American Review* (1993): 165–87; René Millar Carvacho, "Las confiscaciones de la Inquisición de Lima a los comerciantes de origen judío-portugués de la 'gran complicidad' de 1635" *Revista de Indias* XLIII/171 (1983): 27–58; Nathan Wachtel, *La Foi du souvenir. Labyrinthes marranes* (Paris: Seuil, 2001); Daviken Studnicki-Gizbert, *A Nation Upon the Ocean Sea: Portugal's Atlantic Diaspora and the Crisis of the Spanish Empire, 1492–1640* (Oxford, UK, and New York: Oxford University Press, 2007). Another recent account that highlights the role of the Mañozcas has just come to my attention; see Ricardo Escobar Quevedo, *Inquisición y Judaizantes en América Española (Siglos XVI–XVII)* (Bogotá: Editorial Universidad del Rosario, 2008).

momentum in years perceived as those of crisis. And they were bound up with tensions around social mobility and with anxieties about collapsing royal finances, declining silver revenues, contraband, and the dangers of trading with enemies of the monarchy. In addition to their religious motivations, they might thus be read as part of broader disputes about acceptable commercial practices and economic models. Suspicion of such merchants was nothing new. For example, a 1614 junta expressed concern that the activity of Portuguese *conversos* in the slave trade might harm efforts to evangelize indigenous people in the Americas. Yet the status of the Portuguese in the Spanish monarchy deteriorated in the 1630s. In the summer of 1632, for the first time, one of the Portuguese financiers who had been an ally of Olivares was imprisoned by inquisitors in Madrid. Libels filled with stock anti-Jewish charges appeared in the vicinity of Court. An inquisitorial deputy was sent clandestinely to Rouen to investigate Portuguese trading networks, and Toledo's tribunal initiated more Judaizing trials.[70]

The conspiracy was plausible in a number of ways. Lima's inquisitors charted the business networks and family ties of Portuguese merchants to cities in enemy polities, some of which were known for their toleration of openly practicing Jewish communities. They drew upon a notion that heresy was taught in families and in networks of affiliates, and that an individual's associates reflected on his or her honor. They worked in an age particularly concerned about imposture; through such trials, inquisitors could portray themselves as experts in discerning who moved about the world with masks covering their true nature. To reason this way was to assume that there were dissemblers motivated by malicious intent to be found. When inquisitors classified Portuguese men and women in the 1630s as enemies of the Church hiding in plain sight within it, plotting harm, leading their own souls to perdition, and dangerous to the souls of those around them, they refitted very old ideas about heresy to contemporary anxieties. Thus, many historians have seen in these trials a powerful

---

[70] Castillo Mathieu, *Llave de las Indias*, 214–16; Studnicki-Gizbert, *A Nation Upon the Ocean Sea*; Bernardo J. López Belinchón, *Honra, Libertad y Hacienda (Hombres de Negocios y Judíos Sefardíes)* (Alcalá de Henares: Instituto Internacional de Estudios Sefardíes y Andalusíes, Universidad de Alcalá, 2001); Juan Ignacio Pulido Serrano, *Injurias a Cristo. Religión, política y antijudaísmo en el siglo XVII. Análisis de las corrientes antijudías durante la Edad Moderna* (Alcalá de Henares: Instituto Internacional de Estudios Sefardíes y Andalucíes, Universidad de Alcalá, 2002); C. Roth, "Les Marranes à Rouen. Un chapitre ignoré de l'histoire des Juifs de France," *Revue des études juives* 88 (1929): 113–55.

revival and refiguring of anti-Semitism, and, more recently, evidence exposing the processes by which colonial administrators promoted and regularized pejorative racial categorization.[71] For an inquisitor such as Mañozca, the discovery of a heretical conspiracy, and especially one with such substantial political dimensions, made him and his colleagues into the protagonists of one of the great dramas of their time, defenders of the monarchy's spiritual health. There were also considerable financial incentives, especially for a tribunal short of money and facing diminishing royal funding. Although some of those tried had few assets, others had notable wealth and so the confiscation of their goods might enrich the court.

In this atmosphere, the three inquisitors – Mañozca, Gaitán, and Antonio de Castro y Castillo (who had also arrived in the late 1620s) – opened numerous Judaizing trials and found many witnesses. They seized papers and sent inquiries to other Inquisition tribunals. As they began to imprison defendants, they confiscated silver and mercantile goods. The most prominent figure implicated in Lima's Great Complicity was Manuel Bautista Pérez, imprisoned on August 11, 1635, then about age forty-five. Considered part of the Portuguese nation, Pérez had emigrated from Lisbon to Seville as a youth, and then to Lima in 1618. The shipment of slaves he had invested in that year – over which he had been accused of bribing officials in Cartagena de Indias – provided the basis for his subsequent merchant ventures. By 1635, he was one of the wealthiest and most prominent residents of Lima. He had, however, one previous brush with the Inquisition, in 1624, when he was briefly arrested and investigated after a placard posted in the city's central plaza accused him of being a Jewish authority offering secret religious instruction. If Mañozca knew something about Pérez's history, the accused was also aware of elements of the senior inquisitor's past. In one interview, as Pérez refuted a piece of the testimony, he remarked that Mañozca must know about cola and its use, given the time he had spent in Cartagena.[72]

---

[71] Irene Silverblatt has considered as parallel processes these trials and the episcopal pursuit of witches in Peru, which collected evidence about indigenous practices and substances presumed to be dangerous; see her *Modern Inquisitions*. Cf. the examination of another case in which decades of debates about conversion ultimately gave way to violence (in that instance, to expulsion), in Benjamin Ehlers, *Between Christians and Moriscos: Juan de Ribera and Religious Reform in Valencia, 1568–1614* (Baltimore, MD: The Johns Hopkins University Press, 2006).

[72] Here I follow the excellent work on Pérez in Newson and Minchin, *From Capture to Sale*; Silverblatt, *Modern Inquisitions*; and Studnicki-Gizbert, *A Nation Upon the Ocean Sea*; the last opens with a perceptive consideration of what "nation" meant in this context. See also Medina, *Inquisición en Lima*, 2:113ff.

The trials shaped the estimation of Mañozca by two of his principal patrons: Luis Jerónimo Fernández de Cabrera y Bobadilla, Count of Chinchón, and García de Haro y Avellaneda, Count of Castrillo. Chinchón expressed his approval, noting the discovery of "a great harm from heretical Judaizing Portuguese," the implications of which spiraled further with each passing month; the news was seen as so significant that it led to consultations involving the Councils of State, Portugal, the Inquisition, and the Indies, in which it was noted that the trials would have commercial repercussions, given the incrimination of notable members of the merchant community. Writing to the Council of the Indies in May 1636, the viceroy praised the procedures of all three inquisitors, words that might have held particular weight in years when Peru managed briefly to reelevate its silver remittances to Seville.[73] The same month, Mañozca reported to Castrillo. He claimed there had been a sharp increase over the previous decade in the number of "Jews" from Portugal who had immigrated to Peru by way of Seville; he sharply criticized the "ostentation" that he perceived in this new population. Mañozca also gave a revealing account of the tribunal's methods: they first tried to determine the organization of the Portuguese community and identify its "heads," soon classifying Pérez as such, even as they disparaged its lack of firm hierarchical organization. Throughout, they also corresponded extensively with the *Suprema*.[74]

The trials had a rapid effect on Mañozca's fortunes. He was nominated to the *Suprema* on February 24, 1637; on April 1, the council composed a letter to the Lima tribunal notifying it of the senior inquisitor's new status and providing instructions for him to swear his oath of office while still in Lima. He did so on July 29, 1637, although he continued to act as the tribunal's chief judge, acquiring an unusual dual status as royal councillor and district inquisitor. Mañozca had skillfully timed his release of information about cases in progress. He had not been the only inquisitor seeking a seat on the *Suprema*. Andrés de Rueda Rico – formerly a visitor in Milan and inquisitor of Córdoba – also lobbied for promotion; Philip IV advocated the appointment of both men while Sotomayor opposed it on the grounds that it would put more members on the council than had ever

---

[73] "un gran daño de Portugueses hereges Judaiçantes," Chinchón to Council of the Indies, May 13, 1636, AGI, Lima, 47, Govierno no. 44. On Chinchón, see also Elliott, *The Count-Duke of Olivares*, 517.

[74] Mañozca to Castrillo, May 18, 1636, AHN, Inq., leg. 4797, exp. 1. In 1636, for example, the judges reported testimony about Judaizing from numerous natives of Seville, AHN, Inq., lib. 1041, fols. 150–239.

been customary, burdening its finances and slowing its execution of business. Still, he relented under pressure.[75] The members of the Portuguese financial elite in Madrid knew they were living in increasingly dangerous times, as the tribunal in Cartagena had also begun investigating Portuguese merchants, and there are hints that they sought to forestall further prosecutions. In 1637, as Castrillo was receiving reports from Mañozca and Chinchón and the councils were conferring, the financier Manuel de Cortizos – who would be the butt of Adam de la Parra's ill-advised poem – was lavishly fêting the king and queen.[76]

Lima's inquisitors attempted to use their new political capital in other ways. They sought funds for more secretaries given the volume of trials underway. They informed the *Suprema* that they planned to gather evidence against those who had lived in a state of excommunication for more than a year or who spoke or acted against the Church. Yet the attitude of the council was already changing. Upon receipt of this information, in January 1638, it urged caution, ordering that the inquisitors "proceed in these cases with great temperance, without reaching the point of taking the people to the secret jails."[77] Whether this advice stemmed from growing doubts about the procedure used in the Great Complicity trials or from the notion, rather, that those trials demanded the tribunal's full attention or from some other cause is not clear. In the spring, inquisitors Gaitán and Castro y Castillo wrote to the Inquisitor General, hoping that more honors would follow Mañozca's elevation to the *Suprema*, to no effect.[78]

The Great Complicity was exposed to public view in an *auto de fe* of unusual drama, held in Lima on January 23, 1639. The prosecutions culminated in the display of seventy-three people, of whom sixty-three were found to be Judaizers, and eleven of them – including Manuel Bautista Pérez – given capital sentences and relaxed. The inquisitors had

---

[75] Roberto López Vela uses this as evidence of changing patterns of bureaucratic advancement and to show the potential for "friction" between the king, his favorite, and the Inquisitor General, "Sociología de los Cuadros Inquisitoriales," *HIEA* 2:714–15. Rueda Rico was nominated February 4, 1638, and retired in the dramatic days of May 1643; Sánchez Rivilla, "Inquisidores," 367, 407; July 29, 1637, AHN, Inq., lib. 1041, fols. 394–95. Mañozca also pursued – and failed to acquire – the seat of the bishop of Trujillo in 1636 and 1637, AHN, Inq., lib. 1041, fols. 301–3 and leg. 4797, exp. 1.

[76] Studnicki-Gizbert, *A Nation Upon the Ocean Sea*, 151.

[77] *Suprema*'s marginalia: "procedan en estas causas con gran templanca, sin llegar aponer alas personas en carceles secretas," on Mañozca, Gaitán, and Castro, May 15, 1637, AHN, Inq., lib. 1041, fol. 298; see also fol. 299.

[78] April 30 and May 26, 1638, AHN, Inq., lib. 1041, fols. 375–76. In February 1637, public celebration reportedly greeted Alonso Sánchez Chaparro's release from the Holy Office, Suardo, *Diario*, 2:160.

disagreed about some of the cases. Gaitán voted to suspend the trial of doña Mencía de Luna, whereas the others voted to sentence her; in a gruesome turn of events, this was a posthumous deliberation, as she had died following an aborted session of interrogative torture.[79] Just two days before the *auto*, Mañozca – differing from the other inquisitors – decided that the sentence of a Portuguese bigamist should be softened, that his reconciliation should be in private rather than in the *auto*, and that the penalty of ten years in the galleys and exile from Peru was sufficient without also sentencing him to lashes. Rather than explaining his reasoning in a letter, he invoked his stature as a councillor and wrote that he had altered his opinion "for reasons and causes that he would propose orally in his council." His colleagues also noted that Mañozca would soon be able to explain, in person, their positions on a variety of affairs. Not long after, the inquisitor left to take his place on the *Suprema*; sailing from Callao on June 23, he had reached the coast of Spain by the end of November.[80]

A remarkable piece of publicity followed Mañozca out of Lima. The *auto de fe* had been written up in an elaborate printed history, dedicated to the tribunal. The author, a priest named Fernando de Montesinos, depicted the event as one of seminal importance.[81] He melded Páramo's historical vision with that of chroniclers who theorized that the Americas were the cradle of humankind. Thus, he began: "Two *autos de fe*, the greatest, have been celebrated in America. One God, the first inquisitor, made against the apostasy of Adam and Eve, in the theater of paradise. (The opinion is probable which puts it in this land.)" He described Adam and Eve's crime as "infecting" all of humankind with original sin. He then applied the same language to recent events, emphasizing the punishment in Lima of two "rabbis" for the crime of teaching apostasy and Mosaic law and so endangering many. He coupled the *auto* just celebrated with the first divine lesson.[82]

---

[79] One of those taken into custody in 1635, the tribunal finally decided her case in 1664, when she was burned in effigy at an *auto*. Silverblatt, *Modern Inquisitions*, 34–40.

[80] "por razones y causas que aboca propondra en su consejo," *consulta*, January 21, 1639; also May 31 and November 30, 1639, AHN, Inq., lib. 1041, fols. 419, 428–30, 461–62.

[81] Fernando de Montesinos, *Auto de la Fe Celebrado en Lima a 23 de Enero De 1639* (Lima: Pedro de Cabrera, 1639). On Montesinos, see Sabine Hyland, *The Quito Manuscript: An Inca History Preserved by Fernando de Montesinos* (New Haven, CT: Yale University Press, 2007).

[82] "Dos autos de la Fe, los Mayores, se an celebrado en la Hamerica. El uno hizo Dios, primer Inquisidor contra la Apostasia de Adam y Eva, en el Teatro del Paraisso. (Probable es la opinio[n] q[ue] le pone en esta tierra.)" He specifically cited Páramo's *De Origine et progressu*, Montesinos, *Auto de la Fe*, fol. 3v.

A particularly lengthy example of the genre, Montesinos's history enumerated the preparations for the *auto*, the processions, the authorities involved, and the criminal histories of those who appeared in the event, dwelling on lists of supposed secret Jewish practices. Sáenz de Mañozca issued the formal approval for its publication in Lima; with the other tribunal attorney, he was recorded as having directed the procession on the day of the *auto*, notable in its pomp and ceremony, and as having joined other officials in reading the trial summaries to the assembled public. Two days before, Mañozca – identified as a member of the *Suprema* – reportedly instructed the members of the tribunal how to conduct themselves, bearing with him the added authority of that distant council:

[He] made an argument to them with serious words, exhorting them that they attend to their offices with love and precision, and because this was the first day that in this city of Lima the habits of the officials and ministers of the Holy Office were seen, that they show them off with great luster, putting on costly liveries.[83]

In the opening procession, officials carried the sentences in a silver chest. Mañozca was a focal point of the event, occupying the place of honor beside the viceroy in both the procession and the seating arrangement in the plaza. At the *auto*'s culmination, it was he who absolved the reconciled heretics.[84] The printed account projected the image of Mañozca as an authority on inquisitorial procedure, instructing those on the edge of the Pacific how to behave with appropriate gravity. The grandeur of the event was a visible counter to the ostentation Mañozca had perceived in Pérez and others; during the *auto*, silver caskets were to be seen as put into the service of the justice and mercy meted out by God's Church. Mañozca had orchestrated an event in which the Inquisition produced a kind of righteous ostentation designed to remedy worldly corruption and to warn the populace away from impostors and their heresies.

[83] "les hizo vn raçonamiento con palabras graues exortandolos a que acudiessen con amor y puntualidad a sus oficios, y porque fuè este el primer dia q[ue] se vieron en esta Ciudad de Lima los abitos de los oficiales y ministros del santo Oficio, que ostentaron con grande lustre, echando costosas libreas," ibid., fol. B1v. Sáenz de Mañozca's approbation was dated February 1, 1639.

[84] Ibid., fols. B3v, C2v, G4v. On the calculated symbolism of the *auto* and the account, see also Bodian, *Dying in the Law*, 144–47; Ana Schaposchnik, "Exemplary Punishment in Colonial Lima: The 1639 *Auto de Fe*," in *Death and Dying in Colonial Spanish America*, ed. Martina Will de Chaparro and Miruna Achim (Tucson: The University of Arizona Press, 2011), 121–41. And Suardo, *Diario*, 2:196–98.

MONOPOLY IN MEXICO CITY

In Castile, Mañozca was less visible. His starring role in unveiling the Great Complicity was not inevitably an asset and the politics at Court in the early 1640s were especially difficult to navigate. Following the start of war with France in 1635 and the rising tensions in 1640, which saw significant Dutch gains in American waters and revolt in Catalonia and Portugal, theories of economic and religious conspiracy and opposition to policies of toleration and trade with northern Europe were increasingly persuasive. The Lima trials and the printed history of the 1639 *auto* provided fodder for pamphleteers such as Adam de la Parra, whereas the arrival of Mañozca and his entourage in Madrid likely made the events in faraway Peru seem even more tangible. Mañozca took up his seat on the *Suprema*, taking his oath of office a second time, and Sáenz de Mañozca, who had likely accompanied his cousin from Lima to Court, was elevated from attorney of the Peruvian tribunal to *fiscal* of the Mexican Inquisition in 1640, a promotion perhaps facilitated by his councillor cousin. He would arrive from Spain to his new post late in the spring of 1642. Inquisitorial pursuit of the Portuguese in Mexico began in 1641 and 1642, spurred in part by events in both Lima and Madrid. As Adam de la Parra's career attests, there was lobbying in Madrid in 1640 to continue to pursue evidence of heretical and commercial complicity, predicated on the belief that the trials in Lima and Cartagena had not ended the threat, a view given further immediacy by the rebellion in Portugal. To wit, in 1640, the Council of the Indies charged the viceroy of New Spain to investigate the number and situation of the Portuguese in the kingdom and to assess that population's loyalty.[85]

As a councillor of the *Suprema*, Mañozca participated in the appellate review of affairs in which he had been involved in Lima, in addition to more universal attempts at reform, such as the council's determination that district tribunals should endeavor to increase the prestige of the office of *fiscal*.[86] A Lima official petitioned the *Suprema* to restore his honor and his job to him, claiming that before his recent displacement, he had been the

---

[85] AGI, Mexico, 4, doc. 202. On the revolt as context for the *converso* trials of the 1640s, see Israel, *Race, Class, and Politics*; May 6, 1642, AHN, Inq., lib. 1054, fol. 30; López Belinchón, *Honra, Libertad y Hacienda*, 312; and "Olivares contra los portugueses. Inquisición, conversos y guerra económica," *HIEA* 3:516; and my Chap. 4.

[86] May 2, 1642, AHN, Inq., lib. 1231, fol. 60r. He was a junior signatory to much of the *Suprema*'s correspondence in Madrid in 1640, 1641, and 1642, for example, BNE MS 2827, fols. 24, 25, 43.

tribunal's *alcalde* (warden of the jails) for twenty years. He recounted how, after long service and without any formal charge of misconduct, he had been dismissed because Mañozca – whom he labeled a "declared enemy of the Galician nation," with which the claimant identified – was disinclined toward him and wanted to appoint Juan de Yturgoyen, his own retainer, to the post, "for his particular ends."[87] Written in June 1639, the petition arrived in Madrid around the same time as Mañozca's retinue. Hence Yturgoyen could present his case in person in 1640. He recalled making signal arrests in Cuzco and transporting the criminals to Lima during the Great Complicity, and that he was made warden because previous officials had not guarded the prisons well, thus tapping into inquisitors' recurrent anxieties about escapes. He made the extraordinary nature of the recent cases further justification for his appointment; they required more competent officials, who would prevent communications among prisoners and protect the secrecy of the tribunal. Finally, he recalled his family's history of service to the Holy Office, demonstrating his honor through his father's and brother's statuses as familiars in Guipúzcoa, and his nephew's as criminal *fiscal* in Lima's Chancery and legal consultant to the Inquisition there. Yturgoyen appears to have won at least an interim victory.[88]

The Lima cases were also contested, and protests regarding goods confiscated in the 1630s continued for decades. Between July and September 1642, Mañozca was among the signatories to the *Suprema*'s review of the ongoing trial of Diego de Ovalle, identified as a wine trader of the Portuguese nation. Doña Isabel de Ovalle y Pizarro, a resident of Lima, traveled to Court to appeal on her father's behalf, approaching the *Suprema* in Madrid in early July, and – apparently not satisfied with the result – Sotomayor in Zaragoza in early September; the Inquisitor General remitted the petition to the council. Doña Isabel described how she had come to throw herself on the mercy of the court, speaking for her ten siblings, two of them – she was careful to emphasize – priests, all of them and her own four children disconsolate and afflicted. She recounted how her father, some seventy years old, had been swept up in the imprisonments of 1635, but his case had lingered, still unresolved, after the *auto de fe* and now jailed for seven years, he would be so for at least eight by the time any decision made its way back to Lima. In addition to being affecting, her petition showed marked legal savvy.

---

[87] "enemigo declarado dela nacion Gallega," "por sus fines particulares," Bartolomé del Yglesia y Pradeda, June 20, 1639, AHN, Inq., lib. 1041, fols. 466, 468.

[88] March 30, 1640, AHN, Inq., lib. 1041, fol. 470.

She recalled how after the *auto*, many of those who had been punished for bearing false witness had come to her and her siblings personally to ask their forgiveness (and to express their hope for God's) for having accused their father of following the law of Moses. She suggested that those who had not formally recanted their testimony had been too afraid of being whipped to do so, and that enmity had moved others to testify. She contended that her marriage to a native of Navarre with prominent relatives in Peru, rather than to a Portuguese, had been controversial. She begged the council to act on anything in the trial that awaited a decision from its members but indicated no awareness of the tribunal's "secret" business. In July, after reviewing the trial, the councillors – with Mañozca as the most junior of seven signatories – ruled that Ovalle's sentence should be read publicly in Lima's next *auto de fe* or in a church, that he should make a minor abjuration of his crimes, and be condemned to a fine of two thousand pesos for the expenses of the Holy Office. In September – with Mañozca then the sixth of seven – they revised their decision: the sentence would be read and Ovalle abjure secretly, within the tribunal, with only the inquisitors, *fiscal*, and notary present. Dr. don Isidoro de San Vicente wrote the council's harsh rebuke, finding that Lima's court had hampered Ovalle's defense by not properly handling the revocations of witnesses' testimony. Far worse, however, was that it had tortured the prisoner despite disagreement in the judges' votes, and even then following the minority opinion, rather than appealing for advice at that juncture. There never had been grounds to vote on a capital sentence, as the tribunal had done, especially given Ovalle's fortitude and lack of confession under torture; the *Suprema* judged the case to be markedly out of conformity with inquisitorial procedure.[89] Mañozca's role in these deliberations, their effect on his practice or opinions, and the extent to which the misconduct in the Ovalle trial reflected on his reputation as a judge remain unclear. It was probably Gaitán who had the most to lose, as the trial transcript recorded him as often the sole inquisitor presiding in the relevant audiences of 1635 and 1636.

Involvement in the Great Complicity trials was no guarantee of future success, as Adam de la Parra's 1643 disgrace – following his poetic insults to the Cortizos family – would demonstrate. Inquisitor Castro y Castillo was still writing from Lima about the affair in 1641, seeking to translate his service into some reward and focusing on the military danger the

---

[89] AHN, Inq., leg. 1648, exp. 4, [fols. 208–214]. San Vicente was made *fiscal* of the council October 6, 1638, and councillor July 16, 1642; Sánchez Rivilla, "Inquisidores," 412.

Portuguese had posed in their attempts, he insisted, to aid the Dutch. Gaitán also wrote that year to the Inquisitor General, claiming that Mañozca owed money to the receiver of the Lima tribunal and implicating friar Domingo de Irigoyen, of the order of Saint John of God, who had allegedly received the silver in question. Gaitán sued and appointed an agent to pursue the case in Madrid in his stead; Mañozca responded that Irigoyen – who would later accompany him to Mexico – had merely helped him care for his household in Peru.[90] The *Suprema* judged that Mañozca should pay a nominal sum, but the negotiations about payment followed him to Granada and then to Mexico, without clear resolution. Meanwhile, Mañozca's succession of promotions continued. While retaining his seat on the *Suprema*, Philip IV appointed him president of the Chancery of Granada on January 11, 1642. He resided there for scarcely more than a year, from November 1642 to early 1644.[91] It was not a bad time to be out of Madrid, as Olivares fell late in the spring of 1643, followed by Sotomayor not long after. Castrillo and Chinchón, on the other hand, managed political survival, and Mañozca too weathered the changing climate, avoiding the kind of reverses Adam de la Parra, for example, encountered.

I have found scant evidence about his time in the Andalusian city. It is possible that Mañozca crossed paths then with the count of Salvatierra, before their collaboration in Mexico, as the grandee, who would soon become viceroy of New Spain, was in Seville in 1642.[92] A scandal had recently broken in Granada involving a libel – praising a combination of heresies, including those of the "sect of Calvin," and deprecating the Immaculate Conception – that had been affixed to the door of the Chancery in April 1640. The appearance of several such libels provoked a dramatic response, as the Inquisition and Chancery launched investigations, and processions were deployed as a salve for the Virgin's honor. The city council presumed that Portuguese "Hebrews" were the most likely culprits, although the Inquisition tribunal soon found a hermit to be the perpetrator, sentencing him to ten years in the galleys. In 1642, the Chancery's *fiscal* was trying to preserve jurisdiction over an inquisitorial official accused of the crime of dueling; each side printed pamphlets to

---

[90] Silverblatt, *Modern Inquisitions*, 149; Gaitán, May 29, 1641, AHN, Inq., lib. 1042, fol. 62; Mañozca, May 7 and 18, 1640, Madrid, AHN, Inq., leg. 1636, exp. 3, fols. 3r-11v.

[91] Mañozca, May 22, 1643, February 26, 1644, and May 16, 1648, AHN, Inq, leg. 1636, exp. 3, fols. 96r, 122, 144r.

[92] RAH 9/3663, exp. 27.

advance its claim.[93] Yet I know of no involvement by Mañozca in either affair.

But in the midst of the tumult at Court, he gained an even more significant office. With Castrillo presiding, the Council of the Indies proposed him as the next archbishop of Mexico in June 1643. In a further act of patronage, it granted a third of his archiepiscopal rents to fund his travel and expenses.[94] Again, he retained his place on the *Suprema*. A year later, the new archbishop sailed across the Atlantic for the last time, carrying with him to New Spain considerable authority both inquisitorial and episcopal; his influence was even more substantial as his cousin Juan Sáenz de Mañozca was already there in the tribunal, working as both *fiscal* and inquisitor.

Over his career, Mañozca became known for protecting Basque associates, aligning himself with that national faction.[95] He acquired a reputation as a patron on both sides of the Atlantic and supported his Creole and peninsular relatives. In 1643, another Marquina native dedicated a treatise in defense of a Franciscan tertiary order in Bilbao to him.[96] When he sailed in 1644, all eight members of his retinue were seemingly Basque, most from Marquina or the surrounding villages. Two were clerics, at least one of whom – Irigoyen – had also been with him in Lima. One, Juan Fernández de Muguertegui y Mañozca, was a relative for whose benefit

[93] Francisco Rodin de Marenzo, *Decisio Granatensis Tribunalis Sancti Officii* (Granada: Baltasar de Bolívar and Francisco Sánchez, 1641), copies in RAH 9/3663, exp. 80; AHN, Inq., lib. 1231, fol. 378r. As in Cartagena de Indias, there had been contentious disputes about the Immaculate Conception in the later 1610s. In A. Katie Harris's analysis, then, the libel brought an old controversy to a head; see her *From Muslim to Christian Granada: Inventing a City's Past in Early Modern Spain* (Baltimore, MD: The Johns Hopkins University Press, 2007), 137–48. On the familiar: *Por la Iurisdicion de la Inquisicion* (Granada: Baltasar de Bolívar and Francisco Sánchez, 1642), RAH 9/3663, exp. 94. About 1620, the declining practice of dueling saw a new spike, on this see Scott Taylor, *Honor and Violence in Golden Age Spain* (New Haven, CT, and London: Yale University Press, 2008), 28–29.

[94] He was the first choice, before Pedro de Oviedo, bishop of Quito, and Antonio Calderón, June 12, 1643, AGI, México, 4/201 and see 4/214; indexed in Heredia Herrera, dir., *Catálogo de Consultas*, 7:571, 595. For his appointment, see also *HC*, 4:241; AGI, Contratación, 5789, lib. 1, fols. 490v-91, Indiferente, 455, lib. A25, fols. 131v-32, and Patronato, 4, no. 29.

[95] Israel, *Race, Class and Politics*, 114–17; Phelan, *Kingdom of Quito*, 244.

[96] It was addressed to Juan Sáenz de Mañozca, but clearly meant the archbishop; Gabriel de Guillixtegui, *Apologia en Defensa de la Orden de Penitencia de San Francisco* (Bilbao: Pedro de Huydobro, 1643).

Mañozca may even have founded an entail.[97] Sáenz de Mañozca likewise maintained ties to his father's and cousin's native land. One of the two retainers granted passage to Mexico with him in 1641 was from Berriatúa, a mere hour or two walk from Marquina.[98]

Another two young relatives, don Joseph and don Cristóbal Mañozca Bonilla Bastida, natives of Mexico City, were made familiars of the Inquisition in Mexico on April 24, 1643. Sons of the late María Sáenz de Mañozca, Pedro's daughter and Juan's sister, their elevation may have been intended, in part, to protect them from doubts about their purity of blood. They were appointed the same day as their father, don Nicolás Bonilla Bastida – the constable of the tribunal's jails (*alguacil mayor*) – as well as his son from his second marriage, don Bartolomé de Bonilla Bastida Estupiñán. The genealogical investigations raised questions about their father's side of the family; it appeared that the Inquisition might have penanced one of his great-grandparents. On their mother's side, the inquisitors in Logroño readily attested to their fitness for office, as grandsons of a distinguished official.[99] There were other irregular elements: the three brothers were single and younger than twenty-five, both of which were usually impediments to obtaining an appointment as a familiar. Nevertheless, the Mexican tribunal, on which their uncle then sat, admitted them into the Inquisition's service and jurisdiction. The path was paved for Cristóbal's admission as a knight into the military order of Santiago a few years later.[100]

---

[97] On his license were Lic. Marcos de Zárate, chaplain (of Alava); Domingo de Irigoyen, friar of San Juan de Dios (Marquina); and as *criados*, Muguertegui y Mañozca (Berriatúa), Juan Fernández de Gamboa (Alava), Andrés de Munibe (Marquina), Antonio de Aguirre (Mallabia), Gabriel de Ibarrolaza and his brother José (Marquina), March 23, 1644, AGI, Contratación, 5427, no. 1, r. 42. Muguertegui y Mañozca was the son of Nicolás de Muguertegui and Graciana de Mañozca (perhaps Mañozca's sister). There are files (which I have not consulted) relating to his proofs for the order of Calatrava (1644) in AHN, OM, Caballeros Calatrava, exp. 939, and one recounting a judgment of 74,700 maravedís in his favor from the *mayorazgo* in AGS, Contaduría Mayor de Hacienda, 1406, 42. Indexed at http://pares.mcu.es/.

[98] Domingo de Arriola (Berriatúa) and Pedro González de Trejo (Toledo), June 4, 1641, AGI, Contratación, 5424, no. 1, r. 21.

[99] AHN, Inq., leg. 1213, exp. 10 and leg. 1278, exp. 32; Alberro, *Inquisition et Société*, 343, 364. As *alguacil*, Nicolás testified in some of the Inquisition's 1646 proceedings about libels that Palafox's supporters had reportedly spread around Mexico City, AGN, Inq., vol. 424, fols. 5rff. Juan de Mañozca did not sign the *Suprema*'s approval of the investigation, November 10, 1642, AGN, Inq., vol. 417, exp. 9, fols. 380–90.

[100] October 14, 1646, AHN, OM, Caballeros Santiago, Expedientillos, no. 2854. For a detailed consideration of similar issues, see James E. Wadsworth, *Agents of Orthodoxy: Honor, Status and the Inquisition in Colonial Pernambuco, Brazil* (Lanham, MD: Rowman and Littlefield, 2007).

Two other probable relatives were approved as familiars of the tribunal in 1649: Ensigns don Pedro and don Joseph Sáenz de Mañozca, of Manila.[101]

Arriving in Mexico City late in 1644, Mañozca took possession of his archdiocese on January 23, 1645, ending a term of vacancy during which feuds had split the cathedral chapter.[102] Perhaps as a nod to his principal patron, he preached a sermon that year, which was then printed, in honor of Queen Isabel, who had died the previous autumn; Castrillo had been a close ally of Philip IV's late consort and the vicereine had once been her lady-in-waiting.[103] Before long, Inquisitor General Diego de Arce y Reinoso, seeking to establish his credentials as a reformer and suspecting malpractice, ordered a visitation of New Spain's tribunal and appointed Mañozca as the visitor, directing him in September 1645 to investigate "excesses and crimes."[104] Relationships between authorities in the vice-regal capital were fractured. Sáenz de Mañozca held the title to the office of *fiscal*, but also, unusually, instructions that he should exercise the role of inquisitor in matters of "government." In practice, he worked in both capacities and appeared publicly as one of the three inquisitors by decade's end; complaints about this arrangement – implicating Mañozca – were quick in coming. The other *fiscal*, don Antonio de Gaviola, appealed to Madrid, implying that the visitor had nudged him out in order to give his cousin greater latitude. Gaviola spent the later 1640s deprived of much of his authority, though still doing some of the *fiscal*'s work; Mañozca claimed that he had acted ineffectively, not introducing new business and neglecting the Great Complicity trials. In another departure from custom-ary practice, Mañozca used his authority as visitor to act, in effect, as the tribunal's president. As he had done in Quito, he utilized his power to

---

[101] They were the sons of Captain Lucas Sáenz de Mañozca and doña María de Chávez y Sotomayor; March 23, 1649, AGN, Inq., vol. 503, exp. 65, fols. 409r-18r.

[102] Gabriela Oropeza Tena, "Las Actas del Cabildo de la Catedral Metropolitana en Sede Vacante, 1637–1644" (PhD diss., UNAM, 2004), 119.

[103] I have not been able to locate a copy of Mañozca, *Oración fúnebre en las solemnes exequias que hizo México a la Reyna de España Doña Isabel de Borbón* (Mexico, 1645), of which there is a notice in Antonio Palau y Dulcet, *Manual de Librero Hispano-Americano* (Barcelona: A. Palau, 1948–77). On the connections between Castrillo and the queen, see Elliott, *The Count-Duke of Olivares*, 642–43, 653.

[104] AHN, Inq., lib. 1054, fols. 372–73. On the Inquisition tribunal in Mexico in this era, see especially Alberro, *Inquisition et Société*; Israel, *Race, Class, and Politics*; José Toribio Medina, *Historia del Tribunal del Santo Oficio de la Inquisición en México* (Santiago de Chile: Imprenta Elzeveriana, 1905; facsimile repr., Mexico City: Miguel Ángel, Porrúa, 1998). For the tribunal's correspondence in Mañozca's years there, see AHN, Inq., libs. 1054–55.

deprive others of the exercise of their office, suspending the senior inquisitor, Domingo de Asas y Argos, for several months.[105]

More pressing, however, were the contests that swirled around Palafox. One of Olivares's rising stars at Court in the 1630s – and a collaborator with Adam de la Parra on the 1635 junta of historians – he was made Visitor General of New Spain in the spring of 1639 and bishop of Puebla de los Angeles that December, landing in the same fleet as the new viceroy, the duke of Escalona, who reached Mexico City in late summer 1640. Palafox quickly fell out with Escalona and engineered his dismissal from office in 1642 on the grounds that he was insufficiently guarding against the threats posed by the Portuguese revolt, word of which had reached Mexico in April 1641. In the process, Palafox acquired the mitre of archbishop of Mexico in mid-1642 (resigning it in March 1643); he was the interim viceroy from June to November 1642. His reforming program was wide ranging and included spurring the Inquisition to begin trying Portuguese in Mexico in 1642.[106] His actions found support among the Creole elite, as he advocated allowing direct commerce between Mexico and the Philippines and increasing appointments of Creoles to the ecclesiastical hierarchy. He initiated significant reforms of the orders, striving to move indigenous populations away from the mendicants to the jurisdiction of the secular clergy.

Palafox ran afoul of the next viceroy, the count of Salvatierra, and his vicereine soon after their installation at the end of 1642, and he was also at odds with most of the Jesuits in the province and the judges of Mexico's *audiencia*.[107] Palafox consecrated Mañozca as archbishop, but the two

[105] AHN, Inq., lib. 1054, fols. 223–26, 356, 357–62, 433–34. Appointments to the tribunal: Dr. don Francisco de Estrada y Escobedo (*fiscal*, 1634; inquisitor, 1640), Lic. don Domingo Vélez de Asas y Argos (inquisitor, 1637), Sáenz de Mañozca (*fiscal*, 1640), Dr. don Antonio de Gaviola (*fiscal*, 1642), Lic. don Bernabé de la Higuera y Amarilla (inquisitor, 1643). There were no further appointments made until 1660. Alberro noted a bit fewer than two thousand cases between 1571 and 1700, which she deems lesser activity than many peninsular tribunals. Alberro, *Inquisition et Société*, 45–46, 84, 333. Jonathan Israel termed Sáenz de Mañozca "possibly the most virulent inquisitor to serve in Mexico in the seventeenth century," *Race, Class and Politics*, 232.

[106] On this point, and for the observation that tensions had been building from the autumn of 1641, see Israel, *Empires and Entrepots*, 311–31.

[107] Israel, *Race, Class and Politics*, 224–47; R. Olaechea, "El venerable Palafox y la Inquisición," *HIEA* 1:1131–32. Doña Antonia María de Acuña y Guzmán, the countess of Salvatierra, was no minimal player on the political field, either; one diarist at Court reported that she had tried to warn Olivares of French troop movements in 1638, to no avail; Elliott, *The Count-Duke of Olivares*, 538. The count, don García Sarmiento de Sotomayor y Enríquez de Luna, was a very well-connected grandee, a nephew of the count

became bitter opponents, the new prelate seeing Palafox as a menace to his authority. Ironically, Palafox had judged the state of the Inquisition in Mexico in 1641 not so differently from the Mañozcas, finding "corruption and failure to impart moral discipline."[108] Nor were the factions static. The Inquisition *fiscal* Gaviola transferred his loyalties from Salvatierra to Palafox in 1647. Although Palafox had once been closely aligned with Olivares, by the time of the count-duke's fall, he perceived himself as neglected and diverged from his policies; like Mañozca, he identified Castrillo as a stronger patron in those years, though the count's influence was also waning. The crown, moreover, was soon seemingly more interested in strong figures of authority in its viceroyalties and revenues for its war-drained coffers than in a reforming ethos. In 1646 and 1647, the inquisitor Bernabé de la Higuera y Amarilla reported to Palafox that he would prefer to support him, but that he was prevented from doing so by fear of the cousins Mañozca and their threats to deprive him of his office or jail him. The conflict reached such a pitch by late 1646 that a secret meeting at the viceregal palace, in which both Mañozcas were included, considered how to oust the bishop.[109]

To consolidate his position in New Spain, Mañozca honed his skills in directing public display. Supporters of Palafox printed broadsheets and composed verses ridiculing the viceroy and his countess; they railed against the archbishop and the Inquisition tribunal. Mañozca responded with edicts and judicial tools, even imprisoning an agent of Palafox.[110] In 1647, they engaged each other in writing. The cousins composed what they framed as a defense of the archbishop's reputation. In response, Palafox appealed directly to the Inquisitor General about what he called an infamous libel designed to assault him, or, alternately, a satire; placing greater blame on Sáenz de Mañozca, he contended that the archbishop "because of the obligation of blood, and also by inclination, follows so openly the passion of his cousin."[111] The Inquisitor General ordered an inquiry, but the string of retorts and appeals continued. The two prelates

of Alba; he was made viceroy of New Spain on November 13, 1642, then of Peru on May 13, 1648. He resigned the latter in February 1655 and died in Lima, June 26, 1659; *Memorias de los Virreyes del Perú: Marqués de Mancera y Conde de Salvatierra*, ed. José Toribio Polo (Lima: Imprenta del Estado, 1899), xix-xxi.

[108] Quoted in Álvarez de Toledo, *Politics and Reform*, 160–63.

[109] They reputedly considered armed action and charges of sedition. Here, and in the Palafox affair generally, I follow Álvarez de Toledo, *Politics and Reform*, especially pp. 159–63, 193–95, 200–203, 213.

[110] Israel, *Race, Class and Politics*, 230–39.

[111] "y asi por la obligacion de la sangre, è inclinacion sigue tan abiertamente la pasion de su Primo," BNE, MS 12054, fol. 208v.

shared a common idiom, each lambasting the other for perverting royal justice, ecclesiastical virtue, and the administration of their offices.[112] In Palafox's telling, Mañozca created a scandal when he allowed the libel to circulate; he had compromised the dignity of all bishops and sabotaged the decrees of the Council of Trent by making their quarrels a matter for public discussion. Mañozca returned the volley, alleging that the bishop's household spewed libels; Palafox, instead, became the author of clerical conflict and the corruptor of Trent by imposing harsh reforms where none were needed and upsetting the religious orders of his diocese and the kingdom's government. Similarly, Palafox argued that the archbishop exemplified corrupt counsel. He depicted Mañozca and the vicereine as his most implacable foes and insinuated that they led the viceroy astray with their plotting.[113] When the arrows flew in the other direction, the Mañozcas papered Palafox in the tropes of the demonic: he hid his slander, maintaining an appearance of virtue while laying his eggs of "malicious venom." They likened his attacks to those of a snake coiled inside the mouth of a statue.[114] The serpentine aspersions could summon a rich array of associations, as the bishop became a cloaked repository of heretical venom; the ancient enemy of Genesis plotting once again; the viper drawn out of St. John the Evangelist's poisoned cup; the inversion, in sum, of clerical virtue.

Sáenz de Mañozca's manuscript apologia claimed to respond to rumors that the bishop had spread about the archbishop; it juxtaposed Mañozca's virtues to Palafox's passions. He described his cousin's care for his archdiocese as prefigured by his earlier conduct; rather than being enamored of silver, Mañozca, he asserted, had actually contributed his own funds to administrative costs in Quito's visitation, Lima's tribunal, and even Granada's Chancery. He sketched the archbishop's shocked return to Mexico, finding the cathedral in a poor state and the hospital of San Salvador "so dismantled and destroyed."[115] According to his cousin's report, Mañozca repaired the hospital and brokered peace between many of the religious orders. Such praise did dual duty as criticism of

---

[112] The letter from Palafox, August 10, and retort from Mañozca, November 30, 1647, are treated briefly in Huerga, "Tribunal de Mexico," 1:1120–30. See also *Suprema*, July 8 and December 4, 1647, AHN, Inq., lib. 1054, fols. 374, 390–91; Palafox to Mañozca and vice versa, November 12 and 14, 1647, RB, MS II/1989, fols. 53–54, also fol. 55; BNE, MS 12054, fols. 190r-215v.

[113] BNE, MS 12054, fol. 194r.

[114] "veneno malicioso," ibid., fol. 216v.

[115] "tan desmantelado y destruido," in another copy of the libel, BUS, MS 2065 (*Causa de Palafox*), fol. 12r, see also fol. 11r.

Palafox's administration of the archdiocese. Moreover, by having his cousin mount the defense, Mañozca maintained an elegant distance from writing polemic and publicizing the affair.

Simultaneously, Mañozca fired off letters to his superiors, several written in his own hand. Appealing to the viceroy, he first praised his temperance, pious intent, admirable service, and protection of the public good, especially in such difficult times. The archbishop then summoned his long experience to discredit Palafox, recalling that he had spent fifty-two years in the Indies, thirty-seven of them in various official capacities. He claimed that he had observed nine *audiencias*, and that he had never seen a Visitor General incite judges to challenge a viceroy, as had recently happened. Mañozca allowed that Palafox's zeal was praiseworthy, but that his manner of pursuing reforms endangered souls and the political order. He presented Palafox as an innovator – a word with negative connotations in the seventeenth century – and himself as a measured and experienced observer.[116] He also sent the king a lengthy report of the state of the archdiocese. He located the origins of the present conflicts in Palafox's "despoiling" of the Franciscan order in Puebla even as he protested that he remained sympathetic to his subordinate bishop, "remembering the calumnies that the religious attempted against me when I was Your Majesty's visitor in the kingdom of Quito in Peru."[117] He combined a defense of his own record with an attack on Palafox, who, he explained, had quickly come into conflict with both the Dominicans and Augustinians as well, choosing ill advisedly to support a young Dominican who preached against the secular authorities even as his superiors sought to silence him. Mañozca described the conflicts as growing progressively larger, characterizing the Jesuits as initially peaceful, even as the bishop created scandals with the other orders. Over time, though, Mañozca reasoned that Palafox had provoked the Jesuits not merely with lawsuits about tithes, but also because he treated them discourteously. Worse, Palafox involved the uneducated populace in such matters, irreparably damaging the credibility of all the orders and particularly the Jesuits. Mañozca described Palafox's zeal for reform as so excessive that it brought affliction even to obedient nuns, as the bishop allegedly cloistered six convents in Puebla too strictly, prohibiting communication between the women and their relatives.[118]

---

[116] Mañozca to Salvatierra, November 18, 1646, BUS, MS 2065, fols. 18r-19r.
[117] "acordarme las calumnias que intentaron contra mi los Religiosos siendo Vissitador de V[uestra] M[agesta]d en el Reyno de Quito en el Piru." Mañozca to the king, May 9, 1647, RB, MS II/1989, fol. 133r.
[118] Ibid., fol. 138v.

Palafox's accusations, on the other hand, led the Inquisitor General and the *Suprema* to reassign the tribunal visitation to the bishop of Oaxaca, don Bartolomé Benavides, in 1648. Mañozca counter-maneuvered and recused the bishop; he and his cousin assembled various proofs of Benavides's enmity, passions, and ambitions. In Sáenz de Mañozca's telling, Benavides widely publicized how "he was coming to burn the Mañozcas, and to be archbishop and to remove [the] three inquisitors and make Dr. don Antonio de Peralta [an associate of Palafox] an inquisitor … and to exile the other three to the Philippines."[119] Mañozca engineered another survival. In late 1647, Palafox was dismissed as Visitor General; Salvatierra was appointed viceroy in Peru – leaving the capital after several more skirmishes in May 1648; and the bishop of Yucatán, don Marcos de Torres y Rueda, was made interim governor.

In the year or so that followed the relocation of Tepeapulco's cross, the archbishop projected his newly consolidated authority through carefully managed and elaborate spectacle. Mañozca's initiatives were celebrated in at least five pamphlets printed in the vernacular in Mexico City in 1648 and 1649. As had been the case with Lima's 1639 *auto de fe*, these publications served to associate their authors with Mañozca, the archdiocese, and the Inquisition. The printed history of the stone cross was graced by poetic praise.[120] The sermon preached at its installation at the cathedral was also published, and Mañozca had chosen the preacher – Matías de Bocanegra (1612–68) – with particular care.[121] A member of the Society of Jesus, a native of Puebla, a poet, and a playwright, Bocanegra had been involved in the controversies; inclined toward Palafox in 1646, by 1648, he reversed course and supplied testimony against Benavides – Mañozca's proposed replacement – to Sáenz de Mañozca.[122] The following spring, Bocanegra delivered the sermon at another exceptionally elaborate *auto de fe*, held in Mexico City on April 11, 1649. He also composed a printed account that related details of the trials, histories, and condemnations of 109 people, all but one identified as Judaizing Portuguese, of whom

---

[119] "venia a quemar a los Mañozcas, y à ser Arcobispo, y quitar tres Inq[uisido]res y hacer Inq[uisid]or al D[octo]r Don Antonio de Peralta … y desterrar à otros tres a Filipinas," Sáenz de Mañozca, holograph, [1648], AGN, Inq., Vol. 430, exp. 4, fol. 417r.

[120] This has been reprinted as Ambrosio de Solís Aguirre, "'Tercetos' de la Cruz de Mañozca," in Alfonso Méndez Plancarte, *Poetas Novohispanos. Segundo Siglo (1621–1721). Parte Primera* (Mexico City: UNAM, 1944), 84–86.

[121] Matías de Bocanegra, S.J., *Sermón a la Solemne colocación de la Santa Cruz de piedra,* consulted BNE, VC/999/24, fols. 15–26.

[122] Sáenz de Mañozca [1648] and Bocanegra, June 26, 1648, AGN, Inq., vol. 430, exp. 4, fols. 417r-18v, 420v.

twenty-six were reconciled at the *auto* and another thirteen relaxed in person (i.e., burned at the stake); the rest were deceased and so punished exhumed or in effigy.[123] The culmination of the trials of Portuguese in Mexico that had begun in 1641 and 1642, it followed smaller *autos*, in which no capital sentences were given, held in 1646, 1647, and 1648.

Bocanegra dedicated his narrative to the Inquisitor General and portrayed Mañozca as the author of reforms throughout the American Inquisitions, an exemplary defender of true religion. He turned the archbishop's trail of experience into a mark of divine election:

[Mañozca's] calling befits him and he was elected by God to be a minister of the Inquisition. He was called and chosen for this task when he was thirty years of age. It is now over forty years that he has functioned with so much steadfastness as can be verified by the Inquisition of Cartagena. He founded it. He developed the Inquisition of Lima and served on the Supreme Council. He aided the Inquisition of Mexico.[124]

Unusual in its extensive emphasis on posthumous punishment, the account of the 1649 *auto* closely aligned the inquisitors with divine judgment; it showed them as so diligent that their inquiries transcended the present moment, and the convicted heretics as belonging to a well-established hidden society of long standing. Mañozca, it suggested, like

---

[123] One man was listed as a penanced Protestant. Twenty-one men and five women abjured, six women and seven men were relaxed. Another two women had their sentences of relaxation commuted at the last minute; they were reconciled in private later that month. The remaining sixty-seven (twenty-one women and forty-six men) were deceased; two of them were reconciled in that fashion and all the others relaxed. Bocanegra, *Auto general de la fee* (Mexico City: Antonio Calderón, [1649]). Translated as Bocanegra, *Jews and the Inquisition of Mexico: The Great Auto de Fe of 1649*, ed. and trans. Seymour B. Liebman (Lawrence, KS: Coronado Press, 1974). The inquisitors claimed that they punished 207 people, 190 of them for the crime of Judaizing, in the four *autos* between 1646 and 1649; Huerga, "Tribunal de Mexico," 1:1126. The language of "complicidad" was omnipresent in the tribunal's earlier correspondence, see July 23 and September 22, 1642, January 19, 1644, AHN, Inq., lib. 1054, fols. 25–28, 31, 116. Several historians have commented on the connections between events in Lima and Mexico and attributed the persistence of the 1640s trials, in large part, to the Mañozca cousins. See also Alejandro Cañeque, "Theater of Power: Writing and Representing the Auto de Fe in Colonial Mexico," *The Americas* 52 (1996): 321–43; Seymour Liebman, "The Great Conspiracy in New Spain," *The Americas* 30 (1973): 18–31; Alberro, *Inquisition et Société*, 249, 291–97; *Inquisitorial Inquiries: Brief Lives of Secret Jews and Other Heretics*, ed. and trans. Richard L. Kagan and Abigail Dyer (Baltimore, MD, and London: The Johns Hopkins University Press, 2004), 152–88; Matthew D. Warshawsky, "Inquisitorial Prosecution of Tomás Treviño de Sobremonte, a Crypto-Jew in Colonial Mexico," *Colonial Latin American Review* 17 (2008): 101–23.

[124] Translation in Liebman, *Jews and the Inquisition*, 61.

Heliodorus – who had experienced and testified to God's wrath – might bear witness "that God was a vengeful Visitor, who directed His anger to the punishment of the lost."[125] The *auto de fe* projected both the archbishop's honor and that of his family, which by the 1640s stretched from Vizcaya to Manila. Mañozca commissioned one of Mexico City's tailors to make costly habits for two of his nephews, Juan Fernández de Muguertegui y Mañozca (the same young man brought from Vizcaya five years before), by then a knight of the order of Calatrava, and Cristóbal de Bonilla y Mañozca, knight of the order of Santiago.[126] Bocanegra's history soon recorded their knightly status, their relationship to the archbishop, their elegant new dress, and their prominent role in the processions of April 10 and April 11, 1649.[127] Of course Sáenz de Mañozca – identified as one of three tribunal inquisitors – also featured in both the events and the printed report of them.

Such spectacles were part of a duel of sorts. On April 11, Mañozca presided over the *auto de fe* in Mexico City; on April 18, Palafox presided over festivities for the consecration of Puebla's new cathedral, whose construction he had overseen, dedicated to the Virgin of the Conception. Yet 1649 was a triumphant year for the archbishop, as he watched Palafox sail for Spain in June.[128] Both prelates worked in the long shadow of Trent, each striving to show that he maintained the council's spirit. Mañozca attended the cathedral chapter, negotiated with the orders, heard petitions and ecclesiastical cases, dedicated significant time to visiting the district, and attempted to impose reforms on both male and female religious houses. He fielded numerous appeals from Mexico's convents and ordered those repeatedly accused of laxity to conform to the rules of

[125] "que era Dios Visitador vengativo, que enderezò su enojo al suplicio de los perdidos," Bocanegra, *Auto general*, dedication. Here he cited 2 Machabees 3:39: "For he that hath his dwelling in the heavens is the visitor and protector of that place: and he striketh and destroyeth them that come to do evil to it."

[126] A memorandum (April 1, 1649) put the cost, paid from the archbishop's household, of the two "vestidos enteros" at slightly more than 286 pesos; this included the habits of the orders, Canton crape, silk stockings, black silk, black taffeta from Granada, and buttons. On August 14, he ordered similar clothes made for his other nephew, Joseph de Bonilla, AHAM, Cabildo, Museo Catedral, caja 184, exps. 14, 15.

[127] The framing of the procession of the Green Cross (April 10) was significant: "It was not profane vanity by which Christianity displayed itself. The honorable cognizance of power was more than an emulation of piety." Liebman, *Jews and the Inquisition*, 52. The pair also rode with the inquisitors in the procession of the prisoners, ibid., 66–67.

[128] Álvarez de Toledo, *Politics and Reform*, 241–59.

cloistration.[129] Print became a crucial tool for both imposing reform and appearing as a reformer. Thus, Mañozca arranged the publication of acts he concluded with the provincial of the Dominican order that summer, memorializing their negotiations about how the order's administration of doctrine conformed to the requirements of the archbishop and the crown; how to license friars to perform the sacraments had long been a source of conflict.[130]

The archbishop displayed his support for the Society of Jesus in similar fashion. Writing to the king in the midst of Palafox's disputes with the order, he argued "that although it is the newest [order] in this kingdom, it equals and even is superior to the others for the large retinue that it has, with respect to that very affectionate love that stems from its teaching in the schools that they have in their colleges for minor and major studies."[131] During the first three weeks of Advent 1649, Mañozca dedicated a cycle of praise to Jesuit ministries in Mexico City. The subsequent pamphlet began with a history of the order's good works in the Americas, giving center stage to the collaboration between Mañozca – as "zealous prelate and attentive pastor" – and Andrés de Rada, the provincial of the Society in New Spain.[132] Timing the festivities in the holy season of renewal both elevated the order and sought to give special direction to that year's celebrations with pomp, music, processions, and preaching. Mañozca declared a jubilee and had broadsheets posted and edicts read in the city's churches. The Society staffed extra confessors and incorporated the capital's parishes and other religious foundations into the events. According to the pamphlet, the sacraments and grand liturgical celebrations "produced effects so above all human persuasion," and so it was a

---

[129] He spent the first five months of 1646 visiting areas to the south and west of Mexico City, inspecting religious foundations, celebrating confirmations, and censuring irregular practices; see Magnus Lundberg, "Relación de la visita pastoral del arzobispado de México de Juan de Mañozca y Zamora, 1646," *Historia Mexicana* 58.2 (2008): 861–90. See the edict probably directed at the Convent of Jesús María, October 4, 1645, AGN, Templos y Conventos, vol. 158B, exp. 95, fol. 1022r. He also instructed the convent of Santa María de Gracia about their upcoming election, urging them to observe their vow of obedience, October 27, 1645, AHAM, Fondo Episcopal, caja 5, exp. 50.

[130] *Avtos fechos . . . En Cvmplimiento de la Cedula de Sv Magestad* [1649], AHN, Diversos-Colecciones, 27, no. 11.

[131] "que aunque es la mas nueua eneste Reyno iguala y aun esta supperior alas demas por el grande sequito que tiene, respecto de aquel amor tan entrañable que nace de su enseñanza enlas escuelas q[ue] tienen en sus collexios de estudios menores y maiores," RB, MS II/1989, fol. 134.

[132] "zeloso Prelado, y atento Pastor," *Relacion del Solemne Jubileo de las Missiones* (Mexico City: widow of Bernardo Calderón, 1650), fol. 1v.

great success: "this new world had not seen Lents or Holy Weeks with such admirable progresses, or holy jubilee years with such frequency of the sacraments: everything in the city was fervor, piety, tears, mending of lives, improvement of customs, devotion in those who saw it, and admiration in those that heard it."[133]

Under Mañozca's administration, the cathedral devoted significant effort to crafting such displays. The archbishop sought to provide richer trappings for the principal feast days. In 1649, he and the chapter resolved to melt down the cathedral's old silver in order to make new liturgical vessels for use on the high altar during important occasions.[134] He extended his dispute with Palafox into such terrain, pursuing the bishop even after he left Mexico. Thus, in 1650 Mañozca began an investigation of the devices displayed in the royal chapel of Puebla's new cathedral. He judged the coats of arms to be shockingly improper: "and even in my long age and experiences I had not seen nor heard that any vassal would have imagined meddling in such a sovereign subject."[135] Attacking the monument Palafox had built, he sought to leave a lingering image of the departed bishop as a sower of scandal whose excesses verged on sedition, exposing a harmful innovation to public view.

Still visitor of the tribunal and councillor of the *Suprema*, the archbishop fell sick that October and died, in Mexico City, on Monday, December 12, 1650. According to custom, two chaplains of the cathedral choir went with some friars to the archiepiscopal palace; there, they sang masses for his soul. The archbishop of Manila gave the funeral sermon, and Mañozca was buried in the crypt below the floor of the cathedral's royal chapel.[136] He left an abundance of treasures, so valuable that the

[133] "producia efectos tan sobre toda persuasion humana," and "No viò este nuevo mundo Quaresmas, ni semanas Santas, con tan admirables progressos, ni años de jubileo Santo, con tal frequencia de Sacramentos: todo en la Ciudad era fervor, piedad, lagrimas, emmienda de vidas, mejora de costumbres, devocion en los que lo vian, y admiracion en los que lo escuchavan," ibid., fols. 4v, 7r.

[134] August 17, 1649, AHAM, Fondo Episcopal, caja 5, exp. 48.

[135] "Y aunque en mi larga edad y experiencias no hauia visto ni oydo que vassallo algunos huuiesse imajinado poner la mano en materia tan soberana," Mañozca to the king, July 15, 1650, RB, MS II/1992, fol. 43r. For more on the coats of arms – Palafox's enemies accused him of elevating Aragon's arms over those of Castile; Álvarez de Toledo, *Politics and Reform*, 259–60; Israel, *Race and Class*, 248–49. Palafox had been attentive to such displays; at his urging, in 1642, Mexico's city council replaced its eagle and snake device with a host and chalice, and a new motto; *Politics and Reform*, 145.

[136] He was the only dignitary interred there in the colonial period. Manuel Toussaint, *La Catedral de Mexico y el Sagrario Metropolitano, su Historia, su Tesoro, su Arte* (Mexico City: Editorial Porrúa, 1973), 127.

chapter hired a guard just to protect them. Over the years that followed, the chapter took inventory and testified that the archbishop had been seen using the objects; it kept some pieces and sold others, reinvesting the money in the cathedral's upkeep. Mañozca had possessed luxurious garments, from embroidered silk gloves to three mitres, two of white wool and one of amber wool sewn with pearls, and opulent liturgical objects, such as a silver chalice and a chalice cloth worked in silver and gold. In addition to rich vestments, he had collected carpets, furniture, and paintings, some nine of which he willed to the cathedral.[137] All this suggested a particular theory behind his work, that he inhabited his offices with a show of pious ostentation, countering displays made by those he considered enemies of the Church with a rival exhibit of the wealth, in every sense, of God's temporal ministers.

Yet Mañozca's term in office was soon subjected to scrutiny. Although he had completed several acts of the visitation, he had petitioned to end his commission in 1648, preferring not to investigate the tribunal's finances – protesting that it would consume too much time – and instead vouching for the character, skill, and personal wealth of the treasurer. Rather than relieve him of duty or conclude the inspection, the *Suprema* resumed it after his death. The new visitor, Pedro Medina Rico, had already conducted a visitation of the Inquisition in Cartagena de Indias; he reached Mexico in the summer of 1654.[138] Reassessing the era of the Great Complicity trials, Medina Rico noticed numerous irregularities. Among them, the appointment of the two Mañozca Bonilla Bastida brothers as familiars drew his attention. Only their descent from their maternal grandfather, Pedro Sáenz de Mañozca, and his purity of blood had been sufficiently described, and Medina Rico noted that their father had not submitted a report of his genealogy at all. There appeared to have been very little investigation, and no commentary on the quality of their genealogical proofs. The visitor railed that "the act is so indistinct and so without reference to proof for that which touches the said don Nicolás de

---

[137] ACM, Libro de Actas 11, fols. 1r-6r. Inventory in "Pontificales del Ill[ustrísi]mo S[eño]r Arcob[is]po Mañosca difunto," July 14, 1656, ACM, Libro de Correspondencia 8, pages unnumbered; other acts recorded June 17, 1657.

[138] Mañozca to *Suprema* and to Inquisitor General, October 10, 1648, AHN, Inq., lib. 1054, fols. 461, 502. Medina Rico worked in Cartagena from December 1647 until 1650; nominated to the *visita* in Mexico in May 1651, it was not concluded until 1662. He was the nephew of Andrés Rueda Rico, who was appointed to the *Suprema* with Mañozca; López Vela used the two families to demonstrate the passing of inquisitorial office through families, in "La elección y los rasgos sociológicos de inquisidores y fiscales," *HIEA* 2:777–78.

Bonilla in this city, that it does not seem possible that His Highness approved it this way, or that there was [not] a failing in the secretary who wrote it."[139] In 1657, the visitor revoked their status; he ordered that they not be called or treated as familiars until their genealogies were investigated, under penalty of a fine.

Finally, in 1658, Medina Rico issued charges against the tribunal inquisitors, Sáenz de Mañozca still among them. Evidence even suggested that he and his colleagues had devised a scheme in the early 1640s whereby they could turn a personal profit from the auctions of confiscated goods. The judges defended themselves zealously.[140] Reminiscent of his cousin's strategies – asserting the authority gained from experience and construing himself as the true reformer – Sáenz de Mañozca sought to justify his conduct, describing how he had found a somnolent tribunal and the inquisitorial jails virtually empty upon his arrival in 1642. He deemed it impossible that there were no heresies to be found in such a large district and noted that "with lesser beginnings," the tribunal in Lima had made the "glorious discovery of the complicity of Peru at which [he] had been present and served Your Highness [the Inquisitor General] with the care and example that is notorious."[141] He took significant credit for a dramatic increase in the Mexican court's activity, and especially for the trials of Portuguese *conversos*. In spite of the charges against him, Sáenz de Mañozca's career was not ruined. He left the tribunal only when he was elevated to the episcopate, made the bishop of Santiago de Cuba on September 5, 1661, and transferred to Guatemala in February 1668. His final promotion, in June 1675, was to the diocese of Puebla – once Palafox's see – but he died before the year's end, never taking office. Like

---

[139] "es el auto tan indistinto y tan sin referida de prueba para lo tocante al d[ic]ho don Nicolas de bonilla enesta ciud[ad] q[ue] no parece posible que su Alteça lo prouiesse asi, o que fue falta del secretario que lo escribio," September 20, 1657, AGN, Inq., vol. 417, exp. 9, fols. 388v-89v.

[140] Those charged included the inquisitors Higuera, Sáenz de Mañozca, and Estrada y Escobedo, and the officials Eugenio Saravia and Tomás López de Erenchun. Huerga judged that Mañozca accomplished virtually nothing in his visitation, despite producing numerous acts, and delayed some investigations that the *Suprema* specifically requested; he characterized Medina Rico's performance as one of great diligence; see his "La Dinámica de las Estructuras en America. El Caso de Nueva España," *HIEA* 1:1177; see also Tejado Fernández, "La Primera Mitad," 1143; M. Ballesteros Gaibrois, "Los Fondos Inquisitoriales Americanísticos," *HIEA* 1:109, 112; for extensive analysis of the *visita*, see Alberro, *Inquisition et Société*.

[141] "con menores principios … glorioso descubrimiento á la complicidad del Perú á que me había hallado presente y servido á Vuestra Alteza con el cuidado y ejemplo que es notorio." Quoted in Medina, *Inquisición en México*, 222.

many administrators in the Americas in the seventeenth century, his promotions did not take him to the other side of the Atlantic. Still, he rose higher than many Creoles. He applied to enter the order of Santiago in 1660; he was one of only four Creoles nominated to Mexico's tribunal as *fiscal* or inquisitor between 1570 and 1679.[142]

One of the strangest episodes to occur in Mexico's Holy Office in these years was the saga of don Guillén de Lombardo de Guzmán, or William Lamport, an Irishman who, after a life of intrigue, languished in the tribunal's prison for nearly twenty years. Seemingly a creature of Olivares's, he had probably been sent to New Spain as a spy during the crises of the early 1640s. In Mexico, however, he was soon suspected of plotting a rebellion. The Inquisition arrested him on October 26, 1642, and would eventually sentence him to be relaxed to the secular arm, a judgment carried out following the November 1659 *auto de fe*.[143] The years of his trial charted Sáenz de Mañozca's career in the tribunal, and that jurist handled much of the case, especially in its later years, proceedings in which anxieties around imposture recurred repeatedly. Eventually convicted of an assortment of heresies, from astrology and divination to a variety of Protestant propositions, Lombardo's case was made even more dramatic by the writings he produced during his imprisonment and by the events following Mañozca's death.

Early in the morning of December 26, 1650 – two weeks after the archbishop died – Lombardo and another prisoner, Diego Pinto, escaped from the Inquisition's prison. The porter brought the unwelcome news to Sáenz de Mañozca: the two had broken their wooden window, tried to burn their cell door, and somehow managed to flee. Soon, more reports filtered in. At about seven thirty in the morning, there was a knock on the

---

[142] *HC* 4:199, 206, 5:215, 382; AGI, Patronato, 5, nos. 17, 25. Elena Postigo Castellanos terms his parents "villanos," that is, not nobles; for her, he typifies seventeenth-century applicants who rapidly ascended the social ladder through officeholding and then sought to solidify their new status with a more established mark of honor. In a notable exception to this trend, Portuguese in Madrid who applied to the orders after 1640 were generally refused; *Honor y Privilegio en la Corona de Castilla. El Consejo de las Órdenes y los Caballeros de Hábito en el s. XVII* (Almazán, Soria: Junta de Castlla y León, Consejería de Cultura y Bienestar Social, 1988), 115–16, 162, 198–201. Cf. Escandell Bonet, "Sociología Inquisitorial Americana," *HIEA* 2:855.

[143] Five others were also executed, another in effigy. Troncarelli reports the initial denunciation – by Captain Felipe Méndez Ortiz, who had fought with Lombardo in Flanders and lived in the same building in Mexico – occurred on October 16, 1642; *El mito del 'Zorro'*, 111. See also Huerga, "Tribunal de Mexico," 1126; Álvarez de Toledo, *Politics and Reform*, 129–30, 146; Ryan Crewe, "Brave New Spain: An Irishman's Independence Plot in Seventeenth-Century Mexico," *Past and Present* 207 (2010): 53–87.

tribunal's door. Sáenz de Mañozca was advised that Lic. Pedro de Salinas, of the cathedral chapter, was waiting outside. Once admitted, he presented the inquisitor with the papers – soon discerned to be Lombardo's – that had been found that morning at a quarter past six, "affixed to the principal door of the said cathedral, which gives onto the *plaza mayor* and faces the holy cross of stone."[144] After his jailbreak, the fugitive had posted manuscripts on the doors of the cathedral that faced the so-called cross of Mañozca as well as on those of the viceroy's palace. His placards denounced the tribunal's inquisitors and claimed that the late archbishop had been the "principal author" of the Inquisition's abuses: "Visitor that he was of the said Inquisition, not only did he conceal the abominable horrors of the said inquisitors, but he committed with them the same."[145] Moreover, he implied that Mañozca repented of his sins, asserting that the evening he died, the archbishop had appeared to Lombardo in his cell, and that both the angels and his cellmate were witness to the truth of this. The archbishop, Lombardo explained, had then returned to his cell a second time the night before – significantly, Christmas – and broken him out of jail; the author of his abuse became the author of his escape. For Lombardo, it was the sign of God's goodness for which he had waited. After escaping, Pinto fled to Guanajuato and there turned himself in to inquisitor Estrada, whom he knew to be in that city. Lombardo's flight lasted little more than a day, although his writings continued to pass from hand to hand; the inquisitors were still publishing edicts against their circulation on December 31.[146] Lombardo used the same tools to defame Mañozca that the inquisitor had acquired such skill in deploying.

Like many of their contemporaries – including such fellow inquisitors as Adam de la Parra – the Mañozca cousins found an avenue of significant social mobility in legal training, the calculated use of print, and the offices of the Spanish Inquisition. Although the arc of Mañozca's career was exceptional in many respects, it demonstrated well how a politically adept inquisitor could best navigate Habsburg imperial administration, promoting both himself and his institution. Over his forty years as an inquisitor, a visitor, a royal councillor, and an archbishop, Mañozca amassed a remarkable familiarity with the tribunals of the Spanish

---

[144] "fixados enla puerta principal de d[ic]ha catedral q[ue] cae ala placa maior frente de la s[an]ta cruz de piedra," AGN, Inq., vol. 1497, fols. 1v-2r.

[145] "Visitador que fue de d[ic]ha ynq[uisici]on no solo occultò los horrores abominables delos d[ic]hos ynq[uisid]ores, sino que cometiò con ellos los mismos," AGN, Inq., vol. 1497, fols. 1r, 2r, 17r.

[146] Troncarelli, *El mito del 'Zorro'*, 233, 250–51.

FIGURE 6. This anonymous painting, likely from the second half of the eighteenth century, shows the cathedral of Mexico (still under construction), and the prominent placement of the "Cross of Mañozca" in front of it. The cross was significantly altered (much of its ornamentation was removed), and it was relocated to its current, less central position in the early nineteenth century. © 360611 CONACULTA.INAH. SINAFO.FN.MÉXICO.

world. His professional survival from so many conflicts provided him with valuable experience, and he learned which tools were most effective in making the case for his own rectitude and good conduct. He planned public celebrations and sponsored strategic printed accounts, full of well-turned allusions and pointed invective; he presented his arguments on paper and in person, as the situation required; he cultivated patrons, describing his work in ways that suited their needs, and built and sustained a network of clients. He framed his actions as simultaneously part of the spiritual and practical defense of the populace and the realm. The various official charges he exercised were tied together by a common conviction that the route to uncovering both heretical conspiracy and official corruption lay in the careful examination of account books and correspondence and of individual histories, relationships, and remembered conversations.

Mañozca's successes might best be attributed, however, to timing and to his ability to make his work as an inquisitor intelligible to a broad audience. In naming the Great Complicity and in strategically informing authorities of its investigations as they progressed, he and his colleagues

FIGURE 7. An anonymous seventeenth-century portrait of Juan de Mañozca, as archbishop of Mexico. It records his education and his officeholding as inquisitor in Cartagena and Lima, member of the *Suprema* and president of Granada's Chancery. © 365306 CONACULTA.INAH.SINAFO.FN.MÉXICO.

made a place for the Inquisition in some of the most pressing conflicts of their era, offering their contemporaries the images both of a terrifying enemy in the Judaizing Portuguese and of a heroic triumph in the tribunals' uncovering and dismantling of their purported conspiracy. In orchestrating and presiding over two of the most dramatic *autos de fe* of the Spanish Inquisition's history – held a decade apart in two viceregal capitals, Lima in 1639, Mexico City in 1649 – and in sponsoring printed accounts of these events, he publicized inquisitorial actions on a broader scale than his predecessors had done. In all those Atlantic crossings, he developed a strategy to bridge the distances within the Catholic Monarchy with spectacle. Akin to Páramo and the inquisitors of Palermo, Mañozca was able to offer to courtiers in Castile the intermediary knowledge of an administrator with a foot in their world and also with years of experience in multiple colonial locales, mainly as a judge, but also from his youth in Mexico City and relationships with his Creole kin. Yet his combination of skills was most effective in the Americas, where his status as a peninsular Spaniard, the authority of his degree from Salamanca, and his acquaintance with life at Court were rarer commodities.

CHAPTER 6

Building Careers, Making a Legal Culture

Toward an Appraisal of Inquisitorial Office

Provide out of all the people able men, such as fear God, in whom there is truth, and that hate avarice: and appoint them rulers, who may judge the people at all times.

Prudence is in some degree divination.[1]

In the spring of 1633, the inquisitor Juan de Mañozca composed an appeal and sent it to the new Inquisitor General, friar Antonio de Sotomayor. Although he had resumed his residence in Lima's tribunal in 1627, Mañozca was still seeking to build his authority in that viceregal capital, and to discredit accusations that had been levied against him during his recent tenure as visitor of the *audiencia* in Quito. He likened himself to a servant accustomed to one master whom death or other adverse circumstances had forced to work in the house of another. He pushed the analogy further, noting that even a newcomer acting skillfully and in good faith was likely to be mistreated by the established cohort of servants. He tailored this example to his specific circumstances, explaining: "as I was serving Your Highness in Cartagena, with complete satisfaction of my conduct, by your mandate I changed masters, and occupation."[2] He emphasized the difficulties of transferring to a new place, with its particular human geography, as well as the disjuncture between his experience as an inquisitor and the talents required in a Visitor General. Mañozca borrowed words

---

[1] Paraphrase of Exodus 18:21–22; from the life of Pomponius Atticus, Diego de Simancas, *Collectaneorum de Republica Libri IX* (Salamanca: heirs of Matías Gast, 1582), 271, 288.

[2] "estaua yo siruiendo a V[uestra] A[lteza] en Cartagena con entera satisfacion de mi proçeder Por mandato suyo mude de amo, y de ocupacion," Mañozca to Inquisitor General, May 10, 1633, AHN, Inq., lib. 1040, fols. 230–31.

from Cato the Elder, using them as his missive's governing motif. Just as an elderly Cato had been required to respond to false charges in the Roman senate, so too was he obliged to "exclaim" that "It is most wretched for one who has lived among men of one generation, to make his defense before those of another." Mañozca had found himself, he claimed, treated as a stranger among those with little knowledge of the "care and fidelity" that characterized the Inquisition's officials.[3] His appeal exemplified the persuasive strategies to which Spanish inquisitors turned to legitimate their actions. To effectively correspond with his superiors on the other side of the Atlantic, Mañozca aligned himself with his official identity as an inquisitor and, simultaneously, sought to develop a unique image of himself and his worth in order to attract the attention of the Inquisitor General.[4]

In his revisionist study of the Spanish Inquisition, Henry Kamen contended that – contrary to the persisting caricatural image – inquisitors must be seen as a bureaucratic elite.[5] Drawing from the close examination of five inquisitors' lives in the preceding chapters, this chapter explores how individual Spanish inquisitors demonstrated their membership in an elite group and acted to build the authority of that group. In any given year in the later sixteenth or early seventeenth century, it can be estimated that

---

[3] More fully: "y veome necesitado a decir lo que Caton quando ya viejo acussado enel senado de crimenens q[ue] no cometio, exclamo, con aquellas memorables palabras. miserrimum est (Patres conscripti) cum apud alios vixeris. apud alios causam dicere. han me tratado como a estrano, por el poco conocimiento, que tienen del cuidado y fidelidad conque los ministros siruen a V[uestra] A[lteza]." Ibid. He apparently drew this from Plutarch's life of Marcus Cato, 15.4. I have adapted the translation in *Plutarch's Lives*, trans. Bernadotte Perrin (London: William Heinemann; New York: The Macmillan Co., 1928), vol. 2. Mañozca may also have amplified the strength of the words he attributed to Cato. His *miserrimum est* differs, for example, from the passage in one sixteenth-century Latin edition: "*Difficile esse* eum qui apud alios vixerit homines, apud alios de causa sua respondere" (emphasis mine). *Plutarchi Chaeronensis, Summi et Philosophi et Historici Parallela, id est Vitae illustrium Virorum Graecorum et Romanorum* (Frankfurt am Main: Sigmund Feyerabend, 1580), fol. 107r.

[4] Francisco Bethencourt has also given particular attention to the form, organization, and contents of inquisitorial correspondence. On missives like Mañozca's, cf. his comments about the letters of Portuguese inquisitors in Goa: "They are long, as if distance had the effect of amplifying written communication (those of the local tribunals of the Iberian Peninsula are much more circumspect)." *The Inquisition: A Global History, 1478–1834*, trans. Jean Birrell (Cambridge, UK, and New York: Cambridge University Press, 2009), 59.

[5] "Contrary to the image – still widely current – of inquisitors as small-minded clerics and theologians fanatically dedicated to the extirpation of heresy, in the sixteenth and seventeenth centuries, the inquisitors were an elite bureaucracy." Henry Kamen, *The Spanish Inquisition: A Historical Revision* (New Haven, CT, and London: Yale University Press, 1997), 144.

from around forty to perhaps as many as seventy men were holding office
as judges in the Spanish Inquisition's district tribunals and as councillors of
the *Suprema*. The five men I selected for study met with a range of success
in their career trajectories, and all can be classified – in contrast to some of
their judicial colleagues – as taking an active approach to their inquisitorial
work. Although each left a substantial written record and made some
appearance in print, only three published substantive treatises; none
became Inquisitors General, but three ascended to the episcopate and the
Suprema. To reappraise sixteenth- and seventeenth-century Spanish
inquisitors is to seek to see them simultaneously as individuals and as
officials interested in building a corporate identity.[6] Thus, this chapter
charts the processes by which inquisitors built their authority – as
Mañozca did in his careful construction of letters – illuminating how
they could develop formidable persuasive skills and suggesting the kinds
of strategies they adopted to more or less successfully navigate their
judicial environments, the religious initiatives of a reforming Church,
and the Catholic Monarchy's administrative culture. In this way, Spanish
inquisitors, who have so often been summoned as a class apart, might be
woven more meaningfully back into the fabric of their society, not just by
their origins but also by their interactions as members of an educated elite.
To reframe Francisco Bethencourt's conclusion, the remarkably long survival of an institution as controversial as the Spanish Inquisition might be
partially explained by the political adroitness and the argumentative ability of some of these men.[7]

Mañozca's repertoire did not stop with Cato. He further amplified the
tenor of his 1633 letter, refuting those who murmured against him in
Madrid by closing with a line from Tacitus: "It is a principle of human
nature to hate those whom you have injured."[8] Moreover, he adopted

---

[6] On the interplay between the corporate and the individual in constituting identities in early
modern Europe, see John Jeffries Martin, *Myths of Renaissance Individualism*
(Houndmills, Basingstoke, Hampshire, UK, and New York: Palgrave Macmillan, 2004).
For a recent reconsideration of such issues, see Hannah Chapelle Wojciehowski, *Group
Identity in the Renaissance World* (Cambridge, UK, and New York: Cambridge University
Press, 2011).

[7] "The longevity of inquisitorial activity over nearly three centuries was due in large part to
the ability of the tribunals to adapt to circumstances and to different political, social and
cultural contexts," Bethencourt, *The Inquisition*, 442.

[8] Mañozca wrote: "como dijo Tacito Proprium est humani ingenii odisse, quem laeseris."
AHN, Inq., lib. 1040, fol. 231. I have used the translation of Tacitus, *Agricola*, 42.4 from
Agricola. Tacitus in Five Volumes, trans. M. Hutton, rev. R. M. Ogilvie (London: William
Heinemann Ltd.; Cambridge, MA: Harvard University Press, 1970).

Cato's exclamation as a refrain; it reappeared in 1647, used to open another polemic and so to immediately invoke the Roman statesman's experience as a fit model for Mañozca's own career. Seventeenth-century Spanish readers encountered Cato the Elder (234–149 BCE) as the progenitor of the *Origines* as a mode of historical writing and in the writings of Cicero, among other places.[9] Plutarch's life of Marcus Cato – from which the inquisitor had plucked his maxim – suggests why this particular Roman figure made such a powerful motif for Mañozca. A "new man," he embodied meritorious rise from virtuous but not noble Italian stock, earning his name of "wise and prudent, *catus*." He built his career around the empire, in Spain and in Athens as in Rome, well regarded for his conduct of military campaigns and for his oratory and work in affairs of state, though "he always clung to his native ways." Plutarch several times remarked on his long tenure as a statesman, "even in his hoary age, after consulship and triumph. Then, like some victorious athlete, he persisted in the regimen of his training, and kept his mind unaltered to the last." The biographer emphasized the man's severity, his sharp correcting tongue, and a kind of abstemious virtue on display even as he celebrated official triumphs; he related his devotion to a family that went on to serve the state over four generations. Throughout, Plutarch reported Cato's perpetual initiation of prosecutions, his involvement in lawsuits, and his skill in arguing them, often winning as plaintiff, never losing as a defendant. He was praised for restoring a Roman state in decline, as one who "plainly threatened wrong-doers in his speeches, and loudly cried that the city had need of a great purification," while characterizing such correction as that of an earnest physician.[10] Thus, when the 1647 polemic, seemingly a collaboration of Mañozca and his younger cousin, began with the contention that having been a minister for thirty-seven years, "the archbishop of Mexico [Mañozca] could well say with Marcus Cato" his maxim, it suggested a rich array of meanings through which to understand Mañozca and his career.[11]

---

[9] The *Disticha Catonis* – third-century didactic poetry long believed to be Cato's work – also circulated widely in Latin and in Spanish. Sabine MacCormack, *On the Wings of Time: Rome, the Incas, Spain, and Peru* (Princeton, NJ: Princeton University Press, 2007), 49, 63–64.

[10] *Plutarch's Lives*, trans. Perrin, 2:303, 315, 337, 349, 359.

[11] "bien pudiera decir el Arz[obispo] de Mexico, con Marco Caton," BNE, MS 12054, fol. 217r. The reference reappeared in the midst of disputes in viceregal Mexico between Juan de Palafox y Mendoza, Bishop of Puebla de los Angeles and Mañozca, writing here in collaboration with his younger cousin Juan Sáenz de Mañozca.

The summoning of such motifs was hardly unusual. In the first half of the sixteenth century, Cato the Elder was among those Romans noted by Juan Ginés de Sepúlveda for their prudence; the humanist also insisted that their pursuit of glory did not diminish their virtue.[12] He likewise appeared as an exemplar in Juan Luis Vives's manual on feminine education. There, the censor became a dignified and wise defender of public morality, sobriety in dress and affect, and judicious household management.[13] In the first part of *Don Quixote*, Cato's association with prudence joined a litany of ancient figures and their signal virtues.[14] In the same years, he was part of the cast from Greco-Roman antiquity included in the chronicle of the Andean Guaman Poma de Ayala. The Inca Garcilaso de la Vega identified Plutarch's *Parallel Lives* as a model for his comparison of Francisco Pizarro and Diego de Almagro and drew upon the life of Cato the Younger as a precedent for sponsoring public funerals for captains who died in penury.[15] When Michel de Montaigne began one of his essays with a comparison of the two Catos, however, he recognized the virtue and notable public service of the elder but found him also marked by his envy and ambition; moreover, he judged his activities in old age as excessively worldly.[16]

For Spanish inquisitors, the power of invoking such examples lay precisely in their fame and common usage. When Juan Adam de la Parra aimed to catch Inquisitor General Sotomayor's eye in the spring of 1634, his polemic, too, included Plutarch's lives among its constellation of proof texts, but without specific mention of either

[12] Here I follow David A. Lupher, *Romans in a New World: Classical Models in Sixteenth-Century Spanish America* (Ann Arbor: University of Michigan Press, 2003), 112–22.

[13] He drew from Cato's writings and from Livy's report that Cato, "a man of great dignity, spoke out against it in a speech full of widsom." Juan Luis Vives, *The Education of a Christian Woman: A Sixteenth-Century Manual*, ed. and trans. Charles Fantazzi (Chicago and London: University of Chicago Press, 2000), 102, 196, 240, 262, 279.

[14] In addition, the sayings of the pseudo-Cato also made an appearance (pt. 1, chaps. 42, 47, and pt. 2, chap. 33), Miguel de Cervantes, *Don Quijote de la Mancha. Edición del Instituto Cervantes 1605–2005*, dir. Francisco Rico (Barcelona: Galaxia Gutenberg, 2004), 1:544, 602, 994.

[15] MacCormack, *On the Wings of Time*, 63; Garcilaso de la Vega, El Inca, *Royal Commentaries of the Incas and General History of Peru, Abridged*, ed. Karen Spalding, trans. Harold V. Livermore (Indianapolis, IN: Hackett Publishing Company, Inc., 2006), bk. 3, chap. 8, pp. 145–46.

[16] "That man is learning to speak [Greek] when he needs to learn to be silent forever . . . If we must study, let us study something suitable to our condition." He praised the younger Cato, then, for studying Plato's writings on the eternity of the soul. See essay 28, "All Things Have Their Season," in *The Complete Essays of Montaigne*, trans. Donald M. Frame (Stanford, CA: Stanford University Press, 1965), 531–32.

Cato.[17] Mañozca's borrowing of Cato's "memorable words" – as he termed them – allowed him to tap into a commonly held reservoir of knowledge, as well as to develop a specific portrait of himself. It was in noticeable and strategic silences and in the inclusion and recombining of well-worn allusions and citations that such men advanced original arguments fitted to particular cases.[18] Sotomayor had not been the Inquisitor General when Mañozca was promoted out of his post in Cartagena de Indias. The 1647 polemic, moreover, was addressed to the next Inquisitor General, Diego de Arce y Reinoso. Such narratives thus functioned as introductions of sorts; Mañozca's 1633 letter reached an Inquisitor General who had just taken office in the summer of 1632, with a long career already behind him and a reforming mandate.[19] The central motif was one that might not only characterize the letter's author – the judge in his fifties – but also appeal to the experiences of its recipient, a courtier in his seventies. It summoned a specific model of imperial servant, one concerned with reform amid fears of decline, who risked his career and person in the service of justice and the republic. It also spoke to a specific kind of political culture. Plutarch had described Cato's management of his household: "He was always contriving that his slaves should have feuds and dissensions among themselves; harmony among them made him suspicious and fearful of them."[20] Mañozca wrote, he claimed, against those deceived or moved by hatred to murmur against him, a common enough occurrence in a model of government that held overlapping claims to authority, inspections, disputes, and lawsuits as checks against corruption and engines of reform.

---

[17] Juan Adam de la Parra, *Conspiración Herético-Cristianísima*, trans. Angeles Roda Aguirre (Madrid: CSIC, 1943), 189, 201.

[18] Cf. Warren Boutcher, "Unoriginal Authors: How to Do Things with Texts in the Renaissance," in *Rethinking the Foundations of Modern Political Thought*, ed. Annabel Brett and James Tully with Holly Hamilton-Bleakley (Cambridge, UK: Cambridge University Press, 2006), 73–92; cf. also, the idea of Plutarch's work forging "legitimating elite political authority" in the early Roman empire; Rebecca Preston, "Roman Questions, Greek Answers: Plutarch and the Construction of Identity," in *Being Greek under Rome. Cultural Identity, the Second Sophistic and the Development of Empire*, ed. Simon Goldhill (Cambridge, UK: Cambridge University Press, 2001), 86–119.

[19] The letter was marked received March 15, 1634. Sotomayor (1557–1648) took office July 17, 1632, Arce y Reinoso (1587–1665) in 1643. Teresa Sánchez Rivilla, "Inquisidores Generales y Consejeros de la Suprema: Documentación Biográfica," *HIEA* 3:239–40, 272–73.

[20] *Plutarch's Lives*, trans. Perrin, 2:367.

As scholars have shown, throughout the sixteenth and seventeenth centuries, Spanish actors in the Americas used motifs from classical antiquity to make their experiences of empire comprehensible.[21] Inquisitors were no exception to this. Judges posted throughout the Spanish world, from Palermo to Peru, used such references to make their exercise of disparate charges into an organic whole, and to seek to carve out space for particular legal arguments, for individual careers, and for their office. So Cato became a plausible means of communication both between individuals and between occupants of offices whose authority was meant to transcend the individuals who passed through them. For a letter that took ten months from its signing in Lima to be marked as received in Madrid, Mañozca chose – in the allusions to Cato and Tacitus, via Latin quotations – to emphasize a shared intellectual vocabulary. He reminded an audience at Court that he was not a "stranger," that judges in faraway Lima had attended the same universities and read the same books.

Sixteenth- and seventeenth-century Spanish inquisitors sought to attach a variety of such meanings to their work, individually and collectively. The remainder of this chapter explores some of the ways inquisitors simultaneously participated in practices and debates common to their educated contemporaries and sought to differentiate their office from others and characterize it as uniquely valuable. Their official lives were marked by their educational formation as jurists and by the mobility of careers that required them to navigate between the universal and the particular in a variety of ways. When inquisitors argued for the rectitude of their actions and the justice of their cases, they turned to a range of forms of publicity available to them. As they crafted their arguments, they often drew from a repertoire of figures (like Cato) in order to forge and strengthen their corporate identity; to augment the authority of their office; and to carve out intellectual, legal, and political space for it within their society. They sought to demonstrate their learning and make their way into lettered circles, even as they were preoccupied with the potential dangers of speech and writing, of spectacle and artifice.

---

[21] For avenues into the excellent scholarship on this issue, see MacCormack, *On the Wings of Time*; Lupher, *Romans in a New World*; J. H. Elliott, "The Mental World of Hernán Cortés," in *Spain and Its World, 1500–1700: Selected Essays* (New Haven, CT, and London: Yale University Press, 1989), 27–41.

TRAVELING JURISTS

When inquisitors set out to establish a new tribunal, they brought the procedural building blocks of the Inquisition with them. In the late sixteenth century, the first inquisitor and the *fiscal* in Lima's tribunal owned manuals of law and inquisitorial practice, printed in Europe. When his ship wrecked just off the Canaries, Mexico's first inquisitor grabbed the inquisitorial records as he made his escape. This inquisitor and the *fiscal* were not the only ones who sailed from Castile with cargo precious to their official missions. For example, the twenty Jesuits who departed the peninsula in 1620, bound for Cartagena de Indias, lamented the attack from Muslim pirates they suffered en route, even more so because the brigands burned the books and relics they were transporting to their new American foundations. Similar misfortunes befell those officials who traversed the Mediterranean; one of the *Suprema*'s delegates to Rome in the midst of the Carranza affair had been lost in a shipwreck with – a colleague noted – his negotiated dispatches.[22] Inquisitors carried records and regulations on more local travels as well; Cristóbal Fernández de Valtodano reported taking papers from the Toledo tribunal archives along with him when he went to visit the inquisitorial district in the early 1550s. Such tales from official journeys suggest how Spanish inquisitors, like other royal and ecclesiastical administrators, were conduits between the courts and councils in Madrid and Rome and the distant posts around the Catholic Monarchy to which they were sent.

Their careers could be highly mobile. Some judges moved between several tribunals over the course of their official lives. Even those whose trajectories were more sedentary were theoretically expected to go out of the tribunal seat on visitations of their districts (even if this requirement could be avoided or delayed in practice). In their correspondence and in their discharge of official duties in the tribunal, they communicated both local conditions to their superiors and regulations and reforms to the inhabitants of varied places. As judges who operated in a court of hybrid mandate and who were almost

---

[22] Teodoro Hampe Martínez, *Santo Oficio e Historia Colonial: Aproximaciones al Tribunal de la Inquisición de Lima (1570–1820)* (Lima: Ediciones del Congreso del Perú, 1998), 77, 78, 82; Stafford Poole, *Pedro Moya de Contreras: Catholic Reform and Royal Power in New Spain, 1571–1591* (Berkeley: University of California Press, 1987), 29–30; Nicolás del Castillo Mathieu, *La Llave de las Indias* (Bogotá: Ediciones El Tiempo, 1981), 67; Diego de Simancas, "Vida y Cosas Notables," in *Autobiografías y Memorias*, ed. Manuel Serrano y Sanz (Madrid: Bailly, Bailliére, S. B., 1905), 160, 165; Sánchez Rivilla, "Inquisidores," 352.

always clerics, they were theoretically conduits of both divine grace and earthly justice. They were magistrates charged to uphold the laws of the republic and give access to justice as well as local arbiters in a tribunal whose highest court of appeal – beyond the council at the royal Court in Madrid – was arguably in Rome. Given the particular nature of inquisitorial courts, an inquisitor was a sort of pastor-judge, who sought to procure the confession of the accused and who offered reconciliation to the body of the Church to the penitent confessed criminal. The ideals of their office were both judicial and pastoral, even as their disciplinary formation became increasingly uniform.

One of the most commented upon aspects of how a distinctly Spanish approach to inquisitorial practice developed during the sixteenth century was in the increasing preference for jurists rather than theologians to serve as inquisitors and councillors of the Inquisition. This transition was part of the intensifying legality of sixteenth-century Spanish culture, as more universities turned out more graduates in law and a growing royal administration turned to jurists to fill its offices. Perhaps more than anything, this meant that those at the helm of the Inquisition argued that legal reasoning and judicial tools were the best means available to pursue religious objectives. They contended that law degrees equipped inquisitors to be able administrators, to advocate for the Inquisition's standing in a legalistic society, against other authorities, and within the legal and institutional structures of crown and Church.[23] They applied legal reasoning to make sense of the environments around them, turning to assessments of jurisdiction and proof to form opinions and resolve conflicts. Inquisitors thus participated in – and contributed to – an increasing inclination toward jurisprudence and toward writing inflected by legal reasoning in the shaping of the administrative culture of the Catholic Monarchy; their official writings were infused with legal practices of weighing and sifting evidence and building cases and were bounded by legal procedures.[24]

---

[23] On legal education, see Richard Kagan, *Students and Society in Early Modern Spain* (Baltimore, MD, and London: The Johns Hopkins University Press, 1974); On the polemic between jurists and theologians, see Stefania Pastore, *Il Vangelo e la Spada. L'Inquisizione di Castiglia e i Suoi Critici (1460–1598)* (Rome: Edizioni di Storia e Letteratura, 2003); on the roles and approaches of censors, as consulting theologians in tribunals, see Martin Austin Nesvig, *Ideology and Inquisition: The World of the Censors in Early Mexico* (New Haven, CT, and London: Yale University Press, 2009).

[24] Several recent studies have examined, in a host of contexts, how those in the early modern Iberian world grappled with sorting and transmitting large amounts of information, and with how to make that information comprehensible and persuasive to their interlocutors.

It was precisely this expertise and experience that made inquisitors attractive candidates for a multiplicity of tasks. They were frequently delegated to investigate other branches of their own institution, to visit other arms of the royal government, and to inspect universities. Some were even made into bishops.[25] Among the most dramatic of such cases, Charles V dispatched Lic. Pedro de la Gasca, a member of the *Suprema* (trained in both law and theology), to Peru in 1546, giving him special powers as president of the *audiencia*. In the telling of the Inca Garcilaso de la Vega – in whose early seventeenth-century history de la Gasca, his affiliation with the *Suprema* noted, played a prominent role – the councillor restored order in Peru and became a model for the "gentle, kindly, prudent, experienced, astute, and resourceful person who would be able to conduct peaceful affairs, or warlike ones if necessary." De la Gasca's actions – investigating and bringing charges – were rendered as the legal equivalent of valiant deeds of arms.[26]

When inquisitors sought to construe themselves as prudent reformers and champions of the monarchy and the faith, they could turn to such examples and to instances in which the Inquisition had been depicted as an important tool for enacting reforms. As early as 1516, the famous Dominican friar Bartolomé de las Casas petitioned Cardinal Cisneros to "send the Holy Inquisition to those islands of the Indies," reasoning that successful conversion required good examples of Christian behavior and that places where the faith had only recently been established could be even more easily sabotaged by heretics.[27] Although the first two tribunals of the

See the approaches taken in María Portuondo, *Secret Science: Spanish Cosmography and the New World* (Chicago: University of Chicago Press, 2009); Daviken Studnicki-Gizbert, *A Nation Upon the Ocean Sea: Portugal's Atlantic Diaspora and the Crisis of the Spanish Empire, 1492–1640* (Oxford, UK, and New York: Oxford University Press, 2007); Orietta Filippini, "Verso 'Roma locuta.' Questioni teologiche, corte madrilena, e Santa Sede alla metà del Seicento," *Roma moderna e contemporanea* 18.1–2 (2010): 231–74; David Tavárez, "Legally Indian: Inquisitorial Readings of Indigenous Identity in New Spain," in *Imperial Subjects: Race and Identity in Colonial Latin America*, ed. Andrew B. Fisher and Matthew D. O'Hara (Durham, NC, and London: Duke University Press, 2009), 81–100.

[25] John Leddy Phelan observed that inquisitors were favored choices as visitors; *The Kingdom of Quito in the Seventeenth Century; Bureaucratic Politics in the Spanish Empire* (Madison: University of Wisconsin Press, 1967).

[26] Garcilaso, *General History*, ed. Spalding, bk. 5, chaps. 2, 4, pp. 187–89; Sánchez Rivilla, "Inquisidores," 358–59.

[27] "que mande enviar a aquellas islas de Indias la Santa Inquisición," Quoted in A. Huega, "La Pre-Inquisición Hispanoamericana (1516–1568)," *HIEA* 1:662. See also Richard Greenleaf, *The Mexican Inquisition of the Sixteenth Century* (Albuquerque: University of New Mexico Press, 1969).

Spanish Inquisition in the Americas were not ordered until 1569, and then excluded the indigenous population from their jurisdiction, these were the sorts of precursors to which Mañozca laid claim when he went into the field to found a new tribunal and to remake two others in the early seventeenth century. In Cartagena de Indias, he and his senior colleague railed against friars who caused scandal, setting poor examples for converts. The image of himself as a reformer that he crafted in New Spain in the 1640s was of a prudent administrator of the law reviving the reforming spirit of both the Council of Trent and of the first years of missionary activity in the Indies; when Mañozca brought a stone cross from Tepeapulco – the site of an early Franciscan foundation – to the viceregal capital, he summoned the first generations of friars and their dedication to the faith to support seventeenth-century causes.

These patterns did not apply just in the Americas. Many historians have argued that all of the Spanish Inquisition tribunals outside of Castile, as those in Aragon and Valencia, were essentially colonial incursions. Galicia's tribunal was finally instituted, after failed attempts, a short while after those in Mexico and Lima, as was the court's outpost in the Canaries. A specific juridical ideal lay behind this theory of administration, one that strove to use a universal legal structure to contain diverse environments.[28] The safeguard of the common good – the *bonum commune* – was the application of the *ius commune*, that is, the collective corpus of civil and canon law. Inquisitorial law was part of this same cloth, woven together from earlier precedents and commentaries, resting on both papal and royal authority, and sustained by the remarkable boom in legal publishing of the later sixteenth century, even as its Spanish theorists – Diego de Simancas and Luis de Páramo among them – worked to carve out a discrete space for their judicial practice in that field of print.[29] Both in

[28] On their use as instruments of "Castilianization," see especially William Monter, *Frontiers of Heresy: The Spanish Inquisition from the Basque Lands to Sicily* (Cambridge, UK, and New York: Cambridge University Press, 1990); Jaime Contreras, *El Santo Oficio de la Inquisición de Galicia, 1560–1700: poder, sociedad y cultura* (Madrid: Akal, 1982). On the political organization of this world, see Elliott, *Spain and Its World*, 7; and "A Europe of Composite Monarchies," *Past and Present* 137 (1992): 48–71.

[29] On these questions, see Edward Peters, "Editing Inquisitors' Manuals in the Sixteenth Century: Francisco Peña and the *Directorium Inquisitorum* of Nicholas Eymeric," *The Library Chronicle* 40 (1974): 95–107; Pastore, *Il Vangelo e la Spada*; Andrea Errera, *Processus in Causa Fidei: L'Evoluzione dei Manuali Inquisitoriali nei Secoli XVI-XVIII e il Manuale Inedito di un Inquisitore Perugino* (Bologna: Monduzzi, 2000); Adriano Prosperi, *L'Inquisizione Romana: Letture e Richerche* (Rome: Edizioni di Storia e Letteratura, 2003); Kenneth Stow, *Catholic Thought and Papal Jewry Policy*,

symbolic action and in legal print, inquisitors continually sought to breathe new life into the mythology of the Inquisition as bulwark of royal and religious reform.

Yet inquisitorial activity often rested on the presence or absence of a single magistrate and on the authority the judges were able to command. Serván de Cerezuela described the ceremony surrounding his founding of the Lima tribunal in 1570: the inquisitor, holding the symbols of the Holy Office, was between the viceroy and the members of the *audiencia* and the city council while a *Te Deum* was sung and an edict was read.[30] The inquisitor – as the Holy Office incarnate – was publicly consecrated as a pillar of the social order. The composite monarchy of the Habsburgs was predicated on a balance between the universal administration of royal justice and the protection of special privileges and negotiated relationships between crown and locality. Tridentine reforms involved similar acts of juggling.[31] Each cohort of administrators and would-be reformers, inquisitors among them, brought pronouncements, procedures, and laws with them to jurisdictions that often existed more in theory than in practice; then, they began to fill their letters back to the metropole with laments about the distance, harsh terrain, financial woes, odd behaviors, and local politics. In such circumstances, inquisitors often sought to link the worth of their work to the level of threat they encountered. Judges in Palermo enumerated Sicily's "bad neighbors" – Calabria was riddled with heresies and Turks and Protestant corsairs eyed the island as a stepping-stone into Spain. Reporting on the newly founded tribunal in Cartagena de Indias, Mañozca and his senior colleague chose a similar tone. Such ports were potential entry points for foreign heretics and their heresies, in the flesh and in print. The reading of their first edict of faith – "with [all] the solemnity possible" – had turned chaotic when the soldiers of the garrison and those of the galleys started to brawl, causing the authorities to leave the cathedral mid-event to pacify their subordinates. Local elites, they complained, did not greet them with deference; although they may have carried the Inquisition's procedural codes in tact, building the local authority to execute them was a different proposition.[32]

1555–1593 (New York: Jewish Theological Seminary of America, 1977); Thomas Izbicki, *Friars and Jurists: Selected Studies* (Goldbach: Keip Verlag, 1997).

[30] Pedro Guibovich Pérez, *En Defensa de Dios: Estudios y Documentos Sobre la Inquisición en el Perú* (Lima: Ediciones del Congreso del Perú, 1998), 25–26.

[31] See, in particular, Simon Ditchfield, *Liturgy, Sanctity and History in Tridentine Italy* (Cambridge, UK: Cambridge University Press, 1995).

[32] Salcedo and Mañozca, December 18, 1610, and July 14, 1612, AHN, Inq., lib. 1008, fols. 2r, 34r. These were also persistent themes in the correspondence of the first inquisitor in

As jurists with mobile careers, inquisitors operated in a world where their actions were circumscribed by law, procedure, and their standing in an institutional hierarchy, and in places where the exercise of official authority was an ongoing process of creating authority with local populations, other colonial elites, and distant superiors.[33] That mobility also created a circulation of experience and knowledge among university faculties, royal and papal courts, Chanceries, *audiencias*, cathedrals, and Inquisition tribunals. In the early seventeenth century, Juan Gutiérrez Flores's inquisitorial career took him from Sicily to Mallorca, Mexico, and eventually Lima; a few decades later, Pedro Medina Rico followed an inspection of the tribunal in Cartagena de Indias with one in Mexico. Inquisitors' trajectories sometimes crisscrossed over long careers, and their perspectives were informed by experiences with their colleagues and by the other networks of communication that ran alongside official channels.

Those involved in Bartolomé Carranza's trial had long and complicated histories with one another that developed in even more complicated ways over the seventeen years of the trial, the result of their postings to a host of offices and locales; the pope who finally sentenced Carranza in 1576, Gregory XIII, had even seen the early stages of the controversy surrounding it when Pius IV sent him as a legate to Spain to intervene in the case in the early 1560s.

As the minutes of Córdoba's cathedral chapter showed, family correspondence – like that of the Simancas clan – could quickly move inside information about ecclesiastical and inquisitorial matters. And the expectations of inquisitors could well have been shaped by the experiences of their relatives. Simancas's brother, for instance, had been a bishop in Cartagena de Indias, a brother of the Inquisitor General Fernando de Valdés y Salas had lived in Cuzco in the middle of the sixteenth century, and Páramo's brother had been an inquisitor in Toledo's tribunal when he began his own career with the Holy Office in Sicily.[34] Hundreds of such examples could be noted, all to suggest that a barely glimpsed array of experiences, conversations, and human interactions lay behind each inquisitorial action, dressed in legal form.

Mexico, Pedro Moya de Contreras, Greenleaf, *The Mexican Inquisition*, 175; Poole, *Moya de Contreras*.

[33] Cf. the extraordinary mobility of some Portuguese clerical careers, A. J. R. Russell-Wood, *The Portuguese Empire, 1415–1808. A World on the Move* (Baltimore, MD, and London: The Johns Hopkins University Press, 1992), 87–94.

[34] Garcilaso, *General History*, ed. Spalding, bk. 7, chap. 9, p. 70.

THE THEATER OF THE WORLD

Both its secrecy and the dramatic displays of its more elaborate *autos de fe* remain among the most storied elements of the Spanish Inquisition. Attending to those elements of the institution's reputation as well as to such practices as the proclamation of edicts of faith, many scholars have characterized inquisitors as utilizing a "pedagogy of fear." And the staging of *autos de fe* exemplified inquisitorial officials' ability to create spectacle. The processions, sermons, accounts of crimes, displays of penitence, and the public *autos* were both performed for an assembled viewing public and further disseminated in written accounts. As many historians have observed, inquisitorial practice was keenly attuned to publicity; inquisitors manipulated the use of secrecy and of public displays, of powerful symbols and images, and of print in order to authorize and legitimate their institution.[35] Thus, inquisitors may also be considered as orchestrators of publicity campaigns.

Certainly, theorists of inquisition, such as Simancas, argued that heresy ought to be feared. It was the homicide of souls. Heretics, they reasoned, jeopardized not only their own salvation but also that of others, as human perception might so easily be deceived.[36] And heretics were the deceivers *par excellence*, as Luther most dramatically could be shown to be, disseminating error under the guise of piety and ultimately going so far as to alter the laws and customs of polities that came under their sway.[37] A wider swath of sixteenth-century Spanish observers noted the destruction wrought by heresy in Germany, in England's "schism," in France's wars,

---

[35] See especially the sophisticated analysis in Bethencourt, *The Inquisition*; in addition, Edward Peters, *Inquisition* (Berkeley and Los Angeles: University of California Press, 1989). See also, for instance, Bartolomé Bennassar, *L'Inquisition espagnole, XVe – XIXe siècle* (Paris: Hachette, 1979), 78–87; and "Modelos de la Mentalidad Inquisitorial: Métodos de su 'Pedagogía del Miedo,'" in *Inquisición Española y Mentalidad Inquisitorial*, ed. Ángel Alcalá (Barcelona: Editorial Ariel, 1984), 174–81; on *autos*, see the comparative analysis in Bethencourt, *The Inquisition*; Maureen Flynn, "Mimesis of the Last Judgment: The Spanish *Auto de fe*," *Sixteenth Century Journal* 22 (1991): 281–97; Alejandro Cañeque, "Theater of Power: Writing and Representing the Auto de Fe in Colonial Mexico," *The Americas* 52 (1996): 321–43.

[36] "No[n] animaduertu[n]t perditi homines, quàm sit fragilis i[n]tellectus humanus, & quàm facilis ad errorem. sicut se habet oculus noctuae ad lumen solis, sic & intellectus noster ad notissima naturae, vt verè inquit Aristoteles libro secundo Metaphysicae." In "De Haeretics," chap. 31, par. 14, Simancas, *Institutiones Catholicae* (Valladolid: Egidio de Colomies, 1552), fol. 113v.

[37] On heretics as deceivers, see, for example, Simancas, *Institutiones Catholicae* (1552), fol. 112v. Cf. chap. 16 of the 1561 Instructions, in Miguel Jiménez Monteserín, *Introducción a la Inquisición española* (Madrid: Editoria Nacional, 1980), 206.

and in the Netherlands' revolt and ultimately wrote these events into their histories as lessons to be well heeded.[38] And so, Simancas contended, all heresies must be publicly abominated and Catholic truth proclaimed, and staunch legal tools brought to aid this endeavor.[39] Such theorists engaged in the construction of both national and professional identities around Spain's reputed, and singular, freedom from heresy. Inquisitors, they reasoned, were defenders of the republic and its souls against heretics, those rapacious wolves.[40] Panics about fifth columns – Lutheran, Muslim, Jewish, or Portuguese – were likewise intertwined with such assertions of Spanish purity and exemplarity in having uniquely admitted the "ministry" of the Inquisition. As Adam de la Parra phrased it in the early 1630s, to silence this exceptional history of Spain would be an act of negligence.[41] To theorize about heresy in such ways could also be a path into fighting against it in the courtroom; both Adam de la Parra and Simancas composed these arguments when they were not yet inquisitors but rather young jurists in pursuit of promotions.

Each was well aware, as were other inquisitors, that they were negotiating a complex terrain of public opinion. It does not seem accidental, to take another example, that Mañozca engineered two of the most remarked *autos de fe* of the seventeenth century. In short, publicity campaigns – and

[38] On England, for example, see Diego de Yepes, *Historia particular de la persecucion de Inglaterra, y de los martirios mas insignes que en ella ha auido, desde el año del Señor 1570* (Madrid: Luis Sánchez, 1599); Pedro de Ribadeneyra, *Hystoria Ecclesiastica del Scisma del Reino de Inglaterra* (Lisbon: Manoel de Lyra, 1589).

[39] For instance: "Is qvi solenniter abivrat haereses, tria potissimu[m] in abiuratione facere debet: scilicet, omnes haereses publicè detestari, orthodoxam veritatem erroribus suis contrariam firmiter asserere, ad fidem catholicam perpetuò tenendam iure iura[n]do, & obligatione poenali se adstringere: vnde facilè intelliges, quid sit haec abiuratio. Nempe solennis quaeda[m] est haeresum detestatio, cum assertione catholicae veritatis, & iusta obligatione permanendi in fide Christiana." In "De Abivratione Canonica," chap. 1, Simancas, *Institutiones Catholicae* (1552), fol. 1r. Although it was logical, in an alphabetical organization, to begin the manual with the abjuration of error, I think there was additional significance in the choice. Cf. Friar Jacobus de Voragine's explanation of the ordering of the Church's liturgical year: "She does not wish to start from error, for she puts reality before the sequence of time, just as the Evangelists often do; and besides, the renewal of all things came with the coming of Christ"; Jacobus de Voragine, *The Golden Legend: Readings on the Saints*, trans. William Granger Ryan (Princeton, NJ: Princeton University Press, 1993), 1:3.

[40] Simancas made these associations, for instance, in his dedication to Prince Philip, *Institutiones Catholicae* (1552).

[41] With his emphasis on negligence, he invoked its opposite, the important ideal of diligence. Adam de la Parra, *Conspiración*, 175–77. On one political crisis tinged with charges of heresy, see Stuart Schwartz, "Panic in the Indies: The Portuguese Threat to the Spanish Empire, 1640–1650," *Colonial Latin American Review* 2 (1993): 165–87.

their complicated relationship to injunctions about secrecy – were an integral piece of inquisitorial work.[42] They were waged in print and in manuscript, in processions and in correspondence. Inquisitors and their associates advertised *autos de fe* and publicized their jurisdictional competitions with other authorities, their representations of the grandeur of inquisitorial work supporting pleas for funding and coexisting with the fragility and contingency of affairs within inquisitorial courts, as in other early modern institutions.

Inquisitors argued that secrecy about their investigations, trials, archives, and jails – including the suppression of the names of witnesses – was necessary to create conditions in which testimony might be obtained, to guard against fear of reprisal and to protect the honor of those involved in trials. The 1561 instructions gave a hint of what inquisitors saw that needed reform, as, for instance, when they decreed that only one name should appear in each order for arrest, to prevent the loss of secrecy (and so presumably to avoid the flight of suspects). Evidence of the rupture of inquisitorial secrecy, however, was legion. A scandal around prison communications, with messages smuggled in and out in foodstuffs, had erupted in the 1530s in Toledo's tribunal; in the 1540s, there was a dramatic prison break. The inquisitors in Palermo at the century's end reported myriad obstacles to the maintenance of secrecy, from their subjection to the viceroy's soldiers, housed as they were in the port's primary military installation, to the comingling of jail space with that of the viceregal courts, to instances of those on trial conversing – through the window of the tribunal's audience room – with people on passing ships. A crisis of revoked testimony and ruptured secrecy rocked the Lima Portuguese trials in the 1630s. Isabel de Ovalle's reports of some of those who had been penanced visiting her and her siblings to apologize for denouncing her still imprisoned father – whose trial was ongoing – are even more suggestive of the social realities that belied proclamations of the Inquisition's secrecy.[43]

---

[42] For approaches to political culture and the possibility of dissent in early modern Spain, see Michele Olivari, *Entre el trono y la opinión: la vida política castellana en los siglos XVI y XVII*, prologue by Ricardo García Cárcel, trans. Jesús Villanueva (Valladolid: Junta de Castilla y León); Stefania Pastore, *Il Vangelo e la Spada*.

[43] AHN, Inq., leg. 1648, exp. 4. For the 1561 instructions, see Jiménez Monteserín, *Introducción*, 201, 212, 230, 235. On Toledo in the 1530s, see Lu Ann Homza, *Religious Authority in the Spanish Renaissance* (Baltimore, MD, and London: The Johns Hopkins University Press, 2000), chap. 1; on Lima, Miriam Bodian, *Dying in the Law of Moses: Crypto-Jewish Martyrdom in the Iberian World* (Bloomington: Indiana University Press, 2007), chap. 5.

In sum, these were the sorts of concerns that inquisitors might have had on their minds when they decided how to publicize their institution and when to turn to extrajudicial tools to seek to influence trials. Even the Inquisition's instructions betrayed a certain flexibility about the guarding of the institution's confidences; those of 1561, for example, enjoined secrecy around trials unless permission had been given to break that seal, thus suggesting the existence and even likelihood of such exceptions. Simancas – who claimed to have helped compose that watershed set of instructions – displayed a sharp awareness of how inquisitorial affairs played out in public arenas. His autobiographical *Vida* of the late 1570s was in large part an account of his view of the Carranza trial, rearguing the justice of the Inquisition's prosecution of the archbishop. In his vernacular commentary on a just concluded trial, he was careful to note that Gregory XIII had granted him express permission to break his secrecy about the Carranza proceedings on his return from Rome, following the end of the trial and the archbishop's subsequent death.[44] Many manuscript accounts circulated of Carranza's sentence of light abjuration and his much remarked penance, reconciliation, and seemingly holy death in Rome in the spring of 1576, each seeking to advance a version of the events for posterity. Martín de Azpilcueta, the archbishop's defense attorney, folded references to the case into his Latin treatises. In the 1580s, a jurist and cleric in Toledo offered another account in his biography of Carranza, seeking to repair the reputation of both the Spanish Inquisition and the archiepiscopal see by rendering the trial as an aberration, the popes and king as models of justice, inquisitorial procedure as sound, and the archbishop as a man of great sanctity, merely undermined by a few singular enemies. Like those of his collaborators and his opponents, Simancas's writings, sometimes in the vernacular, sometimes in Latin, sometimes in manuscript, sometimes in print, or – when he published in favor of the Toledo cathedral's purity of blood statutes – under a pseudonym, pointed to an acute sensitivity to which information should be aired in which forum.

Ample evidence suggests that inquisitors perceived their trials as occurring not just in the courtroom, but also as requiring them to build support for their institution and its prosecutions before and during the process, and to seek to arbitrate public response afterward. Tribunals were a locus of

---

[44] Even during the trial, the *Suprema* likewise ruled that he might communicate with the Spanish ambassador in Rome (Zúñiga) about the proceedings, in contravention of customary procedure, *Suprema* (Castro, Busto de Villegas, Soto, Ovando, Vega) to Lic. Salgado, July 16, 1569, AHN, lib. 325, fol. 152r.

patronage; thus, inquisitors might, for example, petition the *Suprema* to fund the dowries of their officials' daughters.[45] Páramo and his colleagues reported the insults and jokes about inquisitors that circulated in Sicily, speech that they claimed undermined their ability to try heretics. They entered into conflict with viceroys in letters, council deliberations, and printed tracts; through their symbolic actions and those of their partisans; and even when they sought – with trouble – to find lodging suitable for an inquisitor in Messina while the viceroy was in residence there.

As the Inquisition's *fiscal* in Murcia, Adam de la Parra likewise had a hand in such affairs, printing pamphlets to support the tribunal's jurisdictional claims. In his contests with the bishop of Cartagena in the early 1630s, at stake were both the local projection of authority and much longer-standing debates about the correct manner to prevent and prosecute heresy and about whether that was still the province of bishops as well as inquisitorial tribunals. Construing himself as the champion of the Inquisition's honor, his complaints to the *Suprema* and to the Inquisitor General reveal some of the ways in which he measured inquisitorial authority.[46] He denounced the bishop for dividing the region's clerics into factions, for "perturbing the peace," and for protecting his partisans and defending their pompous behavior. He described how one such associate traveled in a mule litter – although this was unheard of in Murcia – and, from it, accosted the Inquisition's officials, even harassing the *fiscal* himself on his way from his house to the tribunal. Even worse, he alleged that the bishop sabotaged the Inquisition during the celebration of Saint Dominic's feast day and "has banished the tribunal from the principal church." He usurped the selection of the preacher and chose one who was discourteous to the point that "all of the sermon was a satire against the tribunal." Adam de la Parra claimed that the Inquisition was "disauthorized by means of his [partisans] under whose cloak the bishop spills out his venom in order to better conceal his emulation."[47] The *fiscal* was particularly concerned with the bishop's presumption as an "emulator," or a deceptive rival, of the Holy Office; Mañozca and Bishop Palafox leveled

---

[45] Toledo's inquisitor Horozco intervened on behalf of the warden, January 26, 1554, AHN, Inq., leg. 3067, no. 74.

[46] On the central importance of protocol and corporate expressions of identity see, among others, Phelan, *Kingdom of Quito*, 229.

[47] "tiene desterrado el tribunal de la Ygl[esi]a maior," and "todo el sermon fue una satira contra el tribunal." Also, "desautorizado por medio de los suios con cuia capa derrama el obispo su veneno para paliar mas la emulacion." Adam de la Parra to Inquisitor General [August 23, 1634?], AHN, Inq., leg. 2810.

similar charges against each other in Mexico little more than a decade later.

Inquisitorial authority was thus asserted, refuted, and negotiated in the arena of public opinion. Guillén Lombardo's resistance to the inquisitors in Mexico City in 1650 – expressed in placards posted in symbolic sites following his jailbreak – turned the judges' language against them; he excoriated the Mexican tribunal for having betrayed the Inquisition's own standards for just practice, among other offenses. Adam de la Parra's focus on suppressing the trappings of devotion that grew up around the *beata* Mother Luisa can be explained in much the same way.[48] To attempt to stop the circulation of images of her and accounts of her visions and miracles, while her trial was ongoing, was to publicly contest perceived heresy. Turned another way, the persisting circulation of those devotional objects was a public challenge to the Inquisition's right to discern holiness. The poems of João Pinto Delgado, composed from the 1610s into the 1640s, were likewise a challenge to inquisitors issued in the same idioms they employed, rendering them the opposite of the merciful holy ministers they claimed to be and the biblical figures they claimed to follow, while lauding as a martyr Isaac de Castro (who was burned following the conclusion of his trial by the Portuguese Inquisition in Lisbon in December 1647).[49] That language of martyrdom was among the most powerful indictments of inquisitorial action. Across the sixteenth and seventeenth centuries, some exceptional individuals portrayed themselves – and were revered in a variety of communities – as martyrs who died at the inquisitors' hands. Although inquisitors came to be characterized as the latter-day persecutors of martyrs, they simultaneously claimed to have martyrs – Peter of Verona, Pedro Arbués – among their own number.[50]

---

[48] This directive circulated to tribunals as far afield as Lima, where the inquisitors reported reading an edict against devotion to the *beata* in the cathedral in 1638, AHN, Inq., lib. 1041, fol. 387.

[49] His 1627 collection was dedicated to Cardinal Richelieu. See I. S. Révah, "Autobiographie d'un Marrane. Édition partielle d'un manuscrit de João (Moseh) Pinto Delgado," *Revue des études juives* 119 (1961): 41–130; João Pinto Delgado, *Poema de la Reina Ester. Lamentaciones del profeta Jeremías. Historia de Rut y varias poesías*, ed. Révah (Rouen: David du Petit Val, 1627; repr. Lisbon: Institut Français au Portugal, 1954).

[50] For approaches to the subject, see Brad S. Gregory, *Salvation at Stake: Christian Martyrdom in Early Modern Europe* (Cambridge, MA: Harvard University Press, 1999); on two instances of martyrdom intersecting with Mañozca's career, see Bodian, *Dying in the Law*, chaps. 3, 5. Early anti-Inquisition tracts also included martyrologies; see Reginaldus Gonsalvius Montanus, *A Discovery and playne Declaration of sundry subtill practises of the Holy Inquisition of Spayne* (London: John Day, 1568).

BETWEEN CATO AND CICERO

In the fashion of Mañozca's invocation of Cato the Elder, inquisitors – and those who wrote on their behalf – summoned a series of figures to aid them in asserting their authority. They drew from a catalog of historical templates to shape both corporate and individual identities. Cicero (106–43 BCE) was a particular favorite. Simancas repeatedly cited Cicero's works in his compilation of aphoristic advice on the republic and in his legal commentary on the Inquisition. Cicero made an especially valuable model as a philosopher who was also involved in the practical work of the state, renowned for his oratory and for his epistolary rhetoric, a legal practitioner who was also a commentator on jurisprudence.[51] When Simancas quoted from the life of Atticus that "prudence is in some degree divination," he selected a passage in praise of Cicero.[52] In the lines that surrounded the aphorism that he had plucked out, the biography recounted the affinity of the great men of the day for Atticus, the many rolls of letters Cicero had sent to him, and the evidence of Cicero's prudence and diligence that those letters contained.[53]

Elsewhere, Simancas paraphrased Plutarch's life of Cato the Younger. He stressed Cato's diligence in the senate, always the first to arrive and the last to leave, not working for glory or gain but purely for the defense of the republic, inveighing that good men "ought to be more attentive to

---

[51] Dedication, Simancas, *De Republica Libri IX* (Venice: Bolognino Zaltieri, 1569). For the characterization of the Catholic Monarchy as an "empire of towns" that looked toward Cicero's *De Officiis* – often filtered through earlier Renaissance thinkers – as a source of civic ideals, see Richard L. Kagan, with the collaboration of Fernando Marías, *Urban Images of the Hispanic World 1493–1793* (New Haven, CT, and London: Yale University Press, 2000), chap. 2.

[52] "Prudentia quodam modo diuinatio est." This passage is customarily translated into English using "wisdom" in place of "prudence." I have chosen the latter, given its omnipresence in Simancas's epoch, when it conveyed not just the reasoned exercise of a particular kind of knowledge, but also the ability to judge based on practical experience. He placed the aphorism under the subheading "De Prudentia Magistratuum," in bk. 10, chap. 5, *Collectaneorum de Republica* (1582), 288, and attributed it to "Plutarchus in Pomponio Attico"; it is, however, from Cornelius Nepos, Atticus 16.4. Simancas was aware of Nepos, given that he cites him on Themistocles in the same subsection; the confusion may have stemmed from the frequent printing together of Nepos' Atticus and Plutarch's lives. For the passage in question – linked to Cicero in the marginalia – *Plvtarchi Cheronei Graecorvm Romanorvmqve Illvstrvm Vitae* (Basel: Michele Isingrino, 1542), fol. 380r. (Available at http://adrastea.ugr.es/tmp/_webpac2_1111598.84001)

[53] I refer, primarily, to Atticus 15.3–17.1; English translation available in Cornelius Nepos, *A Selection, including the Lives of Cato and Atticus*, trans. Nicholas Horsfall (Oxford, UK: Clarendon Press, 1989), 24–25.

the common interests than the bee to its honey." He recounted how Cicero
had thanked Cato the Younger for defending his wife's sister; the latter
responded that thanks ought to be offered to the republic, instead, in
whose defense the work had been done.[54] Simancas made this pair templates not just for the virtuous magistrate, in general, but for the ideal
inquisitor, in particular. Thus, he drew from Cicero's *De Officiis* when
explaining what should govern the selection and comportment of inquisitors, that, for example, friendship for a defendant should not lead a judge
astray; at most, he might be permitted to schedule such a case at a
favorable hour.[55] In later manuals, he cast the punishment of heretics as
a practice that could be found in the laws of all peoples. To adduce proof of
how the impious had been punished in antiquity, he turned to Plutarch's
writings on superstition, an oration of Demosthenes, and Cicero's *De
Legibus*, among other precedents.[56]

Adam de la Parra chose similar material to open the diatribe against the
French crown that he wrote in the early 1630s. He began with a pair of
dramatic epigraphs, the first presented as a command from Isocrates to
Demosthenes to "guard the religion that you received from your elders."
He followed this with one attributed to Claudian, a writer of the late
Roman Empire, which bemoaned how a single incompetent traitor could
fell a great empire in no time at all.[57] Within the first pages of the book, he
cited Cicero – invoked more familiarly as "Tullius" – to the effect that
sowers of discord and fomenters of civil war should be stripped of their
rights and homes.[58] The orations of Demosthenes and Cicero recurred in

---

[54] "ratus non minus operae, diligentiaeq[ue]; rebus co[m]munibus impendendum, quàm apes
favo solent." He cited the source as "Plutarchus in Catone Vticensi" – as it was a paraphrase of chap. 19 of that text – and placed it under the subheading "Pro Repvblica Omnia
esse Facienda," in bk. 2, chap. 7, *De Republica recte instituenda, conservanda, et amplificanda libri IX* (Cologne: Lazare Zetzner, 1609), 77.

[55] He paraphrased these parts of Cicero's *De Officiis* 4.43 in his "De Inquisitoribus,"
chap. 34, par. 4, *Institutiones Catholicae* (1552), fol. 121. His debt to Cicero was
immediately evident; the first words of the first chapter – "De Abiuratione" – of his final
inquisitorial manual were "Apud Ciceronem & Plautum." Simancas, *De catholicis institutionibus* (Rome: in aedibus Populi Romani, 1575), 2.

[56] He utilized these authorities in the first chapter – there "De Punitione Impiorum" – of his
abridged manual (not alphabetically ordered); Simancas, *Enchiridion Iudicum Violatae
Religionis* (Venice: Giordano Ziletti, 1569), fols. 1r-2r. See also Kimberly Lynn Hossain,
"Was Adam the First Heretic? Luis de Páramo, Diego de Simancas, and the Origins of
Inquisitorial Practice," *Archive for Reformation History* 97 (2006): 193–96.

[57] "Isocrates a Demostenes. Guarda la Religión que recibiste de tus mayores." He reprised
the Claudian, later, in a chapter on pressing threats to the Holy Roman Empire; Adam de la
Parra, *Conspiración*, front matter, 202.

[58] Ibid., 14.

his citations throughout the book, along with the parallel lives of Plutarch. He praised the great Spanish contribution to the global work of propagating the faith, remarking, "It would look for a Cicero or a Demosthenes and even then could lack eloquence to praise it and embellish it."[59] Antonio Domínguez Ortiz has argued, moreover, that Adam de la Parra imitated Cicero's rhetoric, adopting a Ciceronian style of oratory for the Latin treatise he composed in favor of the purity of blood statutes.[60]

Whereas Páramo, too, cited a range of Greek and Latin works, he used an alternate set of paradigms to order the first sections of his *De Origine*. There, he argued that inquisition was coeval with the world, evident in each of six theological ages; in the sixth, Christ became the greatest of the inquisitors and "today is head of the Inquisition," enacted by earthly delegates. Fully the first seventeen chapters of the book were consumed by a close reading of God's supposed work as inquisitor of Adam and Eve, shaped as presaging the specific practices of late-sixteenth-century inquisitions. There followed a veritable catalog of inquisitors of biblical time, offered as lessons, models, and precedent to Páramo's contemporaries. Simancas, too, used the punishment of religious offenses in the Old Testament to legitimize the work of inquisitors, but in a far less detailed manner. Moses became a particular focus, with inquisitors claiming him as originator of a line of priests and judges and identifying him as an exemplar of judicial practice in the old law.[61]

Simancas turned again and again to Moses as paradigmatic judge as he crafted genealogies of inquisitorial practice and of the republic's magistrates more broadly, drawing both on biblical text and on Philo's first-century life of Moses. He was particularly inclined to cite Exodus 18, through which he located active and virtuous judges and their tribunals

---

[59] More fully: "El español atravesó el peligroso mar de incesante oleaje, lleno de amenazas, con desprecio de su vida y salud, para llevar a los pueblos envueltos en la noche de la infidelidad, la luz con que se iluminan también las tinieblas egipcias. ¿Quién no se admira? ¿Qué lengua, qué elocuencia o qué elegancia y fluidez del discurso serán suficientes para ensalzar este hecho conforme a su dignidad y mérito? Buscaría un Cicerón o un Demóstenes y aun le podría faltar elocuencia para alabarlo y embellecerlo." Ibid., 177.

[60] Even if he added neologisms to describe the statutes; Antonio Domínguez Ortiz, "Una obra desconocida del Inquisidor Adam de la Parra" *Revista Bibliográfica y Documental* 5 (1951): 98–99.

[61] For Páramo's description of the first inquisitorial proceeding, see his "Ad Lectorem," and the first forty-five pages of his *De Origine et progressu officii Sanctae Inquisitionis* (Madrid: Juan Flandro, 1598). Although Páramo also depicted Moses as progenitor of a lineage of judges, and so occupier of a pivotal role in the inquisitorial succession, his lengthy treatment of Moses was more ambiguous than that of Simancas, see pp. 48–60. See also my "Was Adam the First Heretic?"

at the heart of a godly society. In one of many such paraphrases, he quoted the injunction to "provide out of all the people able men, such as fear God, in whom there is truth, and that hate avarice: and appoint them rulers ... who may judge the people at all times."[62] Similarly, when the Jesuit Matías de Bocanegra preached a sermon in honor of the translation of the stone cross to Mexico City, he proposed Archbishop Mañozca as the city's new Moses, leading a populace afflicted by drought, illness, poverty, and bad weather in a new exodus.[63] In his history of the 1649 *auto de fe*, he invoked biblical justice by citing the book of Kings: "and so when [Jehu] entered to punish the Apostate Joram, and the immodest Jezabel, he not only gave them to understand that he was going to kill her for obscenity, but rather as a witch."[64] In this analogy, the inquisitors were made the new Jehus, those they had convicted, a lineage of apostates, like Joram and his mother Jezabel. Bocanegra also noted that this condemnation had occurred at Jehu's coronation, thus indicating that Mexico's inquisitors were engaging in the delegated work of kings.

Signal Dominicans were another set of figures around whom affiliates of the Spanish Inquisition sought to forge a collective identity. Páramo dedicated significant space in his *De Origine* to early members of the Dominican order, claiming in them direct antecedents for his own judicial work. Confraternities for inquisition officials dedicated to Saint Peter Martyr (the thirteenth-century Dominican Peter of Verona) expanded throughout the Catholic Monarchy from the late sixteenth century. The saint was adopted as a symbol not only by associates of the Spanish Inquisition; Pius V also sought to develop the cult – and its resonance for the Roman Inquisition – in the late 1560s, and confraternities associated with the Portuguese Inquisition experienced similar growth well into the eighteenth century. The cult was reflected in the physical space of tribunals. Lima's

---

[62] "Prouide de omni plebe viros sapientes, & timentes Deum, in quibus sit veritas, & qui oderint auaritiam; & constitue ex eis tribunos, qui iudicent populum omne tempore." Here Simancas paraphrased and slightly reworded the Vulgate's Exodus 18:21–22 (switching sapientes for potentes, for instance), cited simply as "Exodus 18." He placed it under the subheading "Quales esse debeant Magistratvs," in bk. 5, chap. 4; a lengthier paraphrase (with "potentes," instead) appeared later, at the start of his section "De Magistratibus Hispaniae," bk. 7, chap. 2, *Collectaneorum de Republica* (1582), 271, 399. Among the many uses of Moses as precedent in his inquisitorial manuals, see *Institutiones Catholicae* (1552), chap. 18.

[63] Matías de Bocanegra, *Sermón a la Solemne colocación de la Santa Cruz de piedra* [Mexico, 1648?], BNE, VC/999/24, fol. 26r.

[64] "pues quando [Iehù] entrò a castigar al Apostata Ioran, y à la desonesta Iezabel, no solo diò a entender que la iba a matar por torpe, sino por hechizera." Bocanegra, *Auto general de la fee* (Mexico City: Antonio Calderón [1649]), dedication. Cf. 4 Kings 9:22.

inquisitors, for instance, reported to the *Suprema* that they had conducted an *auto* in the Holy Office's chapel of Saint Peter Martyr at the end of February 1631; the same year, one of their number was interred there. They also sought funds from the council to improve that chapel, "with the vocation of our patron," which they reported had been founded in 1583 by a bishop of Quito who was also a Dominican friar. They had already begun the work, supported in part by alms solicited from the district's familiars, notaries, and commissaries.[65]

The promotion of the cause for sainthood of Pedro Arbués – the inquisitor assaulted in Zaragoza's cathedral in 1485 – further suggests how attempts to forge a connection between inquisitorial office and holy martyrdom were linked to the circumstances of individual careers. The canon's beatification in 1664 was greeted with celebrations and sermons, as well as the reprinting of tracts about the inquisitor, such as Diego García de Trasmiera's. As an inquisitor in Sicily, García de Trasmiera had written about other holy lives, as well as a commentary on inquisitorial law and a theoretical consideration of polygamy. He first published his hagiography of Arbués in Palermo in 1647 – dedicating it to Inquisitor General Arce y Reinoso – during years of revolt in Spanish Sicily and Naples.[66] Following the revolt in Portugal and an era of suspicion about Portuguese orthodoxy, the book offered a dramatic account of the perfidy of *conversos* and the danger they might pose to civic order; it suggested Arbués as a heavenly combatant against such religious threats and as a special advocate against plague. García de Trasmiera further made his case for Arbués's election by arguing that divine providence had guided his parents to choose the name

---

[65] Páramo, *De Origine et progressu*, 95–111; Lima tribunal to *Suprema*, June 8, 1632, AHN, Inq., lib. 1040, fol. 208; cf. fol. 240; Juan Antonio Suardo, *Diario de Lima de Juan Antonio Suardo (1629–1639)*, ed. Ruben Vargas Ugarte S.J. (Lima: Universidad Católica del Perú, Instituto de Investigaciones Históricas, 1936), 1:185–86; Bethencourt, *L'Inquisition à l'époque moderne: Espagne, Portugal, Italie XVe-XIXe siècle* (Paris: Fayard, 1995), 85–115. On processions honoring Peter Martyr in colonial Mexico, see María Águeda Méndez, ed., *Secretos del Oficio: Avatares de la Inquisición novohispana* (Mexico City: El Colegio de Mexico, UNAM, 2001), 27–39.

[66] On García de Trasmiera (1604–61), inquisitor in Valencia, Aragon, and Sicily, and ultimately on the *Suprema* (in 1658), see Sánchez Rivilla, "Inquisidores," 344. On the revolt and the prominence of García de Trasmiera in the tribunal, see Manuel Rivero Rodríguez, "La Inquisición Española en Sicilia," *HIEA* 3:1183–1200; and "Técnica de un golpe de Estado: el inquisidor García de Trasmiera en la revuelta siciliana de 1647," in *La Declinación de la Monarquía Hispánica en el Siglo XVII*, ed. Francisco José Aranda Pérez (Cuenca: Ediciones de la Universidad de Castilla-La Mancha, 2004), 129–53.

Peter in the "holy fount" of baptism, showing his continuation of the work of the Peters of Galilee and of Verona.[67]

García de Trasmiera stitched together a history of Spanish combat against purported enemies of the faith. He centered one chapter on Ferdinand and Isabel's 1492 expulsion of the Jews, tying that act to the "prudent" Philip III's expulsion of *moriscos* from his realms. He argued that history, medieval and more recent, showed that "it is not so dangerous to live with the serpent in the bosom, as in the mixture of unfaithful neighbors," always disposed to harm. That is, he depicted false converts as even more harmful to a Christian polity than the toleration of non-Christians.[68] Simancas and Adam de la Parra had also adopted this argumentative device, playing to anxieties about imposture while in no way advocating policies of toleration. In developing the villainy of Arbués's killers – and, by implication, *conversos* of the later 1640s – García de Trasmiera reworked stock anti-Jewish invective. To give further shape to his narrative, he bifurcated the symbolic meanings of Moses. On the one hand, he reprised the logic of other inquisitor-theorists, claiming that "all nations" established judges of religion and listing Moses among those who "in the people of God were zealots for the purity of the faith (exercising office of inquisitors)."[69] On the other hand, he made Moses' leading of the exodus out of Egypt a parable of cowardice, marveling that so many able-bodied men "did not have the valor to oppose the army of Pharaoh." From there, he fabricated a long sweep of Jewish history (to which he aggregated *conversos*), alleging an eternal national character of "pusillanimity and lowness of spirit."[70] Like other inquisitors, he drew upon a succession of multivalent events and epochs – from biblical times to the contests of medieval Iberia to 1492, from evangelization in the Americas to the Council of Trent to Luther's threat – to supply meaning and drama to depictions of contemporary events. He reinforced and perpetuated criminal archetypes that could be used to justify the persecution of individuals and groups. Such commentators turned

---

[67] Diego García de Trasmiera, *Epitome de la Santa Vida, y Relacion de la Gloriosa Muerte del Venerable Pedro de Arbues, Inquisidor Apostolico de Aragon* (Madrid: Diego Díaz de la Carrera, 1664), 7. The reprint included the brief of beatification and the papal decrees of 1652 and 1663, and mentioned the decrees of 1625, 1631, and 1634.

[68] "No es tan peligroso vivir con la Vivora en el seno, como en la mezcla de vezinos infieles," ibid., 40.

[69] "En el pueblo de Dios fueron zeladores de la pureza de la Ley (exercie[n]do oficio de Inquisidores)." Ibid., 43–44.

[70] "Y su pusilanimidad, y baxeza de animo, que siempre conservan, fue tal, que sie[n]do tan crecido numero, no tuvieron valor para oponerse al exercito de Farao[n], que los seguia, siendo tanto inferior en numero, como se dexa conocer de la prisa con que saliero[n] en su alcance," ibid., 38.

to historical exempla to bind a global network of inquisition tribunals with the institution's fifteenth-century foundation, with two waves of expulsions and a supposedly universal and eternal succession of inquisitors.

When inquisitors and their affiliates described their actions in letters, reports, commentaries, and histories, they adhered their particular experience to famous motifs. They sought to use broadly held ideals as a means to grant authority to specific models of practice or to the conduct of particular affairs, offering a rich array of allusions to elevate, explain, and justify their work. When Adam de la Parra adopted Ciceronian rhetoric to argue for purity of blood statutes, he assumed for himself the stance of the Roman orator, and for the councils at the seventeenth-century royal Court in Madrid, the model of deliberation and the authority of the Roman senate. When Mañozca aligned himself with Cato the Elder, he performed much the same imaginative act. These inquisitors engaged in a specific kind of historical thinking – evident in liturgical practice as well – wherein ancient models were made to authorize present action while present action claimed to revive an idealized ancient time.[71] Moreover, their choice of motifs likened them not only to the ancients they invoked but also to more recent literati – such as humanists in the tradition of Petrarch – who had chosen the same historical models and ancient interlocutors. When they summoned Cicero or Moses to their cause, inquisitors sought both to write themselves into learned circles and to appropriate these figures to their interpretation of truth.

AMONG THE LETTERED ELITE

Particularly with regard to the sixteenth century, historians have charted the participation of Spanish intellectuals in broader learned networks – often with Rome as their hub – and the creation of such circles in the peninsula itself, even as they have tended not to enumerate inquisitors as part of these groups.[72] Yet in order to understand how the men who held

---

[71] There is a large literature on such issues of memory and history. See, among others, Yosef Yerushalmi, *Zakhor. Jewish History and Jewish Memory* (Seattle: University of Washington Press, 1982).

[72] See the approaches taken in Katherine Elliot van Liere, "'Shared Studies Foster Friendship': Humanism and history in Spain," in *The Renaissance World*, ed. John Jeffries Martin (New York and London: Routledge, 2007), 242–61; "Vitoria, Cajetan, and the Conciliarists," *Journal of the History of Ideas* 58 (1997): 597–616; and "After Nebrija: Academic Reformers and the Teaching of Latin in Sixteenth-Century Salamanca," *Sixteenth Century Journal* 34 (2003): 1065–105; Ronald Truman, *Spanish Treatises on*

office as inquisitors built their social and political capital and constructed their institutional identity, it is important to recognize that they were among their society's intellectual elite. Usually graduates of prestigious legal faculties, their education and their intellectual activities shared much with those of their lettered contemporaries; all this did not, of course, preclude disagreements and harsh conflict among inquisitors and between inquisitors and their contemporaries, not least about the legitimacy of the Spanish Inquisition and its practices.[73]

Inquisitors voiced ideals and anxieties akin to those of other Catholic intellectuals. As officials, they dealt in words, and they took sustenance from the letters and praise of their peers; vested in the written and spoken word, they were also deeply suspicious of the heretical content it might contain and its potential for deception.[74] As judges in a court that took confession as the most valuable of proofs, they were charged both to seek truthful speech as judicially and spiritually efficacious and simultaneously to be wary of its veracity. They were also participants in a religious culture that elevated spiritual conversation, a practice associated with Tridentine reformers and virtuous bishops. Thus, a life of Carranza recounted how he had enjoyed conversation with Valtodano, then his inquisitorial judge, on a range of subjects. In his autobiography, Simancas emphasized how in Rome he had promoted only virtuous entertainments in his episcopal household. An Augustinian friar took a similar tack defending Mañozca in 1620, describing the inquisitor's recreation as reading widely, choosing books rather than games. Praise of both Simancas and Mañozca emphasized their facility and knowledge both within and beyond their own discipline of jurisprudence; descriptions of how they shared their long experience and wide reading in conversation with friends and colleagues sought to tie them to a learned ideal.[75]

Government, Society and Religion in the Time of Philip II: The 'de regimine principum' and Associated Traditions (Leiden: Brill, 1999); Guy Lazure, "To Dare Fame: Constructing a Cultural Elite in Sixteenth-Century Seville" (PhD diss., The Johns Hopkins University, 2003); A. Katie Harris, *From Muslim to Christian Granada: Inventing a City's Past in Early Modern Spain* (Baltimore, MD: The Johns Hopkins University Press, 2007), 48–50.

[73] For an intricate examination of this terrain, see Pastore, *Il Vangelo e la Spada*.

[74] See the consideration of these issues – referencing Simancas – in Nesvig, *Ideology and Inquisition*.

[75] Pedro Salazar de Mendoza, *Vida, causa, y sucesos, prósperos, y adversos del Ilustrísimo y Reverendísimo Señor Don Fray Bartolomé de Carranza, y Miranda*, chap. 23, in Spanish History MSS, Lilly Library, Indiana University; Juan de Verzosa, *Epístolas*, ed. and trans. Eduardo del Pino González (Alcañiz and Madrid: CSIC, Centro de Estudios Humanísticos, 2006), 3:860; Simancas, *Vida*, 187; AHN, Inq., lib. 1009, fol. 193. Cf. Homza, *Religious*

Inquisitors' ties of patronage and clientage left traces in print. The prominent humanist Benito Arias Montano offered praise as recompense to Valtodano, his early patron, memorializing Valtodano among a cohort of virtuous men as a combatant against Lutheran deception in his treatise on rhetoric, a work in Latin verse that paid homage to Cicero. In so doing, both men entered the lettered realm as collaborators, defending their republic and providing it with spiritual sustenance. The younger Franciscan who Valtodano sent to the Council of Trent's final sessions in his place, Francisco de Orantes, behaved in similar fashion. When Orantes published the sermon he delivered at Trent in 1562, he dedicated it to Valtodano, identifying him as a councillor of the *Suprema*, and praising his prudence, mercy, and candor of spirit; his pastoral care; and his ardent love of the Church as mother and spouse. Orantes opened his sermon under the twin signs of Francis, his order's founder, and Cicero, whose eloquence he framed as a unifying force.[76] Not long after, he published an extensive theological refutation of Jean Calvin. In the dedication to Philip II's son Carlos, he described his tract as a defense of the Christian republic and again praised Valtodano as possessing the most brilliant virtues, recounting how he had gone to Trent in his place, and there encountered Calvin's *Institutio Christiana*, or "more truly the destruction of Christian instruction."[77]

Simancas's affiliations left similar traces. Arias Montano seems to have served as his intermediary with the Plantin press in Antwerp, enabling the jurist to publish there and writing approbations for his books. The two men had crossed paths in Rome in 1572, sharing a circle of associates. Arias Montano reported to Plantin, moreover, that he had traveled from Rome back to Spain with Simancas in 1576.[78] In the commentary on Joshua he completed in 1581, a theological treatise attuned to

Authority, chap. 4; Constance M. Furey, *Erasmus, Contarini and the Religious Republic of Letters* (Cambridge, UK: Cambridge University Press, 2006).

[76] María Violeta Pérez Custodio, ed. and trans., *Los* Rhetoricorum Libri Qvattvor *de Benito Arias Montano* (Badajoz-Cádiz: Diputación Provincial de Badajoz-Universidad de Cádiz, 1995), 305–7; Francisco de Orantes, *Oratio* (Venice: Giordano Ziletti, 1563).

[77] "seu ueriùs Christianae institutionis destructio," Orantes, *Locorum Catholicorum ... Pro Orthodoxa, et Vetere Fide Retinenda, Libri Septem* (Venice: Giordano Ziletti, 1564), dedication.

[78] I thank Guy Lazure for kindly supplying me with evidence, from the Biblioteca Juan March, that in 1572 Pedro Vélez de Guevara, canon in Seville's cathedral chapter, friend of Arias Montano and associate of Inquisitor General Valdés, sent a Latin letter to Simancas. See also Leon Voet, *The Plantin Press (1555–1589): A Bibliography of the Works Printed and Published by Christopher Plantin at Antwerp and Leiden* (Amsterdam: Van Hoeve, 1980), 5:2090–94.

contemporary politics, he praised Spanish learning and particular expertise in judgment; the book's last lines credited Simancas for providing inspiration for the work. Another figure who orbited around Simancas's household in Rome was Pablo de Céspedes, the painter, humanist, and cleric educated first in his uncle's household in Córdoba and then at the theologically focused University of Alcalá. Perhaps traveling in the inquisitor's company to and from Rome, he was active in Andalusian humanist circles in the decades that followed his return to Spain in 1576 and appointment to a prebend in Córdoba's cathedral.[79]

Inquisitor-prelates sought to sustain their ties to communities far and near through such exchanges and through extensions of patronage and works of charity. With these actions, they also contributed to particular religious devotions. Simancas brought relics of Saints Stephen and Lawrence to Badajoz; with his brothers, he commissioned paintings of the baptism of Christ and the crucifixion – perhaps executed by Céspedes – to hang in their newly constructed chapel of the Holy Spirit in Córdoba's cathedral. At his death, Valtodano left in the cathedral in Santiago de Compostela tapestries of the histories of Solomon and Joseph; perhaps as many as thirty-two oil paintings; and panels of Saint John the Baptist, Saint John the Evangelist, and one of the Virgin with his coat of arms. The inventory of goods left by Mañozca in Mexico City's cathedral listed nine paintings: a portrait of Pope Urban VIII, the martyrdom of Saint Sebastian, the beheading of Saint John the Baptist and another of the saint, a painting of Saint Jerome, one of the creation of light, the death of Christ, Our Lady of Begoña (originally a Vizcayan devotion), and Our Lady of Anguish (to whom there was a chapel dedicated in Mexico's cathedral).[80]

---

[79] Arias Montano noted: "incoeptum ante duos annos Mantuae Carpentanorum suasu & monitu optimi & studiosissimi uiri Iacobi Simancae, tunc Pacensium, nunc Zamorensium episcopi, absolutum in nostro secessu Aracenensis rupis, mense Augusto, [1581]." *De Optimo Imperio Sive In Lib. Iosvae Commentarium* (Antwerp: Christophe Plantin, 1583), 713. See also ibid., fols. 2v–3r; cf. Voet, *Plantin Press*, 1:170–72. On Céspedes (born in the province of Toledo, likely in 1538, and likely student of Ambrosio de Morales at Alcalá), see Priscilla E. Muller, "Pablo de Céspedes: A Letter of 1577," *The Burlington Magazine* 138 (1996): 89–91; Fernando Marías, *El Largo Siglo XVI: los usos artísticos del renacimiento español* (Madrid: Taurus, 1989); Jesús Rubio Lapaz, *Pablo de Céspedes y su Círculo. Humanismo y Contrarreforma en la Cultura Andaluza del Renacimiento al Barroco* (Granada: Universidad de Granada, 1993).

[80] María Angeles Raya Raya, *Catálogo de las pinturas de la Catedral de Córdoba* (Córdoba: Publicaciones del Monte de Piedad y Caja de Ahorros de Córdoba, 1988); José García Oro and María José Portela Silva, "El arzobispo Valtodano (1570–1572). Un recuento de su Testamentaría" *Compostellanum* 50 (2005): 713, 715; "Pontificales del Ill[ustrísi]mo

Inquisitors also mirrored the practices of courtiers and other learned contemporaries in their patterns of correspondence and exchange of books. Simancas enlisted the aid of the interim governor of the Toledan archdiocese, Lic. Busto de Villegas (who was also a member of the *Suprema*) in publishing his works while he was in Rome. In these letters, news of official business was augmented with reports on the health of Spaniards in Rome (Simancas reported that he had had to eat meat for most of Lent as the result of a kidney infection) or on the weather (he remarked on the drought in Spain and a spate of rain in Rome). Simancas sent copies of his books to friends and to those whose eyes and ears he hoped to catch, popes among them. Likewise, Páramo sent some of his books – in a rather clear lobbying effort – to the duke of Feria when he arrived as the newly appointed viceroy of Sicily.[81]

Inventories of inquisitors' libraries furnish additional evidence of how they pursued their intellectual lives. Although it is notoriously difficult to assess what it meant that an individual owned a particular book, the books inquisitors possessed might point to some of their intellectual inclinations, and to the authors with whom they sought to associate themselves. Reference books designed for lawyers and ecclesiastics – resources that they drew upon in their judicial work – were significant components of their collections. Lima's first inquisitor, Serván de Cerezuela, left 105 books, inventoried in Cartagena de Indias in 1583, when he died before reaching that city, en route back to Spain. He had many legal digests and decretals, and Giovanni Andrea's work was noted twice in particular; there was also a volume of Cicero and at least four of Plato's works. He owned a tract on usury, a Roman breviary, a summa of councils, another volume of the Council of Trent's decrees, and one in defense of that council. He had an anti-Lutheran treatise on purgatory and unnamed books of Vives and Alfonso de Castro; among several anti-heretical treatises were two copies of Simancas's *Institutiones* listed at the inventory's start.[82]

S[eño]r Arcob[is]po Mañosca difunto," July 14, 1656, ACM, Libro de Correspondencia 8. On connections between Basque and Mexican cults of the Virgin, see Juan Javier Pescador, *The New World Inside a Basque Village: The Oiartzun Valley and Its Atlantic Emigrants, 1550–1800* (Reno: University of Nevada Press, 2004), 111–25.

[81] For example, Simancas to Busto de Villegas, September 9, 1567, and March 8, 1568, RAH 9/1811, fols. 158r, 161v; Duke of Feria to Inquisitor General, July 8, 1602, AHN, Inq., lib. 883, fols. 17–18, 22–23. Sánchez Rivilla, "Inquisidores," 314.

[82] The anti-heretical works also included a *Directorium Inquisitorum*, Albertini, Castro, Calderinus, and Ugolini. AGI, Contratación, leg. 222, n. 2, r. 1, fols. 24–26. Two *fiscales* of the tribunal, Lic. Juan Alcedo de la Rocha and Lic. Tomás de Solarana, had 116 and 100 books inventoried in Lima in 1583 and 1606, respectively. Teodoro Hampe Martínez,

The councillor of the *Suprema* Dr. Isidoro de San Vicente left behind more than three hundred books, inventoried in Madrid in June 1650. He also had many Latin law books, several works about Aragonese politics and history, devotional works on the feasts of Zaragoza and Saint Teresa, a copy of Thomas à Kempis, and a manual in the genre of the *ars moriendi*. There was a volume of the collected works of Cicero and two translations of Seneca into the vernacular. He, too, had numerous anti-heretical and inquisitorial tracts, among them vernacular instructions of the Spanish Inquisition; a life of Saint Peter Martyr; and titles by Castro, Albertini, and Rojas, among a wide array of other topics.[83] Valtodano's roughly three hundred books were likewise recorded in an inventory made after his death in 1572. The majority of the books were in Latin, and those in the vernacular inclined toward history: historical works of Xenophon and of Eusebius and histories of the battle of Pavia, of Peru, and of the exploits of Álvaro Núñez Cabeza de Vaca in the Indies. There were chronicles, among them those of Alfonso X, Antonio de Nebrija, and Florián de Ocampo, along with two works of Paolo Giovio's in Spanish translation. His library contained traces of his career's itinerary: seemingly a copy of Orantes's *Locorum Catholicorum*, two Palencian missals, and constitutions of the dioceses of Palencia and Badajoz.

Valtodano possessed what might be expected of a jurist and elite ecclesiastic: a wide variety of legal material, civil, canon, and specifically inquisitorial, from early decretals and digests to contemporary theory, some of it by those often termed legal humanists, such as Andrea Alciato. He had three volumes by Simancas: two editions of the *Institutiones* and one of the *De Republica*. Along with instructions of the Spanish Inquisition were an index of prohibited books and works of Castro, Villadiego, and Albertini. Among a range of ecclesiastical tracts, from fathers of the Church to councils to the lives of the saints, were sermons of Augustine and those of John Chrysostom on the Pauline epistles. He had collected works of Tertullian, Ambrose, Jerome, and Chrysostom. There was a work by Philo, and seemingly two by Josephus. His collection was wide

<hr>

"The Diffusion of Books and Ideas in Colonial Peru: A Study of Private Libraries in the Sixteenth and Seventeenth Centuries," *The Hispanic American Historical Review* 73.2 (1993): 211–33; and *Santo Oficio e Historia Colonial: Aproximaciones al Tribunal de la Inquisición de Lima (1570–1820)* (Lima: Ediciones del Congreso del Perú, 1998), 77–82.

[83] There were also a *Directorium Inquisitorum* and a *Repertorium Inquisitorum*; other holdings even included León Pinelo's writings on chocolate. I am grateful to James Amelang for sharing with me his notes on the inventory in AHPM, 4499, fols. 261r-71r. See also Gustav Henningsen, *The Salazar Documents: Inquisitor Alonso de Salazar Frías and others on the Basque witch persecution* (Leiden and Boston: Brill, 2004), 8–9, 450.

ranging: from Ptolemy's geography to the venomous fifteenth-century *Fortalitium fidei* to works of Vitoria and Soto and polemical literature against Luther. Cerezuela, San Vicente, and Valtodano all owned copies of the *Malleus Maleficarum*, and the latter two had at least another volume on *maleficium* each.[84] Valtodano owned books by former colleagues, not just Simancas but also a tract of the mid-1560s by Cristóbal de Rojas – with whom he had collaborated at the Toledan council – of episcopal advice to the clerics of his Cordoban diocese, as well as works of Dr. Navarro – that is, Azpilcueta, the accomplished intellectual who was defending Carranza in Rome when Valtodano died – including his treatise on consecration. Perhaps most suggestive were three works of Erasmus in his library – annotations on the New Testament, the *Paraphrases*, and the *Adages* – and Carranza's own treatise on episcopal residence.[85] As his former judge, Valtodano could investigate Carranza on suspicion of Lutheran heresy and still preserve a copy of his views on pastoral reform; the former inquisitor kept both an index of prohibited books and tracts of Erasmus that had sparked controversy.

To borrow Edward Peters's observation about the writings of Francisco Peña, there were also "libraries" within the books inquisitors wrote.[86] Inquisitorial manuals interwove the citation and weighing of legal precedents and a host of other authoritative texts with commentary that sometimes drew from judicial experience. Through such manuals, jurists, in essence, argued theoretical cases before one another. They cited one another extensively. And even as they often used the same authorities to argue their points, century after century, commentator after commentator, their subtle alterations in argument were significant. When they wrote in this way, they claimed membership in a learned community of legal commentators; moreover, in a certain sense, they designed their own communities within their books. When they chose whom and what to cite, they sometimes revealed which predecessors and contemporaries they sought to associate themselves with and which they did not, whom they hoped to claim as their interlocutors and intellectual kin and whom they disagreed with, dismissed, or reviled. In examining Catholic thinkers of the earlier sixteenth century – Erasmus, Thomas More,

---

[84] San Vicente also had a "Tractatus dibersorum de maleficiis," AHPM, 4499, fol. 269v; Valtodano had a treatise described as "Angelo de maleficis"; García Oro and Portela Silva, "El arzobispo Valtodano," 726. An *Angelus* [*Aretinus*] *De Maleficiis* saw several Lyon and Venice editions from the 1530s to the 1550s.

[85] García Oro and Portela Silva, "El arzobispo Valtodano," 719, 725–31.

[86] Peters, "Editing Inquisitors' Manuals," 101.

Margaret More Roper, Gasparo Contarini – Constance Furey explored how in a climate of uncertainty and anxiety, such literati turned to friendship as a way to create an intellectual community imbued with "spiritual meaning," and to elevate scholarly writing as a religious ideal. Epistolary exchanges, reading, and the writing of associates into one's own work created a non-monastic religious community and established a relationship between the author and those physically distant or who had lived in other ages. Through such activities, these figures tried to counterbalance the artifice and exchange inherent in their political and institutional lives and their experiences as clients there; they explored a tense relationship with written words and eloquence, which could both persuade to virtue and so easily deceive or lead astray.[87]

Simancas, as a prolific writer, provides a fruitful case study of how an inquisitor sought to construct an intellectual community for himself, although Páramo or Adam de la Parra could be examined in the same manner. His autobiographical *Vida* consistently aimed to depict him as part of a larger learned elite, recording the praise he had reportedly received in letters from respected nobles, clerics, and intellectuals of various stripes. In numerous ways, the choice to write a *Vida* also reflected his inquisitorial career; it was in large part a defense of the prosecution of Carranza. And it was not uncommon for inquisitors to compose brief sketches of their life histories as part of their tribunal correspondence, often in response to directives from the *Suprema*. It was the 1561 Inquisition instructions, which Simancas had partly composed, moreover, that spurred the eliciting and recording of life histories from defendants called before Spanish Inquisition tribunals. The first lines of Simancas's work echoed the phrases used to instruct inquisitors about what they should ask of defendants (*discurso de mi vida*).[88]

---

[87] Furey also notes that Erasmus supposed that "texts were valuable not because words signify ideas, but because words can convey presence and enable the reader to encounter the author (be it Christ, Cicero, or a distant contemporary friend) as if in person." *Religious Republic of Letters*, 5, 11, 114, 118–45. Cf. Robert Mayhew's argument that it might be possible to reconstruct a scheme of the republic of letters in similar fashion, suggesting that his charting of the citations of two seventeenth-century (Protestant) British geographers might enable an imagining – in the vein of Benedict Anderson – of early modern intellectual communities, in his "British Geography's Republic of Letters: Mapping an Imagined Community, 1600–1800," *Journal of the History of Ideas* 65.2 (2004): 251–76.

[88] On such issues see Richard Kagan "Autobiografie inquisitoriali (*trazas de la vida*)," *DSI* 1:122–23; James Amelang, "Tracing Lives: The Spanish Inquisition and the Act of Autobiography," in *Controlling Time and Shaping the Self: Developments in Autobiographical Writing Since the Sixteenth Century*, ed. Arianne Baggerman,

In his *De Republica*, Simancas engaged in an even more intricate process of creating a learned circle to which he attached himself by implication. He offered the book to his readers, in turn, as a repertoire of knowledge for their use. Moreover, as he added to it over the years of his career, it became a kind of record of the assimilation of his reading into his written theory.[89] The aphorisms pointed to a theory of social interaction. He selected parts of the chapter in the life of Atticus that described how, even as a younger man, Atticus was esteemed by the older generation, noting Cicero's particular affection for him, holding him as close as his own brother. It recounted the extent and detail of Cicero's epistolary correspondence with his protégé. It elevated the work of public administration and care for family. Simancas offered models to imitate and chose passages that showed the interconnections among his universe of authorities. For instance, he followed a quotation from Cicero's *De Republica* with a passage drawn from Augustine's *City of God* directly citing the former and glossing Cicero's definition of the republic.[90] Simancas wrote himself into that conversation, opening his chapter: "the republic is not just the order of so many magistrates, but the common and universal good of the city and the state, that we call our *res publica*."[91] He asserted as his primary community a class of magistrates, working for the common good and the defense of the faith, precisely what he implied he was doing by compiling his own *De Republica*.

Simancas turned not only to ancient templates. He frequently cited the sixteenth-century Italian bishop and poet Marco Girolamo Vida's tract on

Rudolf Dekker, and Michael Mascuch (Leiden and Boston: Brill, 2011), 33–48. For an example of an autobiographical sketch designed for the Inquisition's internal use, see Henningsen, "Alonso de Salazar Frías: Ese famoso inquisidor desconocido," in *Homenaje a Caro Baroja*, ed. Antonio Carreira, Jesús Antonio Cid, Manuel Gutiérrez Esteve, and Rogelio Rubio (Madrid: Centro de Investigaciones Sociológicas, 1978), 581–86.

[89] Simancas, *Vida*, 154, 182.

[90] His citations moved from Cicero, *Pro Sestio* to Cicero, lib. 3 *De Republica* to Augustine, *De Civitate Dei* 19.21. Under the subheading "De aliis reipublicae significationibus," bk. 2, chap. 2, Simancas, *De Republica* (1569), 23.

[91] "Non ordo tantum magistratuum republica est, sed utilitatem co[m]munem & ciuitatem uniuersam, patriamq; nostram rem publicam appellamus." This opened the same section, ibid., 22. The "ordo" that Simancas chose could have many uses, resonating also with the language of monastic order, a sense that Furey observes Erasmus played upon when he sought an "order" for scholarly spiritual friendship, precisely not within the confines of the regular clergy; see Furey, *Religious Republic of Letters*, 23.

the dignity of the republic.[92] He raised Petrarch, Vives, and Thomas More in numerous places. The last, perceived as a very recent martyr for the faith (and so also proof of King Henry VIII's tyranny), a minister, a jurist, and an intellectual of great repute, was a particularly advantageous alliance for Simancas to pursue in print.[93] Simancas proclaimed an even tighter bond with some Spaniards. He sometimes referred to "our Sepúlveda," and, once, "my [fellow] citizen Sepúlveda." In inquisitorial treatises, Simancas frequently referred to "our Castro" and singled out Covarrubias with added words of praise. The Roman philosopher Seneca – reputedly of Cordoban family – also sometimes garnered such possessives; before a quotation praising the men of Spain, he too became "my [fellow] citizen."[94] This culture of citation allowed sixteenth-century jurists to suggest that they sustained an ancient republican ideal and were its rightful heirs.

Other writers, in turn, wrote Simancas into their books. Juan de Verzosa, the Spanish humanist who resided for a time in Rome, made Simancas the subject of one of his Latin letters of praise, thus placing him among other well-known contemporaries. The 1569 Venetian edition of Simancas's *De Republica* was subsequently prefaced by Verzosa's epistle. Páramo's *De Origine* likewise contained a universe of citations, drawing on Simancas, among other inquisitorial commentators. When he listed Juan de Rojas among the inquisitors who had served in Palermo, Páramo noted Rojas's erudition, demonstrated in the many treatises he had written against heresy. Thus, honor redounded both to Páramo's own district court and to inquisitorial law. His wide range of sources encompassed ancient and modern authorities, and he devoted an entire chapter to a list of famous men who he claimed had praised the Inquisition. Citation of inquisitorial jurisprudence extended, moreover, into other arenas of law, as branches of legal commentary cross-pollinated. The writings of Simancas and Peña, among others, were included in the voluminous reediting of canon law commentaries, sponsored by Gregory XIII and printed in Venice in the early 1580s. The Jesuit Pedro de Ribadeneyra augmented his litany of references prohibiting association between heretics and Catholics with citations from the heresy-fighting

---

[92] It appeared in the mid-1540s; see M. Gerolamo Vida, *Elogio dello Stato (De rei publicae dignitate)*, trans. Antonio Altamura, appendix in Giuseppe Toffanin, *L'Umanesimo al Concilio di Trento* (Bologna: Nicola Zanichelli Editore, 1955), 75–228.

[93] He repeatedly cited both More's epigrams and his *De optimo reipublica statu*, that is, his famous *Utopia*. With Vives, he favored his *De anima, In Satellitio* (or *Satellitium animi*), and *Introductio ad sapientam*; he did not claim him as a fellow Spaniard anywhere I have seen.

[94] Simancas, *De Republica* (1569), 37, 104, 170, 376.

manuals of Castro and Simancas.[95] Azpilcueta drew upon Simancas in his *responsa* and in his *consilia*, whereas later sixteenth-century commentators on criminal prosecution in canon law cited and disputed with Simancas, engaging him on such issues as when the confiscation of goods was an appropriate penalty. Perhaps the most prominent manual of civil law, moreover, turned to Simancas – praising his learning – when it weighed legal opinions on the status of children of heretics and the material consequences of that status.[96]

In sum, like other educated contemporaries, early modern Spanish inquisitors participated in the primary intellectual and cultural activities of their day, patronizing the work of painters, building libraries, and engaging in spiritual conversation and learned correspondence. Furthermore, the Spanish Inquisition's investigative practices provide additional evidence that inquisitors thought such practices and networks mattered. Their combination of esteem for the written word and unease about the soul-endangering deceptions that books could transmit led them to advocate the practice of censorship, even when they had doubts or disagreements with other authorities about what exactly should be censored. Exchanges of books and information, the contents of conversations, and the quality of relationships were also precisely what inquisitors were attuned to track as investigators, as potential evidence of religious affinities and beliefs, affirming orthodoxy or betraying heresy. When, for example, Adam de la Parra worked to compile evidence against Portuguese men of affairs in Madrid, in the margins of the trial record he assiduously noted the cities and correspondents implicated in their letters and statements. Libraries of the accused were also among the goods confiscated and inventoried after an inquisitorial arrest, and the investigation of reading material litters trials.[97]

[95] Páramo, *De Origine et progressu*, 216, 273ff.; Gaetano Colli, *Per Una Bibliografia dei Trattati Giuridici Pubblicati nel XVI Secolo: Indici dei Tractatus Universi Iuris* (Milan: Giuffrè Editore, 1994); Thomas Izbicki, "Problems of Attribution in the *Tractatus Universi Iuris* (Venice 1584)" in *Friars and Jurists*, 413–27; Truman, *Spanish Treatises on Government*, 287, 331.

[96] Diego de Covarrubias y Leyva, *Omnia Opera* (Venice: heirs of Girolamo Scoto, 1597), 2:162; there are multiple citations of Simancas in Francisco Sarmiento, *Interpretationvm Selectarvm Libri Octo* (Antwerp: Ioannes Keerbergius, 1616); Ignacio López de Salcedo, *Practica Criminalis Canonica* (Antwerp: Arnold Coninx, 1593); "Ivris Responsum D. Martini De Azpilcueta. Doctoris Nauarri," May 27, 1566, AHN, Inq., lib. 1231, fols. 754v, 755v; Martín de Azpilcueta, *Opera Omnia* (Venice: Domenico Nicolini, 1601), vol. 2, fols. 85r-96v.

[97] AHN, Inq., leg. 54, exp. 10. On censorship see Virgilio Pinto Crespo, *Inquisición y control ideológico en la España del siglo XVI* (Madrid: Taurus, 1983); Nesvig, *Ideology and Inquisition*.

THINKING WITH INQUISITORS

Although – as the careers of Simancas, Páramo, and Adam de la Parra suggest – too much (or impolitic) writing and publication could hinder professional ascent, inquisitors who were successful in their official work learned how to adapt key elements of their intellectual culture to the particular business of their office. They used a repertoire of common practices, historical models, metaphors, and motifs to seek to communicate the value of their work to other authorities, and to defend the approaches they had taken to address a variety of cases and environments.[98] There were recurring themes in disputes within the Spanish Inquisition, in how inquisitors framed their efforts to carve out administrative space and authority for their courts, and in dissent against the institution of various kinds and degrees. One such refrain was the ongoing polemic between jurists and theologians, often mobilized to critique inquisitorial practices, other times used to elevate their work and so to depict partnership between the disciplines in the combat against heresy.

Another common tactic was the comparison of the Spanish Inquisition to other tribunals. Inquisitors favorably compared their court to other royal and ecclesiastical forums. In rewriting the Carranza case, Simancas repeatedly elevated the practices of Spanish over Italian inquisitions, proposing the former as a model to reform the latter. When the *Suprema* reprimanded the Lima tribunal in 1642, San Vicente adopted a similar tactic, noting that the style of all inquisitions – save that of Portugal – was to not admit singular witnesses as sufficient proof of crime; he sought to shame the inquisitors as having behaved in a manner more Portuguese than Spanish.[99] Páramo took the opposite approach in his *De Origine*, writing anything that could conceivably be classified as an inquisitorial tribunal into a universal history of the Inquisition's origin and progress, drawing them together as unified and eternal rather than differentiating them as a means to indicate malpractice (even as he implied that the Toledo tribunal was a model for others). Similarly, when inquisitors evaluated cases or explained their judicial decisions, they measured the situation at hand against available precedent and referenced the Spanish Inquisition's

---

[98] The title of this subsection is indebted to Stuart Clark, *Thinking with Demons: The Idea of Witchcraft in Early Modern Europe* (Oxford, UK, and New York: Oxford University Press, 1997).

[99] San Vicente, September 15 (July 10 crossed out), 1642, AHN, Inq., leg. 1648, exp. 4. See also the deprecation of the Portuguese Inquisition in Adam de la Parra, *Comercio impedido* (Madrid, 1640), fol. 10v.

governing regulations. San Vicente cast the *Suprema*'s 1642 ruling as customary practice by explicitly invoking the standards of the 1561 instructions. In 1643, in the midst of a high-profile case, the *Suprema*'s councillors read the account of the Carranza trial that they found in Simancas's *Vida* as offering precedent for recusing the Inquisitor General.[100] Aware of a range of persuasive sources to which they might turn, when inquisitors cited such examples, they not only engaged in standard argumentative practice, but also suggested their connection to earlier figures, binding contemporary action to a recognizable history.

They also sought to align their working habits with an ideal of diligence. In this fashion, the traces of Adam de la Parra's career are indicative of larger patterns. He frequently annotated trial records in his own hand, creating a judicial marginalia that tracked the information he would use to render judgments and to spur additional investigations. In January 1640, he reviewed correspondence confiscated from Portuguese merchants, preparing for the audiences that would follow and deciding what evidence could serve other ongoing cases. This review was the judge's preparation for interrogations; he clearly based questions on his observations about the correspondence and even recorded showing a defendant one of the letters in the course of the audience. He had behaved similarly in the case of Mother Luisa. In correspondence about her trial, much of it from 1636, he drew from his experience to opine that the affair had been mishandled from the start. He evaluated and annotated the assembled evidence, and his handwriting is evident in the marginalia in many instances. When still a *fiscal*, he fully glossed a little parchment volume of devotion to the *beata* that had been confiscated; significantly, a note was added to credit him with that work. These habits of mind were evident not only in the Inquisition's judicial business. One copy of Adam de la Parra's 1630 treatise on purity of blood appears to have been extensively annotated in his hand, perhaps with an eye to a revised second edition that seems never to have appeared. Simancas, too, persistently revised his publications over his career, framing and interpreting his judicial experience through continual reading, writing, and assimilation of new sources. Adam de la Parra even offered a rationale to explain why such careful

---

[100] This occurred during the trial of Jerónimo de Villanueva, Protonotary of Aragon, who had been a close associate of the count-duke of Olivares. *Consulta* (Alarcón, Riaño, Contreras, Robles), March 25, 1647, AHN, Inq., lib. 1231, fols. 291r-92r. See also the analysis of the Inquisition's processes of deliberation in James Amelang, "Between Doubt and Discretion: Revising the Rules for Prosecuting Spanish Witches," in *Making, Using and Resisting the Law in European History*, ed. Günther Lottes, Eero Medijainen, and Jón Viðar Sigurðsson (Pisa: Pisa University Press, 2008), 77–92.

attention, diligent annotation, and tracking of evidence mattered; he began a 1636 report on the *beata*'s case with a Latin epigraph: "he who does not condemn error approves it."[101]

In sum, one of the capacities that made Spanish inquisitors successful in their social, political, and religious worlds was their ability to draw upon a repertoire of recognizable practices and exemplary predecessors in order to make their actions and aspirations intelligible to their contemporaries. They turned their learning to the service of inquisitorial office: seeking to create successful narratives of their own actions, to elicit narratives from witnesses and those they suspected as heretics, and to judge what was or was not criminal in the narratives of the accused. They argued that their procedures were consonant with widely held ideals – good judicial brevity, diligence, conscience, prudence, and justice. They and their theorists built a flexible but coherent body of legal reasoning and a corpus of available arguments as part of the work of making their careers, promoting a particular vision of pastoral reform that took heresy inquisitions as an efficacious remedy for worldly ills and spiritual harm, and sustaining their judicial office and its place in the administration of the Catholic Monarchy. When they filtered their appeals through Cicero or Cato the Elder, they asserted that they were the Christian fulfillment of a Roman republican ideal: honorable statesmen who did not turn their backs on their families yet who served the public good through diligent activity, judging, prosecuting, arguing, speaking, conversing, reading, and writing, to virtuous ends. Inquisitors such as the five who have been considered in this book thus drew on a storehouse of common metaphors and practices, of widely used authorities and historical figures, to justify their official decisions and to articulate their individual ambitions, ideals, and opinions. They employed their persuasive capacities to build an official identity for inquisitors that both shared much with other contemporary juridical and ecclesiastical posts and was recognizably specific to their office. They navigated the relationship between the particular and the universal in various ways – reconciling their own ambitions with the requirements of an office, assessing the individual on trial against the available categories of criminality, and adapting standardized procedures to diverse places. As they did so, they built the theory of their office out of the peculiarities of individual careers and their particular experiences and exigencies.

---

[101] "errorem qui non damnat, approbat," Adam de la Parra, July 11, 1636, leg. 3704, caja 1, no. 1, fol. 120r. See also AHN, Inq., leg. 54, exp. 10 and leg. 3708, caja 1, nos. 1–2; BNE, MS 6157, fols. 141rff.

The Afterlife of Spanish Inquisitors

[I]t has been for only a short time, and still with difficulty, that it is permissible to laugh and to be outraged about them.[1]

He who does not condemn error approves it.[2]

When Philipp van Limborch published his *History of the Inquisition* in Amsterdam in 1692, he cited his principal sources in the front matter of the book. Thus, thumbing through the first pages, his readers would immediately encounter a list – a *syllabus* – of authors whom he had drawn upon to produce his history. Part of a program of tolerationist arguments, Limborch's history was composed, in large part, to cast inquisitions from the fourteenth century to the present as an aberration in Christian history, an abuse to be corrected and avoided. Twenty-seven volumes appeared on his *syllabus*, a course of reading that began with medieval and early modern manuals of inquisition, Peña, Simancas, and Páramo among them, and then proceeded to indictments of inquisitorial practice, including the famous exposé of the Portuguese Inquisition in Goa that had recently been printed in Paris. As a participant in that late seventeenth-century "republic of letters," Limborch identified a set of books that promoted a way of thinking opposed to his own. He used a careful reading of his sources to combat an inquisitorial vision of history. His aim was

---

[1] In "Postscriptum de l'Editeur," Nicolau Eymeric, *Le manuel des inquisiteurs, à l'usage des inquisitions d'Espagne & de Portugal . . . On y a joint une courte Histoire de l'établissement de l'inquisition dans le royaume de Portugal, tirée du latin de Louis à Páramo*, ed. abbé André Morellet (Lisbon [Paris?], 1762), 197–98.

[2] "errorem qui non damnat, approbat," Adam de la Parra, July 11, 1636, AHN, Inq. leg. 3704, caja 1, no. 1, fol. 120r.

clear: the first book of his history was titled as a retort to Páramo, as "the history and progress of the Inquisition." His first chapter heading – that the doctrine of Jesus Christ is opposed to all religious persecution – made the thrust of his argument even clearer. Heresy inquisitions were no longer allowed to originate with humankind with God as inquisitor. Each element of Limborch's treatise, proceeding through sections that addressed the Inquisition's officials, criminal charges, and procedures, was designed to disrupt the kind of universality Páramo had claimed for the Holy Office.[3] The same year, Simancas's collected works were reprinted in Ferrara, depicted as still useful and relevant for tribunals of faith. Not long before, Nicolás Antonio had published in Rome his extensive bibliographies of Spanish authors, ancient and modern – which also included Peña, Simancas, and Páramo – placing them in a "library" that might bind together his contemporaries and their literary predecessors.

In assigning signal inquisitorial theorists to a "history" rather than to a "library," Limborch proposed a future in which inquisitors might be a thing of the past.[4] The use of the Inquisition and inquisitors as a stand-in for intolerance became a mainstay of Enlightenment critiques. In the 1760s, a book that included excerpts of Páramo's *De Origine* and of Eymeric's inquisition manual was published, purportedly in Lisbon (likely in Paris), in French translation. The editor's postscript that closed the volume reveals the tenor of its critique:

It may happen that honest people and sensitive souls will blame us for having put before their eyes the frightful pictures we have just presented; they might ask what advantage or pleasure can be found in halting their gaze over such revolting objects. To counter these reproaches, it will suffice for us to remark that it is precisely because these pictures are revolting that it is necessary to show them to them, to

---

[3] Philipp van Limborch, *Historia Inquisitionis* (Amsterdam: Henricus Wetstenius, 1692). See also his *The History of the Inquisition*, trans. Samuel Chandler (London: J. Gray, 1731). His syllabus included the 1560s Latin tract against the Inquisition published under the pseudonym Reginaldus Gonsalvius Montanus, and an exposé of Goa that was presumably the 1687 work of Charles Dellon. Nicolás Antonio, *Bibliotheca Hispana Nova: sive Hispanorum scriptorum qui ab anno MD. ad MDCLXXXIV. floruere notitia*, ed. Mario Ruffini (Turin: Bottega d'Erasmo, 1963). There are similar observations in Francisco Bethencourt, *The Inquisition: A Global History, 1478–1834*, trans. Jean Birrell (Cambridge, UK, and New York: Cambridge University Press, 2009), 5–8; Edward Peters, *Inquisition* (Berkeley and Los Angeles: University of California Press, 1989). On Limborch's intellectual and religious contexts, see John Marshall, *John Locke, Toleration, and Early Enlightenment Culture: Religious Intolerance and Arguments for Religious Toleration in Early Modern and "Early Enlightenment" Europe* (Cambridge, UK: Cambridge University Press, 2006).

[4] Cf. Constantin Fasolt, *The Limits of History* (Chicago: University of Chicago Press, 2004).

inspire horror; after all, these cruelties were applauded for several centuries by nations that we call civilized (*polies*), and who pretended to have morality, [and] in many countries of Europe these horrible maxims are still regarded as sacred; in others it has been for only a short time, and still with difficulty, that it is permissible to laugh and to be outraged about them … it is thus still useful to write about the Inquisition.[5]

Such lines of critique were not wholly novel, as polemic had surrounded the Spanish Inquisition from its conception. Nevertheless, the remarkable frequency with which Enlightenment authors used the words "Inquisition" and "inquisitor" was noteworthy. The Inquisition became an image of crucial importance, one that aided in conceptualizing social and political problems, and one that opposition could rally around.[6] It is that figure of the inquisitor – the inquisitor as thought experiment, summoned to make a variety of arguments – that has eclipsed the diversity of individual inquisitors.

In recent years, historians have dedicated considerable attention to investigating the boundaries of republics of letters, sometimes alleging them and their citizenries as heralding a new kind of public space. They have been approached as fora important for the sharing and production of scientific knowledge and for affording women some space for intellectual activity. The sociability of republics of letters – particularly in the eighteenth century – has been asserted as an oppositional force in society, challenging social and political hierarchies with its privileging of friendship and conversation and its presumptions of equality within the republic's confines. That republic, as it took shape in the final decades of the seventeenth century, represented a minority view in European thought, taking universal religious toleration as an aim of paramount importance. As John Marshall has demonstrated, its principal figures – Pierre Bayle, Philipp van Limborch, and John Locke – defined the Inquisition as the opposite of their republic, with its tolerationist agenda and its ideals of conversational and

---

[5] Eymeric, *Le manuel des inquisiteurs* (1762), 196–98.

[6] On this point – and for the observation that Montesquieu used "the word *Inquisition* and its variants" sixty times in the *Lettres juives* – see Ronald Schechter, *Obstinate Hebrews. Representations of Jews in France, 1715–1815* (Berkeley, Los Angeles, and London: University of California Press, 2003), 7, 40–44. See also the remarks of John Renwick: "To give some idea of Voltaire's vehemence concerning these matters, in the *Essai sur les moeurs* (1741–69), he pillories 'that foul Inquisition' ('cette infâme Inquisition', *Ode sur le fanatisme*, 1736) sixty times; in the *Dictionnaire philosophique* (1764–9), forty-six times; in the *Questions sur l'Encyclopédie* (1770–2), fifty-seven times. Between 1723 and 1776, the term occurs on more than four hundred occasions in over seventy of his works." "Voltaire and the Politics of Toleration," in *The Cambridge Companion to Voltaire*, ed. Nicholas Cronk (Cambridge, UK: Cambridge University Press, 2009), 186.

open intellectual exchange. The inquisitors were, by extension, their antitheses.[7]

Although it is clear why the Spanish Inquisition was an institution antithetical to the values of the republicans of letters, it seems likely that their focus on inquisitors was not purely as a stand-in for the institution they served. In individual Spanish inquisitors, they could see men who, with the benefit of impressive educations, read many of the same books they did and revered many of the same authorities. Their revulsion toward inquisitors, then, was also toward men who had sought to appropriate their cherished books and ideals to serve ends opposite those the republicans of letters hoped to pursue. Each group claimed to aspire to a republican ideal to which its reading of Cicero was pivotal; good citizens had an obligation to serve the republic and were not only persistently engaged in public life but also in reading and writing.[8] Yet inquisitors then argued that those very ideals supported their conviction that Catholic orthodoxy offered the only path to salvation, that major heresies posed an existential danger to any ordered, virtuous political community, and that censorship of heretical books and conducting trials of faith were sound uses of law and among the best means to safeguard the common good and the souls of their fellow citizens.

The polemics against and about inquisitors were deeply intertwined with the images inquisitors had projected of their work and the procedures they had drafted to order it. Critiques such as Limborch's drew an image of the inquisitor, in no small part, from the writings those judges had produced to create and to sustain the authority of their office. Some of the most famous renderings of inquisitors played upon a certain inquisitorial ideal, that in his judicial work, the individual's particular passions and enmities should fall away. This idea – and the injunction that inquisitorial judges should keep their disputes behind closed doors – contributed to the perception of inquisitors as faceless and interchangeable figures, rather than as individuals whose particular ideas and capacities might

---

[7] Marshall, *John Locke, Toleration*, 1–14, 469–535. For other avenues into this scholarship, see Robert Mayhew, "British Geography's Republic of Letters: Mapping an Imagined Community, 1600–1800," *Journal of the History of Ideas* 65.2 (2004): 251–76; Dena Goodman, *The Republic of Letters: A Cultural History of the French Enlightenment* (Ithaca, NY: Cornell University Press, 1994), 1–11; Orest Ranum, "Book review of *The Republic of Letters: A Cultural History of the French Enlightenment*, by Dena Goodman," *AHR* 103.1 (1998): 193–94.

[8] Marshall, *John Locke, Toleration*, 507–13; Constance M. Furey, *Erasmus, Contarini and the Religious Republic of Letters* (Cambridge, UK: Cambridge University Press, 2006), 23, 32, 44.

significantly change the course of trials or the tenor of the court. In a related series of representations, inquisitors became emblems of capricious, cruel, and irrational punishment, acting without regard for law or, alternately, so zealous in its application as to be deaf to human suffering.

So William Hickling Prescott (1796–1859), the first American historian of such matters, described the monstrosity and the power of the Inquisition under Philip II; he wrote of Spain's suffering "under the malign influence of an eye that never slumbered, of an unseen arm ever raised to strike."[9] The Inquisitor General Fernando de Valdés was made to embody this villainy, as he "readily availed himself of the terrible machinery placed under his control. Careful not to alarm the suspected parties, his approaches were slow and stealthy. He was the chief of a tribunal which sat in darkness and which dealt by invisible agents."[10] Prescott's Inquisition was a faceless, secretive, unpredictable, and efficient machine. For him, it became one of the chief forces that had impeded progress in Spain. In this, he followed other liberal critiques, such as that prepared by Juan Antonio Llorente, an Inquisition secretary, whose *Critical History of the Inquisition of Spain* first appeared in Paris in 1817 and 1818. Contained therein was an Inquisition read as diametrically opposed to the views of most learned men, and "arresting the progress of arts, sciences, industry, and commerce."[11] Llorente indicted inquisitors for forgetting Saint Peter's example that there should be perpetual forgiveness of sins.

Perhaps the most famous literary portrait of an inquisitor is that of Fyodor Dostoevsky, who included his "Grand Inquisitor" interlude, set in sixteenth-century Seville, in his novel *The Brothers Karamazov* (1881): "He is an old man, almost ninety, tall and straight, with a gaunt face and sunken eyes from which a glitter still shines like a fiery spark."[12] He possessed two personas: as a cardinal in his robes, he presided over the

---

[9] William H. Prescott, *History of the Reign of Philip II of Spain* (Boston: Phillips, Sampson, 1855), 2:446. On Prescott's crucial role in shaping the study of Spanish history in the United States, see Richard L. Kagan, "Prescott's Paradigm: American Historical Scholarship and the Decline of Spain," *AHR* 101 (April 1996): 423–46.

[10] William H. Prescott, *Philip II*, in *The Works of William H. Prescott* (Philadelphia: J. B. Lippincott Company, 1904), 17:39.

[11] Juan Antonio Llorente, *A Critical History of the Inquisition of Spain* (1826; repr. Williamstown, MA: The John Lilburne Company, 1967), xvi.

[12] The interlude is Pt. II, bk. 5, chap. 5. Fyodor Dostoevsky, *The Brothers Karamazov. A Novel in Four Parts with Epilogue*, trans. Richard Pevear and Larissa Volokhonsky (New York: Farrar, Straus and Giroux, 1990), 249. Dostoevsky owned Prescott's history of Philip II, and he seemingly drew heavily from Prescott's vision of Valdés, see Peters, *Inquisition*, 254–62, 285–87.

public display and burning of heretics; as a monk in his habit, he interrogated prisoners and exuded ascetic rigor. The austere inquisitor exercised complete control over an obedient crowd. Dostoevsky imagined that the Grand Inquisitor witnessed Jesus – who had returned merely for a visit and whom the populace immediately recognized – performing miracles among the people; he quickly took Jesus into custody. After accepting Jesus' identity, the Grand Inquisitor rebuked him for having revealed teachings so contrary to human nature. The inquisitor saw humankind as utterly base; people were only happy without freedom. The populace, he argued, needed a strong Inquisition to control it and to decipher and impose religion upon it. In sum, the Grand Inquisitor turned away from the opportunity to converse with Jesus and toward the authority he was accustomed to exercise.

Thus, the Spanish inquisitor, as a symbol, has supplied fertile ground for later thinkers.[13] The image of the inquisitor has also served as an effective political rallying cry. This was already true for Dutch rebels in the 1560s and for the Neapolitans who resisted the establishment of a tribunal of the Spanish Inquisition in their city in the sixteenth century. Guillén Lombardo attempted to mobilize public opinion on similar grounds when he broke out of the Inquisition's prison in Mexico City at Christmas 1650 and posted his placards accusing the inquisitors of cruel miscarriages of justice. Two of the inquisitors implicated, the cousins Mañozca, would even be revived in the polemical histories that circulated around the time of the Mexican Revolution in the early twentieth century. Their legend in particular (and the Inquisition in general) was reworked as a symbol of the abuses of the *ancien regime*, proof of what deserved to be overthrown.[14] Inquisitorial archives and buildings, too, held their symbolic valence. They were a focus of political action in the eighteenth and

---

[13] There are a multitude of examples that might still be raised here. In the realm of fiction, António Lobo Antunes's novel, *The Inquisitors' Manual* (1996), or Leonardo Sciascia's short story or essay *Death of the Inquisitor* (1964). Commenting on contemporary political life is the very interesting meditation of Carlo Ginzburg, *The Judge and the Historian: Marginal Notes on a Late-Twentieth-Century Miscarriage of Justice*, trans. Antony Shugaar (London and New York: Verso, 1999). Or, to take a brief example from a recent article: "But [Paul] Berman reads volumes into [Tariq] Ramadan's silences and pursues him with inquisitorial zeal." Pankaj Mishra, "Islamismism: How Should Western Intellectuals Respond to Muslim Scholars?" *The New Yorker*, June 7, 2010, 72.

[14] For a detailed example of this, see Alberto Lombardo, *Injusticias Históricas. Olvido del Primero que concibió é Intentó la Independencia de México* (Mexico City: Tipografía Económica, 1901), 14–23. See also Fabio Troncarelli, *El mito del 'Zorro' y la Inquisición en México. La aventura de Guillén Lombardo (1615–1659)*, trans. Pau Oliva (Lleida: Editorial Milenio, 2003), 9. Juan de Mañozca was also turned into a principal character in

nineteenth centuries; for example, when Palermo's tribunal was disbanded, its records were deliberately burned.[15]

The records, practices, and writings of inquisitors have left other legacies. Over the past several decades, some scholars have turned their attention to analyzing Spain's imperial administration as a bureaucracy. In this vein, John Leddy Phelan examined the use of visitations – and their interest in financial corruption, judicial abuses, and adherence to procedures – and termed this apparatus essentially "the Spanish bureaucratic system of checks and balances."[16] Much of the outpouring of revisionist work and scouring of the Inquisition's archives over the past forty years has explained a process of system building, of constructing an institution in practice and in theory. Henry Kamen summed up the judgment of inquisitors that resulted from this work, characterizing them as "an elite bureaucracy."[17] Thus, one important strand of analysis has approached inquisitors as quintessential bureaucrats in the making. Irene Silverblatt's study, centered on seventeenth-century Peru, has taken this approach further. Presenting inquisitors as part of a "national mission," she argues that their practices were a fundamental part of initiating such modern practices as the institutionalization of race thinking. In this, she adds to a line of analyses that have fitted inquisitors into trajectories of persecuting behavior and of racist thought, policy, and action. She reads the inquisitors' interest in rules and procedures to show how "imperial ends were realized, first and foremost, through a modern bureaucracy"; thus, inquisitors have also come to be read as agents pivotal in creating that which is dehumanizing and violent in the bureaucracies of modern states.[18]

The extensive work of elaborating procedure; of codifying crimes and practices; and of generating records, archives, and commentaries produced a host of results with which scholars are just beginning to grapple. The practices and writings of early modern inquisitors are increasingly being read as intertwined with the investigative and descriptive efforts of their

a Colombian novel; Germán Espinosa, *Los Cortejos del Diablo: balada de tiempos de brujas* (Montevideo: Editorial Alfa, 1970).

[15] The tribunal was suppressed in 1782, and at the conclusion of the process the following year, in 1783, the inquisitorial symbols were effaced from the buildings and the records nearly completely destroyed; Manuel Rivero Rodríguez, "La Inquisición Española en Sicilia," *HIEA* 3:1209.

[16] John Leddy Phelan, *The Kingdom of Quito in the Seventeenth Century; Bureaucratic Politics in the Spanish Empire* (Madison: University of Wisconsin Press, 1967), 286.

[17] Henry Kamen, *The Spanish Inquisition: A Historical Revision* (New Haven, CT, and London: Yale University Press, 1997), 144.

[18] Irene Silverblatt, *Modern Inquisitions: Peru and the Colonial Origins of the Civilized World* (Durham, NC, and London: Duke University Press, 2004), 57–58, 227.

contemporaries, as connected, for example, to the development of anthro-pological modes of thought.[19] In significant and complicated ways, the debates in which inquisitors engaged are mirrored in the questions that continue to be asked about them. They served – and were shaped by – an institution whose existence was predicated on the conviction that heresy murdered souls, that heretics were existential threats to their society, and that salvation was possible only through the Church. They treated heret-ical belief as a criminal act. They persecuted many. Yet they must still be seen as more than bi-dimensional figures, capable of reasoned deliberation, of doubt, of change over time, and of inconsistency.

As scholars such as Lu Ann Homza have persuasively shown, early modern Spanish authorities elude the categories into which they have often been too neatly placed. The men who were inquisitors, like their colleagues in royal, ecclesiastical, and academic posts, could also adopt arrays of argumentative stances and pursue working methods that were seemingly contradictory.[20] They argued about how to define purity of faith and purity of blood and whether the pursuit of that purity was ultimately harmful or beneficial to their political order. They argued about whether toleration endangered souls or was sensible policy. They argued about the balance between the individual and the communal in matters of salvation and in the prevention of what they deemed criminal. They argued about how and who best to define and promote truth, about which matters were appropriately resolved in legal courts and which in the confessional, about what was best publicized and what was best silenced. They argued about how to investigate and discern truth and how best to serve their ideals of justice. They argued, moreover, about the reliability of human language, about the mutability of words and the danger that they could so easily be used to deceive. And above all, they argued about how to interpret human behavior, about what actions, relationships, speech, and writing said and did not say about belief and about intention. Inquisitorial office offered income, prestige, power, and the possibility of substantial social mobility; it allowed judges the sense that they were serving a religious mission of

---

[19] See here Adriano Prosperi, *L'Inquisizione Romana: Letture e Richerche* (Rome: Edizioni di Storia e Letteratura, 2003); Carlo Ginzburg, "The Inquisitor as Anthropologist," in *Clues, Myths, and the Historical Method*, trans. John and Anne C. Tedeschi (Baltimore, MD: The Johns Hopkins University Press, 1989), 156–64.

[20] See the careful investigation of the potential for intellectual flexibility and argumentative complexity evident in the writings and careers of other sixteenth-century Spanish clerics in Lu Ann Homza, *Religious Authority in the Spanish Renaissance* (Baltimore, MD, and London: The Johns Hopkins University Press, 2000).

paramount importance and were important protagonists in some of the greatest struggles of their day. In a world they perceived as inherently sinful, inquisitors could believe that they were serving the common good by finding the dangerous deceivers they assumed were lurking in any society, by rendering justice according to the law, and by offering pastoral care. To grapple wholeheartedly with the Spanish Inquisition as a moral, social, and historical problem thus requires complicating the image of the Spanish inquisitor, looking beyond caricatural versions of those judges and so grappling with inquisitors in their full human diversity and complexity.

To respond, finally, to Julio Caro Baroja's half-century-old critique, what does an Inquisition *with* inquisitors look like?[21] Above all, it is one in which inquisitorial actions were not inevitable. As the best scholarship has demonstrated, the course of trials and the decisions to open or close them were profoundly shaped by political, social, legal, economic, and religious dynamics occurring on multiple overlapping levels. Inquisitors elaborated and respected procedure and they were well aware of the many constraints on their possible actions, yet they also perceived their judicial work as possessing a certain autonomy, requiring reasoning in the operation of discernment, and implicating both their consciences and those of the accused. They were simultaneously deeply invested in working within the law, well aware of its mutability and inability to fit all situations, and savvy about how to use it to their own advantage. They were concerned to promote a powerful image of their office, but to attend to the inquisitors is to see the Inquisition much less like a machine, or certainly as a highly imperfect one, in which procedures were contingent on the people applying them and the authority they could command, and in which the gaps between inquisitors' theories and what their working environments really looked like could be vast. As recently published evidence from a 1597 visitation of the Córdoba Inquisition tribunal amply demonstrates, inquisitors were part and parcel of their social worlds. Accusations against the senior inquisitor sketched, among other things, an unchaste judge who had moved a woman who seemed like a common-law wife – involved in managing his household and receiving inquisitorial officials – with him from post to post for twenty years. The charges also suggested that the inquisitor's relationships affected his conduct of inquisitorial business. At the same time, the very existence of the affidavit indicated the established

---

[21] Cf. Julio Caro Baroja, *El Señor Inquisidor y otras vidas por oficio* (Madrid: Alianza Editorial, 1968), 15.

place of the Inquisition in early modern Spanish society, that there were expectations about how an inquisitor should act and the dignity of the office and that visitations were perceived as a potentially effective way to compel local authorities to reform their behavior.[22] As early modern elites well knew, inquisitions operated well within the realm of human politics, even as they dealt with matters of religious belief and its regulation and correction; their projections of authority were part of those politics. Like administrators of other early modern institutions, inquisitors were deeply tied to networks of patronage and clientage, family, and learned friendship, as well as to their official duties; their institutional lives were profoundly shaped by such personal ties.

And inquisitors were not simply interchangeable. Considerable variation can be found not only in their career trajectories, but also in their abilities; their particular devotions; their visions of reform; and their approaches to their judicial, pastoral, and administrative work. The stances of individuals were profoundly important to policy decisions within the Inquisition, even though their differences of opinion were precisely not what inquisitors were interested in preserving in the institution's archives. An Inquisition with inquisitors is one in which conditions and events in localities throughout the Habsburg world influenced policy and action in other places, not only through institutional channels and the decrees of royal councils but also as officials were influenced by their prior experiences; by other human ties; and by what they read, saw, and heard. It is one in which neither the judges nor the victims existed in a vacuum, but rather in which both lived in complex social worlds that permeated the courtroom.

---

[22] *Góngora y el Señor Inquisidor. Un autógrafo inédito de Don Luis en edición facsímil,* presented and transcribed by Amelia de Paz (Madrid: Ministerio de Educación, Cultura y Deporte-Sociedad Estatal de Acción Cultural, 2012).

Bibliography

Primary Sources

ARCHIVAL COLLECTIONS AND MANUSCRIPTS

Córdoba, *Archivo de la Catedral*
  Actas Capitulares 20, 21
London, *British Library*
  Add. 16176, 19319, 28336, 28343, 28371, 28403, 28410, 28412
  Egerton 339, 343, 345, 1508
Madrid, *Archivo y Biblioteca de Francisco Zabálburu*
  Altamira, 9, doc. 23; 39, GD 15, doc. 80; 149, doc. 12; 219, doc. 68; 453,
    doc. 12
Madrid, *Archivo Histórico Nacional*
  Diversos-Colecciones, 27, no. 11
  Órdenes Militares, Caballeros de Santiago, exp. 2854; Religiosos Alcántara,
    exp. 315; Religiosas Santiago, exp. 577 and 578
  Inquisición, libros 100, 248, 325, 500, 575, 878–84, 1008–9, 1039–42,
    1054–55, 1231–32, 1252; legajos 54, exp. 10; 69, exp. 31; 100, 496, exp.
    3; 512, exp. 17; 1213, exp. 10; 1258, exp. 1; 1278, exp. 32; 1306, exp. 14;
    1636, exp. 3; 1648, exp. 4; 2120, exp. 5; 2124, exp. 4; 2136, exp. 2; 2809–
    10, 2960, 3067, exp. 2, nos. 1–91; 3109–12, 3189, nos. 74, 76; 3704, 3708,
    4436, no. 2; 4797, exp. 1
Madrid, *Archivo Histórico de Protocolos*
  protoc. 3.823 de Diego de Escobar de 2 de marzo de 1624
Madrid, *Biblioteca Nacional de España*
  Iconografía Hispana 8933, ER/574 (44)
  MSS 1332, 1555, 2592, 2612, 2666–68, 2792, 2827, 6035, 6157, 8851,
    9393, 12054
Madrid, *Instituto Valencia Don Juan*
  Envíos 80, caja 106, doc. 745; 89, caja 1, docs. 268–303, 329; 111, docs. 186,
    251, 317

Madrid, *Real Academia de la Historia*
9/302; 9/826; 9/1809–13 (Carranza Trial XVII-XXI); 9/3572; 9/3663
Madrid, *Real Biblioteca*
MSS II/265, II/1989, II/1992, II/2334
Mexico City, *Archivo del Cabildo Catedral Metropolitano de México*
Libros de Actas 10, 11
Libro de Correspondencia 8
Libro de Fábrica Material 16
Mexico City, *Archivo General de la Nación*
Inquisición, vols. 204, exp. 6; 223, exp. 28; 318, exp. 8G; 417, exp. 9; 424;
430, exp. 4; 503, exp. 65; 1497
Templos y Conventos, vol. 158B, exp. 95
Mexico City, *Archivo Histórico del Arzobispado de México*
Cabildo, Museo Catedral, caja 184
Fondo Episcopal, caja 5
Palencia, *Archivo de la Catedral*
Armario I, leg. 1, doc. 15; IV, leg. 1, estatutos, no. 20; leg. 5; leg. 8, nos. 7–8;
XIV, caja 3A, no. 1
Salamanca, *Biblioteca General Universitaria de Salamanca*
MSS 1925, 2065
Santiago de Compostela, *Archivo de la Catedral*
Espolios, IG 174
Actas Capitulares, lib. 16 (IG 516); lib. 17 (IG 517)
Santiago de Compostela, *Archivo Histórico Diocesano*
no. 298 antiguo, exp. 6, Cabildo de Santiago; visita pastoral, 1.52.2 (antigua
1262)
Santiago de Compostela, *Biblioteca Universitaria*
RSE Espino, Foll. 3–21, Dn Cristobal Fernández Valtodano
Simancas, *Archivo General de Simancas*
Estado, legajos 137, 148, 153, 158, 161, 918, 919, 1061, 1155, 1160–62
Patronato Real 8, doc. 61; 22, docs. 21, 35; 23, doc. 127; 57, docs. 23, 27, 28,
89; 62, docs. 94, 95, 127–28, 147
Seville, *Archivo General de Indias*
Contratación, 5243, no. 2, r. 54, 60, 61; 5247, no. 2, r. 79; 5320, nos. 32–36;
5379, no. 17; 5424, no. 1, r. 21; 5427, no. 1, r. 42; 5788, lib. 1; 5789, lib. 1;
5793, lib. 1
Indiferente, 455, lib. A25; 754
Lima, 5; 47, nos. 41, 44
México, 4, nos. 201, 202, 214
Pasajeros, lib. 7, exp. 3344, 3348; lib. 9, exp. 1944–47, 1971; lib. 10, exp.
2794, 2796
Patronato, 4, no. 29; 5, nos. 17, 25
Quito 209, lib. 2
Santa Fe 38, r. 4, no. 120; r. 5, no. 140; 63, no. 34; 243
Seville, *Biblioteca Capitular*
MS 84-6-29 (Microfiche 58-5-23)
Zamora, *Archivo Catedralicio*

orden no. 1427, leg. 19, no. 1

leg. 152(1), exp. 4

Zamora, *Archivo de la Diputación Provincial*

orden 1776, leg. 86, exp. 1

Primary Sources

PRINTED WORKS

Adam de la Parra, Juan. *Apologetico contra el Tirano y Rebelde Verganza, y Conivrados Arzobispo de Lisboa, y sus Parciales, en Respuesta a los Doze Fundamentos del Padre Mascareñas.* Zaragoza: Diego Dormer, 1642.

Comercio impedido. Madrid, 1640.

Conspiración Herético-Cristianísima. Translated by Angeles Roda Aguirre. Madrid: CSIC, 1943.

Conspiratio Haeretico-Christianissima in Religionem Imperivm, Hispanvm Austriacos & fiduciales eorum Iure sacro, Oeconomico Politico Canonico Ciuili, & à temporum euentibus damnata. Arma Austriaca Germano-Hispanica Pro Religione & Imperio Hispano Austriacis, & eorum fiducialibus. Iure sacro, Oeconomico Politico Canonico Ciuili, & à temporum euentibus defensa. Murcia: Luis Berós, 1634.

Pro Cautione Christiana in supremis Senatibus sanctae Inquisitionis, & Ordinum, Ecclesia Toletana, & coetibus scholarium obseruata Adversus Christianorvm Proselytos, & sabbatizantes, nomine, & specie Christianorum. Declamat Ad Serenissmvm Dominvm Ferdinandum Austriacum, uniuersalis Ecclesia Purpuratum, Toletanae Primatem, & Religionis Supremum Censorem. Madrid, 1630.

Súplica de la muy noble y muy leal ciudad de Tortosa, En ocasion de las alteraciones del Principado de Cataluña, y Condados de Rosellon, Zerdaña, & c. Para Que V. Magestad se sirua, como tan Catolico y Magno, perdonar a sus hermanos, admitiendolos con benignidad a su gracia, En Honor De su fidelidad, y de Prouincias tan leales, y de tanta nobleza. Tortosa: Pedro Martorell, 1640.

Antiche Consuetudini delle Città di Sicilia. Edited by Vito la Mantia. Palermo: Alberto Reber, 1900.

Antonio, Nicolás. *Bibliotheca Hispana Nova: sive Hispanorum scriptorum qui ab anno MD. ad MDCLXXXIV. floruere notitia.* Edited by Mario Ruffini. 2 vols. Turin: Bottega d'Erasmo, 1963.

Araujo, Leonardo de. *Relacion de las cosas que svcedieron en la civdad de Quito, Reyno del Pirù, con las Ordenes de Santo Domingo, y san Agustin, por mano del Licenciado Iuan de Mañosca, Visitador de la Real Audiencia de la dicha ciudad, y Oydores de dicha Real Audiencia, y Comissario del santo Oficio della.* [1627].

Arias Montano, Benito. *De Optimo Imperio, Sive In Lib. Iosvae Commentarium.* Antwerp: Christophe Plantin, 1583.

De Varia Repvblica, sive Commentaria in Librvm Ivdicvm. Antwerp: Plantin, 1592.

Los *Rhetoricorum* Libri Qvattvor *de Benito Arias Montano*. Edited and translated by María Violeta Pérez Custodio. Badajoz and Cádiz: Diputación Provincial de Badajoz, Universidad de Cádiz, 1995.

Avtos fechos por el Ilmo. y Revmo. Señor Don Iuan de Mañozca, del Consejo de su Magestad, y de la S. y General Inquisicion, Visitador della en este Tribunal de Mexico, y Arçobispo de dicha Ciudad. En Cvmplimiento de la Cedula de Sv Magestad y Patente del Reuerendissimo P. M. General de la Orden de Santo Domingo: Tocante à los examenes, y aprobacion de los Ministros de Doctrina de la dicha Orden, en este Arçobispado de Mexico. [Mexico, 1649].

Azpilcueta, Martín de. *Enchiridion sive Manvale Confessariorvm, et Paenitentivm.* Venice: heirs of Francesco Ziletti, 1589.

Opera Omnia. 3 vols. Venice: Domenico Nicolini, 1601.

Bocanegra, Matias de, S. J. *Auto general de la fee: celebrado por los señores . . . Don Iuan de Mañozca, Arçobispo de Mexico . . . Francisco de Estrada, y Escobedo, Doct. D. Iuan Saenz de Mañozca, Licenciado D. Bernabè de la Higuera, y Amarilla, y el señor fiscal Doct. D. Antonio de Gabiola, en la . . . ciudad de Mexico . . . Dominica in albis 11 de abril de 1649.* Mexico City: Antonio Calderón, Impresor del Santo Oficio. [1649].

Jews and the Inquisition of Mexico: The Great Auto de Fe of 1649. Edited and translated by Seymour B. Liebman. Lawrence, KS: Coronado Press, 1974.

Sermón a la Solemne colocación de la Santa Cruz de piedra, que el Ilustrissimo Señor don Iuan de Mañozca Arçobispo de Mexico, trasladó, y dedicò en el atrio de su Iglesia Cathedral, dia de la Exaltacion de la misma Cruz, Año de 1648. [Mexico, 1648].

Botero, Giovanni. *The Reason of State.* Translated by P. J. and D. P. Waley. New Haven, CT: Yale University Press, 1956.

Canons and Decrees of the Council of Trent. Translated by Rev. H. J. Schroeder, O. P. Rockford, IL: Tan Books and Publishers, Inc., 1978.

Castro, Alfonso de, O. F. M. *De iusta haereticorum punitione libri tres, opus nunc recens, & nunquam antea impressum.* Salamanca: Juan de Junta, 1547.

Aduersus omnes haereses Libri XIII. In quibus recensentur & reuincuntur omnes haereses, quarum memoria extat, quae ab Apostolorum tempore ad hoc usque seculum in Ecclesia ortae sunt. Cologne: Melchior von Neuss, 1539.

Carranza de Miranda, Bartolomé. *Controversia sobre la necesaria residencia personal de los obispos y de los otros pastores inferiores.* Edited by José Ignacio Tellechea Idígoras. Madrid: Fundación Universitaria Española, Universidad Pontificia de Salamanca, 1993.

Castrillo Benito, Nicolás, ed. *El "Reginaldo Montano": Primer Libro Polémico contra la Inquisición Española.* Madrid: CSIC, Centro de Estudios Inquisitoriales, 1991.

Catalogvs librorvm reprobatorvm ex ivdicio Academiæ Lovaniensiscvm edicto Caesareae Maiestatis evvlgatvs . . . Toledo: Juan de Ayala, 1551. Reprint, New York: De Vinne Press, 1896.

Catena, Girolamo. *Vita del Gloriosissimo Papa Pio Quinto.* Rome: Vincenzo Accolti, 1586.

Cervantes Saavedra, Miguel de. *Don Quixote.* Translated by Edith Grossman. New York: Ecco, 2003.

Don Quijote de la Mancha. Edición del Instituto Cervantes 1605–2005. Directed by Francisco Rico. 2 vols. Barcelona: Galaxia Gutenberg, 2004.

Concilium Prouinciale Compostellanum à Gaspare à Çuñiga, & Auellaneda Archiepiscopo, & totius Prouinciae Compostellanae Metropolitano Salimanticae congregatum, & celebratum sub Pio quarto, & Pio quinto pontificibus maximis, & regnante Catholico, & Inuictissimo Rege nostro Philippo secundo. Salamanca: Andrea Portonari, 1566.

Constituciones synodales del Obispado de Palencia, hechas y ordenadas por ... Don Christoval Fernandez de Valtodano, Obispo de dicho obispado ... en el año de mil y quinientos y sesenta y seys. Palencia: Sebastián Martínez, 1567.

Covarrubias y Leyva, Diego de. *Opera Omnia.* Venice: heirs of Girolamo Scoto, 1597.

Covarrubias Orozco, Sebastián de. *Tesoro de la lengua castellana o española.* Edited by Felipe C. R. Maldonado. Madrid: Editorial Castalia, 1995.

A Defence and True Declaration of the Things Lately Done in the Low Country. London: John Day, 1571. In *The Dutch Revolt*, edited and translated by Martin van Gelderen, 1–77. Cambridge, UK: Cambridge University Press, 1993.

Elliott, J. H., and José F. de la Peña, eds. *Memoriales y Cartas del Conde Duque de Olivares.* 2 vols. Madrid: Ediciones Alfaguara, 1978–80.

Enzinas, Francisco de. *Epistolario.* Edited by Ignacio J. García Pinilla. Geneva: Librairie Droz, 1995.

Les Memorables de Francisco de Enzinas. Edited and translated by Jean de Savignac. Brussels: Éditions de la Librairie Encyclopédique, 1963.

Exorcismi sive adivrationes ad usum Palentinae Diocesis quondam iussu a D. D. Christophoro Baltodano Episcopi eiusdem ciuitatis excusii nunc vero denuo recognito & iterum editi. [Valladolid?, 1628?].

Eymeric, Nicolau. *Directorivm Inquisitorvm F. Nicolai Eymerici Ordinis Praedicatorum. Cvm Commentariis Francisci Pegñae Sacrae Theologiae ac Iuris Vtriusque Doctoris.* Venice: Marc'Antonio Zaltieri, 1595.

Le manuel des inquisiteurs, à l'usage des inquisitions d'Espagne & de Portugal.... On y a joint une courte Histoire de l'établissement de l'inquisition dans le royaume de Portugal, tirée du latin de Louis à Paramo. Edited by abbé André Morellet. Lisbon [Paris?], 1762.

Eymeric, Nicolau, and Francisco Peña. *El manual de los inquisidores.* Edited and translated by Luis Sala-Molins. Barcelona: Muchnik, 1996.

Fuenmayor, Antonio de. *Vida y Hechos de Pío Quinto Pontífice Romano. con algunos notables sucessos dela Christiandad del tiempo de su Pontificado.* Third Edition. Madrid: widow of Juan Sánchez, 1639.

Gabutius, Joannes Antonius. *De Vita et Rebus Gestis Pii V. Pont. Max. Libri Sex.* Rome: Aloisius Zannetti, 1605.

García de Trasmiera, Diego. *Epitome de la Santa Vida, y Relacion de la Gloriosa Muerte del Venerable Pedro de Arbues, Inquisidor Apostolico de Aragon.* Madrid: Diego Díaz de la Carrera, 1664.

Góngora y el Señor Inquisidor. Un autógrafo inédito de Don Luis en edición facsímil. Presented and transcribed by Amelia de Paz. Madrid: Ministerio de Educación, Cultura y Deporte- Sociedad Estatal de Acción Cultural, 2012.

González Dávila, Gil. *Teatro Eclesiástico de España*. 4 vols. Madrid: Francisco Martínez, 1645.

Teatro Eclesiástico de la Primitiva Iglesia de Indias Occidentales. 2 vols. Madrid: Diego Díaz de la Carrera, 1649–55.

Guevara, Alonso de. *Menosprecio de Corte y Alabanza de Aldea*. Edited by Asunción Rallo Gruss. Madrid: Cátedra, 1984.

Guillixtegui, Gabriel de. *Apologia en Defensa de la Orden de Penitencia de San Francisco*. Bilbao: Pedro de Huydobro, 1643.

Institoris, Heinrich, and Jakob Sprenger. *Malleus Maleficarum, Maleficas et Earum haeresim frameâ conterens, ex variis auctoribus compilatus, & in quatuor Tomos iustè distributus*. Lyon: Claude Bourgeat, 1669.

Instrucciones del Santo Oficio de la Inquisición, sumariamente, antiguas, y nueuas. Puestas por Abecedario por Gaspar Isidro de Arguello, Oficial del Consejo. Madrid: Imprenta Real, 1630.

Jiménez Monteserín, M. *Introducción a la Inquisición española. Documentos básicos para el estudio del Santo Oficio*. Madrid: Editora Nacional, 1980.

Limborch, Philipp van. *Historia Inquisitionis*. Amsterdam: Henricus Wetstenius, 1692.

Llorente, Juan Antonio. *A Critical History of the Inquisition of Spain*. 1826. Reprinted with an introduction by Gabriel H. Lovett. Williamstown, MA: The John Lilburne Company, 1967.

López de Salcedo, Ignacio. *Practica Criminalis Canonica*. Antwerp: Arnold Coninx, 1593.

Memorias de Sevilla (1600–1678). Edited by Francisco Morales Padrón. Córdoba: Publicaciones de Monte de Piedad y Caja de Ahorros de Córdoba, 1981.

Memorias de los Virreyes del Perú: Marqués de Mancera y Conde de Salvatierra. Edited by José Toribio Polo. Lima: Imprenta del Estado, 1899.

Methodus consecrationis sacri Chrismatis ex mandato Illustrissimi ac Reuerendissimi Domini sui Christophori a Valtodano Episcopi Pallan. Comitisq[ue] Perniae & c. Valladolid: Sebastián Martínez, 1563.

Missale Pallantinum, Iussu Illmi. D.D. Christophori fernandez a Valtodano. Epi. Pallan., Perniae Comitis. Palencia: Sebastián Martínez, 1567.

Missale Pallantinvm. Iussu Illustrissimi D. D. Christophori Fernandez a Valtodano . . . Secundo excussum. Palencia: Sebastián Martínez, 1568.

Montaigne, Michel de. *The Complete Essays of Montaigne*. Translated by Donald M. Frame. Stanford, CA: Stanford University Press, 1965.

Montanus, Reginaldus Gonsalvius. *A Discovery and playne Declaration of sundry subtill practises of the Holy Inquisition of Spayne*. London: John Day, 1568.

Montesinos, Fernando de. *Auto de la Fe Celebrado en Lima a 23 de Enero De 1639*. Lima: Pedro de Cabrera, 1639.

Orantes, Francisco de, O. F. M. *Locorum Catholicorum Tum Sacrae Scripturae, tum etiam antiquorum patrum, Pro Orthodoxa, et Vetere Fide Retinenda, Libri Septem*. Venice: Giordano Ziletti, 1564.

Oratio Francisci Orantii Hispani, Habita in sacra oecumenica Synodo Tridentina, die celeberrimo Sanctorum omnium, anno 1562. Venice: Giordano Ziletti, 1563.

Páramo, Luis de. *Ad Sanctissimvm D.N.D Pavlvm V. Pontficem Max. Confutationes decretorum, quae à Venetorum Duce aduersus immunitatem Ecclesiasticam temerè atq[ue] impiè edita sunt.* Palermo: Gio. Antonio de Franciscis, 1606.

    De Origine et progressu officii Sanctae Inquisitionis eiusque dignitate et utilitate; de Romani Pontificis potestate et delegata Inquisitorum: edicto Fidei, et ordine judicario sancti officii, quaestiones decem. Libri tres. Madrid: Typographia Regia, Juan Flandro, 1598.

    Responsum D. Ludovicii a Paramo, adversus obiectiones secundo loco, excitatas contra iurisdictionem sancti Officii Regni Siciliae. Madrid: Pedro Madrigal, 1599.

    Responsvm D. Ludouici de Paramo, Inquisitoris Regni Siciliae, pro defensione jurisdictionis Sancti Officii, aduersus oppositiones & capitula iudicum secularium eiusdem Regni. Madrid: Luis Sánchez, 1594.

Parrino, Domenico Antonio. *Teatro Eroico, e Politico De'Governi de'Vicere del Regno di Napoli dal tempo del Re Ferdinando el Cattolico fino al Presente.* Naples: Nuova Stampa del Parrino, e del Mutti, 1692.

Pellicer de Tovar, José. *Avisos: 17 de Mayo de 1639–29 de Noviembre de 1644.* Edited by Jean-Claude Chevalier and Lucien Clare. 2 vols. Paris: Éditions Hispaniques, 2003.

Pérez de Ayala, Martín. "Discurso de la Vida del Ilustrísimo y Reverendísimo Señor don Martín de Ayala." In *Autobiografías y Memoriales,* edited by Manuel Serrano y Sanz, 211–38. Madrid: Bailly, Bailliére, S. B., 1905.

Pinto Delgado, João. *Poema de la Reina Ester. Lamentaciones del profeta Jeremiás. Historia de Rut y varias poesías.* Edited by I. S. Révah. Rouen: David du Petit Val, 1627. Reprint, Lisbon: Institut Français au Portugal, 1954.

    The Poem of Queen Esther. Translated by David R. Slavitt. New York and Oxford, UK: Oxford University Press, 1999.

Por la Iurisdicion de la Inquisicion de la Ciudad y Reyno de Granada, en el Caso de Competencia, Sobre el Desacato que se imputa auer cometido Don Gomez de Montalvo Familiar del Santo Oficio. Granada: Imprenta Real, Baltasar de Bolívar, Francisco Sánchez, 1642.

Procesos de Luis de Carvajal (el Mozo). Edited by Luis González Obregón. Mexico City: Talleres Gráficos de la Nación, 1935.

Relación de la Pompa Festiva, y Solemne colocación de una santa, y hermosa cruz de piedra, que el Ilustrissimo Señor D. Juan de Mañozca, Arzobispo de Mexico, del Consejo de su Magestad, y del General de la Inquisicion, Visitador de su Tribunal en esta Nueva España, & c. Traslado al Cementerio de esta Iglesia Cathedral de Mexico el Año de 1648. Y celebre Novenario, Jubileo de quarenta horas, y procession de sangre, que se tuvo por la peste, y necessidades publicas de la Monarquia, y de este Reyno. Mexico City: Hipolyto de Ribera, 1648. Reprint, Mexico City: widow of Joseph Bernardo de Hogal, 1748.

Relacion del Solemne Jubileo de las Missiones, que los Padres de la Compañia de Iesvs Celebraron, y Administraron este Año de 1649. en la Ciudad de Mexico. Por orden, è instancia del Ilustrissimo, y Reuerendissimo señor D. Iuan de Mañozca, Arçobispo desta Metropoli del Consejo de su Magestad, y del de la

Santa General Inquisicion, su Visitador en esta Nueua España, & c. Mexico City: widow of Bernardo Calderón, 1650.

Ribadeneyra, Pedro de. *Hystoria Ecclesiastica del Scisma del Reino de Inglaterra.* Lisbon: Manoel de Lyra, 1589.

Obras del Padre Pedro de Ribadeneyra de la Compañia de Iesus, agora de nueuo reuistas y acrecentadas. Madrid: Luis Sánchez, 1605.

Rodin de Marenzo, Francisco. *Decisio Granatensis Tribunalis Sancti Officii, In Causa Famosi Libelli, adversùs sacrosanctam Iesu Christi Legem, & incorruptam Deiparae Virginitatem.* Granada: Baltasar de Bolívar, Francisco Sánchez, 1641.

Sarmiento, Francisco. *Interpretationvm Selectarvm Libri Octo. De Ecclesiasticis Redditibvs Liber Vnvs.* Antwerp: Ioannes Keerbergius, 1616.

Simancas, Diego de. *Collectaneorum de Republica libri nouem. Opus studiosis omnibus utile: Viris autem politicis necessarium.* Valladolid: Adrian Ghemart, 1565.

Collectaneorum de Republica Libri IX. Ex illustribus Theologis, Legum latoribus, Iurisconsultis, Medicis, Philosophis, Poëtis, Historicis, aliisque bonarum artium peritis. Opus studiosis omnibus vtile, viris autem politicis necessarium. Antwerp: Plantin, 1574.

Collectaneorum de Republica libri IX. Salamanca: heirs of Matías Gast, 1582.

Collectaneorum de Republica libri IX. Salamanca: Diego de Cusio, 1598.

Collectaneorum de Republica libri IX. Salamanca: Diego de Cusio, 1600.

De catholicis institutionibus Iacobi Simancae Pacensis Episcopi: de catholicis institutionibus liber, ad praecauendas & extirpandas haereses admodum necessarius. Alcalá de Henares: Andrea de Angulo, 1569.

De catholicis institutionibus liber ad praecauendas & extirpandas haereses admodum necessarius. Rome: in aedibus Populi Romani, 1575.

De Dignitate Episcoporum Summarium. Antwerp: Plantin, 1575.

De Episcopis iuris peritis, opusculum. Antwerp: Plantin, 1574.

De episcoporum dignitate, scriptorum veterum auctoritates Iacobi Simancae … opera collectae. Rome: Bartolomeo Bonfadino, 1592.

De primogenitis Hispaniae libri quinque. Salamanca: Juan María de Terranova, 1566.

De Repvblica Libri IX. Opus collectum ex omnibus, qui de ea optime scripserunt, auctoribus. Venice: Bolognino Zaltieri, 1569.

De Republica recte instituenda, conservanda, et amplificanda libri IX … sunt in hac postrema editione plures quam mille loci memorabiles ab ipso auctore adjecti. Cologne: Lazare Zetzner, 1609.

Enchiridion iudicum violatae religionis ad extirpandas h[a]ereses theoricen & praxim summa breuitate complectens…: cui accesserunt, eiusdem auctoris [et] argumenti, opuscula duo hactenus non impresa: vnum annotationum in Zanchinum, alterum, de patre haeretico. Venice: Giordano Ziletti, 1569.

Enchiridion Iudicvm violatae religionis, ad extirpandas haeredes [sic], theoricen & praxim … complectens…. Cui accesserunt eiusdem auctoris opuscula duo: Vnum, Annotationum in Zanchinum; Alterum de dignitate Episcopali. Antwerp: Plantin, 1573.

Institutiones Catholicae quibus ordine ac brevitate diseritur quicquid ad praecauendas & extirpandas haereses necessarium est. Valladolid: Egidio de Colomies, 1552.

Liber Disceptationvm: In Qvo de Primogeniis Hispaniae, ac potissimè de illorum publicatione disputatur. Antwerp: Plantin, 1575.

Opera Jacobi Simancae Episcopi Pacensis, et Postmodum Zamorensis Juriscons. Praestantiss. hoc est. De Catholicis Institutionibus Liber ad praecavendas, & extirpandas haereses admodum necessarius. Theorice, et Praxis Haereseos, Sive Enchiridion Judicum violatae Religionis. Annotationes in Zanchinum, Cum animadversionibus in Campegium, Et Liber Singularis de Patre Haeretico. Ferrara: Bernardino Pomatelli, 1692.

Praxis haereseos siue Enchiridion iudicum violatae religionis. Venice: Giordano Ziletti, 1568.

[   ]. *Promptuarium Politicum ad Regulas Prudentiae formatum*. Strasburg: Georg Andreas Dolhopff; Johann Eberhard Zetzner, 1664.

Theorice et praxis haereseos, sive Enchiridion Ivdicvm violatae religionis. Cui nunc primum accesserunt opuscula duo eiusdem argumenti, scilicet Annotationum, in Zanchinum, cum animaduersionibus, in Campegium, liber singularis. De patre haeretico, liber singularis, eodem auctore. Venice: Giordano Ziletti, 1573.

Vida y Cosas Notables del Señor Obispo de Zamora Don Diego de Simancas. In *Autobiografías y Memorias*, edited by Manuel Serrano y Sanz, 151–210. Madrid: Bailly, Bailliére, S. B., 1905.

Solano de Figueroa y Altamirano, don Juan. *Historia Eclesiástica de la Ciudad y Obispado de Badajoz*. 4 vols. Badajoz: Imprenta del Hospicio provincial, 1929.

Suardo, Juan Antonio. *Diario de Lima de Juan Antonio Suardo (1629–1639)*. 2 vols. Edited by Ruben Vargas Ugarte S. J. Lima: Universidad Católica del Perú, Instituto de Investigaciones Históricas, 1936.

Tellechea Idígoras, José Ignacio. *Fray Bartolomé Carranza, documentos históricos*. 7 vols. Madrid: RAH, 1962–94.

Trejo, Antonio de, O. F. M. *Legatio Philippi III et IV Catholicorum Hispaniae Regum ad SS. DD. NN. Paulum PP. V et Gregorium XV De definiendâ Controuersiâ Immacullatae Conceptionis B. Virginis Mariae*. Louvain: Henricus Hastenius, 1624.

Vega, Garcilaso de la, El Inca. *Royal Commenatries of the Incas and General History of Peru, Abridged*. Edited by Karen Spalding and translated by Harold V. Livermore. Indianapolis, IN: Hackett Publishing Company, Inc., 2006.

Velásquez, Didacus. [Simancas, Diego de.] *Defensio statuti Toletani a Sede Apostolica saepe confirmati, pro his, qui bono et incontaminato genere nati sunt*. Antwerp: Plantin, 1575.

Verzosa, Juan de. *Epístolas*. Edited and translated by Eduardo del Pino González. 3 vols. Alcañiz and Madrid: CSIC, Centro de Estudios Humanísticos, 2006.

Vida, M. Gerolamo. "Elogio dello Stato (De rei publicae dignitate)." Translated by Antonio Altamura. In Giuseppe Toffanin, *L'Umanesimo al Concilio di Trento*, 75–228. Bologna: Nicola Zanichelli Editore, 1955.

Vives, Juan Luis. *Ioannis Lodovici Vivis, Valentini, Commentarii ad Divi Avrelii Avgvstini de Civitate Dei.* Edited by F. Jorge Pérez Durà and José María Estellés González. Valencia: Universitat de València, 2004.

    De concordia et discordia in human genere ad Carolum V. Caesarem, libri 4. . . . De Pacificatione, liber unus. Antwerp: Michael Hillenius, 1529.

    The Education of a Christian Woman: A Sixteenth-Century Manual. Edited and translated by Charles Fantazzi. Chicago and London: University of Chicago Press, 2000.

Voragine, Jacobus de, O.P. *The Golden Legend: Readings on the Saints.* 2 vols. Translated by William Granger Ryan. Princeton, NJ: Princeton University Press, 1993.

Yepes, Diego de. *Historia particular de la persecucion de Inglaterra, y de los martirios mas insignes que en ella ha auido, desde el año del Señor 1570.* Madrid: Luis Sánchez, 1599.

Secondary Sources

Abulafia, David. *The Western Mediterranean Kingdoms 1200–1500: The Struggle for Domination.* London and New York: Longman, 1997.

Albaret, Laurent, ed. *Les Inquisiteurs: Portraits de défenseurs de la foi en Languedoc.* Toulouse: Éditions Privat, 2001.

Alcalá, Ángel. "El control inquisitorial de intelectuales en el Siglo de Oro. De Nebrija al 'Índice' de Sotomayor de 1640." In *HIEA* 3: 829–958.

Águeda Méndez, María, ed. *Secretos del Oficio: Avatares de la Inquisición novohispana.* Mexico City: El Colegio de México, UNAM, 2001.

    dir. *Catálogo de Textos Marginados Novohispanos. Inquisición: siglo XVII Archivo General de la Nación (México).* Mexico City: Colegio de México, Centro de Estudios Lingüísticos y Literarios, Archivo General de la Nación, Fondo Nacional para la Cultura y las Artes, 1997.

Ahlgren, Gillian. "Francisca de los Apóstoles: A Visionary Voice for Reform in Sixteenth-Century Toledo." In *Women in the Inquisition: Spain and the New World*, edited by Mary E. Giles, 119–33. Baltimore, MD: The Johns Hopkins University Press, 1999.

Alberro, Solange. *Inquisition et Société au Mexique, 1571–1700.* Mexico City: Centre d'Études Mexicaines et Centramericaines, 1988.

Alcocer, Mariano, and Saturnino Rivera. *Historia de la Universidad de Valladolid: Bio-Bibliografías de Juristas Notables.* Valladolid: Imprenta de la Casa Social Católica, 1924.

Aldea Vaquero, Quintín, and Tomás Marín Martínez, eds. *Diccionario de Historia Eclesiástica de España.* 4 vols. Madrid: Instituto Enrique Florez, CSIC, 1972–75.

Allen, Paul. *Philip III and the Pax Hispanica, 1598–1621: The Failure of Grand Strategy.* New Haven, CT: Yale University Press, 2000.

Álvarez Alonso, Fermina. *La Inquisición en Cartagena de Indias durante el siglo XVII.* Madrid: Fundación Universitaria Española, 1999.

Alvarez Reyero, Antonio. *Crónicas Episcopales Palentinas ó Datos y apuntes biográficos, necrológicos, bibliográficos é históricos de los Señores Obispos de Palencia, desde los primeros siglos de la Iglesia Católica hasta el día; materia precisa para escribir la historia de dicha ciudad.* Palencia: Abundo Z. Menéndez, 1898.

Álvarez de Toledo, Cayetana. *Politics and Reform in Spain and Viceregal Mexico: The Life and Thought of Juan de Palafox 1600–1659.* Oxford, UK: Clarendon Press, 2004.

Amelang, James S. "Between Doubt and Discretion: Revising the Rules for Prosecuting Spanish Witches." In *Making, Using and Resisting the Law in European History*, edited by Günther Lottes, Eero Medijainen, and Jón Viðar Sigurðsson, 77–92. Pisa: Pisa University Press, 2008.

"Ethnographies of Error." In *L'Europa divisa e i nuovi mondi. Per Adriano Prosperi*, edited by Massimo Donattini, Giuseppe Marcocci, and Stefania Pastore, 2:105–15. Pisa: Edizioni della Normale, 2011.

"Exchanges between Italy and Spain: Culture and Religion." In *Spain in Italy: Politics, Society and Religion 1500–1700*, edited by Thomas James Dandalet and John A. Marino, 433–55. Leiden & Boston: Brill, 2007.

The Flight of Icarus: Artisan Autobiography in Early Modern Europe. Stanford, CA: Stanford University Press, 1998.

"Tracing Lives: The Spanish Inquisition and the Act of Autobiography." In *Controlling Time and Shaping the Self: Developments in Autobiographical Writing Since the Sixteenth Century*, edited by Arianne Baggerman, Rudolf Dekker, and Michael Mascuch, 33–48. Leiden & Boston: Brill, 2011.

Ames, Christine Caldwell. "Does the Inquisition Belong to Religious History?" *American Historical Review* 110 (2005): 11–37.

Righteous Persecution: Inquisition, Dominicans and Christianity in the Middle Ages. Philadelphia: University of Pennsylvania Press, 2009.

Amezaga, Elias. *Auto de Fe en Valladolid.* Buenos Aires: Gráficas Ellacuría, 1966.

Arendt, Hannah. *Eichmann in Jerusalem. A Report on the Banality of Evil.* New York and London: Penguin Books, 1994.

Aron-Beller, Katherine. "Disciplining Jews: The Papal Inquisition of Modena, 1598–1630." *Sixteenth Century Journal* 41 (2010): 713–29.

Arredondo Sirodey, María Soledad. "Armas de Papel: Quevedo y sus contemporáneos ante la guerra de Cataluña." *La Perinola: Revista de investigación quevediana* (1998): 117–54.

Literatura y Propaganda en Tiempo de Quevedo: Guerras y Plumas Contra Francia, Cataluña y Portugal. Frankfurt and Madrid: Iberoamericana Vervuert, 2011.

"Noticia de la *Súplica de Tortosa* (1640), atribuida al Inquisidor Juan Adam de la Parra. *Cuadernos de Historia Moderna* 22 (1999): 139–56.

Baernstein, P. Renée. *A Convent Tale: A Century of Sisterhood in Spanish Milan.* New York: Routledge, 2002.

Ballesteros Gaibrois, Manuel. "La Instalación del Tribunal del Santo Oficio en Cartagena de Indias. Nuevas Noticias." In *HIEA* 3: 1025–29.

"Los Fondos Inquisitoriales Americanísticos." In *HIEA* 1: 90–135.

Bataillon, Marcel. *Erasme et l'Espagne. 1937.* Edited by Daniel Devoto and Charles Amiel. 3 vols. Geneva: Droz, 1991.

Benigno, Francesco. "Integration and Conflict in Spanish Sicily." In *Spain in Italy: Politics, Society and Religion 1500–1700*, edited by Thomas James Dandelet and John A. Marino, 23–44. Leiden and Boston: Brill, 2007.

La sombra del rey: Validos y lucha política en la España del siglo XVII. Translated by Esther Benítez. Madrid: Alianza Editorial, 1994.

Bennassar, Bartolomé. *L'Inquisition espagnole, XVe – XIXe siècle.* Paris: Hachette, 1979.

"La Inquisición o La Pedagogía del Miedo." In *Inquisición española: poder político y control social*, edited by Bartolomé Bennassar, 94–125. Barcelona: Editorial Crítica, 1981.

"Modelos de la Mentalidad Inquisitorial: Métodos de su 'Pedagogía del Miedo.'" In *Inquisición Española y Mentalidad Inquisitorial*, edited by Ángel Alcalá, 174–81. Barcelona: Editorial Ariel, 1984.

Valladolid au siècle d'or, une ville de Castille et sa campagne au XVIe siècle. Paris: La Haye, Mouton et Cie, 1967.

Bergin, Joseph. *The Making of the French Episcopate 1589–1661.* New Haven, CT, and London: Yale University Press, 1996.

Bethencourt, Francisco. *L'Inquisition à l'époque moderne: Espagne, Portugal, Italie XVe-XIXe siècle.* Paris: Fayard, 1995.

The Inquisition: A Global History, 1478–1834. Translated by Jean Birrell. Cambridge, UK, and New York: Cambridge University Press, 2009.

Bilinkoff, Jodi. *The Avila of Saint Teresa: Religious Reform in a Sixteenth-Century City.* Ithaca, NY: Cornell University Press, 1989.

Related Lives: Confessors and Their Female Penitents, 1450–1750. Ithaca, NY: Cornell University Press, 2005.

Bireley, Robert. *The Counter-Reformation Prince. Anti-Machiavellianism or Catholic Statecraft in Early Modern Europe.* Chapel Hill and London: The University of North Carolina Press, 1990.

Bodian, Miriam. *Dying in the Law of Moses: Crypto-Jewish Martyrdom in the Iberian World.* Bloomington, IN: Indiana University Press, 2007.

Hebrews of the Portuguese Nation: Conversos and Community in Early Modern Amsterdam. Bloomington, IN: Indiana University Press, 1997.

Borromeo, A. "Eymerich, Nicolau." In *DSI* 2: 568–70.

Boutcher, Warren. "Unoriginal Authors: How to Do Things with Texts in the Renaissance." In *Rethinking the Foundations of Modern Political Thought*, edited by Annabel Brett and James Tully with Holly Hamilton-Bleakley, 73–92. Cambridge, UK: Cambridge University Press, 2006.

Bouza Álvarez, Fernando. *Corre manuscrito. Una historia cultural del Siglo de Oro.* Madrid: Marcial Pons Historia, 2001.

Del Escribano a la Biblioteca. Madrid: Síntesis, 1992.

Imagen y propaganda. Capítulos de Historia Cultural del Reinado de Felipe II. Madrid: Akal Ediciones, 1998.

Boyd, Maurice. *Cardinal Quiroga Inquisitor General of Spain.* Dubuque, IA: William C. Brown Co., 1954.

Braudel, Fernand. *The Mediterranean and the Mediterranean World in the Age of Philip II.* Translated by Siân Reynolds. 2 vols. New York: Harper and Row, 1972.

Briggs, Robin. *Witches and Neighbors: The Social and Cultural Context of European Witchcraft*. New York: Viking, 1996.

Brundage, James A. *Medieval Canon Law*. London and New York: Longman, 1995.

Brunelle, Gayle K. "Migration and Religious Identity: The Portuguese of Seventeenth-Century Rouen." *Journal of Early Modern History* 7, nos. 3–4 (2003): 283–311.

　The New World Merchants of Rouen 1559–1630. Kirksville, MO: Sixteenth Century Journal Publishers, 1991.

Burgos, Alonso. *El Luteranismo en Castilla Durante el S. XVI. Autos de fe de Valladolid de 21 de mayo y de 8 de octubre de 1559*. San Lorenzo de El Escorial: Editorial Swan, 1983.

Cañeque, Alejandro. *The King's Living Image: The Culture and Politics of Viceregal Power in Colonial Mexico*. London and New York: Routledge, 2004.

　"Theater of Power: Writing and Representing the Auto de Fe in Colonial Mexico," *The Americas* 52 (1996): 321–43.

Caro Baroja, Julio. *El Señor Inquisidor y otras vidas por oficio*. Madrid: Alianza Editorial, 1968.

Castañeda Delgado, Paulino, and Pilar Hernández Aparicio. *La Inquisición de Lima*. 3 vols. Madrid: Editorial Deimos, 1989.

del Castillo Mathieu, Nicolas. *La Llave de las Indias*. Bogotá: Ediciones El Tiempo, 1981.

Cavarzere, Marco. *La Prassi della Censura nell'Italia del Seicento*. Rome: Edizioni di Storia e Letteratura, 2011.

Ceballos Gómez, Diana Luz. *Hechicería, brujería, e Inquisición en el Nuevo Reino de Granada. Un duelo de imaginarios*. Bogotá: Editorial Universidad Nacional, 1995.

Christian, William. *Local Religion in Sixteenth-Century Spain*. Princeton, NJ: Princeton University Press, 1981.

Chuchiak, John F. "*In Servitio Dei:* Fray Diego de Landa, the Franciscan Order, and the Return of the Extirpation of Idolatry in the Colonial Diocese of Yucatán, 1573–1579." *The Americas* 61.4 (2005): 611–46.

Clark, Stuart. *Thinking with Demons: The Idea of Witchcraft in Early Modern Europe*. Oxford, UK, and New York: Oxford University Press, 1997.

Clavero, Bartolomé. *Mayorazgo: Propiedad Fedual en Castilla (1369–1836)*. Madrid: Siglo Veintiuno Editores, 1974.

Clendinnen, Inga. *Ambivalent Conquests: Maya and Spaniard in Yucatan, 1517–1570*. Cambridge, UK, and New York: Cambridge University Press, 1987.

Colli, Gaetano. *Per Una Bibliografia dei Trattati Giuridici Pubblicati nel XVI Secolo: Indici dei Tractatus Universi Iuris*. Milan: Giuffrè Editore, 1994.

Contreras, Jaime. *El Santo Oficio de la Inquisición de Galicia, 1560–1700: poder, sociedad y cultura*. Madrid: Akal, 1982.

　"The Social Infrastructure of the Inquisition: Familiars and Commissioners." In *The Spanish Inquisition and the Inquisitorial Mind*, edited by Angel Alcalá, 133–58. Boulder, CO: Social Science Monographs, distr. Columbia University Press, 1987.

Sotos contra Riquelmes: regidores, inquisidores, y criptojudíos. Madrid: Anaya & M. Muchnik, 1992.

Contreras, Jaime, and Jean Pierre Dedieu. "Estructuras Geográficas del Santo Oficio en España." In *HIEA* 2: 3–47.

Contreras, Jaime, and Gustav Henningsen. "Cases of the Spanish Inquisition (1540–1700): Analysis of a Historical Data Bank." In *The Inquisition in Early Modern Europe: Studies on Sources and Methods*, edited by Gustav Henningsen and John Tedeschi, 100–129. DeKalb: Northern Illinois University Press, 1986.

Cotarelo Valledor, D. Armando. *El Cardenal Don Rodrigo de Castro y su fundación en Monforte de Lemos*. Madrid: Imprenta de Editorial Magisterio Español, 1945.

Crewe, Ryan. "Brave New Spain: An Irishman's Independence Plot in Seventeenth-Century Mexico." *Past and Present* 207 (2010): 53–87.

Crosby, James O., ed. *Nuevas Cartas de la Última Prisión de Quevedo*. Woodbridge, Suffolk, and Rochester, NY: Tamesis, 2005.

Curcio-Nagy, Linda A. *The Great Festivals of Colonial Mexico City: Performing Power and Identity*. Albuquerque: University of New Mexico Press, 2004.

Dandelet, Thomas James. *Spanish Rome, 1500–1700*. New Haven, CT, and London: Yale University Press, 2001.

and John A. Marino, eds. *Spain in Italy: Politics, Society and Religion 1500–1700*. Leiden and Boston: Brill, 2007.

Davis, Natalie Zemon. *Fiction in the Archives: Pardon Tales and Their Tellers in Sixteenth- Century France*. Stanford, CA: Stanford University Press, 1987.

Women on the Margins: Three Seventeenth-Century Lives. Cambridge, MA: Harvard University Press, 1995.

De Boer, Wietse. *The Conquest of the Soul: Confessions, Discipline, and Public Order in Counter-Reformation Milan*. Leiden and Boston: Brill, 2001.

Del Col, Andrea. "Inquisitore." In *DSI* 2: 800–3.

L'Inquisizione in Italia. Dal XII al XXI secolo. Milan: Mondadori, 2006.

Dedieu, Jean-Pierre. *L'Administration de la foi: l'Inquisition de Tolède, XVI-XVII siècle*. Madrid: Casa de Velázquez, 1989.

"Les inquisiteurs de Tolède et la visite du district. La sédentarisation d'un tribunal (1550–1630)." *Mélanges de la Casa de Velázquez* 13 (1977): 235–56.

"Inquisitore di distretto, Spagna." In *DSI* 2: 803–4.

Dedieu, Jean-Pierre, and René Millar Carvacho. "Entre histoire et mémoire. L'Inquisition à l'époque moderne: dix ans d'historiographie." *Annales HSS* 57 (2002): 349–72.

Diefenderfer, Lara Mary. "Making and Unmaking Saints in Seventeenth-Century Madrid." PhD diss., University of Virginia, 2003.

Diehl, Peter. "An Inquisitor in Manuscript and in Print: The *Tractatus super materia haereticorum* of Zanchino Ugolini." In *The Book Unbound: Editing and Reading Medieval Manuscripts and Texts*, edited by Siân Echard and Stephen Partridge, 58–77. Toronto: University of Toronto Press, 2004.

Ditchfield, Simon. "Alla ricerca di un genere: come leggere la 'Cronica dell'origine di Piacenza' dell'inquisitore piacentino Umberto Locati (1503–1587)." *Bollettino Storico Piacentino* 82 (1987): 145–67.

Liturgy, Sanctity and History in Tridentine Italy. Cambridge, UK, and New York: Cambridge University Press, 1995.

"Of Dancing Cardinals and Mestizo Madonnas: Reconfiguring the History of Roman Catholicism in the Early Modern Period." *Journal of Early Modern History* 8 (2004): 386–408.

"Umberto Locati, O. P. (1503–1587): Inquisitore, Vescovo e Storico – un profilo bio-bibliografico." *Bollettino Storico Piacentino* 84 (1989): 205–21.

Domínguez Ortiz, Antonio. *Los Conversos de origen judío después de la expulsión.* Madrid: CSIC, 1957.

"Las Presuntas 'Razones' de la Inquisición." In *HIEA* 3: 57–82.

"Regalismo y Relaciones Iglesia-Estado en el Siglo XVII." In *Historia de la Iglesia de España*, edited by Ricardo García-Villoslada, 4:73–121. Madrid: Biblioteca de Autores Cristianos, 1979–1982.

"Una obra desconocida del Inquisidor Adam de la Parra." *Revista Bibliográfica y Documental* 5 (1951): 97–114.

and Bernard Vincent, *Historia de los Moriscos. Vida y tragedia de una minoría.* Madrid: Alianza, 1978.

Domínguez Salgado, María del Pilar. "Inquisidores y fiscales de la Inquisición de Corte (1580–1700)." *Revista de la Inquisición* 4 (1995): 205–48.

Donattini, Massimo, ed. *L'Italia dell'Inquisitore: storia e geografia dell'Italia del Cinquecento nella Descrittione di Leandro Alberti.* Bologna: Bononia University Press, 2007.

Duke, Alastair. *Dissident Identities in the Early Modern Low Countries.* Edited by Judith Pollmann and Andrew Spicer. Farnham, UK and Burlington, VT: Ashgate, 2009.

Edwards, John. *The Inquisitors: The Story of the Grand Inquisitors of the Spanish Inquisition.* Stroud, UK: Tempus, 2007.

and Ronald Truman, eds. *Reforming Catholicism in the England of Mary Tudor. The Achievement of Friar Bartolomé Carranza.* Aldershot, UK, and Burlington, VT: Ashgate, 2005.

Ehlers, Benjamin. *Between Christians and Moriscos: Juan de Ribera and Religious Reform in Valencia, 1568–1614.* Baltimore, MD: The Johns Hopkins University Press, 2006.

"La Esclava y El Patriarca: Las Visiones de Catalina Muñoz en la Valencia de Juan de Ribera." *Estudis* 23 (1997): 101–16.

Eire, Carlos M. N. *From Madrid to Purgatory: The Art and Craft of Dying in Sixteenth-Century Spain.* Cambridge, UK: Cambridge University Press, 1995.

Elliott, J. H. *The Count-Duke of Olivares: The Statesman in an Age of Decline.* New Haven, CT, and London: Yale University Press, 1986.

Imperial Spain, 1469–1716. New York: St. Martin's Press, 1964.

"Nueva luz sobre la prisión de Quevedo y Adam de la Parra." *Boletín de la Real Academia de la Historia* 169 (1972): 171–82.

The Revolt of the Catalans: A Study in the Decline of Spain, 1598–1643. Cambridge, UK: Cambridge University Press, 1963.

"A Europe of Composite Monarchies." *Past and Present* 137 (1992): 48–71.

Spain and Its World, 1500–1700: Selected Essays. New Haven, CT, and London: Yale University Press, 1989.

Entrambasaguas, Joaquín de. "El Inquisidor Juan Adam de la Parra." In *Estudios y ensayos de investigación y crítica*. Madrid: CSIC, 1973.

Prologue to *Conspiración Herético-Cristianísima*, by Juan Adam de la Parra. Translated by Angeles Roda Aguirre, vii–lii. Madrid: CSIC, 1943.

Varios Datos Referentes al Inquisidor Juan Adam de la Parra. Madrid: Tipografía de Archivos, 1930.

Errera, Andrea. "Manuali per inquisitori." In *DSI* 2: 975–81.

Processus in Causa Fidei: L'Evoluzione dei Manuali Inquisitoriali nei Secoli XVI-XVIII e il Manuale Inedito di un Inquisitore Perugino. Bologna: Monduzzi, 2000.

"*Repertorium inquisitorum*." In *DSI* 3: 1313.

Escandell Bonet, Bartolomé. "Las adecuaciones estructurales: establecimiento de la Inquisición en Indias." In *HIEA* 1: 713–30.

"Hacia una prosopografía inquisitorial." In *HIEA* 3: 225–28.

"Estructuras económicas de la Inquisición indiana." In *HIEA* 2: 1077–1105.

"Sociología Inquisitorial Americana." In *HIEA* 2: 841–82.

Escobar Quevedo, Ricardo. *Inquisición y judaizantes en América española (siglos XVI–XVII)*. Bogotá: Editorial Universidad del Rosario, 2008.

Escudero, José Antonio. *Los orígenes del "Consejo de la Suprema Inquisición."* In *Inquisición Española y Mentalidad Inquisitorial*, edited by Ángel Alcalá, 81–122. Barcelona: Editorial Ariel, 1984.

Fallay d'Este, Lauriane. *L'art de la peinture: Peinture et théorie à Séville au temps de Francisco Pacheco (1564–1644)*. Paris: Honoré Champion, 2001.

Fasolt, Constantin. "Visions of Order in the Canonists and Civilians." In *Handbook of European History, 1400–1600: Late Middle Ages, Renaissance and Reformation*, edited by Thomas A. Brady, Heiko Oberman, and James Tracy, 2:31–59. Leiden and New York: Brill, 1995.

The Limits of History. Chicago: University of Chicago Press, 2004.

Feitler, Bruno Guilherme. "Teoria e Prática na Definição da Jurisdição e da Práxis Inquisitorial Portuguesa: da 'Prova' como Objeto de Análise." In *O Império por escrito. Formas de transmissão da cultura letrada no mundo ibérico. Séculos XVI-XIX*, edited by Leila Mezan Algranti and Ana Paula Torres Megiani, 73–93. São Paulo: Alameda, 2009.

"Usos Políticos del Santo Oficio Portugués en el Atlántico (Brasil y África Occidental). El Período Filipino." *Hispania Sacra* LIX/119 (2007): 269–91.

Fernández Álvarez, Manuel, ed. *La Universidad de Salamanca II: Docencia e Investigación*. Salamanca: Acta Salamanticensia, Europa Artes Gráficas, 1990.

Fernández Duro, Cesáreo. *Memorias Históricas de la Ciudad de Zamora: su provincia y obispado*. Madrid: Establecimiento tipográfico de los sucesores de Rivadeneyra, 1882–83.

Fernández Terricabras, Ignasi. *Felipe II y el clero secular: la aplicación del concilio de Trento*. Madrid: Sociedad Estatal para la Conmemoración de los Centenarios de Felipe II y Carlos V, 2000.

Philippe II et la Contre-Réforme: L'Église Espagnole à l'Heure du Concile de Trente. Paris: Éditions Publisud, 2001.

Feros, Antonio. *Kingship and Favoritism in the Spain of Philip III, 1598–1621.* Cambridge, UK: Cambridge University Press, 2000.

Filippini, Orietta. *La coscienza del re: Juan de Santo Tomás, confessore di Filippo IV di Spagna, 1643–1644.* Florence: Olschki, 2006.

"Juan de Santo Tomás O.P., Confessore di Filippo IV di Spagna (1643–1644), e la Nascente Questione Giansenista." *Nouvelles de la République des Lettres* 2 (2002): 63–84.

"Verso 'Roma locuta.' Questioni teologiche, corte madrilena, e Santa Sede alla metà del Seicento." *Roma moderna e contemporanea* 18.1–2 (2010): 231–74.

Flynn, Maureen. "Mimesis of the Last Judgment: The Spanish *Auto de fe.*" *Sixteenth Century Journal* 22 (1991): 281–97.

Sacred Charity: Confraternities and Social Welfare in Spain, 1400–1700. Ithaca, NY: Cornell University Press, 1989.

Fox-Genovese, Elizabeth, and Eugene D. Genovese. *The Mind of the Master Class: History and Faith in the Southern Slaveholders' Worldview.* Cambridge, UK, and New York: Cambridge University Press, 2005.

Fuentes Caballero, José Antonio. *Concilios y Sínodos en la Diócesis de Palencia.* Palencia: Imprenta Provincial, 1980.

Furey, Constance. *Erasmus, Contarini, and the Religious Republic of Letters.* New York and Cambridge, UK: Cambridge University Press, 2006.

Galván Rodríguez, Eduardo. *El Inquisidor General.* Madrid: Dykinson, 2010.

García-Arenal, Mercedes. "Religious Dissent and Minorities: The Morisco Age." *Journal of Modern History* 81 (2009): 888–920.

and Gerard Albert Wiegers. *A Man of Three Worlds: Samuel Pallache, a Moroccan Jew in Catholic and Protestant Europe.* Translated by Martin Beagles. Baltimore, MD: The Johns Hopkins University Press, 2003.

García Barriuso, Patrocinio. "El Milagrismo. Sor Luisa de la Ascensión, La Monja de Carrión. Fr. Froilán Díaz y el Inquisidor Mendoza." In *HIEA* 1: 1089–113.

La Monja de Carrión. Sor Luisa de la Ascensión Colmenares Cabezón. Madrid and Zamora: Ediciones Monte Casino, 1986.

García Cárcel, Ricardo, and Doris Moreno Martínez. *Inquisición. Historia Crítica.* Madrid: Ediciones Temas de Hoy, 2000.

Herejía y sociedad en el siglo xvi. La Inquisición en Valencia, 1530–1609. Barcelona: Ediciones Península, 1980.

García Oro, José, and María José Portela Silva. "El arzobispo Valtodano (1570–1572). Un recuento de su Testamentaría." *Compostellanum* 50 (2005): 701–49.

Las Reformas Hospitalarias del Renacimiento en la Corona de Castilla: Del Gran Hospital de Santiago a los Hospitales Generales. Santiago de Compostela: Editorial del Eco Franciscano, 2005.

"La visita de Cristóbal de Valtodano y el proceso de codificación académica." *Liceo Franciscano* 55 (2003): 71–80.

Garufi, Carlo Alberto. *Fatti e personaggi dell'Inquisizione in Sicilia.* 1917. Reprint, Palermo: Sellerio editore, 1978.

Gerhard, Peter. *A Guide to the Historical Geography of New Spain,* rev. ed. Norman: University of Oklahoma Press, 1993.

Ginzburg, Carlo. "The Inquisitor as Anthropologist." In *Clues, Myths, and the Historical Method*, translated by John and Anne C. Tedeschi, 156–64. Baltimore, MD: The Johns Hopkins University Press, 1989.

Giordano, Silvano, ed. *Istruzioni di Filippo III ai suoi ambasciatori a Roma, 1598–1621*. Preface by Maria Antonietta Visceglia. Rome: Ministero per i beni e le attività culturali, 2006.

Goldhagen, Daniel Jonah. *Hitler's Willing Executioners: Ordinary Germans and the Holocaust*. New York: Vintage Books, 1997.

Gómez Rivas, León. "Roma y Madrid: correspondencia del cardenal Espinosa con el embajador Luis de Requesens." In *Madrid, Felipe II, y Las Ciudades de la Monarquía*, edited by Enrique Martínez Ruiz. Madrid: Actas Editorial, 2000.

González Novalín, José Luis. *El Inquisidor General Fernando de Valdés (1483–1568): Su vida y su obra*. 2 vols. Oviedo: Universidad de Oviedo, 1968.

"Reorganización valdesiana de la Inquisición española." In *HIEA* 1: 613–48.

González-Raymond, Anita. *La croix et le croissant: les inquisiteurs des îles face à l'islam, 1550–1700*. Paris: Éditions du Centre national de la recherche scientifique, 1993.

Goodman, Dena. *The Republic of Letters: A Cultural History of the French Enlightenment*. Ithaca, NY: Cornell University Press, 1994.

Goosens, Aline. *Les Inquisitions modernes dans les pays-bas méridionaux, 1520–1633*. 2 vols. Brussels: Éditions Université de Bruxelles, 1997–98.

Gracia Boix, Rafael. *Colección de Documentos para la Historia de la Inquisición de Córdoba*. Córdoba: Publicaciones del Monte de Piedad y Caja de Ahorros de Córdoba, 1982.

Green, Anna. *Cultural History*. New York: Palgrave Macmillan, 2008.

Greenblatt, Stephen. *Renaissance Self-Fashioning From More to Shakespeare*. Chicago and London: The University of Chicago Press, 1980.

Greenleaf, Richard. "The Inquisition Brotherhood: Cofradía de San Pedro Mártir of Colonial Mexico," *The Americas* 40.2 (1983): 171–207.

The Mexican Inquisition of the Sixteenth Century. Albuquerque: University of New Mexico Press, 1969.

Greer, Margaret R., and Elizabeth Rhodes. "Volume Editors' Introduction" and "A Note on the Translations." In María de Zayas y Sotomayor, *Exemplary Tales of Love and Tales of Disillusion*, edited and translated by Margaret R. Greer and Elizabeth Rhodes, 1–42. Chicago: University of Chicago Press, 2009.

Gregory, Brad S. *Salvation at Stake: Christian Martyrdom in Early Modern Europe*. Cambridge, MA: Harvard University Press, 1999.

Grice-Hutchinson, Marjorie. *The School of Salamanca: Readings in Spanish Monetary Theory 1544–1605*. Oxford, UK: Clarendon Press, 1952.

Griffin, Clive. *The Crombergers of Seville: The History of a Printing and Merchant Dynasty*. Oxford, UK: Clarendon Press, 1988.

Journeymen-Printers, Heresy, and the Inquisition in Sixteenth-Century Spain. Oxford, UK, and New York: Oxford University Press, 2005.

Guibovich Pérez, Pedro. *En Defensa de Dios: Estudios y Documentos Sobre la Inquisición en el Perú*. Lima: Ediciones del Congreso del Perú, 1998.

Guitarte Izquierdo, Vidal. *Episcopologio Español (1500–1699): Españoles obispos en España, América, Filipinas y otros países*. Rome: Instituto Español de Historia Eclesiástico, 1994.

Gutiérrez, C., S. J. *Españoles en Trento*. Valladolid: CSIC, Instituto Jerónimo Zurita, 1951.

Haliczer, Stephen, ed. *Inquisition and Society in Early Modern Europe*. London and Sydney: Croom Helm, 1987.

The Inquisition in the Kingdom of Valencia (1478–1834). Berkeley: University of California Press, 1984.

Hallman, Barbara McClung. *Italian Cardinals, Reform, and the Church as Property*. Berkeley, Los Angeles, and London: University of California Press, 1985.

Hampe Martínez, Teodoro. "The Diffusion of Books and Ideas in Colonial Peru: A Study of Private Libraries in the Sixteenth and Seventeenth Centuries." *The Hispanic American Historical Review* 73.2 (1993): 211–33.

Santo Oficio e Historia Colonial: Aproximaciones al Tribunal de la Inquisición de Lima (1570–1820). Lima: Ediciones del Congreso del Perú, 1998.

Harline, Craig. *The Burdens of Sister Margaret: Inside a Seventeenth-Century Convent*. New Haven, CT, and London: Yale University Press, 2000.

and Eddy Put. *A Bishop's Tale*. New Haven, CT, and London: Yale University Press, 2000.

Harris, A. Katie. "Forging History: The *Plomos* of Sacromonte of Granada in Francisco Bermúdez de Pedraza's *Historia Eclesiástica*." *Sixteenth Century Journal* 30 (1999): 945–66.

From Muslim to Christian Granada: Inventing a City's Past in Early Modern Spain. Baltimore, MD: The Johns Hopkins University Press, 2007.

Hauben, Paul J. *Three Spanish Heretics and the Reformation: Antonio del Corro, Cassiodoro de Reina, Cypriano de Valera*. Geneva: Librairie Droz, 1967.

Harvey, L. P. *Muslims in Spain, 1500 to 1614*. Chicago: University of Chicago Press, 2005.

Henningsen, Gustav. "Alonso de Salazar Frías: Ese famoso inquisidor desconocido." In *Homenaje a Caro Baroja*. Edited by Antonio Carreira, Jesús Antonio Cid, Manuel Gutiérrez Esteve, and Rogelio Rubio, 581–86. Madrid: Centro de Investigaciones Sociológicas, 1978.

The Salazar Documents: Inquisitor Alonso de Salazar Frías and Others on the Basque Witch Persecution. Leiden and Boston: Brill, 2004.

The Witches' Advocate: Basque Witchcraft and the Spanish Inquisition (1609–1614). Reno: University of Nevada Press, 1980.

Hernández Vegas, Mateo. *Ciudad Rodrigo: La Catedral y La Ciudad*. 2 vols. Ciudad Rodrigo: Excmo. Cabildo de la Catedral de Ciudad Rodrigo, 1982.

Heredia Herrera, Antonio, dir. *Catálogo de las Consultas de Consejo de Indias*. 12 vols. Seville: Diputación Provincial, 1983.

Herrejón Peredo, Carlos. "El Sermón Barroco en el Mundo Hispánico: Estudio de dos Latitudes." In *México en el mundo hispánico*, edited by Óscar Mazín Gómez, 1:343–51. Zamora, Michoacán: El Colegio de Michoacán, 2000.

Herzog, Tamar. *Defining Nations: Immigrants and Citizens in Early Modern Spain and Spanish America*. New Haven, CT: Yale University Press, 2003.

Hillgarth, J. N. *The Mirror of Spain, 1500–1700: The Formation of a Myth*. Ann Arbor: University of Michigan Press, 2000.

Homza, Lu Ann. "How to Harass an Inquisitor-General: The Polyphonic Law of Friar Francisco Ortíz." In *A Renaissance of Conflicts: Visions and Revisions of Law and Society in Italy and Spain*, edited by John A. Marino and Thomas Kuchn, 299–336. Toronto: Centre for Reformation and Renaissance Studies, 2004.

"The Merits of Disruption and Tumult: New Scholarship on Religion and Spirituality in Spain during the Sixteenth Century." *Archive for Reformation History* 100 (2009): 212–28.

Religious Authority in the Spanish Renaissance. Baltimore, MD, and London: The Johns Hopkins University Press, 2000.

ed. and trans. *The Spanish Inquisition 1478–1614. An Anthology of Sources*. Indianapolis, IN, and Cambridge: Hackett Publishing Company, 2006.

Honores, Renzo. "*Pleytos*, letrados y cultura legal en Lima y en Potosí, 1540–1640." Paper presented at Instituto Riva-Agüero, Lima, July 15, 2008.

Hossain, Kimberly Lynn. "Arbiters of Faith, Agents of Empire: Spanish Inquisitors and Their Careers, 1550–1650." PhD diss., The Johns Hopkins University, 2006.

"Unraveling the Spanish Inquisition: Inquisitorial Studies in the Twenty-First Century." *History Compass* 5/4 (2007): 1280–93.

"Was Adam the First Heretic? Luis de Páramo, Diego de Simancas, and the Origins of Inquisitorial Practice." *Archive for Reformation History* 97 (2006): 184–210.

Huerga, A. "La Pre-Inquisición Hispanoamericana (1516–1568)." In *HIEA* 1: 662–700.

"La Dinámica de las Estructuras en América. El Caso de Nueva España." In *HIEA* 1: 1177–79.

"Los hechos inquisitoriales en Indias. Tribunal de México," In *HIEA* 1: 1124–30.

"El Tribunal de México en la Época de Felipe II." In *HIEA* 1: 937–69.

"El Tribunal de México en la Época de Felipe III." In *HIEA* 1: 969–78.

Hyland, Sabine. *The Quito Manuscript: An Inca History Preserved by Fernando de Montesinos*. New Haven, CT: Yale University Press, 2007.

Israel, Jonathan I. *Empires and Entrepots: The Dutch, The Spanish Monarchy and the Jews, 1585–1713*. London and Ronceverte: The Hambledon Press, 1990.

European Jewry in the Age of Mercantilism 1550–1750. Oxford, UK, and Portland, OR: The Littman Library of Jewish Civilization, 1998.

Race, Class and Politics in Colonial Mexico, 1610–1670. London: Oxford University Press, 1975.

Izbicki, Thomas. "The Immaculate Conception and Ecclesiastical Politics from the Council of Basel to the Council of Trent: The Dominicans and Their Foes." *Archive for Reformation History* 96 (2005): 145–70.

"Problems of Attribution in the Tractatus Universi Iuris (Venice 1584)." In *Friars and Jurists: Selected Studies*, 413–27. Goldbach: Keip Verlag, 1997.

"When the Judge Is Not a Judge: Nicholas Eymeric on the Office of the Inquisitor." Unpublished conference paper, Newberry Library, 1985.

Jaraulde Pou, Pablo. *Francisco de Quevedo (1580–1645)*. Madrid: Editorial Castalia, 1998.

Jover, José María. *1635: Historia de una Polémica y Semblanza de una Generación*. Madrid: CSIC, Instituto Jerónimo Zurita, 1949.

Juliá Martínez, Eduardo. *La Amistad entre Quevedo y Adam de la Parra*. Madrid: Anales de la Universidad de Madrid, 1932.

Kagan, Richard L. "Autobiografie inquisitoriali (*trazas de la vida*)." In *DSI* 1: 122–23.

Clio and the Crown: The Politics of History in Medieval and Early Modern Spain. Baltimore, MD: The Johns Hopkins University Press, 2009.

"Clio and the Crown: Writing History in Habsburg Spain." In *Spain, Europe, and the Atlantic World: Essays in Honour of John H. Elliott*, edited by Richard L. Kagan and Geoffrey Parker, 73–99. Cambridge, UK, and New York: Cambridge University Press, 1995.

"A Golden Age of Litigation: Castile, 1500–1700." In *Disputes and Settlements: Law and Human Relations in the West*, edited by John Bossy, 145–66. Cambridge, UK: Cambridge University Press, 1983.

Lawsuits and Litigants in Castile, 1500–1700. Chapel Hill: The University of North Carolina Press, 1981.

Lucrecia's Dreams: Politics and Prophecy in Sixteenth-Century Spain. Berkeley, Los Angeles, and Oxford, UK: University of California Press, 1990.

"Prescott's Paradigm: American Historical Scholarship and the Decline of Spain." *AHR* 101 (1996): 423–46.

"La Salamanca del Siglo de Oro." In *Salamanca en la Edad de Oro*, edited by Conrad Kent, 287–305. Salamanca and Delaware, OH: Ohio Wesleyan University and Librería Cervantes, 1993.

Spain in America: The Origins of Hispanism in the United States. Urbana and Chicago: University of Illinois Press, 2002.

Students and Society in Early Modern Spain. Baltimore, MD, and London: The Johns Hopkins University Press, 1974.

and Abigail Dyer, eds. and trans. *Inquisitorial Inquiries. Brief Lives of Secret Jews and Other Heretics*. Baltimore, MD, and London: The Johns Hopkins University Press, 2004.

with the collaboration of Fernando Marías. *Urban Images of the Hispanic World 1493–1793*. New Haven, CT, and London: Yale University Press, 2000.

Kamen, Henry. "A Crisis of Conscience in Golden Age Spain: The Inquisition against limpieza de sangre." In *Crisis and Change in Early Modern Spain*, 1–27. Aldershot, UK, and Brookfield, VT: Variorum, 1993.

Inquisition and Society in Spain in the Sixteenth and Seventeenth Centuries. Bloomington: Indiana University Press, 1985.

Philip of Spain. New Haven, CT: Yale University Press, 1997.

The Spanish Inquisition: A Historical Revision. New Haven, CT, and London: Yale University Press, 1997.

Keitt, Andrew Wannamaker. "'Inventing the Sacred': Religious Enthusiasm and Imposture in Mid-Seventeenth Century Madrid." PhD diss., University of California, Berkeley, 1998.
   Inventing the Sacred: Imposture, Inquisition, and the Boundaries of the Supernatural in Golden Age Spain. Leiden & Boston: Brill, 2005.
Keniston, Hayward. *Francisco de los Cobos, Secretary of the Emperor Charles V.* Pittsburgh, PA: University of Pittsburgh Press, 1960.
Koenigsberger, H. G. *The Practice of Empire.* Ithaca, NY: Cornell University Press, 1969.
Kuttner, Stephan. "Introduction." In *Ioannis Andreae In Quinque Decretalium Libros Novella Commentaria,* 1: v–xiv. 1581. Facsimile, Turin: Bottega d'Erasmo, 1963.
Lamadrid, Lázaro, O.F.M., ed. "Report on the Missions by the Franciscan Commissary General of the Indies (1612)." *The Americas* 2.4 (1946): 489–97.
La Mantia, Vito. *Origine e vicende dell'Inquisizione in Sicilia.* 1886. Reprint, Palermo: Sellerio editore, 1977.
Lane, Kris. *Quito 1599. City and Colony in Transition.* Albuquerque: University of New Mexico Press, 2002.
Lavenia, Vincenzo. "Albert, Arnau (Arnaldo Albertini)." In *DSI* 1: 26.
   "Peña, Francisco de." In *DSI* 3: 1186–89.
   "Salazar Frías, Alonso de." In *DSI* 3: 1358–60.
Lazure, Guy. "To Dare Fame: Constructing a Cultural Elite in Sixteenth-Century Seville." PhD diss., The Johns Hopkins University, 2003.
Lea, Henry Charles. *A History of the Inquisition of Spain.* 4 vols. New York: Macmillan, 1906–7.
Lehfeldt, Elizabeth. *Religious Women in Golden Age Spain: The Permeable Cloister.* Aldershot, UK, and Burlington, VT: Ashgate, 2005.
León-Portilla, Miguel. *Bernardino de Sahagún, First Anthropologist.* Translated by Mauricio J. Mixco. Norman: University of Oklahoma Press, 2002.
Levi, Giovanni. *Inheriting Power: The Story of an Exorcist.* Translated by Lydia G. Cochrane. Chicago and London: The University of Chicago Press, 1988.
Levin, Michael. *Agents of Empire: Spanish Ambassadors in Sixteenth-Century Italy.* Ithaca, NY: Cornell University Press, 2005.
Liebman, Seymour. "The Great Conspiracy in New Spain." *The Americas* 30 (1973): 18–31.
   "The Great Conspiracy in Peru." *The Americas* 28 (1971): 176–90.
Lombardo, Alberto. *Injusticias Históricas. Olvido del Primero que concibió é Intentó la Independencia de México.* Mexico City: Tipografía Económica, 1901.
Lope Toledo, José María. "Un Hermano del Célebre Inquisidor Riojano Juan Adam de la Parra." *Berceo* 33 (1954): 473–74.
López Belinchón, Bernardo. *Honra, Libertad y Hacienda (Hombres de Negocios y Judíos Sefardíes).* Alcalá de Henares: Instituto Internacional de Estudios Sefardíes y Andalusíes, Universidad de Alcalá, 2001.
   "Olivares contra los portugueses. Inquisición, conversos y guerra económica." In *HIEA* 3: 499–530.

López Ferreiro, D. Antonio. *Historia de la Santa A. M. Iglesia de Santiago de Compostela.* Santiago de Compostela: Seminario Conciliar Central, 1905.

López García, María Trinidad. "El auge del dogma de la Inmaculada Concepción auspiciado por el franciscano fray Antonio de Trejo, obispo de Cartagena, y la implicación del concejo de Murcia, a principios del siglo XVII." In *La Inmaculada Concepción en España: religiosidad, historia y arte: actas del simposium, 1/4-IX-2005,* edited by Francisco Javier Campos y Fernández de Sevilla, 1:119–38. San Lorenzo de El Escorial: Ediciones Escurialenses, Real Centro Universitario Escorial-María Cristina, 2005.

López-Salazar Codes, Ana Isabel, "'Che Si Riduca al Modo di Procedere di Castiglia.' El Debate Sobre el Procedimiento Inquisitorial Portugués en Tiempos de los Austrias." *Hispania Sacra* LIX/119 (2007): 243–68.

López de Toro, José. "Respuesta del cardenal Trejo a una carta de Tomás Campanella." *Revista de Estudios Políticos* 122 (1962): 161–78.

López Vela, Roberto. "Estructuras administrativas del Santo Oficio." In *HIEA* 2: 63–274.

"Inquisitore generali, Spagna." In *DSI* 2: 807–8.

"Sociología de los Cuadros Inquisitoriales." In *HIEA* 2: 669–840.

Lorenzo Pinar, F. J. "Monjas disidentes. Las resistencias a la clausura en Zamora tras el Concilio de Trento." In *Disidencias y exilios en la España Moderna,* edited by A. Mestre Sanchís and E. Giménez López, 71–80. Alicante: Caja de Ahorros del Mediterráneo, Universidad de Alicante, AEHM, 1997.

Lundberg, Magnus. "Relación de la visita pastoral del arzobispado de México de Juan de Mañozca y Zamora, 1646." *Historia Mexicana* 58.2 (2008): 861–90.

Lupher, David A. *Romans in a New World: Classical Models in Sixteenth-Century Spanish America.* Ann Arbor: University of Michigan Press, 2003.

MacCormack, Sabine. *On the Wings of Time: Rome, the Incas, Spain, and Peru.* Princeton, NJ: Princeton University Press, 2007.

"Visions of the Roman Past in Late Medieval and Early Modern Spain." In *Genesis and Regeneration: Essays on Conceptions of Origins,* edited by Shaul Shaked, 77–109. Jerusalem: Israel Academy of Sciences and Humanities, 2005.

Mann, Richard G. *El Greco and His Patrons. Three Major Projects.* Cambridge, UK: Cambridge University Press, 1986.

Marías, Fernando. *El Largo Siglo XVI: los usos artísticos del renacimiento español.* Madrid: Taurus, 1989.

Marshall, John. *John Locke, Toleration and Early Enlightenment Culture: Religious Intolerance and Arguments for Religious Toleration in Early Modern and 'Early Enlightenment' Europe.* Cambridge, UK: Cambridge University Press, 2006.

Martin, John Jeffries. *Myths of Renaissance Individualism.* Houndmills, Basingstoke, Hampshire, UK, and New York: Palgrave Macmillan, 2004.

Venice's Hidden Enemies: Italian Heretics in a Renaissance City. Baltimore, MD, and London: The Johns Hopkins University Press, 2004.

Martín de la Hoz, José Carlos. *Inquisición y Confianza.* Madrid: Homo Legens, 2010.

Martínez Bujanda, J. "Índices de libros prohibidos del siglo XVI." In *HIEA* 3: 773–828.

Martínez Millán, José. "Las elites de poder durante el reinado de Carlos V a través de los miembros del Consejo de Inquisición (1516–1558)." *Hispania* 48/168 (1988): 103–67.

"Estructura de la hacienda de la Inquisición." In *HIEA* 2: 885–1075.

"Grupos de Poder en la Corte Durante el Reinado de Felipe II: La Facción Ebolista, 1554–1573." In *Instituciones y Elites de Poder en la Monarquía Hispana Durante el Siglo XVI*, edited by José Martínez Millán, 137–97. Madrid: Ediciones de la Universidad Autónoma, 1992.

"Las fuentes impresas." In *HIEA* 1: 136–69.

La hacienda de la Inquisición (1478–1700). Madrid: CSIC, 1984.

Maryks, Robert A. *The Jesuit Order as a Synagogue of Jews: Jesuits of Jewish Ancestry and Purity-of-Blood Laws in the Early Society of Jesus*. Leiden: Brill, 2009.

Matilla Tascón, A. *Guía-inventario delos Archivos de Zamora y su Provincia*. Madrid: Dirección General de Archivos y Bibliotecas, Diputación Provincial de Zamora, Ayuntamiento de Zamora, 1964.

Mayer, Thomas F., and D. R. Woolf, eds. *The Rhetorics of Life-Writing in Early Modern Europe: Forms of Biography from Cassandra Fedele to Louis XIV*. Ann Arbor: University of Michigan Press, 1995.

Mayhew, Robert. "British Geography's Republic of Letters: Mapping an Imagined Community, 1600–1800." *Journal of the History of Ideas* 65.2 (2004): 251–76.

Mazín Gómez, Óscar, dir. *Archivo del Cabildo Catedral Metropolitano de México*. 2 vols. Mexico City: El Colegio de Michoacán y Condumex, 1999.

Mazur, Peter. "Negotiating with the Inquisition. *Conversos*, the Holy Office, and the Viceroy of Naples, 1569–1582." *Archivio Italiano per la storia della pietà* 20 (2007): 39–54.

Medina, José Toribio. *Biblioteca Hispano-Americana, 1493–1810*. Santiago de Chile: Fondo Histórico y Bibliográfico José Toribio Medina, 1958.

Historia del Tribunal del Santo Oficio de la Inquisición en Cartagena de Indias. Imprenta Elzeviriana: Santiago de Chile, 1899.

Historia del Tribunal del Santo Oficio de la Inquisición en Lima, 1569–1820. Santiago de Chile: Fondo Histórica y Bibliográfico J. T. Medina, 1956.

Historia del Tribunal del Santo Oficio de la Inquisición en México. Santiago de Chile: Imprenta Elzeveriana, 1905. Facsimile reprint, Mexico City: Miguel Ángel, Porrúa, 1998.

Melammed, Renée Levine. *Heretics or Daughters of Israel? The Crypto-Jewish Women of Castile*. New York: Oxford University Press, 1999.

Méndez Plancarte, Alfonso. *Poetas Novohispanos. Segundo Siglo (1621–1721). Parte Primera*. Mexico City: UNAM, 1944.

Menéndez Pelayo, Marcelino. *Historia de los Heterodoxos Españoles*, 4th ed. 2 vols. Madrid: Biblioteca de Autores Cristianos, 1987.

Meseguer Fernández, J. "El Periodo Fundacional (1478–1517)." *HIEA* 1: 281–370.

"Las primeras estructuras del Santo Oficio." *HIEA* 1: 370–405.

Messana, Maria Sofia. *Inquisitori, negromanti e streghe nella Sicilia moderna, 1500–1782*. Palermo: Sellerio, 2007.

Miguel González, María Luisa de. "El Problema de los Conflictos Jurisdiccionales (Memorial de Antonio Trejo a Felipe IV)." In *La Inquisición Española: Nueva visión, nuevos horizontes*, edited by Joaquín Pérez Villanueva, 83–88. Madrid: Siglo Veintiuno, 1980.

Millar Carvacho, René. "Las confiscaciones de la Inquisición de Lima a los comerciantes de origen judío-portugués de la 'gran complicidad' de 1635." *Revista de Indias* 43/171 (1983): 27–58.

Inquisición y sociedad en el virreinato peruano: Estudios sobre el tribunal de Lima. Lima: Instituto Riva-Agüero, Pontificia Universidad Católica del Perú, 1988.

Miller, Kathryn. *Guardians of Islam: Religious Authority and Muslim Communities of Late Medieval Spain*. New York: Columbia University Press, 2008.

Mills, Kenneth. *Idolatry and Its Enemies: Colonial Andean Religion and Extirpation, 1614–1750*. Princeton, NJ: Princeton University Press, 1997.

Mínguez Cornelles, Víctor. *Los Reyes Distantes: Imágenes del Poder en el México Virreinal*. Castelló: Biblioteca de les Aules, 1995.

Monter, William. *The Frontiers of Heresy: The Spanish Inquisition from the Basque Lands to Sicily*. Cambridge, UK: Cambridge University Press, 1990.

Judging the French Reformation: Heresy Trials by Sixteenth-Century Parlements. Cambridge, MA: Harvard University Press, 1999.

Moralejo, Macarena. "El Obispo Diego de Simancas y su Papel como Virrey en Nápoles." *Librosdelacorte.es* 4 (2012): 141–53

Morales, Alfredo J. *Hernán Ruiz "el Joven."* Madrid: Akal, 1996.

Moreno Martínez, Doris. *La invención de la Inquisición*. Madrid: Marcial Pons Historia, 2004.

Moore, R.I. *The Formation of a Persecuting Society: Power and Deviance in Western Europe, 950–1250*. Oxford, UK: Blackwell Publishers, 1987.

Muldoon, James. *The Americas in the Spanish World Order: The Justification for Conquest in the Seventeenth Century*. Philadelphia: University of Pennsylvania Press, 1994.

Muller, Priscilla E. "Pablo de Céspedes: A Letter of 1577." *The Burlington Magazine* 138 (1996): 89–91.

Nadal Iniesta, Javier. "Fray Antonio de Trejo: El Primer Príncipe Contrarreformista de la Diócesis de Cartagena." In *Congreso Internacional Imagen Apariencia. Noviembre 19, 2008 – Noviembre 21, 2008*. Murcia: Universidad de Murcia, 2009.

Nader, Helen. *Liberty in Absolutist Spain: The Habsburg Sale of Towns, 1516–1700*. Baltimore, MD: The Johns Hopkins University Press, 1990.

Nalle, Sara Tilghman. *God in La Mancha: Religious Reform and the People of Cuenca, 1500–1650*. Baltimore, MD: The Johns Hopkins University Press, 1992.

"Inquisitors, Priests, and the People during the Catholic Reformation in Spain." *Sixteenth Century Journal* 18 (1987): 557–87.

Mad for God: Bartolomé Sánchez, the Secret Messiah of Cardenete. Charlottesville: University of Virginia Press, 2001.

Navarrete, María Cristina. *Historia Social del Negro en la Colonia Cartagena, siglo XVII*. Santiago de Cali: Universidad del Valle, 1995.

Netanyahu, Benzion. *The Origins of the Inquisition in Fifteenth-Century Spain*. New York: Random House, 1995.

Newson, Linda A., and Susie Minchin. *From Capture to Sale: The Portuguese Slave Trade to Spanish South America in the Early Seventeenth Century*. Leiden and Boston: Brill, 2007.

Nieto Cumplido, Manuel. *La Catedral de Córdoba*. Córdoba: Publicaciones de la Obra Social y Cultural de Cajasur, 1998.

Nirenberg, David. *Communities of Violence: Persecution of Minorities in the Middle Ages*. Princeton, NJ: Princeton University Press, 1996.

"Figures of Thought and Figures of Flesh: Jews and Judaism in Late-Medieval Spanish Poetry and Politics," *Speculum* 81 (2006): 398–426.

"Mass Conversion and Genealogical Mentalities: Jews and Christians in Fifteenth-Century Spain." *Past and Present* 174 (2002): 3–41.

Olaechea, Rafael. "El venerable Palafox y la Inquisición." In *HIEA* 1: 1131–32.

Olin, John C. *The Catholic Reformation. Savonarola to Ignatius Loyola*. New York: Fordham University Press, 1992.

Olivari, Michele. *Entre el trono y la opinión: la vida política castellana en los siglos XVI y XVII*. Prologue by Ricardo García Cárcel, translated by Jesús Villanueva. Valladolid: Junta de Castilla y León, 2004.

Olsen, H. Eric R. *The Calabrian Charlatan, 1598–1603: Messianic Nationalism in Early Modern Europe*. New York: Palgrave Macmillan, 2003.

Oropeza Tena, Gabriela. "Las Actas del Cabildo de la Catedral Metropolitana en Sede Vacante, 1637–1644". PhD diss., UNAM, 2004.

Padgen, Anthony, and Jeremy Lawrance, eds. *Political Writings of Francisco de Vitoria*. New York and Cambridge, UK: Cambridge University Press, 1991.

Palau y Dulcet, Antonio. *Manual del librero hispano-americano; bibliografía general española e hispano-americana desde la invención de la imprenta hasta nuestros tiempos, con el valor comercial de los impresos*. Barcelona: A. Palau, 1948–1977.

Parker, Geoffrey. *The Grand Strategy of Philip II*. New Haven, CT: Yale University Press, 1998.

Philip II. Chicago: Open Court, 2002.

"Some Recent Work on the Inquisition in Spain and Italy." *Journal of Modern History* 54.3 (1982): 519–32.

Parrado del Olmo, Jesús María. "Datos Inéditos de Entalladores Palentinos del Siglo XVI." *Publicaciones de la Institución Tello Téllez de Meneses* 54 (1986): 264–65.

Parry, J. H. *The Audiencia of New Galicia in the Sixteenth Century: A Study in Spanish Colonial Government*. Cambridge, UK: Cambridge University Press, 1948.

Pastore, Stefania. "Simancas, Diego de." In *DSI* 3: 1430–31.

Il Vangelo e la Spada. L'Inquisizione di Castiglia e i Suoi Critici (1460–1598). Rome: Edizioni di Storia e Letteratura, 2003.

Pazos, Manuel R., O.F.M, *Episcopado Gallego. Tomo I: Arzobispos de Santiago (1550–1850).* Madrid: CSIC & Instituto Jerónimo Zurita, 1946.

Pennington, Kenneth. *Popes, Canonists and Texts, 1150–1550.* Brookfield, VT, and Aldershot, UK: Variorum, 1993.

Perez, Béatrice. *Inquisition, Pouvoir, Société. La province de Séville et ses judéoconvers sous les Rois Catholiques.* Paris: Honoré Champion Éditeur, 2007.

Pérez, Joseph. *The Spanish Inquisition. A history.* Translated by Janet Lloyd. New Haven, CT, and London: Yale University Press, 2005.

Pérez Canto, María del Pilar. "Tribunal de Lima." In *HIEA* 1: 1133–41.

Pérez Pastor, Cristóbal. *Bibliografía Madrileña, o descripción de las obras impresas en Madrid.* 3 vols. 1891. Reprint, Pamplona: Analecta, 2000.

Pérez Villanueva, Joaquín, and Bartolomé Escandell Bonet, eds. *Historia de la Inquisición en España y América.* 3 vols. Madrid: Biblioteca de Autores Cristianos, Centro de Estudios Inquisitoriales, 1984–2000.

Pérez Villanueva, Joaquín. "Felipe IV y su política." In *HIEA* 1: 1006–78.

Perry, Mary Elizabeth. *Gender and Disorder in Early Modern Seville.* Princeton, NJ: Princeton University Press, 1990.

Pescador, Juan Javier. *The New World Inside a Basque Village: The Oiartzun Valley and Its Atlantic Emigrants, 1550–1800.* Reno: University of Nevada Press, 2004.

Peters, Edward. "Editing Inquisitors' Manuals in the Sixteenth Century: Francisco Peña and the *Directorium Inquisitorum* of Nicholas Eymeric." *The Library Chronicle* 40 (1974): 95–107.

    Inquisition. Berkeley and Los Angeles: University of California Press, 1989.

    Torture. Philadelphia: University of Pennsylvania Press, 1996.

Pcytavin, Mireille. *Visite et gouvernement dans le royaume de Naples, XVIe-XVIIe siècles.* Madrid: Casa de Velázquez, 2003.

Phelan, John Leddy. *The Hispanization of the Philippines: Spanish Aims and Filipino Responses 1565–1700.* Madison, Milwaukee, and London: University of Wisconsin Press, 1967.

    The Kingdom of Quito in the Seventeenth Century; Bureaucratic Politics in the Spanish Empire. Madison: University of Wisconsin Press, 1967.

Pinto Crespo, Virgilio. *Inquisición y control ideológico en la España del siglo XVI.* Madrid: Taurus Ediciones, 1983.

    "La Justificación Doctrinal del Santo Oficio." In *HIEA* 1: 880–86.

Pizarro Llorente, Henar. *Un gran patrón en la corte de Felipe II: don Gaspar de Quiroga.* Madrid: Universidad Pontificia Comillas, 2004.

    "Las relaciones de patronazgo a través de los inquisidores de Valladolid durante el siglo XVI." In *Instituciones y Elites de Poder en la Monarquía Hispana Durante el Siglo XVI,* edited by José Martínez Millán, 223–52. Madrid: Ediciones de la Universidad Autónoma, 1992.

Poole, Stafford. *Juan de Ovando: Governing the Spanish Empire in the Reign of Philip II.* Norman: University of Oklahoma Press, 2004.

    Pedro Moya de Contreras: Catholic Reform and Royal Power in New Spain, 1571–1591. Berkeley: Univeristy of California Press, 1987.

Portuondo, María. *Secret Science: Spanish Cosmography and the New World.* Chicago: University of Chicago Press, 2009.

Postigo Castellanos, Elena. *Honor y Privilegio en la Corona de Castilla. El Consejo de las Ordenes y los Caballeros de Hábito en el s. XVII.* Almazán, Soria: Junta de Castilla y León, Consejería de Cultura y Bienestar Social, 1988.

Prado Moura, Ángel de. *Inquisición e Inquisidores en Castilla: El Tribunal de Valladolid Durante el Crisis de Antiguo Régimen.* Valladolid: Universidad de Valladolid, 1995.

Prescott, William H. *The Works of William H. Prescott.* 22 vols. Philadelphia, PA: J. B. Lippincott Company, 1904.

Preston, Rebecca. "Roman Questions, Greek Answers: Plutarch and the Construction of Identity." In *Being Greek under Rome. Cultural Identity, the Second Sophistic and the Development of Empire*, edited by Simon Goldhill, 86–119. Cambridge, UK: Cambridge University Press, 2001.

Price Zimmerman, T. C. "Paolo Giovio and the Rhetoric of Individuality." In *The Rhetorics of Life-Writing in Early Modern Europe: Forms of Biography from Cassandra Fedele to Louis XIV*, edited by Thomas F. Mayer and D. R. Woolf, 39–62. Ann Arbor: University of Michigan Press, 1995.

Prosperi, Adriano, ed., with the collaboration of Vincenzo Lavenia and John Tedeschi. *Dizionario storico dell'Inquisizione.* 4 vols. Pisa: Edizioni della Normale, 2010.

Prosperi, Adriano. "Campeggi, Camillo." In *DSI* 1: 252–53.

   L'Inquisizione Romana: Letture e Richerche. Rome: Edizioni di Storia e Letteratura, 2003.

   Tribunali della coscienza: Inquisitori, confessori, missionari. Turin: G. Einaudi, 1996.

Pulido Serrano, Juan Ignacio. "La expulsión frustrada. Proyectos para la erradicación de la herejía judaica en la Monarquía Hispana." In *La Declinación de la Monarquía Hispánica en el Siglo XVII*, 891–904, edited by Francisco José Aranda Pérez. Cuenca: Ediciones de la Universidad de Castilla-La Mancha, 2004.

   Injurias a Cristo. Religión, política y antijudaísmo en el siglo XVII. Análisis de las corrientes antijudías durante la Edad Moderna. Alcalá de Henares: Instituto Internacional de Estudios Sefardíes y Andalucíes, Universidad de Alcalá, 2002.

Pullapilly, Cyriac K. *Caesar Baronius: Counter-Reformation Historian.* Notre Dame, IN, and London: University of Notre Dame Press, 1975.

Puyol Buil, Carlos. *Inquisición y Política en el reinado de Felipe IV: los procesos de Jerónimo de Villanueva y las monjas de San Plácido.* Madrid: CSIC, 1993.

Quiroz Norris, Alfonso. "La expropiación inquisitorial de cristianos nuevos portugueses en Los Reyes, Cartagena y México, 1635–1649." *Histórica* 10 (1986): 237–303.

Ranum, Orest. "Book review of *The Republic of Letters: A Cultural History of the French Enlightenment*, by Dena Goodman." *AHR* 103.1 (1998): 193–94.

Raphael, David. *The Expulsion 1492 Chronicles: An Anthology of Medieval Chronicles Relating to the Expulsion of the Jews from Spain and Portugal.* North Hollywood, CA: Carmi House Press, 1992.

Rawlings, Helen. "The Secularisation of Castilian Episcopal Office under the Habsburgs, 1516–1700." *Journal of Ecclesiastical History* 38 (1987): 53–79.

The Spanish Inquisition. Malden, MA, and Oxford, UK: Blackwell Publishing, 2006.

Raya Raya, María Angeles. *Catálogo de las pinturas de la Catedral de Córdoba*. Córdoba: Publicaciones del Monte de Piedad y Caja de Ahorros de Córdoba, 1988.

El retablo barroco cordobés. Córdoba: Publicaciones del Monte de Piedad y Caja de Ahorros de Córdoba, 1987.

Redondo Moreno, Conchi. "Adam de la Parra, el inquisidor indomable." In *Hijos Ilustres del Camero Viejo*, edited by R. Calvo Torre and C. Redondo Moreno, 20–27. Soto en Cameros: A.R.C.E.S., 2005.

Renda, Francesco. *L'Inquisizione in Sicilia: I fatti. Le persone*. Palermo: Sellerio editore, 1997.

Renwick, John. "Voltaire and the Politics of Toleration." In *The Cambridge Companion to Voltaire*, edited by Nicholas Cronk, 179–91. Cambridge, UK: Cambridge University Press, 2009.

Révah, I.S. "Autobiographie d'un Marrane. Édition partielle d'un manuscrit de João (Moseh) Pinto Delgado," *Revue des études juives* 119 (1961): 41–130.

del Rey Fajardo, José, S.J. *Los Jesuitas en Cartagena de Indias 1604–1767*. Bogotá: Centro Editorial Javeriano (Pontificia Universidad Javeriana), 2004.

del Río Barredo, María José. *Madrid, Urbs Regia: La capital ceremonial de la Monarquía Católica*. Madrid: Marcial Pons Historia, 2000.

"Representaciones Dramáticas en Casa de un Artesano del Madrid de Principios del Siglo XVII." In *Teatros y Vida Teatral en el Siglo de Oro a Través de las Fuentes Documentales*, edited by Luciano García Lorenzo and J.E. Varey, 245–58. London: Tamesis Books Limited, 1991.

Rivero Rodríguez, Manuel. "El Consejo de Italia y el gobierno de los dominios italianos de la monarquía hispana durante el reinado de Felipe II (1556–1598)." PhD diss., Universidad Autónoma, Madrid, 1992.

Felipe II y el Gobierno de Italia. Madrid: Sociedad Estatal para la Conmemoración de los Centenarios de Felipe II y Carlos V, 1998.

"La Inquisición Española en Sicilia," In *HIEA* 3: 1031–222.

"Páramo, Luis de." In *DSI* 3: 1170–71.

"Técnica de un golpe de Estado: el inquisidor García de Trasmiera en la revuelta siciliana de 1647." In *La Declinación de la Monarquía Hispánica en el Siglo XVII*, edited by Francisco José Aranda Pérez, 129–53. Cuenca: Ediciones de la Universidad de Castilla–La Mancha, 2004.

Rodríguez Besné, Ramón. *El Consejo de la Suprema Inquisición: Perfil jurídico de una institución*. Madrid: Editorial Complutense, 2000.

Rodríguez González, Ángel. "Notas al Episcopologio Compostelano: Relaciones del Arzobispo D. Cristóbal Fernández Valtodano con la Ciudad de Santiago." *Compostellanum: Revista Trimestral de la Archidiócesis de Santiago de Compostela* 14 (1969): 671–82.

Romeo, Giovanni. *Inquisitori, esorcisti e streghe nell'Italia della Controriforma*. Florence: Sansoni, 1990.

Roth, C. "Les Marranes à Rouen. Un chapitre ignoré de l'histoire des Juifs de France." *Revue des études juives* 88 (1929): 113–55.

Rowe, Erin K. *Saint and Nation: Santiago, Teresa of Ávila, and Plural Identities in Early Modern Spain.* University Park: Pennsylvania State University Press, 2011.

Rubio Lapaz, Jesús. *Pablo de Céspedes y su Círculo. Humanismo y Contrarreforma en la Cultura Andaluza del Renacimiento al Barroco.* Granada: Universidad de Granada, 1993.

Russell-Wood, A. J. R. *The Portuguese Empire, 1415–1808. A World on the Move.* Baltimore, MD, and London: The Johns Hopkins University Press, 1992.

Sala-Molins, Louis. "Utilisation d'Aristote en droit inquisitorial." In *Platon et Aristote à la Renaissance*, 191–99. Paris: Librairie Philosophique J. Vrin, 1976.

Sánchez, Magdalena. "Spain, Austria, and the Bohemian and Hungarian Successions." *Sixteenth Century Journal* 25 (1994): 887–903.

Sánchez de Madariaga, Elena. "Familiares de la Inquisición e Integración Social: la Cofradía de San Pedro Mártir de Madrid en el Siglo XVII." In *Integrazione ed Emarginazione. Circuiti e Modelli: Italia e Spagna nei Secoli XV-XVIII*, edited by Laura Barletta, 53–89. Naples: Istituto Suor Orsola Benincasa, 2002.

Sánchez Rivilla, Teresa. "Inquisidores Generales y Consejeros de la Suprema: documentación biográfica." In *HIEA* 3: 228–437.

"Sociología de inquisidores generales y Consejeros." In *HIEA* 2: 715–30.

Sanchiz, Javier. "Funcionarios Inquisitoriales en el Tribunal, Siglo XVI." In *Inquisición Novohispana.* Edited by Noemí Quezada, Martha Eugenia Rodríguez, and Marcela Suárez, 2 vols. Mexico City: UNAM, Instituto de Investigaciones Antropológicas, Universidad Autónoma Metropolitana Azcapotzalco, 2000, 1: 165–95.

Santiago Vela, P. Gregorio de. *Ensayo de una Biblioteca Ibero-Americana de la Orden de San Agustín.* 8 vols. Madrid: Imprenta del Asilo de Huérfanos del S. C. de Jesús, 1913.

Scalisi, Lina. *Il controllo del sacro. Poteri e istituzioni concorrenti nella Palermo del Cinque e Seicento.* Rome: Viella, 2004.

Schaposchnik, Ana. "Exemplary Punishment in Colonial Lima: The 1639 Auto de Fe." In *Death and Dying in Colonial Spanish America*, edited by Martina Will de Chaparro and Miruna Achim, 121–41. Tucson: The University of Arizona Press, 2011.

Schaub, Jean-Frédéric. *Les juifs du roi d'Espagne.* Paris: Hachette, 1999.

Le Portugal au temps du Comte-Duc d'Olivares, 1621–1640: le conflit de juridictions comme exercice de la politique. Madrid: Casa de Velázquez, 2001.

Schechter, Ronald. *Obstinate Hebrews. Representations of Jews in France, 1715–1815.* Berkeley, Los Angeles, and London: University of California Press, 2003.

Schutte, Anne Jacobson. *Aspiring Saints: Pretense of Holiness, Inquisition, and Gender in the Republic of Venice, 1618–1750.* Baltimore, MD, and London: The Johns Hopkins University Press, 2001.

Pier Paolo Vergerio: the making of an Italian reformer. Geneva: Droz, 1977.

Schwartz, Stuart. *All Can Be Saved: Religious Tolerance and Salvation in the Iberian Atlantic World.* New Haven, CT: Yale University Press, 2008.

"Panic in the Indies: The Portuguese Threat to the Spanish Empire, 1640–50." *Colonial Latin American Review* (1993): 165–87.

Seidel Menchi, Silvana. "The Inquisitor as Mediator." Translated by John Jeffries Martin. In *Heresy, Culture, and Religion in Early Modern Italy: Contexts and Contestations*, edited by Ronald K. Delph, Michelle M. Fontaine, and John Jeffries Martin, 173–92. Kirksville, MO: Truman State University Press, 2006.

Sicroff, Albert A. *Les Controverses des Statuts de 'Pureté de Sang' en Espagne du XVe au XVIIe Siècle*. Paris: Didier, 1960.

Sigaut, Nelly. "Procesión de Corpus Christi: La Muralla Simbólica en un Reino de Conquista Valencia y México-Tenochtitlan." In *México en el mundo hispánico*, edited by Óscar Mazín Gómez, 1:363–93. Zamora, Michoacán: El Colegio de Michoacán, 2000.

Silverblatt, Irene. *Modern Inquisitions: Peru and the Colonial Origins of the Civilized World*. Durham, NC: Duke University Press, 2004.

Skinner, Quentin. *The Foundations of Modern Political Thought: The Age of Reformation*. 1978. Reprint, Cambridge, UK: Cambridge University Press, 2002.

Splendiani, Anna María. *Cincuenta Años de Inquisición en el Tribunal de Cartagena de Indias, 1610–1660*. 4 vols. Bogotá: Centro Editorial Javeriano, Instituto Colombiano de Cultura Hispánica, 1997.

Starr-LeBeau, Gretchen. *In the Shadow of the Virgin: Inquisitors, Friars, and Conversos in Guadalupe, Spain*. Princeton, NJ: Princeton University Press, 2003.

Stow, Kenneth. *Catholic Thought and Papal Jewry Policy, 1555–1593*. New York: Jewish Theological Seminary of America, 1977.

Studnicki-Gizbert, Daviken. *A Nation Upon the Ocean Sea: Portugal's Atlantic Diaspora and the Crisis of the Spanish Empire, 1492–1640*. Oxford, UK, and New York: Oxford University Press, 2007.

Taín Guzmán, Miguel. *Dibujos históricos, epigráficos, y heráldicos del archivo de la catedral de Santiago*. A Coruña: Editorial Diputación Provincial, 2002.

Tausiet, María. *Ponzoña en los ojos: brujería y superstición en Aragón en el siglo XVI*. Madrid: Turner, 2004.

Tavárez, David. "Legally Indian: Inquisitorial Readings of Indigenous Identity in New Spain." In *Imperial Subjects: Race and Identity in Colonial Latin America*, edited by Andrew B. Fisher and Matthew D. O'Hara, 81–100. Durham, NC, and London: Duke University Press, 2009.

Tavuzzi, Michael M. *Renaissance Inquisitors: Dominican Inquisitors and Inquisitorial Districts in Northern Italy, 1474–1527*. Leiden and Boston: Brill, 2007.

Taylor, Bruce. "The Enemy Within and Without: An Anatomy of Fear on the Spanish Mediterranean Littoral." In *Fear in Early Modern Society*, edited by W. G. Naphy and P. Roberts, 78–99. New York: Manchester University Press, 1997.

Taylor, Scott K. *Honor and Violence in Golden Age Spain*. New Haven, CT, and London: Yale University Press, 2008.

Tedeschi, John. *The Prosecution of Heresy: Collected Studies on the Inquisition in Early Modern Italy*. Binghamton, NY: Medieval and Renaissance Texts and Studies, 1991.

"Rojas, Juan de." In *DSI* 3: 1337.

Tejado Fernández, Manuel. "La Ampliación del Dispositivo: Fundación del Tribunal de Cartagena de Indias." In *HIEA*, 1: 984–95.

Aspectos de la Vida Social en Cartagena de Indias durante el Seiscientos. Seville: Escuela de Estudios Hispano-Americanos, 1954.

"Las Modificaciones Estructurales en Cartagena de Indias." In *HIEA* 1: 1189–95.

"El Tribunal de Cartagena de Indias. La Primera Mitad del Siglo XVII (1621–1650)." In *HIEA* 1: 1141–45.

Tellechea Idígoras, José Ignacio. *El arzobispo Carranza y su tiempo*. 2 vols. Madrid: Ediciones Guadarrama, 1968.

El Arzobispo Carranza, "Tiempos Recios," 4 vols. Salamanca: Publicaciones Universidad Pontificia, Fundación Universitaria Española, 2003–7.

"Cartas inéditas de un inquisidor por oficio. El Dr. Simancas y el proceso romano de Carranza." In *Homenaje a Julio Caro Baroja*, edited by Antonio Carreira, Jesús Antonio Cid, Manuel Gutiérrez Esteve, and Rogelio Rubio, 965–99. Madrid: Centro de Investigaciones Sociológicas, 1978.

"Documentación cifrada y diplomacia inquisitorial." In *HIEA* 3: 41–56.

"Inquisición española e Inquisición romana, ¿dos estilos?" In *Perfiles jurídicos de la Inquisición Española*, edited by José Antonio Escudero, 17–48. Madrid: Instituto de la Historia de la Inquisición, 1988.

El Obispo ideal en el siglo de la Reforma. Rome: Iglesia Nacional Española, 1963.

"El Proceso del Arzobispo Carranza." In *HIEA* 1: 556–99.

Tiempos Recios: Inquisición y Heterodoxias. Salamanca: Ediciones Sígueme, 1977.

Thomas, Werner. *La represión del protestantismo en España, 1517–1648*. Leuven: Leuven University Press, 2001.

Toussaint, Manuel. *La Catedral de Mexico y el Sagrario Metropolitano, su Historia, su Tesoro, su Arte*. Mexico City: Editorial Porrúa, 1973.

Troncarelli, Fabio. *El mito del 'Zorro' y la Inquisición en México. La aventura de Guillén Lombardo (1615–1659)*. Translated by Pau Oliva. Lleida: Editorial Milenio, 2003.

Truman, Ronald. "Pedro Salazar de Mendoza and the First Biography of Carranza." In *Reforming Catholicism in the England of Mary Tudor: The Achievement of Friar Bartolomé Carranza*, edited by John Edwards and Ronald Truman, 177–205. Aldershot, UK, and Burlington, VT: Ashgate, 2005.

Spanish Treatises on Government, Society and Religion in the Time of Philip II: the 'de regimine principum' and Associated Traditions. Leiden: Brill, 1999.

Valente, Michaela. *Contro L'Inquisizione. Il dibattito europeo secc. XVI-XVIII*. Turin: Claudiana, 2009.

van der Vekene, Emil. *Bibliotheca bibliographica historiae Sanctae Inquisitionis.* 3 vols. Vaduz: Topos, 1982–92.

van Gulik, Guglielmus, O.M. Conv., and Conrad Eubel, O.M. Conv., eds. *Hierarchia Catholica Medii et Recentioris Aevi.* 8 vols. Münster: Libreria Regensbergiana, 1913–68.

van Liere, Katherine Elliot. "After Nebrija: Academic Reformers and the Teaching of Latin in Sixteenth-Century Salamanca." *Sixteenth Century Journal* 34 (2003): 1065–105.

"Diego de Covarrubias y Leyva." In *Encyclopedia of the Renaissance*, edited by Paul F. Grendler et al., 2: 96–97. New York: Charles Scribner's Sons, 1999.

"'Shared Studies Foster Friendship': Humanism and History in Spain." In *The Renaissance World*, edited by John Jeffries Martin, 242–61. New York and London: Routledge, 2007.

"Vitoria, Cajetan, and the Conciliarists." *Journal of the History of Ideas* 58 (1997): 597–616.

Vermaseren, B. A. "Who Was Reginaldus Gonsalvius Montanus?" *Bibliothèque d'Humanisme et Renaissance* 47.1 (1985): 47–77.

Vigiano, Valentina. *L'esercizio della politica. La città di Palermo nel Cinquecento.* Rome: Viella, 2004.

Vila Vilar, Enriqueta. Introduction to *Un tratado sobre la esclavitud*, by Alonso de Sandoval, edited and translated by Enriqueta Vila Vilar, 15–44. Madrid: Alianza Editorial, 1987.

Villa-Flores, Javier. "Wandering Swindlers: Imposture, Style, and the Inquisition's Pedagogy of Fear in Colonial Mexico." *Colonial Latin American Review* 17 (2008): 251–72.

Villanueva López, Jesús. *Política y Discurso Histórico en la España del Siglo XVII. Las polémicas sobre los orígenes medievales de Cataluña.* Alicante: Universidad de Alicante, 2004.

Vivo, Filippo de. *Information and Communication in Venice: Rethinking Early Modern Politics.* Oxford, UK, and New York: Oxford University Press, 2007.

Voet, Leon. *The Plantin Press (1555–1589): A Bibliography of the Works Printed and Published by Christopher Plantin at Antwerp and Leiden.* 6 vols. Amsterdam: Van Hoeve, 1980.

Voigt, Lisa. *Writing Captivity in the Early Modern Atlantic: Circulations of Knowledge and Authority in the Iberian and English Imperial Worlds.* Chapel Hill: Omohundro Institute, University of North Carolina Press, 2009.

Von Germeten, Nicole. "Introduction." In *Treatise on Slavery. Selections from De instauranda Aethiopum salute*, by Alonso de Sandoval, S. J., edited and translated by Nicole von Germeten, ix–xxx. Indianapolis, IN, and Cambridge: Hackett Publishing Co., 2008.

Wachtel, Nathan. *La Foi du souvenir. Labyrinthes marranes.* Paris: Seuil, 2001.

La logique des bûchers. Paris: Seuil, 2009.

Wadsworth, James E. *Agents of Orthodoxy: Honor, Status and the Inquisition in Colonial Pernambuco, Brazil.* Lanham, MD: Rowman & Littlefield, 2007.

Walsh, William Thomas. *Characters of the Inquisition.* Rockford, IL: Tan Books and Publishers, 1987.

Warsh, Molly A. "Enslaved Pearl Divers in the Sixteenth-Century Caribbean." *Slavery and Abolition* 31.3 (2010): 345–62.

Warshawsky, Matthew D. "Inquisitorial Prosecution of Tomás Treviño de Sobremonte, a Crypto-Jew in Colonial Mexico." *Colonial Latin American Review* 17 (2008): 101–23.

Watson Marrón, Gustavo, Gilberto González Merlo, Berenise Bravo Rubio, and Marco Antonio Pérez Iturbe. *Guía de Documentos Novohispanos del Archivo Histórico del Arzobispado de México*. Mexico City: AHAM, 2002.

Weber, Alison. *Teresa of Ávila and the Rhetoric of Femininity*. Princeton, NJ: Princeton University Press, 1990.

Wickersham, J. "Castro, Alfonso de." In *DSI* 1: 301–2.

Williams, Patrick. "A Jewish Councillor of Inquisition? Luis de Mercado, the Statutes of *limpieza de sangre* and the Politics of Vendetta (1598–1601)." *Bulletin of Hispanic Studies* 67 (1990): 253–64.

Wojciehowski, Hannah Chapelle. *Group Identity in the Renaissance World*. Cambridge, UK, and New York: Cambridge University Press, 2011.

Wright, A. D. "Church and State in Post-Tridentine Spain." In *Catholic Times and Tastes: Essays in Honour of Michael E. Williams*, edited by Margaret Rees, 303–62. Leeds: Trinity & All Saints' College, 1987.

   Federico Borromeo and Baronius: A Turning-Point in the Development of the Counter-Reformation Church. Reading, UK: Department of Italian Studies, University of Reading, 1974.

Wright, Elizabeth. *Pilgrimage to Patronage: Lope de Vega and the Court of Philip III, 1598–1621*. Lewisburg, PA: Bucknell University Press, 2001.

Wunder, Amanda. "Murillo and the Canonisation Case of San Fernando, 1649–52." *The Burlington Magazine* 143 (2001): 670–75.

Yerushalmi, Yosef. *Zakhor. Jewish History and Jewish Memory*. Seattle: University of Washington Press, 1982.

Zen, Stefano. *Baronio storico: Controriforma e crisi del metodo umanistico*. Naples: Vivarium, 1994.

Index

Notes: Locators followed by 'n' refer to note numbers.

CPSIA information can be obtained
at www.ICGtesting.com
Printed in the USA
LVHW032314070722
722990LV00001B/67